BIO 115 CONCEPTS IN BIOLOGY

Selected Chapters From

BIOLOGY

Seventh Edition

Sylvia S. Mader

For Northland College

The McGraw-Hill Companies, Inc.
Primis Custom Publishing

New York St. Louis San Francisco Auckland Bogota
Caracas Lisbon London Madrid Mexico Milan Montreal
New Delhi Paris San Juan Singapore Sydney Tokyo Toronto

McGraw-Hill Higher Education

A Division of The McGraw·Hill Companies

Bio 115 Concepts in Biology
Selected Chapters in
BIOLOGY

This book contains selected material from *Biology*, Seventh Edition, by Sylvia S. Mader. Copyright © 2001 by The McGraw-Hill Companies, Inc. Reprinted with permission of the publisher.

234567890 QSR QSR 098765432

ISBN 0-07-252331-X

Printer/Binder: Quebecor World

TABLE OF CONTENTS

History of Biology

Antonie van Leeuwenhoek

Charles Darwin

Louis Pasteur

Robert Koch

Ivan Pavlov

Year	Name	Country	Contribution
1628	William Harvey	Britain	Demonstrates that the blood circulates and the heart is a pump.
1665	Robert Hooke	Britain	Uses the word *cell* to describe compartments he sees in cork under the microscope.
1668	Francesco Redi	Italy	Shows that decaying meat protected from flies does not spontaneously produce maggots.
1673	Antonie van Leeuwenhoek	Holland	Uses microscope to view living microorganisms.
1735	Carolus Linnaeus	Sweden	Initiates the binomial system of naming organisms.
1809	Jean B. Lamarck	France	Supports the idea of evolution but thinks there is inheritance of acquired characteristics.
1825	Georges Cuvier	France	Founds the science of paleontology and shows that fossils are related to living forms.
1828	Karl E. von Baer	Germany	Establishes the germ layer theory of development.
1838	Matthias Schleiden	Germany	States that plants are multicellular organisms.
1839	Theodor Schwann	Germany	States that animals are multicellular organisms.
1851	Claude Bernard	France	Concludes that a relatively constant internal environment allows organisms to survive under varying conditions.
1858	Rudolf Virchow	Germany	States that cells come only from preexisting cells.
1858	Charles Darwin	Britain	Presents evidence that natural selection guides the evolutionary process.
1858	Alfred R. Wallace	Britain	Independently comes to same conclusions as Darwin.
1865	Louis Pasteur	France	Disproves the theory of spontaneous generation for bacteria; shows that infections are caused by bacteria, and develops vaccines against rabies and anthrax.
1866	Gregor Mendel	Austria	Proposes basic laws of genetics based on his experiments with garden peas.
1882	Robert Koch	Germany	Establishes the germ theory of disease and develops many techniques used in bacteriology.
1900	Walter Reed	United States	Discovers that the yellow fever virus is transmitted by a mosquito.
1902	Walter S. Sutton Theodor Boveri	United States Germany	Suggest that genes are on the chromosomes, after noting the similar behavior of genes and chromosomes.
1903	Karl Landsteiner	Austria	Discovers ABO blood types.
1904	Ivan Pavlov	Russia	Shows that conditioned reflexes affect behavior, based on experiments with dogs.
1910	Thomas H. Morgan	United States	States that each gene has a locus on a particular chromosome, based on experiments with *Drosophila*.
1922	Sir Frederick Banting Charles Best	Canada	Isolate insulin from the pancreas.
1924	Hans Spemann Hilde Mangold	Germany	Show that induction occurs during development, based on experiments with frog embryos.
1927	Hermann J. Muller	United States	Proves that X rays cause mutations
1929	Sir Alexander Fleming	Britain	Discovers the toxic effect of a mold product he called penicillin on certain bacteria.

History of Biology

Year	Name	Country	Contribution.
1937	Konrad Z. Lorenz	Austria	Founds the study of ethology and shows the importance of imprinting as a form of early learning.
1937	Sir Hans A. Krebs	Britain	Discovers the reactions of a cycle that produces carbon dioxide during cellular respiration.
1940	George Beadle Edward Tatum	United States	Develop the one gene–one enzyme theory, based on red bread mold studies.
1944	O. T. Avery Maclyn McCarty Colin MacLeod	United States	Demonstrate that DNA alone from virulent bacteria can transform nonvirulent bacteria.
1945	Melvin Calvin Andrew A. Benson	United States	Discover the individual reactions of a cycle that reduces carbon dioxide during photosynthesis.
1950	Barbara McClintock	United States	Discovers transposons (jumping genes) while doing experiments with corn.
1952	Alfred D. Hershey Martha Chase	United States	Find that only DNA from viruses enters cells and directs the reproduction of new viruses.
1953	James Watson Francis Crick Rosalind Franklin	United States Britain	Establish that the molecular structure for DNA is a double helix.
1953	Harold Urey Stanley Miller	United States	Demonstrate that the first organic molecules may have arisen from the gases of the primitive atmosphere.
1954	Linus Pauling	United States	States that disease-causing abnormal hemoglobins are due to mutations.
1954	Jonas Salk	United States	Develops a vaccine that protects against polio.
1958	Matthew S. Meselson Franklin W. Stahl	United States	Demonstrate that DNA replication is semiconservative.
1961	Francois Jacob Jacques Monod	France	Discover that genetic expression is controlled by regulatory genes.
1964	Marshall W. Nirenberg Philip Leder	United States	Produce synthetic RNA, enabling them to break the DNA code.
1967	Christiaan Barnard	South Africa	Performs first human heart transplant operation.
1973	Stanley Cohen	United States	Uses recombinant DNA technique (genetic engineering) to place plant and animal genes in *Escherichia coli*.
1976	Georges Kohler Cesar Milstein	Britain	Fuse mouse leukemia cells with lymphocytes, developing clones, each of which produces only one type of "monoclonal" antibody.
1977	Carl Woese	United States	Based on differences in ribosomal RNA sequences, proposes the three domain system of clasifications.
1978	Peter Mitchell	Britain	Determines chemiosmotic mechanism by which ATP is produced in chloroplasts and mitochondria.
1982	William De Vries	United States	Performs first complete replacement of human heart with artificial heart on Dr. Barney B. Clark at University of Utah.
1989	Sidney Altman Thomas R. Check	United States	Independently discover that some RNA molecules can act as enzymes.
1990	R. Michael Blaese W. French Anderson Kenneth W. Culver	United States	Develop procedure to infuse genetically engineered blood cells for treatment of immune system disorder–first gene therapy used in a human.
1997	Ian Wilmut	Britain	Clones an adult mammal for the first time.

Konrad Z. Lorenz

Barbara McClintock

Rosalind Franklin

Linus Pauling

Metric System

Unit and Abbreviation	Metric Equivalent	Approximate English-to-Metric Equivalents	
Length			
nanometer (nm)	$= 10^{-9}$ m		
micrometer (µm)	$= 10^{-6}$ m		
millimeter (mm)	$= 0.001\ (10^{-3})$ m		
centimeter (cm)	$= 0.01\ (10^{-2})$ m	1 inch	= 2.54 cm
		1 foot	= 30.5 cm
meter (m)	$= 100\ (10^{2})$ cm	1 foot	= 0.30 m
	$= 1{,}000$ mm	1 yard	= 0.91 m
kilometer (km)	$= 1{,}000\ (10^{3})$ m	1 mi	= 1.6 km
Weight (mass)			
nanogram (ng)	$= 10^{-9}$ g		
microgram (µg)	$= 10^{-6}$ g		
milligram (mg)	$= 10^{-3}$ g		
gram (g)	$= 1{,}000$ mg	1 ounce	= 28.3 g
		1 pound	= 454 g
kilogram (kg)	$= 1{,}000\ (10^{3})$ g		= 0.45 kg
metric ton (t)	$= 1{,}000$ kg	1 ton	= 0.91 t
Volume			
microliter (µl)	$= 10^{-6}\ l\ (10^{-3}$ ml)		
milliliter (ml)	$= 10^{-3}$ liters	1 tsp	= 5 ml
	$= 1\ cm^{3}$ (cc)	1 fl oz	= 30 ml
	$= 1{,}000\ mm^{3}$		
liter (l)	$= 1{,}000$ ml	1 pint	= 0.47 liters
		1 quart	= 0.95 liters
		1 gallon	= 3.79 liters
kiloliter (kl)	$= 1{,}000$ liters		

Units of Temperature

To convert temperature scales:

$$°C = \frac{5(°F-32)}{9}$$

$$°F = \frac{9°C}{5} + 32$$

°C	°F	
100	212	Water boils at standard temperature and pressure
71	160	Flash pasteurization of milk
57	134	Highest recorded temperature in the United States, Death Valley, July 10, 1913
41	105.8	Average body temperature of a marathon runner in hot weather
37	98.6	Human body temperature
20.3	68.6	Lowest recorded body temperature to be survived by a human
0	32.0	Water freezes at standard temperature and pressure

Periodic Table of the Elements

Legend:
- Atomic number
- Atomic weight
- Chemical symbol

| 1 — 1 — H — hydrogen |

group Ia	IIa	IIIb	IVb	Vb	VIb	VIIb	VIIIb			Ib	IIb	IIIa	IVa	Va	VIa	VIIa	VIIIa
1 1 H hydrogen																	2 4 He helium
3 7 Li lithium	4 9 Be beryllium											5 11 B boron	6 12 C carbon	7 14 N nitrogen	8 16 O oxygen	9 19 F fluorine	10 20 Ne neon
11 23 Na sodium	12 24 Mg magnesium											13 27 Al aluminum	14 28 Si silicon	15 31 P phosphorus	16 32 S sulfur	17 35 Cl chlorine	18 40 Ar argon
19 39 K potassium	20 40 Ca calcium	21 45 Sc scandium	22 48 Ti titanium	23 51 V vanadium	24 52 Cr chromium	25 55 Mn manganese	26 56 Fe iron	27 59 Co cobalt	28 59 Ni nickel	29 64 Cu copper	30 65 Zn zinc	31 70 Ga gallium	32 73 Ge germanium	33 75 As arsenic	34 79 Se selenium	35 80 Br bromine	36 84 Kr krypton
37 85 Rb rubidium	38 88 Sr strontium	39 89 Y yttrium	40 91 Zr zirconium	41 93 Nb niobium	42 96 Mo molybdenum	43 98 Tc technetium	44 101 Ru ruthenium	45 103 Rh rhodium	46 106 Pd palladium	47 108 Ag silver	48 112 Cd cadmium	49 115 In indium	50 119 Sn tin	51 122 Sb antimony	52 128 Te tellurium	53 127 I iodine	54 131 Xe xenon
55 133 Cs cesium	56 137 Ba barium	57 139 La lanthanum	72 178 Hf hafnium	73 181 Ta tantalum	74 184 W tungsten	75 186 Re rhenium	76 190 Os osmium	77 192 Ir iridium	78 195 Pt platinum	79 197 Au gold	80 201 Hg mercury	81 204 Tl thallium	82 207 Pb lead	83 209 Bi bismuth	84 210 Po polonium	85 210 At astatine	86 222 Rn radon
87 223 Fr francium	88 226 Ra radium	89 227 Ac actinium	104 261 Rf rutherfordium	105 260 Ha hahnium													

Lanthanides:

58 140 Ce cerium	59 141 Pr praseodymium	60 144 Nd neodymium	61 147 Pm promethium	62 150 Sm samarium	63 152 Eu europium	64 157 Gd gadolinium	65 159 Tb terbium	66 163 Dy dysprosium	67 165 Ho holmium	68 167 Er erbium	69 169 Tm thulium	70 173 Yb ytterbium	71 175 Lu lutetium

Actinides:

90 232 Th thorium	91 231 Pa protactinium	92 238 U uranium	93 237 Np neptunium	94 242 Pu plutonium	95 243 Am americium	96 247 Cm curium	97 247 Bk berkelium	98 249 Cf californium	99 254 Es einsteinium	100 253 Fm fermium	101 256 Md mendelevium	102 254 No nobelium	103 257 Lr lawrencium

When I write *Biology* I always feel that I am speaking directly to you, the reader. This occurs, no doubt, because I taught biology before I began to write about it. During those years, I began to develop techniques for making science-shy students successful in their study of biology. The first edition of *Biology* had a learning system that has continued to improve through feedback from both students and instructors. The end result is the seventh edition you hold in your hands. The major topics in *Biology* are now numbered. This allows instructors to assign just certain portions of the chapter and permits study in terms of the concepts listed in the chapter outline. With the advent of the computer it became possible for me to page the text so that each illustration is on the same or facing page as the reference.

Most illustrations in this edition are new or revised to improve their student appeal and educational design. Each type of molecule (fat, protein, nucleic acids) is colored the same, not just in the chemistry chapters but throughout the book. Each type organelle is colored the same in the cell chapter and also in all chapters. The addition of icons relates the part to the whole and the addition of micrographs relates art to an actual structure. Icons occur in the cell, ecology, diversity, and systems chapters. A cell icon shows the usual location of organelles. A cellular respiration icon depicts the connections between various pathways. Phylogenetic tree icons remind students of the evolutionary relationship among groups of organisms.

The emphasis on the scientific process has been strengthened in this edition of *Biology*. The first chapter has an improved description of the scientific process using a more appealing experiment from literature. The end matter of each chapter now contains *Thinking Scientifically* questions and these give students an opportunity to participate in the scientific process and learn to think critically. The *Science Focus* readings are more varied this edition. Some of these are written by contemporary biologists who tell how they go about doing their research and how these findings can be applied to human beings.

A *Bioethical Issue* section has been added to the end of most chapters. These issues pertain to a wide range of topics that require thoughtful consideration by society at this time. The issues end with appropriate questions to help students center their thoughts and arrive at an opinion. The myriad of topics considered include genetic disease testing, human cloning, AIDS vaccine trials, animal rights, responsibility for one's health, and fetal research.

New Chapters and Sections

Biology is an introductory text that covers the concepts and principles of biology from the structure and function of the cell to the organization of the biosphere. It draws upon the entire world of living things to bring out an evolutionary theme that is introduced from the start. The concept of evolution is necessary to understanding the unity and diversity of life and serves as a background for the study of ecological principles and modern ecological problems.

Every chapter of *Biology* has been revised and skillfully updated so that this edition has not grown in page length. These chapters are new:

Chapter 9, Cellular Reproduction and the Cell Cycle, has been reorganized and now ends with a discussion of the relationship between the cell cycle and cancer.
Chapter 27, Conservation Biology, is a new chapter which discusses the current biodiversity crisis including why we should care, the root causes, and how to preserve species and prevent extinctions.
Chapter 30, The Protists, was thoroughly updated to better reflect modern concepts regarding protist diversity.
Chapter 37, Nutrition and Transport in Plants, now begins with a section that includes a discussion of soil formation and its nutritional functions. In this chapter, new figures support an improved discussion of xylem and phloem transport.
Chapter 46, Neurons and Nervous Systems, has been reorganized and rewritten for better flow. The more thorough discussion of the central nervous system includes a new section on learning and memory.
Chapter 49, Hormones and Endocrine Systems, better emphasizes the role of hormones in homeostasis and the effects of imbalance on the human phenotype.

A more complete list of updates for the seventh edition is available on the *Biology* website.

Readings

The readings are organized into four types. The *Science Focus* readings are often written by contemporary scientists who tell us about their particular type of research and how they became interested in this field of biology. The *Health Focus* readings usually give practical information concerning some particular topic of interest, such as proper nutrition and how to prevent cancer. The *Ecology Focus* readings draw attention to some particular environmental problem such as the need to preserve tropical rain forests and the relationship between ozone holes and skin cancer. The *Closer Look* readings are designed to expand, in an interesting way, on the core information presented in each chapter.

Science Focus

Ecology Focus

Health Focus

A Closer Look

The Learning System

Each chapter in *Biology* is comprised of basic features that serve as the pedagogical framework for the chapter. Before you begin reading the text, spend a little time looking over these pages. They provide a quick guide to the learning tools found throughout the text that have been designed to enhance your understanding of biology.

Chapter Concepts

The chapter begins with an integrated outline that numbers the major topics of the chapter and lists the concepts for each topic.

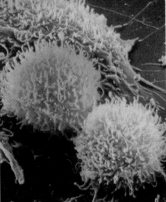

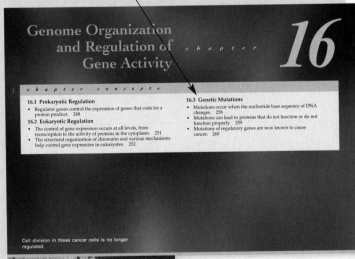

Genome Organization and Regulation of Gene Activity
chapter
16

chapter concepts

16.1 Prokaryotic Regulation
- Regulator genes control the expression of genes that code for a protein product. 248

16.2 Eukaryotic Regulation
- The control of gene expression occurs at all levels, from transcription to the activity of proteins in the cytoplasm. 251
- The structural organization of chromatin and various mechanisms help control gene expression in eukaryotes. 252

16.3 Genetic Mutations
- Mutations occur when the nucleotide base sequence of DNA changes. 258
- Mutations can lead to proteins that do not function or do not function properly. 259
- Mutations of regulatory genes are now known to cause cancer. 260

Cell division in these cancer cells is no longer regulated.

We all begin life as a one-celled zygote that has 46 chromosomes, and these same chromosomes are passed to all the daughter cells during mitosis. Yet cells become specialized in structure and function. The genes for digestive enzymes are expressed only in digestive tract cells and the genes for muscle proteins are expressed only in muscle cells. This shows it is possible to control transcription and translation of genes in each particular type cell.

In this chapter we will see that regulation of gene activity extends from the nucleus (whether a gene is transcribed) to the cytoplasm (whether an enzyme is functioning). Complete knowledge of how gene expression is controlled has far-ranging applications. Only then will we understand how development progresses and what causes the occurrence of various disorders, including cancer. Cancer develops when genes that promote cell division are expressed and when genes that suppress cell division are not expressed. It has become increasingly apparent that the regulation of gene expression is of major importance to the health of all species, including human beings.

The Essential Study Partner CD-ROM

An icon has been placed throughout the text to alert you to topics that are also discussed in detail on the Essential Study Partner CD-ROM that accompanies their text.

chapter 16 Genome Organization and Regulation of Gene Activity 16–5 251

16.2 Eukaryotic Regulation

The **genome** is all of a cell's DNA including all of its genes that code for a protein product. As we have seen in prokaryotes, the genome is organized into regulators and operons that control the expression of structural genes. In eukaryotes, there is no universal regulatory mechanism that controls the activity of coding genes. Instead regulation is possible at any point in the pathway from gene to functional protein. These four levels of gene expression are commonly seen in eukaryotes (Fig. 16.4):

1. **Transcriptional control:** In the nucleus a number of mechanisms serve to control which structural genes are transcribed or the rate at which transcription of the genes occurs. These include the organization of chromatin and the use of transcription factors that initiate transcription, the first step in the process of gene expression.

2. **Posttranscriptional control:** Posttranscriptional control occurs in the nucleus after DNA is transcribed and primary mRNA is formed. Differential processing of preliminary mRNA before it leaves the nucleus, and also the speed with which mature mRNA leaves the nucleus, can affect the ultimate amount of gene product.

3. **Translational control:** Translational control occurs in the cytoplasm after mRNA leaves the nucleus and before there is a protein product. The life expectancy of mRNA molecules (how long they exist in the cytoplasm) can vary, as can their ability to bind ribosomes. It is also possible that some mRNAs may need additional changes before they are translated at all.

4. **Posttranslational control:** Posttranslational control, which also takes place in the cytoplasm, occurs after protein synthesis. The polypeptide product may have to undergo additional changes before it is biologically functional. Also, a functional enzyme is subject to feedback control—the binding of an end product can change the shape of an enzyme so that it is no longer able to carry out its reaction.

We will see that regulation of gene expression in eukaryotes means there is cellular control of the amount and activity of a gene product.

Control of gene expression occurs at four levels in eukaryotes. In the nucleus there is transcriptional and posttranscriptional control; in the cytoplasm there is translational and posttranslational control.

Figure 16.4 Levels of gene expression control in eukaryotic cells.
Transcriptional and posttranscriptional control occur in the nucleus. Translational and posttranslational control occur in the cytoplasm.

Internal Summary Statements

Internal summaries stress the chapter's key concepts. These appear at the ends of major sections and help you focus their study efforts on the basics.

Connecting Concepts

These appear at the close of the text portion of the chapter, and they stimulate critical thinking by showing how the concepts of the chapter are related to others in the text.

Summary

The major headings are repeated in the summary because it is organized according to the major sections of the chapter. The summary helps you review the important concepts and topics discussed in each chapter.

Reviewing the Chapter

These are a series of page-referenced study questions that follow the sequence of the chapter.

Thinking Scientifically

New this edition, these critical thinking questions give you an opportunity to reason as a scientist. Detailed answers to these questions are found on the Online Learning Center.

Testing Yourself

This section consists of objective questions that allow you to test your ability to answer recall-based questions. Answers to *Testing Yourself* questions are given in Appendix A.

Bioethical Issue

A *Bioethical Issue* has been added to the end of many chapters this edition. These short readings discuss a variety of controversial topics that our society continues to confront. The reading ends with appropriate questions to help you fully consider the issue and arrive at an opinion.

Web Connections

This section directs you to the Online Learning Center, and informs you of links that are available for further study of the topics discussed in the chapter.

Essential Study Partner CD-ROM

A free study partner that engages, investigates, and reinforces what you are learning from your textbook. You'll find the **Essential Study Partner** for *Biology* to be a complete, interactive student study tool packed with hundreds of animations and learning activities. From quizzes to interactive diagrams, you'll find that there has never been a better study partner to ensure the mastery of core concepts. Best of all, it's **FREE** with your new textbook purchase.

The topic menu contains an interactive list of the available topics. Clicking on any of the listings within this menu will open your selection and will show the specific concepts presented within this topic. Clicking any of the concepts will move you to your selection. You can use the UP and DOWN arrow keys to move through the topics.

The unit pop-up menu is accessible at any time within the program. Clicking on the current unit will bring up a menu of other units available in the program.

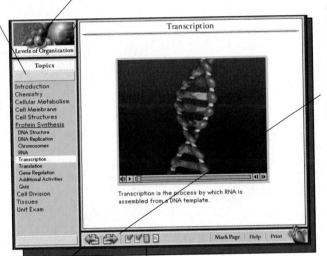

To the right of the arrows is a row of icons that represent the number of screens in a concept. There are three different icons, each representing different functions that a screen in that section will serve. The screen that is currently displayed will highlight yellow and visited ones will be checked.

The film icon represents an animation screen.

Along the bottom of the screen you will find various navigational aids. At the left are arrows that allow you to page forward and backward through text screens or interactive exercise screens. You can also use the LEFT and RIGHT arrows on your keyboard to perform the same function.

The activity icon represents an interactive learning activity.

The page icon represents a page of informational text.

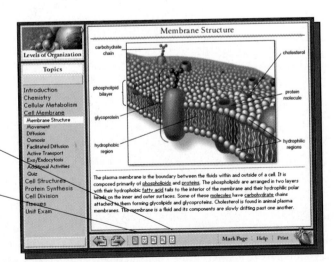

Contact your McGraw-Hill sales representative for more information or visit *www.mhhe.com.*

The Online
Learning Center
Your Password to Success

www.mhhe.com/biosci/genbio/maderbiology7

This text-specific website allows students and instructors from all over the world to communicate. Instructors can create a more interactive course with the integration of this site, and students will find tools that help them improve their grades and learn that biology can be fun.

Student Resources

Study questions
Quizzing with immediate feedback
Links to chapter-related websites
Case studies
Interactive art labeling exercises
Critical thinking exercises

Instructor Resources

Instructor's Manual
Activities that can be assigned
  as coursework
Links to related websites to expand on
  particular topics
Classroom activities
Lecture outlines
Case studies

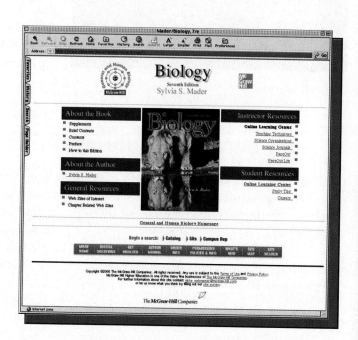

Imagine the advantages of having so many
learning and teaching tools
all in one place—all at your fingertips—FREE.

Contact your McGraw-Hill sales
representative for more information
or visit *www.mhhe.com*.

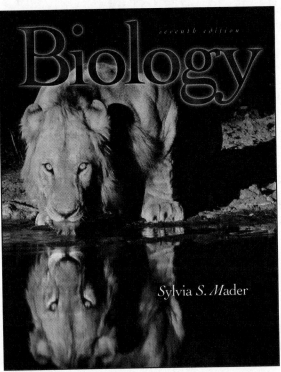

Visual Resource Library CD-ROMs

These CD-ROMs are electronic libraries of educational presentation resources that instructors can use to enhance their lectures. View, sort, search, and print catalog images, play chapter-specific slideshows using PowerPoint, or create customized presentations when you:

- Find and sort thumbnail image records by name, type, location, and user-defined keywords
- Search using keywords or terms
- View images at the same time with the Small Gallery View
- Select and view images at full size
- Display all the important file information for easy file identification
- Drag and place or copy and paste into virtually any graphics, desktop publishing, presentation, or multimedia application

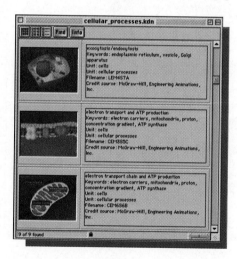

Life Science Animations Visual Resource Library CD-ROM

This instructor's tool, containing more than 125 animations of important biological concepts and processes—found in the *Essential Study Partner* and *Dynamic Human CD-ROMs*—is perfect to support your lecture. The animations contained in this library are not limited to subjects covered in the text, but include an expansion of general life science topics.

Biology Visual Resource Library CD-ROM

This helpful CD-ROM contains ALL 1,500 photographs and illustrations from *Biology*. You'll be able to create interesting multimedia presentations with the use of these images, and students will have the ability to easily access the same images in their texts to later review the content covered in class.

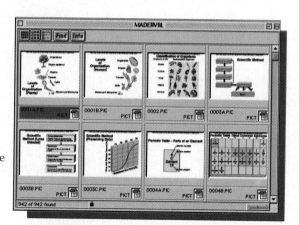

Contact your McGraw-Hill sales representative for more information or visit *www.mhhe.com*.

PageOut
Proven. Reliable. Class-tested.

More than 6,000 professors have chosen **PageOut** to create course websites. And for good reason: **PageOut** offers powerful features, yet is incredibly easy to use.

Now you can be the first to use an even better version of **PageOut**. Through class-testing and customer feedback, we have made key improvements to the grade book, as well as the quizzing and discussion areas. Best of all, **PageOut** is still free with every McGraw-Hill textbook. And students needn't bother with any special tokens or fees to access your **PageOut** website.

Customize the site to coincide with your lectures.

Complete the **PageOut** templates with your course information and you will have an interactive syllabus online. This feature lets you post content to coincide with your lectures. When students visit your **PageOut** website, your syllabus will direct them to components of McGraw-Hill web content germane to your text, or specific material of your own.

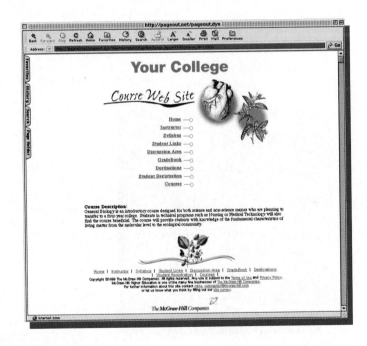

New Features based on customer feedback:

- Specific question selection for quizzes

- Ability to copy your course and share it with colleagues or use as a foundation for a new semester

- Enhanced grade book with reporting features

- Ability to use the **PageOut** discussion area, or add your own third party discussion tool

- Password protected courses

Short on time? Let us do the work.

Send your course materials to our McGraw-Hill service team. They will call you for a 30 minute consultation. A team member will then create your **PageOut** website and provide training to get you up and running. Contact your McGraw-Hill representative for details.

Contact your local McGraw-Hill sales representative for more information or visit *www.mhhe.com*.

Course Solutions

Simplify your life.

Course Solutions 2000 is the answer to your teaching needs. With a full range of multimedia products and special services married to our market-respected, time-tested textbooks, the *Course Solutions 2000* program is designed to make your life easier. Everything you need for effective, interactive teaching is at your fingertips.

WHY USE COURSE SOLUTIONS?

- **McGraw-Hill Learning Architecture** Each *McGraw-Hill Online Learning Center* is ready to be imported into our *McGraw-Hill Learning Architecture*—a full course management software system for *Local Area Networks* and *Distance Learning Classes*. Developed in conjunction with Top Class software, *McGraw-Hill Learning Architecture* is a powerful course management system available upon special request.

- **Course Consultant Service** In addition to the *Course Integration Guide*, instructors using Course Solutions textbooks can access a special curriculum-based Course Consultant Service via a web-based threaded discussion list within each *Online Learning Center*.

- **Instructor Syllabus Service** For *new* adopters of *Course Solutions* textbooks, McGraw-Hill will help correlate all text, supplementary, and appropriate materials and services to your course syllabus. Simply call your McGraw-Hill representative for assistance.

- **PageOut** Use this intuitive software to create your own course website.

- **Other Delivery Options** *Online Learning Centers* are also compatible with a number of full-service online course delivery systems or outside educational service providers.

- **Student Tutorial Service** Within each *Online Learning Center* resides a free student tutorial service.

- **e-BOOKS** Each *Course Solutions* title will feature its own e-book—an on-screen version of the actual textbook with numerous in-text links to other valuable digital resources. E-books—which are extremely valuable and very affordable—are available in one of three formats, depending on the textbook:
  - Interactive e-Source CD-ROM
  - e-Text CD-ROM
  - Online Learning Center

- **Web CT Linkage** Specially prepared *Online Learning Centers*, available with *Course Solutions* textbooks, load easily into any *Web CT Course Management* system.

- **Enhanced New Media Integration Guide** Each *Course Solutions* title features a valuable *Integration Guide* for instructors, significantly improved over past Integration Guides. Each guide indicates where and how to use available media resources with the text. Each now includes detailed descriptions of the content of each relevant new media module or exercise.

- **Online Animations** Selected *Course Solutions* titles now include high-quality animations in their *Online Learning Centers*.

Contact your local McGraw-Hill sales representative for more information or visit *www.mhhe.com*.

New Technology

 Essential Study Partner CD-ROM
This interactive student study tool is packed with over 100 animations and more than 200 learning activities. From quizzes to interactive diagrams, your students will find that there has never been a more exciting way to study biology. A self-quizzing feature allows students to test their knowledge of a topic before moving on to a new module. Additional unit exams give students the opportunity to review an entire subject area. The quizzes and unit exams hyperlink students back to tutorial sections so they can easily review coverage for a more complete understanding. The text-specific *Essential Study Partner CD-ROM* supports and enhances the material presented in **Biology** and is correlated with the text.

Biology Online Learning Center
McGraw-Hill text-specific websites allow students and instructors from all over the world to communicate. By visiting this site, students can access additional study aids—including quizzes—explore links to other relevant biology sites, and catch up on current information. Log on today!

www.mhhe.com/biosci/genbio/mader

 **McGraw-Hill Course Solutions**
Designed specifically to help you with your individual course needs, *Course Solutions* will assist you in integrating your syllabus with **Biology,** and state-of-the-art new media tools.

At the heart of *Course Solutions* you'll find integrated multimedia, a full-scale Online Learning Center, and an enhanced Integration Guide. These unparalleled services are also available as a part of *Course Solutions:* e-Books, Web CT linkage, Online animations, McGraw-Hill Learning Architecture, McGraw-Hill Course Consultation Service, Visual Resource Library Image Licensing, McGraw-Hill Student Tutorial Service, McGraw-Hill Instructor Syllabus Service, PageOut Lite, PageOut: The Course Website Development Center, and other delivery options.

PageOut™ Put together your own customized website with the use of PageOut, a program designed specifically for instructors wanting to put course information on the web. No experience in web publishing is necessary, just choose from a collection of templates to create your class website.

 Visual Resource Library CD-ROM
This helpful CD-ROM contains approximately 1,500 images and select animations that can be easily imported into PowerPoint to create multimedia presentations. Or, you may use the already prepared PowerPoint presentations.

 Life Science Animations CD-ROM
This two CD-ROM set contains more than 125 animations of important biological concepts and processes.

 Classroom Testing Software (MicroTest)
This helpful testing software—available in either Macintosh or Windows format—provides well-written and researched book-specific questions featured in the Test Item File.

 **Life Science Animations Videotape Series**
Animations of key biological processes are available on seven videotapes. The animations bring visual movement to biological processes that are difficult to understand on the text page.

 **Microbes in Motion CD-ROM, Version 2.0**
This interactive CD-ROM allows students to actively explore microbial structure and function. Great for self-study, preparation for class or exams, or for classroom presentations.

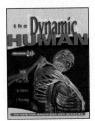 **The Dynamic Human CD-ROM, Version 2.0**
This guide to anatomy and physiology interactively illustrates the complex relationships between anatomical structures and their functions in the human body. Realistic, three-dimensional visuals are the premier feature of this exciting learning tool.

Dynamic Human Videodisc
Enhance your classroom presentations with movement, sound, and motion of internal organs, cells, and systems. More than 80 premier 3-D animations covering all body systems from the outstanding *Dynamic Human CD-ROM* are included.

Other Available Supplements

Instructor's Manual

The *Instructor's Manual* is designed to assist instructors as they plan and prepare for classes using **Biology.** The *Instructor's Manual* contains both an extended lecture outline and lecture enrichment ideas, which together review in detail the contents of the text chapter. The technology section lists videos and computer software items that are available from outside sources and also those that are available from McGraw-Hill.

Student Study Guide

To ensure close coordination with the text, the author Dr. Sylvia S. Mader has written the *Student Study Guide* that accompanies the text. Each text chapter has a corresponding study guide chapter that includes a listing of objectives, study questions, and a chapter test. Answers to the study questions and the chapter tests are provided to give students immediate feedback.

The concepts in the study guide are the same as those in the text, and the study questions in the study guide are sequenced according to these concepts. Instructors who make their choice of concepts known to the students can thereby direct student learning in an efficient manner. Instructors and students who make use of the *Student Study Guide* should find that student performance increases dramatically.

Laboratory Manual

Dr. Mader has also written the **Laboratory Manual** to accompany **Biology.** With few exceptions, each chapter in the text has an accompanying laboratory exercise in the manual (some chapters have more than one accompanying exercise). In this way, instructors are better able to emphasize particular portions of the curriculum, if they wish. The 35 laboratory sessions in the manual are designed to further help students appreciate the scientific method and to learn the fundamental concepts of biology and the specific content of each chapter. All exercises have been tested for student interest, preparation time, and feasibility. This lab manual can be customized to fit your lab course, contact your McGraw-Hill representative for details.

Transparencies

This set of transparency acetates to accompany the text, has been expanded to *650* full-color acetates.

Micrograph Slides

This ancillary provides a boxed set of 100 color slides of photomicrographs and electron micrographs in the text.

HealthQuest CD-ROM
ISBN 0-697-29723-3 (Windows)
ISBN 0-07-039335-4 (Macintosh)

Virtual Biology Laboratory CD-ROM
ISBN 0-697-37991-4

Life Science Living Lexicon CD-ROM
ISBN 0-697-37993-0

How to Study Science, Third Edition
ISBN 0-697-36051-2

Basic Chemistry for Biology, Second Edition
ISBN 0-697-36087-3

Schaum's Outlines: Biology
ISBN 0-07-022405-6

Understanding Evolution, by Volpe and Rosenbaum
ISBN 0-697-05137-4

AIDS Booklet
ISBN 0-697-29428-5

The Internet Primer
ISBN 0-07-303203-4

Critical Thinking Case Study Workbook
ISBN 0-697-14556-5

How Scientists Think, by George Johnson
ISBN 0-697-27875-1

To order any of these great study tools, contact your bookstore manager or call our Customer Service Department at 800-338-3987.

Acknowledgments

Biology has always been a team effort and it is fitting to acknowledge all those who worked so diligently on this edition. My publisher Michael Lange was always there to offer advice and my editor Patrick Reidy stepped in when needed to encourage us all. The clear, steady directives of my developmental editor, Anne Melde, were very much appreciated. She also contributed heavily to the success of the multimedia that accompanies the text.

Those in production also worked unfailingly toward the success of this edition. Marilyn Sulzer was pleasant, efficient, and cooperative while balancing a multitude of tasks. Marilyn doubled as the art coordinator and Lori Hancock was the photo research coordinator. And I especially want to thank Wayne Harms for the beautiful book he designed for all of us to enjoy.

In my office, Evelyn Jo Hebert has consistently provided steadfast and proficient support through several editions of the text. Everyone on the book team remained cheerful and helpful while going beyond the call of duty. My thanks to them all.

The Reviewers

Many instructors have contributed not only to this edition of *Biology* but also to previous editions. I am extremely thankful to each one, for they have all worked diligently to remain true to our calling and provide a product that will be the most useful to our students.

In particular, it is appropriate to acknowledge the help of the following individuals for the seventh edition:

Christine Tachibana
University of Washington

Larry Frederick
Southeastern Louisiana University

Dennis Bakewicz
New York City Technical College

Linda Smith-Staton
Pellissippi State Technical Community College

Shirley Porteous-Gafford
Fresno City College

Jerald Dosch
College of Visual Arts

Todd Christian Yetter
Cumberland College

Rita Hoots
Woodland College

Gary Greer
West Virginia State College

Bernard Wood
George Washington University

Robert Grammer
Belmont University

Beth Montelone
Kansas State University

Howard Duncan
Norfolk State University

Peter I. Ekechukwu
Horry-Georgetown Technical College

Lynne Lohmeier
Mississippi Gulf Coast Community College

Brian Hagenbuch
Holyoke Community College

Thomas J. Montagno
Simmons College

Margaret Nordlie
University of Mary

Brenda Zink
Northeastern Junior College

Jun Tsuji
Siena Heights University

Ralph C. Goff
Mansfield University of Pennsylvania

Judy Bluemer
Morton College

Tammy J. Liles
Lexington Community College

Marjorie Miller
Greenville Technical College

Angela Mason
Beaufort County Community College

Lyndell Robinson
Lincoln Land Community College

Andy Neill
Joliet Junior College

Debbie Firak
McHenry County College

Richard Bounds
Mount Olive College

John Mathwig
College of Lake County

Terry F. Werner
Harris-Stowe State College

Suzanne Kempke
Armstrong Atlantic State University

Thurman Wilson
Prairie State College

Stephen A. Miller
College of the Ozarks

R. Douglas Lyng
Indiana University–Purdue University at Fort Wayne

Andrew Goliszek
North Carolina Agricultural and Technical State University

James Enderby Bidlack
University of Central Oklahoma

Billy Williams
Dyersburg State Community College

Timothy Metz
Campbell University

George Williams, Jr.
Southern University and Agricultural and Mechanical College of Baton Rouge

James Fitch
Jones Junior College

Suzzette F. Chopin
Texas A&M University–Corpus Christi

Sue Trammell
Rend Lake College

Anton Lawson
Arizona State University–Main

Philip Snider
University of Houston

Robert David Allen
University of Nevada–Las Vegas

Jane Aloi
Saddleback College

Carol St. Angelo
Hofstra University

George W. Cox
San Diego State University

A View of Life

chapter

1

Snakes and humans, like all living things, have many characteristics in common.

From bacteria to bats, toadstools to trees, whippoorwills to whales—the diversity of the living world boggles the mind. Yet, all organisms, over all of time, are united by a common bond. Just as you are descended from your parents, grandparents, and so forth, going back for many generations, all forms of life that ever lived are tied together by an unbroken lineage that can be traced back through time to the infancy of our planet. Humans and snakes share many similarities because they have a recent common ancestor. Both have a heart, a liver, intestines, and backbone. Why? Because they are both descended from the first vertebrates that ever existed.

Through adaptation to particular environments, groups of organisms diversified. Now the diversity of life including tigers, lions, gorillas, and elephants is threatened by human activities. What evolution has accomplished over billions of years can be destroyed in a much shorter length of time. What do we want to do—preserve or destroy diversity? We are in the driver's seat, but which road will we choose to take? The future of life is in our hands.

Courtesy of J. William Schopf, Director, UCLA Center for the Study of Evolution and the Origin of Life.

chapter 1

1.1 How to Define Life

You intuitively know that the cat and not the couch where the cat snuggles is alive. But it would most likely be difficult for you to come up with a one-line definition of life. The same is true for biologists; they can't easily define life either. Therefore, they rely on listing certain characteristics shared by all living things.

Living Things Are Organized

The complex organization of living things begins with the cell, the basic unit of life. Cells are made up of molecules that contain atoms, which are the smallest units of matter that can enter into chemical combination. In multicellular organisms, similar cells combine to form a tissue—nerve cells form nerve tissue, for example. Tissues make up organs, as when various tissues combine to form the brain. Organs, in turn, work together in systems; for example, the brain works with the spinal cord and a network of nerves to form the nervous system. A multicellular individual has several other organ systems also.

There are levels of biological organization that extend beyond the individual organism. All organisms of one type in a particular area belong to a population. In a temperate deciduous forest, there is a population of gray squirrels and a population of oak trees. The populations of various animals and plants in the forest make up a community (Fig. 1.1). The populations interact among themselves and with the physical environment (soil, atmosphere, etc.) forming an ecosystem.

Summing the Parts

In the living world, the whole is more than the sum of its parts. Each new level of biological organization has emergent properties that are due to interactions between the parts making up the whole. For example, when cells are broken down into bits of membrane and oozing liquids, these parts themselves cannot carry out the business of living. Slice a frog and arrange the slices, and the frog cannot flick out its tongue and catch flies.

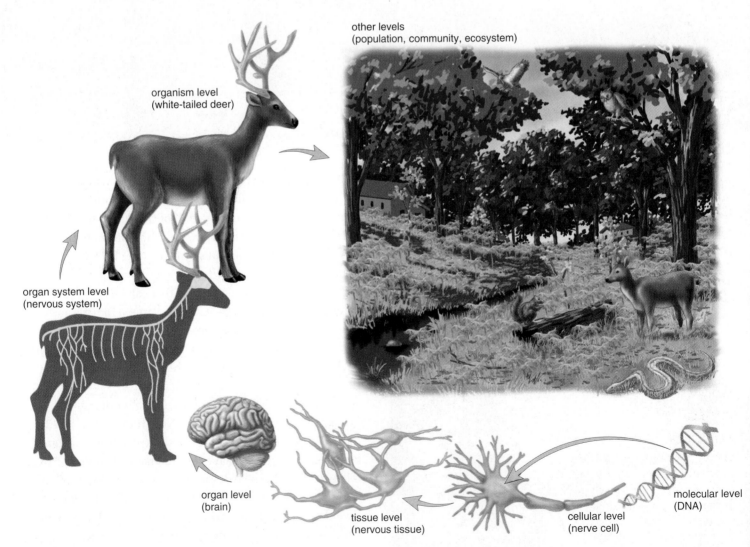

Figure 1.1 Levels of biological organization.

a.

b.

Figure 1.2 Acquiring nutrient materials and energy.
Plants and other types of photosynthesizers are able to produce organic
nutrients; animals feed directly on photosynthesizers or other animals.
a. A lioness charges her prey, a group of zebras. **b.** One zebra of the herd
is taken and becomes a meal for hungry lionesses.

Living Things Acquire Materials and Energy

Living things cannot maintain their organization or carry on
life's activities without an outside source of materials and energy (Fig. 1.2). Food provides nutrient molecules, which are
used as building blocks or for energy. **Energy** is the capacity
to do work, and it takes work to maintain the organization of
the cell and the organism. When cells use nutrient molecules
to make their parts and products, they carry out a sequence
of chemical reactions. **Metabolism** [Gk. *meta,* implying
change] is all the chemical reactions that occur in a cell.

The ultimate source of energy for nearly all life on
earth is the sun. Plants and certain other organisms are able
to capture solar energy and carry on **photosynthesis,** a
process that transforms solar energy into chemical energy
in the bonds of organic nutrient molecules. Animals and
plants get energy by metabolizing the nutrient molecules
made by photosynthesizers.

Remaining Homeostatic

For metabolic processes to continue, living things need to
keep themselves stable in temperature, moisture level, acidity, and other physiological factors. This is **homeostasis** [Gk.
homoios, like, resembling, and *stasis,* standing]—the maintenance of internal conditions within certain boundaries.

Many organisms depend on behavior to regulate their
internal environment. A chilly lizard may raise its internal

temperature by basking in the sun on a hot rock. When it
starts to overheat, it scurries for cool shade. Other organisms have control mechanisms that do not require any con-
scious activity. When a student is so engrossed in her textbook that she forgets to eat lunch, her liver releases stored
sugar to keep the blood sugar level within normal limits.
Hormones regulate sugar storage and release, but in other
instances the nervous system is involved in maintaining
homeostasis.

Living Things Respond

Living things find energy and/or nutrients by interacting
with their surroundings. Even unicellular organisms can respond to their environment. In some, the beating of microscopic hairs, and in others, the snapping of whiplike tails,
moves them toward or away from light or chemicals. Multicellular organisms can manage more complex responses. A
vulture can smell meat a mile away and soar toward dinner.
A monarch butterfly can sense the approach of fall and begin
its flight south where resources are still abundant.

The ability to respond often results in movement: the
leaves of a plant turn toward the sun and animals dart
toward safety. Appropriate responses help ensure survival
of the organism and allow it to carry on its daily activities.
All together, we call these activities the behavior of the
organism.

Figure 1.3 Adaptations of rockhopper penguins, *Eudyptes.*
Male and female rockhoppers with their offspring. The stubby forelimbs of penguins are modified as flippers for fast swimming. Only a little over a half meter tall, rockhopper penguins are named for their skill in leaping from rock to rock.

Living Things Have Adaptations

Adaptations [L. *ad,* toward, and *aptus,* fit, suitable] are modifications that make organisms suited to their way of life. For example, penguins are adapted to an aquatic existence in the Antarctic (Fig. 1.3). Most birds have forelimbs proportioned for flying, but a penguin has stubby, flattened wings suitable for swimming. Their feet and tails serve as rudders in the water, but the flat feet also allow them to walk on land. Rockhopper penguins have a bill adapted to eating small shellfish. Their eggs—one, or at most two—are carried on their feet, where they are protected by a pouch of skin. This allows the birds to huddle together for warmth while standing erect and incubating eggs.

Organisms become modified over time by a process called **natural selection.** Certain members of a **species** [L. *species,* model, kind], defined as a group of interbreeding individuals, may inherit a genetic change that causes them to be better suited to a particular environment. These members can be expected to produce more surviving offspring who also have the favorable characteristic. In this way, the attributes of the species' members change over time.

Living Things Reproduce and Develop

Life comes only from life. Every type of living thing can **reproduce,** or make another organism like itself (Fig. 1.3). Bacteria, protozoa, and other unicellular organisms simply split in two. In most multicellular organisms, the reproductive process begins with the pairing of a sperm from one partner and an egg from the other partner. The union of sperm and egg, followed by many cell divisions, results in an immature individual, which grows and develops through various stages to become the adult.

An embryo develops into a sperm whale or a yellow daffodil because of a blueprint inherited from its parents. The blueprint or instructions for their organization and metabolism are encoded in the genes. The **genes,** which contain specific information for how the organism is to be ordered, are made of long molecules of DNA (deoxyribonucleic acid). All cells have a copy of the hereditary material, DNA, whose shape resembles a spiral staircase with millions of steps.

Descent with Modification

All living things share the same basic characteristics discussed in this chapter. They are all composed of cells organized in a similar manner. Their genes are composed of DNA, and they carry out the same metabolic reactions to acquire energy and maintain their organization. This unity suggests that all living things are descended from a common ancestor—the first cell or cells. However, **evolution** [L. *evolutio,* an unrolling] is descent with modification. One species can give rise to several species, each adapted to a particular set of environmental conditions. Specific adaptations allow species to play particular roles in an ecosystem. The diversity of life-forms is best understood in terms of the many different ways in which organisms carry on their life functions within an ecosystem where they live, acquire energy, and reproduce.

Descent from a common ancestor explains the unity of life. Adaptations to different ways of life account for the great diversity of life-forms.

1.2 How the Biosphere Is Organized

Individual organisms belong to a **population,** all the members of a species within a **community.** All communities taken together make up the **biosphere** [Gk. *bios,* life, and L. *sphaera,* ball], a thin layer of life that encircles earth. One of the most interesting discoveries about communities is that they are highly dynamic. The number of species, kinds of species, and size of populations within most communities is constantly changing due to disturbances and climatic variability. Because species composition is so variable, ecologists often concentrate on studying the movement of energy and nutrients through communities. Such a study involves the physical environment. The populations within a community interact among themselves and with the physical environment (soil, atmosphere, etc.), forming an **ecosystem** [Gk. *oikos,* home, house, and *systema,* ordered arrangement].

A major feature of the interactions between populations of a community pertains to who eats whom. Plants produce organic nutrients for themselves, and the animals that eat plants are food for other animals. Such a sequence of organisms is called a food chain (Fig. 1.4).

Both plants and animals interact with the physical environment. Plants take in inorganic nutrients, like carbon dioxide and water; both plants and animals return carbon dioxide to the atmosphere when they respire. When organisms die and decay, inorganic nutrients are made available to plants once more. The blue arrows in Figure 1.4 show how chemicals cycle through the various populations of an ecosystem.

In contrast, the yellow to red arrows in Figure 1.4 show how energy flows through an ecosystem: solar energy used by plants to produce organic nutrients is eventually converted to heat when organisms, including plants, use organic nutrients as an energy source. Therefore, a constant supply of solar energy is required for an ecosystem and for life to exist.

The ecosystems that make up the biosphere are classified first as terrestrial or aquatic. Among the terrestrial ecosystems, tropical rain forests are of extreme interest at present because of their great diversity and the threat of their imminent destruction as discussed in the reading on page 7.

In ecosystems, the same nutrients keep cycling through populations, but energy flows because it is eventually converted to heat.

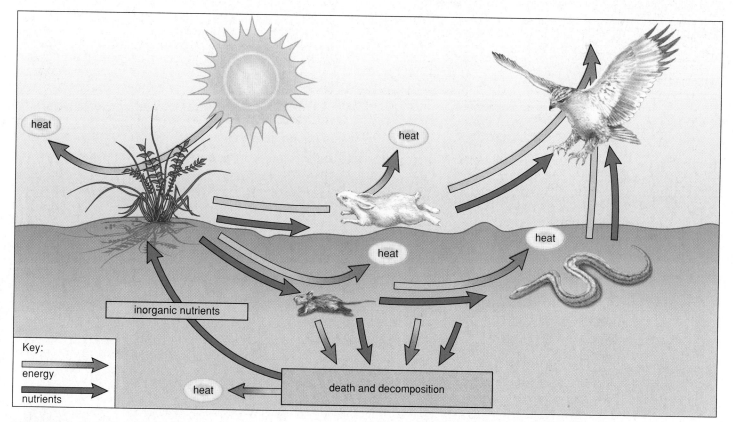

Figure 1.4 Ecosystem organization.
Within an ecosystem, nutrients cycle (see blue arrows): from plants, which use solar energy and inorganic nutrients to produce organic nutrients, to decomposers, which make inorganic nutrients available to plants once more. Energy flows (see yellow to red arrows) from the sun through all populations and eventually is converted to heat which dissipates.

Tropical Rain Forest, a Terrestrial Ecosystem

Of all the ecosystems, the greatest diversity of species occurs in tropical rain forests. They are found near the equator where there is plentiful sun and rainfall the entire year. Major rain forests are located in South America (Fig. 1.5), central and west Africa, and Southeast Asia. Rain forests have a multilayered canopy which consists of broad-leaved evergreen trees of different heights. Most animal populations live in the canopy where they interact with each other. Typically, brightly colored birds, such as toucans and macaws, fly around eating fruits, buds, and pollen. Other birds, such as long-billed hummingbirds feed on nectar often taken from small plants that grow independently on the trees. Tree sloths and spider monkeys are mammals that live in the canopy and are preyed upon by jaguars. Other canopy animals include butterflies, tree frogs, and dart-poison frogs. Many canopy animals, such as bats, are active only at night. Snakes, spiders, and ants are animals that live on or near the ground and not in the canopy.

morpho butterfly, *Morpho*

toco toucan, *Ramphastos*

jaguar, *Panthera*

dart-poison frog, *Dendrobates*

epiphytic orchid, *Lycaste*

Figure 1.5 Tropical rain forest populations interact in the manner described in Figure 1.4.

Tropical Rain Forests: Can We Live Without Them?

So far, nearly 2 million species of organisms have been discovered and named. Two-thirds of the plant species, 90% of the nonhuman primates, 40% of birds of prey, and 90% of the insects live in the tropics. Many more species of organisms (perhaps as many as 30 million) are estimated to live in the tropical rain forests but have not yet been discovered.

Ten years ago tropical forests spanned the planet on both sides of the equator and covered 6–7% of the total land surface of the earth—an area roughly equivalent to our contiguous forty-eight states. Every year humans destroy an area of forest equivalent to the size of Oklahoma. At this rate, these forests and the species they contain will disappear completely in just a few more decades. If the forest areas now legally protected survive, 56–72% of all tropical forest species would still be lost.

The loss of tropical rain forests results from an interplay of social, economic, and political pressures. Many people already live in the forest, and as their numbers increase, more of the land is cleared for farming. People move to the forests because internationally financed projects build roads and open the forests up for exploitation. Small-scale farming accounts for about 60% of tropical deforestation, and this is followed by commercial logging, cattle ranching, and mining. International demand for timber promotes destructive logging of rain forests in Southeast Asia and South America. A market for low-grade beef encourages the conversion of tropical rain forests to pastures for cattle. The lure of gold draws miners to rain forests in Costa Rica and Brazil.

The destruction of tropical rain forests produces only short-term benefits but is expected to cause long-term problems. The forests soak up rainfall during the wet season and release it during the dry season. Without them, a regional yearly regime of flooding followed by drought is expected to destroy property and reduce agricultural harvests. Worldwide, there could be changes in climate that would affect the entire human race. On the other hand, the preservation of tropical rain forests offers benefits. For example, the rich diversity of plants and animals would continue to exist for scientific and pharmacological study. One-fourth of the medicines we currently use come from tropical rain forests. The rosy periwinkle from Madagascar has produced two potent drugs for use against Hodgkin's disease, leukemia, and other blood cancers. It is hoped that many of the still-unknown plants will provide medicines for other human ills.

Studies show that if the forests were used as a sustainable source of nonwood products, such as nuts, fruits, and latex rubber, they would generate as much or more revenue while continuing to perform their various ecological functions. And biodiversity could still be preserved. Brazil is exploring the concept of "extractive reserves," in which plant and animal products are harvested but the forest itself is not cleared. Ecologists have also proposed "forest farming" systems, which mimic the natural forest as much as possible while providing abundant yields. But for such plans to work maximally, the human population size and the resource consumption per person must be stabilized.

Preserving tropical rain forests is a wise investment. Such action promotes the survival of most of the world's species—indeed, the human species, too.

The Human Population

The human population tends to modify existing ecosystems for its own purposes. As more and more ecosystems are converted to towns and cities, fewer of the natural cycles are able to function adequately to sustain an ever growing human population. It is important to do all we can to preserve ecosystems, because only then can we be assured that we will continue to exist. The recognition that natural ecosystems need to be conserved is one of the most important developments of our new ecological awareness.

We now know that tropical rain forests perform many services for us. For example, they act like a giant sponge and absorb carbon dioxide, a pollutant that pours into the atmosphere from the burning of fossil fuels such as oil and coal. If rain forests continue to be depleted as they are now, an increased amount of carbon dioxide in the atmosphere is expected to cause an increase in the average daily temperature. Problems with acid rain are also expected to increase, since carbon dioxide combines with water to form carbonic acid, a component of acid rain.

The present **biodiversity** (number and size of populations in a community) of our planet is being threatened. It has been estimated that the number of species in the biosphere may be as high as 80 million species, but only about 2 million have been identified and named. We may never have a chance to identify all there are because we may be presently losing from 24 to even 100 species a day due to human activities. The existence of the species featured in Figure 1.5 is threatened because tropical rain forests are being reduced in size. Most biologists are alarmed over the present rate of extinction and believe the rate may eventually rival the mass extinctions that have periodically occurred during our planet's history.

Because all living things are dependent upon the normal functioning of the biosphere, the wisest approach is to conserve ecosystems as much as possible.

1.3 How Living Things Are Classified

Since life is so diverse it is helpful to have a classification system to group organisms according to their similarities (see Appendix B). **Taxonomy** [Gk. *tasso*, arrange, classify, and *nomos*, usage, law] is the discipline of identifying and classifying organisms according to certain rules. Biologists give each living thing a binomial [L. *bis*, two, and *nomen*, name] or two-part name. For example, the scientific name for the garden pea is *Pisum sativum*. The first word is the genus and the second word is the specific epithet of a species within a genus. Species are grouped into ever more inclusive categories: genera, families, orders, classes, phyla, kingdoms, and finally domains.

It has been common practice the past few years to recognize five kingdoms (called Monera, Protista, Fungi, Plantae, and Animalia) but biochemical evidence now suggests that kingdoms should be organized into three higher categories called domains. Further, both domain Bacteria and domain Archaea contain unicellular prokaryotes which are structurally simple but metabolically complex. They lack a membrane bounded nucleus found in the eukaryotes of domain Eukarya. Domain Eukarya contains the kingdoms most familiar to most (Fig. 1.6). Protists (kingdom Protista) range from unicellular to multicellular organisms and include the algae and protozoans. Among the fungi (kingdom Fungi) are the familiar molds and mushrooms. Plants (kingdom Plantae) are well known as multicellular photosynthesizers of the world while animals (kingdom Animalia) are multicellular and ingest their food.

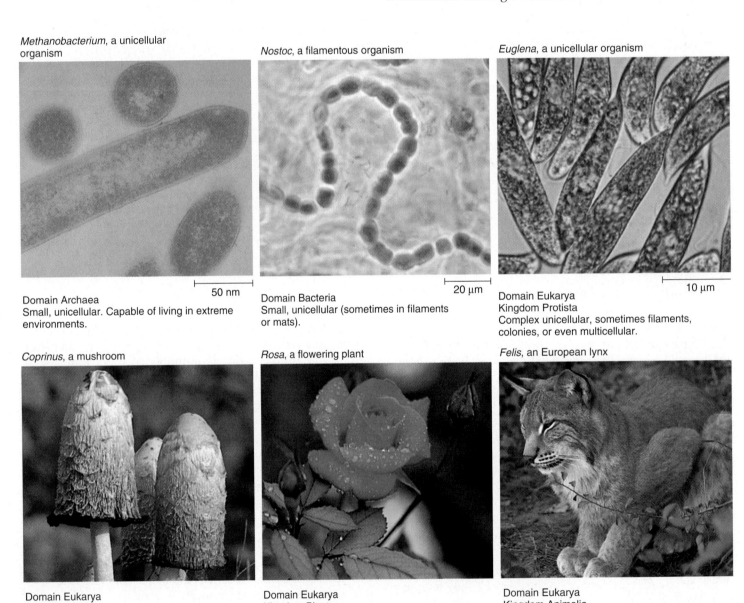

Methanobacterium, a unicellular organism

50 nm

Domain Archaea
Small, unicellular. Capable of living in extreme environments.

Nostoc, a filamentous organism

20 μm

Domain Bacteria
Small, unicellular (sometimes in filaments or mats).

Euglena, a unicellular organism

10 μm

Domain Eukarya
Kingdom Protista
Complex unicellular, sometimes filaments, colonies, or even multicellular.

Coprinus, a mushroom

Domain Eukarya
Kingdom Fungi
Multicellular and absorb food.

Rosa, a flowering plant

Domain Eukarya
Kingdom Plantae
Multicellular and photosynthesize.

Felis, an European lynx

Domain Eukarya
Kingdom Animalia
Multicellular and ingest food.

Figure 1.6 **Pictorial representation of the three domains of life.**

1.4 The Process of Science

Biology is the scientific study of life. Religion, aesthetics, ethics, and, science, are all ways that human beings have of finding order in the natural world. Science differs from other human ways of knowing and learning by its process. **Science** considers only what is observable by the senses or by instruments that extend the ability of the senses as a way to understand the natural world. Microscopes extend the ability of sight way beyond what can be seen by the naked eye, for example. Observations can be made by any one of our five senses; we can observe with our noses that dinner is almost ready; observe with our fingertips that a surface is smooth and cold; and observe with our ears that a piano needs tuning. Observations help scientists conduct various types of investigations.

Once a scientist becomes interested in an observable event, called a **phenomenon,** he or she will most likely study up on it. The goal will be to find any past studies by using the Internet, the library, or other scientists to discover what ideas there may be about this phenomenon. Then a scientist uses inductive reasoning to formulate a hypothesis. **Inductive reasoning** occurs when a person uses isolated facts and creative thinking to come up with a possible explanation. In this case, the possible explanation is called a **hypothesis.** All past experiences of the individual no matter what they be, will most likely influence the formulation of a hypothesis. Einstein said that aesthetic qualities like beauty and simplicity helped him to formulate his hypotheses about the workings of the universe. Indeed, most every scientist looks favorably upon the simplest hypothesis for a phenomenon and tests that one first.

Science only considers hypotheses that can be tested. Moral and religious beliefs while very important to our lives differ between cultures and through time and they are not always testable by further observations and/or experimentation. Hypotheses are tested either in the laboratory setting or in a natural setting. The laboratory is a place that lends itself to carrying on **experiments,** which are artificial situations devised to test hypotheses. Experiments can also be carried out in a natural setting, called the field.

A Field Investigation

David P. Barash, who was observing the mating behavior of mountain bluebirds, decided to perform an experiment to test the hypothesis that aggression of the male varies during the reproductive cycle (Fig. 1.7). Once the hypothesis has been stated, deductive reasoning comes into play. **Deductive reasoning** begins with a general statement that infers a specific conclusion. It often takes the form of an "if, then" statement. In this case, if male aggression varies during the reproductive cycle, then aggression may change after the nest is built, after the first egg is laid, and after the hatching of the eggs.

a. Scientist makes observations, studies previous data, and formulates a hypothesis.

b. Scientist performs experiment and collects objective data.

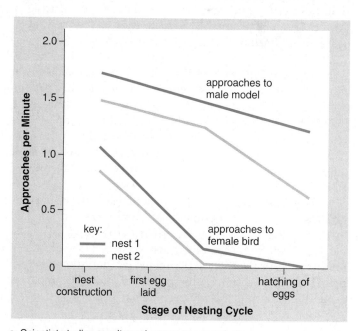

c. Scientist studies results and comes to a conclusion.

Figure 1.7 An experiment in the field.
a. Observation of male bluebird behavior allowed David Barash to formulate a testable hypothesis. Then, he **(b)** collected data and **(c)** displayed in a graph. Finally, he came to a conclusion.

Barash posted a male bluebird model near nests while the resident male was out foraging. The behavior of the male toward the model and toward his female mate were noted during the first ten minutes of the male's return. Aggression was most severe when the male model was presented before the first egg was laid, less severe when the model was presented after an egg was laid, and least severe after the eggs had hatched (see Fig. 1.7).

Experiments are considered more rigorous when they include a control group. Control in this context does not refer to the power of the experimenter—rather it refers to the validity of the experimental results. A **control group** experiences all the steps in the experiment but does not contain the variable being tested. Barash used a control group. He posted a male robin instead of a male bluebird near certain nests. (The male bluebirds did not respond at all to the robin model.) When an experiment has a control group, we know that the results are due to the variable being tested and not due to some nonidentifiable chance event that occurred during the experiment.

The Experimental Results

The results of an experiment are referred to as the **data.** Data often take the form of a table or a graph that allows one to see the results in an organized manner. Barash's data are shown in Figure 1.7. Data should be objective rather than subjective, and mathematical data are conducive to objectivity. For example, Barash didn't report that it seemed to him that the male bluebirds were more aggressive before the eggs were laid (subjective); rather, he defined aggression as the "number of approaches per minute" (objective) and reported that number. When Mendel, the father of genetics, did a pea cross concerning height, he didn't report that he could tell at a glance there were more tall than short plants; he reported that the ratio was three tall to every short plant. In fact, Mendel repeated one particular experiment so many times that he counted 7,324 peas!

To ensure that the results are not due to chance or some unknown variable, experiments are often repeated not only by the original scientist but by others in the same area of expertise. Therefore, scientists must keep careful records of how they perform their experiments so that others can repeat them. If the same results are not obtained over and over again, the experiment is not considered valid.

The Conclusion

After studying the results, the experimenter comes to a **conclusion** whether the results support or **falsify** (show to be untrue) the hypothesis. The data allowed Barash to conclude that aggression in male bluebirds is related to their reproductive cycle. Therefore, his hypothesis was supported. If male bluebirds were always aggressive even toward male robin models, his hypothesis would have been proven false.

Science progresses and any hypothesis may have to be modified in the future. There is always the possibility that a more sophisticated experiment using perhaps more advanced technology might falsify the hypothesis. Therefore, a scientist never says that the data "prove" the hypothesis to be "true." Because of this feature, some think of science as what is left after alternative hypotheses have been rejected.

Scientists report their findings in scientific journals so that their methodology and results are available to the scientific community. Barash reported his experiment in the *American Naturalist*.[1] The reporting of experiments results in accumulated data that will help other scientists formulate hypotheses. Also, it results in a body of information that is made known to the general public through the publishing of books, such as this biology textbook.

A Laboratory Investigation

When scientists are studying a phenomenon, they often perform experiments in a laboratory where conditions can be kept constant. A **variable** in a controlled experiment is a factor that can cause an observable change during the experiment. The component in an experiment being tested is called the **experimental variable;** in other words, the investigator deliberately manipulates this step of the experiment. Then the investigator observes the effects of the experiment. In other words, he or she observes the **dependent variable:**

Experimental Variable	Dependent Variable
Component of the experiment being tested	Result or change that occurs due to the experimental variable

Suppose, for example, physiologists want to determine if sweetener S is a safe food additive. On the basis of available information, they formulate a hypothesis that sweetener S is a safe food additive even when 50% of diet is sweetener S. They decide on testing these two groups:

Test group: 50% of diet is sweetener S

Control group: diet contains no sweetener S

[1] Barash, D. P. 1976. The male responds to apparent female adultery in the mountain bluebird, *Sialia currucoides:* An evolutionary interpretation. *American Naturalist* 110: 1097–1101.

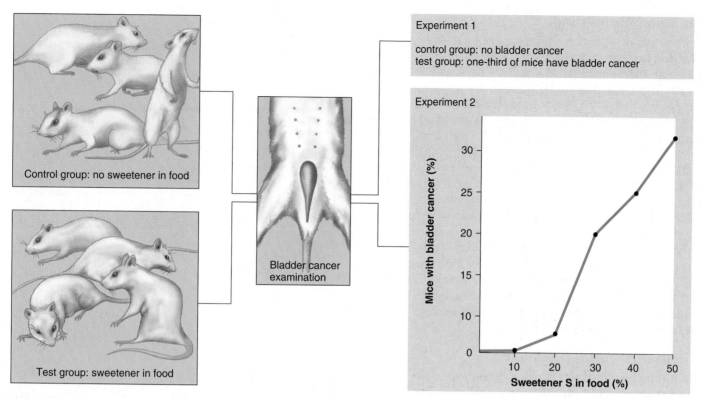

Figure 1.8 A controlled experiment.
Genetically similar mice are randomly divided into a control group and (a) test group(s) that contain 100 mice each. All groups are exposed to same conditions, such as housing, temperature, and water supply. The control group is not subjected to sweetener S in the food. At the end of an experiment all mice are examined for bladder cancer. The results of experiment 1 and experiment 2, which are described in the text, are shown on the far right.

To help ensure that the two groups are identical, the researchers place a certain number of randomly chosen inbred (genetically identical) mice into the various groups—say, 100 mice per group. If any of the mice are different from the others, it is hoped random selection has distributed them evenly among the groups. The researchers also make sure that all conditions, such as availability of water, cage setup, and temperature of the surroundings, are the same for both groups. The food for each group is exactly the same except for the amount of sweetener S.

At the end of the experiment, both groups of mice are to be examined for bladder cancer. Let's suppose that one-third of the mice in the test group are found to have bladder cancer, while none in the control group have bladder cancer. The results of this experiment do not support the hypothesis that sweetener S is a safe food additive when 50% of diet is sweetener S.

Continuing the Experiment

Science is ongoing, and one experiment frequently leads to another. Physiologists might now wish to hypothesize that sweetener S is safe if the diet contains a limited amount of sweetener S. They feed sweetener S to groups of mice at ever-greater concentrations:

Group 1: diet contains no sweetener S (the control)

Group 2: 5% of diet is sweetener S

Group 3: 10% of diet is sweetener S

↓

Group 11: 50% of diet is sweetener S

Again the data is presented in the form of a table or a graph (Fig. 1.8). Researchers might run a statistical test to determine if the difference in the number of cases of bladder cancer between the various groups is significant. After all, if a significant number of mice in the control group develop cancer, the results are invalid. Scientists prefer mathematical data because such data lends itself to objectivity.

On the basis of the data, the experimenters try to develop a recommendation concerning the safety of sweetener S in the food of humans. They might caution, for example, that the intake of sweetener S beyond 10% of the diet is associated with too great a risk of bladder cancer.

Laboratory experiments have a control group, which is not exposed to the experimental variable.

The Scientific Method

The process of science is often described in terms of the **scientific method.** Some scientists object to outlining the steps of the scientific method as is done in Figure 1.9 because such a diagram suggests a rigid methodology. Actually, scientists approach their work in many different ways and even sometimes make discoveries by chance. The most famous case pertains to penicillin. When examining a petri dish in 1928, Alexander Fleming noticed an area around a mold that was free of bacteria. Upon investigating, Fleming found that the mold produced an antibacterial substance he called penicillin. Penicillin was later mass produced and is still a successfully used antibiotic in humans today.

A discussion of the scientific process is not complete without an admission that scientists do have to accept certain assumptions. They have to believe, for example, that nature is real and understandable and knowable by observing it; that nature is orderly and uniform; that measurements yield knowledge of the thing measured; and that natural laws are not affected by time.

Scientific Theories in Biology

The ultimate goal of science is to understand the natural world in terms of **scientific theories,** which are concepts that join together well-supported and related hypotheses. In a movie, a detective may claim to have a theory about the crime. Or you may say that you have a theory about the won-lost record of your favorite baseball team. But in science, the word *theory* is reserved for a conceptual scheme that is supported by a broad range of observations, experiments, and data.

Some of the basic theories of biology are:

Name of Theory	Explanation
Cell	All organisms are composed of cells.
Biogenesis	Life comes only from life.
Evolution	All living things have a common ancestor and are adapted to a particular way of life.
Gene	Organisms contain coded information that dictates their form, function, and behavior.

Evolution is the unifying concept of biology because it pertains to many different aspects of living things. For example, the theory of evolution enables scientists to understand the history of life, the variety of living things, and the anatomy, physiology, and development of organisms—even their behavior.

Barash gave an evolutionary interpretation to his results. It was adaptive, he said, for male bluebirds to be less aggressive after the first egg is laid because by that time the male bird is "sure the offspring is his own" and maladaptive for the male bird to waste time and energy being too aggressive toward a rival and his mate after hatching because his offspring are already present. (When an organism is adapted to its environment, it is better able to survive and produce offspring.)

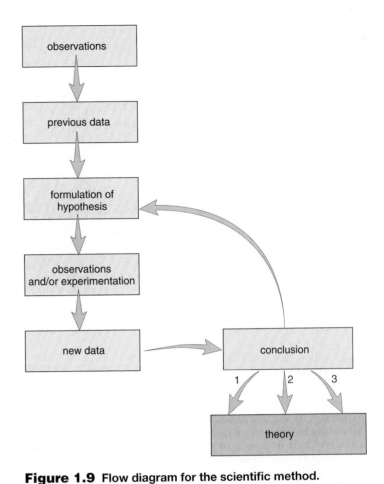

Figure 1.9 Flow diagram for the scientific method. On the basis of observations and previous data, a scientist formulates a hypothesis. The hypothesis is tested by further observations or a controlled experiment, and new data either support or falsify the hypothesis. The return arrow indicates that a scientist often chooses to retest the same hypothesis or to test a related hypothesis. Conclusions from many different but related experiments may lead to the development of a scientific theory. For example, studies pertaining to development, anatomy, and fossil remains all support the theory of evolution.

Fruitful theories are ones that help scientists generate new hypotheses, and the theory of evolution has been a very fruitful theory. In fact, it probably helped Barash develop the hypothesis he chose to test. Because the theory of evolution has been supported by so many observations and experiments for over 100 years, some biologists refer to the **principle** of evolution, suggesting that this is the appropriate term for theories that are generally accepted by an overwhelming number of scientists. The term **law** instead of principle is preferred by some. In another chapter concerning energy relationships, for example, we will examine the laws of thermodynamics.

The scientific process eventually enables biologists to arrive at a theory that is generally accepted by all.

Connecting Concepts

What we know about biology and what we'll learn in the future results from objective observation and testing of the natural world. The ultimate goal of science is to understand the natural world in terms of theories—conceptual schemes supported by abundant research and not yet found lacking. Evolution is a theory that accounts for the differences that divide and the unity that joins all living things. All living things have the same levels of organization and function similarly because they are related—even back to the first living cells on earth.

Scientific creationism, which states that God created all species as they are today, cannot be considered science because creationism upholds a supernatural cause rather than a natural cause for events. When faith is involved, a hypothesis cannot be tested in a purely objective way. Just as science does not test religious beliefs, it does not make ethical or moral decisions. The general public may want scientists to label certain research as "good" or "bad" and to predict whether any resulting technology will primarily benefit or harm. Yet science, by its very nature, is impartial and simply attempts to study natural phenomena.

Scientists should provide the public with as much information as possible when such issues as recombinant DNA technology or various methods to preserve the environment are being debated. Then, they, along with other citizens, can help make decisions about what is most likely best for society. All men and women have a responsibility to decide how to use scientific knowledge so that it benefits all living things, including the human species.

This textbook was written to help you understand the scientific process and learn the basic concepts of general biology so that you will be better informed. This chapter introduced you to the levels of biological organization from the cell to the biosphere. The cell, the simplest of living things, is composed of nonliving molecules. Therefore, we must begin our study of biology with a brief look at cellular chemistry. In the next two chapters, you will study some important inorganic and organic molecules in the cell. Then, you will learn how the cell makes use of energy and materials in order to maintain itself and reproduce.

Summary

1.1 How to Define Life

Although living things are diverse, they share certain characteristics in common. Living things (a) are organized, and there are levels of organization from the cell to ecosystems, (b) need an outside source of materials and energy, (c) respond to external stimuli, (d) reproduce, passing on genes to their offspring, and (e) have adaptations suitable to their way of life in a particular environment.

The process of evolution explains both the unity and the diversity of life. Descent from a common ancestor explains why all organisms share the same characteristics, and adaptation to various ways of life explains the diversity of life-forms.

1.2 How the Biosphere Is Organized

Within an ecosystem, populations interact with one another and with the physical environment. Nutrients cycle within and between ecosystems, but energy flows unidirectionally, and eventually becomes heat. Adaptations of organisms allow them to play particular roles within an ecosystem, as when the trees within a tropical rain forest photosynthesize and provide a home for other organisms.

1.3 How Living Things Are Classified

Each living thing is given an italicized binomial name that consists of the genus and specific epithet. For example, *Pisum sativum* is the name of the garden pea. Each species belongs to genus, family, order, class, phylum, kingdom, and finally domain from the least inclusive to the most inclusive category. The three domains of life are Archaea, Bacteria, and Eukarya. The first two domains contain unicellular organisms which are structurally simple but metabolically complex. Domain Eukarya contains the kingdoms Protista, Fungi, Plantae, and Animalia. Protists range from unicellular to multicellular organisms and include the protozoans and algae. Among the fungi are the familiar molds and mushrooms. Plants are well known as multicellular photosynthesizers of the world while animals are multicellular and ingest their food.

1.4 The Process of Science

When studying the world of living things, biologists and other scientists use the scientific process. Observations along with previous data are used to formulate a hypothesis. New observations and/or experiments are carried out in order to test the hypothesis.

Scientists often do controlled experiments. In a controlled experiment, the experimental variable is that portion of the experiment being manipulated and the dependent variable is the change due to the experimental variable. The control group is not exposed to the experimental variable.

New data may support a hypothesis or they may prove it false. Hypotheses cannot be proven true. Several conclusions in a particular area may allow scientists to arrive at a theory—such as the cell theory, gene theory, or the theory of evolution. The theory of evolution is a unifying theory of biology.

Reviewing the Chapter

1. What evidence can you cite to show that living things are organized? 2
2. Why do living things require an outside source of materials and energy? 3
3. What are the common characteristics of life listed in the text? 3–4
4. What is passed from generation to generation when organisms reproduce? What has to happen to the hereditary material DNA in order for evolution to occur? 4
5. How does evolution explain both the unity and the diversity of life? 4
6. What is an ecosystem, and why should human beings preserve ecosystems? 5, 7
7. Explain the scientific name of an organism. What are the categories of classification? What four kingdoms are in the domain Eukarya? 8
8. Describe the series of steps involved in the scientific process. Which of the steps requires the use of inductive reasoning? deductive reasoning? 9
9. Give an example of a laboratory experiment. Name the experimental variable and the dependent variable. 10
10. What is the ultimate goal of science? Give an example that supports your answer. 12

Testing Yourself

Choose the best answer for each question. For questions 1–4, match the statements in the key with the sentences below.

Key:

    a. Living things are organized.
    b. Living things metabolize.
    c. Living things respond.
    d. Living things reproduce.
    e. Living things evolve.

1. Genes made up of DNA are passed from parent to child.
2. Zebras run away from approaching lions.
3. Cells use materials and energy for growth and repair.
4. There are many different kinds of living things.
5. Evolution from the first cell(s) best explains why
    a. ecosystems have populations of organisms.
    b. photosynthesizers produce food.
    c. diverse organisms share common characteristics.
    d. human activities are threatening the biosphere.
    e. All of these are correct.
6. Adaptation to a way of life best explains why living things
    a. display homeostasis.
    b. are diverse.
    c. began as single cells.
    d. are classified into three domains.
    e. mate with their own kind.
7. Into which kingdom would you place a multicellular land organism that carries on photosynthesis?
    a. Protista   d. Animalia
    b. Fungi   e. Archaea
    c. Plantae
8. Which is the experimental variable in the experiment concerning sweetener S?
    a. Conditions like temperature and housing are the same for all groups.
    b. The amount of sweetener S in food.
    c. Two percent of the group fed food that was 10% sweetener S got bladder cancer, and 90% of the group fed food that was 50% sweetener S got bladder cancer.
    d. The data were presented as a graph.
    e. The use of a control versus a test group.
9. Which is the control group in this same experiment?
    a. All mice in this group died because a lab assistant forgot to give them water.
    b. All mice in this group received food that was 10% sweetener S.
    c. All mice in this group received no sweetener S in food.
    d. Some mice in all groups got bladder cancer; therefore, there was no control group.
    e. All of these are correct.
10. With which of these steps in the scientific method do you associate inductive reasoning?
    a. experimentation
    b. conclusion
    c. researching the scientific literature
    d. formulating the hypothesis
    e. Both b and d are correct.
11. An investigator spills dye on a culture plate and then notices that the bacteria live despite exposure to sunlight. He hypothesizes that the dye protects bacteria against death by ultraviolet (UV) light. To test this hypothesis, he decides to expose two hundred culture plates to UV light. One hundred plates contain bacteria and dye; the other hundred plates contain only bacteria. Result: after exposure to UV light, the bacteria on both plates die. Fill in the right-hand portion of this diagram.

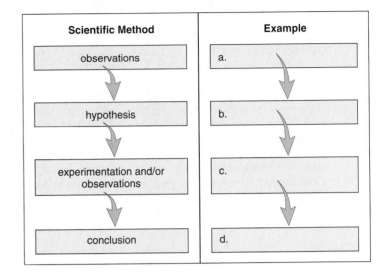

Thinking Scientifically

1. You were part of a study testing a new drug to treat migraine headaches. Some 25% of the control group, which had been given a placebo[2], and 46% of the experimental group reported an improvement in their symptoms. Would you conclude that this is an effective drug? What variables in study participants might have influenced which of them benefited from the new drug?
2. Viruses are small, infectious particles. They have a genome of either DNA or RNA, but no organelles characteristic of cells. They do not divide by mitosis but are duplicated by having their constituent parts produced and assembled by the infected cell. Viruses can evolve in the same way as living things. Genome changes due to random mutations is followed by selection. Would a virus be considered alive? What are the criteria on which you base your answer?

Bioethical Issue

The Endangered Species Act requires the federal government to identify endangered and threatened species and to protect their habitats, even to the extent of purchasing the land where they live. Developers feel that the act protects wildlife at the expense of jobs for U.S. citizens. In an effort to allow development in sensitive areas, it is now possible to move forward after a Habitat Conservation Plan (HCP) is approved. An HCP permits, for instance, new home construction or logging on a part of the land if wildlife habitat is conserved on another part. Habitat conservation can also mean helping the government buy suitable land someplace else.

    The nation's first HCP was approved in 1980. It permitted housing construction on San Bruno Mountain, near San

---

[2] A placebo is an inert substance that looks like the medication taken by the experimental group.

Francisco, if 97% of the living space for the endangered mission blue butterfly was preserved. That sounds pretty good, but over time, hundreds of HCPs have been approved, and the conservation requirement has slipped a bit. Tim Cullinan, a director of the National Audubon Society, recently found that logging companies in the Pacific Northwest are proposing the exchange of habitat on public land for the right to log privately owned, old forests. In other words, nothing has been given up. Today, there are so many HCPs presented, they are rubber-stamped by government officials with no public review at all.

Do you favor development over preservation of habitats or vice versa? Do you think the federal government should be in the business of trying to preserve endangered species? Do you think that public review of HCPs should be allowed, even if it slows down the approval process? Is it the public's responsibility to remain vigilant or is governmental review of HCPs sufficient?

Understanding the Terms

adaptation 4	homeostasis 3
biodiversity 7	hypothesis 9
biology 9	inductive reasoning 9
biosphere 5	law 12
community 5	metabolism 3
conclusion 10	natural selection 4
control group 10	phenomenon 9
data 10	photosynthesis 3
deductive reasoning 9	population 5
dependent variable 10	principle 12
ecosystem 5	reproduce 4
energy 3	science 9
evolution 4	scientific method 12
experiment 9	scientific theory 12
experimental variable 10	species 4
falsify 10	taxonomy 8
gene 4	variable 10

Match the terms to these definitions:

a. _____ All of the chemical reactions that occur in a cell during growth and repair.

b. _____ Changes that occur among members of a species with the passage of time, often resulting in increased adaptation to the prevailing environment.

c. _____ Component in an experiment that is manipulated as a means of testing it.

d. _____ Process by which plants utilize solar energy to make their own organic food.

e. _____ Sample that goes through all the steps of an experiment except the one being tested; a standard against which results of an experiment are checked.

Web Connections

Exploring the Internet

http://www.mhhe.com/biosci/genbio/mader
(click on *Biology 7/e*)

The *Biology 7/e* Online Learning Center provides many resources for studying the material in this chapter including links to the following sites:

Links to Many Specific Career Descriptions. At least 200 links to websites can be found through this site which is updated frequently. An alphabetical listing of occupations in biology allows the user to see websites under many of the listings that include detailed descriptions of careers.

http://www.furman.edu/~snyder/careers/careerlist.html

The Tree of Life explores the phylogenetic relationships between great numbers of organisms and is continually updated.

http://phylogeny.arizona.edu/tree/phylogeny.html

Microscopy Society of America with current information about the society and information on many kinds of microscopy.

http://www.msa.microscopy.com/

National Biological Information Infrastructure. This is a gateway site to biological information from a myriad of sources, both governmental and private. Links abound.

http://www.nbii.gov/index.html

New Scientist. Science and technology news is the focus of this website. Internet Magazine called this the best website in 1995. A must-see site for amateur and professional scientists.

http://www.newscientist.com/

Further Readings for Chapter One

Balick, M. J., and Cox, P. A. 1996. *Plants, people, and culture: The science of ethnobotany.* New York: Scientific American Library. Discusses the importance of rain forest conservation.

Carey, S. S. 1997. *A beginner's guide to scientific method.* 2d ed. Belmont, Calif.: Wadsworth Publishing. The basics of scientific method are explained.

Cox, G. W. 1997. *Conservation biology.* Dubuque, Ia.: Wm. C. Brown Publishers. This text examines the field of conservation, surveys basic principles of ecology, and considers steps to preserve biodiversity.

Dobson, A. P. 1996. *Conservation and biodiversity.* New York: Scientific American Library. Attempts to manage endangered species and preserve biodiversity are presented.

Drewes, F. 1997. *How to study science.* 2d ed. Dubuque, Ia.: Wm. C. Brown Publishers. This supplement shows students how to study, take notes, and interpret text figures.

Johnson, G. B. 1996. *How scientists think.* Dubuque, Ia.: Wm. C. Brown Publishers. Presents 21 fundamental experiments in genetics and molecular biology.

Kellert, S. R. 1996. *The value of life: Biological diversity and human society.* Washington D.C.: Island Press/Shearwater Books. The importance of biological diversity to the well-being of humanity is explored.

Marchuk, W. N. 1992. *A life science lexicon.* Dubuque, Ia.: Wm. C. Brown Publishers. Helps students master life science terms.

Minkoff, E. C., and Baker, P. J. 1996. *Biology today: An issues approach.* New York: The McGraw-Hill Companies, Inc. This introductory text emphasizes understanding of selected biological issues, and discusses each issue's social context.

Primak, R. B. 1995. *A primer of conservation biology.* Sunderland, Mass.: Sinauer Associates. Addresses the loss of biological diversity throughout the world, and suggests remedies.

part

i The Cell

A cell is the basic unit of life, and all living things are composed of cells. Therefore, our knowledge of the structure and function of a cell can be applied directly to the organism. Our study of the cell begins with the atoms and molecules that make up the structure and carry on the functions of cells. Cellular organization requires an ongoing input of matter and energy. Metabolic pathways carry out the transformations needed to keep the cell operational. In most ecosystems, the energy of the sun maintains life. Plant cells, and other types of photosynthetic cells, capture solar energy and store it in molecules that later are a source of matter and energy for all living things.

Cells come from preexisting cells. A better understanding of the regulation of cellular reproduction has contributed greatly to cancer research. Knowledge of chemistry, energy transformations, metabolic pathways, and cellular reproduction increases our ability to keep ourselves healthy and our world fit to live in.

Basic Chemistry

chapter

2

Eastern gray kangaroo, *Macropus giganteus*

A hundred years ago, scientists believed that only nonliving things, like rocks and metals, consisted of chemicals. They thought that living things like kangaroos and sunflowers had a special force, called a vital force, which was necessary for life. Scientific investigation, however, has repeatedly shown that both nonliving and living things have the same physical and chemical bases. Although living things contain molecules not found in inanimate objects, such molecules must still be understood by studying basic chemical properties.

Suppose you have a special interest in kangaroos, and you read books about them and even go to Australia to watch kangaroos in the wild. Still, it would be necessary for you to study chemistry in order to fully understand kangaroos. We perceive the world in terms of whole objects like kangaroos, sunflowers, mushrooms, and humans, but in this chapter you will discover that all organisms consist of atoms and molecules linked together in specific ways that give them properties different from nonliving things. In order to understand how kangaroos jump, the kangaroo expert must study the physical and chemical nature of the kangaroo's muscular system.

2.1 Chemical Elementse

Matter refers to anything that takes up space and has mass. It is helpful to remember that matter can exist as a solid, a liquid, or a gas. Then we can realize that not only are we matter but so too are the water we drink and the air we breathe.

All matter, both nonliving and living, is composed of certain basic substances called **elements.** It is quite remarkable that there are only 92 naturally occurring elements. We know these are elements because they cannot be broken down to substances with different properties (a property is a chemical or physical characteristic, such as density, solubility, melting point, and reactivity).

Both the earth's crust and organisms are made up of elements, but they differ as to which ones are predominant (Fig. 2.1). Only six elements—carbon, hydrogen, nitrogen, oxygen, phosphorus, and sulfur—make up most (about 98%) of the body weight of most organisms. The acronym CHNOPS helps us remember these six elements. The properties of these elements are essential to the uniqueness of living things from cells to organisms.

All living and nonliving things are matter composed of elements. Six elements in particular are commonly found in living things.

Figure 2.1 Elements of earth's crust and organisms. The earth's crust primarily contains the elements oxygen, silicon, and aluminum. Organisms primarily contain the elements hydrogen, oxygen, carbon, and nitrogen. Along with phosphorus and sulfur, these elements make up most biological molecules.

Atomic Structure

In the early 1800s, the English scientist John Dalton proposed that elements actually contain tiny particles called **atoms** [Gk. *atomos*, uncut, indivisible]. He also deduced that there is only one type of atom in each type of element. You can see why, then, the name assigned to each element is the same as the name assigned to the type of atom it contains. Some of the names we use for the elements (atoms) are derived from English and some are derived from Latin. One or two letters create the **atomic symbol,** which stands for this name. For example, the symbol H stands for a hydrogen atom, and the symbol Na (for *natrium* in Latin) stands for a sodium atom. Table 2.1 gives the atomic symbols for the other elements (atoms) commonly found in living things.

From our discussion of elements, we would expect each atom to have a certain mass. The mass of an atom is in turn dependent upon the presence of certain subatomic particles. Although physicists have identified a number of subatomic particles, we will consider only the most stable of these: **protons, neutrons,** and **electrons** [Gk. *elektron*, amber, electricity]. Protons and neutrons are located within the nucleus of an atom, and electrons move about the nucleus. Figure 2.2 shows the arrangement of the subatomic particles in helium, an atom that has only two electrons. In Figure 2.2*a*, the stippling shows the probable location of electrons, and in Figure 2.2*b*, the circle represents the average location of electrons.

Table 2.1

Common Elements in Living Things

Element*	Atomic Symbol	Atomic Number	Atomic Mass**
Hydrogen	H	1	1
Carbon	C	6	12
Nitrogen	N	7	14
Oxygen	O	8	16
Sodium	Na	11	23
Magnesium	Mg	12	24
Phosphorus	P	15	31
Sulfur	S	16	32
Chlorine	Cl	17	35
Potassium	K	19	39
Calcium	Ca	20	40

The atomic number gives the number of protons (and electrons in electrically neutral atoms). The number of neutrons is equal to the atomic mass minus the atomic number.

* In the Periodic Table of the Elements (see inside back cover) and here, elements are arranged in order of ascending atomic number and mass.

** Average of most common isotopes.

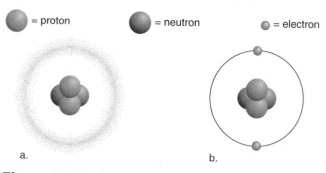

Figure 2.2 Model of helium (He).
Atoms contain subatomic particles, which are located as shown. Protons and neutrons are found within the nucleus, and electrons are outside the nucleus. **a.** The stippling shows the probable location of the electrons in the helium atom. **b.** The average location of electrons is sometimes represented by a circle.

Our concept of an atom has changed greatly since Dalton's day. If we could draw an atom the size of a football field, the nucleus would be like a gumball in the center of the field and the electrons would be tiny specks whirling about in the upper stands. Most of an atom is empty space. We should also realize that we can only indicate where the electrons are expected to be most of the time. In our analogy, the electrons may even stray outside the stadium at times.

In effect, the **atomic mass** of an atom is just about equal to the sum of its protons and neutrons. Protons and neutrons are assigned one atomic mass unit each. Electrons are so small that their mass is assumed to be zero in most calculations (Table 2.2). The term atomic mass is preferred over the term atomic weight because mass is constant while weight changes according to the gravitational force of a planet. The gravitational force of the earth is greater than that of the moon, therefore substances weigh less on the moon even though their mass has not changed.

All atoms of an element have the same number of protons. This is called the atom's **atomic number.** In Table 2.1, atoms are listed according to increasing atomic number, as they are in the periodic table of the elements found inside the back cover. This indicates that it is the number of protons (i.e., the atomic number) that makes an atom unique. The atomic number is often written as a subscript to the lower left of the atomic symbol. The atomic mass is often written as a superscript to the upper left of the atomic symbol. For example, the carbon atom can be noted in this way:

$$\text{atomic mass} \longrightarrow {}^{12}_{6}\mathbf{C} \longleftarrow \text{atomic symbol}$$
atomic number

Atoms have an atomic symbol, mass, and number. The subatomic particles (protons, neutrons, and electrons) determine the characteristics of atoms.

Table 2.2

Subatomic Particles

Particle	Electric Charge	Atomic Mass	Location
Proton	+1	1	Nucleus
Neutron	0	1	Nucleus
Electron	−1	0	Electron shells

Isotopes

The atomic mass given in Table 2.1 is the average mass of each type of atoms listed. This is because atoms of the same element may differ in the number of neutrons. Atoms of the same element that have the same number of protons, and differ only in the number of neutrons, are called **isotopes** [Gk. *isos*, equal, and *topos*, place]. Three isotopes of carbon can be written in the following manner:

$$ {}^{12}_{6}\mathbf{C} \quad {}^{13}_{6}\mathbf{C} \quad {}^{14}_{6}\mathbf{C} $$

Carbon 12 has six neutrons, carbon 13 has seven neutrons, and carbon 14 has eight neutrons. Unlike the other two isotopes, carbon 14 is unstable; it breaks down into elements with lower atomic numbers. When it decays, it emits radiation in the form of radioactive particles or radiant energy. Therefore carbon 14 (^{14}C) is called a **radioactive isotope.**

Isotopes have many uses. Because proportions of isotopes in various food sources are known, biologists can now determine the proportion of isotopes in mummified or fossilized human tissues to know what ancient peoples ate. Radioactive isotopes are used as tracers in biochemical experiments. For example, ^{14}C was used to detect the sequential biochemical steps that occur during photosynthesis. And because ^{14}C decays at a known rate, the amount of ^{14}C remaining is often used to determine the age of fossils.

Radioactive isotopes are also used in medicine. If a patient is injected with radioactive iodine, the thyroid gland will take it up, and a scan of the thyroid will indicate if any abnormality is present. Glucose labeled with a radioactive isotope can be injected into the body and will be taken up by metabolically active tissues. In PET (positron emission tomography), the radiation given off is used by a computer to generate cross-sectional images that indicate the metabolic activity of various tissues.

Atoms of the same element that have the same number of protons but a different number of neutrons and a different mass are called isotopes.

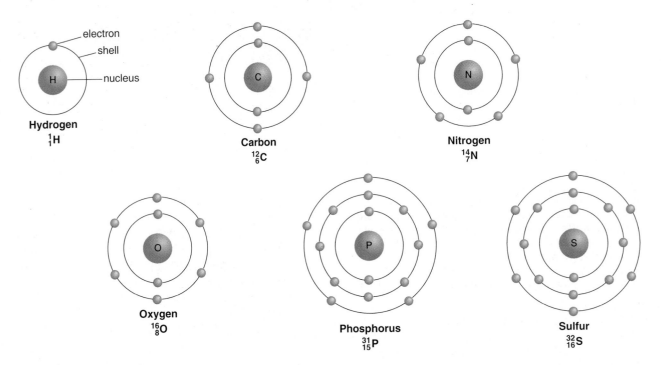

Figure 2.3 Bohr models of atoms.
Electrons are placed in energy levels (electron shells) according to certain rules: the first shell can contain up to two electrons, and each shell thereafter can contain up to eight electrons as long as we consider only atoms with an atomic number of 20 or below. Each shell is to be filled before electrons are placed in the next shell.

Energy Levels

Protons and electrons carry a charge; protons have a positive (+) electrical charge, and electrons have a negative (−) electrical charge. When an atom is electrically neutral, the number of protons equals the number of electrons. Therefore, in electrically neutral atoms, the atomic number tells you the number of protons and the number of electrons. For example, a carbon atom has six protons, and when electrically neutral, it also has six electrons.

In 1913, the Danish physicist Niels Bohr proposed that electrons orbit in concentric energy levels (called **electron shells**) about the nucleus. He based his model on a previous discovery that although electrons have the same mass and charge, they vary in energy content. **Energy** is defined as the ability to do work. Electrons differ in the amount of their potential energy, that is, stored energy ready to do work. The electron shells indicate the relative amounts of stored energy electrons have. Electrons with the least amount of potential energy are located in the shell closest to the nucleus, called the *K* shell. Electrons in the next higher shell, called the *L* shell, have more energy, and so forth, as we proceed from shell to shell outside the nucleus.

An analogy may help you appreciate that the farther electrons are from the nucleus, the more potential energy they possess. Falling water has energy, as witnessed by how it can turn a waterwheel connected to a shaft that transfers the energy to machinery for grinding grain, cutting wood, or weaving cloth. The higher the waterfall, the greater the amount of energy released per unit amount of water. The potential energy possessed by electrons is not due to gravity; it is due to the attraction between the positively charged protons and the negatively charged electrons. It takes energy to keep an electron farther away from the nucleus as opposed to closer to the nucleus. You have often heard that sunlight provides the energy for photosynthesis in green plants, but it may come as a surprise to learn that when a pigment such as chlorophyll absorbs the energy of the sun, electrons move to higher energy levels about nuclei.

Figure 2.3 shows you how the Bohr model helps you determine how many electrons are in the outer shell of an atom. For atoms up to an atomic number of 20 (i.e., calcium), the first shell can contain as many as two electrons; thereafter, each additional shell can contain eight electrons. For these atoms, each lower shell is filled with electrons before the next higher shell contains any electrons. The sulfur atom, with an atomic number of 16, has three shells (two electrons in the first shell, eight electrons in the second shell, and six electrons in the third, or outer, shell).

In the periodic table (see inside back cover), elements are arranged in rows according to the number of electrons in the outer shell. If an atom has only one shell, the outer shell

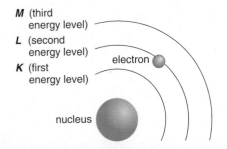

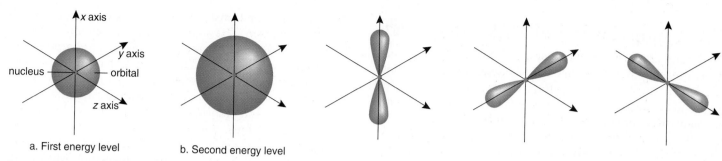

a. First energy level   b. Second energy level

Figure 2.4 Electron orbitals.
Each electron energy level (see Fig. 2.3) has one or more orbitals, a volume of space in which the rapidly moving electrons are most likely found. The nucleus is at the intersection of *x*, *y*, and *z* axes. **a.** The first energy level (electron shell) has only one orbital, which has a spherical shape. Two electrons can occupy this orbital. **b.** The second energy level has one spherically-shaped orbital and three dumbbell-shaped orbitals at right angles to each other. Since two electrons can occupy each orbital, there are a total of eight electrons in the second electron shell. **c.** The orbitals of the second shell superimposed on one another. **d.** When the orbitals of the second shell hybridize, teardrop-shaped orbitals point toward the corners of a tetrahedron (a triangular pyramid).

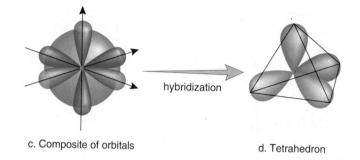

c. Composite of orbitals   d. Tetrahedron

is complete when it has two electrons. Otherwise, the **octet rule,** which states that the outer shell is most stable when it has eight electrons, holds. Atoms with eight electrons in the outer shell do not ordinarily react; they are said to be inert. Atoms with fewer than eight electrons in the outer shell react with other atoms in such a way that after the reaction, each has a stable outer shell. Atoms can give up, accept, or share electrons in order to have a stable outer shell.

Electron orbitals. The Bohr model was later modified because it is not actually possible to pinpoint the location of an electron. Rather than an orbit, an electron occupies an **orbital,** which is a volume of space where a rapidly moving electron is statistically predicted to be found. An orbital has a characteristic energy state and a characteristic shape. At the first energy level, there is only a single spherical orbital, where at most two electrons are found about the nucleus (Fig. 2.4*a*). The space is spherical shaped because the most likely location for each electron is a fixed distance in all directions from the nucleus. At the second energy level, there are four orbitals; one of these is spherical shaped but the other three are dumbbell shaped (Fig. 2.4*b*). This is the shape that allows the electrons to be most distant from one another. Since each orbital can hold two electrons, there are a maximum of eight electrons in the L shell (Fig. 2.4*c*). When bonding occurs, the orbitals of this shell sometimes hybridize, forming teardrop-shaped orbitals that point to the corners of a triangular pyramid called a tetrahedron (Fig. 2.4*d*).

The number of electrons in the outer shell determines the manner in which atoms react with one another.

Chemical Formulas and Equations
When writing chemical formulas, atomic symbols are used to represent the atoms, and subscripts are used to indicate how many atoms of each type there are in a substance. For example, the chemical formula H_2O (read as H-two-O) indicates that a water molecule contains two hydrogen atoms and one oxygen atom. The chemical formula for glucose contains many atoms:

one molecule
$$C_6 H_{12} O_6$$
indicates 6 atoms of carbon   indicates 12 atoms of hydrogen   indicates 6 atoms of oxygen

Formulas are used in chemical equations to represent chemical reactions that occur between atoms and molecules:

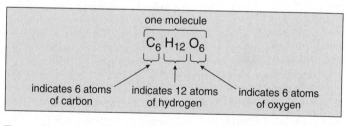

$$6CO_2 + 6H_2O \longrightarrow C_6H_{12}O_6 + 6O_2$$
carbon dioxide   water   glucose   oxygen

In this equation, which is often used to represent photosynthesis, six molecules of carbon dioxide react with six molecules of water to yield one glucose molecule and six molecules of oxygen. The reactants (molecules that participate in the reaction) are shown on the left of the arrow, and the products (molecules formed by the reaction) are shown on the right. Notice that the equation is "balanced," that is, there are the same number of each type of atom on both sides of the arrow.

2.2 Compounds and Molecules

Molecules can form when two or more atoms of the same element react with one another. For example, oxygen does not exist in nature as a single atom, O; instead, two oxygen atoms are joined as O_2. When atoms of two or more different elements react or bond together, a **compound** results. Water (H_2O) is a compound that contains the elements hydrogen and oxygen. We can also speak of H_2O as a **molecule** [L. *moles,* mass], because a molecule is the smallest part of a compound that still has the properties of that compound.

Electrons possess energy and the bonds that exist between atoms contain energy. Organisms are dependent upon chemical-bond energy to maintain their organization. When a chemical reaction occurs, electrons shift in their relationship to one another and energy may be given off. This is the energy that we make use of to carry on our daily lives.

Ionic Bonding

Ionic bonds form when electrons are transferred from one atom to another. For example, sodium (Na), with only one electron in its third shell, tends to be an electron donor (Fig. 2.5*a*). Once it gives up this electron, the second shell, with eight electrons, becomes its outer shell. Chlorine (Cl), on the other hand, tends to be an electron acceptor. Its outer shell has seven electrons, so it needs only one more electron to have a completed outer shell. When a sodium atom and a chlorine atom come together, an electron is transferred from the sodium atom to the chlorine atom. Now both atoms have eight electrons in their outer shells.

This electron transfer, however, causes a charge imbalance in each atom. The sodium atom has one more proton than it has electrons; therefore, it has a net charge of $+1$ (symbolized by Na^+). The chlorine atom has one more electron than it has protons; therefore, it has a net charge of -1 (symbolized by Cl^-). Such charged particles are called **ions.** Sodium (Na^+) and chlorine (Cl^-) are not the only biologically important ions. Some, such as potassium (K^+), are formed by the transfer of a single electron to another atom; others, such as calcium (Ca^{2+}) and magnesium (Mg^{2+}), are formed by the transfer of two electrons.

Ionic compounds are held together by an attraction between the charged ions called an **ionic bond.** When sodium reacts with chlorine, an ionic compound called sodium chloride (NaCl) results, and the reaction is called an ionic reaction. Sodium chloride is a salt commonly known as table salt because it is used to season our food (Fig. 2.5*b*). Salts can exist as dry solids, but when such a compound is placed in water, the ions separate as the salt dissolves, as when NaCl separates into Na^+ and Cl^-. Ionic compounds are most commonly found in this dissociated (ionized) form in biological systems because these systems are 70–90% water.

The transfer of electron(s) between atoms results in ions that are held together by an ionic bond, the attraction of negative and positive charges.

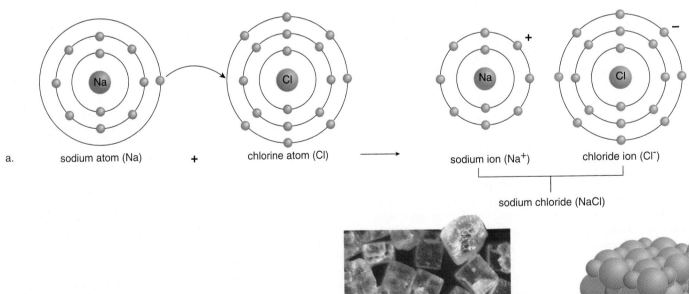

a. sodium atom (Na)   +   chlorine atom (Cl)   ⟶   sodium ion (Na^+)   chloride ion (Cl^-)

sodium chloride (NaCl)

Figure 2.5 Ionic reaction.

a. During the formation of sodium chloride, an electron is transferred from the sodium atom to the chlorine atom. At the completion of the reaction, each atom has eight electrons in the outer shell, but each also carries a charge as shown. **b.** In a sodium chloride crystal, ionic bonding between Na^+ and Cl^- causes the atoms to assume a three-dimensional lattice in which each sodium ion is surrounded by six chlorine ions, and each chlorine ion is surrounded by six sodium ions.

Na^+ ———

Cl^- ———

b. ⊢—⊣ 1 mm

Covalent Bonding

A **covalent bond** [L. *co*, together, with, and *valens*, strength] results when two atoms share electrons in such a way that each atom has an octet of electrons in the outer shell (or two electrons, in the case of hydrogen). In a hydrogen atom the outer shell is complete when it contains two electrons. If hydrogen is in the presence of a strong electron acceptor, it gives up its electron to become a hydrogen ion (H^+). But if this is not possible, hydrogen can share with another atom and thereby have a completed outer shell. For example, a hydrogen atom can share with another hydrogen atom. In this case, the two orbitals overlap and the electrons are shared between them (Fig. 2.6*a*). Because they share the electron pair, each atom has a completed outer shell. When a reaction results in a covalent molecule, it is called a covalent reaction.

A more common way to symbolize that atoms are sharing electrons is to draw a line between the two atoms, as in the structural formula H—H. In a molecular formula, the line is omitted and the molecule is simply written as H_2.

Like a single bond between two hydrogen atoms, a double bond can also allow two atoms to complete their octets. In a double covalent bond, two atoms share two pairs of electrons (Fig. 2.6*b*). In order to show that oxygen gas (O_2) contains a double bond, the molecule can be written as O=O.

It is even possible for atoms to form triple covalent bonds as in nitrogen gas (N_2), which can be written as N≡N. Single covalent bonds between atoms are quite strong, but double and triple bonds are even stronger.

Shape of Molecules

Structural formulas make it seem as if molecules are one dimensional but actually molecules have a three dimensional shape that often determines their biological function. Molecules consisting of only two atoms are always linear but a molecule like methane with five atoms (Fig. 2.6*c*) has a tetrahedral shape. Why? Because each of carbon's four hybrid orbitals is sharing with a hydrogen atom. The space-filling model comes closest to the actual shape of the molecule (Fig. 2.6*d*).

The shapes of molecules are necessary to the structural and functional roles they play in living things. For example, hormones have shapes that allow them to be recognized by the cells in the body. One form of diabetes occurs when the receptors of cells fail to recognize the hormone insulin. On the other hand, AIDS occurs when certain blood cells have receptors that bind to the HIV virus, allowing it to enter, multiply, and destroy the cell.

In a covalent molecule, atoms share electrons; the final shape of the molecule often determines the role it plays in cells and organisms.

Electron Model	Structural Formula	Molecular Formula
a. (H—H electron model)	H−H	H_2
b. (O=O electron model)	O=O	O_2
c. (methane electron model)	H−C−H with H above and below	CH_4

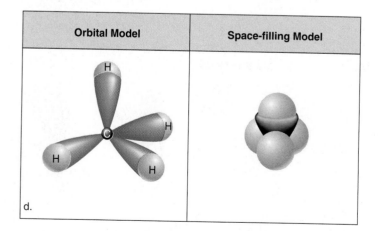

Orbital Model	Space-filling Model
d.	

Figure 2.6 Covalently bonded molecules.
In a covalent bond, atoms share electrons and each atom has a completed outer shell. **a.** A molecule of hydrogen (H_2) contains two hydrogen atoms sharing a pair of electrons. This single covalent bond can be represented in any of the three ways shown. **b.** A molecule of oxygen (O_2) contains two oxygen atoms sharing two pairs of electrons. This results in a double covalent bond. **c.** A molecule of methane (CH_4) contains one carbon atom bonded to four hydrogen atoms. By sharing pairs of electrons, each has a completed outer shell. **d.** When carbon binds to four other atoms as in methane, the orbitals of the outer shell hybridize forming a tetrahedron. The space-filling model is also a three-dimensional representation of the molecule.

Nonpolar and Polar Covalent Bonds

When the sharing of electrons between two atoms is fairly equal, the covalent bond is said to be a **nonpolar covalent bond.** All the molecules in Figure 2.6, including methane (CH_4), are nonpolar. In the case of water (H_2O), however, the sharing of electrons between oxygen and each hydrogen is not completely equal. The larger oxygen atom, with the greater number of protons, dominates the H_2O association. The attraction of an atom for the electrons of a covalent bond is called its **electronegativity.** The oxygen atom is more electronegative than the hydrogen atom, and it can attract the electron pair to a greater extent. In a water molecule, this causes the oxygen atom to assume a slightly negative charge (δ^-), and it causes the hydrogen atoms to assume a slightly positive charge (δ^+). The unequal sharing of electrons in a covalent bond creates a **polar covalent bond,** and, in the case of water, the molecule itself is a polar molecule (Fig. 2.7*a*).

Hydrogen Bonding

Polarity within a water molecule causes the hydrogen atoms in one molecule to be attracted to the oxygen atoms in other polar molecules (Fig. 2.7*b*). This attractive force creates a weak bond called a **hydrogen bond.** This bond is often represented by a dotted line because a hydrogen bond is easily broken. Hydrogen bonding is not unique to water. A biological molecule can contain many polar covalent bonds involving hydrogen and usually oxygen or nitrogen. An electropositive hydrogen atom can be attracted to an electronegative oxygen or nitrogen atom within the same molecule or in another molecule.

Although a hydrogen bond is more easily broken than a covalent bond, many hydrogen bonds taken together are quite strong. Hydrogen bonds between parts of cellular molecules help maintain their proper structure and function. We will see that some of the important properties of water are also due to hydrogen bonding.

The water molecule is a polar molecule and has a symmetric distribution of charge: one end of the molecule (the oxygen atom) carries a slightly negative charge, and the other ends of the molecule (the hydrogen atoms) carry slightly positive charges.

A hydrogen bond occurs between a slightly positive hydrogen atom of one molecule and a slightly negative atom of another molecule or between parts of the same molecule.

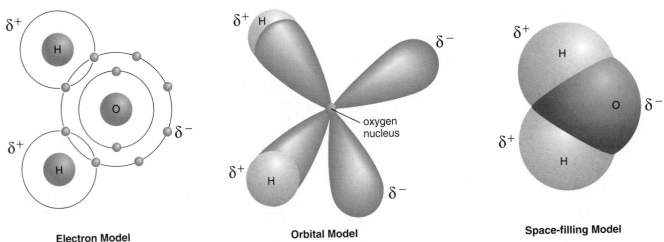

a. **Electron Model**   **Orbital Model**   **Space-filling Model**

b.   hydrogen bond

Figure 2.7 **Water molecule.**
a. Three models for the structure of water. The electron model does not indicate the shape of the molecule. The orbital model shows that the four orbitals of the outer shell (see Fig. 2.4*b*) have hybridized so that they point toward the corners of a tetrahedron. In water only two of these orbitals are utilized in covalent bonding. The space-filling model shows the V shape of a water molecule. Water is a polar molecule; the oxygen attracts the electrons more strongly than do the hydrogens, and there is a slightly positive charge on each hydrogen and a slightly negative charge on the oxygen. b. Hydrogen bonding between water molecules. A hydrogen bond is the attraction of a slightly positive hydrogen to a slightly negative atom in the vicinity. Each water molecule can bond to four other molecules in this manner. When water is in its liquid state, some hydrogen bonds are forming and others are breaking at all times.

2.3 Chemistry of Water

The first cell(s) evolved in water, and all living things are 70–90% water. What are the unique properties of water that make water essential to the continuance of life? Water is a polar molecule and water molecules are hydrogen bonded to one another (Fig. 2.7). A hydrogen bond is much weaker than a covalent bond within a water molecule, but taken together, hydrogen bonds cause water molecules to cling together. Without hydrogen bonding between molecules, water would boil at −80°C and freeze at −100°C, making life as we know it impossible. But because of hydrogen bonding, water is a liquid at temperatures suitable for life. It boils at 100°C and freezes at 0°C.

Properties of Water

The temperature of water rises and falls more slowly than other liquids under the same conditions. A calorie is the amount of heat energy needed to raise the temperature of one gram of water 1°C. In comparison, other covalently bonded liquids require only about half this amount of energy to rise in temperature 1°C. The many hydrogen bonds that link water molecules help water absorb heat without a great change in temperature.

When water cools down, heat is released. Converting one gram of the coldest liquid water to ice requires the loss of 80 calories of heat energy (Fig. 2.8). However, water holds heat, and its temperature falls more slowly than other liquids. This property of water is important not only for aquatic organisms but also for all living things. Water protects organisms from rapid temperature changes and helps them maintain their normal internal temperatures.

Water has a high heat of vaporization. Converting one gram of the hottest water to steam requires an input of 540 calories of heat energy. This high heat of vaporization means that water has a high boiling point. Because water boils at 100°C, it is in a liquid state at temperatures suitable to living things (Fig. 2.8).

Hydrogen bonds must be broken to change water to steam; this accounts for the very large amount of heat needed for evaporation. This property of water helps moderate the earth's temperature and keep it suitable to living things. It also gives animals in a hot environment an efficient way to release excess body heat. When an animal sweats, body heat is used to vaporize the sweat, thus cooling the animal.

a.

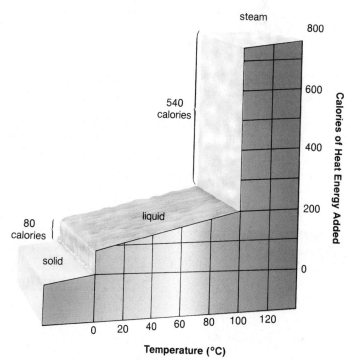

b.

Figure 2.8 Temperature and water.
a. Water has a high heat of vaporization; therefore, splashing water on the body when temperatures rise keeps animals cool. b. Water is the only common molecule that can be a solid, a liquid, or a gas according to naturally occurring environmental temperatures. At ordinary temperatures and pressure, water is a liquid, and it takes a large input of heat to change it to steam. In contrast, water gives off heat when it freezes, and this heat will keep the environmental temperature higher than expected. Can you see why there are less severe changes in temperature along the coasts?

Water facilitates chemical reactions both outside of and within living systems. Water dissolves a great number of solutes because it is a polar molecule. When a salt, such as sodium chloride (NaCl), is put into water, the negative ends of the water molecules are attracted to the sodium ions, and the positive ends of the water molecules are attracted to the chloride ions. This causes the sodium ions and the chloride ions to separate and to dissociate in water:

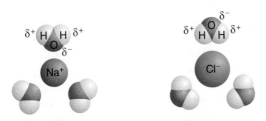

The salt NaCl dissolves in water

Water is also a solvent for larger molecules that contain ionized atoms or are polar molecules:

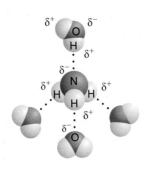

A polar molecule dissolves in water

When ions and molecules disperse in water, they move about and collide, allowing reactions to occur. Those molecules that can attract water are said to be **hydrophilic** [Gk. *hydrias*, of water, and *phileo*, love]. Nonionized and nonpolar molecules that cannot attract water are said to be **hydrophobic** [Gk. *hydrias*, of water, and *phobos*, fear].

Water molecules are cohesive and adhesive. Cohesion is apparent because water flows freely, yet water molecules do not separate from each other. They cling together because of hydrogen bonding. Because water molecules have a positive and negative pole, they adhere to surfaces, particularly polar surfaces; therefore, water exhibits adhesion. Because water can fill a tubular vessel and still flow, dissolved and suspended molecules are evenly distributed throughout a system. For these reasons, water is an excellent transport system both outside of and within living organisms. One-celled organisms rely on external water to transport nutrient and waste molecules, but multicellular organisms often contain internal vessels in which water serves to transport nutrients and wastes. For example, the liquid portion of our blood is 90% water that contains dissolved and suspended substances.

Cohesion and adhesion both contribute to the transport of water in plants. Plants have their roots anchored in the soil where they absorb water, but the leaves are uplifted and exposed to solar energy. How is it possible for water to rise to the top of even very tall trees (Fig. 2.9)? The properties of water account for the transport of water in plants. A plant contains a system of vessels that reaches from the roots to the leaves. Water evaporating from the leaves is immediately replaced with water molecules from the vessels. Because water molecules are cohesive, a tension is created that pulls water up from the roots. Adhesion of water to the walls of the vessels also helps prevent the water column from breaking apart.

Water has a high surface tension. It's possible to skip rocks on water because it has a high surface tension. Surface tension is measured by determining how difficult it is to break the surface of a liquid. As with cohesion, hydrogen bonding causes water to have a high surface tension. A water strider can even walk on the surface of a pond without breaking the water's surface. Table 2.3 summarizes the properties of water.

Table 2.3

Water

Properties	Chemical Reason	Effect
Resists change of state (from liquid to ice and from liquid to steam)	Hydrogen bonding	Moderates earth's temperature
Resists changes in temperature	Hydrogen bonding	Helps keep body temperatures constant
Universal solvent	Polarity	Facilitates chemical reactions
Is cohesive and adhesive	Hydrogen bonding; polarity	Serves as transport medium
Has a high surface tension	Hydrogen bonding	Difficult to break surface
Less dense as ice than as liquid water	Hydrogen bonding changes	Ice floats on water

Unlike most substances, frozen water is less dense than liquid water. As water cools, the molecules come closer together. They are densest at 4 °C, but they are still moving about (Fig. 2.10). At temperatures below 4 °C, there is only vibrational movement, and hydrogen bonding becomes more rigid but also more open. This means that water expands as it freezes, which is why cans of soda burst when placed in a freezer or why frost heaves make northern roads bumpy in the winter. It also means that ice is less dense than liquid water, and therefore ice floats on liquid water. If ice did not float on water, ice would sink, and once it began to accumulate at the bottom of ponds, lakes, and perhaps even the ocean,

they would freeze solid and never melt, making life impossible in the water and also on land.

Instead, bodies of water always freeze from the top down. When a body of water freezes on the surface, the ice acts as an insulator to prevent the water below it from freezing. This protects many aquatic organisms so that they can survive the winter. As ice melts in the spring, it draws heat from the environment, helping to prevent a sudden change in temperature that might be harmful to life.

> **Water has unique properties that allow cellular activities to occur and that make life on earth possible.**

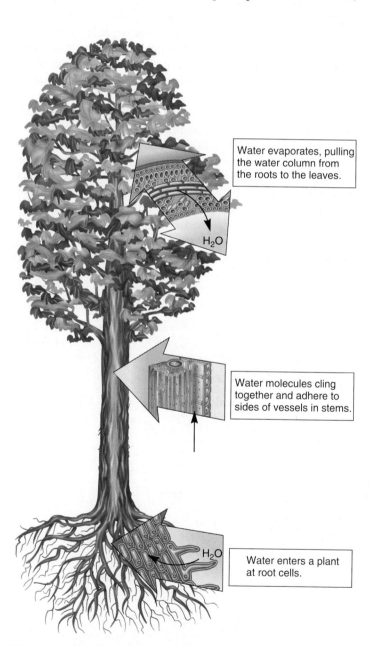

Figure 2.9 Water as a transport medium.
How does water rise to the top of tall trees? Vessels are water-filled open pipelines from the roots to the leaves. When water evaporates from the leaves, this water column is pulled upward due to the cohesion of water molecules with one another and the adhesion of water molecules to the sides of vessels.

Water evaporates, pulling the water column from the roots to the leaves.

H_2O

Water molecules cling together and adhere to sides of vessels in stems.

Water enters a plant at root cells.

H_2O

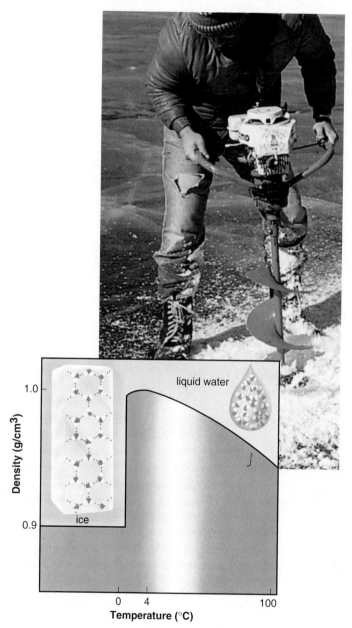

Figure 2.10 Water as ice.
Most substances contract when they solidify, but water expands because the water molecules in ice form a lattice in which the hydrogen bonds are farther apart than in liquid water. Water is more dense at 4 °C than at 0 °C; therefore, water freezes from the top down, making it necessary to drill a hole in order to go ice fishing.

Acids and Bases

When water ionizes, it releases an equal number of **hydrogen ions (H^+)** and **hydroxide ions (OH^-):**

$$H-O-H \rightleftharpoons H^+ + OH^-$$
water　　hydrogen　hydroxide
ion　　　ion

Only a few water molecules at a time are dissociated, and the actual number of these ions is very small (10^{-7} moles/liter).[1]

Acids (High H^+ Concentration)

Lemon juice, vinegar, tomatoes, and coffee are all familiar acids. What do they have in common? **Acids** are molecules that dissociate in water, releasing hydrogen ions (H^+).[2] For example, an important inorganic acid is hydrochloric acid (HCl), which dissociates in this manner:

$$HCl \longrightarrow H^+ + Cl^-$$

Dissociation is almost complete; therefore, this is called a strong acid. If hydrochloric acid is added to a beaker of water, the number of hydrogen ions (H^+) increases greatly.

Bases (Low H^+ Concentration)

Milk of magnesia and ammonia are common bases that most people have heard of. **Bases** are molecules that either take up hydrogen ions (H^+) or release hydroxide ions (OH^-). For example, an important inorganic base is sodium hydroxide (NaOH), which dissociates in this manner:

$$NaOH \longrightarrow Na^+ + OH^-$$

Dissociation is almost complete; therefore, sodium hydroxide is called a strong base. If sodium hydroxide is added to a beaker of water, the number of hydroxide ions increases.

pH Scale

The **pH scale**[3] is used to indicate the acidity and basicity (alkalinity) of a solution. A pH of exactly 7 is neutral pH. Pure water has an equal number of hydrogen ions (H^+) and hydroxide ions (OH^-), and therefore, one of each is released when water dissociates. One mole of pure water contains only 10^{-7} moles/liter of hydrogen ions, which is the source of the pH value for neutral solutions.

The pH scale was devised to simplify discussion of the hydrogen ion concentration [H^+] and consequently of the hydroxide ion concentration [OH^-]; it eliminates the use of cumbersome numbers.

For example,

	[H^+] (moles per liter)		pH
0.000001	=	1×10^{-6}	6
0.0000001	=	1×10^{-7}	7
0.00000001	=	1×10^{-8}	8

Each pH unit has 10 times the amount of hydrogen ions (H^+) as the next higher unit.

In order to understand the relationship between hydrogen ion concentration and pH, consider the following question. Of the two other values listed above, which indicates a higher hydrogen ion concentration than pH 7 (neutral pH) and therefore refers to an acidic solution? A number with a smaller negative exponent indicates a greater quantity of hydrogen ions (H^+) than one with a larger negative exponent. Therefore, pH 6 is an acidic solution.

Bases add hydroxide ions (OH^-) to solutions and increase the hydroxide ion concentration [OH^-] of water. Basic (also called alkaline) solutions, then, have fewer hydrogen ions (H^+) compared to hydroxide ions. The pH 8 refers to a basic solution because it indicates a lower hydrogen ion concentration [H^+] (greater hydroxide ion concentration) than pH 7.

The pH scale (Fig. 2.11) ranges from 0 to 14. It is a logarithmic scale as opposed to an exponential scale. As we move toward a lower pH, each unit has 10 times the acidity of the previous unit, and as we move toward a higher pH,

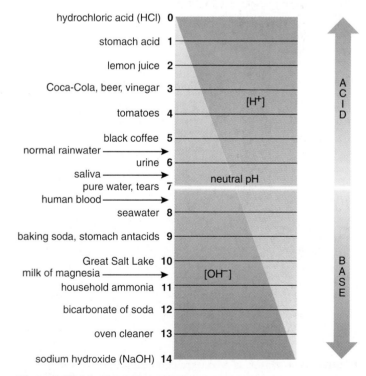

Figure 2.11 The pH scale.
The proportionate amount of hydrogen ions to hydroxide ions is indicated by the diagonal line. Any pH above 7 is basic, while any pH below 7 is acidic.

---

[1] In chemistry, a mole is defined as the amount of matter that contains as many objects (atoms, molecules, ions) as the number of atoms in exactly 12 grams of ^{12}C.

[2] A hydrogen atom contains one electron and one proton. A hydrogen ion has only one proton, so is often called a proton.

[3] pH is defined as the negative log of the hydrogen ion concentration [H^+]. A log is the power to which 10 must be raised to produce a given number.

Normally, rainwater has a pH of about 5.6 because the carbon dioxide in the air combines with water to give a weak solution of carbonic acid. Rain falling in northeastern United States and southeastern Canada now has a pH between 5.0 and 4.0. We have to remember that a pH of 4 is ten times more acidic than a pH of 5 to comprehend the increase in acidity this represents.

There is very strong evidence that this observed increase in rainwater acidity is a result of the burning of fossil fuels, like coal and oil, as well as gasoline derived from oil. When fossil fuels are burned, sulfur dioxide and nitrogen oxides are produced, and they combine with water vapor in the atmosphere to form the acids sulfuric acid and nitric acid. These acids return to earth contained in rain or snow, a process properly called wet deposition, but more often called acid rain. Dry particles of sulfate and nitrate salts descend from the atmosphere during dry deposition.

Unfortunately, regulations that require the use of tall smokestacks to reduce local air pollution only cause pollutants to be carried far from their place of origin. Acid deposition in southeastern Canada is due to the burning of fossil fuels in factories and power plants in the Midwest.

Acid deposition adversely affects lakes, particularly in areas where the soil is thin and lacks limestone (calcium carbonate, $CaCO_3$), a buffer to acid deposition. It leaches aluminum from the soil, carries aluminum into the lakes, and converts mercury deposits in lake bottom sediments to soluble and toxic methyl mercury. Lakes not only become more acidic, but they also show accumulation of toxic substances. The increasing deterioration of thousands of lakes and rivers in southern Norway and Sweden during the past two decades has been attributed to acid deposition. Some lakes contain no fish and others have decreasing amounts of fish. The same phenomenon has been observed in Canada and the United States (mostly in the Northeast and upper Midwest).

In forests, acid deposition weakens trees because it leaches away nutrients and releases aluminum. By 1988, most spruce, fir, and other conifers atop North Carolina's Mt. Mitchell were dead from being bathed in ozone and acid fog for years. The soil was so acidic, new seedlings could not survive. Many countries in northern Europe have also reported woodland and forest damage most likely due to acid deposition (see photograph).

Lake and forest deterioration aren't the only effects of acid deposition. Reduction of agricultural yields, damage to marble and limestone monuments and buildings, and even illnesses in humans have been reported. Acid deposition has been implicated in the increased incidence of lung cancer and possibly colon cancer in residents of the East Coast. Tom McMillan, former Canada Minister of the Environment, says that acid rain is "destroying our lakes, killing our fish, undermining our tourism, retarding our forests, harming our agriculture, devastating our heritage, and threatening our health."

---

each unit has 10 times the basicity of the previous unit. A pH of 7 has an equal concentration of hydrogen ions (H^+) and hydroxide ions (OH^-). Above pH 7 there are more hydroxide ions than hydrogen ions, and below pH 7 there are more hydrogen ions than hydroxide ions.

Buffers

In living things, pH needs to be maintained within a narrow range or there are health consequences. The pH of our blood when we are healthy is always about 7.4, that is, just slightly basic (alkaline). Normally, pH stability is possible because the body has built-in mechanisms to prevent pH changes. **Buffers** are the most important of these mechanisms. Buffers help keep the pH within normal limits because they are chemicals or combinations of chemicals that take up excess hydrogen ions (H^+) or hydroxide ions (OH^-). For example, carbonic acid (H_2CO_3) is a weak acid that minimally dissociates and then reforms in the following manner:

$$\underset{\text{carbonic acid}}{H_2CO_3} \;\overset{\text{dissociates}}{\underset{\text{re-forms}}{\rightleftarrows}}\; \underset{\text{bicarbonate ion}}{H^+ + HCO_3^-}$$

Blood always contains a combination of some carbonic acid and some bicarbonate ions. When hydrogen ions (H^+) are added to blood, the following reaction occurs:

$$H^+ + HCO_3^- \longrightarrow H_2CO_3$$

When hydroxide ions (OH^-) are added to blood, this reaction occurs:

$$OH^- + H_2CO_3 \longrightarrow HCO_3^- + H_2O$$

These reactions prevent any significant change in blood pH.

Acids have a pH that is less than 7, and bases have a pH that is greater than 7. Buffers, which can combine with both hydrogen ions and hydroxide ions, help to keep the pH of internal body fluids near pH 7 (neutral).

Connecting Concepts

The methods of science applied to the structure of matter have revealed that all substances consist of various combinations of the same set of 92 elements. Living things consist primarily of just six of these elements—carbon, hydrogen, nitrogen, oxygen, phosphorus, and sulfur (CHNOPS for short). These elements combine to form the unique types of molecules found in living cells. Many other elements exist in smaller amounts in organisms as ions, and their functions are dependent on their charged nature. Cells consist largely of water, a molecule that contains only hydrogen and oxygen. Co-valent bonding between the atoms and hydrogen bonding between the molecules give water properties that sustain life. No other planet we know of has liquid water.

In the next chapter, we will learn that carbon combines covalently with the other five elements (i.e., HNOPS) to form the organic molecules of cells. It is these unique molecules that set living forms apart from nonliving objects. Carbon-containing molecules can be modified in numerous ways and this accounts for the diversity of life. In a cheetah, for example, such molecules are modified to become its black and beige fur. Another molecule called chlorophyll, which is necessary for photosynthesis, gives plants their green color.

It is difficult for us to visualize that a kangaroo, cheetah, or a pine tree is a combination of molecules and ions, but later in this book we will learn that even our thoughts of these organisms are simply the result of molecules flowing from one brain cell to another. An atomic, ionic, and molecular understanding of the variety of processes unique to life provides a deeper understanding of the definition of life and offers tools for the improvement of its quality, preservation of its diversity, and appreciation of its beauty.

Summary

2.1 Chemical Elements

Both living and nonliving things are composed of matter consisting of elements. Each element contains atoms of just one type. The acronym CHNOPS tells us the most common elements (atoms) found in living things: carbon, hydrogen, nitrogen, oxygen, phosphorus, and sulfur. Atoms contain subatomic particles. Protons and neutrons in the nucleus determine the atomic mass of an atom. The atomic number indicates the number of protons and the number of electrons in electrically neutral atoms. Protons have a positive charge and electrons have a negative charge. Isotopes are atoms of the same type that differ in their number of neutrons. Radioactive isotopes are used as tracers in biological experiments and medical procedures.

Electrons occupy energy levels (electron shells) at discrete distances from the nucleus. The number of electrons in the outer shell determines the reactivity of an atom. The first shell is complete when it has two electrons. In atoms up through calcium, number 20, every shell thereafter is complete with eight electrons. The octet rule states that atoms react with one another in order to have a stable outer shell that contains eight electrons. Most atoms, including those common to living things, do not have stable outer shells. This causes them to react with one another to form compounds and/or molecules. Following the reaction, the atoms have stable outer shells.

Electron shells have orbitals. The first shell has a single spherical-shaped orbital. The second shell has four orbitals: the first is spherical shaped and the others are dumbbell shaped. When hybridization occurs, the orbitals of the second shell are teardrop shaped and point to the corners of a tetrahedron. Atoms have a three-dimensional shape which determines the shape of molecules.

2.2 Compounds and Molecules

Ionization is the loss or addition of one or more electrons from an atom's outer shell and a more stable atomic configuration results. An ionic bond is an attraction between oppositely charged ions. When a covalent reaction occurs, atoms share electrons. A covalent bond is the sharing of these electrons. There are single, double, and triple covalent bonds.

When carbon combines with four other atoms, the resulting molecule has a tetrahedral shape because the orbitals of carbon's outer shell have hybridized. The shape of a molecule is important to its biological role. Hormones and other molecules, for example, are recognized by a cell's receptors because of their specific shapes.

In polar covalent bonds, the sharing of electrons is not equal; one of the atoms exerts greater attraction for the electrons than the other and a slight charge results on each atom. A hydrogen bond is a weak attraction between a slightly positive hydrogen atom of one molecule and a slightly negative oxygen or nitrogen atom within the same or a different molecule. Hydrogen bonds help maintain the structure and function of cellular molecules.

2.3 Chemistry of Water

Water is a polar molecule. The polarity of water molecules causes hydrogen bonding to occur between water molecules. These two features account for the unique properties of water, which are summarized in Table 2.3. These features allow cellular activities to occur and life to exist on Earth.

A small fraction of water dissociates to produce an equal number of hydrogen ions and hydroxide ions. This is termed neutral pH. In acidic solutions, there are more hydrogen ions than hydroxide ions; these solutions have a pH less than 7. In basic solutions, there are more hydroxide ions than hydrogen ions; these solutions have a pH greater than 7. Cells are sensitive to pH changes. Biological systems often contain buffers that help keep the pH within a normal range.

Reviewing the Chapter

1. Name the kinds of subatomic particles studied; list their mass, charge, and location in an atom. Which of these varies in isotopes?   18–19
2. Using the Bohr model draw an atomic structure for a carbon atom that has six protons and six neutrons.   20
3. Draw an atomic representation for the molecule $MgCl_2$. Using the octet rule, explain the structure of the compound.   21
4. State the number of orbitals per energy level. With reference to the second energy level, explain how a tetrahedral shape comes about.   21

5. Explain whether CO_2 (O=C=O) is an ionic or a covalent compound. Why does this arrangement satisfy all atoms involved? 22–23
6. Show that the shape of methane is dependent on the shape of carbon's orbitals. Of what significance is the shape of molecules in organisms? 23
7. Explain why water is a polar molecule. What is the relationship between the polarity of the molecule and the hydrogen bonding between water molecules? 24
8. Name six properties of water and relate them to the structure of water, including its polarity and hydrogen bonding between molecules. 25–27
9. Define an acid and a base. On the pH scale, which numbers indicate an acid, a base, and a neutral pH? 28
10. What are buffers, and why are they important to life? 29

Testing Yourself

Choose the best answer for each question.

1. An atom, such as calcium, which has two electrons in the outer shell, would most likely
   a. share to acquire a completed outer shell.
   b. lose these two electrons and become a negatively charged ion.
   c. lose these two electrons and become a positively charged ion.
   d. bind with carbon by way of hydrogen bonds.
   e. bind with another calcium to satisfy its energy needs.
2. The atomic number tells you the
   a. number of neutrons in the nucleus.
   b. number of protons in the atom.
   c. mass of the atom.
   d. the number of its electrons when neutral.
   e. Both b and d are correct.
3. Orbitals
   a. have the same volume and charge as an electron shell.
   b. always occupy the same space and have the same energy content.
   c. are the volume of space most likely occupied by an electron.
   d. influence the shape of atoms.
   e. Both c and d are correct.
4. A covalent bond is indicated by
   a. plus and minus charges attached to atoms.
   b. dotted lines between hydrogen atoms.
   c. concentric circles about a nucleus.
   d. overlapping electron shells or a straight line between atomic symbols.
   e. the touching of atomic nuclei.
5. The shape of a molecule
   a. is dependent in part on the shape of orbitals.
   b. influences their biological function.
   c. is dependent on its electronegativity.
   d. is dependent on its place in the periodic table.
   e. Both a and b are correct.
6. In which of these are the electrons shared unequally?
   a. double covalent bond
   b. triple covalent bond
   c. hydrogen bond
   d. polar covalent bond
   e. ionic and covalent bonds

7. In the molecule

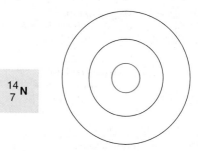

   a. all atoms have eight electrons in the outer shell.
   b. all atoms are sharing electrons.
   c. carbon could accept more hydrogen atoms.
   d. the orbitals point to the corners of a square.
   e. All of these are correct.
8. Which of these properties of water is not due to hydrogen bonding between water molecules?
   a. stabilizes temperature inside and outside cell
   b. molecules are cohesive
   c. is a solvent for many molecules
   d. ice floats on water
   e. Both b and c are correct.
9. Acids
   a. release hydrogen ions.
   b. have a pH value above 7.
   c. take up hydroxide ions and become neutral.
   d. increase the number of water molecules.
   e. Both a and b are correct.
10. Complete this diagram of a nitrogen atom by placing the correct number of protons and neutrons in the nucleus and electrons in the shells. Explain why the correct formula for ammonia is NH_3 and not NH_4.

Thinking Scientifically

1. Natural antifreeze molecules allow many animals to exist in conditions cold enough to freeze the blood (or equivalent fluid) of animals without these additives. The usual explanation about how these molecules work is that they bind to tiny ice crystals in the blood and prevent them from getting larger. However, the exact mechanism is still not completely understood. Knowing the role of hydrogen bonding in the transition from liquid water to ice, how might these "natural antifreeze" molecules interact with ice/water to prevent crystal growth?
2. DNA is a large molecule that is made of two long, thin strands. All of the atoms within each strand are held together by covalent bonds, but the two strands are held together by hydrogen bonds only. Knowing that individual hydrogen bonds are weaker than covalent bonds, but that many hydrogen bonds together make a strong connection, what would you predict about the stability of the DNA molecule?

Bioethical Issue

Like a well-tuned system, your body constantly balances acidic and basic chemicals to keep your pH level at a steady state. Normally, this system works fine.

But when a person gets sick or endures physical stress—as in, for example, childbirth—pH levels may dip or rise too far, endangering that person's life. In most American hospitals, doctors routinely administer IVs, or intravenous infusions, of certain fluids to maintain a patient's pH level.

However, some people oppose IVs for philosophical reasons. For example, women preferring a natural childbirth may refuse an IV. That's relatively safe, as long as the woman is healthy.

Problems arise when hospital policy dictates an IV, even though a patient does not want one. Should a patient be allowed to refuse an IV? Or does a hospital have the right to insist, for health reasons, that patients accept IV fluids? And what role should doctors play—patient advocates or hospital representatives?

Understanding the Terms

acid 28	hydrophilic 26
atom 18	hydrophobic 26
atomic mass 19	hydroxide ion 28
atomic number 19	ion 22
atomic symbol 18	ionic bond 22
base 28	isotope 19
buffer 29	matter 18
compound 22	molecule 22
covalent bond 23	neutron 18
electron 18	nonpolar covalent bond 24
electron shells 20	octet rule 21
electronegativity 24	orbital 21
element 18	pH scale 28
energy 20	polar covalent bond 24
hydrogen bond 24	proton 18
hydrogen ion 28	radioactive isotope 19

Match the terms to these definitions:

a. _____ Bond in which the sharing of electrons between atoms is unequal.

b. _____ Charged particle that carries a negative or positive charge(s).

c. _____ Molecules tending to raise the hydrogen ion concentration in a solution and to lower its pH numerically.

d. _____ Union of two or more atoms of the same element; also the smallest part of a compound that retains the properties of the compound.

e. _____ Measurement scale for the hydrogen ion concentration [H^+] of a solution.

Web Connections

Exploring the Internet

http://www.mhhe.com/biosci/genbio/mader
(click on *Biology 7/e*)

The *Biology 7/e* Online Learning Center provides many resources for studying the material in this chapter including links to the following sites:

Chemist's Art Gallery. This site consists of a series of visualizations and animations of various chemicals and chemical processes. This is a huge site with many links.

http://www.csc.fi/lul/chem/graphics.html

Water and Ice Module is a site with online activities for students to learn more about the structure of water and ice.

http://cwis.nyu.edu/pages/mathmol/modules/water/water_teacher.html

Learn more about the elements, their structures, and properties in Chemicool, a periodic table of the elements produced by MIT.

http://www-tech.mit.edu/Chemicool/

ChemCenter, a site sponsored by the American Chemical Society, includes information on graduate programs, chemistry related news, and events.

http://www.chemcenter.org/

Visual Elements is a site designed by the Chemistry Society and has much text and visual images for all elements in the periodic table.

http://www.chemsoc.org/viselements/pages/periodic_table.html

The Chemistry of Organic Molecules

chapter

Normal red blood cell compared to a sickled red blood cell.

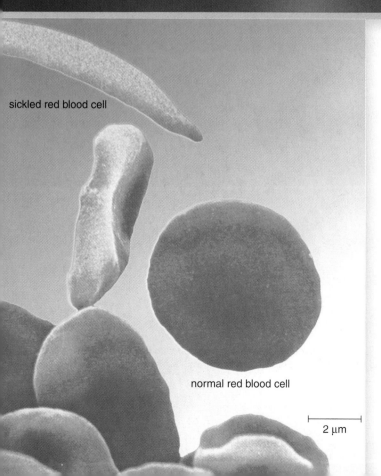

sickled red blood cell

normal red blood cell

2 µm

Normal red blood cells are biconcave disks that easily change shape as they squeeze along tiny blood vessels. A person with sickle-cell disease has sickle-shaped red blood cells that aren't as flexible. Their inflexibility causes them to either break down or clog small blood vessels. Typically, the individual suffers from anemia, poor circulation, and lack of resistance to infection. Internal hemorrhaging leads to jaundice, episodic pain of the abdomen and joints, and damage to internal organs.

Red blood cells contain the respiratory pigment hemoglobin. The chemistry of sickle-cell hemoglobin is different from that of normal hemoglobin. Sickle-cell hemoglobin isn't as soluble as normal hemoglobin. It stacks up into long semirigid rods that distort the red blood cells into a sickle shape. The molecule acts this way because a different chemical (amino acid) is found at one tiny spot compared to normal hemoglobin. This one difference accounts for abnormally shaped red blood cells and the symptoms of sickle-cell disease. Sickle-cell disease reminds us that the structure and shape of organic chemicals making up our bodies can influence our health.

3.1 Organic Molecules

The most common elements in living things are carbon, hydrogen, nitrogen, and oxygen, which constitute about 95% of your body weight. But we will see that both the sameness and the diversity of life are dependent upon the chemical characteristics of carbon, an atom whose chemistry is essential to living things.

The bonding of hydrogen, oxygen, nitrogen, and other atoms to carbon creates the molecules known as **organic molecules.** Laypeople sometimes use the word organic to mean wholesome. To biologists, organic molecules are those that always contain carbon and hydrogen. It is the organic molecules that characterize the structure and the function of living things like the primrose, the blueshell crab, and the bacterium in Figure 3.1. **Inorganic molecules** constitute nonliving matter, but even so, inorganic molecules like salts (e.g., NaCl) also play important roles in living things. Table 3.1 contrasts inorganic and organic molecules.

Living things are highly organized; therefore, it is easy for us to differentiate between the plant, the animal, and the bacterium in Figure 3.1. Despite their diversity all living things contain the same classes of primary molecules: carbohydrates, proteins, lipids, and nucleic acids. But within these classes there is molecular diversity. For example, the plant, the animal, and the bacterium all utilize a carbohydrate molecule for structural purposes, but the exact carbohydrate is different in each of them.

Of the elements most common to living things, the chemistry of carbon allows the formation of varied organic molecules. This accounts for both the sameness and the diversity of living things.

Table 3.1

Inorganic Versus Organic Molecules

Inorganic Molecules	Organic Molecules
Usually contain positive and negative ions	Always contain carbon and hydrogen
Usually ionic bonding	Always covalent bonding
Always contain a small number of atoms	May be quite large with many atoms
Often associated with nonliving matter	Usually associated with living organisms

a.   b.   c.

250 nm

Figure 3.1 Carbohydrates as structural materials.
a. Plants are held erect partly by the incorporation of the polysaccharide cellulose into the cell wall, which surrounds each cell. **b.** The shell of crabs contains chitin, a different type of polysaccharide. **c.** Most bacterial cells, like plant cells, are enclosed by a cell wall, but in this case the wall is strengthened by another type of polysaccharide known as peptidoglycan.

Carbon Skeletons and Functional Groups

Carbon has four electrons in its outer shell, and this allows it to bond with as many as four other atoms. Moreover, because these bonds are covalent, they are quite strong. Usually carbon bonds to hydrogen, oxygen, nitrogen, or another carbon atom. The ability of carbon to bond to itself results in carbon chains of various lengths and shapes. Long chains containing 50 or more carbon atoms are not unusual in living systems. Carbon can also share two pairs of electrons with another atom, giving a double covalent bond. Carbon-to-carbon bonding sometimes results in ring compounds of biological significance.

Carbon chains make up the skeleton or backbone of organic molecules. **Functional groups,** which are clusters of certain atoms that always behave in a certain way, can be attached to the carbon chain. The organic molecules in living things—sugars, fatty acids, amino acids, and nucleotides—all have a carbon backbone, and in addition, they often have one or more of the functional groups listed in Figure 3.2.

Molecules composed only of carbon and hydrogen, are **hydrophobic** (not attracted to water). But the addition of a functional group like —OH, or —C=O makes the molecule polar and able to interact with other polar molecules. In particular, polar molecules are **hydrophilic** (attracted to water). Since cells are 70–90% water, the ability to interact with and be soluble in water profoundly affects the function of organic molecules in cells.

Organic molecules containing carboxyl groups (—COOH) are both polar and acidic. They tend to ionize and release hydrogen ions in solution:

$$-COOH \longrightarrow -COO^- + H^+$$

Functional groups determine the polarity of an organic molecule and also the types of reactions it will undergo. We will see that alcohols react with carboxyl groups when a fat forms, and amino groups react with carboxyl groups during protein formation.

Isomers

Isomers also contribute to the diversity of organic molecules. **Isomers** [Gk. *isos,* equal, and *meros,* part, portion] are molecules that have identical molecular formulas, but they are different molecules because the atoms in each are arranged differently. For example, the compounds in Figure 3.3 are isomers.

Functional Groups			
Name	**Structure**	**Found in**	**Chemical characteristics**
hydroxyl (alcohol)	R—OH	some amino acids, nucleotides, sugars	polar, forms hydrogen bonds
carboxyl (acid)	R—C(=O)OH	fats amino acids	polar, acidic
ketone	R—C(=O)—R	some sugars	polar
aldehyde	R—C(=O)H	some sugars	polar
amino	R—N(H)(H)	amino acids proteins	polar, basic, forms hydrogen bonds
sulfhydryl	R—SH	some amino acids proteins	forms disulfide bonds
phosphate	R—O—P(=O)(OH)—OH	phospholipids nucleotides nucleic acids	polar, acidic
R = remainder of molecule			

Figure 3.2 Functional groups.
Molecules with the same type of backbone can still differ according to the type of functional group attached to the backbone. Many of these functional groups are polar, helping to make the molecule soluble in water. In this illustration, the remainder of the molecule (aside from the functional groups) is represented by an *R*.

a. Glyceraldehyde   b. Dihydroxyacetone

Figure 3.3 Isomers.
Isomers have the same molecular formula but different configurations. Both of these compounds have the formula $C_3H_6O_3$. **a.** In glyceraldehyde, oxygen is double-bonded to an end carbon. **b.** In dihydroxyacetone, oxygen is double-bonded to the middle carbon.

Organic molecules are diverse. Carbon skeletons vary in size and shape; functional groups have various chemical characteristics, and isomers occur.

Building Polymers

The four classes of organic compounds in living things are carbohydrates, lipids, proteins, and nucleic acids. Among the carbohydrates, polysaccharides are **polymers:** they are long chains of unit molecules called **monomers.** Simple sugars (monosaccharides) are the monomers within polysaccharides, amino acids join to form the polypeptides of proteins, and nucleotides are the monomers of nucleic acids:

Polymer	Monomer
Polysaccharide	Monosaccharide
Polypeptide	Amino acid
Nucleic acid	Nucleotide

Each type of monomer comes in different varieties because functional groups attached to monomers and/or the placement of functional groups can vary. Also the bonding between monomers can differ according to the particular polymer. For these reasons even polymers that contain the same type monomer can have different chemical characteristics and functions. In the pages that follow, note the names of unit molecules and how they join to form large molecules. You will also want to know the functions of each type of organic molecule discussed.

Polymers are long chains of unit molecules called monomers. Even polymers that contain the same type monomer can vary because monomers come in modified form and bonding between monomers is characteristic of the polymer.

Condensation and Hydrolysis

Polymers can be so large that they are called macromolecules. A polypeptide can contain hundreds of amino acids, and a nucleic acid can contain millions of nucleotides. How do polymers get so large? Cells use the modular approach when constructing polymers. Just as a train increases in length as box cars are hitched together one by one, so a polymer gets longer as monomers bond to one another.

Regardless of the type of bond that holds monomers join by an identical mechanism. During **condensation synthesis,** when monomers join, a hydroxyl (—OH) group is removed from one monomer and a hydrogen (—H) is removed from the other. Notice in Figure 3.4*a* that water is given off during condensation synthesis. Water is removed (*condensation*) and a bond is made (*synthesis*). Condensation synthesis does not take place unless the proper enzyme (a molecule that speeds a chemical reaction in cells) is present and the monomers are in an activated energy-rich form.

Polymers are broken down by **hydrolysis,** which is essentially the reverse of condensation synthesis. Notice in Figure 3.4*b* that water is added during hydrolysis: an —OH group from water attaches to one monomer and an —H from water attaches to the other monomer. In other words, during hydrolysis, water is used to break a bond.

Organic molecules are routinely built up in cells by the removal of water (H_2O) during condensation synthesis. They are broken down in cells by the addition of water during hydrolysis.

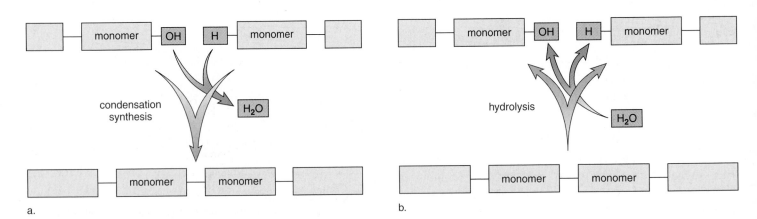

a.

b.

Figure 3.4 Condensation synthesis and hydrolysis of polymers.
a. In cells, synthesis often occurs when monomers bond following condensation (removal of H_2O). **b.** Hydrolysis occurs when the monomers in a polymer separate after the addition of H_2O.

3.2 Carbohydrates

The formula CH_2O is sometimes used to represent **carbohydrates** [L. *carbo*, charcoal, and Gk. *hydatos*, water], molecules that bear many hydroxyl groups (Fig. 3.5). Carbohydrates include monosaccharides (one sugar), disaccharides (two sugars bonded together), and polysaccharides (many sugars bonded together). Sugars and some polysaccharides (starches and glycogen) serve as energy storage compounds. Cellulose, a polysaccharide, is the most abundant organic compound on Earth because it supports plant cell walls. The carbohydrates attached to the surfaces of animal cells are specific to the individual and antigenic to certain other individuals.

Monosaccharides are simple sugars with a carbon backbone of three to seven carbon atoms. The best known sugars are those that have six carbons **(hexoses)**. **Glucose** [Gk. *glykys*, sweet, and *osus*, full of] is in the blood of animals, and **fructose** is frequently found in fruits. These sugars are isomers of each other. They both have the molecular formula $C_6H_{12}O_6$, but they differ in structure (Fig. 3.5). Structural differences cause molecules to vary in shape, which is best seen by using space-filling models. Shape is very important in determining how molecules interact with one another.

Ribose and **deoxyribose** are two five-carbon sugars **(pentoses)** of significance because they are found respectively in the nucleic acids RNA and DNA. RNA and DNA are discussed later in the chapter.

A **disaccharide** contains two monosaccharides that have joined by condensation. **Lactose** is a disaccharide that contains galactose and glucose and is found in milk. **Maltose** (composed of two glucose molecules) is a disaccharide of interest because it is found in our digestive tract as a result of starch digestion (Fig. 3.6).

Sucrose is a disaccharide that contains glucose and fructose. Sugar is transported within the body of a plant in the form of sucrose, and this is the sugar we use at the table to sweeten our food. We acquire this sugar from plants, such as sugarcane and sugar beets.

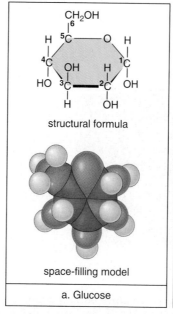
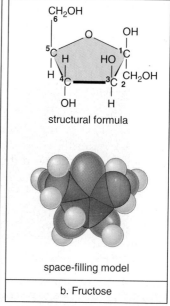

Figure 3.5 Two common six-carbon sugars.
a. Glucose is a six-carbon sugar that usually exists as a ring compound in cells. The shape of glucose is indicated in the space-filling model.
b. Fructose is an isomer of glucose. It too has the molecular formula $C_6H_{12}O_6$. Notice, though, that the atoms are bonded in a slightly different manner. The carbon atoms in glucose and fructose are numbered.

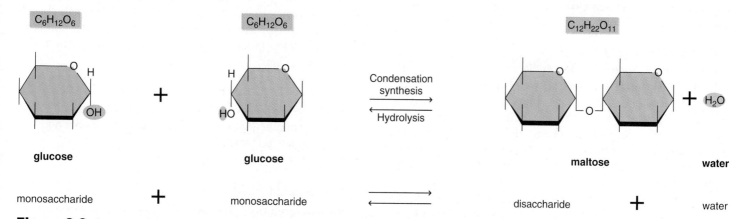

Figure 3.6 Condensation synthesis and hydrolysis of maltose, a disaccharide.
During condensation synthesis of maltose, a bond forms between two glucose molecules and the components of water are removed. During hydrolysis, the components of water are added and the bond is broken. This illustration uses a simplified way to represent glucose, only the bonds between the carbon atoms and bonds between attached groups are indicated.

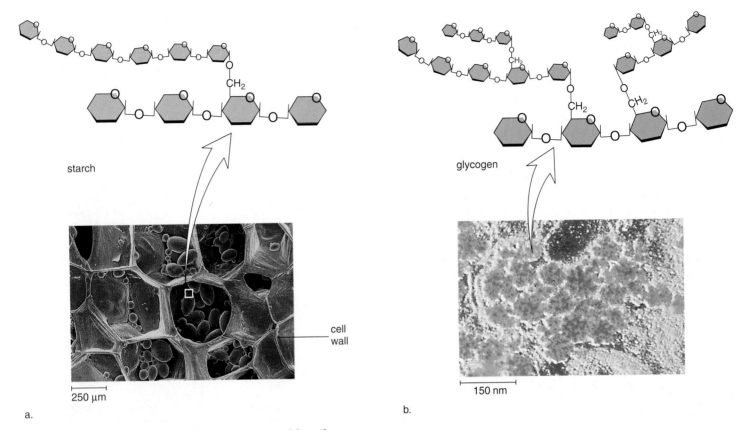

Figure 3.7 Starch and glycogen structure and function.
a. Starch is a chain of glucose molecules that branches as shown. The electron micrograph shows the location of starch in plant cells. Glucose is stored in plants as starch. **b.** Glycogen is a highly-branched polymer of glucose molecules. The electron micrograph shows glycogen deposits in a portion of a liver cell. Glucose is stored in animals as glycogen.

Polysaccharides

Polysaccharides are long polymers of monosaccharides formed by condensation synthesis. The most common polysaccharides in living things are starch, glycogen, and cellulose, which are chains of glucose molecules. Chitin is a polysaccharide that contains a modified glucose molecule.

Starch and Glycogen

The structures of starch and glycogen differ only slightly (Fig. 3.7). **Glycogen** [Gk. *glykys,* sweet, and *genitus,* producing] is characterized by many branches, which are side chains of glucose that go off from the main chain. **Starch** has fewer branches. Branching allows the breakdown of starch and glycogen to proceed at several points simultaneously. Once glucose is released, it is used directly as an energy source for cells.

The orientation of the bond in starch and glycogen allows these polymers to form compact spirals, making these polymers suitable as storage compounds. When leaf cells are actively producing sugar by photosynthesis, they store some of this sugar within the cell as starch (Fig. 3.7*a*). Otherwise, roots store sugar as starch, and so do seeds. During seed germination, starch is broken down into maltose and then glucose, which provides energy for growth.

Animal cells store extra carbohydrates as glycogen, sometimes called "animal starch." After we eat, the muscles and liver join glucose molecules to form glycogen (Fig. 3.7*b*). Between meals, the liver releases glucose to keep the blood concentration of glucose near the normal 0.1%. Glucose moves from the blood into cells where it participates in cellular metabolism.

Cells use sugars, especially glucose, as an immediate energy source. Glucose is stored as starch in plants and as glycogen in animals.

Cellulose and Chitin

Cellulose contains glucose molecules that are joined together differently than they are in starch and glycogen. The orientation of the bond between glucose molecules in cellulose causes the polymers to be straight and fibrous, making cellulose suitable as a structural compound.

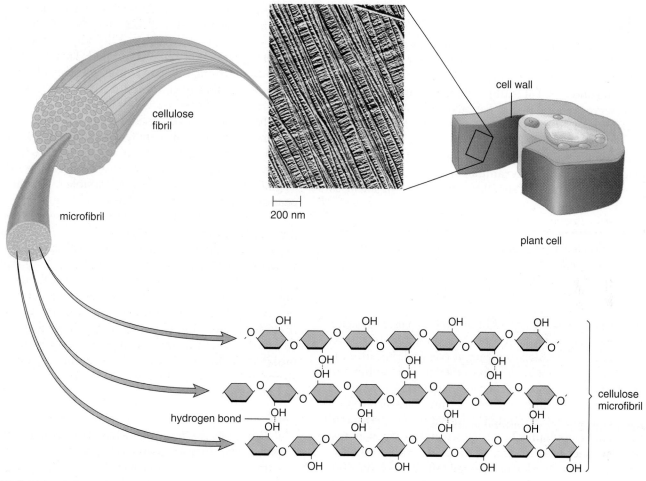

Figure 3.8 Cellulose fibrils.
In plant cell walls, each cellulose fibril contains several microfibrils. Each microfibril contains many polymers of glucose hydrogen-bonded together. Three such polymers are shown.

As shown in Figure 3.8, the long, unbranched polymers of glucose in cellulose are held together by hydrogen bonding within microfibrils. Several microfibrils, in turn, make up a cellulose fibril. Layers of cellulose fibrils occur in plant cell walls; fibrils are parallel in each layer, and the layers lie at angles to one another. This arrangement makes plant cell walls stronger. Humans have found many uses for cellulose and cotton fibers which are almost pure cellulose. We often wear cotton clothing. Furniture and buildings are made from wood, which contains a high percentage of cellulose.

Most animals, including humans, digest little cellulose because digestive enzymes are unable to break the linkage between the glucose molecules in cellulose. Even so, cellulose is a recommended part of our diet because it provides bulk (also called fiber or roughage) that helps the body maintain regularity of elimination.

Cattle and sheep receive nutrients from grass because they have a special stomach chamber, the rumen, where bacteria live that can digest cellulose. Unfortunately, cattle are often kept in feedlots, where they are fed grains instead of grass. This practice wastes fossil fuel energy because it takes energy to grow the grain, to process it, to transport it, and finally to feed it to the cattle. Also, range-fed cattle move about and produce a leaner meat than do cattle raised in a feedlot. There is growing evidence that lean meat is healthier for humans than fatty meat.

Chitin [Gk. *chiton,* tunic], which is found in the exoskeleton of crabs and related animals like lobsters and insects, is also a polymer of glucose. Each glucose unit, however, has an amino group attached to it. The linkage between the glucose molecules is like that found in cellulose; therefore, chitin is not digestible by humans. Recently, scientists have discovered how to turn chitin into thread that can be used as suture material. They hope to find other uses for treated chitin. If so, all those discarded crab shells that pile up beside crabmeat processing plants will not go to waste.

Plant cell walls contain cellulose. The shells of crabs and related animals contain chitin.

3.3 Lipids

A variety of organic compounds are classified as **lipids** [Gk. *lipos*, fat]. Many of these are insoluble in water because they lack any polar groups. The most familiar lipids are those found in fats and oils. Fat is utilized for both insulation and energy reserves by organisms. Fat below the skin of whales is called blubber; in humans it is given slang expressions such as "spare tire" and "love handles."

Phospholipids and steroids are also important lipids found in living things. For example, they are components of the plasma membrane, a sheetlike structure that encloses the cell.

Lipids are quite varied in structure, but they tend to be insoluble in water.

Fats and Oils

Fats and **oils** contain two types of unit molecules: fatty acids and glycerol. Each **fatty acid** consists of a long hydrocarbon chain with a carboxyl (acid) group at one end. Because the carboxyl group is a polar group, fatty acids are soluble in water. Most of the fatty acids in cells contain 16 to 18 carbon atoms per molecule, although smaller ones are also found. Fatty acids are either saturated or unsaturated. **Saturated** fatty acids have no double bonds between the carbon atoms. The carbon chain is saturated, so to speak, with all the hydrogens that can be held. **Unsaturated** fatty acids have double bonds in the carbon chain wherever the number of hydrogens is less than two per carbon atom:

saturated   unsaturated

Glycerol is a compound with three hydroxyl (—OH) groups. Hydroxyl groups are polar; therefore, glycerol is soluble in water. When a fat is formed, the acid portions of three fatty acids react with these hydroxyl groups. Aside from a fat molecule, three molecules of water result. This is condensation synthesis reaction and a fat can be hydrolyzed to its components (Fig. 3.9*a*). Because there are three fatty acids per glycerol molecule, fats and oils are sometimes called a **triglyceride.** Notice that unlike fatty acids, triglycerides lack polar groups; therefore they do not mix with water. Despite the liquid nature of both cooking oils and water, cooking oils separate out of water even after shaking.

Triglycerides containing fatty acids with unsaturated bonds melt at a lower temperature than those containing fatty acids with saturated bonds. This is because a double bond makes a kink that prevents close packing between the hydrocarbon chains (Fig. 3.9*b* and *c*). We can reason that butter, a fat, which is solid at room temperature, must be saturated while corn oil, which is a liquid even when placed in the refrigerator, must be unsaturated. This difference is useful to living things. For example, the feet of reindeer and penguins contain unsaturated triglycerides, and this helps protect these exposed parts from freezing.

In general, however, fats, which are most often of animal origin, are solid at room temperature and oils, which are liquid at room temperature, are of plant origin. Diets high in animal fat have been associated with circulatory disorders. Replacement of fat whenever possible with oils such as peanut oil and sunflower oil has been suggested.

Nearly all animals use fat in preference to glycogen for long-term energy storage. Gram per gram, fat stores more energy than glycogen. The C—H bonds of fatty acids makes them a richer source of chemical energy than glycogen, which has many C—OH bonds. Also, fat droplets, being nonpolar, do not contain water. Small birds, like the broad-tailed hummingbird, store a great deal of fat before they start their long spring and fall migratory flights. About 0.15 gram of fat per gram of body weight is accumulated each day. If the same amount of energy were stored as glycogen, a bird would be so heavy it would not be able to fly.

Fats and oils are triglycerides (one glycerol plus three fatty acids). They are used as long-term energy-storage compounds in plants and animals.

Waxes

In **waxes,** a long-chain fatty acid bonds with a long-chain alcohol.

fatty acid

long-chain alcohol

Waxes are solid at normal temperatures because they have a high melting point. Being hydrophobic, they are also waterproof and resistant to degradation. In many plants, waxes form a protective cuticle (covering) that retards the loss of water for all exposed parts. In animals, waxes are involved in skin and fur maintenance. In humans, wax is produced by glands in the outer ear canal. Here its function is to trap dust and dirt particles, preventing them from reaching the eardrum.

A honeybee produces wax in glands on the underside of its abdomen. The wax is used to make the six-sided cells of the comb where honey is stored. Honey contains the sugars fructose and glucose, breakdown products of the sugar sucrose.

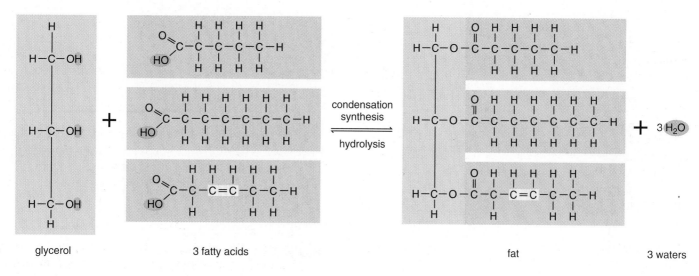

glycerol   3 fatty acids   condensation synthesis / hydrolysis   fat   3 waters

a. Formation of a fat.

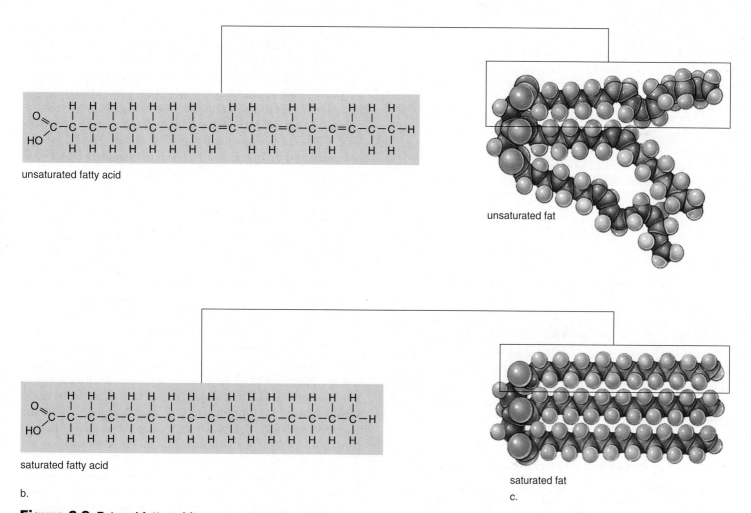

unsaturated fatty acid

unsaturated fat

saturated fatty acid

saturated fat

b.

c.

Figure 3.9 Fat and fatty acids.

a. During condensation synthesis of a fat, glycerol combines with three fatty acid molecules. During hydrolysis, the components of water are added, and the bonds are broken. **b.** A fatty acid has a carboxyl group attached to a long hydrocarbon chain. If there are double bonds between some of the carbons in the chain, the fatty acid is unsaturated. If there are no double bonds, the fatty acid is saturated. **c.** Space-filling models of an unsaturated fat and a saturated fat.

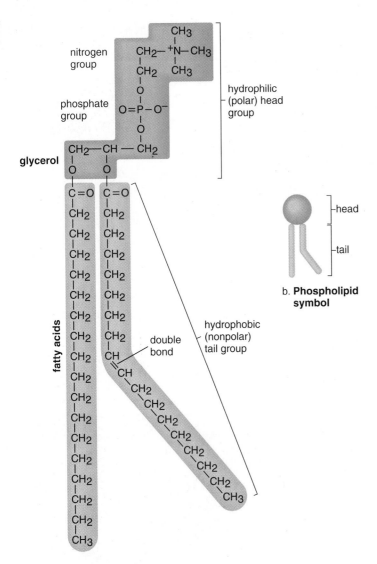

a. **Lecithin, a phospholipid**

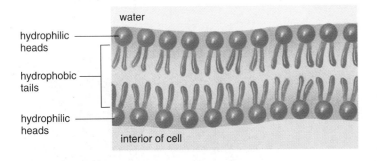

c. **Phospholipid bilayer in plasma membrane**

Figure 3.10 **Phospholipid structure and shape.**
a. Phospholipids are constructed like fats, except that they contain an ionized phosphate group. Lecithin also contains an ionized nitrogen-containing group. **b.** The hydrophilic (polar) head group is soluble in water, whereas the two hydrophobic (nonpolar) tail groups are not. **c.** This causes the molecules to arrange themselves as a bilayer in the plasma membrane which surrounds cells.

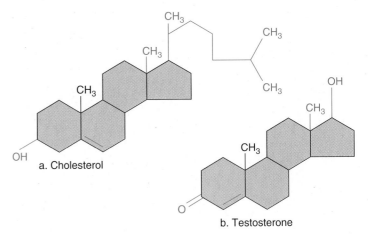

Figure 3.11 **Steroid diversity.**
a. Cholesterol, like all steroid molecules, has four adjacent rings, but their effects on the body largely depend on the attached groups indicated in red. **b.** Testosterone is the male sex hormone.

Phospholipids

Phospholipids [Gk. *phos*, light, and *lipos*, fat], as implied by their name, contain a phosphate group. Essentially, phospholipids are constructed like neutral fats, except that in place of the third fatty acid, there is a phosphate group or a grouping that contains both phosphate and nitrogen. This group becomes the polar head of the molecule, while the hydrocarbon chains of the fatty acids become the nonpolar tails (Fig. 3.10). The plasma membrane which surrounds cells is a phospholipid bilayer in which the polar heads face outward into a watery medium and the tails face each other because they are water repelling.

Steroids

Steroids are lipids that have an entirely different structure from that of fats. Steroid molecules have a backbone of four fused carbon rings, but each one differs primarily by the type of functional groups attached to the rings. Cholesterol is a component of an animal cell's plasma membrane and is the precursor of several other steroids, such as the sex hormones estrogen and testosterone (Fig. 3.11).

We know that a diet high in saturated fats and cholesterol can lead to circulatory disorders. This type of diet causes fatty material to accumulate inside the lining of blood vessels and blood flow is reduced. As discussed in the Health Focus reading on page 43, nutrition labels are now required to list the calories from fat per serving and the percent daily value from saturated fat and cholesterol.

Phospholipids, unlike other lipids, are soluble in water because they have a hydrophilic group. Steroids are ring compounds that have a similar backbone but vary according to the attached functional groups.

Since May 1994, packaged foods have been labeled as depicted in Figure 3A. The nutrition information given here is based on the serving size (i.e., 1¼ cup, 57 grams) of the cereal. A Calorie* is a measurement of energy. One serving of the cereal provides 220 Calories, of which 20 are from fat. It's also of interest that the cereal provides no cholesterol nor saturated fat. The suggestion that we study nutrition labels to determine how much cholesterol and fat (whether saturated or nonsaturated) they contain is based on innumerable statistical and clinical studies of three types:

(1) Clinical trials that show an elevated blood cholesterol level is a risk factor for coronary heart disease (CHD). The Framingham Heart Study conducted in Framingham, Massachusetts, concludes that as the blood cholesterol level in over 5,000 men and women rises so does the risk of CHD. Elevated blood cholesterol appears to be one of the three major CHD risk factors along with smoking and high blood pressure. Other studies have shown the same. The Multiple Risk Factor Intervention Trial followed more than 360,000 men and found also that there was a direct relationship between an increasing blood cholesterol level and the risk of a heart attack.

(2) Clinical trials indicate that lowering high blood cholesterol levels will reduce the risk of CHD. For example, the Coronary Primary Prevention Trial found that 9% reduction in total blood cholesterol levels produced a 19% reduction in CHD deaths and nonfatal heart attacks. The Cholesterol Lowering Atherosclerosis Study collected X-ray evidence that substantial cholesterol lowering produces slowed progression and regression of plaque in coronary arteries. Plaque is a buildup of soft fatty material including cholesterol

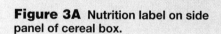

Nutrition Facts

Serving Size: 1¼ cup (57 g)
Servings per container: 8

Amount per Serving	Cereal
Calories	220
Calories from Fat	20

	% Daily Value
Total fat: 2 g	3%
Saturated fat: 0g	0%
Cholesterol: 0 mg	0%
Sodium: 320 mg	13%
Total Carbohydrate: 46 g	15%
Soluble fiber: less than 1 g	
Insoluble fiber: 6 g	
Sugars: 11 g	
Other carbohydrates: 28 g	
Protein: 5 g	

Vitamin A — 0% • Vitamin C — 10%
Calcium — 0% • Iron — 80%

		2,000 Calories	2,500 Calories
Total fat	Less than	65 g	80 g
Saturated fat	Less than	20 g	25 g
Cholesterol	Less than	300 mg	300 mg
Sodium	Less than	2,400 mg	2,400 mg
Total carbohydrate		300 mg	375 mg
Dietary fiber		25 g	30 g

Calories per gram:
Fat 9 • carbohydrate 4 • protein 4

Figure 3A Nutrition label on side panel of cereal box.

beneath the inner linings of arteries. Plaque can accumulate to the point that blood can no longer reach the heart and a heart attack occurs.

(3) Clinical studies show that there is a relationship between diet and

blood cholesterol levels. The national Research Council reviewed all sorts of scientific studies before concluding that the intake of saturated fatty acids raises blood cholesterol levels, while the substitution of unsaturated fats and carbohydrates in the diet lowers the blood cholesterol level. An Oslo Study, a Los Angeles Veterans Administration study, and a Finnish Mental Hospital Study showed that diet alone can produce 10–15% reductions in blood cholesterol level.

The desire of consumers to follow dietary recommendations led to the development of the type of nutrition label shown in 3A, which shows the amount of total fat, saturated fat, and cholesterol in a serving of food. The carbohydrate content in a food is of interest because carbohydrates aren't usually associated with health problems. In fact, carbohydrates should compose the largest proportion of the diet. Breads and cereals containing complex carbohydrates are preferable to candy and ice cream containing simple carbohydrates because they are likely to contain dietary fiber (nondigestible plant material). Insoluble fiber has a laxative effect and may reduce the risk of colon cancer; soluble fiber combines with the cholesterol in food and prevents the cholesterol from entering the body proper.

The amount of dietary sodium (as in table salt) is of concern because excessive sodium intake has been linked to high blood pressure in some people. It is recommended that the intake of sodium be no more than 2,400 mg per day. A serving of this cereal provides what percent of this maximum amount?

Vitamins are essential requirements needed in small amounts in the diet. Each vitamin has a recommended daily intake, and the food label tells what percent of the recommended amount is provided by a serving of this cereal.

*A calorie is the amount of heat required to raise the temperature of 1 gram of water 1°C. A Calorie (capital C), which is used to measure food energy, is equal to 1,000 calories.

3.4 Proteins

A **protein** is composed of one or more polypeptides, which are polymers of amino acids. Proteins perform many functions, and only a few functions can be discussed here.

Support   Some proteins such as keratin, which makes up hair and nails, and collagen, which lends support to ligaments, tendons, and skin are structural proteins.

Enzymes   Enzymes bring reactants together and thereby speed chemical reactions in cells. They are specific for one particular type of reaction and can function at body temperature.

Transport   Channel proteins in the plasma membrane allow substances to enter and exit cells. Carrier proteins in the membrane actually transport molecules into and out of the cell. Some other proteins transport molecules in the blood of animals; hemoglobin is a complex protein that transports oxygen.

Defense   Antibodies are proteins. They combine with foreign substances, called antigens. In this way they prevent antigens from destroying cells and upsetting homeostasis.

Hormones   Hormones are regulatory proteins. They serve as intercellular messengers that influence the metabolism of cells. Insulin regulates the content of glucose in the blood and in cells; the presence of growth hormone determines the height of the individual.

Motion   The contractile proteins actin and myosin allow parts of cells to move and cause muscles to contract. Muscle contraction accounts for the movement of animals from place to place.

Vertebrate cells function differently according to the type of protein they contain; muscle cells contain actin and myosin; red blood cells contain hemoglobin; support cells contain collagen, and so forth.

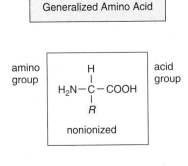

Figure 3.12 Amino acids.
a. Generalized amino acid showing the amino group, the acid (carboxyl) group and the *R* group. Both the nonionized and ionized form are shown.
b. Polypeptides contain 20 different kinds of amino acids, of which only eight are shown here. Amino acids differ by the particular *R* group (yellow) attached to the central carbon. Some *R* groups are nonpolar and hydrophobic, some are polar and hydrophilic, and some are ionized and hydrophilic.

Amino Acids

An **amino acid** has a carbon atom bonded to one hydrogen atom and in addition three groups of atoms. The name of the molecule is appropriate because one of these groups is an amino group ($-NH_2$) and another is an acidic group ($-COOH$). The last group is called an *R* group because it is the *Remainder* of the molecule (Fig. 3.12).

Amino acids differ according to their particular *R* group. The *R* groups range in complexity from a single hydrogen atom to a complicated ring compound. The unique chemical properties of an amino acid depend on those of the *R* group. For example, some *R* groups are polar and some are not. Also, the amino acid cysteine has an *R* group that ends with a sulfhydryl ($-SH$) group that often serves to connect one chain of amino acids to another by a disulfide bond, $-S-S-$. There are 20 different amino acids commonly found in cells, of which Figure 3.12 gives several examples.

Peptides

Figure 3.13 shows how two amino acids join by a condensation reaction between the carboxyl group of one and the amino group of another. The resulting covalent bond between two amino acids is called a **peptide bond.** The atoms associated with the peptide bond share the electrons unevenly because oxygen is more electronegative than nitrogen. Therefore, the hydrogen attached to the nitrogen has a slightly positive charge, while the oxygen has a slightly negative charge.

The polarity of the peptide bond means that hydrogen bonding is possible between the $-CO$ of one amino acid and the $-NH$ of another amino acid in a polypeptide.

A **peptide** is two or more amino acids bonded together, and a **polypeptide** is a chain of many amino acids joined by peptide bonds. A protein may contain more than one polypeptide chain; therefore, you can see why a protein could have a very large number of amino acids.

Levels of Protein Structure

The final shape of a protein, in large measure, determines the function of a protein in the cell and body of an organism. A protein can have up to four levels of structure but not all proteins have all four levels. Fibrous proteins have no specific tertiary structure and many proteins have no quaternary structure.

Primary Structure

The primary structure of a protein is the sequence of the amino acids joined by peptide bonds. When amino acids join together a polypeptide results. In other words, the primary structure is a polypeptide with its own particular sequence of amino acids. Therefore, polypeptides differ by the number of amino acids they contain and the sequence of their *R* groups. The chemical characteristics of the *R* groups are important to other levels of structure.

In 1953, Frederick Sanger determined the amino acid sequence of the hormone insulin, the first protein to be sequenced. He did it by first breaking insulin into fragments and then determining the amino acid sequence of the fragments before determining the sequence of the fragments themselves. It was a laborious ten-year task, but it established for the first time that each polypeptide has a particular sequence of amino acids. Today, there are automated sequencers that tell scientists the sequence of amino acids in a polypeptide within a few hours.

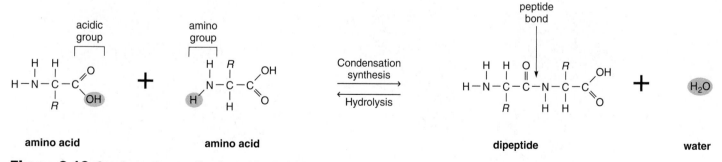

Figure 3.13 Condensation synthesis and hydrolysis of a dipeptide.
As two amino acids join, a peptide bond forms and a water molecule is given off. During hydrolysis, water is added and the peptide bond is broken.

Secondary Structure

The secondary structure of a protein occurs when segments of a polypeptide coil or fold in a particular way (Fig. 3.14).

Linus Pauling and Robert Corey, who began studying the structure of amino acids in the late 1930s, concluded that a coiling, they called an α helix, and a pleated sheet, they

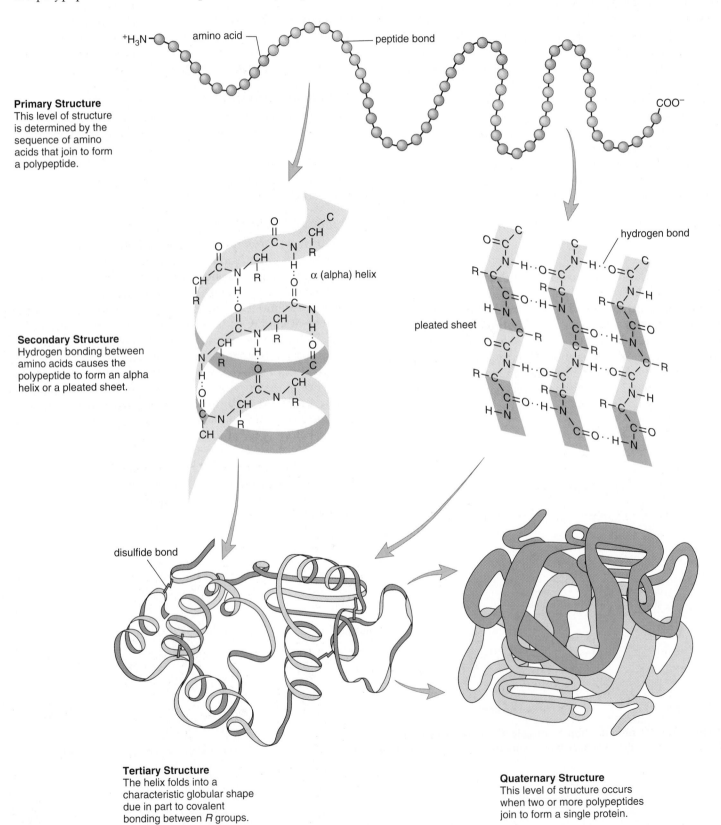

Primary Structure
This level of structure is determined by the sequence of amino acids that join to form a polypeptide.

Secondary Structure
Hydrogen bonding between amino acids causes the polypeptide to form an alpha helix or a pleated sheet.

Tertiary Structure
The helix folds into a characteristic globular shape due in part to covalent bonding between *R* groups.

Quaternary Structure
This level of structure occurs when two or more polypeptides join to form a single protein.

Figure 3.14 Levels of protein organization.

called the β (beta) sheet, were two basic patterns of amino acids within a polypeptide. They called it the α helix because it was the first pattern they discovered, and the β sheet because it was the second pattern they discovered.

Hydrogen bonding often holds the secondary structure of a polypeptide in place. Hydrogen bonding between every fourth amino acid accounts for the spiral shape of the helix. In a β sheet, the polypeptide turns back upon itself and hydrogen bonding occurs between extended lengths of the polypeptide. In keratin, α helices are covalently bonded to one another by disulfide linkages (—S—S—) between two cysteine amino acids. When you get a permanent, the hair is rolled and a reducing agent is used to break the present disulfide bonds. Each —S—S— bond becomes two —SH groups instead. When the reducing agent is removed, newly formed disulfide bonds make the hair curly.

Tertiary Structure

The tertiary structure is a folding and twisting that results in the final three-dimensional shape of a polypeptide.

Various types of bonding between the *R* groups of the amino acids bring about the tertiary structure. Hydrogen bonds, ionic bonds, and covalent bonds all contribute to the tertiary structure of a polypeptide. Strong disulfide linkages in particular help maintain the tertiary shape. Hydrophobic *R* groups do not bond with other *R* groups, and they tend to collect in a common region where they are not exposed to water. These are called hydrophobic interactions. Although hydrophobic interactions are not bonds, they are very important in creating and stabilizing the tertiary structure.

Quaternary Structure

Some proteins have a quaternary structure because they consist of more than one polypeptide. Hemoglobin is a much-studied globular protein that consists of four polypeptides and therefore has a quaternary structure. Each polypeptide in hemoglobin has a primary, secondary, and tertiary structure.

Denaturation of Proteins

Both temperature and pH can bring about a change in polypeptide shape. For example, we are all aware that the addition of acid to milk causes curdling; heating causes egg white, which consists mainly of a protein called albumin, to congeal, or coagulate. When a protein loses its normal configuration, it is said to be **denatured.** Denaturation occurs because the normal bonding patterns between parts of a molecule have been disturbed. Once a protein loses its normal shape, it is no longer able to perform its usual function.

Each type of enzyme is specific to the reaction it speeds. The shape of an enzyme is suitable for receiving its substrate(s) so that an enzyme-substrate complex forms. When an enzyme is denatured its shape changes and it can no longer bring the substrates, which are the reactants, together for the reaction to occur. Enzymes work best at body temperature and each one also has an optimal pH at which the rate of the reaction is highest. At this pH value, the enzyme has its normal shape. A change in pH can change the polarity of *R* groups and disrupt the normal interactions that maintain the normal shape of the enzyme.

If the conditions which caused denaturation were not too severe, and if these are removed, some proteins regain their normal shape and biological activity. This shows that it is simply the sequence of amino acids that cause the levels of structure and the protein's final shape (Fig. 3.15).

The sequence of amino acids in a polypeptide determines its final shape because various *R* groups interact differently. The function of a protein is dependent on its shape.

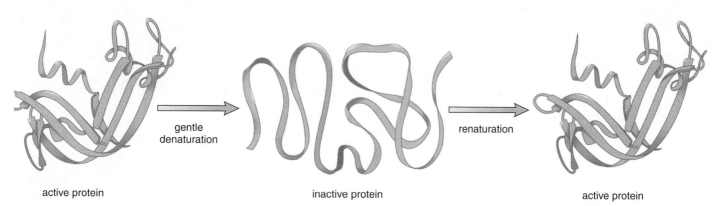

Figure 3.15 Denaturation and renaturation of a protein.
When a protein is denatured, it loses its normal shape and activity. If denaturation is gentle and if the original conditions are restored, some proteins regain their normal shape. This shows that the normal conformation of the molecule is due to the various interactions among a set sequence of amino acids. Each type of protein has a particular sequence of amino acids.

active protein   inactive protein   active protein

gentle denaturation   renaturation

3.5 Nucleic Acids

Nucleic acids are polymers of nucleotides with very specific functions in cells. **DNA (deoxyribonucleic acid)** is the genetic material that stores information regarding its own replication and the order in which amino acids are to be joined to make a protein. **RNA (ribonucleic acid)** is another type of nucleic acid. An RNA molecule called messenger RNA (mRNA) is an intermediary in the process of protein synthesis, conveying information from DNA regarding the amino acid sequence in a protein.

Some nucleotides have independent metabolic functions in cells. For example, some are components of coenzymes, which facilitate enzymatic reactions. **ATP (adenosine triphosphate)** is a nucleotide that supplies energy for synthetic reactions and for various other energy-requiring processes in cells.

Structure of DNA and RNA

Every **nucleotide** is a molecular complex of three types of molecules: phosphate (phosphoric acid), a pentose sugar, and a nitrogen-containing base (Fig. 3.16*a*). In DNA the pentose sugar is deoxyribose, and in RNA the pentose sugar is ribose. A difference in the structure of these 5-carbon sugars accounts for their respective names because deoxyribose lacks an oxygen atom found in ribose (Fig. 3.16*b*).

There are four types of nucleotides in DNA and four types of nucleotides in RNA (Fig. 3.16*c*). The base of a nucleotide can be a pyrimidine with a single ring or a purine with a double ring. In DNA, the pyrimidine bases are cytosine and thymine; in RNA, the pyrimidine bases are cytosine and uracil. In both DNA and RNA, the purine bases are adenine or guanine. These molecules are called bases because their presence raises the pH of a solution.

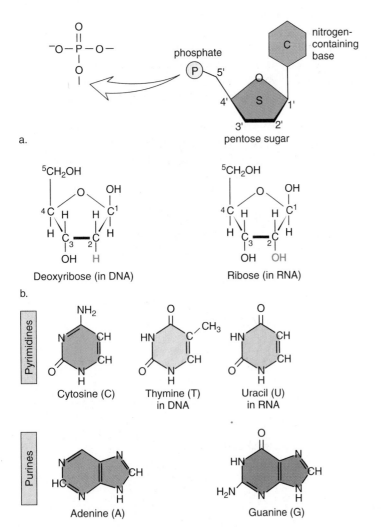

Figure 3.16 Nucleotides.
a. A nucleotide consists of a phosphate molecule, a pentose sugar, and a nitrogen-containing base. **b.** RNA contains the sugar ribose and DNA contains the sugar deoxyribose. **c.** RNA contains the bases C, U, A, and G. DNA contains the bases C, T, A, and G.

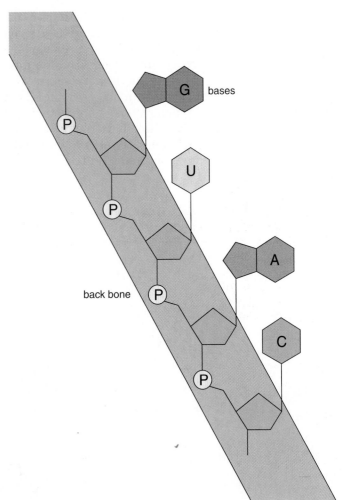

Figure 3.17 RNA structure.
RNA is a single-stranded polymer of nucleotides. When the nucleotides join, the phosphate group of one is bonded to the sugar of the next. The bases project out to the side of the resulting sugar-phosphate backbone.

Nucleotides join in a definite sequence when DNA and RNA form by condensation synthesis. The polynucleotide is a linear molecule called a strand in which the backbone is made up of a series of sugar-phosphate-sugar-phosphate molecules. The bases project to one side of the backbone. Since the nucleotides occur in a definite order, so do the bases. RNA is single stranded (Fig. 3.17).

DNA is double stranded, with the two strands usually twisted about each other in the form of a double helix. The two strands are held together by hydrogen bonds between pyrimidine and purine bases. The bases can be in any order within a strand, but between strands, thymine (T) is always paired with adenine (A), and guanine (G) is always paired with cytosine (C). This is called **complementary base pairing.** Therefore, regardless of the order or the quantity of any particular base pair, the number of purine bases (A + G) always equals the number of pyrimidine bases (T + C) (Fig. 3.18). Table 3.2 summarizes the differences between RNA and DNA.

Table 3.2

DNA Structure Compared to RNA Structure

	DNA	RNA
Sugar	Deoxyribose	Ribose
Bases	Adenine, guanine, thymine, cytosine	Adenine, guanine, uracil, cytosine
Strands	Double stranded with base pairing	Single stranded
Helix	Yes	No

The nucleic acids DNA and RNA are polymers of nucleotides. DNA is the genetic material and RNA is an intermediary during the process of protein synthesis.

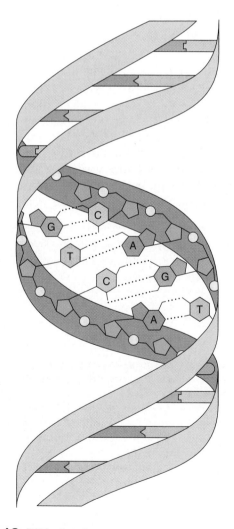

a.

b.

Figure 3.18 DNA structure.
DNA is a double helix in which the two nucleotide strands twist about each other. **a.** There are hydrogen bonds (dotted lines) between the complementarily paired bases: C is always paired with G and A is always paired with T. **b.** Space-filling model.

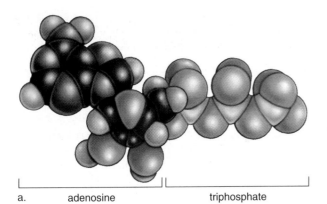

Figure 3.19 ATP

ATP, the universal energy currency of cells, is composed of adenosine and three phosphate groups. **a.** Space-filling model of ATP. **b.** When cells require energy, ATP usually becomes ADP + Ⓟ and energy is released.

a.   adenosine   triphosphate

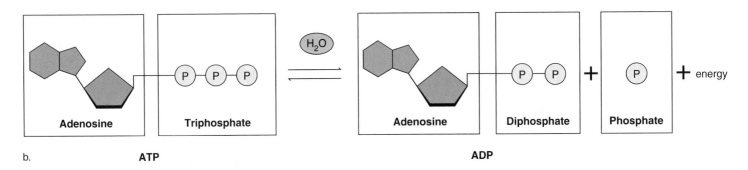

b.   **ATP**   **ADP**

ATP (Adenosine Triphosphate)

ATP is a nucleotide in which **adenosine** is composed of adenine and ribose. Triphosphate stands for the three phosphate groups that are attached to ribose, the pentose sugar (Fig. 3.19). ATP is a high-energy molecule because the last two phosphate bonds are unstable and are easily broken. Usually in cells the terminal phosphate bond is hydrolyzed to give the molecule **ADP (adenosine diphosphate)** and a molecule of inorganic phosphate Ⓟ.

The energy that is released by ATP breakdown is coupled to energy-requiring processes in cells, such as the synthesis of macromolecules like carbohydrates and proteins. In muscle cells, the energy is used for muscle contraction, and in nerve cells, it is used for the conduction of nerve impulses. Just as you spend money when you pay for a prod-

uct or a service, cells "spend" ATP in the same way. Therefore ATP is called the energy currency of cells.

Because energy is released when the last phosphate bonds of ATP are hydrolyzed, it is sometimes called a high-energy bond, symbolized by a wavy line. But this terminology is misleading—the breakdown of ATP releases energy because the products of hydrolysis (ADP and Ⓟ) are more stable than ATP. It is the entire molecule that releases energy and not a particular bond.

ATP is a high-energy molecule. ATP breaks down to ADP + Ⓟ, releasing energy, which is used for all metabolic work done in a cell.

Connecting Concepts

What does the term organic mean? For some, organic means that food products have been grown without the use of chemicals or have been minimally processed. But you now know that biochemically speaking, organic refers to molecules containing carbon and hydrogen. In biology, organic also refers to living things or anything that has been alive in the past. Therefore, the food we eat and the wood we burn are organic substances. Fossil fuels (coal and oil) formed over 300 million years ago from plant and animal life that, by chance, did not decompose, are also organic. When burned,

they release carbon dioxide into the atmosphere just as we do when we breathe!

Although living things are very complex, their macromolecules are simply polymers of small organic molecules. Simple sugars are the monomers of complex carbohydrates; amino acids are the monomers of proteins; nucleotides are the monomers of nucleic acids. Fats are composed of fatty acids and glycerol.

This system of forming macromolecules still allows for diversity. Monomers exist in modified forms and can combine in slightly different ways; therefore, a variety of macromolecules can come about.

In cellulose, a plant product, glucose monomers are linked in a slightly different way from glucose monomers in glycogen, an animal product. One protein differs from another by the sequence of the same 20 amino acids.

There is no doubt that the chemistry of carbon is the chemistry of life. The groups of molecules discussed in this chapter, as well as other small molecules and ions, are assembled into structures that make up cells. As discussed in the next chapter, each structure has a specific function necessary to the life of a cell.

Summary

3.1 Organic Molecules

The chemistry of carbon accounts for the diversity of organic molecules found in living things. Carbon can bond with as many as four other atoms. It can also bond with itself to form both chains and rings. Differences in the carbon backbone and attached functional groups cause organic molecules to have different chemical properties. The chemical properties of a molecule determine how it interacts with other molecules and the role the molecule plays in the cell. Some functional groups are hydrophobic and some are hydrophilic.

There are four classes of organic compounds in cells: carbohydrates, lipids, proteins, and nucleic acids (Table 3.3). Polysaccharides, the largest of the carbohydrates, are polymers of simple sugars called monosaccharides. The polypeptides of proteins are polymers of amino acids and nucleic acids are polymers of nucleotides. Polymers are formed by the joining together of monomers. For each bond formed during condensation synthesis, a molecule of water is removed, and for each bond broken during hydrolysis, a molecule of water is added.

3.2 Carbohydrates

Monosaccharides, disaccharides, and polysaccharides are all carbohydrates. Therefore, the term carbohydrate includes both the monomers (e.g., glucose) and the polymers (e.g., starch, glycogen, and cellulose). Glucose is the immediate energy source of cells. Polysaccharides like starch, glycogen, and cellulose are polymers of glucose. Starch in plants and glycogen in animals are energy-storage compounds, but cellulose in plants and chitin in arthropods have structural roles. Chitin's monomer is glucose with an attached amino group.

3.3 Lipids

Lipids include a wide variety of compounds that are insoluble in water. Fats and oils, which allow long-term energy storage, contain one glycerol and three fatty acids. Both glycerol and fatty acids have polar groups but fats and oils do not have polar groups and this accounts for the insolubility of fats and oils. Fats tend to contain saturated fatty acids, and oils tend to contain unsaturated fatty acids. Saturated fatty acids do not have double bonds but unsaturated fatty acids do have double bonds in their hydrocarbon chain.

In a phospholipid, one of the fatty acids is replaced by a phosphate group. In the presence of water, phospholipids form a double layer because the head of each molecule is ionized and the tails are not.

Waxes are composed of a long fatty acid bonded to an alcohol with a long hydrocarbon chain. Steroids have the same four-ring structure as cholesterol but each differs by the groups attached to these rings.

3.4 Proteins

Proteins are polymers of amino acids. Proteins carry out many diverse functions in cells and organisms. Various ones play a support, enzymatic, defensive, transport, motion, and regulatory function.

Table 3.3

Organic Molecules in Cells

	Categories	Elements	Examples	Functions
Carbohydrates	Monosaccharides 　6-carbon sugar 　5-carbon sugar	C, H, O	 Glucose Deoxyribose, ribose	 Immediate energy source Structure of DNA, RNA
	Disaccharides 　12-carbon sugar	C, H, O	Sucrose	Transport sugar in plants
	Polysaccharides 　polymer of glucose	C, H, O	Starch, glycogen Cellulose	Energy storage in plants, animals Plant cell wall structure
Lipids	Triglycerides 　1 glycerol + 3 fatty acids	C, H, O	Fats, oils	Long-term energy storage
	Waxes 　fatty acid + alcohol	C, H, O	Cuticle Ear wax	Protective covering in plants Protective wax in ears
	Phospholipids 　like triglyceride except 　the head group 　contains phosphate	C, H, O, P	Lecithin	Plasma membrane component
	Steroids 　backbone of 4 fused rings	C, H, O	Cholesterol Testosterone	Plasma membrane component Male sex hormone
Proteins	Polypeptides 　polymer of amino acids	C, H, O, N, S	Enzymes Myosin and actin Insulin Hemoglobin Collagen	Speed up cellular reactions Muscle cell components Regulates sugar content of blood Oxygen carrier in blood Fibrous support of body parts
Nucleic Acids	Nucleic acids 　polymer of nucleotides	C, H, O, N, P	DNA RNA	Genetic material Protein synthesis
	Nucleotides		ATP Coenzymes	Energy carrier Assist enzymes

A polypeptide is a long chain of amino acids joined by peptide bonds. There are 20 different amino acids in cells that differ only by their *R* groups. Polarity and nonpolarity are important aspects of the *R* groups. A protein has three levels of structure: the primary level is the sequence of the amino acids; the secondary level contains α helices and β (pleated) sheets held in place by hydrogen bonding between amino acids along the polypeptide chain; and the tertiary level is the final folding and twisting of the polypeptide that is held in place by bonding and hydrophobic interactions between *R* groups. Proteins that contain more than one polypeptide have a quaternary level of structure, as well.

A protein can be denatured and lose its normal shape and activity, but if renaturation occurs, it assumes both again. This shows that the final shape of a protein is dependent upon the primary sequence of amino acids.

3.5 Nucleic Acids

The nucleic acids DNA and RNA are polymers of nucleotides. Each nucleotide has three components: a phosphate (phosphoric acid), a 5-carbon sugar, and a nitrogen-containing base.

DNA, which contains the sugar deoxyribose, is the genetic material that stores information for its own replication and for the order in which amino acids are to be sequenced in proteins. DNA, with the help of mRNA, specifies protein synthesis. DNA contains phosphate, the sugar deoxyribose, the bases A, T, C, and G and is a double-stranded helix. RNA contains phosphate, the sugar ribose, the bases A, U, C, and G and is single stranded.

ATP, with its unstable phosphate bonds, is the energy currency of cells. Hydrolysis of ATP to ADP + Ⓟ releases energy that is used by the cell to make a product or do any other type of metabolic work.

Reviewing the Chapter

1. How do the chemical characteristics of carbon affect the characteristics of organic molecules?   34–35
2. Give examples of functional groups, and discuss the importance of their being hydrophobic or hydrophilic.   35
3. What molecules are monomers of the polymers studied in this chapter? How do monomers join to produce polymers, and how are polymers broken down to monomers?   36
4. Name several monosaccharides, disaccharides, and polysaccharides, and give a function of each. How are these molecules structurally distinguishable?   37–38
5. What is the difference between a saturated and unsaturated fatty acid? Explain the structure of a fat molecule by stating its components and how they join together.   40–41
6. How does the structure of a phospholipid differ from that of a fat? How do phospholipids form a bilayer in the presence of water?   42
7. Describe the structure of a generalized steroid. How does one steroid differ from another?   42
8. Draw the structure of an amino acid and a dipeptide, pointing out the peptide bond.   44

9. Discuss the four possible levels of protein structure and relate each level to particular bonding patterns.   46
10. How is the tertiary structure of a polypeptide related to its primary structure? Mention denaturation as evidence of this relationship.   44–46
11. How do nucleotides bond to form nucleic acids? State and explain several differences between the structure of DNA and that of RNA.   48–49
12. Discuss the structure and function of ATP.   49

Testing Yourself

Choose the best answer for each question.

1. Which of these is not a characteristic of carbon?
   a. forms four covalent bonds
   b. bonds with itself
   c. is sometimes ionic
   d. forms long chains
   e. sometimes shares two pairs of electrons with another atom
2. The functional group —COOH is
   a. acidic.
   b. basic.
   c. never ionized.
   d. found only in nucleotides.
   e. All of these are correct.
3. A hydrophilic group is
   a. attracted to water.
   b. a polar and/or ionized group.
   c. found in fatty acids.
   d. the opposite of a hydrophobic group.
   e. All of these are correct.
4. Which of these is an example of hydrolysis?
   a. amino acid + amino acid ⟶ dipeptide + H_2O
   b. dipeptide + H_2O ⟶ amino acid + amino acid
   c. denaturation of a polypeptide
   d. Both a and b are correct.
   e. Both b and c are correct.
5. Which of these makes cellulose nondigestible in humans?
   a. a polymer of glucose subunits
   b. a fibrous protein
   c. the linkage between the glucose molecules
   d. the peptide linkage between the amino acid molecules
   e. The carboxyl groups ionize.
6. A fatty acid is unsaturated if it
   a. contains hydrogen.
   b. contains double bonds.
   c. contains an acidic group.
   d. bonds to glycogen.
   e. bonds to a nucleotide.
7. Which of these is not a lipid?
   a. steroid
   b. fat
   c. polysaccharide
   d. wax
   e. phospholipid

8. The difference between one amino acid and another is found in the
   a. amino group.
   b. carboxyl group.
   c. *R* group.
   d. peptide bond.
   e. carbon atoms.
9. The shape of a polypeptide is
   a. maintained by bonding between parts of the polypeptide.
   b. important to its function.
   c. ultimately dependent upon the primary structure.
   d. necessary to its function.
   e. All of these are correct.
10. Which of these contains a peptide bond?

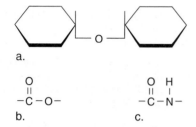

a.

$$\begin{matrix} O \\ \| \\ -C-O- \end{matrix} \qquad \begin{matrix} O\ \ H \\ \|\ \ \ | \\ -C-N- \end{matrix}$$
b.   c.

11. Nucleotides
    a. contain a sugar, a nitrogen-containing base, and a phosphate molecule.
    b. are the monomers for fats and polysaccharides.
    c. join together by covalent bonding between the bases.
    d. are present in both DNA and RNA.
    e. Both a and d are correct.
12. ATP
    a. is an amino acid.
    b. has a helical structure.
    c. is a high-energy molecule that can break down to ADP and phosphate.
    d. provides enzymes for metabolism.
    e. is most energetic when in the ADP state.
13. Label the following diagram using the terms monomer, hydrolysis, condensation, and polymer, and explain the diagram:

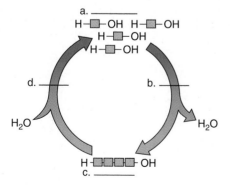

Thinking Scientifically

1. You are studying the fat content of different types of seeds. You have discovered that some types of seeds have a much higher percentage of saturated fatty acids than others. You know the property difference (solid versus liquid) and the structural difference (more hydrogen versus less) between saturated and unsaturated fatty acids. How might these fatty acid differences correlate with climate (tropical compared to temperate), the size of seeds (small compared to large) and environmental conditions for germination (favorable compared to unfavorable)?
2. You are investigating molecules that inhibit a bacterial enzyme. You discovered that the addition of several phosphate groups to an inhibitor improves its effectiveness. Why would knowledge of the three-dimensional structure of the bacterial enzyme help you understand why the phosphate groups improve the inhibitor's effectiveness?

Bioethical Issue

Eric Stevenson and more than 110,000 veterans of the Gulf War are mysteriously ill. They complain of conditions like skin rashes, breathing difficulties, fatigue, diarrhea, muscle and joint pain, headaches, and loss of memory. While the Pentagon doesn't recognize what is called the Gulf War Syndrome (GWS), it does admit that soldiers were exposed to at least four categories of organic chemicals:

- Petroleum products such as kerosene, diesel fuel, leaded gasoline, and smoke from oil-well fires.
- Pesticides and insect repellents. These were applied to clothing and sprayed into the air.
- Drugs and vaccines. Pyridostigmine bromide was given to protect against nerve gas. Vaccines against anthrax and botulism were given in case of biological warfare.
- Biological and chemical weapons. Reluctantly, the Pentagon estimates that hundreds of thousands of soldiers may have been exposed to nerve gas released into the air when Iraqi ammunition depots were bombed.

While the military says that exposure can make you sick, they cling to the idea that toxic chemicals either kill you outright or you recover completely. Therefore, they suggest that the veterans are suffering from post-traumatic stress disorder. Lingering symptoms of stress are to be expected in a certain number of soldiers that come home from war.

Epidemiologist Robert Haley, however, has studied the effects of these chemicals on chickens, and found that their combination does produce Gulf War Syndrome symptoms. He says, "The Defense Department should agree that this is a physical injury, a brain injury, aided and abetted by acute stress."

For what reasons might the Pentagon be reluctant to accept the possibility that GWS is due to exposure of troops to organic chemicals? In so doing are they shirking their responsibility to Gulf War veterans?

Understanding the Terms

adenosine 50	inorganic molecule 34
ADP (adenosine diphosphate) 50	isomer 35
amino acid 45	lactose 37
ATP (adenosine triphosphate) 48, 50	lipid 40
carbohydrate 37	maltose 37
cellulose 38	monomer 36
chitin 39	monosaccharide 37
complementary base pairing 49	nucleic acid 48
condensation synthesis 36	nucleotide 48
denatured 47	oil 40
deoxyribose 37	organic molecule 34
disaccharide 37	pentose 37
DNA (deoxyribonucleic acid) 48	peptide 45
fat 40	peptide bond 45
fatty acid 40	phospholipid 42
fructose 37	polymer 36
functional group 35	polypeptide 45
glucose 37	polysaccharide 38
glycerol 40	protein 44
glycogen 38	ribose 37
hexose 37	RNA (ribonucleic acid) 48
hydrolysis 36	saturated 40
hydrophilic 35	starch 38
hydrophobic 35	steroid 42
	sucrose 37
	triglyceride 40
	unsaturated 40
	wax 40

Match the terms to these definitions:

a. _____ Class of organic compounds that includes monosaccharides, disaccharides, and polysaccharides.

b. _____ Class of organic compounds that tend to be soluble in nonpolar solvents such as alcohol.

c. _____ Macromolecule consisting of covalently bonded monomers.

d. _____ Molecules that have the same molecular formula but a different structure and, therefore, shape.

e. _____ Two or more amino acids joined together by covalent bonding.

Web Connections

Exploring the Internet

http://www.mhhe.com/biosci/genbio/mader
(click on *Biology 7/e*)

The *Biology 7/e* Online Learning Center provides many resources for studying the material in this chapter including links to the following sites:

Amino Acids. This site lists the 20 different amino acids, presents their structure, and discusses their abbreviations.

http://www.chemie.fu-berlin.de/chemistry/bio/amino-acids.html

Large Molecule Review. The chapters that follow are from a hypertextbook. They cover lipids, sugars, and nucleic and amino acids.

http://esg-www.mit.edu:8001/esgbio/lm/lmdir.html

and

http://esg-www.mit.edu:8001/esgbio/lm/lipids/lipids.html
http://esg-www.mit.edu:8001/esgbio/lm/sugars/sugars.html
http://esg-www.mit.edu:8001/esgbio/lm/proteins/aa/aminoacids.html
http://esg-www.mit.edu:8001/esgbio/lm/nucleicacids/nucleicacids.html

Library of 3-D Molecular Structures. Both organic and inorganic molecular structures are seen.

http://www.nyu.edu/pages/mathmol/library/

Cell Structure and Function

chapter

4

Micrograph of a plant cell. *Arabidopsis thaliana.*

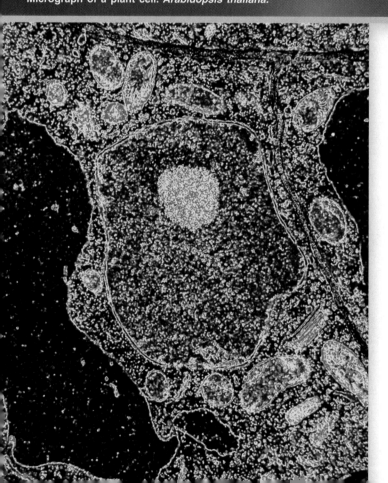

Today we are accustomed to thinking of living things as being constructed of cells. But the word cell didn't come into use until the seventeenth century. Antonie van Leeuwenhoek of Holland is famous for observing tiny, unicellular living things that no one had seen before. Leeuwenhoek sent his findings to an organization of scientists called the Royal Society in London. Robert Hooke, an Englishman, confirmed Leeuwenhoek's observations and was the first to use the term cell. The tiny chambers he observed in the honeycomb structure of cork reminded him of the rooms, or cells, in a monastery. Naturally, he referred to the boundaries of these chambers as walls.

Even today, a light micrograph of a cell is not overly impressive. You can make out the nucleus and its nucleolus near the cell's center but that's about it. The rest of the cell seems to contain only an amorphous matrix. Through electron microscopy and biochemical analysis it was discovered that the cell actually contains organelles, tiny specialized structures performing specific cellular functions. Further, the nucleus contains numerous chromosomes and thousands of genes!

◐ 4.1 Cellular Level of Organization

In the 1830s, Matthias Schleiden stated that all plants are composed of cells and Theodor Schwann stated that all animals are composed of cells. These Germans based their ideas not only on their own work but on the work of all who had studied tissues under microscopes. Today we recognize that all the organisms we see about us are made up of cells. Figure 4.1 illustrates that in our daily lives we observe the whole organism, but if it were possible to view them internally with a microscope, we would then see their cellular nature. A **cell** is the smallest unit of living matter.

There are unicellular organisms but most, including ourselves, are multicellular. A cell is not only the structural unit, it is also the functional unit of organs and, therefore, organisms. This is very evident when you consider certain illnesses of the human body such as diabetes or prostate cancer. It is the cells of the pancreas or the prostate that are malfunctioning, rather than the organ itself.

All organisms are made up of cells, and a cell is the structural and functional unit of organs and, ultimately, organisms.

Cells reproduce. Once a growing cell gets to a certain size, it divides. Unicellular organisms reproduce themselves when they divide. Multicellular organisms grow when their cells divide. Cells are also involved in the reproduction of multicellular organisms. Therefore, there is always a continuity of cells from generation to generation. Soon after Schleiden and Schwann had presented their findings, another German scientist, Rudolf Virchow, used a microscope to study the life of cells. He came to the conclusion that cells do not arise on their own accord; rather, "every cell comes from a preexisting cell." By the middle of the nineteenth century, biologists clearly recognized that all organisms are composed of self-reproducing cells.

Cells are capable of self-reproduction, and cells come only from preexisting cells.

The previous two highlighted statements are often called the **cell theory**. The cell theory is one of the unifying concepts of biology. There are extensive data to support its two basic principles and it is universally accepted by biologists.

Figure 4.1 Organisms and cells.
All organisms, whether plants or animals, are composed of cells. This is not readily apparent because a microscope is usually needed to see the cells. **a.** Corn. **b.** Light micrograph of corn leaf showing many individual cells. **c.** Rabbit. **d.** Light micrograph of a rabbit's intestinal lining showing that it, too, is composed of cells. The dark-staining bodies are nuclei.

a. Corn, *Zea mays*

c. Rabbit, *Oryctolagus* sp.

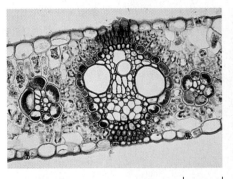

b.   20 µm

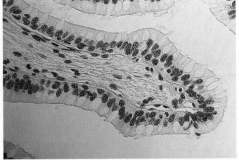

d.   200 µm

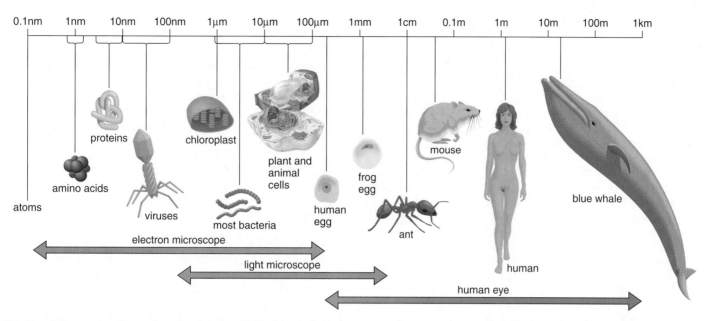

Figure 4.2 The sizes of living things and their components.
Whales', humans', mice's, and even frogs' eggs can be seen by the human eye. It takes a microscope to see most cells and lower levels of biological organization. Cells are visible with the light microscope, but not in much detail. It takes an electron microscope to see organelles in detail and to make out viruses and molecules. Notice that in this illustration each higher unit is 10 times greater than the lower unit. (In the metric system, see inside back cover, 1 meter = 10^2 cm = 10^3 mm = 10^6 mm = 10^9 nm.)

Cell Size

Cells are quite small. A frog's egg, at about one millimeter (mm) in diameter, is large enough to be seen by the human eye. Most cells are far smaller than one millimeter; some are even as small as one micrometer (μm)—one thousandth of a millimeter. Cell inclusions and macromolecules are even smaller still than a micrometer and are measured in terms of nanometers (nm).

Why are cells so small? To answer this question consider that a cell needs a surface area large enough to allow adequate nutrients to enter and to rid itself of wastes. A small cube that is 1 mm tall has a surface area of 6 mm² and a volume of 1 mm³. This is a ratio of surface area to volume of 6:1. But a cube that is 2 mm tall has a surface area of 24 mm² and a volume of 8 mm³. This is a ratio of only 3:1. Therefore a small cell has more surface area per volume than does a large cell:

small cell—
more surface area
per volume

large cell—
less surface area
per volume

Small cells, not large cells, are likely to have an adequate surface area for exchange of wastes for nutrients. We would expect, then, a size limitation for an actively metabolizing cell. A chicken's egg is several centimeters in diameter, but the egg is not actively metabolizing. Once the egg is incubated and metabolic activity begins, the egg divides repeatedly without growth. Cell division restores the amount of surface area needed for adequate exchange of materials. Further, cells that specialize in absorption have modifications that greatly increase the surface area per volume of the cell. The columnar cells along the surface of the intestinal wall have surface foldings called microvilli (sing., microvillus), which increase their surface area.

A cell needs a surface area that can adequately exchange materials with the environment. Surface-area-to-volume considerations require that cells stay small.

Figure 4.2 outlines the visual range of the eye, light microscope, and electron microscope. The discussion of microscopy in the reading on pages 58–59 explains why the electron microscope allows us to "see" so much more detail than the light microscope does.

Microscopy of Today

Cells were not discovered until the invention of the microscope in the seventeenth century. Since that time, various types of microscopes have been developed for the study of cells and their components.

In the *bright-field light microscope*, light rays passing through a specimen are brought into focus by a set of glass lenses, and the resulting image is then viewed by the human eye. In the *transmission electron microscope*, electrons passing through a specimen are brought into focus by a set of magnetic lenses, and the resulting image is projected onto a fluorescent screen or photographic film. In the *scanning electron microscope* (*SEM*), a narrow beam of electrons is scanned over the surface of the specimen, which is coated with a thin metal layer. The metal gives off secondary electrons that are collected by a detector to produce an image on a television screen. The SEM permits the development of three-dimensional images (Fig. 4A).

Magnification, Resolution, and Contrast

Almost everyone knows that the magnifying capability of a transmission electron microscope is greater than that of a light microscope. A light microscope can magnify objects a few thousand times, but an electron microscope can magnify them hundreds of thousands of times. The difference lies in the means of illumination. The path of light rays and electrons moving through space is wavelike, but the wavelength of electrons is much shorter than the wavelength of light. This difference in wavelength accounts for the electron microscope's greater magnifying capability and its greater resolving power. The greater the resolving power, the greater the detail eventually seen. Resolution is the minimum distance between two objects at which they can still be seen, or resolved, as two separate objects. If oil is placed between the sample and the objective lens of the light microscope, the resolving power is increased, and if ultraviolet light is used instead of visible light, it is also increased. But typically, a light microscope can resolve down to 0.2 μm, while the electron microscope can resolve down to 0.0002 μm. If the resolving power of the average human eye is set at one, then that of the typical light microscope is about 500, and that of the electron microscope is 100,000. This means that the electron microscope distinguishes much greater detail (Fig. 4A).

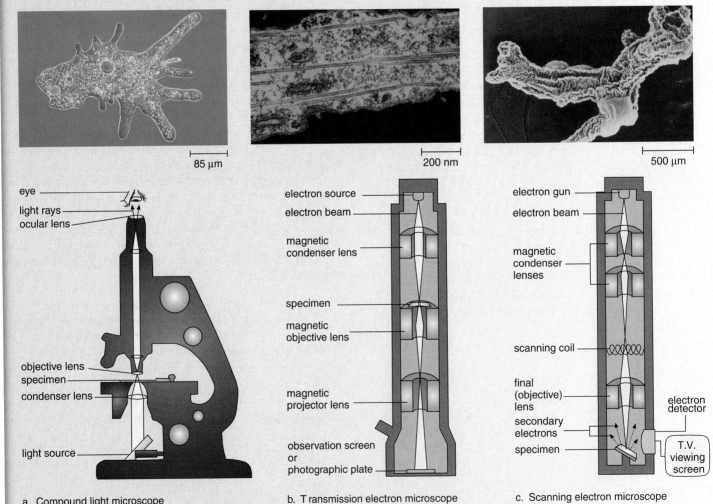

85 μm

200 nm

500 μm

eye
light rays
ocular lens

objective lens
specimen
condenser lens

light source

a. Compound light microscope

electron source
electron beam

magnetic
condenser lens

specimen
magnetic
objective lens

magnetic
projector lens

observation screen
or
photographic plate

b. Transmission electron microscope

electron gun
electron beam

magnetic
condenser
lenses

scanning coil

final
(objective)
lens
secondary
electrons
specimen

electron
detector

T.V.
viewing
screen

c. Scanning electron microscope

Figure 4A Diagram of microscopes with accompanying micrographs of *Amoeba proteus.*

Some microscopes view living specimens, but often specimens are treated prior to observation. Cells are killed, fixed so they do not decompose, and embedded into a matrix. The matrix strengthens the specimen so that it can be thinly sliced. These sections are often stained with colored dyes (light microscopy) or with electron-dense metals (electron microscopy) to provide contrast. Another way to increase contrast is to use optical methods such as phase contrast and differential interference contrast (Fig. 4B). In addition to optical and electronic methods for contrasting transparent cells, a third very prominent research tool is called *immunofluorescence microscopy,* because it uses fluorescent antibodies to reveal the location of a protein in the cell (see Fig. 4.14). The importance of this method is that the cellular distribution of a single type of protein can be examined.

Illumination, Viewing, and Recording

Light rays can be bent (refracted) and brought to a focus as they pass through glass lenses, but electrons do not pass through glass. Electrons have a charge that allows them to be brought into a focus by magnetic lenses. The human eye utilizes light to see an object but cannot utilize electrons for the same purpose. Therefore, electrons leaving the specimen in the electron microscope are directed toward a screen or a photograph plate that is sensitive to their presence. Humans can view the image on the screen or photograph.

A major advancement in illumination has been the introduction of *confocal microscopy,* which uses a laser beam scanned across the specimen to focus on a single shallow plane within the cell.

The microscopist can "optically section" the specimen by focusing up and down, and a series of optical sections can be combined in a computer to create a three-dimensional image, which can be displayed and rotated on the computer screen.

An image from a microscope may be recorded by replacing the human eye with a television camera. The television camera converts the light image into an electronic image, which can be entered into a computer. In *video-enhanced contrast microscopy,* the computer makes the darkest areas of the original image much darker and the lightest areas of the original much lighter. The result is a high-contrast image with deep blacks and bright whites. Even more contrast can be introduced by the computer if shades of gray are replaced by colors.

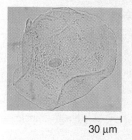

30 μm

Bright-field. Light passing through the specimen is brought directly into focus. Usually, the low level of contrast within the specimen interferes with viewing all but its largest components.

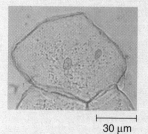

30 μm

Bright-field (stained). Dyes are used to stain the specimen. Certain components take up the dye more than other components, and therefore contrast is enhanced.

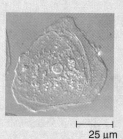

25 μm

Differential interference contrast. Optical methods are used to enhance density differences within the specimen so that certain regions appear brighter than others. This technique is used to view living cells, chromosomes, and organelle masses.

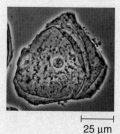

25 μm

Phase contrast. Density differences in the specimen cause light rays to come out of "phase." The microscope enhances these phase differences so that some regions of the specimen appear brighter or darker than others. This technique is widely used to observe living cells and organelles.

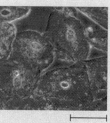

25 μm

Darkfield. Light is passed through the specimen at an oblique angle so that the objective lens receives only light diffracted and scattered by the object. This technique is used to view organelles, which appear quite bright against a dark field.

Figure 4B **Cheek cells.**
Photomicrographs of cheek cells, illustrating different types of light microscopy.

4.2 Bacterial Cells

Bacteria [Gk. *bacterion,* rod] are **prokaryotic cells**[1] [Gk. *pro,* before, and *karyon,* kernel, nucleus] in the domain Bacteria. Most bacteria are between 1–10 µm in size; therefore, they are just visible with the light microscope.

Figure 4.3 illustrates the main features of bacterial anatomy. The **cell wall** contains peptidoglycan, a complex molecule with chains of a unique amino disaccharide joined by peptide chains. In some bacteria, the cell wall is further surrounded by a **capsule** and/or gelatinous sheath called a **slime layer.** Motile bacteria usually have long, very thin appendages called flagella (sing., **flagellum**) that are composed of subunits of the protein called flagellin. The flagella, which rotate like propellers, rapidly move the bacterium in a fluid medium. Some bacteria also have fimbriae, which are short appendages that help them attach to an appropriate surface.

A membrane called the **plasma membrane** regulates the movement of molecules into and out of the cytoplasm, the interior of the cell. **Cytoplasm** in a prokaryotic cell consists of **cytosol,** a semifluid medium, and thousands of **ribosomes,** small bodies that coordinate the synthesis of proteins. In prokaryotes, most genes are found within a single chromosome (loop of DNA) located within the **nucleoid** [L. *nucleus,* nucleus, kernel and Gk. *-eides,* like], but they may also have small accessory rings of DNA called **plasmids.** In addition,

the photosynthetic cyanobacteria have light-sensitive pigments, usually within the membranes of flattened disks called **thylakoids.**

Although bacteria seem structurally simple, they are actually metabolically diverse. Bacteria are adapted to living in almost any kind of environment and are diversified to the extent that almost any type of organic matter can be used as a nutrient for some particular bacterium. Given an energy source, most bacteria are able to synthesize any kind of molecule they may need. Therefore, the cytoplasm is the site of thousands of chemical reactions and bacteria are more metabolically competent than are human beings. Indeed, the metabolic capability of bacteria is exploited by humans who use them to produce a wide variety of chemicals and products for human use.

Bacteria are prokaryotic cells. Prokaryotic cells have these constant features.

Outer boundary	cell wall
	plasma membrane
Cytoplasm	ribosomes
	thylakoids (cyanobacteria)
Nucleoid	innumerable enzymes
	chromosome (loop of DNA)

---

[1] Archaea (domain Archaea) are another type of prokaryote. Chapter 29 discusses archaea, and also bacteria in more detail.

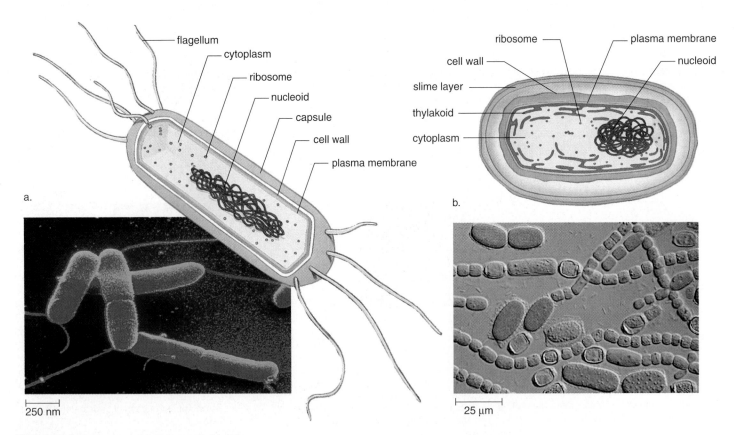

Figure 4.3 Bacterial (prokaryotic) cells.
a. Nonphotosynthetic bacterium. b. Cyanobacterium, a photosynthetic bacterium, formerly called a blue-green alga.

4.3 Eukaryotic Cells

In general, eukaryotic cells are larger than prokaryotic cells. In contrast to prokaryotic cells, **eukaryotic cells** [Gk. *eu,* true, and *karyon,* kernel, nucleus] have a true nucleus. A nucleus is a membrane-bounded structure where DNA is housed within threadlike structures called chromatin.

Eukaryotic cells have a membrane-bounded nucleus, and prokaryotic cells lack a nucleus.

A membrane is a phospholipid bilayer with embedded proteins.

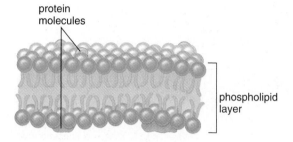

In eukaryotic cells, **organelles** are small bodies, each with a specific structure and function (Table 4.1). Many organelles are membrane-bounded. The cytosol, which is a semifluid medium outside the nucleus, is divided up and compartmentalized by the organelles. Compartmentalization keeps the cell organized and keeps its various functions separate from one another. The cytosol in eukaryotic cells has an organized lattice of protein filaments called the cytoskeleton.

Eukaryotic cells, like prokaryotic cells, have a plasma membrane that separates the contents of the cell from the environment and regulates the passage of molecules into and out of the cell. Some eukaryotic cells, notably plant cells, also have an outer boundary called a **cell wall.** A plant cell wall contains cellulose fibrils and therefore has a different composition than the cell wall of bacteria. A cell wall supports and protects the cell but does not interfere with the movement of molecules across the plasma membrane.

Notice in Figures 4.4 and 4.5, both animal and plant cells contain mitochondria while only plant cells have chloroplasts. Animal cells, but not plant cells, have centrioles. The color chosen to represent each structure in the plant and animal cell is used for that structure throughout the chapters of this part and throughout the text.

Eukaryotic cells have a number of organelles and prokaryotic cells lack membrane-bounded organelles.

Table 4.1

Structures in Eukaryotic Cells

Name	Composition	Function
Cell wall	Contains cellulose fibrils	Support and protection
Plasma membrane	Phospholipid bilayer with embedded proteins	Define cell boundary; regulation of molecule passage into and out of cell
Nucleus	Nuclear envelope surrounding nucleoplasm, chromatin, and nucleoli	Storage of genetic information; synthesis of DNA and RNA
Nucleolus	Concentrated area of chromatin, RNA, and proteins	Ribosomal formation
Ribosome	Protein and RNA in two subunits	Protein synthesis
Endoplasmic reticulum (ER)	Membranous flattened channels and tubular canals	Synthesis and/or modification of proteins and other substances, and transport by vesicle formation
Rough ER	Studded with ribosomes	Protein synthesis
Smooth ER	Having no ribosomes	Various; lipid synthesis in some cells
Golgi apparatus	Stack of membranous saccules	Processing, packaging, and distribution of proteins and lipids
Vacuole and vesicle	Membranous sacs	Storage of substances
Lysosome	Membranous vesicle containing digestive enzymes	Intracellular digestion
Peroxisomes	Membranous vesicle containing specific enzymes	Various metabolic tasks
Mitochondrion	Membranous cristae bounded by an outer membrane	Cellular respiration
Chloroplast	Membranous grana bounded by two membranes	Photosynthesis
Cytoskeleton	Microtubules, intermediate filaments, actin filaments	Shape of cell and movement of its parts
Cilia and flagella	9 + 2 pattern of microtubules	Movement of cell
Centriole	9 + 0 pattern of microtubules	Formation of basal bodies

protein molecules

phospholipid layer

Figure 4.4 Animal cell anatomy.
a. Generalized drawing. b. Transmission electron micrograph. See
Table 4.1 for a description of these structures, along with a listing of
their functions.

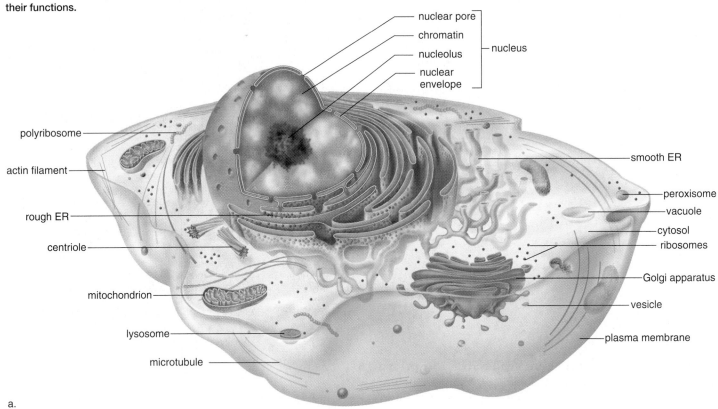

nuclear pore
chromatin ⎫
nucleolus ⎬ nucleus
nuclear
envelope ⎭

polyribosome

actin filament

rough ER

centriole

mitochondrion

lysosome

microtubule

smooth ER

peroxisome

vacuole

cytosol

ribosomes

Golgi apparatus

vesicle

plasma membrane

a.

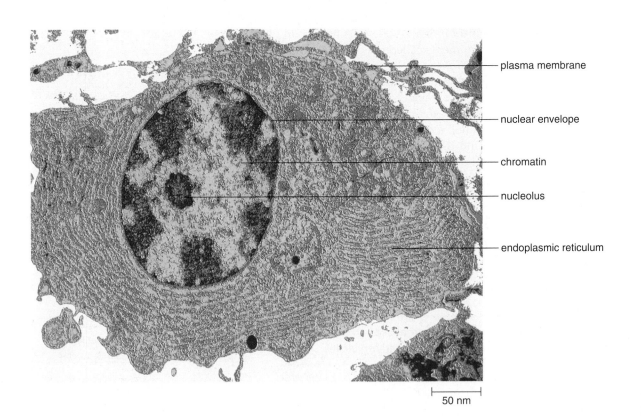

plasma membrane

nuclear envelope

chromatin

nucleolus

endoplasmic reticulum

50 nm

b.

Figure 4.5 Plant cell anatomy.
a. Generalized drawing. b. Transmission electron micrograph of young leaf cell. See Table 4.1 for a description of these structures, along with a listing of their functions.

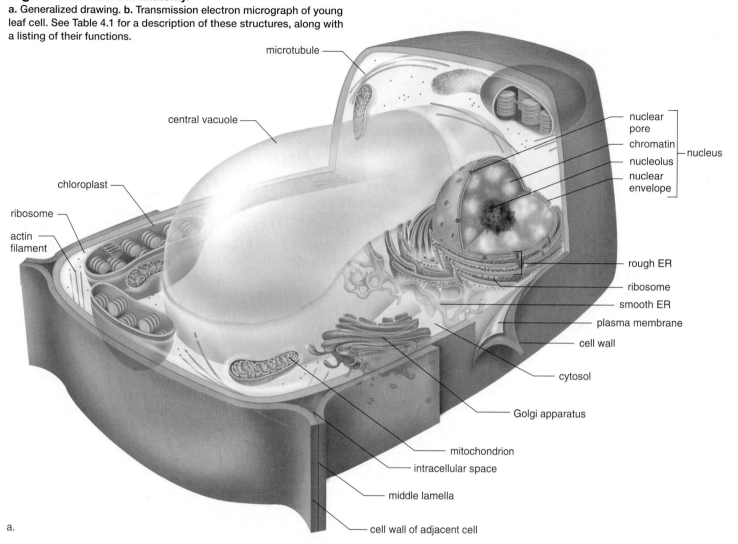

microtubule

central vacuole

chloroplast

ribosome

actin filament

nuclear pore

chromatin

nucleolus — nucleus

nuclear envelope

rough ER

ribosome

smooth ER

plasma membrane

cell wall

cytosol

Golgi apparatus

mitochondrion

intracellular space

middle lamella

cell wall of adjacent cell

a.

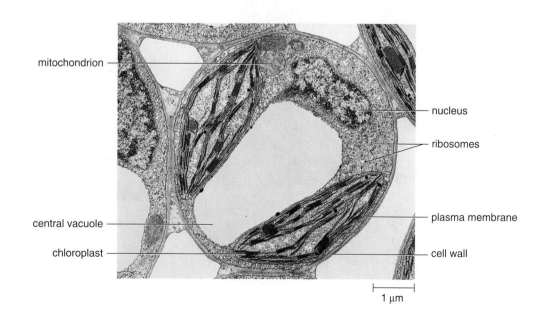

mitochondrion

central vacuole

chloroplast

nucleus

ribosomes

plasma membrane

cell wall

1 μm

b.

The Evolution of the Eukaryotic Cell

How did the eukaryotic cell arise? Invagination of the plasma membrane might explain the origination of the nucleus and certain other organelles, such as the endoplasmic reticulum and the Golgi apparatus. Some believe that the rest of the organelles could also have arisen in this manner.

Another hypothesis has gained recognition and acceptance by many. In the laboratory, it has been observed that an amoeba infected with bacteria can become dependent upon them so that the bacteria remain within the cell. Some investigators, especially Lynn Margulis, believe that mitochondria and chloroplasts are derived from bacteria that were taken up by a much larger cell that already had a nucleus (Fig. 4.6). Perhaps mitochondria were originally aerobic bacteria that take in oxygen and chloroplasts were originally cyanobacteria that photosynthesize. The host cell would have benefited from an ability to utilize oxygen and/or make its own organic food if by chance the bacteria were not destroyed. In other words, after these prokaryotes entered by *endocytosis,* a *symbiotic* relationship was established. Some of the evidence for the **endosymbiotic hypothesis** is as follows:

1. Mitochondria and chloroplasts are similar to bacteria in size and in structure.
2. Both organelles are bounded by a double membrane—the outer membrane may be derived from the engulfing vesicle, and the inner one may be derived from the plasma membrane of the original prokaryote.
3. Mitochondria and chloroplasts contain a limited amount of genetic material and divide by splitting. Their DNA is a circular loop like that of bacteria.
4. Although most of the proteins within mitochondria and chloroplasts are now produced by the eukaryotic host, they do have their own ribosomes and they do produce some proteins. Their ribosomes resemble those of bacteria.
5. The RNA (ribonucleic acid) composition of their ribosomes suggests a eubacterial origin for chloroplasts and mitochondria.

Margulis even suggests that the flagella of eukaryotes are derived from a spirochete prokaryote that became attached to a host cell (Fig. 4.6). However, it is important to remember that the flagella of eukaryotes but not prokaryotes are composed of structures called microtubules. In any case, the acquisition of microtubules by eukaryotes would have led to the ability to form a spindle which separates the chromosomes during cell division. The type of cell division called meiosis is associated with sexual reproduction of eukaryotes and sexual reproduction contributes to variation among members of a population and the evolution of new species.

According to the endosymbiotic hypothesis, aerobic bacteria became mitochondria and cyanobacteria became chloroplasts after being taken up by precursors to modern-day eukaryotic cells.

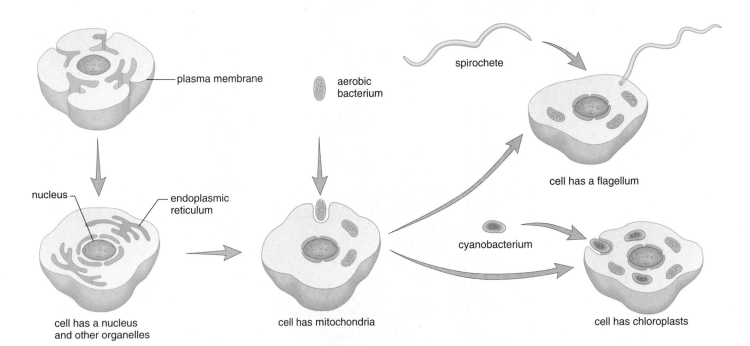

Figure 4.6 Evolution of the eukaryotic cell.
Invagination of the plasma membrane could account for the formation of the nucleus and certain other organelles. The endosymbiotic hypothesis suggests that mitochondria, chloroplasts, and flagella are derived from prokaryotes that were taken up by a much larger eukaryotic cell.

The Nucleus

The **nucleus** [L. *nucleus,* kernel], which has a diameter of about 5 μm, is a prominent structure in the eukaryotic cell (Fig. 4.7). The nucleus contains **chromatin** [Gk. *chroma,* color, and *teino,* stretch] in a semifluid medium called the **nucleoplasm.** Chromatin looks grainy, but actually it is a network of strands that undergoes coiling into rodlike structures called **chromosomes** [Gk. *chroma,* color, and *soma,* body], just before the cell divides. Chemical analysis shows that chromatin, and therefore chromosomes, contains DNA and much protein, and some RNA (ribonucleic acid).

All forms of RNA, of which there are several, are produced in the nucleus. Some dark regions of chromatin are nucleoli (sing., **nucleolus**) where a type of RNA, called ribosomal RNA (rRNA), is produced and where rRNA joins with proteins to form the subunits of ribosomes. (Ribosomes are small bodies in the cytoplasm where protein synthesis occurs.)

The nucleus is separated from the cytoplasm by a double membrane known as the **nuclear envelope.** The nuclear envelope has **nuclear pores** of sufficient size (100 nm) to permit the passage of proteins into the nucleus and ribosomal subunits out of the nucleus. High-power electron micrographs show that the pores have nonmembranous components associated with them that form a nuclear pore complex.

The nucleus is of primary importance because it contains DNA, the molecule which stores genetic information and determines the characteristics of a cell and its metabolic functioning. Activated DNA, with the help of messenger RNA (mRNA) acting as an intermediary, specifies the sequencing of amino acids during protein synthesis. The proteins of a cell determine its structure and the functions it can perform.

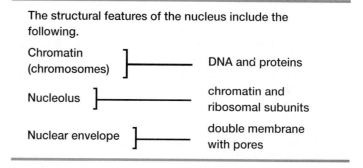

The structural features of the nucleus include the following.

Chromatin (chromosomes)	DNA and proteins
Nucleolus	chromatin and ribosomal subunits
Nuclear envelope	double membrane with pores

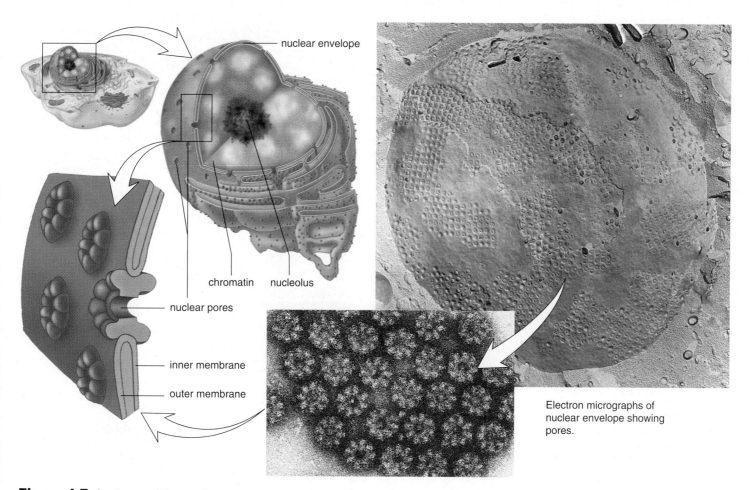

nuclear envelope

chromatin   nucleolus

nuclear pores

inner membrane

outer membrane

Electron micrographs of nuclear envelope showing pores.

Figure 4.7 **Anatomy of the nucleus.**
The nucleus contains chromatin. Chromatin has a special region called the nucleolus, which is where rRNA is produced and ribosomal subunits are assembled. The nuclear envelope contains pores, as is shown in this micrograph of a freeze-fractured nuclear envelope. Each pore is lined by a complex of eight proteins.

Ribosomes

Unlike many of the organelles discussed in this chapter, **ribosomes** are found in both prokaryotes and eukaryotes. In eukaryotes, ribosomes are 20 nm by 30 nm, and in prokaryotes they are slightly smaller. In both types of cells, ribosomes are composed of two subunits, one large and one small (Fig. 4.8*c*). Each subunit has its own mix of proteins and rRNA.

In eukaryotic cells some ribosomes occur free within the cytosol either singly or in groups, called **polyribosomes,** and others are attached to the endoplasmic reticulum (ER), a membranous system of saccules and channels discussed in the next section.

Ribosomes, as mentioned, are sites of protein synthesis. They receive mRNA from the nucleus and this nucleic acid carries a coded message from DNA indicating the correct sequence of amino acids in a protein. Proteins synthesized by cytoplasmic ribosomes are used in the cytosol and those synthesized by attached ribosomes end up in a cellular membrane, stored in a **vesicle** (tiny membranous sacs), or secreted out of the cell.

What causes a ribosome to bind to endoplasmic reticulum? Binding occurs only if the protein being synthesized by a ribosome has an ER signal sequence. An ER signal sequence enables a ribosome to bind to a receptor protein on the endoplasmic reticulum (Fig. 4.8*d*). Receptor proteins are sometimes called "docking proteins" because they form a docking site for a particular molecule.

Ribosomes are small organelles where protein synthesis occurs. Ribosomes occur in the cytosol, both singly and in groups (i.e., polyribosomes). Numerous ribosomes are attached to the endoplasmic reticulum.

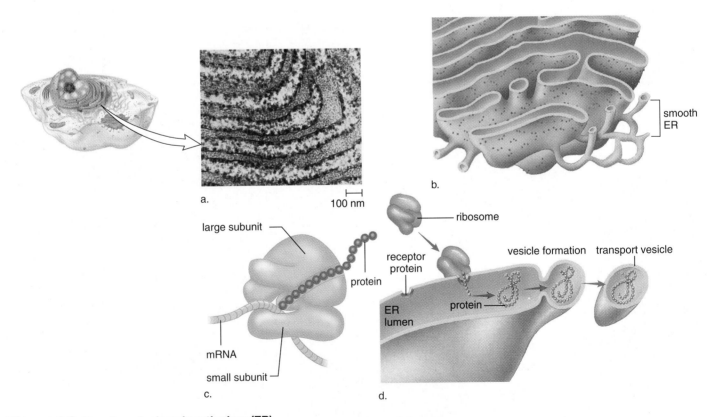

Figure 4.8 Rough endoplasmic reticulum (ER).
a. In this mouse liver cell micrograph, rough ER consists of flattened vesicles studded on the outer surface with ribosomes. **b.** Rough ER is continuous with smooth ER as illustrated. **c.** A ribosome carries out protein synthesis. The messenger RNA (mRNA) molecule, situated between the large subunit and small subunit, contains coded information which specifies the sequence of amino acids in a protein. **d.** When a ribosome attaches to the endoplasmic reticulum the growing protein enters the lumen of the ER. Transport vesicles, which bud from smooth ER, carry protein molecules to other locations in the cell.

The Endomembrane System

The endomembrane system consists of the nuclear envelope, the endoplasmic reticulum, the Golgi apparatus, and several vesicles. This system compartmentalizes the cell so that particular enzymatic reactions are restricted to specific regions. Membranes that make up the endomembrane system are connected by direct physical contact and/or by the transfer of vesicles from one part to the other.

Endoplasmic Reticulum

The **endoplasmic reticulum (ER)** [Gk. *endon*, within, *plasma*, something molded, and L. *reticulum*, net], consisting of a complicated system of membranous channels and saccules (flattened vesicles), is physically continuous with the outer membrane of the nuclear envelope. **Rough ER** is studded with ribosomes on the side of the membrane that faces the cytoplasm; therefore it is correct to say that rough ER synthesizes proteins. It also modifies proteins after they have entered the ER lumen (Fig. 4.8). Certain ER enzymes add carbohydrate (sugar) chains to proteins and then they are called glycoproteins. Others assist the folding process that results in higher levels of protein organization.

   Smooth ER, which is continuous with rough ER, does not have attached ribosomes. Smooth ER synthesizes phospholipids, steroids, and fatty acids. It also has various other functions depending on the particular cell. In the testes, it produces testosterone and, in the liver, it helps detoxify drugs. Regardless of any specialized function, smooth ER also forms vesicles in which large molecules are transported to other parts of the cell. Often these vesicles are on their way to the plasma membrane or the Golgi apparatus.

> Rough ER is involved in protein synthesis and modification. Smooth ER is generally a site for lipid metabolism. Molecules that are produced or modified in the ER are eventually enclosed in transport vesicles.

Research Methods   Modern microscopic techniques can be counted on to reveal the structure of organelles like rough and smooth ER. But researchers have to turn to biochemical analysis in order to discover the function of organelles. Figure 4.9 shows how organelles can be separated out of the cell by a process called cell fractionation. Cell fractionation allows researchers to concentrate on finding the function of particular parts of cell. Microscopy and biochemical analysis has allowed researchers to distinguish the functions of all the different components of the endomembrane system.

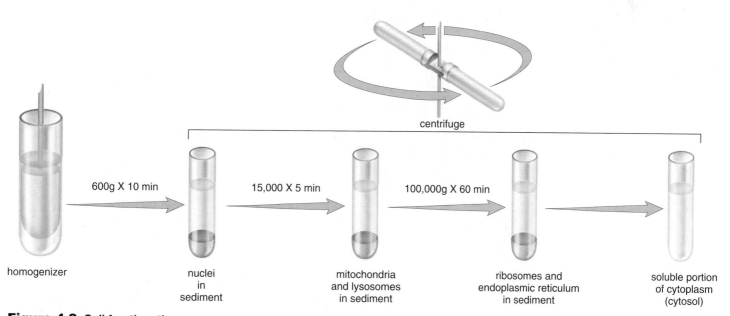

Figure 4.9 Cell fractionation.
Cells are broken open mechanically by the action of the pestle against the side of a centrifuge tube. Then, a centrifuge spins the tubes and this action separates out the contents of the cell. The notations above the arrows indicate the speed and length of time necessary to separate out the structures listed. With ever increasing speed, first the larger and then smaller components of the cell separate out. Once a purified sample of an organelle has been obtained, its proteins can be identified. Also, under the proper conditions, an organelle will continue to work in isolation so that its functions can be determined.

The Golgi Apparatus

The **Golgi apparatus** is named for Camillo Golgi, who discovered its presence in cells in 1898. The Golgi apparatus consists of a stack of three to twenty slightly curved saccules whose appearance can be compared to a stack of pancakes (Fig. 4.10). In animal cells, one side of the stack (the inner face) is directed toward the ER, and the other side of the stack (the outer face) is directed toward the plasma membrane. Vesicles can frequently be seen at the edges of the saccules.

Protein or lipid-filled vesicles that bud from the smooth ER are received by the Golgi apparatus at its inner face. Thereafter, the apparatus carries out its functions as these substances move through its saccules. The Golgi apparatus contains enzymes that alter the carbohydrate chains first attached to proteins in the rough ER. For example, one monomer could be substituted for another or a phosphate might be added to the carbohydrate chain. In some cases the modified carbohydrate chain serves as a signal molecule that determines the protein's final destination in the cell.

The Golgi apparatus packages its products in vesicles that depart the Golgi apparatus at the outer face. Some of these are vesicles called lysosomes, which are discussed next. Some vesicles are on their way to other organelles that have docking sites for them. In that case a glycoprotein with a signaling sequence is a part of the vesicle's membrane. Some vesicles proceed to the plasma membrane, where they discharge their contents as secretion occurs. Secretion is termed exocytosis because the substance exits the cytosol.

The Golgi apparatus receives transport vesicles from the smooth ER. It then modifies, sorts, and packages proteins for use in the cell or secretion from the cell.

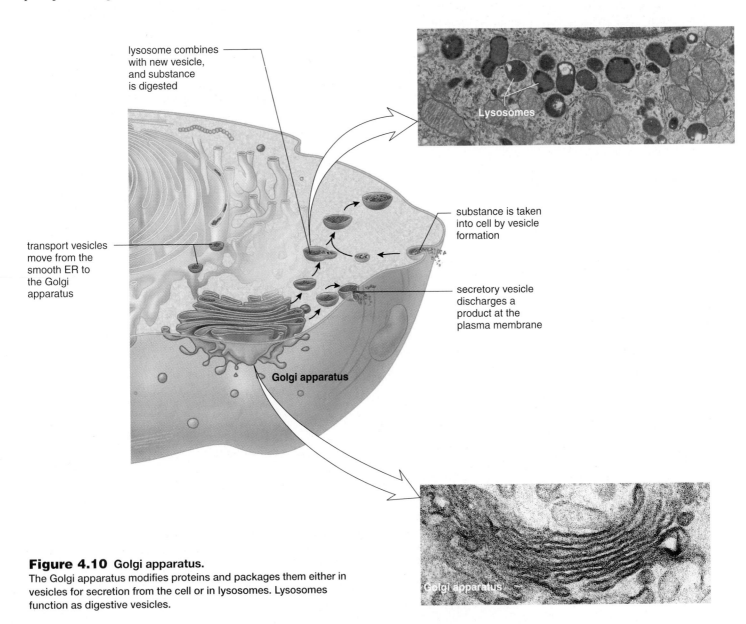

lysosome combines with new vesicle, and substance is digested

Lysosomes

transport vesicles move from the smooth ER to the Golgi apparatus

substance is taken into cell by vesicle formation

secretory vesicle discharges a product at the plasma membrane

Golgi apparatus

Golgi apparatus

Figure 4.10 Golgi apparatus.
The Golgi apparatus modifies proteins and packages them either in vesicles for secretion from the cell or in lysosomes. Lysosomes function as digestive vesicles.

Lysosomes

Lysosomes [Gk. *lyo*, loose, and *soma*, body] are membrane-bounded vesicles produced by the Golgi apparatus. They have a very low pH and contain powerful hydrolytic digestive enzymes.

Sometimes macromolecules are brought into a cell by vesicle formation at the plasma membrane (Fig. 4.10). When a lysosome fuses with such a vesicle, its contents are digested by lysosomal enzymes into simpler subunits that then enter the cytoplasm. Some white blood cells defend the body by engulfing bacteria that are then enclosed within vesicles. When lysosomes fuse with these vesicles, the bacteria are digested. It should come as no surprise, then, that even parts of a cell are digested by its own lysosomes (called autodigestion). Normal cell rejuvenation most likely takes place in this manner, but autodigestion is also important during development. Lysosomes participate in programmed cell death technically termed **apoptosis** which is a normal part of development. When a tadpole becomes a frog, lysosomes digest away the cells of the tail. The fingers of a human embryo are at first webbed, but they are freed from one another as a result of lysosomal action.

Occasionally, a child is born with a metabolic disorder involving a missing or inactive lysosomal enzyme. In these cases, the lysosomes fill to capacity with macromolecules that cannot be broken down. The cells become so full of these lysosomes that the child dies. Someday soon it may be possible to provide the missing enzyme for these children.

Lysosomes are produced by the Golgi apparatus, and their hydrolytic enzymes digest macromolecules from various sources.

Peroxisomes are membrane-bounded vesicles that contain specific enzymes imported from the cytosol (Fig. 4.11). Peroxisomes have enzymes for oxidizing small organic molecules with the formation of hydrogen peroxide (H_2O_2):

$$RH_2 + O_2 \longrightarrow R + H_2O_2$$

Hydrogen peroxide, a toxic molecule, is immediately broken down to water and oxygen by another peroxisomal enzyme called catalase. Peroxisomes are abundant in cells that metabolize lipids; in liver and yeast cells they detoxify alcohol.

Peroxisomes have additional roles in plants. In germinating seeds, peroxisomes, called glyoxysomes, oxidize fatty acids into molecules that can be converted to sugars needed by the growing plant. Peroxisomes also carry out a reaction in leaves that uses up oxygen and releases carbon dioxide that can be used for photosynthesis.

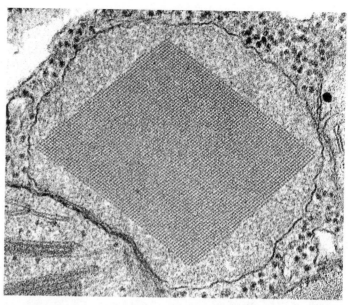

Figure 4.11 **Peroxisome in a tobacco leaf.**
Peroxisomes are vesicles that oxidize organic substances with a resulting build-up of hydrogen peroxide. The crystalline, squarelike core of a peroxisome contains the enzyme catalase, which breaks down hydrogen peroxide (H_2O_2) to water and oxygen.

Vacuoles

A **vacuole** is a large membranous sac. A vesicle is smaller than a vacuole. Typically, plant cells have a large central vacuole so filled with a watery fluid that it gives added support to the cell (see Fig. 4.5).

Vacuoles store substances. Plant vacuoles contain not only water, sugars, and salts but also pigments and toxic molecules. The pigments are responsible for many of the red, blue, or purple colors of flowers and some leaves. The toxic substances help protect a plant from herbivorous animals. The vacuoles present in some protists are quite specialized, and they include contractile vacuoles for ridding the cell of excess water and digestive vacuoles for breaking down nutrients.

The organelles of the endomembrane system are as follows.

Endoplasmic reticulum (ER): synthesis and modification and transport of proteins and other substances
 Rough ER: protein synthesis
 Smooth ER: lipid synthesis, in particular
Golgi apparatus: modifies, sorts, and packages protein molecules
Lysosomes: intracellular digestion
Peroxisomes: metabolize small organic molecules
Vacuoles: storage areas

Energy-Related Organelles

Life is possible only because of a constant input of energy used to maintain the structure of cells. Chloroplasts and mitochondria are the two eukaryotic membranous organelles that specialize in converting energy to a form that can be used by the cell. **Chloroplasts** use solar energy to synthesize carbohydrates, and carbohydrate-derived products are broken down in mitochondria (sing., **mitochondrion**) to produce ATP molecules.

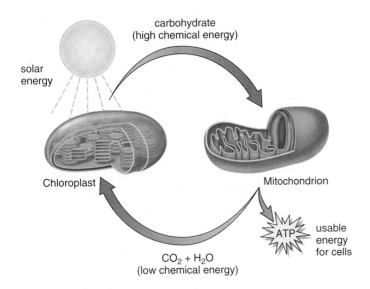

Photosynthesis, which occurs in chloroplasts [Gk. *chloros*, green, and *plastos*, formed, molded], is the process by which solar energy is converted to chemical energy within carbohydrates. Photosynthesis can be represented by this equation:

solar energy + carbon dioxide + water ⟶ carbohydrate + oxygen

Here the word *energy* stands for solar energy, the ultimate source of energy for cellular organization. Only plants, algae, and certain bacteria are capable of carrying on photosynthesis in this manner.

Cellular respiration is the process by which the chemical energy of carbohydrates is converted to that of ATP (adenosine triphosphate). Cellular respiration can be represented by this equation:

carbohydrate + oxygen ⟶ carbon dioxide + water + energy

Here the word *energy* stands for ATP molecules. When a cell needs energy, ATP supplies it. The energy of ATP is used for synthetic reactions, active transport, and all energy-requiring processes in cells. In eukaryotes mitochondria are necessary to the process of cellular respiration, which produces ATP.

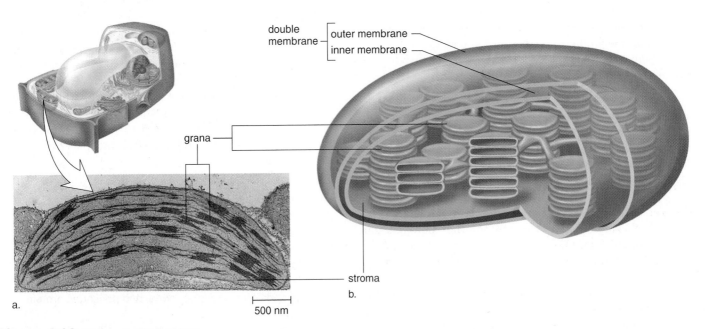

Figure 4.12 Chloroplast structure.
Chloroplasts carry out photosynthesis. **a.** Electron micrograph. **b.** Generalized drawing in which the outer and inner membranes have been cut away to reveal the grana.

Chloroplasts

The photosynthetic cells of algae and plants contain chloroplasts. Chloroplasts are about 4–6 μm in diameter and 1–5 μm in length; they belong to a group of organelles known as plastids. Among the plastids are also the amyloplasts, which store starch, and the chromoplasts, which contain red and orange pigments.

A chloroplast is bounded by two membranes that enclose a fluid called the **stroma.** The stroma contains enzymes that synthesize carbohydrates. It also contains DNA and ribosomes. Chloroplasts are able to synthesize some of the proteins necessary to their function; others are imported into the organelle from the cytosol.

A membrane system within the stroma is organized into interconnected flattened sacs called **thylakoids** [Gk. *thylakos,* sack, and *eides,* like, resembling]. In certain regions, the thylakoids are stacked up in structures called grana (sing., **granum**). There can be hundreds of grana within a single chloroplast (Fig. 4.12). Chlorophyll, a green pigment that is located within the thylakoid membranes of grana, captures solar energy. In chapter 7, you will learn how the organization of a chloroplast allows it to not only capture solar energy but also produce carbohydrates.

Mitochondria

Most eukaryotic cells, whether protists, fungi, plant or animal cells, contain mitochondria. This means that algal and plant cells contain both chloroplasts and mitochondria. The shape and size of mitochondria is variable according to the species but they are usually 0.5–1.0 μm in diameter and 2–5 μm in length.

Mitochondria, like chloroplasts, are bounded by two membranes. The inner membrane invaginates to form **cristae.** Cristae provide a much greater surface area to accommodate the protein complexes and other participants in cellular respiration. The cristae project into the **matrix,** an inner space filled with semifluid medium that contains enzymes. These enzymes break down carbohydrate products, releasing energy that is used for ATP production on the cristae (Fig. 4.13). The matrix also contains DNA and ribosomes. Mitochondria are able to synthesize some of the proteins necessary to their function; others are imported into the organelle from the cytosol.

Chloroplasts and mitochondria are membranous organelles whose structure lends itself to the processes that occur within them.

Figure 4.13 Mitochondrion structure.
Mitochondria are involved in cellular respiration. **a.** Electron micrograph. **b.** Generalized drawing in which the outer membrane and portions of the inner membrane have been cut away to reveal

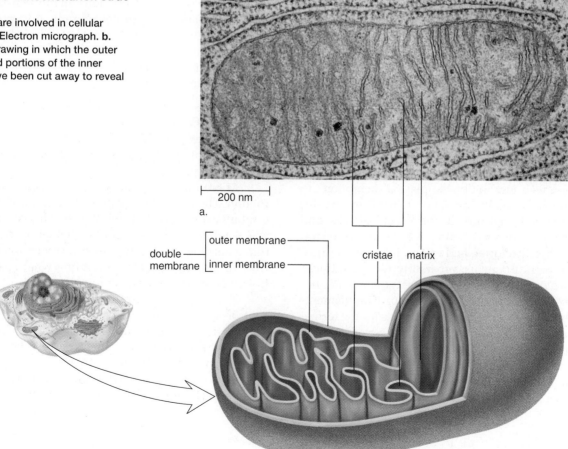

200 nm

a.

double membrane
┌ outer membrane
└ inner membrane

cristae   matrix

b.

The Cytoskeleton

The **cytoskeleton** [Gk. *kytos*, cell, and *skeleton*, dried body] is a network of interconnected filaments and tubules that extends from the nucleus to the plasma membrane in eukaryotic cells. Prior to the 1970s, it was believed that the cytosol was an unorganized mixture of organic molecules. Then, high-voltage electron microscopes, which can penetrate thicker specimens, showed that the cytosol was instead highly organized. The technique of immunofluorescence microscopy identified the makeup of specific protein fibers within the cytoskeletal network (Fig. 4.14).

The name *cytoskeleton* is convenient in that it allows us to compare the cytoskeleton to the bones and muscles of an animal. Bones and muscles give an animal structure and produce movement. Similarly, we will see that the elements of the cytoskeleton maintain cell shape and cause the cell and its organelles to move. The cytoskeleton is dynamic especially because elements can undergo rapid assembly and disassembly. Such changes occur at rates that are measured in seconds and minutes. The entire cytoskeletal network can even disappear and reappear at various times in the life of a cell. Before a cell divides, for instance, the elements disassemble and then reassemble into a structure called a spindle that distributes chromosomes in an orderly manner. At the end of cell division, the spindle disassembles and the elements reassemble once again into their former array.

The cytoskeleton contains three types of elements: actin filaments, intermediate filaments, and microtubules, which are responsible for cell shape and movement.

Actin Filaments

Actin filaments (formerly called microfilaments) are long, extremely thin fibers (about 7 nm in diameter) that occur in bundles or meshlike networks. The actin filament contains two chains of globular actin monomers twisted about one another in a helical manner.

Actin filaments play a structural role when they form a dense complex web just under the plasma membrane, to which they are anchored by special proteins. They are also seen in the microvilli that project from intestinal cells, and their presence most likely accounts for the ability of microvilli to alternately shorten and extend into the intestine. In plant cells, actin filaments apparently form the tracks along which chloroplasts circulate or stream in a particular direction. Also, the presence of a network of actin filaments lying beneath the plasma membrane accounts for the formation of pseudopods, extensions that allow certain cells to move in an amoeboid fashion.

How are actin filaments involved in the movement of the cell and its organelles? They interact with **motor molecules,** which are proteins that can attach, detach, and reattach farther along an actin filament. In the presence of ATP, myosin pulls actin filaments along in this way. Myosin has both a head and a tail. In muscle cells, the tails of several muscle myosin molecules are joined to form a thick filament. In nonmuscle cells, cytoplasmic myosin tails are bound to membranes but the heads still interact with actin:

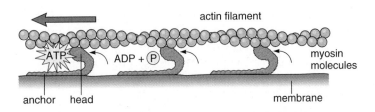

During animal cell division, the two new cells form when actin, in conjunction with myosin, pinches off the cells from one another.

Intermediate Filaments

Intermediate filaments (8–11 nm in diameter) are intermediate in size between actin filaments and microtubules. They are a ropelike assembly of fibrous polypeptides, but the specific type varies according to the tissue. Some intermediate filaments support the nuclear envelope, whereas others support the plasma membrane and take part in the formation of cell-to-cell junctions. In the skin, the filaments, which are made of the protein keratin, give great mechanical strength to skin cells. Recent work has shown intermediate filaments to be highly dynamic. They also assemble and disassemble but need to have phosphate added first by soluble enzymes.

Microtubules

Microtubules [Gk. *mikros*, small, little, and L. *tubus*, pipe] are small hollow cylinders about 25 nm in diameter and from 0.2–25 μm in length.

Microtubules are made of a globular protein called tubulin. There is a slightly different amino acid sequence in α tubulin compared to β tubulin. When assembly occurs, α and β tubulin molecules come together as dimers and the dimers arrange themselves in rows. Microtubules have 13 rows of tubulin dimers surrounding what appears in electron micrographs to be an empty central core.

The regulation of microtubule assembly is under the control of a microtubule organizing center (MTOC). In most eukaryotic cells the main MTOC is in a structure called the **centrosome** [Gk. *centrum*, center, and *soma*, body], which lies near the nucleus. Microtubules radiate from the MTOC, helping to maintain the shape of the cell and acting as tracks along which organelles can move. Whereas the motor

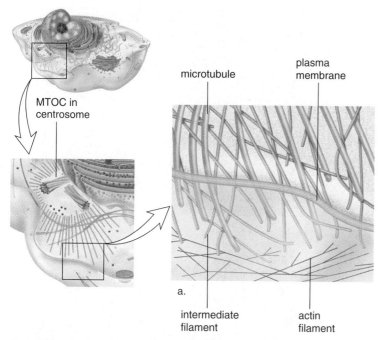

MTOC in
centrosome

microtubule   plasma
                   membrane

a.

intermediate   actin
filament   filament

Figure 4.14 The cytoskeleton.

a. Diagram comparing the size relationship of actin filaments, intermediate filaments, and microtubules. Immunofluorescence, a technique based on the binding of fluorescent antibodies to specific proteins, is used to detect the location of (**b**) actin filaments, (**c**) intermediate filaments, and (**d**) microtubules in the cell.

molecule myosin is associated with actin filaments, the motor molecules kinesin and dynein are associated with microtubules:

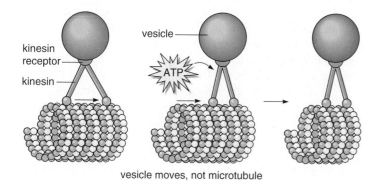

kinesin
receptor

kinesin

vesicle

ATP

vesicle moves, not microtubule

There are different types of kinesin proteins, each specialized to move one kind of vesicle or cellular organelle. Kinesin moves vesicles or organelles in an opposite direction from dynein. Cytoplasmic dynein is closely related to the molecule dynein found in flagella.

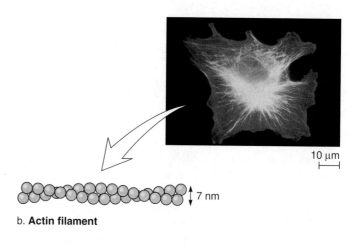

10 μm

7 nm

b. **Actin filament**

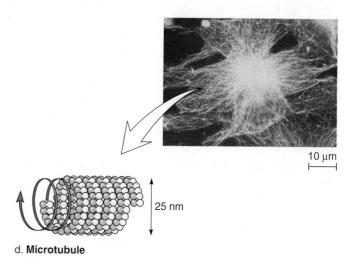

10 μm

10 nm

c. **Intermediate filament**

10 μm

25 nm

d. **Microtubule**

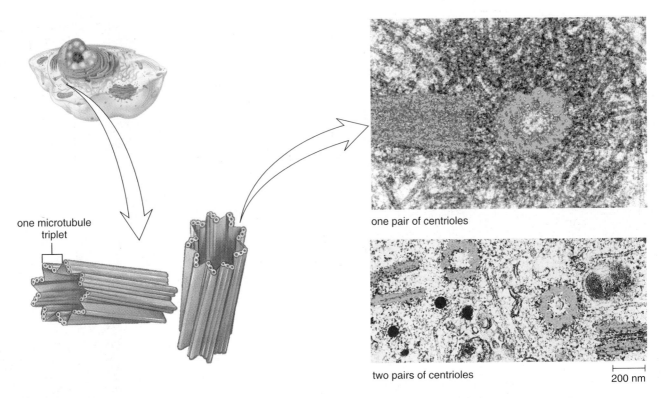

one microtubule triplet

one pair of centrioles

two pairs of centrioles

200 nm

Figure 4.15 Centrioles.
In a nondividing cell there is a pair of centrioles in a centrosome outside the nucleus. Just before a cell divides, the centrioles replicate and there are two pairs of centrioles. During cell division, centrioles in two centrosomes separate so that each new cell has one centrosome containing one pair of centrioles.

Centrioles

Centrioles [Gk. *centrum,* center] are short cylinders with a 9 + 0 pattern of microtubule triplets—that is, a ring having nine sets of triplets with none in the middle. In animal cells and most protists, a centrosome contains two centrioles lying at right angles to each other. A centrosome, you will recall, is the major microtubule organizing center for the cell. Therefore, it is possible that centrioles are also involved in the process by which microtubules assemble and disassemble.

Before an animal cell divides, the centrioles replicate and the members of each pair are at right angles to one another (Fig. 4.15). Then each pair becomes part of a separate centrosome. During cell division the centrosomes move apart and most likely function to organize the mitotic spindle. In any case, each new cell has its own centrosome and pair of centrioles. Plant and fungal cells have the equivalent of a centrosome but it does not contain centrioles, suggesting that centrioles are not necessary to the assembly of cytoplasmic microtubules.

In cells with cilia and flagella, centrioles are believed to give rise to basal bodies that direct the organization of microtubules within these structures. In other words, a basal body may do for a cilium (or flagellum) what the centrosome does for the cell.

Centrioles, which are short cylinders with a 9 + 0 pattern of microtubule triplets, may give rise to the basal bodies of cilia and flagella.

Cilia and Flagella

Cilia [L. *cilium,* eyelash, hair] and **flagella** [L. *flagello,* whip] are hairlike projections that can move either in an undulating fashion, like a whip, or stiffly, like an oar. Cells that have these organelles are capable of movement. For example, unicellular paramecia move by means of cilia, whereas sperm cells move by means of flagella. The cells that line our upper respiratory tract have cilia that sweep debris trapped within mucus back up into the throat, where it can be swallowed. This action helps keep the lungs clean.

In eukaryotic cells, cilia are much shorter than flagella, but they have a similar construction. Both are membrane-bounded cylinders enclosing a matrix area. In the matrix are nine microtubule doublets arranged in a circle around two central microtubules. This is called the 9 + 2 pattern of microtubules. Cilia and flagella move when the microtubule doublets slide past one another (Fig. 4.16).

As mentioned, each cilium and flagellum has a basal body lying in the cytoplasm at its base. Basal bodies have the same circular arrangement of microtubule triplets as centrioles and are believed to be derived from them. It is possible that basal bodies organize the microtubules within cilia and flagella, but this is not supported by the observation that cilia and flagella grow by the addition of tubulin dimers to their tips.

Cilia and flagella, which have a 9 + 2 pattern of microtubules, are involved in the movement of cells.

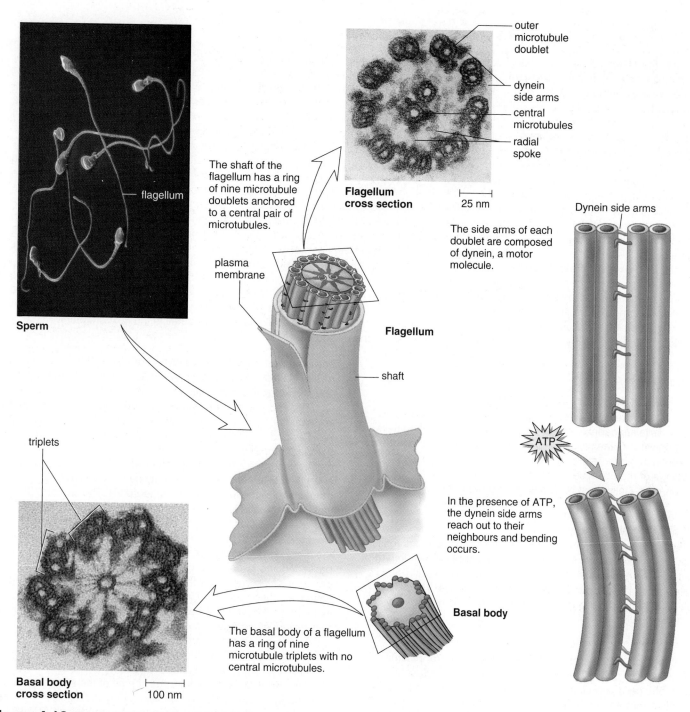

outer microtubule doublet

dynein side arms

central microtubules

radial spoke

Flagellum cross section   ⊢ 25 nm ⊣

The side arms of each doublet are composed of dynein, a motor molecule.

Dynein side arms

The shaft of the flagellum has a ring of nine microtubule doublets anchored to a central pair of microtubules.

plasma membrane

Flagellum

shaft

ATP

In the presence of ATP, the dynein side arms reach out to their neighbours and bending occurs.

Basal body

flagellum

Sperm

triplets

The basal body of a flagellum has a ring of nine microtubule triplets with no central microtubules.

Basal body cross section   ⊢ 100 nm ⊣

Figure 4.16 Structure of cilium or flagellum.
A flagellum has a basal body with a 9 + 0 pattern of microtubule triplets. (Notice the ring of nine triplets, with no central microtubules.) The shaft of the flagellum has a 9 + 2 pattern (a ring of nine microtubule doublets surrounds a central pair of single microtubules). Compare the cross section of the basal body to the cross section of the flagellum shaft and note that in place of the third microtubule, the outer doublets have side arms of dynein, a motor molecule. In the presence of ATP, the dynein side arms reach out and attempt to move along their neighboring doublet. Because of the radial spokes connecting the doublets to the central microtubules, bending occurs.

Connecting Concepts

When the Dutchman Antonie van Leeuwenhoek observed one-celled creatures under his homemade microscope in the 1600s, he probably had no idea the unicellular organisms he found so fascinating had the same basic structure as the cells in his own body. Eukaryotic cells are compartmentalized and therefore can be likened to a miniature factory, where each department has a specific function. The nucleus, which contains the chromosomes, determines the characteristics of the cell. Mitochondria produce high-energy ATP molecules from carbohydrates and oxygen. Proteins are made on the ribosomes and the Golgi apparatus prepares materials to be secreted by the cell. Lysosomes degrade chemical refuse for recycling of molecular subunits. The cytoskeleton is highly organized with protein fibers of different dimension contributing to cell shape and motility as well as movement of structures within the cell.

Unicellular organisms are generalists, while cells from multicellular organisms are specialized for specific functions. Muscle cells, which depend on a ready supply of ATP, are full of mitochondria; pancreatic cells, which secrete insulin, are full of rough ER, a Golgi apparatus and so forth. "Form follows function," a concept developed by architects from designing buildings, applies equally well to cells and even to their organelles. For example, we will see that both chloroplasts and mitochondria rely on membrane compartmentalization to produce ATP. In chloroplasts this ATP is used to produce glucose and in mitochondria the ATP is made available to the cell as an energy source.

Prokaryotic cells lack the compartmentalization seen in eukaryotic cells, but they carry out all the functions of eukaryotic cells. They have a plasma membrane, but their single chromosome is located within a nucleoid region. They lack a true membrane-bounded nucleus. Like eukaryotes, prokaryotes have ribosomes where proteins are synthesized. Despite their simple organization, prokaryotes are among the most adaptable and successful forms on earth. This is largely due to their diverse metabolic capabilities; most any organic molecule can be broken down by some type of prokaryote.

Most cellular processes are more complex than presented here and we will investigate certain cellular processes in more detail in the next chapters.

Summary

4.1 Cellular Level of Organization

All organisms are composed of cells, the smallest units of living matter. Cells are capable of self-reproduction, and existing cells come only from preexisting cells. Cells are very small and are measured in micrometers. The plasma membrane regulates exchange of materials between the cell and the external environment. Cells must remain small in order to have an adequate amount of surface area per cell volume.

4.2 Bacterial Cells

There are two major groups of cells: prokaryotic and eukaryotic. Both types have a plasma membrane and cytoplasm. Prokaryotic cells lack the nucleus of eukaryotic cells. Prokaryotic cells have a nucleoid that is not bounded by a nuclear envelope. They also lack most of the other organelles that compartmentalize eukaryotic cells.

4.3 Eukaryotic Cells

Eukaryotic cells, like prokaryotic cells, have an outer plasma membrane surrounding a cytosol. In addition, the cytosol of eukaryotic cells contains various organelles, each with a specific structure and function. The possible evolution of the eukaryotic cell is of interest. The nuclear envelope most likely evolved through invagination of the plasma membrane, but mitochondria and chloroplasts may have arisen through endosymbiotic events.

The nucleus of eukaryotic cells is bounded by a nuclear envelope containing pores. These pores serve as passageways between the cytoplasm and the nucleoplasm. Within the nucleus, chromatin, which contains DNA, undergoes coiling into chromosomes at the time of cell division. The nucleolus is a special region of the chromatin where rRNA is produced and where proteins from the cytoplasm gather to form ribosomal subunits. These subunits are joined in the cytoplasm.

Ribosomes are organelles that function in protein synthesis. They can be bound to ER or exist within the cytosol singly or in groups called polyribosomes. When protein synthesis occurs a mRNA leaves the nucleus with a coded message from DNA that specifies the sequence of amino acids in that protein.

The endomembrane system includes the ER (both rough and smooth), the Golgi apparatus, the lysosomes, and other types of vesicles and vacuoles. The endomembrane system serves to compartmentalize the cell and keep the various biochemical reactions separate from one another. Newly produced proteins enter the ER lumen, where they may be modified before proceeding to the interior of the smooth ER. The smooth ER has various metabolic functions depending on the cell type, but it also forms vesicles that carry proteins and lipids to different locations, particularly to the Golgi apparatus. The Golgi apparatus modifies, sorts, and repackages proteins. Some proteins are packaged into lysosomes, which carry out intracellular digestion, or into vesicles that fuse with the plasma membrane. Following fusion, secretion occurs. The endomembrane system also includes peroxisomes. When these organelles oxidize molecules they produce hydrogen peroxide that is subsequently broken down. The large single plant cell vacuole not only stores substances but lends support to the plant cell.

Cells require a constant input of energy to maintain their structure. Chloroplasts capture the energy of the sun and carry on photosynthesis, which produces carbohydrate. Carbohydrate-derived products are broken down in mitochondria as ATP is produced. This is an oxygen-requiring process called cellular respiration.

The cytoskeleton contains actin filaments, intermediate filaments, and microtubules. These maintain cell shape and allow it and the organelles to move. Actin filaments, the thinnest filaments, interact with the motor molecule myosin in muscle cells to bring about contraction; in other cells, they pinch off daughter cells and have other dynamic functions. Intermediate filaments support the nuclear envelope and the plasma membrane and probably participate in cell-to-cell junctions. Microtubules radiate out from the centrosome and are present in centrioles, cilia, and flagella. They serve as tracks, along which vesicles and other organelles move, due to the action of specific motor molecules.

Reviewing the Chapter

1. What are the two basic tenets of the cell theory?   56
2. Why is it advantageous for cells to be small?   57
3. Roughly sketch a bacterial (prokaryotic) cell, label its parts, and state a function for each of these.   60
4. What similar features do prokaryotic cells and eukaryotic cells have? What is their major difference?   60–61
5. Describe the endosymbiotic hypothesis and the evidence to support it.   64
6. Describe the structure and the function of the nuclear envelope and the nuclear pores.   65
7. Distinguish between the nucleolus, rRNA, and ribosomes.   65–66
8. Trace the path of a protein from rough ER to the plasma membrane.   66
9. Give the overall equations for photosynthesis and cellular respiration, contrast the two, and tell how they are related.   70
10. What are the three components of the cytoskeleton? What are their structures and functions?   72–73
11. Relate the structure of flagella (and cilia) to centrioles, and discuss the function of both.   74–75

Testing Yourself

Choose the best answer for each question.

1. The small size of cells best correlates with
   a. the fact they are self-reproducing.
   b. their prokaryotic versus eukaryotic nature.
   c. an adequate surface area for exchange of materials.
   d. the fact they come in multiple sizes.
   e. All of these are correct.
2. Which of these is not a true comparison of the light microscope and the transmission electron microscope?

Light	**Electron**
a. uses light to "view" object	uses electrons to "view" object
b. uses glass lenses for focusing	uses magnetic lenses for focusing
c. specimen must be killed and stained	specimen may be alive and nonstained
d. magnification is not as great	magnification is greater
e. resolution is not as great	resolution is greater

3. Which of these best distinguishes a prokaryotic cell from a eukaryotic cell?
   a. Prokaryotic cells have a cell wall, but eukaryotic cells never do.
   b. Prokaryotic cells are much larger than eukaryotic cells.
   c. Prokaryotic cells have flagella, but eukaryotic cells do not.
   d. Prokaryotic cells do not have a membrane-bounded nucleus, but eukaryotic cells do have such a nucleus.
   e. Prokaryotic cells have ribosomes but eukaryotic cells do not have ribosomes.

4. Which organelle would not have originated by endosymbiosis?
   a. mitochondria
   b. flagella
   c. nucleus
   d. chloroplasts
   e. Both b and c are correct.
5. Which of these is not found in the nucleus?
   a. functioning ribosomes
   b. chromatin that condenses to chromosomes
   c. nucleolus that produces rRNA
   d. nucleoplasm instead of cytoplasm
   e. all forms of RNA
6. Vesicles from the smooth ER most likely are on their way to the
   a. rough ER.
   b. lysosomes.
   c. Golgi apparatus.
   d. plant cell vacuole only.
   e. location suitable to their size.
7. Lysosomes function in
   a. protein synthesis.
   b. processing and packaging.
   c. intracellular digestion.
   d. lipid synthesis.
   e. production of hydrogen peroxide.
8. Mitochondria
   a. are involved in cellular respiration.
   b. break down ATP to release energy for cells.
   c. contain grana and cristae.
   d. are present in animal but not plant cells.
   e. All of these are correct.
9. Which organelle releases oxygen?
   a. ribosome
   b. Golgi apparatus
   c. mitochondrion
   d. chloroplast
   e. smooth ER
10. Which of these is not true?
    a. Actin filaments are found in muscle cells.
    b. Microtubules radiate out from the ER.
    c. Intermediate filaments sometimes contain keratin.
    d. Motor molecules use microtubules as tracts.
    e. Eukaryotic cells without centrosomes still produce a spindle.
11. Cilia and flagella
    a. bend when microtubules try to slide past one another.
    b. contain myosin that pulls on actin filaments.
    c. are organized by basal bodies derived from centrioles.
    d. are constructed similarly in prokaryotes and eukaryotes.
    e. Both a and c are correct.

12. Study the example given in (a) below. Then for each other organelle listed, state another that is structurally and functionally related. Tell why you paired these two organelles.
    a. The nucleus can be paired with nucleoli because nucleoli are found in the nucleus. Nucleoli occur where chromatin is producing rRNA.
    b. mitochondria
    c. centrioles
    d. ER
13. Label these parts of the cell that are involved in protein synthesis and modification. Give a function for each structure.

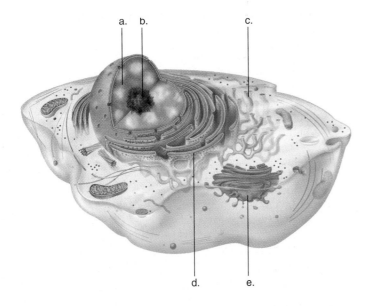

a. b.   c.

d.   e.

Thinking Scientifically

1. Vesicles that leave the Golgi apparatus as lysosomes move to different locations including the plasma membrane and the cytoplasm. What type of system could direct each budding vesicle to its proper location? What role could be played by the cytoskeleton?
2. In a cell biology laboratory students are examining sections of plant cells. Some students report seeing the nucleus, others do not. Some students see a large vacuole, others see a small vacuole. Some see evidence of an extensive endoplasmic reticulum, others see almost none. How can these observations be explained if the students are looking at the same cells?

Understanding the Terms

apoptosis 69
bacteria 60
capsule 60
cell 56
cell theory 56
cell wall 60, 61
centriole 74
centrosome 72
chloroplast 70
chromatin 65
chromosome 65

cilium (pl., cilia) 74
cristae 71
cytoplasm 60
cytoskeleton 72
cytosol 60
endoplasmic reticulum (ER) 67
endosymbiotic hypothesis 64
eukaryotic cell 61
flagellum (pl., flagella) 60, 74
Golgi apparatus 68

granum 71
lysosome 69
matrix 71
microtubule 72
mitochondrion 70
motor molecule 72
nuclear envelope 65
nuclear pore 65
nucleoid 60
nucleolus (pl., nucleoli) 65
nucleoplasm 65
nucleus 65
organelle 61

peroxisome 69
plasma membrane 60
plasmid 60
polyribosome 66
prokaryotic cell 60
ribosome 60, 66
rough ER 67
slime layer 60
smooth ER 67
stroma 71
thylakoid 60, 71
vacuole 69
vesicle 66

Match the terms to these definitions:

a. _____ Organelle consisting of saccules and vesicles that processes, packages, and distributes molecules about or from the cell.
b. _____ Network of strands consisting of DNA and associated proteins observed within a nucleus that is not dividing.
c. _____ Dark-staining, spherical body in the cell nucleus that produces ribosomal subunits.
d. _____ Internal framework of the cell, consisting of microtubules, actin filaments, and intermediate filaments.
e. _____ Membrane-bounded vesicle that contains hydrolytic enzymes for digesting macromolecules.

Web Connections

Exploring the Internet

http://www.mhhe.com/biosci/genbio/mader/
(click on *Biology 7/e*)

The *Biology 7/e* Online Learning Center provides many resources for studying the material in this chapter including links to the following sites:

Cells Alive! is a fun website with downloadable videos and animations of a variety of cell topics, including the cytoskeleton, bacterial mobility, comparative sizes of cells, and much more.

http://www.cellsalive.com/

View a wide variety of different cell types using Histoweb.

http://www.kumc.edu/instruction/medicine/anatomy/histoweb/

Organelles: an overview of cellular organelle structure and function.

http://www.dcn.davis.ca.us/~carl/organell.htm

Prokaryotes, Eukaryotes, & Viruses Tutorial. A discussion of the 6 kingdoms, and the basic functions of the eukaryotic cell organelles.

http://www.biology.arizona.edu/cell_bio/tutorials/pev/main.html

MIT site showing and describing cellular parts. Quite detailed with many links.

http://esg-www.mit.edu:8001/esgbio/cb/cbdir.html

Membrane Structure and Function

c h a p t e r

5

A needle is poised to puncture the plasma membrane of a cell.

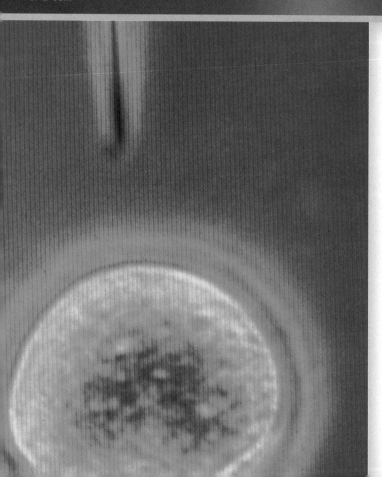

At first glance, a short pygmy, an overweight diabetic, and a young child with a high cholesterol level seem to have little in common. In reality, however, each suffers from a defect of their cells' plasma membrane. The pygmy's cells won't allow growth hormone to enter; the diabetic's cells do not bind to insulin, and the young child's cells prevent the entrance of a lipoprotein. A plasma membrane was essential to the origin of the first cell(s) and its proper functioning is essential to our good health today.

A plasma membrane encloses every cell, whether the cell is a unicellular amoeba or one of many from the body of a cockroach, peony, mushroom, or human. Universally, a plasma membrane protects a cell by acting as a barrier between its living contents and the surrounding environment. It regulates what goes into and out of the cell and marks the cell as being unique to the organism. In multicellular organisms, cell junctions requiring specialized features of the plasma membrane connect cells together in specific ways and pass on information to neighboring cells so that the activities of tissues and organs are coordinated.

5.1 Membrane Models

At the turn of the century, investigators noted that lipid-soluble molecules entered cells more rapidly than water-soluble molecules. This prompted them to suggest that lipids are a component of the plasma membrane. Later, chemical analysis disclosed that the plasma membrane contains phospholipids. In 1925, E. Gorter and G. Grendel measured the amount of phospholipid extracted from red blood cells and determined that there is just enough to form a bilayer around the cells. They further suggested that the nonpolar (hydrophobic) tails are directed inward and the polar (hydrophilic) heads are directed outward, forming a phospholipid bilayer:

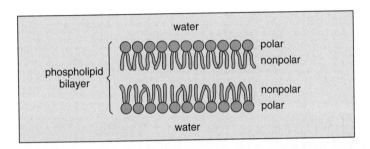

The presence of lipids cannot account for all the properties of the plasma membrane, such as its permeability to certain nonlipid substances. Such observations prompted J. Danielli and H. Davson to suggest in the 1940s that proteins are also a part of the membrane. They proposed a sandwich model in which the phospholipid bilayer is a filling between two continuous layers of proteins. By the late 1950s, electron microscopy had advanced to allow viewing of the plasma membrane and indeed it does have a sandwich appearance (Fig. 5.1*a*). At that time, J. D. Robertson modified the sandwich model and proposed that the outer dark layer (stained with heavy metals) contained protein *plus* the hydrophilic heads of the phospholipids. The interior was assumed to be the hydrophobic tails of these molecules. Robertson went on to suggest that all membranes in various cells have basically the same composition. Therefore his proposal was called the unit membrane model (Fig. 5.1*b*).

After some years, investigators began to doubt the accuracy of the unit membrane model. Not all membranes have the same appearance in electron micrographs and they do not have the same function. For example, the inner membrane of a mitochondrion, which is coated with rows of particles, functions in cellular respiration and it has a far different appearance from the plasma membrane. Finally, in 1972, S. Singer and G. Nicolson introduced the **fluid-mosaic model** of membrane structure, which proposes, in part, that the membrane is a fluid phospholipid bilayer in which protein molecules are either partially or wholly embedded. The proteins are scattered throughout the membrane in an irregular pattern that can vary from membrane to membrane. The mosaic distribution of proteins is supported especially by electron micrographs of freeze-fractured membranes (Fig. 5.1*c* and *d*).

a. Electron micrograph of red blood cell plasma membrane

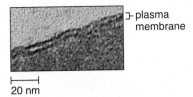

plasma membrane

20 nm

b. Two possible models

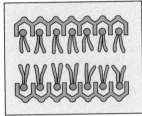

Robertson unit membrane

Singer and Nicolson fluid-mosaic model

c. Freeze-fracture of membrane

protein

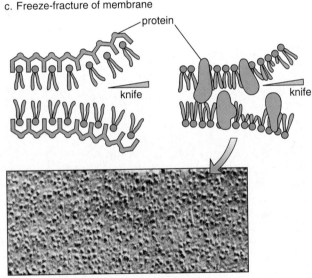

knife

knife

d. Electron micrograph of freeze-fractured membrane shows presence of particles

Figure 5.1 Membrane structure.
a. The red blood cell plasma membrane typically has a three-layered appearance in electron micrographs. **b.** Robertson's unit membrane model proposed that the outer dark layers in electron micrographs were made up of protein and polar heads of phospholipid molecules, while the inner light layer was composed of the nonpolar tails. The Singer and Nicolson fluid-mosaic model put protein molecules within the lipid bilayer. **c.** A technique called freeze-fracture allows an investigator to view the interior of the membrane. Cells are rapidly frozen in liquid nitrogen and then fractured with a special knife. Platinum and carbon are applied to the fractured surface to produce a faithful replica that is observed by electron microscopy. **d.** A fracture in the middle of the bilayer shows the presence of particles, consistent with the fluid-mosaic model.

The fluid-mosaic model of membrane structure is widely accepted at this time.

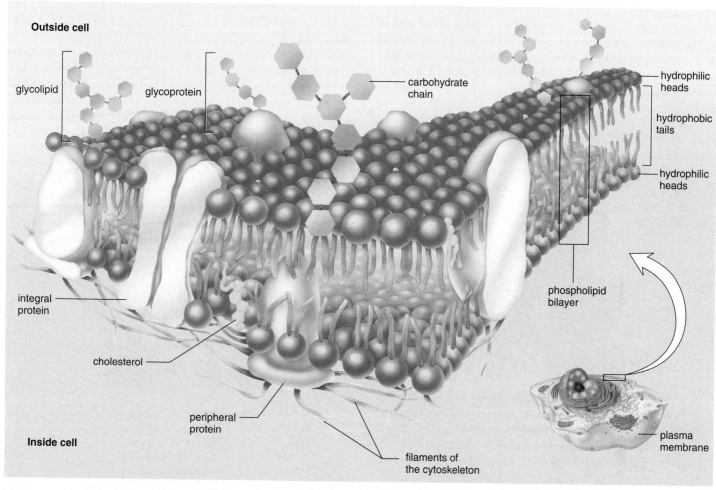

Figure 5.2 **Fluid-mosaic model of plasma membrane structure.**
The membrane is composed of a phospholipid bilayer in which proteins are embedded. The hydrophilic heads of phospholipids are a part of the outside surface and the inside surface of the membrane. The hydrophobic tails make up the interior of the membrane. Note the plasma membrane's asymmetry—carbohydrate chains are attached to the outside surface and cytoskeleton filaments are attached to the inside surface.

5.2 Plasma Membrane Structure and Function

According to the fluid-mosaic model of membrane structure, a membrane has two components: lipids and proteins. Most of the lipids in the plasma membrane are **phospholipids** which are known to arrange themselves spontaneously into a bilayer. The hydrophilic (polar) heads of the phospholipid molecules face the intracellular and extracellular fluids. The hydrophobic (nonpolar) tails face each other (Fig. 5.2).

In addition to phospholipids, there are two other types of lipids in the plasma membrane. **Glycolipids** have a structure similar to phospholipids except that the hydrophilic head is a variety of sugars joined to form a straight or branching carbohydrate chain. Glycolipids have a protective function and also have various other functions to be discussed in this chapter.

Cholesterol is a lipid that is found in animal plasma membranes; related steroids are found in the plasma membrane of plants. Cholesterol reduces the permeability of the membrane to most biological molecules.

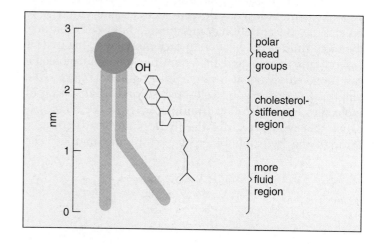

The proteins in a membrane may be peripheral proteins or integral proteins. Peripheral proteins occur either on the outside or the inside surface of the membrane. Some of these are anchored to the membrane by covalent bonding. Still others are held in place by noncovalent interactions that can be disrupted by gentle shaking or by change in the pH.

Integral proteins are found within the membrane. Their hydrophobic regions are embedded within the membrane and their hydrophilic regions project from both surfaces of the bilayer:

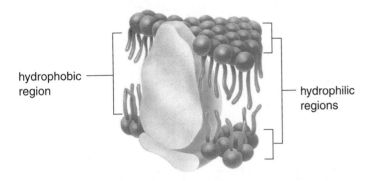

hydrophobic region

hydrophilic regions

Many integral proteins are **glycoproteins,** which have an attached carbohydrate chain. As with glycolipids, the carbohydrate chain of sugars projects externally. Therefore it can be said that the plasma membrane is "sugar-coated."

The plasma membrane is asymmetrical: the two halves are not identical. The carbohydrate chains of the glycolipids and proteins occur only on the outside surface and the cytoskeletal filaments attach to proteins only on the inside surface.

The plasma membrane consists of a phospholipid bilayer. Peripheral proteins are found on the outside and inside surface of the membrane. Integral proteins span the lipid bilayer and often have attached carbohydrate chains.

Fluidity of the Plasma Membrane

At body temperature, the phospholipid bilayer of the plasma membrane has the consistency of olive oil. The greater the concentration of unsaturated fatty acid residues, the more fluid is the bilayer. In each monolayer, the hydrocarbon tails wiggle, and the entire phospholipid molecule can move sideways at a rate averaging about 2 μm—the length of a prokaryotic cell—per second. (Phospholipid molecules rarely flip-flop from one layer to the other, because this would require the hydrophilic head to move through the hydrophobic center of the membrane.) The

fluidity of a phospholipid bilayer means that cells are pliable. Imagine if they were not—the long nerve fibers in your neck would crack whenever you nodded your head!

Although some proteins are often held in place by cytoskeletal filaments, in general, proteins are free to drift laterally in the fluid lipid bilayer. This has been demonstrated by fusing mouse and human cells, and watching the movement of tagged proteins (Fig. 5.3). Forty minutes after fusion, the proteins are completely mixed. The fluidity of the membrane is needed for the functioning of some proteins such as enzymes which become inactive when the membrane solidifies.

The fluidity of the membrane, which is dependent on its lipid components, is critical to the proper functioning of the membrane's proteins.

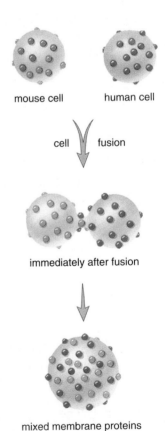

mouse cell   human cell

cell   fusion

immediately after fusion

mixed membrane proteins

Figure 5.3 Experiment to demonstrate lateral drifting of plasma membrane proteins.
After human and mouse cells fuse, the plasma membrane proteins of the mouse (blue circles) and of the human cell (red circles) mix within a short time.

Mosaic Quality of the Membrane

The plasma membranes of various cells and the membranes of various organelles each have their own unique collections of proteins. The proteins form different patterns according to the particular membrane and also within the same membrane at different times. When you consider that the plasma membrane of a red blood cell contains over 50 different types of proteins, you can see why the membrane is said to be a mosaic.

The integral proteins largely determine a membrane's specific functions. As we will discuss in more detail, certain plasma membrane proteins are involved in the passage of molecules through the membrane. Some of these are **channel proteins** through which a substance can simply move across the membrane; others are **carrier proteins** that combine with a substance and help it to move across the membrane. Still others are receptors; each type of **receptor protein** has a shape that allows a specific molecule to bind to it. The binding of a molecule, such as a hormone (or other signal molecule), can cause the protein to change its shape and bring about a cellular response. Some plasma membrane proteins are **enzymatic proteins** that carry out metabolic reactions directly. The peripheral proteins associated with the membrane often have a structural role in that they help stabilize and shape the plasma membrane.

Figure 5.4 depicts the various functions of membrane proteins.

The mosaic pattern of a membrane is dependent on the proteins, which vary in structure and function.

Cell-Cell Recognition

The carbohydrate chains of glycolipids and glycoproteins serve as the "fingerprints" of the cell. The possible diversity of the chain is enormous; it can vary by the number of sugars (15 is usual, but there can be several hundred), by whether the chain is branched, and by the sequence of the particular sugars.

Glycolipids and glycoproteins vary from species to species, from individual to individual of the same species, and even from cell to cell in the same individual. Therefore, they make cell-cell recognition possible. Researchers working with mouse embryos have shown that as development proceeds, the different type cells of the embryo develop their own carbohydrate chains and that these chains allow the tissues and cells of the embryo to sort themselves out.

As you probably know, transplanted tissues are often rejected by the body. This is because the immune system is able to recognize that the foreign tissue's cells do not have the same glycolipids and glycoproteins as the rest of the body's cells. We also now know that a person's particular blood type is due to the presence of particular glycoproteins in the membrane of red blood cells.

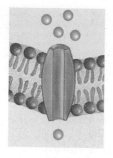

Channel Protein
Allows a particular molecule or ion to cross the plasma membrane freely. Cystic fibrosis, an inherited disorder, is caused by a faulty chloride (Cl^-) channel; a thick mucus collects in airways and in pancreatic and liver ducts.

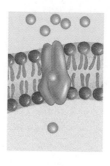

Carrier Protein
Selectively interacts with a specific molecule or ion so that it can cross the plasma membrane. The inability of some persons to use energy for sodium-potassium (Na^+–K^+) transport has been suggested as the cause of their obesity.

Cell Recognition Protein
The MHC (major histocompatibility complex) glycoproteins are different for each person, so organ transplants are difficult to achieve. Cells with foreign MHC glycoproteins are attacked by blood cells responsible for immunity.

Receptor Protein
Is shaped in such a way that a specific molecule can bind to it. Pygmies are short, not because they do not produce enough growth hormone, but because their plasma membrane growth hormone receptors are faulty and cannot interact with growth hormone.

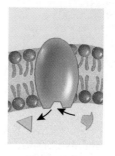

Enzymatic Protein
Catalyzes a specific reaction. The membrane protein, adenylate cyclase, is involved in ATP metabolism. Cholera bacteria release a toxin that interferes with the proper functioning of adenylate cyclase; sodium ions and water leave intestinal cells and the individual dies from severe diarrhea.

Figure 5.4 Membrane protein diversity.
These are some of the functions performed by proteins found in the plasma membrane.

Table 5.1

Passage of Molecules into and out of Cells

	Name	Direction	Requirement	Examples
Passive Transport Means	Diffusion	Toward lower concentration	Concentration gradient only	Lipid-soluble molecules, water, and gases
	Facilitated transport	Toward lower concentration	Carrier and concentration gradient	Some sugars and amino acids
Active Transport Means	Active transport	Toward greater concentration	Carrier plus cellular energy	Other sugars, amino acids, and ions
	Exocytosis	Toward outside	Vesicle fuses with plasma membrane	Macromolecules
	Endocytosis Phagocytosis	Toward inside	Vacuole formation	Cells and subcellular material
	Pinocytosis (includes receptor-mediated endocytosis)	Toward inside	Vesicle formation	Macromolecules

5.3 Permeability of the Plasma Membrane

The plasma membrane is **differentially** (selectively) **permeable.** Some substances can move across the membrane and some cannot (Fig. 5.5). Macromolecules cannot diffuse across the membrane because they are too large. Ions and charged molecules cannot cross the membrane because they are unable to enter the hydrophobic phase of the lipid bilayer.

Noncharged, lipid-soluble molecules such as alcohols and oxygen can cross the membrane with ease. They are able to slip between the hydrophilic heads of the phospholipids and pass through the hydrophobic tails of the membrane.

Small polar molecules such as carbon dioxide and water also have no difficulty crossing through the membrane. These molecules follow their **concentration gradient** which is a gradual decrease in concentration over distance. To take an example, oxygen is more concentrated outside the cell than inside the cell because a cell uses oxygen during cellular respiration. Therefore oxygen follows its concentration gradient as it enters a cell. Carbon dioxide, on the other hand, which is produced when a cell carries on cellular respiration, is more concentrated inside the cell than outside the cell, and therefore it moves down its concentration gradient as it exits a cell.

Special means are sometimes used to get ions and charged molecules into and out of cells. Macromolecules can cross a membrane when they are taken in or out by vesicle formation (Table 5.1). Ions and molecules, like amino acids and sugars, are assisted across by one of two classes of transport proteins. Carrier proteins combine with an ion or molecule before transporting it across the membrane. Channel proteins form a channel that allows an ion or charged molecule to pass through. Our discussion in this chapter is largely restricted to carrier proteins. Carrier proteins are specific for the substances they transport across the plasma membrane.

Ways of crossing a plasma membrane are classified as passive or active (Table 5.1). Passive ways, which do not use chemical energy, involve diffusion or facilitated transport. These passive ways depend on the motion energy of ions and molecules. Active ways, which do require chemical energy, include active transport, endocytosis, and exocytosis.

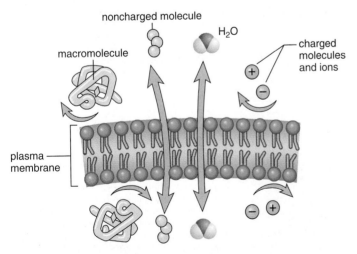

Figure 5.5 How molecules cross the plasma membrane. The curved arrows indicate that these substances cannot cross the plasma membrane and the back and forth arrows indicate that these substances can cross the plasma membrane.

noncharged molecule

macromolecule

H$_2$O

charged molecules and ions

plasma membrane

The plasma membrane is differentially permeable. Certain substances can freely pass through the membrane and others must be transported across either by carrier proteins or by vacuole formation.

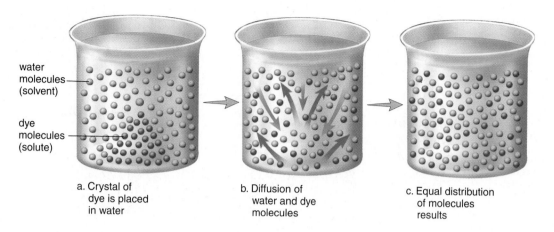

water molecules (solvent)

dye molecules (solute)

a. Crystal of dye is placed in water

b. Diffusion of water and dye molecules

c. Equal distribution of molecules results

Figure 5.6 Process of diffusion.
Diffusion is spontaneous, and no chemical energy is required to bring it about. **a.** When a dye crystal is placed in water, it is concentrated in one area. **b.** The dye dissolves in the water, and there is a net movement of dye molecules from higher to lower concentration. There is also a net movement of water molecules from a higher to a lower concentration. **c.** Eventually, the water and the dye molecules are equally distributed throughout the container.

Diffusion and Osmosis

Diffusion is the movement of molecules from a higher to a lower concentration—that is, down their concentration gradient—until equilibrium is achieved and they are distributed equally. Diffusion is a physical process that can be observed with any type of molecule. For example, when a dye crystal is placed in water (Fig. 5.6), the dye and water molecules move in various directions, but their net movement, which is the sum of their motion, is toward the region of lower concentration. Therefore, the dye is eventually dissolved in the water, resulting in a colored solution. A **solution** contains both a solute, usually a solid, and a solvent, usually a liquid. In this case, the **solute** is the dye and the solvent is the water molecules. Once the solute and **solvent** are evenly distributed, they continue to move about, but there is no net movement of either one in any direction.

As discussed, the chemical and physical properties of the plasma membrane allow only a few types of molecules to enter and exit a cell simply by diffusion. Gases can diffuse through the lipid bilayer; this is the mechanism by which oxygen enters cells and carbon dioxide exits cells. Also, consider the movement of oxygen from the alveoli (air sacs) of the lungs to blood in the lung capillaries (Fig. 5.7). After inhalation (breathing in), the concentration of oxygen in the alveoli is higher than that in the blood; therefore, oxygen diffuses into the blood.

Molecules diffuse down their concentration gradients. A few types of small molecules can simply diffuse through the plasma membrane.

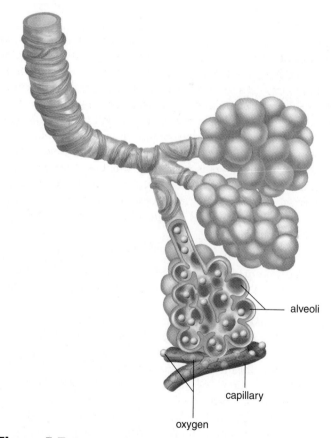

alveoli

capillary

oxygen

Figure 5.7 Gas exchange in lungs.
Oxygen (O_2) diffuses into the capillaries of the lungs because there is a higher concentration of oxygen in the alveoli (air sacs) than in the capillaries.

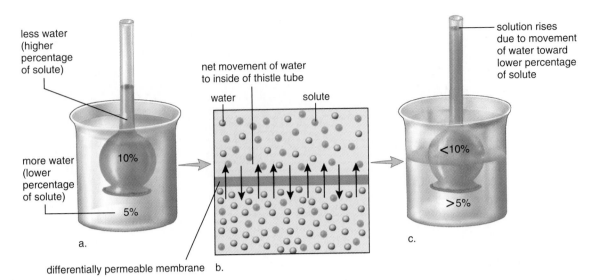

less water (higher percentage of solute)

net movement of water to inside of thistle tube

water   solute

solution rises due to movement of water toward lower percentage of solute

more water (lower percentage of solute)

10%

5%

<10%

>5%

a.

c.

differentially permeable membrane   b.

Figure 5.8 Osmosis demonstration.
a. A thistle tube, covered at the broad end by a differentially permeable membrane, contains a 10% sugar solution. The beaker contains a 5% sugar solution. **b.** The solute (green circles) is unable to pass through the membrane, but the water (blue circles) passes through in both directions. There is a net movement of water toward the inside of the thistle tube, where there are fewer water molecules per volume. **c.** Due to the incoming water molecules, the level of the solution rises in the thistle tube.

Osmosis

Osmosis [Gk. *osmos*, a pushing] is the diffusion of water into and out of cells. To illustrate osmosis, a thistle tube containing a 10% sugar solution[1] is covered at one end by a differentially permeable membrane and is then placed in a beaker containing a 5% sugar solution (Fig. 5.8). The beaker contains more water molecules (lower percentage of solute) per volume, and the thistle tube contains fewer water molecules (higher percentage of solute) per volume (Fig. 5.8*a*). Under these conditions, there is a net movement of water from the beaker to the inside of the thistle tube across the membrane (Fig. 5.8*b*). The solute is unable to pass through the membrane; therefore, the level of the solution within the thistle tube rises (Fig. 5.8*c*).

Notice the following in this illustration of osmosis:

1.   A differentially permeable membrane separates two solutions. The membrane does not permit passage of the solute.
2.   The beaker has more water (lower percentage of solute), and the thistle tube has less water (higher percentage of solute) per volume.
3.   The membrane permits passage of water, and there is a net movement of water from the beaker to the inside of the thistle tube.
4.   In the end, the concentration of solute in the thistle tube is less than 10%. Why? Because there is now less solute per volume. And the concentration of solute in the beaker is greater than 5%. Why? Because there is now more solute per volume.

Water enters the thistle tube due to the osmotic pressure of the solution within the thistle tube. **Osmotic pressure** is the pressure that develops in a system due to osmosis.[2] In

other words, the greater the possible osmotic pressure the more likely water will diffuse in that direction. Due to osmotic pressure, water is absorbed from the human large intestine, is retained by the kidneys, and is taken up by capillaries from tissue fluid.

Tonicity

Tonicity is the degree to which a solution's concentration of solute versus water causes water to move into or out of cells. In the laboratory, cells are normally placed in **isotonic solutions;** that is, the solute concentration is the same on both sides of the membrane, and therefore there is no net gain or loss of water (Fig. 5.9). The prefix *iso* means *the same as,* and the term *tonicity* refers to the strength of the solution. A 0.9% solution of the salt sodium chloride (NaCl) is known to be isotonic to red blood cells. Therefore, intravenous solutions medically administered usually have this tonicity.

Solutions that cause cells to swell, or even to burst, due to an intake of water are said to be **hypotonic solutions.** The prefix *hypo* means *less than,* and refers to a solution with a lower percentage of solute (more water) than the cell. If a cell is placed in a hypotonic solution, water enters the cell; the net movement of water is from the outside to the inside of the cell.

Any concentration of a salt solution lower than 0.9% is hypotonic to red blood cells. Animal cells placed in such a solution expand and sometimes burst due to the buildup of

[1] Percent solutions are grams of solute per 100 ml of solvent. Therefore, a 10% solution is 10 g of sugar with water added to make up 100 ml of solution.

[2] Osmotic pressure is measured by placing a solution in an osmometer and then immersing the osmometer in pure water. The pressure that develops is the osmotic pressure of a solution.

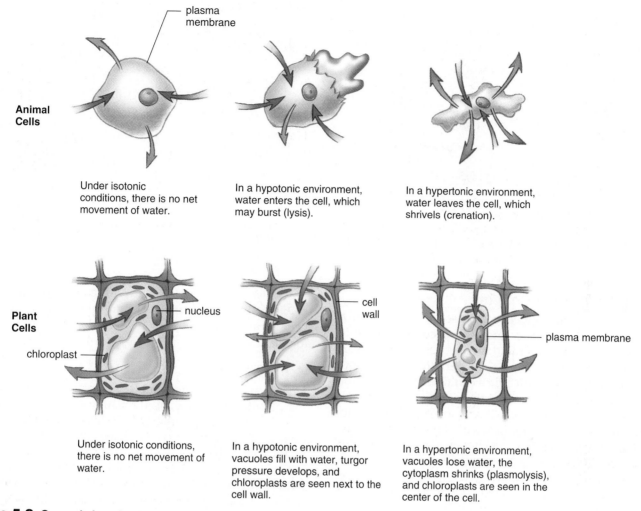

Figure 5.9 Osmosis in animal and plant cells.
The arrows indicate the net movement of water. In an isotonic solution, a cell neither gains nor loses water; in a hypotonic solution, a cell gains water; and in a hypertonic solution, a cell loses water.

pressure. The term *lysis* is used to refer to disrupted cells; hemolysis, then, is disrupted red blood cells.

The swelling of a plant cell in a hypotonic solution creates **turgor pressure** [L. *turgor,* swelling]. When a plant cell is placed in a hypotonic solution, we observe expansion of the cytoplasm because the large central vacuole gains water and the plasma membrane pushes against the rigid cell wall. The plant cell does not burst because the cell wall does not give way. Turgor pressure in plant cells is extremely important to the maintenance of the plant's erect position. If you forget to water your plants they wilt due to decreased turgor pressure.

Solutions that cause cells to shrink or to shrivel due to a loss of water are said to be **hypertonic solutions.** The prefix *hyper* means *more than,* and refers to a solution with a higher percentage of solute (less water) than the cell. If a cell is placed in a hypertonic solution, water leaves the cell; the net movement of water is from the inside to the outside of the cell.

Any solution with a concentration higher than 0.9% sodium chloride is hypertonic to red blood cells. If animal cells are placed in this solution, they shrink. The term **crenation** [L. *cranatus,* notched, wrinkled] refers to red blood cells in this condition. Meats are sometimes preserved by salting them. The bacteria are not killed by the salt but by the lack of water in the meat.

When a plant cell is placed in a hypertonic solution, the plasma membrane pulls away from the cell wall as the large central vacuole loses water. This is an example of **plasmolysis,** a shrinking of the cytoplasm due to osmosis. Dead plants you see along a salted roadside after the winter died because they were exposed to a hypertonic solution.

In an isotonic solution, a cell neither gains nor loses water. In a hypotonic solution, a cell gains water. In a hypertonic solution, a cell loses water and the cytoplasm shrinks.

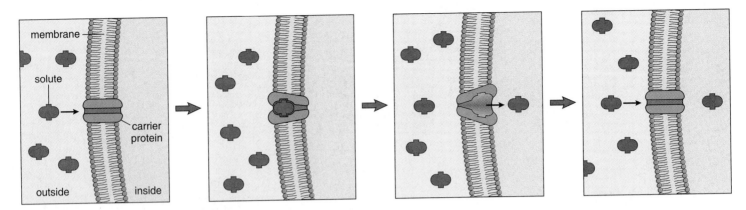

Figure 5.10 Facilitated transport.
During facilitated transport, a carrier protein speeds the rate at which the solute crosses the plasma membrane toward a lower concentration. Note that the carrier protein undergoes a change in shape as it moves a solute across the membrane.

Transport by Carrier Proteins

The plasma membrane impedes the passage of all but a few substances. Yet, biologically useful molecules are able to enter and exit the cell at a rapid rate because there are carrier proteins in the membrane. **Carrier proteins** are specific; each can combine with only a certain type of molecule or ion, which is then transported through the membrane. It is not completely understood how carrier proteins function, but after a carrier combines with a molecule, the carrier is believed to undergo a change in shape that moves the molecule across the membrane. Carrier proteins are required for facilitated transport and active transport (see Table 5.1).

> Some of the proteins in the plasma membrane are carriers. They transport biologically useful molecules into and out of the cell.

Facilitated Transport

Facilitated transport explains the passage of such molecules as glucose and amino acids across the plasma membrane even though they are not lipid-soluble. The passage of glucose and amino acids is facilitated by their reversible combination with carrier proteins, which in some manner transport them through the plasma membrane. These carrier proteins are specific. For example, various sugar molecules of identical size might be present inside or outside the cell, but glucose can cross the membrane hundreds of times faster than the other sugars. As stated earlier, this is the reason that the membrane can be called differentially permeable.

A model for facilitated transport (Fig. 5.10) shows that after a carrier has assisted the movement of a molecule to the other side of the membrane, it is free to assist the passage of other similar molecules. Neither diffusion, explained previously, nor facilitated transport requires an expenditure of energy because the molecules are moving down their concentration gradient in the same direction they tend to move anyway.

Active Transport

During **active transport,** molecules or ions move through the plasma membrane, accumulating either inside or outside the cell. For example, iodine collects in the cells of the thyroid gland; glucose is completely absorbed from the gut by the cells lining the digestive tract; and sodium can be almost completely withdrawn from urine by cells lining the kidney tubules. In these instances, molecules have moved to the region of higher concentration, exactly opposite to the process of diffusion.

Both carrier proteins and an expenditure of energy are needed to transport molecules against their concentration gradient. In this case, chemical energy (ATP molecules usually) is required for the carrier to combine with the substance to be transported. Therefore, it is not surprising that cells involved primarily in active transport, such as kidney cells, have a large number of mitochondria near a membrane where active transport is occurring.

Proteins involved in active transport often are called pumps because, just as a water pump uses energy to move water against the force of gravity, proteins use energy to move a substance against its concentration gradient. One type of pump that is active in all animal cells, but is especially associated with nerve and muscle cells, moves sodium ions (Na^+) to the outside of the cell and potassium ions (K^+) to the inside of the cell. These two events are linked, and the carrier protein is called a **sodium-potassium pump.** A change in carrier shape after the attachment and again after the detachment of a phosphate group allows it to combine alternately with sodium ions and potassium ions (Fig. 5.11). The phosphate group is donated by ATP when it is broken down enzymatically by the carrier.

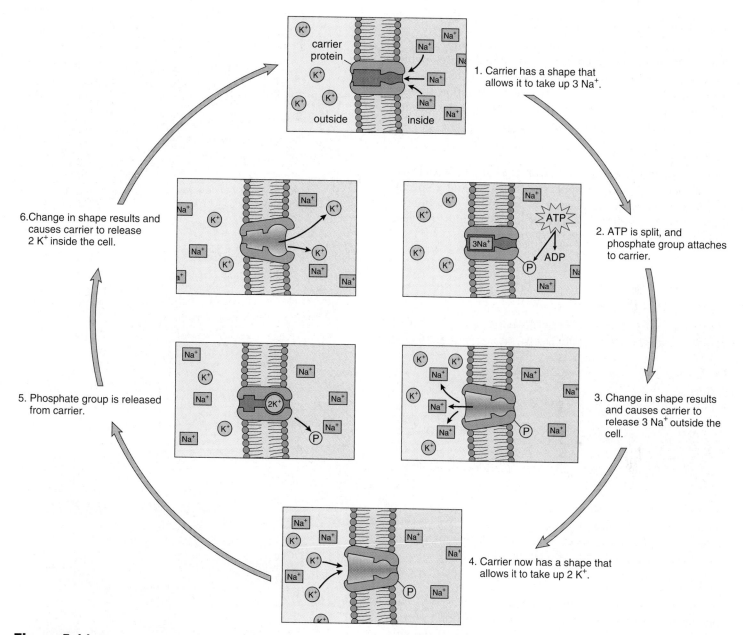

Figure 5.11 The sodium-potassium pump.
The same carrier protein transports sodium ions (Na⁺) to the outside of the cell and potassium ions (K⁺) to the inside of the cell because it undergoes an ATP-dependent change in shape. Three sodium ions are carried outward for every two potassium ions carried inward; therefore, the inside of the cell is negatively charged compared to the outside.

The sodium-potassium pump results in both a concentration gradient and an electrical gradient for these ions across the plasma membrane.

The passage of salt (NaCl) across a plasma membrane is of primary importance in cells. The chloride ion (Cl^-) usually crosses the plasma membrane because it is attracted by positively charged sodium ions (Na^+). First sodium ions are pumped across a membrane and then chloride ions simply diffuse through channels that allow their passage.

As noted in Figure 5.4, the chloride ion channels malfunction in persons with cystic fibrosis, leading to the symptoms of this inherited (genetic) disorder.

During facilitated transport, small molecules follow their concentration gradient. During active transport, small molecules and ions move against their concentration gradient.

Membrane-Assisted Transport

What about the transport of macromolecules such as polypeptides, polysaccharides, or polynucleotides, which are too large to be transported by carrier proteins? They are transported in or out of the cell by vesicle formation, thereby keeping the macromolecules contained so that they do not mix with those in the cytoplasm.

Exocytosis

During **exocytosis** [Gk. *ex*, out of, and *kytos*, cell], vesicles often formed by the Golgi apparatus and carrying a specific molecule, fuse with the plasma membrane as secretion occurs. This is the way that insulin leaves insulin-secreting cells, for instance.

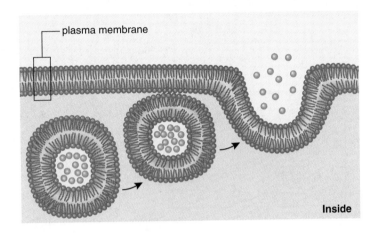

Notice that the membrane of the vesicle becomes a part of the plasma membrane. During cell growth, exocytosis is probably used as a means to enlarge the plasma membrane, whether or not secretion is also taking place.

Endocytosis

During **endocytosis** [Gk. *endon*, within, and *kytos*, cell], cells take in substances by vesicle formation (Fig. 5.12). A portion of the plasma membrane invaginates to envelop the substance, and then the membrane pinches off to form an intracellular vesicle.

When the material taken in by endocytosis is large, such as a food particle or another cell, the process is called **phagocytosis** [Gk. *phagein*, to eat, and *kytos*, cell]. Phagocytosis is common in unicellular organisms like amoebas and in ameboid cells like macrophages, which are large cells that engulf bacteria and worn-out red blood cells in mammals. When the endocytic vesicle fuses with a lysosome, digestion occurs.

Pinocytosis [Gk. *pino*, drink, and *kytos*, cell] occurs when vesicles form around a liquid or very small particles. Blood cells, cells that line the kidney tubules or intestinal wall, and plant root cells all use this method of ingesting substances (solutes). Whereas phagocytosis can be seen with the light microscope, the electron microscope must be used to observe pinocytic vesicles, which are no larger than 1–2 μm.

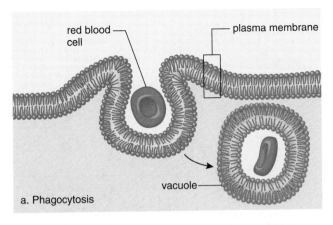

a. Phagocytosis

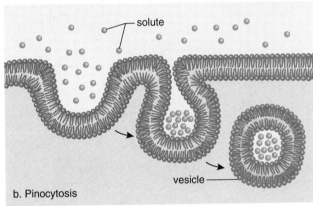

b. Pinocytosis

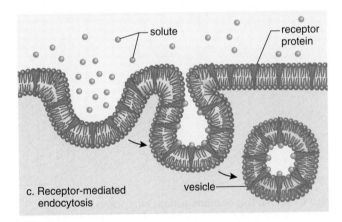

c. Receptor-mediated endocytosis

Figure 5.12 **Three methods of endocytosis.**
a. Phagocytosis occurs when the substance to be transported into the cell is large: white blood cells can engulf bacteria by phagocytosis. Digestion occurs when the resulting vacuole fuses with a lysosome.
b. Pinocytosis occurs when a solute such as a polypeptide is to be transported into the cell. The result is a small vacuole or vesicle.
c. Receptor-mediated endocytosis is a form of pinocytosis. The solute to be taken in first binds to specific receptor proteins which migrate to a pit or are already in a pit. The vesicle that forms contains the solute and its receptors. Sometimes the receptors are recycled, as shown in Figure 5.13.

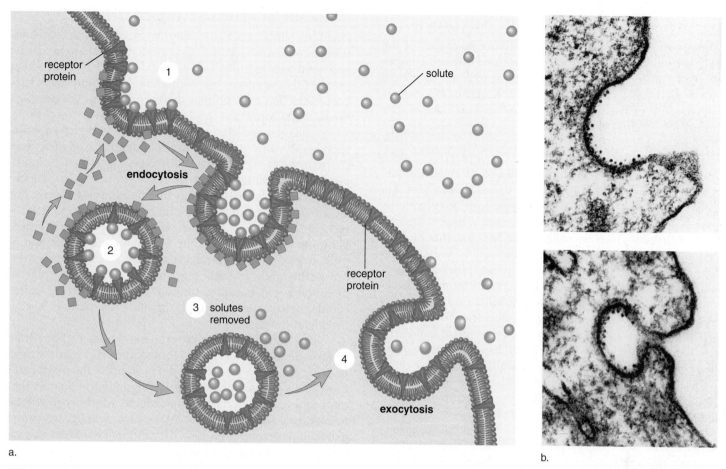

a.

b.

Figure 5.13 Receptor-mediated endocytosis.

a. (1) The receptor proteins (blue triangles) in a pit combine only with a specific solute (green circles). (2) The vesicle that forms is at first coated with a fibrous protein (blue squares), but soon the vesicle loses its coat. (3) Solutes sometimes leave the vesicle undigested. (4) When exocytosis occurs, membrane and therefore receptors are returned to the plasma membrane. **b.** Electron micrographs of a coated pit in the process of forming a vesicle.

Receptor-mediated endocytosis is a form of pinocytosis that is quite specific because it involves the use of a receptor protein shaped in such a way that a specific substance (called a ligand) such as vitamins, peptide hormones, and lipoproteins can bind to it. The binding of a substance to receptor proteins causes the receptors to gather at one location. This location is called a coated pit because there is a layer of fibrous protein on the cytoplasmic side (see step 1, Fig. 5.13). Once the vesicle is formed, the fibrous coat is released and the vesicle appears uncoated (see step 2). The fate of the vesicle and its contents depends on the kind of substance it contains. Sometimes the substance simply enters the cytoplasm (step 3). A spent hormone, on the other hand, may be digested when the vesicle fuses with a lysosome. The membrane of the vesicle and, therefore, the receptor proteins are returned to the plasma membrane (step 4), or the vesicle can go to other membranous locations.

Aside from simply allowing substances to enter cells selectively from an extracellular fluid, coated pits are also involved in the transfer and exchange of substances between cells. Such exchanges take place when the substances move from maternal blood into fetal blood at the placenta, for example.

The importance of receptor-mediated endocytosis is demonstrated by a genetic disorder called familial hypercholesterolemia. Cholesterol is transported in blood by a complex of lipids and proteins called low-density lipoprotein (LDL). Individuals with familial hypercholesterolemia have inherited a gene that causes them to have a reduced number and/or defective receptors for LDL in their plasma membranes. Instead of cholesterol entering cells, it accumulates in the walls of arterial blood vessels, leading to high blood pressure, occluded (blocked) arteries, and heart attacks.

Substances are secreted from a cell by exocytosis. Substances enter a cell by endocytosis. Receptor-mediated endocytosis allows cells to take up specific kinds of molecules and then release them within the cell.

5.4 Modification of Cell Surfaces

The plasma membrane is the outer living boundary of the cell, but many cells have an extracellular surface component that is formed exterior to the membrane. In plants, fungi, algae, and bacteria, the extracellular component is called a cell wall while animal cells have an extracellular matrix.

Plant Cell Walls

In addition to a plasma membrane, plant cells are surrounded by a porous **cell wall** that varies in thickness, depending on the function of the cell (Fig. 5.14). All plant cells have a primary cell wall. The primary cell wall contains cellulose fibrils in which microfibrils are held together by noncellulose substances. Pectins allow the wall to stretch when the cell is growing, and noncellulose polysaccharides harden the wall when the cell is mature. Pectins are especially abundant in the middle lamella, which is a layer of adhesive substances that holds the cells together. Some cells in woody plants have a secondary wall that forms inside the primary cell wall. The secondary wall has a greater quantity of cellulose fibrils than the primary wall, and layers of cellulose fibrils are laid down at right angles to one another. Lignin, a substance that adds strength, is a common ingredient of secondary cell walls in woody plants.

In plant tissues, the cytoplasm of neighboring cells is sometimes connected by **plasmodesmata** (sing., plasmodesma), numerous narrow membrane-lined channels that pass through the cell wall. Cytoplasmic strands within these channels allow direct exchange of materials between neighboring plant cells. Coordination of cellular activities within a tissue occurs because of these linkages.

Extracellular Matrix of Animal Cells

An extracellular matrix is a meshwork of insoluble proteins with carbohydrate chains (glycoproteins) that are produced and secreted by animal cells (Fig. 5.15). The extracellular matrix fills the spaces between animal cells and helps support them. The extracellular matrix influences the development, migration, shape, and function of cells.

Collagen and elastin fibers are two well-known structural components of the extracellular matrix. Collagen gives the matrix strength and elastin gives it resilience. Fibronectins and laminins are two adhesive proteins that seem to play a dynamic role in influencing the behavior of cells. For example, fibronectin and laminin form "highways" that direct the migration of cells during development. Recently, laminins were found to be necessary for the production of milk by mammary gland cells taken from a mouse. Fibronectins and laminins bind to receptors in the plasma membrane and permit communication between the extracellular matrix and the cytoplasm of the cell, perhaps via cytoskeletal connections.

Proteoglycans are glycoproteins whose carbohydrate chains contain amino sugars. Proteoglycans provide a rigid packing gel that joins the various proteins in the matrix and most likely regulate the activity of signaling sequences that bind to receptors in the plasma protein. More work will be needed to determine the functions of proteoglycans in the extracellular matrix and how they influence cellular metabolism via signaling proteins like hormones.

Cells have extracellular structures. Cellulose and noncellulose substances occur in plant cell walls; the extracellular matrix of animal cells is rich in glycoproteins. Certain of these have functions that affect cell behavior.

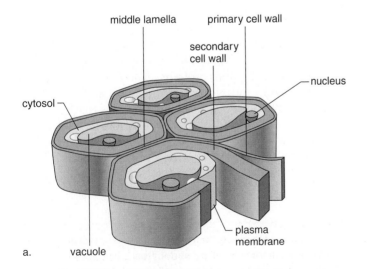

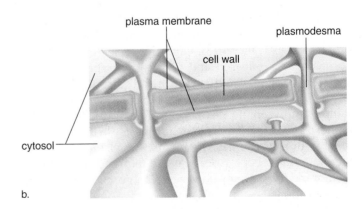

Figure 5.14 Plant cell wall and plasmodesmata.
a. All plant cells have a primary cell wall and some have a secondary cell wall. The cell wall, which lends support to the cell, is freely permeable.
b. Plasmodesmata are strands of cytoplasm that run in membrane-lined channels connecting certain plant cells.

Junctions Between Cells

For the cells of a tissue to act in a coordinated manner, it is beneficial for the plasma membranes of adjoining cells to interact. The plasmodesmata that link adjacent plant cells and the junctions that occur between animal cells are examples of such cellular interactions (Fig. 5.16).

In **adhesion junctions,** internal cytoplasmic plaques, firmly attached to the cytoskeleton within each cell, are joined by intercellular filaments. In some organs—like the heart, stomach, and bladder, where tissues get stretched—adhesion junctions hold the cells together.

Adjacent cells are even more closely joined by **tight junctions,** in which plasma membrane proteins actually attach to each other, producing a zipperlike fastening. The cells of tissues that serve as barriers are held together by tight junctions; in the intestine the digestive juices stay out of the body, and in the kidneys the urine stays within kidney tubules, because the cells are joined by tight junctions.

A **gap junction** allows cells to communicate. A gap junction is formed when two identical plasma membrane channels join. The channel of each cell is lined by six plasma membrane proteins. A gap junction lends strength to the cells, but it also allows small molecules and ions to pass between them. Gap junctions are important in heart muscle and smooth muscle because they permit a flow of ions that is required for the cells to contract as a unit.

Three types of junctions are seen between animal cells: adhesion junctions (desmosomes), tight junctions, and gap junctions.

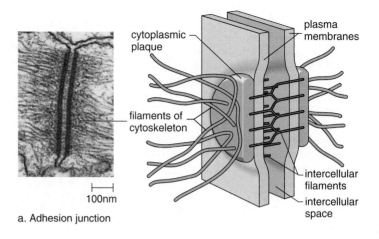

a. Adhesion junction

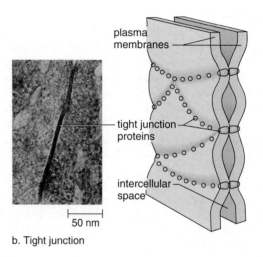

b. Tight junction

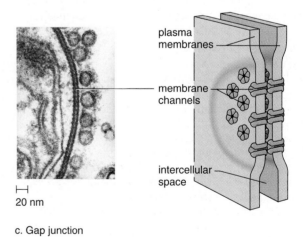

c. Gap junction

Figure 5.16 Junctions between cells of the intestinal wall.
a. In adhesion junctions (desmosomes), intercellular filaments run between two cells. b. Tight junctions between cells form an impermeable barrier because their adjacent plasma membranes are joined. c. Gap junctions allow communication between two cells because adjacent plasma membrane channels are joined.

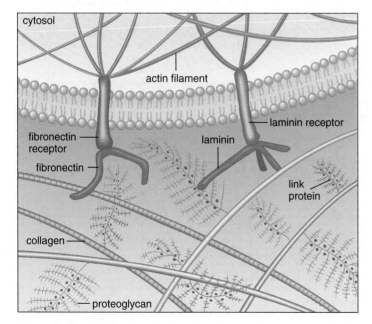

Figure 5.15 Animal cell extracellular matrix.
The glycoproteins in the extracellular matrix support an animal cell and also affect its behavior. Collagen and elastin also have a support function, while fibronectins and laminins bind to receptors in the plasma membrane and most likely assist cell communication processes.

Connecting Concepts

The plasma membrane is quite appropriately called the gatekeeper of the cell because it maintains the integrity of the cell and stands guard over what enters and leaves the cell. But we have seen that the plasma membrane does so much more than this. Its glycoproteins and glycolipids mark the cell as belonging to the organism. Its numerous proteins allow communication between cells and allow tissues to function as a whole. Now it appears that the extracellular material secreted by cells assists the plasma membrane in its numerous functions.

The progression in our knowledge about the plasma membrane illustrates how science works. The concepts and techniques of science evolve and change, and the knowledge we have today is amended and expanded by new investigative work. Basic science has applications that promote the well-being and health of human beings. To know that the plasma membrane is misfunctioning in a person who is diabetic, or those with a high cholesterol count is a first step toward curing these conditions. Even cancer is sometimes due to receptor proteins that signal the cell to divide even when no growth factor is present.

Our ability to understand the functioning of the plasma membrane is dependent on a thorough understanding of the molecules and ions that make up the cell. Today, it is impossible to deny the premise that biology and medicine have a biochemical basis.

Summary

5.1 Membrane Models

The fluid-mosaic model of membrane structure developed by Singer and Nicolson was preceded by several other models. Electron micrographs of freeze-fractured membranes support the fluid-mosaic model, and not Robertson's unit membrane concept based on the Danielli and Davson sandwich model.

5.2 Plasma Membrane Structure and Function

There are two components of the plasma membrane, lipids and proteins. In the lipid bilayer, phospholipids are arranged with their hydrophilic (polar) heads at the surfaces and their hydrophobic (nonpolar) tails in the interior. The lipid bilayer has the consistency of oil but acts as a barrier to the entrance and exit of most biological molecules. Membrane glycolipids and glycoproteins are involved in marking the cell as belonging to a particular individual and tissue.

The hydrophobic portion of a transmembrane protein lies in the lipid bilayer of the plasma membrane, and the hydrophilic portion lies at the surfaces. Proteins act as receptors, carry on enzymatic reactions, join cells together, form channels, or act as carriers to move substances across the membrane.

5.3 Permeability of the Plasma Membrane

Some molecules (lipid-soluble compounds, water, and gases) simply diffuse across the membrane from the area of higher concentration to the area of lower concentration. No metabolic energy is required for diffusion to occur.

The diffusion of water across a differentially permeable membrane is called osmosis. Water moves across the membrane into the area of higher solute (less water) content per volume. When cells are in an isotonic solution, they neither gain nor lose water. When cells are in a hypotonic solution, they gain water, and when they are in a hypertonic solution, they lose water (Table 5.2).

Other molecules are transported across the membrane by carrier proteins that span the membrane. During facilitated transport, a carrier protein assists the movement of a molecule down its concentration gradient. No energy is required.

During active transport, a carrier protein acts as a pump that causes a substance to move against its concentration gradient. The sodium-potassium pump carries Na^+ to the outside of the cell and K^+ to the inside of the cell. Energy in the form of ATP molecules is required for active transport to occur.

Larger substances can enter and exit a membrane by exocytosis and endocytosis. Exocytosis involves secretion. Endocytosis includes phagocytosis, pinocytosis, and receptor-mediated endocytosis. Receptor-mediated endocytosis makes use of receptor proteins in the plasma membrane. Once a specific solute (e.g., ligand) binds to receptors, a coated pit becomes a coated vesicle. After losing the coat, the vesicle can join with the lysosome, or after discharging the substance, the receptor-containing vesicle can fuse with the plasma membrane.

5.4 Modification of Cell Surfaces

Plant cells have a freely permeable cell wall, with cellulose as its main component. Plant cells are joined by small membrane-lined channels called plasmodesmata that span the cell wall and contain strands of cytoplasm that allow materials to pass from one cell to another.

Animal cells have an extracellular matrix that determines their shape and influences their behavior. Junctions between animal cells include adhesion junctions and tight junctions, which help to hold cells together, and gap junctions, which allow passage of small molecules between cells.

Table 5.2

Effect of Osmosis on a Cell

Tonicity of Solution	Concentrations		Net Movement of Water	Effect on Cell
	Solute	Water		
Isotonic	Same as cell	Same as cell	None	None
Hypotonic	Less than cell	More than cell	Cell gains water	Swells, turgor pressure
Hypertonic	More than cell	Less than cell	Cell loses water	Shrinks, plasmolysis

Reviewing the Chapter

1. Describe the fluid-mosaic model of membrane structure as well as the models that preceded it. Cite the evidence that either disproves or supports these models.   80–81
2. Tell how the phospholipids are arranged in the plasma membrane. What other lipids are present in the membrane, and what functions do they serve?   81–82
3. Describe how proteins are arranged in the plasma membrane. What are their various functions? Describe an experiment indicating that proteins can laterally drift in the membrane.   82–83
4. Define diffusion. What substances can diffuse through a differentially permeable membrane?   85
5. Define osmosis. Describe verbally and with drawings what happens to an animal cell when placed in isotonic, hypotonic, and hypertonic solutions.   86–87
6. Describe verbally and with drawings what happens to a plant cell when placed in these solutions.   86–87
7. Why do most substances have to be assisted through the plasma membrane? Contrast movement by facilitated transport with movement by active transport.   88
8. Draw and explain a diagram that shows how the sodium-potassium pump works.   88–89
9. Describe and contrast three methods of endocytosis.   90–91
10. Give examples to show that cell surface modifications help plant and animal cells communicate.   92–93

Testing Yourself

Choose the best answer for each question.

1. Write hypotonic solution or hypertonic solution beneath each cell. Justify your conclusions.

a. _____

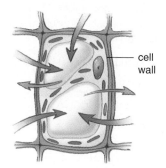

cell wall

b. _____

2. Electron micrographs following freeze-fracture of the plasma membrane indicate that
   a.   the membrane is a phospholipid bilayer.
   b.   some proteins span the membrane.
   c.   protein is found only on the surfaces of the membrane.
   d.   glycolipids and glycoproteins are antigenic.
   e.   there are receptors in the membrane.
3. A phospholipid molecule has a head and two tails. The tails are found
   a.   at the surfaces of the membrane.
   b.   in the interior of the membrane.
   c.   spanning the membrane.
   d.   where the environment is hydrophilic.
   e.   Both a and b are correct.
4. During diffusion,
   a.   solvents move from the area of higher to lower concentration but not solutes.
   b.   there is a net movement of molecules from the area of higher to lower concentration.
   c.   a cell must be present for any movement of molecules to occur.
   d.   molecules move against their concentration gradient if they are small and charged.
   e.   All of these are correct.
5. When a cell is placed in a hypotonic solution,
   a.   solute exits the cell to equalize the concentration on both sides of the membrane.
   b.   water exits the cell toward the area of lower solute concentration.
   c.   water enters the cell toward the area of higher solute concentration.
   d.   solute exits and water enters the cell.
   e.   Both c and d are correct.
6. When a cell is placed in a hypertonic solution,
   a.   solute exits the cell to equalize the concentration on both sides of the membrane.
   b.   water exits the cell toward the area of lower solute concentration.
   c.   water exits the cell toward the area of higher solute concentration.
   d.   solute exits and water enters the cell.
   e.   Both a and c are correct.
7. Active transport
   a.   requires a carrier protein.
   b.   moves a molecule against its concentration gradient.
   c.   requires a supply of chemical energy.
   d.   does not occur during facilitated transport.
   e.   All of these are correct.
8. The sodium-potassium pump
   a.   helps establish an electrochemical gradient across the membrane.
   b.   concentrates sodium on the outside of the membrane.
   c.   utilizes a carrier protein and chemical energy.
   d.   is present in the plasma membrane.
   e.   All of these are correct.
9. Receptor-mediated endocytosis
   a.   is no different from phagocytosis.
   b.   brings specific solutes into the cell.
   c.   helps to concentrate proteins in vesicles.
   d.   results in high osmotic pressure.
   e.   All of these are correct.

10. Plant cells
    a. always have a secondary cell wall, even though the primary one may disappear.
    b. have channels between cells that allow strands of cytoplasm to pass from cell to cell.
    c. develop turgor pressure when water enters the nucleus.
    d. do not have cell-to-cell junctions like animal cells.
    e. All of these are correct.

Thinking Scientifically

1. The mucus in bronchial tubes must be thin enough for cilia to move bacteria and viruses up into the throat away from the lungs. Which way would Cl⁻ normally cross the plasma membrane (see Fig. 5.4, top) of bronchial tube cells in order for mucus to be thin? Use the concept of osmosis to explain your answer.
2. Winter wheat is planted in the early fall, grows over the winter when the weather is colder, and is harvested in the spring. As the temperature drops, the makeup of the plasma membrane of winter wheat changes. Unsaturated fatty acids replace saturated fatty acids in the phospholipids of the membrane. Why is this a suitable adaptation?

Understanding the Terms

active transport 88
adhesion junction 93
carrier protein 83, 88
cell wall 92
channel protein 83
cholesterol 81
concentration gradient 84
crenation 87
differentially permeable 84
diffusion 85
endocytosis 90
enzymatic protein 83
exocytosis 90
facilitated transport 88
fluid-mosaic model 80
gap junction 93
glycolipid 81
glycoprotein 82
hypertonic solution 87

hypotonic solution 86
isotonic solution 86
osmosis 86
osmotic pressure 86
phagocytosis 90
phospholipid 81
pinocytosis 90
plasmodesmata 92
plasmolysis 87
receptor-mediated
  endocytosis 91
receptor protein 83
sodium-potassium pump 88
solute 85
solution 85
solvent 85
tight junction 93
tonicity 86
turgor pressure 87

Match the terms to these definitions:

a. _____ Type of plasma membranes that regulates the passage of substances into and out of the cell, allowing some to pass through and preventing the passage of others.
b. _____ Diffusion of water through the plasma membrane of cells.
c. _____ Higher solute concentration (less water) than the cytosol of a cell; causes cell to lose water by osmosis.
d. _____ Causes an increase in liquid on the side of the membrane with higher solute concentration.
e. _____ One of the major lipids found in animal plasma membranes; makes the membrane impermeable to many molecules.

Web Connections

Exploring the Internet

http://www.mhhe.com/biosci/genbio/mader/
(Click on *Biology 7/e*)

The *Biology 7/e* Online Learning Center provides many resources for studying the material in this chapter including links to the following sites:

Membrane Structure contains a thorough, well-illustrated discussion of membrane structure.

http://cellbio.utmb.edu/cellbio/membrane.html

Cell Membrane Structure and Composition. This site describes the fluid-mosaic model of membrane structure.

http://esg-www.MIT.EDU:8001/esgbio/cb/membranes/structure.html

Cell Membranes. This site discusses the structure and function of proteins in cell membranes.

http://esg-www.MIT.EDU:8001/esgbio/cb/membranes/intro.html

Membrane Transport Mechanisms. This site describes the mechanisms of cellular transport. Examples include diffusion, active transport, and the sodium-potassium pump.

http://esg-www.MIT.EDU:8001/esgbio/cb/membranes/transport.html

Electron Microscopic View of Membranes. A large number of electron microscopic photos of cell membranes, showing gap junctions, integral and peripheral proteins, and text to describe.

http://cellbio.utmb.edu/cellbio/membrane3.htm#polarized cells

Metabolism: Energy and Enzymes

c h a p t e r

Painted lady butterfly, *Vanessa cardui*, on purple coneflower, *Echinacea purpurea*

Living things cannot maintain their organization nor carry on life's other activities without a source of organic food. Green plants utilize solar energy, carbon dioxide, and water to make organic food for themselves and all living things. Animals, such as butterflies and human beings, feed on plants or other animals that have eaten plants.

Food provides nutrient molecules, which are used as a source of energy and building blocks. Energy is the capacity to do work, and it takes work to maintain the organization of a cell and the organism, including the beautiful wings of this butterfly. When nutrients are broken down, they provide the necessary energy to make ATP (adenosine triphosphate). ATP fuels chemical reactions in cells such as the synthetic reactions that produce cell parts and products. The use of ATP in cells is substantial evidence of the relatedness of all life-forms.

Metabolism is all the chemical reactions that occur in a cell. Enzymes are protein molecules that speed metabolic reactions in cells at a relatively low temperature. This chapter deals with energy and enzymes, two essential requirements for cellular metabolism.

6.1 Energy

Living things can't grow, reproduce, or exhibit any of the characteristics of life without a ready supply of energy. **Energy,** which is the capacity to do work, occurs in many forms. Light energy comes from the sun; electrical energy powers kitchen appliances; and heat energy warms our houses. **Kinetic energy** is the energy of motion. All moving objects have kinetic energy. Thrown baseballs, falling water, and contracting muscles have kinetic energy. **Potential energy** is stored energy. Water behind a dam, or a rock at the top of a hill, or ATP, has potential energy that can be converted to kinetic energy. **Chemical energy** is in the interactions of atoms, one to the other, in a molecule.

Not only do chemicals have potential energy, they also have varying amounts of potential energy. Glucose has much more energy than its breakdown products, carbon dioxide and water.

Two Laws of Thermodynamics

Early researchers who first studied energy and its relationships and exchanges formulated two **laws of thermodynamics.** *The first law, also called the "law of conservation of energy," says that energy cannot be created or destroyed but can only be changed from one form to another.* Think of the conversions that occur when coal is used to power a locomotive. First, the chemical energy of coal is converted to heat energy and then heat energy is converted to kinetic energy in a steam engine. Similarly, the potential energy of coal or gas is

Figure 6.1 Energy for life.
All of the energy needed to move this athlete is provided by the food he has eaten. Once food has been processed in the digestive tract, nutrients are transported about the body, including to the muscles. The energy of nutrient molecules is converted to that of ATP molecules which power muscle contraction.

converted to electrical energy by power plants. Do energy transformations occur in the human body? Yes, indeed. As an example, consider that the chemical energy in the food we eat is changed to the chemical energy of ATP, and then this form of potential energy is used for, say, muscle contraction (Fig. 6.1).

The second law of thermodynamics says that energy cannot be changed from one form to another without a loss of usable energy. Only about 25% of the chemical energy of gasoline is converted to the motion of a car; the rest is lost as heat. Heat, of course, is a form of energy, but heat is the most random form of energy and quickly dissipates into the environment. When muscles use the chemical energy within ATP to bring about contraction, some of this energy becomes heat right away. With conversion upon conversion, eventually all usable forms of energy become heat that is lost by the organism to the environment. And because heat dissipates, it can never be converted back to a form of potential energy. Organisms abide by laws of thermodynamics but so do larger systems. The reading on the next page discusses how ecosystems also obey the second law of thermodynamics.

Entropy

Entropy [Gk. *entrope*, a turning inward] is a measure of randomness or disorder. An organized, usable form of energy has low entropy, whereas an unorganized, less stable form of energy such as heat has high entropy. A neat room has a much lower entropy than a messy room. We know that a neat room always tends toward messiness. In the same way, energy conversions eventually result in heat, and therefore the entropy of the universe is always increasing.

How does an ordered system such as a neat room or an organism come about? You know very well that it takes an input of usable energy to keep your room neat. In the same way, it takes a constant input of usable energy from the food you eat to keep you organized. This input of energy goes through many energy conversions, and the output is finally heat, which increases the entropy of the universe.

A civilized society such as ours requires a great deal of low entropy energy. Fossil fuel energy, such as coal and oil, is used to grow and process your food and is used to keep your environment ordered. Building houses and schools and roads all require an input of usable energy, which is finally converted to heat. Our civilized society is increasing the entropy of the universe at a much higher rate than any society in the past.

The laws of thermodynamics explain why the entropy of the universe spontaneously increases and why organisms need a constant input of usable energy to maintain their organization.

Ecosystems and the Second Law of Thermodynamics

A cell converts the energy of one chemical molecule into another but ecosystems also convert energy. In an ecosystem, the energy stored in a prey population is used by a predator population. Because of this, energy flows through an ecosystem (Fig. 6A). As transformations of energy occur, useful energy is lost to the environment in the form of heat, until finally useful energy is completely used up. Since energy cannot recycle, there is a need for an ultimate source of energy. This source, which continually supplies almost all living things with energy, is the sun. The entire universe is tending toward disorder, but in the meantime, solar energy is sustaining living things.

Human beings also feed on other organisms. We feed directly on plants, such as corn, or on animals like poultry and cattle that have fed on corn. In the United States, however, much supplemental energy in addition to solar energy is used to produce food. Even before planting time, there is an input of fossil fuel energy for the processing of seeds, and the making of tools, fertilizers, and pesticides. Then, fossil fuel energy is used to transport these materials to the farm. At the farm, fuel is needed to plant the seeds, to apply fertilizers, and pesticides, and to irrigate, harvest, and dry crops. After harvesting, still more fuel is used to process crops to make the neatly packaged products we buy in the supermarket. Most of the food we eat today has been processed in some way. Even farm families now buy at least some of their food from supermarkets in nearby towns.

Since 1940 the amount of supplemental fuel used in the American food system has greatly increased. By now the amount of supplemental energy is at least three or four times that of the caloric content of the food produced! This is partially caused by the trend to produce more food on less land by growing high-yielding hybrid wheat and corn plants. These plants require more care and about twice as much supplemental energy as the tradi-

tional varieties of wheat and corn. Cattle confined to feedlots and fed grain that has gone through the whole production process require about twenty times the amount of supplemental energy as do range-fed cattle. Our food system has been labeled energy-intensive because it requires such a large input of supplemental energy.

Our energy-intensive food system is a matter for concern because it increases the cost of food and the burning of fossil fuels adds pollutants to the atmosphere. What can be done? First of all, we could grow crops that do not require so much supplemental energy. And second, we could eat primarily vegetables and grains. It is estimated that only about 10% of the energy contained in one population is actually taken up by the next population. (About 90% is lost as heat.) This means that about ten times the number of people can be sustained on a diet of vegetables and grain rather than a diet of meat. And when we do eat meat we could depend more on range-fed cattle. Cattle kept close to farmland supply manure that can substitute, in part, for chemical fertilizer. Biological control, the use of natural enemies to control pests, would cut down on pesti-

cide use. Solar and wind energy could be used instead of fossil fuel energy, particularly on the farm. For example, wind-driven irrigation pumps are feasible.

Finally, of course, consumers could help matters. We could overcome our prejudice against vegetables that have slight blemishes. We could avoid processed foods and buy cheaper cuts of beef, which have come from range-fed cattle. And we could avoid using electrically powered gadgets when preparing food at home.

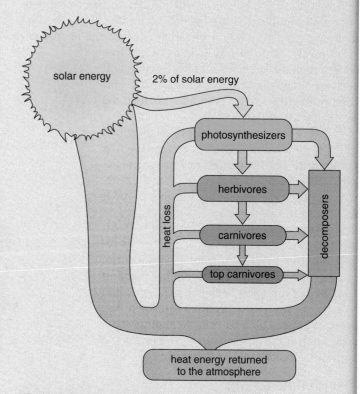

Figure 6A Energy loss in an ecosystem.
Ordinarily about 2% of the solar energy reaching the earth is taken up by photosynthesizers (plants and algae). This is the energy that allows them to make their own food. Herbivores obtain their food by eating plants, and carnivores obtain food by eating other animals. Whenever the energy content of food is used by organisms, it is eventually converted to heat. With death and decay by decomposers, all the energy temporarily stored in organisms returns as heat to the atmosphere. In order to support a very large population, human beings supplement solar energy with fossil fuel energy to grow crops. Usually, humans feed on crops directly or on animals (herbivores) that have been fed on crops.

6.2 Metabolic Reactions and Energy Transformations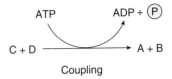

Metabolism is the sum of all the reactions that occur in a cell. **Reactants** are substances that participate in a reaction, while **products** are substances that form as a result of a reaction. In the reaction A + B → C + D, A and B are the reactants while C and D are the products. How would you know that this reaction will occur spontaneously—that is, without an input of energy? Using the concept of entropy, it is possible to state that a reaction will occur spontaneously if it increases the entropy of the universe. But this is not very helpful because in cell biology we don't wish to consider the entire universe. We simply want to consider this reaction. In such instances, cell biologists use the concept of free energy. **Free energy** is the amount of energy available—that is, energy that is still "free" to do work after a chemical reaction has occurred. Free energy is denoted by the symbol G after Josaih Gibbs who first developed the concept. A negative ΔG (change in free energy) means that the products have less free energy than the reactants and the reaction will occur spontaneously. In our reaction, if C and D have less free energy than A and B, then the reaction will "go."

Exergonic reactions are ones in which ΔG is negative and energy is released, while **endergonic reactions** are ones in which the products have more free energy than the reactants. Endergonic reactions can only occur if there is an input of energy.

If the change in free energy in both directions is just about zero, the reaction is reversible and the reaction is at equilibrium. How could you make a reversible reaction "go" in one direction or the other? Very often in cells, as soon as a product is formed, the product is used as a reactant in another reaction. Such occurrences cause the reaction to go in the direction of the product.

Coupled Reactions

Can the energy released by an exergonic reaction be used to "drive" an endergonic reaction? In the body many reactions such as protein synthesis, nerve conduction, or muscle contraction are endergonic: they require an input of energy. On the other hand, the breakdown of ATP to ADP + Ⓟ is exergonic and energy is released (Fig. 6.2).

In **coupled reactions,** the energy released by an exergonic reaction is used to drive an endergonic reaction. ATP breakdown is often coupled to cellular reactions that require an input of energy. Coupling,

which requires that the exergonic reaction and the endergonic reaction be closely tied, can be symbolized like this:

ATP   ADP + Ⓟ

C + D ————————→ A + B

Coupling

When ATP breakdown is coupled to an endergonic reaction, the overall reaction becomes exergonic (Fig. 6.2). Not all the energy of ATP breakdown is captured and some is immediately lost as heat. Eventually it is all lost as heat.

How is a cell assured of a supply of ATP? Recall that glucose breakdown during cellular respiration provides the energy for the buildup of ATP in mitochondria. Only 39% of the free energy of glucose is transformed to ATP; the rest is lost as heat.

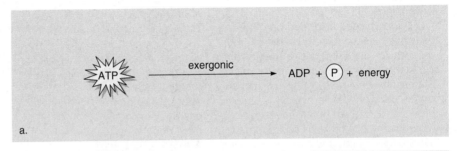

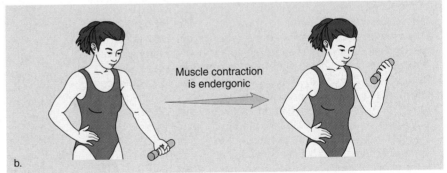

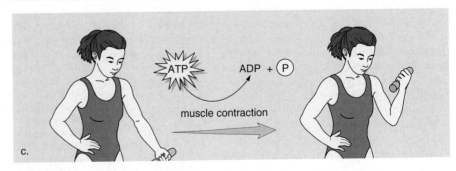

Figure 6.2 Coupled reactions.
a. The breakdown of ATP is exergonic. **b.** Muscle contraction is endergonic and therefore cannot occur without an input of energy. **c.** Muscle contraction is coupled to ATP breakdown, making the overall process exergonic. Now muscle contraction can occur.

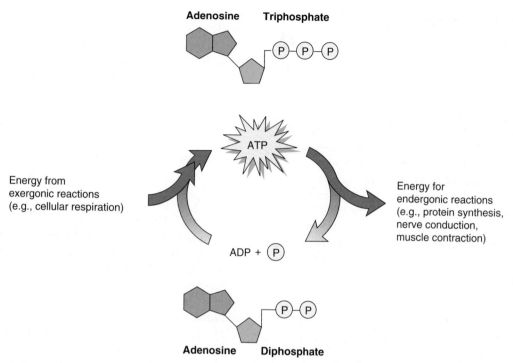

Figure 6.3 **The ATP cycle.**
In cells, the exergonic breakdown of glucose during cellular respiration is coupled to the buildup of ATP, and then the exergonic breakdown of ATP is coupled to various endergonic reactions in cells. When a phosphate group is removed by hydrolysis, ATP releases the appropriate amount of energy for most metabolic reactions. The high-energy content of ATP comes from the complex interaction of the atoms within the molecule.

ATP: Energy for Cells

ATP (adenosine triphosphate) is the common energy currency of cells: when cells require energy, they "spend" ATP. You may think that this causes our bodies to produce a lot of ATP, and it does; however, the amount stored in cells is minimal because ATP is constantly being broken down to **ADP (adenosine diphosphate)** and P (Fig. 6.3).

The use of ATP as a carrier of energy has some advantages: (1) It provides a common energy currency that can be used in many different types of reactions. (2) When ATP becomes ADP + P, the amount of energy released is just about enough for the biological purposes mentioned in the following section, and so little energy is wasted. (3) ATP breakdown is coupled to endergonic reactions in such a way that it minimizes energy loss.

Function of ATP

Recall that at various times we have mentioned at least three uses for ATP.

Chemical work   Supplies the energy needed to synthesize macromolecules that make up the cell.

Transport work   Supplies the energy needed to pump substances across the plasma membrane.

Mechanical work   Supplies the energy needed to permit muscles to contract, cilia and flagella to beat, chromosomes to move, and so forth.

Structure of ATP

ATP is a nucleotide composed of the base adenine and the sugar ribose (together called adenosine) and three phosphate groups. ATP is called a "high-energy" compound because a phosphate group is easily removed. Under cellular conditions, the amount of energy released when ATP is hydrolyzed to ADP + P is about 7.3 kcal per mole.[1]

ATP is a carrier of energy in cells. It is the common energy currency because it supplies energy for many different types of reactions.

---

[1] A mole is the number of molecules present in the molecular weight of a substance (in grams).

6.3 Metabolic Pathways and Enzymes

Reactions do not occur haphazardly in cells; they are usually a part of a **metabolic pathway,** a series of linked reactions. Metabolic pathways begin with a particular reactant and terminate with an end product. While it is possible to write an overall equation for a pathway as if the beginning reactant went to the end product in one step, there are actually many specific steps in between. In the pathway, one reaction leads to the next reaction, which leads to the next reaction, and so forth in an organized, highly structured manner. This arrangement makes it possible for one pathway to lead to several others, because various pathways have several molecules in common. Also, metabolic energy is captured and utilized more easily if it is released in small increments rather than all at once.

A metabolic pathway can be represented by the following diagram:

$$E_1 \quad E_2 \quad E_3 \quad E_4 \quad E_5 \quad E_6$$

$$A \rightarrow B \rightarrow C \rightarrow D \rightarrow E \rightarrow F \rightarrow G$$

In this diagram, the letters A–F are reactants and letters B–G are products in the various reactions. The letters E_1–E_6 are enzymes.

An **enzyme** is a protein molecule[2] that functions as an organic catalyst to speed a chemical reaction. In a crowded ballroom, a mutual friend can cause particular people to interact. In the cell, an enzyme brings together particular molecules and causes them to react with one another.

The reactants in an enzymatic reaction are called the **substrates** for that enzyme. In the first reaction, A is the substrate for E_1 and B is the product. Now B becomes the substrate for E_2, and C is the product. This process continues until the final product G forms.

Any one of the molecules (A–G) in this linear pathway could also be a substrate for an enzyme in another pathway. A diagram showing all the possibilities would be highly branched.

Energy of Activation

Molecules frequently do not react with one another unless they are activated in some way. In the absence of an enzyme, activation is very often achieved by heating the reaction flask to increase the number of effective collisions between molecules. The energy that must be added to cause molecules to react with one another is called the **energy of activation** (E_a). Figure 6.4 compares E_a when an enzyme is not present to when an enzyme is present, illustrating that enzymes lower the amount of energy required for activation to occur.

In baseball, a home-run hitter must not only hit the ball to the fence, but over the fence. When enzymes lower the energy of activation, it is like removing the fence; then it is possible to get a home run by simply hitting the ball as far as the fence was.

---

[2] Catalytic RNA molecules are called ribozymes and are not enzymes.

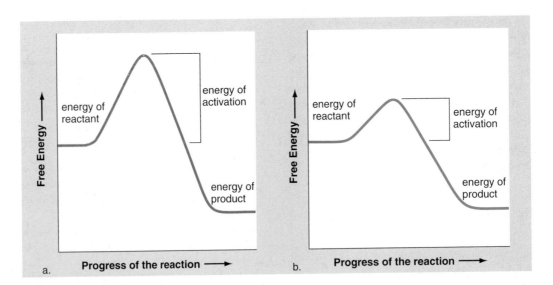

Figure 6.4 Energy of activation (E_a).
Enzymes speed the rate of chemical reactions because they lower the amount of energy required to activate the reactants. **a.** Energy of activation when an enzyme is not present. **b.** Energy of activation when an enzyme is present. Even spontaneous reactions like this one speed up when an enzyme is present.

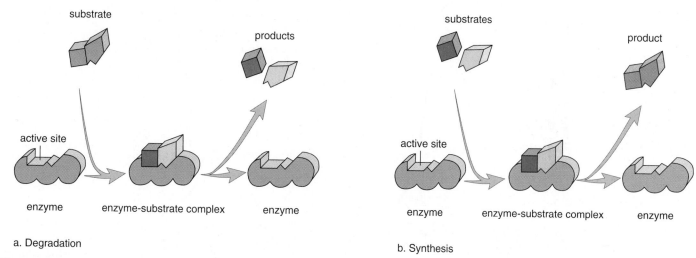

a. Degradation

b. Synthesis

Figure 6.5 Enzymatic action.
An enzyme has an active site, which is where the substrates and enzyme fit together in such a way that the substrates are oriented to react. Following the reaction, the products are released and the enzyme is free to act again. **a.** Some enzymes carry out degradation; the substrate is broken down to smaller products. **b.** Other enzymes carry out synthesis; substrates are combined to produce a larger product.

Enzyme-Substrate Complexes

The following equation, which is pictorially shown in Figure 6.5, is often used to indicate that an enzyme forms a complex with its substrate:

$$\underset{\text{enzyme}}{E} \; + \; \underset{\text{substrate}}{S} \; \rightarrow \; \underset{\substack{\text{enzyme-substrate}\\\text{complex}}}{ES} \; \rightarrow \; \underset{\text{enzyme}}{E} \; + \; \underset{\text{product}}{P}$$

In most instances only one small part of the enzyme, called the **active site,** complexes with the substrate(s). It is here that the enzyme and substrate fit together, seemingly like a key fits a lock; however, it is now known that the active site undergoes a slight change in shape in order to accommodate the substrate(s). This is called the **induced-fit model** because the enzyme is induced to undergo a slight alteration to achieve optimum fit (Fig. 6.6).

The change in shape of the active site facilitates the reaction that now occurs. After the reaction has been completed, the product(s) is released, and the active site returns to its original state, ready to bind to another substrate molecule. Only a small amount of enzyme is actually needed in a cell because enzymes are not used up by the reaction.

Some enzymes do more than simply complex with their substrate(s); they actually participate in the reaction. Trypsin digests protein by breaking peptide bonds. The active site of trypsin contains three amino acids with *R* groups that actually interact with members of the peptide bond—first to break the bond and then to introduce the components of water. This illustrates that the formation of the enzyme-substrate complex is very important in speeding up the reaction.

Sometimes it is possible for (a) particular reactant(s) to produce more than one type of product(s). The presence or

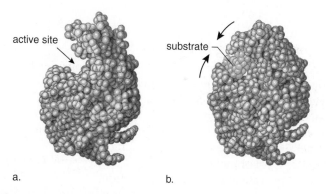

Figure 6.6 Induced fit model.
Computer-generated images of an enzyme called lysozyme that hydrolyzes its substrate, a polysaccharide that makes up bacterial cell walls. **a.** Configuration of enzyme when no substrate is bound to it. **b.** After the substrate binds, the configuration of the enzyme changes so that hydrolysis can better proceed.

absence of an enzyme determines which reaction takes place. If a substance can react to form more than one product, then the enzyme that is present and active determines which product is produced.

Every reaction in a cell requires its specific enzyme. Because enzymes only complex with their substrates, they are named for their substrates. For example, the enzyme that digests lipid molecules is called lipase and the enzyme that digests urea is called urease. Notice that the name of an enzyme ends in "ase."

Enzymes are protein molecules that speed chemical reactions by lowering the energy of activation. They do this by forming an enzyme-substrate complex.

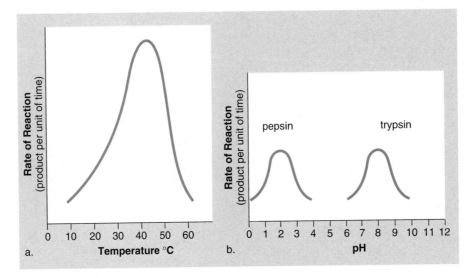

Figure 6.7 Rate of an enzymatic reaction as a function of temperature and pH.
a. At first, as with most chemical reactions, the rate of an enzymatic reaction doubles with every 10°C rise in temperature. In this graph, the rate of reaction is maximum at about 40°C; then it decreases until the reaction stops altogether, because the enzyme has become denatured. **b.** Pepsin, an enzyme found in the stomach, acts best at a pH of about 2, while trypsin, an enzyme found in the small intestine, performs optimally at a pH of about 8. The shape that enables these proteins to bind with their substrates is not properly maintained at other pHs.

Factors Affecting Enzymatic Speed

Enzymatic reactions proceed quite rapidly. Consider, for example, the breakdown of hydrogen peroxide (H_2O_2) as catalyzed by the enzyme catalase: $2\ H_2O_2 \rightarrow 2\ H_2O + O_2$. The breakdown of hydrogen peroxide can occur 600,000 times a second when catalase is present. To achieve maximum product per unit time, there should be enough substrate to fill active sites most of the time. Temperature and optimal pH also increase the rate of an enzymatic reaction.

Substrate Concentration

Generally, enzyme activity increases as substrate concentration increases because there are more collisions between substrate molecules and the enzyme. As more substrate molecules fill active sites, more product results per unit time. But when the enzyme's active sites are filled almost continuously with substrate, the enzyme's rate of activity cannot increase anymore. Maximum rate has been reached.

Temperature and pH

As the temperature rises, enzyme activity increases (Fig. 6.7a). This occurs because as the temperature rises there are more effective collisions between enzyme and substrate. However, if the temperature rises beyond a certain point, enzyme activity eventually levels out and then declines rapidly because the enzyme is **denatured**. An enzyme's shape changes during denaturation, and then it can no longer bind its substrate(s) efficiently.

Each enzyme also has an optimal pH at which the rate of the reaction is highest. Figure 6.7b shows the optimal pH for the enzymes pepsin and trypsin. At this pH value, these enzymes have their normal configurations. The globular shape of an enzyme is dependent on interactions, such as hydrogen bonding, between R groups. A change in pH can alter the ionization of these side chains and disrupt normal interactions, and under extreme conditions of pH, denaturation eventually occurs. Again, the enzyme has an altered shape and is then unable to combine efficiently with its substrate.

Enzyme Concentration

Since enzymes are specific, a cell regulates which enzymes are present and/or active at any one time. Otherwise enzymes may be present that are not needed, or one pathway may negate the work of another pathway.

One way to control enzyme activity after it is present is to activate or deactivate the enzyme. Phosphorylation is one way to activate an enzyme. Signal molecules received by membrane receptors often turn on kinases, which then activate enzymes by phosphorylating them:

Enzyme Inhibition

Enzyme inhibition occurs when an active enzyme is prevented from combining with its substrate. In *competitive inhibition,* another molecule is so close in shape to the enzyme's substrate that it can compete with the true substrate for the enzyme's active site. This molecule inhibits the reaction because only the binding of the true substrate results in a product. In *noncompetitive inhibition,* a molecule binds to an enzyme, but not at the active site. The other binding site is called the **allosteric site** [Gk. *allo,* other, and *steric,* space, structure]. In this instance, inhibition occurs when binding of a molecule causes a shift in the three-dimensional structure so that the substrate cannot bind to the active site.

The activity of almost every enzyme in a cell can be regulated by its product. When a product is in abundance, it binds competitively with its enzyme's active site; as the product is used up, inhibition is reduced and more product can be produced. In this way, the concentration of the product is always kept within a certain range. Most metabolic pathways are regulated by **feedback inhibition,** but the end product of the pathway binds at an allosteric site on the first enzyme of the pathway (Fig. 6.8). This binding shuts down the pathway, and no more product is produced.

In inhibition, a metabolite binds to the active site or binds to an allosteric site on an enzyme.

Poisons are often enzyme inhibitors. Cyanide is an inhibitor for an essential enzyme (cytochrome *c* oxidase) in all cells, which accounts for its lethal effect on humans. Penicillin blocks the active site of an enzyme unique to bacteria. When penicillin is administered, bacteria die but humans are unaffected.

Enzyme Cofactors

Many enzymes require an inorganic ion or organic, but nonprotein, molecule to function properly. These necessary ions or molecules are called **cofactors.** The inorganic ions are metals such as copper, zinc, or iron. The organic, nonprotein molecules are called **coenzymes.** Coenzymes assist the enzyme and may even accept or contribute atoms to a reaction.

It is interesting that vitamins are often components of coenzymes. **Vitamins** are relatively small organic molecules that are required in trace amounts in our diet and in the diet of other animals for synthesis of coenzymes. The vitamin becomes a part of the coenzyme's molecular structure. For example, vitamin niacin is part of the coenzyme NAD^+ and B_{12} is a part of the coenzyme FAD.

A deficiency of any vitamin results in a lack of a coenzyme and therefore enzymatic actions. In humans, this eventually results in vitamin-deficiency symptoms: niacin deficiency results in a skin disease called pellagra, and riboflavin deficiency results in cracks at the corners of the mouth.

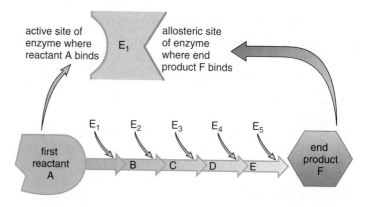

a. Overall view of pathway

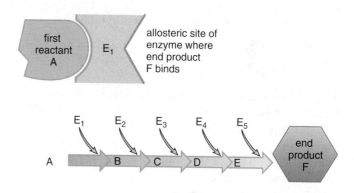

b. View of active pathway

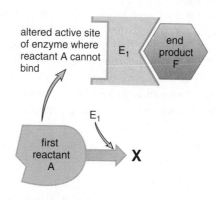

c. View of inhibited pathway

Figure 6.8 **Feedback inhibition.**
a. This hypothetical metabolic pathway is regulated by feedback inhibition. **b.** When reactant A binds to the active site of E_1, the pathway is active and the end product is produced. **c.** Once there is sufficient end product, some binds to the allosteric site of E_1. Now a change of shape prevents reactant A from binding to the active site of E_1 and the end product is no longer produced.

Enzymes speed a reaction by forming a complex with the substrate. Various factors affect enzymatic speed, including substrate concentration, temperature, pH, enzyme concentration, the presence of inhibitors or necessary cofactors.

6.4 Metabolic Pathways and Oxidation-Reduction

In oxidation-reduction (redox) reactions, electrons pass from one molecule to another. **Oxidation** is the loss of electrons and **reduction** is the gain of electrons. Oxidation and reduction always take place at the same time because one molecule accepts the electrons given up by another molecule. Oxidation-reduction reactions occur during photosynthesis and cellular respiration.

Photosynthesis

In living things, hydrogen ions often accompany electrons, and oxidation is a loss of hydrogen atoms ($e^- + H^+$). Reduction is a gain of hydrogen atoms. For example, the overall reaction for photosynthesis can be written like this:

$$6\,CO_2 \; + \; 6\,H_2O \; + \; Energy \; \rightarrow \; C_6H_{12}O_6 \; + \; 6\,O_2$$

Carbon   Water   Glucose   Oxygen
dioxide

This equation shows that when hydrogen atoms are transferred from water to carbon dioxide, glucose is formed. Water has been oxidized and carbon dioxide has been reduced. Since glucose is a high-energy molecule, an input of energy is needed to make the reaction go. Chloroplasts are able to capture solar energy and convert it by way of an electron transport system (discussed in the next section) to the chemical energy of ATP molecules. ATP is then used along with hydrogen atoms to reduce glucose.

A coenzyme of oxidation-reduction called **NADP$^+$** **(nicotinamide adenine dinucleotide phosphate)** is active during photosynthesis. This molecule carries a positive charge, and therefore is written as NADP$^+$. During photosynthesis, NADP$^+$ accepts electrons and a hydrogen ion derived from water and later passes them by way of a metabolic pathway to carbon dioxide, forming glucose. The reaction that reduces NADP$^+$ is:

$$NADP^+ \; + \; 2\,e^- \; + \; H^+ \; \rightarrow \; NADPH$$

Cellular Respiration

The overall equation for cellular respiration is opposite that of photosynthesis:

$$C_6H_{12}O_6 \; + \; 6\,O_2 \; \rightarrow \; 6\,CO_2 \; + \; 6\,H_2O \; + \; Energy$$

Glucose   Oxygen   Carbon   Water
                                dioxide

In this reaction, glucose has lost hydrogen atoms (been oxidized) and oxygen has gained hydrogen atoms (been reduced). When oxygen gains hydrogen atoms it becomes water. Since glucose is a high-energy molecule and water is a low-energy molecule, energy has been released. The organelles called mitochondria use the energy released from glucose breakdown to build ATP molecules by way of an electron transport system that passes electrons to oxygen. Oxygen then becomes water.

In metabolic pathways, most oxidations such as those that occur during cellular respiration involve a coenzyme called **NAD$^+$ (nicotinamide adenine dinucleotide).** This molecule carries a positive charge, and therefore is represented as NAD$^+$. During oxidation reactions, NAD$^+$ accepts two electrons but only one hydrogen ion. The reaction that reduces NAD$^+$ is:

$$NAD^+ \; + \; 2\,e^- \; + \; H^+ \; \rightarrow \; NADH$$

Electron Transport System

As mentioned above, chloroplasts use solar energy to generate ATP and mitochondria use glucose energy to generate ATP by way of an electron transport system. An **electron transport system** is a series of membrane-bound carriers that pass electrons from one carrier to another. High-energy electrons are delivered to the system and low-energy electrons leave it. Every time electrons are transferred to a new carrier, energy is released; this energy is ultimately used to produce ATP molecules (Fig. 6.9).

In certain redox reactions, the result is release of energy, and in others, energy is required. In an electron transport system, each carrier is reduced and then oxidized in turn. The overall effect of oxidation/reduction as electrons are passed from carrier to carrier of the electron transport system is the release of energy for ATP production.

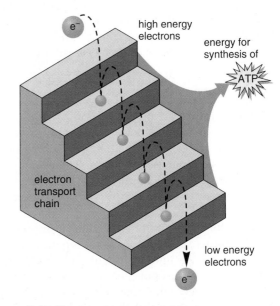

Figure 6.9 Electron transport system.
High-energy electrons enter the system and with each step, as they pass from carrier to carrier, energy is released and used for ATP production.

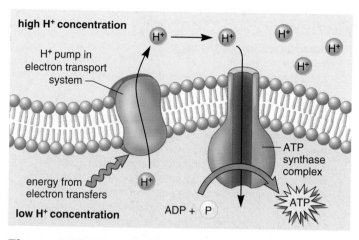

Figure 6.10 Chemiosmosis.
Carriers in the electron transport system pump hydrogen ions (H⁺)
across a membrane. When the hydrogen ions flow back across the
membrane through a protein complex, ATP is synthesized by an
enzyme called ATP synthase. Chemiosmosis occurs in mitochondria
and chloroplasts.

ATP Production

For many years, it was known that ATP synthesis was some-
how coupled to the electron transport system, but the exact
mechanism could not be determined. Peter Mitchell, a
British biochemist, received a Nobel Prize in 1978 for his
chemiosmotic theory of ATP production in both mitochondria and chloroplasts.

In mitochondria and chloroplasts, the carriers of the
electron transport system are located within a membrane.
Hydrogen ions (H⁺), which are often referred to as protons
in this context, tend to collect on one side of the membrane
because they are pumped there by certain carriers of the
electron transport system. This establishes an electrochemical gradient across the membrane that can be used to
provide energy for ATP production. Particles, called **ATP**

synthase complexes, span the membrane. Each complex
contains a channel that allows hydrogen ions to flow down
their electrochemical gradient. The flow of hydrogen ions
through the channel provides the energy for the ATP synthase enzyme to produce ATP from ADP + ⓟ (Fig. 6.10).
Chemiosmosis [Gk. *osmos*, push] is the production of ATP
due to a hydrogen ion gradient across a membrane.

Consider this analogy to understand chemiosmosis.
The sun's rays evaporate water from the seas and help create
the winds that blow clouds to the mountains, where water
falls in the form of rain and snow. The water in a mountain
reservoir has a higher potential energy than that of water in
the ocean. The potential energy is converted to electrical energy when water is released and used to turn turbines in an
electrochemical dam before it makes its way to the ocean.
The continual release of water results in a continual production of electricity.

Similarly, during photosynthesis, solar energy collected by chloroplasts continually leads to ATP production.
ATP is produced because thylakoid membrane acts like a
dam to maintain an energy gradient in the form of a concentration gradient of hydrogen ions. The hydrogen ions flow
through membrane channels that couple the flow of hydrogen ions to the formation of ATP, like the turbines in a
hydroelectric dam system couple the flow of water to the
formation of electricity.

Similarly, during cellular respiration, glucose breakdown provides the energy to establish a hydrogen ion gradient across the inner membrane of mitochondria. And
again hydrogen ions flow through membrane channels that
couple the flow of hydrogen ions to the formation of ATP.

As oxidation-reduction occurs, the electron transport
system deposits hydrogen ions (H⁺) on one side of a
membrane. When the ions flow down an electrochemical
gradient through an ATPase complex, ATP is formed.

Connecting Concepts

All cells use energy. Energy is the ability to
do work, to bring about change, to make
things happen, whether it's a leaf growing
or a human running. The metabolic pathways inside cells utilize the chemical
bond energy of ATP to synthesize molecules, cause muscle contraction, and
even allow us to read these words.

A metabolic pathway consists of a
series of individual chemical reactions,
each with its own enzyme. The cell can
regulate the activity of the very many hundreds of different enzymes taking part in
cellular metabolism. Enzymes are proteins and as such they are sensitive to

environmental conditions, including pH,
temperature, and even certain pollutants
as will be discussed later in this text.

ATP is called the universal energy
"currency" of life. This is an apt analogy—
before we can spend currency (i.e.,
money), we must first make some money.
Similarly, before the cell can spend ATP
molecules, it must make them. Cellular
respiration in mitochondria transforms the
chemical bond energy of carbohydrates
to that of ATP molecules. An ATP is spent
when it is hydrolyzed and the resulting
energy is coupled to an endergonic metabolic reaction. All cells are continually

making and breaking down ATPs. If ATP
is lacking, the organism dies.

What is the ultimate source of energy
for ATP production? Except for a few
deep ocean vents and also certain cave
communities, the answer is the sun. Photosynthesis inside chloroplasts transforms solar energy into the chemical
bond energy of carbohydrates. And then
carbohydrate products are broken down
in mitochondria as ATP is built up. Chloroplasts and mitochondria are the cellular
organelles that permit a flow of energy
from the sun through all living things.

Summary

6.1 Energy

There are two energy laws that are basic to understanding energy-use patterns at all levels of biological organization. The first law states that energy cannot be created or destroyed, but can only be transferred or transformed. The second law states that one usable form of energy cannot be completely converted into another usable form. As a result of these laws, we know that the entropy of the universe is increasing and that only a constant input of energy maintains the organization of living things.

6.2 Metabolic Reactions and Energy Transformations

Metabolism is a term that encompasses all the chemical reactions occurring in a cell. Considering individual reactions, only those that result in a negative free energy difference—that is, the products have less usable energy than the reactants—occur spontaneously. Such reactions, called exergonic reactions, release energy. Endergonic reactions, which require an input of energy, occur only in cells because it is possible to couple an exergonic process with an endergonic process. For example, glucose breakdown is an exergonic metabolic pathway that drives the buildup of many ATP molecules. These ATP molecules then supply energy for cellular work. Thus, ATP goes through a cycle in which it is constantly being built up from, and then broken down, to ADP + ℗.

6.3 Metabolic Pathways and Enzymes

A metabolic pathway is a series of reactions that proceed in an orderly, step-by-step manner. Each reaction requires a specific enzyme. Reaction rates increase when enzymes form a complex with their substrates. Generally, enzyme activity increases as substrate concentration increases; once all active sites are filled, maximum rate has been achieved.

Any environmental factor, such as temperature and pH, affects the shape of a protein and, therefore, also affects the ability of an enzyme to do its job. Cellular mechanisms regulate enzyme quantity and activity. The activity of most metabolic pathways is regulated by feedback inhibition. Many enzymes have cofactors or coenzymes that help them carry out a reaction.

6.4 Metabolic Pathways and Oxidation-Reduction

Photosynthesis is a metabolic pathway in chloroplasts that transforms solar energy to the chemical energy within carbohydrates (e.g., glucose). Cellular respiration is a metabolic pathway completed in mitochondria that transforms this energy into that of ATP molecules.

The overall equation for photosynthesis is the opposite of that for cellular respiration. During photosynthesis, $NADP^+$ is a coenzyme that reduces substrates, and during cellular respiration, NAD^+ is a coenzyme that oxidizes substrates. Redox reactions are a major way in which energy transformation occurs in cells.

Both processes make use of an electron transport system in which electrons are transferred from one carrier to the next one with the release of energy that is ultimately used to produce ATP molecules. Chemiosmosis explains how the electron transport system produces ATP. The carriers of this system deposit hydrogen ions (H^+) on one side of a membrane. When the ions flow down an electrochemical gradient through an ATPase complex, an enzyme utilizes the release of energy to make ATP from ADP and ℗.

Reviewing the Chapter

1. State the first law of thermodynamics and give an example. 98
2. State the second law of thermodynamics and give an example. 98
3. Explain why the entropy of the universe is always increasing and why an organized system like an organism requires a constant input of useful energy. 98
4. What is the difference between exergonic reactions and endergonic reactions? Why can exergonic but not endergonic reactions occur spontaneously? 100
5. Define coupling and write an equation that shows an endergonic reaction being coupled to ATP breakdown. 100
6. Why is ATP called the energy currency of cells? What is the ATP cycle? 101
7. Diagram a metabolic pathway. Label the reactants, products, and enzymes. 102
8. Why is less energy needed for a reaction to occur when an enzyme is present? 102
9. Why are enzymes specific, and why can't each one speed up many different reactions? 103
10. Name and explain the manner in which at least three factors can influence the speed of an enzymatic reaction. How do cells regulate the activity of enzymes? 104–05
11. What are cofactors and coenzymes? 105
12. Describe how oxidation-reduction occurs in cells and discuss the overall equations for photosynthesis and cellular respiration in terms of oxidation-reduction. 106
13. Describe an electron transport system. 106
14. Tell how cells form ATP during chemiosmosis. 107

Testing Yourself

Choose the best answer for each question.

1. Consider this reaction: A + B → C + D + energy.
   a. This reaction is exergonic.
   b. An enzyme could still speed the reaction.
   c. ATP is not needed to make the reaction go.
   d. A and B are reactants; C and D are products.
   e. All of these are correct.
2. The active site of an enzyme
   a. is similar to that of any other enzyme.
   b. is the part of the enzyme where its substrate can fit.
   c. can be used over and over again.
   d. is not affected by environmental factors like pH and temperature.
   e. Both b and c are correct.
3. If you wanted to increase the amount of product per unit time of an enzymatic reaction, do not increase
   a. the amount of substrate.
   b. the amount of enzyme.
   c. the temperature somewhat.
   d. the pH.
   e. All of these are correct.
4. An allosteric site on an enzyme is
   a. the same as the active site.
   b. nonprotein in nature.
   c. where ATP attaches and gives up its energy.
   d. often involved in feedback inhibition.
   e. All of these are correct.

5. During photosynthesis, carbon dioxide
   a. is oxidized to oxygen.
   b. is reduced to glucose.
   c. gives up water to the environment.
   d. is a coenzyme of oxidation-reduction.
   e. All of these are correct.
6. Electron transport systems
   a. are found in both mitochondria and chloroplasts.
   b. release energy as electrons are transferred.
   c. are involved in the production of ATP.
   d. are located in a membrane.
   e. All of these are correct.
7. The difference between NAD^+ and $NADP^+$ is that
   a. only NAD^+ production requires niacin in the diet.
   b. one is an organic molecule and the other is inorganic because it contains phosphate.
   c. one carries electrons to the electron transport system and the other carries them to synthetic reactions.
   d. one is involved in cellular respiration and the other is involved in photosynthesis.
   e. Both c and d are correct.
8. Chemiosmosis is dependent upon
   a. the diffusion of water across a differentially permeable membrane.
   b. an outside supply of phosphate and other chemicals.
   c. the establishment of an electrochemical hydrogen ion (H^+) gradient.
   d. the ability of ADP to join with Ⓟ even in the absence of a supply of energy.
   e. All of these are correct.
9. Use these terms to label this diagram: substrates, enzyme (used twice), active site, product, and enzyme-substrate complex. Explain the importance of an enzyme's shape to its activity.

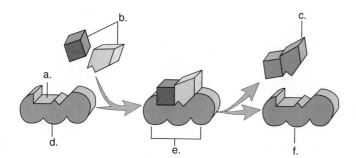

10. Label this diagram describing chemiosmosis.

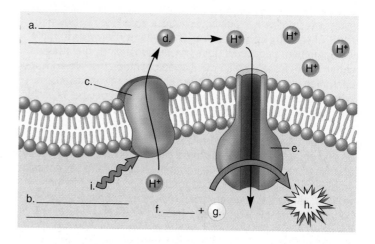

Thinking Scientifically

1. A certain flower generates heat. This heat attracts pollinating insects to the flower. While the evolutionary benefit of attracting insects is obvious, the metabolic cost of this particular adaptation is high. What metabolic mechanism(s) might a plant use to generate heat and under what circumstances would the metabolic cost be high?
2. The free energy of carbon dioxide and water is considerably less than the free energy of sucrose (table sugar). However, the conversion of sucrose to carbon dioxide and water is never spontaneous under normal conditions. How would you explain this observation?

Bioethical Issue

Today, we are very much concerned about emerging diseases caused by parasites. Emerging diseases are ones like AIDS and Ebola, which emerge from their natural host to cause illness in humans. In 1993, the hantavirus strain emerged from the common deer mouse and killed about 60 young people in the Southwest. In the case of hantavirus, we know that climate was involved. An unusually mild winter and wet spring caused piñon trees to bloom well and provide pine nuts to the mice. The increasing deer mouse population came into contact with humans, and the hantavirus leaped easily from mice to humans.

The prediction is that global warming, caused in large part by the burning of fossil fuels, will upset normal weather cycles and result in outbreaks of hantavirus as well as malaria, dengue and yellow fevers, filariasis, encephalitis, schistosomiasis, and cholera. Clearly any connection between global warming and emerging diseases offers another reason why greenhouse gases should be curtailed when fossil fuels like gasoline are consumed. Greenhouse gases are those like carbon dioxide and methane, which allow the sun's rays to pass through but then trap the heat from escaping.

In December of 1997, 159 countries met in Kyoto, Japan, to work out a protocol that would reduce greenhouse gases worldwide. It is believed that the emission of greenhouse gases, especially from power plants, will cause earth's temperature to rise 1.5°–4.5° by 2060. The U.S. Senate does not want to ratify the agreement because it does not include a binding emissions commitment from the less-developed countries that are only now becoming industrialized. While the U.S. presently emits a large proportion of the greenhouse gases, China is expected to pass the United States in about 2020 to become the biggest source of greenhouse emissions.

Negotiations with the less-developed countries is still going on and some creative ideas have been put forward. Why not have a trading program that allows companies to buy and sell emission credits across international boundaries? Accompanying that would be a market in greenhouse reduction techniques. If it became monetarily worth their while, companies in developing countries would have an incentive to reduce greenhouse emissions. If you were a CEO, would you be willing to reduce greenhouse emissions simply because they cause a deterioration of the environment and probably cause human illness? Why or why not? Instead, do you approve of giving companies monetary incentives to reduce greenhouse emissions? Why or why not?

Understanding the Terms

active site   103
ADP (adenosine diphosphate)   101
allosteric site   105
ATP (adenosine triphosphate)   101
ATP synthase complex   107
chemical energy   98
chemiosmosis   107
coenzyme   105
cofactor   105
coupled reactions   100
denatured   104
electron transport system   106
endergonic reaction   100
energy   98
energy of activation   102
entropy   98
enzyme   102
enzyme inhibition   105

exergonic reaction   100
feedback inhibition   105
free energy   100
induced-fit model   103
kinetic energy   98
laws of thermodynamics   98
metabolic pathway   102
metabolism   100
NAD^+ (nicotinamide adenine dinucleotide)   106
$NADP^+$ (nicotinamide adenine dinucleotide phosphate)   106
oxidation   106
potential energy   98
product   100
reactant   100
reduction   106
substrate   102
vitamin   105

Match the terms to these definitions:

a. _____ All of the chemical reactions that occur in a cell during growth and repair.

b. _____ Stored energy as a result of location or spatial arrangement.

c. _____ Essential requirement in the diet, needed in small amounts. They are often part of coenzymes.

d. _____ Measure of disorder or randomness.

e. _____ Nonprotein organic molecule that aids the action of the enzyme to which it is loosely bound.

Web Connections

Exploring the Internet

http://www.mhhe.com/biosci/genbio/mader
(click on *Biology 7/e*)

The *Biology 7/e* Online Learning Center provides many resources for studying the material in this chapter including links to the following sites:

Enzymes Tutorials. Answer questions as you learn more about enzymes, how scientists study enzyme-catalyzed reactions, and enzyme kinetics.

http://biog-101-104.bio.cornell.edu/BioG101_104/tutorials/enzymes.html

Animated GIFs and Protein Chemistry. In a short visit to this site, you can encounter the three-dimensional structure of an enzyme with its substrate bound to the active site.

http://www2.ucsc.edu/people/straycat/cpa.html

Enzymes in the Manufacture of Fruit Juices. Information on the practical uses of enzymes utilized in the commercial manufacture of fruit juices.

http://134.225.167.114/NCBE/FEATURES/juice.html

Enzyme Mechanisms. This chapter is from an MIT hypertextbook. Chemical energetics, enzyme mechanics, enzyme kinetics, and feedback inhibition are covered, and there are feedback regulation problems included.

http://esg-www.mit.edu:8001/esgbio/eb/ebdir.html

Whole Food Formula—Enzymes. Visit this rather scientifically incorrect site to see how many people pay lots of money due to lack of knowledge of enzymes. As a scientist, why can you see that this is just a waste of money? What statements in this ad are correct facts and which are not?

http://www.wimall.com/friend/enzyme.html

Photosynthesis

Giant panda, *Ailuropoda melanoleuca*, feeding on bamboo, *Bambusa arundinacea*.

Why would most life on earth perish without photosynthesis? Through photosynthesis plants and algae produce food for themselves and all other living things. Animals, like giant pandas, feed directly on photosynthesizers while other animals feed indirectly on photosynthesizers.

When photosynthesis occurs, carbon dioxide is absorbed and oxygen is released. Oxygen is required by organisms when they carry on cellular respiration. Oxygen also rises high in the atmosphere and forms the ozone shield that protects terrestrial organisms from the damaging effects of the ultraviolet rays of the sun. Planting trees and saving forests helps purify the air of carbon dioxide which is poisonous to many organisms and contributes to global warming.

The human population feeds on plants, but they are also a source of fabrics, rope, paper, lumber, fuel, and pharmaceuticals. In short, plants make modern society possible. And while we are thanking green plants for human survival, let's not forget the simple beauty of a magnolia bloom or the majesty of an old-growth forest.

7.1 Solar Energy

Solar energy makes our modern way of life possible not only because it can be used directly to heat buildings, but also because the bodies of plants became the fossil fuel coal which we still use today to generate electricity. Photosynthetic organisms, like plants and algae, produce organic food for the biosphere. Organic nutrients serve as an energy source and the building blocks that permit growth and repair. Photosynthesis is carried out in this manner:

$$\text{solar energy} + \text{carbon dioxide} + \text{water} \longrightarrow \text{carbohydrate} + \text{oxygen}$$

Because **photosynthesis** is an energy transformation in which solar energy is converted to the chemical bond energy of carbohydrate molecules, we will examine solar radiation in a little more detail.

Electromagnetic Spectrum

Solar radiation can be described in terms of its energy content and its wavelength. The energy comes in discrete packets called **photons** [Gk. *phos*, light]. So, in other words, you can think of radiation as photons that travel in waves:

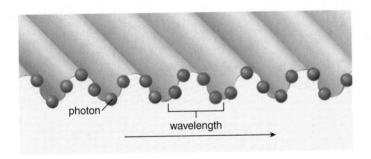

photon
wavelength

Figure 7.1*a* illustrates that solar radiation, or the **electromagnetic spectrum,** can be divided on the basis of wavelength—gamma rays have the shortest wavelength and radio waves have the longest wavelength. The energy content of photons is inversely proportional to the wavelength of the particular type of radiation; that is, short-wavelength radiation has photons of a higher energy content than long-wavelength radiation. High-energy photons, such as those of short-wavelength ultraviolet radiation, are dangerous to cells because they can break down organic molecules. Low-energy photons, such as those of infrared radiation, do not damage cells. They only increase the vibrational or rotational energy of molecules; and do not break bonds. Photosynthesis utilizes only the portion of the electromagnetic spectrum known as **visible light.** (It is called visible light because it is the part of the spectrum that the eye can see.) Photons of visible, or white light, have just the right amount of energy to promote electrons to a higher electron shell in atoms without harming cells. White light is

---

> ### Energy Balance Sheet
> Only 42% of solar energy directed toward earth actually reaches the earth's surface; the rest is absorbed by or reflected into the atmosphere and becomes heat.
> Of this usable portion, only about 2% is eventually utilized by plants; the rest becomes heat.
> Of this, only 0.1–1.6% is ever incorporated into plant material; the rest becomes heat.*
> Of this, only 20% is eaten by herbivores; a large proportion of the remainder becomes heat.*
> Of this, only 30% is ever eaten by carnivores; a large proportion becomes heat.*
> Conclusion: Most of the available energy is never utilized by living things.
>
> * *Plant and animal remains became the fossil fuels that we burn today to provide energy. So eventually this energy becomes heat.*

actually made up of a number of different wavelengths of radiation; when it is passed through a prism (or through raindrops), we see these wavelengths as different colors of light.

Energy Balance Sheet

Only about 42% of solar radiation passes through the earth's atmosphere and reaches its surface. Most of this radiation is within the visible-light range. Higher energy wavelengths are screened out by the ozone layer in the atmosphere, and lower energy wavelengths are screened out by water vapor and carbon dioxide before they reach the earth's surface. The conclusion is, then, that organic molecules and processes within organisms, like vision and photosynthesis, are chemically adapted to the radiation that is most prevalent in the environment—that is, visible light.

The energy balance sheet given on this page shows that most of the available energy reaching the earth is never utilized by living things. Photosynthetic pigments capture less than 2% of the solar energy that reaches the earth. Of this only a small percentage ever becomes a part of living things.

Photosynthesis utilizes the portion of the electromagnetic spectrum (solar radiation) known as visible light.

Photosynthetic Pigments

The pigments found in photosynthesizing cells are capable of absorbing various portions of visible light. This is called their absorption spectrum. Photosynthetic organisms differ by the type of chlorophyll they utilize. In plants, chlorophyll *a* and chlorophyll *b* play a prominent role in photosynthesis. The absorption spectra for chlorophylls *a* and *b* are shown in Figure 7.1*b*. Both chlorophylls *a* and *b* absorb violet, blue, and red light better than the light of other colors. Because green light is only minimally absorbed, plant leaves appear green to us. Other plant pigments such as the carotenoids

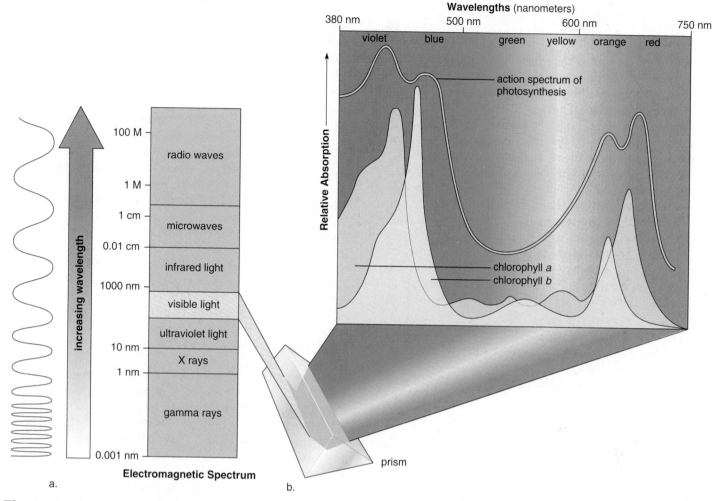

Figure 7.1 The electromagnetic spectrum and chlorophylls *a* and *b*.
a. The electromagnetic spectrum contains forms of energy that differ according to wavelength. Visible light is only a small portion of the electromagnetic spectrum. **b.** Chlorophylls *a* and *b*, significant pigments in plants, absorb certain wavelengths within visible light. This is their absorption spectrum. The action spectrum for photosynthesis in plants—the wavelengths that are used when photosynthesis is taking place—matches well the sum of the absorption spectrums for chlorophylls *a* and *b*.

are shades of yellow and orange and are able to absorb light in the violet-blue-green range. These pigments become noticeable in the fall when chlorophyll breaks down.

How do you determine the absorption spectrum of pigments? To identify the absorption spectrum of a particular pigment, a purified sample is exposed to different wavelengths of light inside an instrument called a spectrophotometer. A spectrophotometer measures the amount of light that passes through the sample, and from this it can be calculated how much was absorbed. The amount of light absorbed at each wavelength is plotted on a graph, and the result is a record of the pigment's absorption spectrum (Fig. 7.1*b*). How do we know that the peaks shown in the absorption spectrum for chlorophyll *a* and *b* indicate which wavelengths plants use for photosynthesis? Because photosynthesis gives off oxygen, we can use the production rate of

oxygen as a means to measure the rate of photosynthesis at each wavelength of light. When such data are plotted, the resulting graph is a record of the action spectrum for photosynthesis in plants. An action spectrum is those portions of the electromagnetic spectrum that are used to perform a function, in this case, photosynthesis. Because the sum of the absorption spectrum for chlorophylls *a* and *b* matches the action spectrum for plant photosynthesis, we are confident that the light absorbed by the chlorophylls does contribute extensively to photosynthesis in plants.

The sum of the absorption spectrums for chlorophylls *a* and *b* matches well the action spectrum for photosynthesis.

7.2 Structure and Function of Chloroplasts

It wasn't until the end of the nineteenth century that scientists understood the photosynthetic process and that, in eukaryotes, it occurs in **chloroplasts** [Gk. *chloros*, green, and *plastos*, formed, molded]. The overall equation for photosynthesis given on page 112 suggests that in the presence of sunlight, carbon dioxide, and water are combined to produce a high-energy food molecule such as carbohydrate.

In 1930, C. B. van Niel of Stanford University found that oxygen given off by photosynthesis comes from water and not from carbon dioxide as had been originally thought. This was proven by two separate experiments. When plants were exposed to carbon dioxide that contained an isotope of oxygen, called heavy oxygen (^{18}O), the O_2 given off by the plant did not contain heavy oxygen. Only when heavy oxygen was a part of water (indicated by the color red in this equation) did this isotope appear in O_2 given off by the plant:

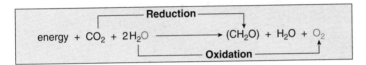

$$\text{energy} + CO_2 + 2H_2O \longrightarrow (CH_2O) + H_2O + O_2$$

Notice that carbon dioxide is reduced and water is oxidized during photosynthesis. This equation is preferred by some because it has the advantage of keeping the chemical arithmetic correct. In this equation CH_2O stands for carbohydrate.

Structure of Chloroplasts

In a chloroplast, a double membrane surrounds a fluid called the **stroma** [Gk. *stroma*, bed, mattress]. The stroma is an enzyme-rich solution where CO_2 is first attached to an organic compound and then is reduced. A membrane system within the stroma forms flattened sacs called **thylakoids** [Gk. *thylakos*, sack, and *eides*, like, resembling], which in some places are stacked to form grana (sing., **granum**), so called because they looked like piles of seeds to early microscopists. The space within each thylakoid is thought to be connected to the space within every other thylakoid, thereby forming an inner compartment within chloroplasts called the thylakoid space. **Chlorophyll** and other pigments are found within the membranes of the thylakoids. These pigments absorb the solar energy, which will energize electrons prior to reduction of CO_2 in the stroma (Fig. 7.2).

Because chlorophyll, within thylakoids, absorbs solar energy, electrons are available for reduction of CO_2 in the stroma.

Function of Chloroplasts

An overall equation tells us the beginning reactants and the end products of a metabolic pathway. What about what goes on in between the first reactants (carbon dioxide and water) and the final products (carbohydrate and water) during photosynthesis?

In 1905, F. F. Blackman suggested that there were probably two sets of reactions involved in photosynthesis because when light is being maximally absorbed, a rise in temperature still increases the rate of photosynthesis. (Enzymatic reactions speed up when temperature is increased.) The first set of photosynthetic reactions is called the **light-dependent reactions** because they cannot take place unless light is present. The second set of reactions is called the **light-independent reactions** because they can take place whether light is present or not.

The light-dependent reactions occur in the thylakoid membrane where the pigments chlorophyll *a* and *b*, plus the carotenoids, are located. Light can be absorbed by (taken up), reflected by (given off), or transmitted (passed through) a pigment. Chlorophyll *a* appears blue-green and chlorophyll *b* appears yellow-green to us because these are the very colors they do not absorb and are instead reflected to our eyes or transmitted through these pigments (see Fig. 7.1). For the same reason, the carotenoids appear as various shades of yellow and orange to our eyes.

The light-dependent reactions are the energy-capturing reactions—low-energy electrons removed from H_2O are energized when thylakoid membrane pigments absorb solar energy. These electrons move from chlorophyll *a* down an electron transport system, which produces ATP from ADP and Ⓟ. Energized electrons are also taken up by $NADP^+$. After $NADP^+$ accepts electrons, it becomes NADPH. This molecule temporarily holds energy, in the form of energized electrons, that will be used to reduce CO_2.

The light-dependent reactions capture solar energy.

The second set of reactions involved in photosynthesis occurs in the stroma of a chloroplast. They are called the light-independent reactions because they can take place in either the light or the dark. The light-independent reactions are the synthesis reactions, which use the ATP and NADPH formed in the thylakoids to reduce CO_2.

The light-independent reactions synthesize carbohydrate.

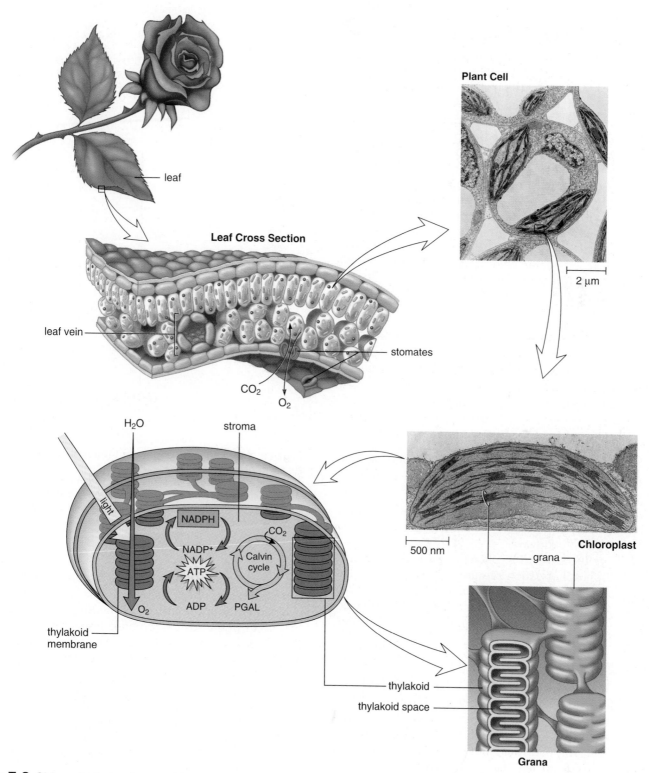

Leaf Cross Section

leaf

leaf vein

stomates

CO$_2$

O$_2$

Plant Cell

2 μm

Chloroplast

500 nm

grana

H$_2$O

stroma

light

NADPH

NADP+

ATP

Calvin cycle

CO$_2$

O$_2$

ADP

PGAL

thylakoid membrane

thylakoid

thylakoid space

Grana

Figure 7.2 Chloroplast structure and function.
The cells that form the bulk of a leaf contain many chloroplasts. Each chloroplast is bounded by a double membrane and contains a fluid called stroma. The membranous thylakoids stacked in grana are interconnected so that there is a single thylakoid space. The light-dependent reactions, which produce ATP and NADPH, occur in the thylakoid membrane. These molecules are used by the light-independent reactions to reduce carbon dioxide during a cyclical series of enzymatic reactions called the Calvin cycle. The Calvin cycle occurs in the stroma.

7.3 Solar Energy Capture

The light-dependent reactions that occur in the thylakoid membranes require the participation of two light-gathering units called photosystem I (PS I) and photosystem II (PS II). The photosystems are named for the order in which they were discovered and not for the order in which they occur in the thylakoid membrane or participate in the photosynthetic process. Each **photosystem** has closely packed molecules of chlorophyll *a* and chlorophyll *b* molecules and accessory pigments, such as carotenoid pigments. These pigment molecules are called an antenna complex because they serve as an "antenna" for gathering solar energy. Solar energy is passed from one pigment to the other until it is concentrated into one of two particular chlorophyll *a* molecules, the reaction-center chlorophylls. Electrons in the reaction-center chlorophyll *a* molecules become so excited that they escape and move to a nearby electron-acceptor molecule.

In a photosystem, the light-gathering antenna complex absorbs solar energy and funnels it to a reaction-center chlorophyll *a* molecule, which then sends energized electrons to an electron-acceptor molecule.

Electron Pathways

Electrons can follow a cyclic electron pathway or a noncyclic electron pathway during the first phase of photosynthesis. The cyclic electron pathway generates only ATP, while the noncyclic pathway results in both NADPH and ATP. The cell regulates the proportion of ATP to NADPH by the relative activity of the two pathways.

ATP production during photosynthesis is sometimes called photophosphorylation because light is involved. The production of ATP during the cyclic electron pathway is called cyclic photophosphorylation whereas ATP production during the noncyclic electron pathway is called noncyclic photophosphorylation.

Cyclic Electron Pathway

The **cyclic electron pathway** (Fig. 7.3) begins after the PS I antenna complex absorbs solar energy. In this pathway, high-energy electrons (e$^-$) leave the PS I reaction-center chlorophyll *a* molecule but eventually return to it. Before they return, however, the electrons enter an **electron transport system,** a series of carriers that pass electrons from one to the other. As the electrons pass from one carrier to the next, energy is released and stored in the form of a hydrogen (H$^+$) gradient. When these hydrogen ions flow down their electrochemical gradient through ATP synthase complexes, ATP production occurs (see page 118).

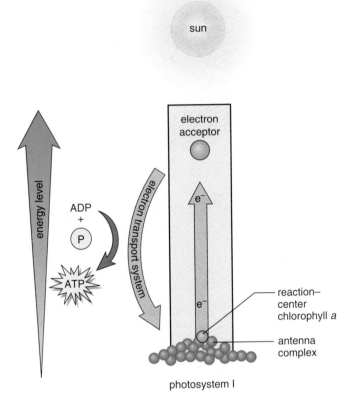

Figure 7.3 The light-dependent reactions: the cyclic electron pathway.
Energized electrons (e$^-$) leave the photosystem I (PS I) reaction-center chlorophyll *a* and are taken up by an electron acceptor, which passes them down an electron transport system before they return to PS I. Only ATP production results from this pathway.

Some photosynthetic bacteria utilize the cyclic electron pathway only; therefore, this pathway probably evolved early in the history of life. In plants the reactions that occur in the stroma can make use of this extra ATP for the Calvin cycle because this cycle requires a larger number of ATP than NADPH. Also, there are other enzymatic reactions aside from those involving photosynthesis occurring in the stroma that can make use of this ATP. It's possible that the cyclic flow of electrons is utilized alone when carbon dioxide is in such limited supply that carbohydrate is not being produced. At this time there would be no need for NADPH, which is produced only by the noncyclic electron pathway.

The cyclic electron pathway, from PS I back to PS I, has only one effect: production of ATP.

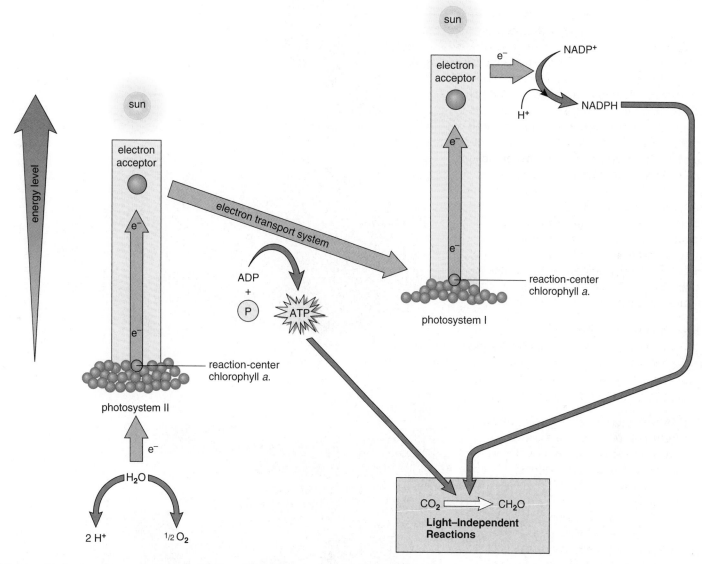

Figure 7.4 The light-dependent reactions: the noncyclic electron pathway.
Electrons, taken from water, move from photosystem II (PS II) to photosystem I (PS I) to NADP$^+$. The ATP and NADPH produced will be used by the light-independent reactions to reduce carbon dioxide (CO_2) to a carbohydrate (CH_2O).

Noncyclic Electron Pathway

During the **noncyclic electron pathway,** electrons move from water (H_2O) through PS II to PS I and then on to NADP$^+$ (Fig. 7.4). This pathway begins when the PS II antenna complex absorbs solar energy and high-energy electrons (e$^-$) leave the reaction-center chlorophyll *a* molecule. PS II takes replacement electrons from water, which splits, releasing oxygen. This oxygen is released from the chloroplast and the plant as oxygen gas. The hydrogen ions (H$^+$) stay in the thylakoid space and contribute to the formation of a hydrogen ion gradient.

The high-energy electrons that leave PS II are captured by an electron acceptor, which sends them to an electron transport system. As the electrons pass from one carrier to the next, energy is released and stored in the form of a hydrogen ion (H$^+$) gradient. When these hydrogen ions flow down their electrochemical gradient through ATP synthase complexes, ATP production occurs (see page 118).

Low-energy electrons leaving the electron transport system enter PS I. When the PS I antenna complex absorbs solar energy, high-energy electrons leave the reaction-center chlorophyll *a* and are captured by an electron acceptor. This time, the electron acceptor passes the electrons on to NADP$^+$. NADP$^+$ now takes on an H$^+$ and becomes NADPH. The NADPH and ATP produced by the noncyclic flow of electrons in the thylakoid membrane are used by enzymes in the stroma during the light-independent reactions.

Results of noncyclic electron flow: water is oxidized (split), yielding H$^+$, e$^-$, and O_2; ATP is produced; and NADP$^+$ becomes NADPH.

ATP Production

The thylakoid space acts as a reservoir for hydrogen ions (H$^+$). First, each time water is oxidized, two H$^+$ remain in the thylakoid space. Second, as the electrons move from carrier to carrier in the electron transport system, they give up energy, which is used to pump H$^+$ from the stroma into the thylakoid space. Therefore, there is a large number of H$^+$ in the thylakoid space compared to the number in the stroma. The flow of H$^+$ (often referred to as protons in this context) from high to low concentration across the thylakoid membrane provides the energy that allows an **ATP synthase** enzyme to enzymatically produce ATP from ADP + Ⓟ. This method of producing ATP is called **chemiosmosis** because ATP production is tied to an electrochemical gradient.

The Thylakoid Membrane

Both biochemical and structural techniques have been used to determine that there are intact complexes (particles) in the thylakoid membrane (Fig. 7.5):

PS II consists of a protein complex and a light-gathering antenna complex shown to one side. PS II oxidizes water and produces oxygen.

The cytochrome complex acts as the transporter of electrons between PS II and PS I. The pumping of H$^+$ occurs during electron transport.

PS I consists of a protein complex and a light-gathering antenna complex to one side. Notice that PS I is associated with the enzyme that reduces NADP$^+$ to NADPH.

ATP synthase complex has an H$^+$ channel and a protruding ATP synthase. As H$^+$ flows down its concentration gradient through this channel from the thylakoid space into the stroma, ATP is produced from ADP + Ⓟ.

The light-dependent reactions that occur in the thylakoid membrane produce ATP and NADPH and oxidize water, giving off oxygen.

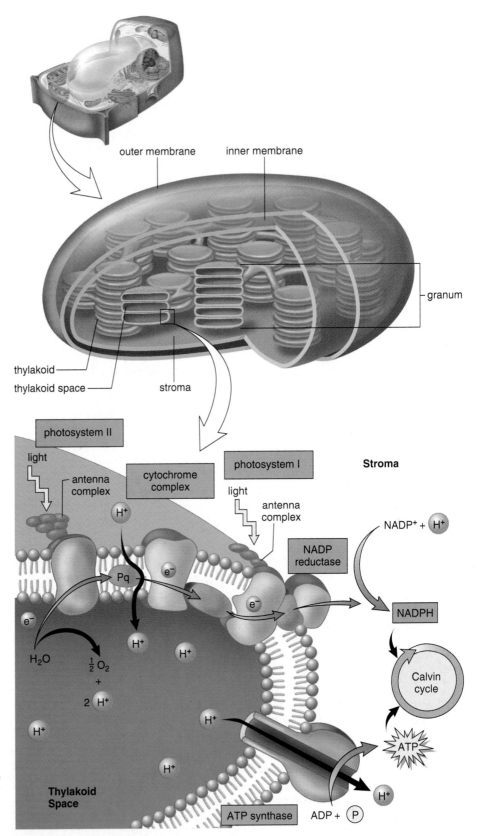

Figure 7.5 Organization of the thylakoid.
Protein complexes within the thylakoid membrane pump hydrogen ions from the stroma into the thylakoid space. *Pq* is a mobile carrier that also transfers hydrogen ions (H$^+$) from the stroma to the thylakoid space. When hydrogen ions flow back out of the space into the stroma through the ATP synthase complex, ATP is produced from ADP + Ⓟ.

7.4 Carbohydrate Synthesis

The light-independent reactions are the second stage of photosynthesis. They take their name from the fact that light is not directly required for these reactions to proceed. These reactions occur when CO_2 has entered the leaf and ATP and NADPH have been produced during the light-dependent reactions. PS I sets in motion a regulatory mechanism by which the enzymes of the light-independent reactions are turned on.

In this stage of photosynthesis, NADPH and ATP are used to reduce carbon dioxide: CO_2 becomes CH_2O within a carbohydrate molecule. Electrons and energy needed for this reduction synthesis are supplied by NADPH and ATP.

The reduction of carbon dioxide occurs in the stroma of a chloroplast by a series of reactions known as the **Calvin cycle.** In a cyclic series of reactions, the final product will also be the first reactant when the cycle of reactions begins again.

The Calvin cycle is named for Melvin Calvin, one of the individuals who was instrumental in identifying the reactions that make up the cycle (Fig. 7.6). Calvin received a Nobel Prize in 1961 for his part in determining these reactions.

The light-independent reactions use the ATP and NADPH from the light-dependent reactions to reduce carbon dioxide.

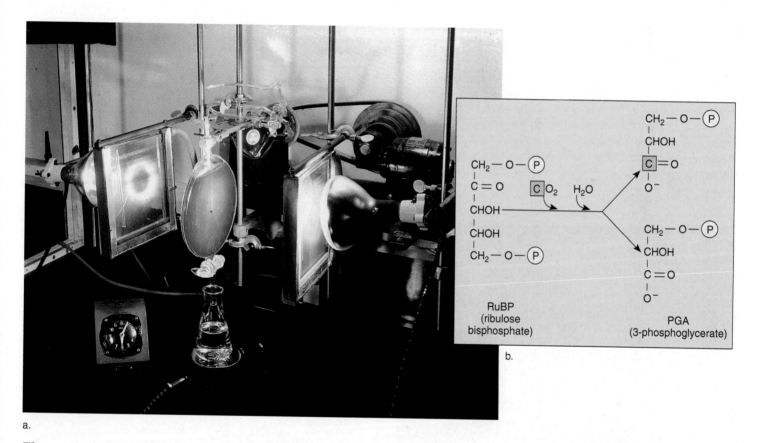

a.

Figure 7.6 Identifying the reactions of the Calvin cycle.

a. Calvin and his colleagues used the apparatus shown; algae (*Chlorella*) were placed in the flat flask, which was illuminated by two lamps. Radioactive carbon dioxide ($^{14}CO_2$) was added, and the algae were killed a short time later by transferring them into boiling alcohol (in the beaker below the flask). This treatment instantly stopped all chemical reactions in the cells. Carbon-based compounds were then extracted from the cells and analyzed. b. By tracing the radioactive carbon, Calvin and his colleagues were able to trace the pathway by which CO_2 was metabolized. They found that the radioactive carbon (gray box) is first added to RuBP and that the resulting molecule splits to form two molecules of PGA. By gradually increasing the time (2 seconds, 5 seconds, and so on) after initial exposure of the algae to $^{14}CO_2$ before killing, they were able to identify the rest of the molecules in the cycle that is now called the Calvin cycle (see Fig. 7.8).

The Importance of PGAL

PGAL (glyceraldehyde-3-phosphate) is the product of the Calvin cycle that can be converted to all sorts of organic molecules. Compared to animal cells, algae and plants have enormous biochemical capabilities. They use PGAL for the purposes described in Figure 7.7.

Notice that glucose phosphate is among the organic molecules that result from PGAL metabolism. This is of interest to us because glucose is the molecule that plants and animals most often metabolize to produce the ATP molecules they require for their energy needs. Glucose is blood sugar in human beings.

Glucose phosphate can be combined with fructose (and the phosphate removed) to form sucrose, the molecule that plants use to transport carbohydrates from one part of the body to the other. Glucose phosphate is also the starting point for the synthesis of starch and cellulose. Starch is the storage form of glucose. Some starch is stored in chloroplasts, but most starch is stored in amyloplasts in roots. Cellulose is a structural component of plant cell walls and becomes fiber in our diet because we are unable to digest it. A plant can utilize the hydrocarbon skeleton of PGAL to form fatty acids and glycerol, which are combined in plant oils. We are all familiar with corn oil, sunflower oil, or olive oil, which we use in cooking. Also, when nitrogen is added to the hydrocarbon skeleton derived from PGAL, amino acids are formed.

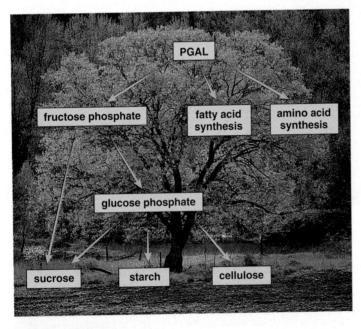

Figure 7.7 Fate of PGAL.
PGAL is the first reactant in a number of plant cell metabolic pathways. Two PGALs are needed to form glucose phosphate: glucose is often considered the end product of photosynthesis. Sucrose is the transport sugar in plants; starch is the storage form of glucose, and cellulose is a major constituent of plant cell walls.

The Calvin Cycle

The reactions of the Calvin cycle are the light-independent reactions that synthesize carbohydrate. The Calvin cycle includes (1) carbon dioxide fixation, (2) carbon dioxide reduction, and (3) regeneration of RuBP (ribulose bisphosphate).

Fixation of Carbon Dioxide

Carbon dioxide (CO_2) fixation, the attachment of carbon dioxide to an organic compound, is the first event in the Calvin cycle. **RuBP (ribulose bisphosphate),** a five-carbon molecule, combines with carbon dioxide (Fig. 7.8). The enzyme that speeds up this reaction, called RuBP carboxylase, is a protein that makes up about 20–50% of the protein content in chloroplasts. The reason for its abundance may be that it is unusually slow (it processes only a few molecules of substrate per second compared to thousands per second for a typical enzyme), and so there has to be a lot of it to keep the Calvin cycle going.

Carbon dioxide fixation occurs when carbon dioxide combines with RuBP.

Reduction of Carbon Dioxide

The six-carbon molecule resulting from carbon dioxide fixation immediately breaks down to form two PGA (3-phosphoglycerate) three-carbon molecules. Each of the two PGA molecules undergoes reduction to PGAL in two steps:

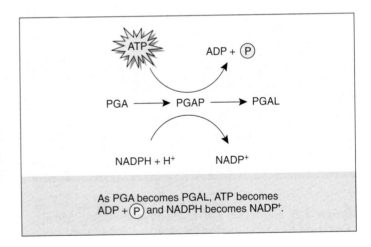

As PGA becomes PGAL, ATP becomes ADP + Ⓟ and NADPH becomes $NADP^+$.

This is the sequence of reactions that uses NADPH from the light-dependent reactions and one of the two sequences that uses ATP from the same source. This sequence signifies the reduction of carbon dioxide (CO_2) to a carbohydrate (CH_2O). Electrons and energy are needed for this reduction reaction, and these are supplied by NADPH and ATP, respectively.

Figure 7.8 Light-independent reactions.

The Calvin cycle is divided into three portions: CO_2 fixation, CO_2 reduction, which requires NADPH and ATP, and regeneration of RuBP. Because five PGAL are needed to re-form three RuBP, it takes three turns of the cycle to have a net gain of one PGAL. Two PGAL molecules are needed to form one glucose ($C_6H_{12}O_6$) molecule.

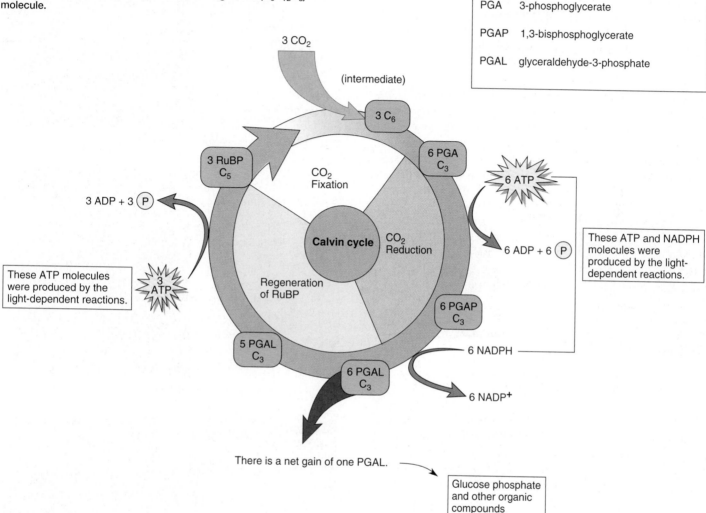

Metabolites of the Calvin Cycle	
RuBP	ribulose bisphosphate
PGA	3-phosphoglycerate
PGAP	1,3-bisphosphoglycerate
PGAL	glyceraldehyde-3-phosphate

Regeneration of RuBP

For every three turns of the Calvin cycle, five molecules of PGAL are used to re-form three molecules of RuBP so that the cycle can continue. Notice that 5×3 (carbons in PGAL) = 3×5 (carbons in RuBP):

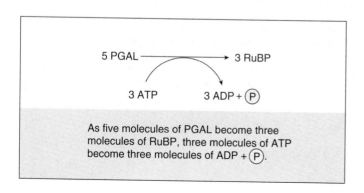

As five molecules of PGAL become three molecules of RuBP, three molecules of ATP become three molecules of ADP + Ⓟ.

The net gain of three turns of the Calvin cycle is one PGAL molecule. This sequence of reactions also utilizes some of the ATP produced by the light-dependent reactions.

Five out of every six PGAL molecules of the Calvin cycle are used to regenerate three RuBP molecules, so the cycle can continue.

The first detectable molecule identified by Melvin Calvin—namely PGA—has three carbons (Fig. 7.8). Therefore the Calvin cycle is also known as the C_3 cycle. Since Melvin Calvin did his research work, it's been discovered that plant species differ in the way they fix carbon dioxide and the first detectable molecule following carbon dioxide fixation is not always a C_3 molecule.

Modes of Photosynthesis

Three modes of photosynthesis are known (Fig. 7.9). In **C_3 plants,** the Calvin cycle fixes carbon dioxide (CO_2) directly, and the first detectable molecule following fixation is PGA, a C_3 molecule. **C_4 plants** fix CO_2 by forming a C_4 molecule prior to the involvement of the Calvin cycle. **CAM plants** fix CO_2 by forming a C_4 molecule at night when stomates can open without much loss of water.

C_4 Photosynthesis

The structure of a leaf from a C_3 plant is different from that of a C_4 plant. In a C_3 plant, the mesophyll cells contain well-formed chloroplasts and are arranged in parallel layers. In a C_4 leaf, the bundle sheath cells, as well as the mesophyll cells, contain chloroplasts. Further, the mesophyll cells are arranged concentrically around the bundle sheath cells:

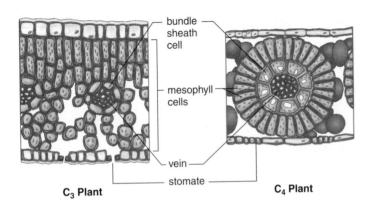

C_3 plants use the enzyme RuBP carboxylase to fix CO_2 to RuBP in mesophyll cells. The first detected molecule following fixation is PGA. C_4 plants use the enzyme PEP carboxylase (PEPCase) to fix CO_2 to PEP (phosphoenolpyruvate, a C_3 molecule). The result is oxaloacetate, a C_4 molecule.

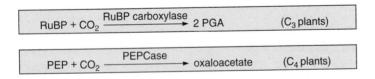

In a C_4 plant, CO_2 is taken up in mesophyll cells and then malate, a reduced form of oxaloacetate, is pumped into the bundle sheath cells (Fig. 7.9). Here, and only here, CO_2 enters the Calvin cycle. It takes energy to pump molecules, and you would think that the C_4 pathway would be disadvantageous. Yet in hot, dry climates, the net photosynthetic rate of C_4 plants such as sugarcane, corn, and Bermuda grass is about two to three times that of C_3 plants such as wheat, rice, and oats. Why do C_4 plants enjoy such an advantage? The answer is they can avoid photorespiration, discussed next.

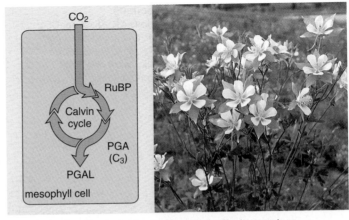

CO_2 fixation in a C_3 plant, blue columbine, *Aquilegia caerulea*

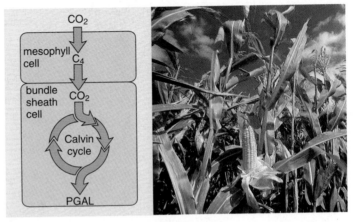

CO_2 fixation in a C_4 plant, corn, *Zea mays*

CO_2 fixation in a CAM plant, pineapple, *Ananas comosus*

Figure 7.9 Carbon dioxide fixation.
Plants can be categorized according to the way carbon dioxide (CO_2) is fixed. **a.** In C_3 plants, CO_2 is taken up by the Calvin cycle directly. **b.** C_4 plants utilize a C_4 molecule prior to releasing CO_2 to the Calvin cycle. **c.** CAM plants use this same C_4 molecule only at night to take up CO_2.

Photorespiration

Notice in the diagrams of leaves on the previous page, there are little openings called stomates (sing., stomate) in the surfaces of leaves through which water can leave and carbon dioxide (CO_2) can enter. If the weather is hot and dry, the stomates close, conserving water. (Water loss might cause the plant to wilt and die.) Now the concentration of CO_2 decreases in leaves, while oxygen, a by-product of photosynthesis, increases. When oxygen rises in C_3 plants, it combines with RuBP carboxylase instead of CO_2. The result is one molecule of PGA and eventually the release of CO_2. This is called **photorespiration** because in the presence of light (*photo*), oxygen is taken up and CO_2 is released (*respiration*).

Photorespiration does not occur in C_4 leaves because PEPCase does not combine with O_2. Even when stomates are closed CO_2 is delivered to the Calvin cycle in the bundle sheath cells. When the weather is moderate, C_3 plants have the advantage, but when the weather becomes hot and dry, C_4 plants have the advantage, and we can expect them to predominate. In the early summer, C_3 plants such as Kentucky bluegrass and creeping bent grass predominate in lawns in the cooler parts of the United States, but by midsummer, crabgrass, a C_4 plant, begins to take over.

> When the weather is hot and dry, photorespiration occurs in C_3 plants but not C_4 plants. This gives C_4 plants an advantage under these conditions.

CAM Photosynthesis

CAM stands for crassulacean-acid metabolism; the Crassulaceae is a family of flowering succulent (water-containing) plants that live in warm, arid regions of the world. CAM was first discovered in these plants, but now it is known to be prevalent among most succulent plants that grow in desert environments, including the cacti.

Whereas a C_4 plant represents partitioning in space—carbon dioxide fixation occurs in mesophyll cells and the Calvin cycle occurs in bundle sheath cells—CAM is partitioning by the use of time. During the night, CAM plants use PEPCase to fix some CO_2 forming C_4 molecules, which are stored in large vacuoles in mesophyll cells. During the day, C_4 molecules (malate) release CO_2 to the Calvin cycle when NADPH and ATP are available from the light-dependent reactions. The primary reason for this partitioning again has to do with the conservation of water. CAM plants open their stomates only at night, and therefore only at that time is atmospheric CO_2 available. During the day, the stomates close to conserve water and CO_2 cannot enter the plant.

Photosynthesis in a CAM plant is minimal because of the limited amount of CO_2 fixed at night, but it does allow CAM plants to live under stressful conditions.

> CAM plants use PEPCase to fix carbon dioxide at night when the stomates are open. During the day, the stored carbon dioxide can enter the Calvin cycle.

Connecting Concepts

"Have You Thanked a Green Plant Today?" is a bumper sticker that you may have puzzled over until now. Plants, you now know, capture solar energy and store it in carbon-based organic nutrients that are passed to other organisms when they feed on plants and/or on other organisms. In this context, plants are called autotrophs because they make their own organic food. Heterotrophs are organisms that take in preformed organic food.

Both autotrophs and heterotrophs contribute to the global carbon cycle. In the carbon cycle, organisms in both terrestrial and aquatic ecosystems exchange carbon dioxide with the atmosphere. Autotrophs, like plants, take in carbon dioxide when they photosynthesize. Carbon dioxide is returned to the atmosphere when autotrophs and heterotrophs carry on cellular respiration. In this way, the very same carbon atoms cycle from the atmosphere to autotrophs, then to heterotrophs, and then back to autotrophs again.

Living and dead organisms contain organic carbon and serve as a reservoir of carbon in the carbon cycle. Some 300 million years ago, a host of plants died and did not decompose. These plants were compressed to form the coal that we mine and burn today. (Oil has a similar origin, but most likely formed in marine sedimentary rocks that included animal remains.)

The amount of carbon dioxide in the atmosphere is increasing steadily because we humans burn fossil fuels to run our modern industrial society. Many fear that this buildup of carbon dioxide will contribute to global warming, because carbon dioxide is a greenhouse gas. Like the glass of a greenhouse, it allows sunlight to pass through, but then traps the resulting heat. Yet while we are pumping carbon dioxide into the atmosphere due to fossil fuel burning, we are destroying vast tracts of tropical rain forests, which soak up carbon dioxide like a sponge. Clearly, these actions are not in our self-interest and it would behoove us to reduce the burning of fossil fuels and preserve tropical rain forests.

Summary

7.1 Solar Energy

Photosynthesis produces carbohydrates and releases oxygen, both of which are utilized by the majority of living things. Photosynthesis uses solar energy in the visible-light range; the photons of this range contain the right amount of energy to energize the electrons of chlorophyll molecules. Specifically, chlorophylls *a* and *b* absorb violet, blue, and red wavelengths best. This causes chlorophyll to appear green to us.

7.2 Structure and Function of Chloroplasts

A chloroplast is bounded by a double membrane and contains two main components: the liquid stroma and the membranous grana made up of membranous thylakoids. The light-dependent reactions take place in the thylakoids, and the light-independent reactions take place in the stroma.

7.3 Solar Energy Capture

In the cyclic electron pathway, electrons energized by the sun leave PS I. They pass down an electron transport system and back to PS I again. Chemiosmosis follows and ATP is generated. In keeping with its name, PS I probably evolved first and is the only photosynthetic pathway present in certain bacteria today. Most photosynthetic cells regulate the activity of the cyclic and noncyclic pathways to suit the needs of the cell.

The noncyclic electron pathway of the light-dependent reactions begins when solar energy enters PS II. PS II energized electrons are picked up by an electron acceptor. The oxidation (splitting) of water replaces these electrons in the reaction-center chlorophyll *a* molecule. Oxygen is released to the atmosphere and hydrogen ions (H^+) remain in the thylakoid space. The acceptor molecule passes electrons to PS I by way of an electron transport (cytochrome) system. When solar energy is absorbed by PS I, energized electrons leave and are ultimately received by $NADP^+$, which also combines with H^+ from the stroma to become NADPH.

The energy made available by the passage of electrons down the electron transport system allows carriers to pump H^+ into the thylakoid space. The buildup of H^+ establishes an electrochemical gradient. When H^+ flows down this gradient through the channel present in ATP synthase complexes, ATP is synthesized from ADP and ⓟ by ATP synthase. This method of producing ATP is called chemiosmosis.

Chemiosmosis requires an organized membrane. The thylakoid membrane is highly organized: PS II functions to oxidize (split) water, the cytochrome complex transports electrons and pumps H^+, PS I is associated with an enzyme that reduces $NADP^+$, and ATP synthase produces ATP.

7.4 Carbohydrate Synthesis

The energy yield of the light-dependent reactions is stored in ATP and NADPH. These molecules are used by the light-independent reactions to reduce carbon dioxide (CO_2) to carbohydrate, namely PGAL, which is then converted to all the organic molecules a plant needs.

During the first stage of the Calvin cycle, the enzyme RuBP carboxylase fixes CO_2 to RuBP, producing a six-carbon molecule that immediately breaks down to two C_3 molecules. During the second stage, CO_2 is incorporated into an organic molecule and is reduced to carbohydrate (CH_2O). This step requires the NADPH and some of the ATP from the light-dependent reactions. For every three turns of the Calvin cycle, the net gain is one PGAL molecule; the other five PGAL molecules are used to re-form three molecules of RuBP. This step also requires ATP for energy. It required two PGAL molecules to make one glucose molecule.

In C_4 plants, as opposed to the C_3 plants just described, the enzyme PEPCase fixes carbon dioxide to PEP to form a four-carbon molecule, oxaloacetate, within mesophyll cells. A reduced form of this molecule is pumped into bundle sheath cells where CO_2 is released to the Calvin cycle. C_4 plants avoid photorespiration by a partitioning of pathways in space: carbon dioxide fixation occurs in mesophyll cells and the Calvin cycle occurs in bundle sheath cells.

During CAM photosynthesis, PEPCase fixes CO_2 to PEP at night. The next day, CO_2 is released and enters the Calvin cycle within the same cells. This represents a partitioning of pathways in time: carbon dioxide fixation occurs at night and the Calvin cycle occurs during the day. The plants that carry on CAM are desert plants, in which the stomates only open at night in order to conserve water.

Reviewing the Chapter

1. Why is it proper to say that almost all living things are dependent on solar energy?   112
2. Discuss the electromagnetic spectrum and the absorption spectrum of chlorophyll. Why is chlorophyll a green pigment?   112–13
3. Name the two major components of chloroplasts and associate each portion with the two sets of reactions that occur during photosynthesis. How are the two pathways related?   114
4. What roles do PS I and PS II play during the light-dependent reactions?   116
5. Trace the cyclic electron pathway, naming and explaining the main events that occur as electrons cycle.   116
6. Trace the noncyclic electron pathway, naming and explaining all the events that occur as the electrons move from water to $NADP^+$.   117
7. Explain what is meant by chemiosmosis, and relate this process to the electron transport system present in the thylakoid membrane.   118
8. How is the thylakoid membrane organized? Name the main complexes in the membrane and give a function for each.   118
9. Describe the three stages of the Calvin cycle. Which stage utilizes the ATP and NADPH from the light-dependent reactions?   120–21
10. Explain C_4 photosynthesis, contrasting the actions of RuBP carboxylase and PEPCase.   122–23
11. Explain CAM photosynthesis, contrasting it to C_4 photosynthesis in terms of partitioning a pathway.   123

Testing Yourself

Choose the best answer for each question.

1. The absorption spectrum of chlorophyll
   a. is not the same as that of carotenoids.
   b. approximates the action spectrum of photosynthesis.
   c. explains why chlorophyll is a green pigment.
   d. shows that some colors of light are absorbed more than others.
   e. All of these are correct.
2. The final acceptor of electrons during the noncyclic electron pathway is
   a. PS I.
   b. PS II.
   c. ATP.
   d. $NADP^+$.
   e. water.
3. A photosystem contains
   a. pigments, a reaction center, and an electron acceptor.
   b. ADP, Ⓟ, and hydrogen ions (H^+).
   c. protons, photons, and pigments.
   d. cytochromes only.
   e. Both b and c are correct.
4. Which of these should not be associated with the electron transport system?
   a. chloroplasts
   b. cytochromes
   c. movement of H^+ into the thylakoid space
   d. formation of ATP
   e. absorption of solar energy
5. PEPCase has an advantage compared to RuBP carboxylase. The advantage is that
   a. PEPCase is present in both mesophyll and bundle sheath cells, but RuBP carboxylase is not.
   b. RuBP carboxylase fixes carbon dioxide (CO_2) only in C_4 plants, but PEPCase does it in both C_3 and C_4 plants.
   c. RuBP carboxylase combines with O_2, but PEPCase does not.
   d. PEPCase conserves energy but RuBP carboxylase does not.
   e. Both b and c are correct.
6. The NADPH and ATP from the light-dependent reactions are used to
   a. split water.
   b. cause RuBP carboxylase to fix CO_2.
   c. re-form the photosystems.
   d. cause electrons to move along their pathways.
   e. convert PGA to PGAL.
7. CAM photosynthesis
   a. is the same as C_4 photosynthesis.
   b. is an adaptation to cold environments in the southern hemisphere.
   c. is prevalent in desert plants that close their stomates during the day.
   d. occurs in plants that live in marshy areas.
   e. stands for chloroplasts and mitochondria.
8. Chemiosmosis
   a. depends on protein complexes in the thylakoid membrane.
   b. depends on an electrochemical gradient.
   c. depends on a difference in H^+ concentration between the thylakoid space and the stroma.
   d. results in ATP formation.
   e. All of these are correct.
9. Label this diagram of a chloroplast.

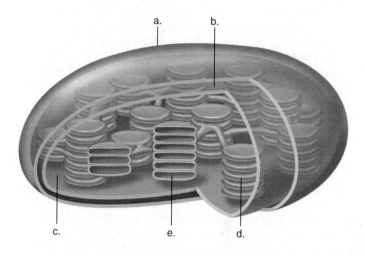

   f. The light-dependent reactions occur in which part of a chloroplast?
   g. The light-independent reactions occur in which part of a chloroplast?
10. Label this diagram using these labels: water, carbohydrate, carbon dioxide, oxygen, ATP, ADP + Ⓟ, NADPH, and $NADP^+$.

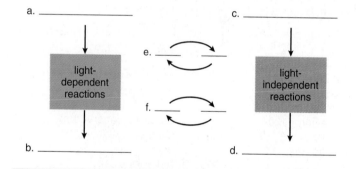

Thinking Scientifically

1. In the fall of the year the leaves of many trees change from green to red or yellow. Two hypotheses can explain this color change: (1) In the fall, chlorophyll degenerates and red or yellow pigments that were earlier masked by chlorophyll become apparent. (2) In the fall, red or yellow pigments are synthesized and they mask the color of chlorophyll. How could you test these two hypotheses?
2. You have discovered a type of bacteria that seems to be capable of photosynthesis but has no chloroplasts. However, there are invaginations of the plasma membrane inside the bacteria. Would photosynthesis be possible with such an arrangement? What would you expect to find in the invaginated membrane if these bacteria were photosynthetic?

Bioethical Issue

Whether there will be enough food to feed the increase in population expected by the middle of the twenty-first century is unknown. Over the past 40 years, the world's food supply has expanded faster than the population, due to the development of high-yielding plants, and the increased use of irrigation, pesticides, and fertilizers. Unfortunately, modern farming techniques result in pollution of the air, water, and land. One of the most worrisome threats to food security is an increasing degradation of agricultural land. Soil erosion in particular is robbing the land of its topsoil and reducing its productivity.

In 1986, it was estimated that humans already use nearly 40% of the Earth's terrestrial photosynthetic production and therefore we should reach maximum capacity in the middle of the twenty-first century when the population is projected to double its 1986 size. Most population growth will occur in the less developed countries in Africa, Asia, and Latin America that are only now becoming industrialized. Even the United States will face an increased drain on its economic resources and increased pollution problems due to population growth. In the developing countries the technical gains needed to prevent a disaster will be enormous.

Some people feel that technology will continue to make great strides for many years to come. They maintain technology hasn't begun to reach the limits of performance and therefore, will be able to solve the problems of increased population growth. Others feel that technology's successes are self-defeating. The newly developed hybrid crops that led to enormous increases in yield per acre also cause pollution problems that degrade the environment. These scientists are in favor of calling a halt to an increasing human population by all possible measures and as quickly as possible. Which of these approaches do you favor?

Understanding the Terms

ATP synthase 118	light-dependent reactions 114
C_3 plant 122	light-independent
C_4 plant 122	reactions 114
Calvin cycle 119	noncyclic electron
CAM plant 122	pathway 117
carbon dioxide (CO_2)	photon 112
fixation 120	photorespiration 123
chemiosmosis 118	photosynthesis 112
chlorophyll 114	photosystem 116
chloroplast 114	RuBP (ribulose
cyclic electron pathway 116	bisphosphate) 120
electromagnetic spectrum 112	stroma 114
electron transport system 116	thylakoid 114
granum 114	visible light 112

Match the terms to these definitions:

a. _____ Energy-capturing portion of photosynthesis that takes place in thylakoid membranes of chloroplasts and cannot proceed without solar energy; it produces ATP and NADPH.

b. _____ Photosynthetic unit where solar energy is absorbed and high-energy electrons are generated; contains an antenna complex and an electron acceptor.

c. _____ Passage of electrons along a series of carrier molecules from a higher to a lower energy level; the energy released is used for the synthesis of ATP.

d. _____ Process usually occurring within chloroplasts whereby chlorophyll traps solar energy and carbon dioxide is reduced to a carbohydrate.

e. _____ Series of photosynthetic reactions in which carbon dioxide is fixed and reduced to PGAL.

Web Connections

Exploring the Internet

http://www.mhhe.com/biosci/genbio/mader
(click on *Biology 7/e*)

The *Biology 7/e* Online Learning Center provides many resources for studying the material in this chapter including links to the following sites:

Introduction to Photosynthesis contains a thorough treatment of the topic and includes the evolution and discovery of photosynthesis, the light and dark reactions, and chloroplast structure, illustrated with diagrams and formulas.

http://esg-www.mit.edu:8001/esgbio/ps/intro.html

For a more detailed account of photosynthesis, choose Photosynthesis—the Light Reactions, which includes sections on the physics of light and the photosystem, the light and dark reactions, and alternate pathways for photosynthesis.

http://esg-www.mit.edu:8001/esgbio/ps/light.html

Photosynthetic Molecules Page. Three-dimensional representations of chlorophyll and other molecules involved in photosynthesis.

http://www.nyu.edu:80/pages/mathmol/library/photo/index.html

Photosynthesis—Other Approaches. This MIT hypertextbook chapter covers C_4 mechanisms as well as chemosynthesis, with both text and diagrams.

http://esg-www.mit.edu:8001/esgbio/ps/other.html

Photosynthesis. This page has links to lectures on photosynthesis and problem sets.

http://mss.scbe.on.ca/DSPHOTOS.HTM

Cellular Respiration

Effort requires energy.

When you go snow boarding, take an aerobics class, or just sit around, ATP molecules allow your muscles to contract. ATP molecules are produced during cellular respiration, a process that requires the participation of mitochondria. There are numerous mitochondria in muscle cells.

The glucose and oxygen for cellular respiration are delivered to cells by the circulatory system, and the end products—water and carbon dioxide—are removed by the circulatory system. Cellular respiration consists of many small steps mediated by specific enzymes. High-energy electrons are removed from glucose breakdown products and are passed down an electron transport system located on the cristae of mitochondria. As the electrons move from one carrier to the next, energy is released and captured for the production of ATP molecules.

One form of chemical energy (glucose) cannot be transformed completely into another (ATP molecules) without the loss of usable energy in the form of heat. When ATP is produced, heat is given off. Since exercise requires plentiful ATP, your body's internal temperature rises and you begin sweating.

8.1 Cellular Respiration

Cellular respiration includes all the various metabolic pathways which break down carbohydrates and other metabolites with the concomitant buildup of ATP. **Cellular respiration,** as implied by its name, is a cellular process that requires oxygen and gives off carbon dioxide (CO_2). Most often it involves the complete breakdown of glucose to carbon dioxide and water (H_2O):

$$C_6H_{12}O_6 + 6O_2 \longrightarrow 6CO_2 + 6H_2O + energy$$

Oxidation (above), Reduction (below); glucose.

Glucose is a high-energy molecule, and its breakdown products, CO_2 and H_2O, are low-energy molecules. Therefore, we expect the process to be exergonic and release energy. As breakdown occurs, electrons are removed from substrates and eventually are received by oxygen atoms, which then combine with H^+ to become H_2O.

The equation shows changes in regard to hydrogen atom (H) distribution. But remember that a hydrogen atom consists of a hydrogen ion plus an electron ($H^+ + e^-$). Therefore when hydrogen atoms are removed from glucose so are electrons. Since oxidation is the loss of electrons, and reduction is the gain of electrons, glucose breakdown is an oxidation-reduction reaction. Glucose is oxidized and O_2 is reduced.

On the other hand, the buildup of ATP is an endergonic reaction that requires energy. The pathways of cellular respiration allow the energy within a glucose molecule to be released slowly so that ATP can be produced gradually. Cells would lose a tremendous amount of energy if glucose breakdown occurred all at once—much energy would become nonusable heat. The step-by-step breakdown of glucose to carbon dioxide and water usually realizes a maximum yield of 36 or 38 ATP molecules dependent on conditions to be discussed later. The energy in these ATP molecules is equivalent to about 39% of the energy that was available in glucose. This conversion is more efficient than many others; for example, only about 25% of the energy within gasoline is converted to the motion of a car.

NAD^+ and FAD

Cellular respiration involves many individual metabolic reactions, each one catalyzed by its own enzyme. Enzymes of particular significance are the redox enzymes that utilize the coenzyme **NAD^+**. When a metabolite is oxidized, NAD^+ accepts two electrons plus a hydrogen ion (H^+) and NADH results. The electrons received by NAD^+ are high-energy electrons that are usually carried to the electron transport system. Figure 8.1 illustrates how NAD^+ carries electrons.

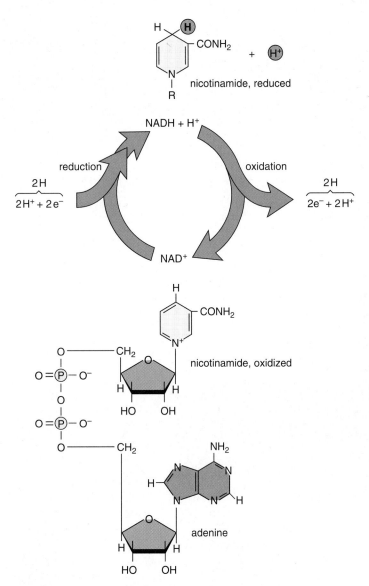

Figure 8.1 The NAD^+ cycle.
The coenzyme NAD^+ is a dinucleotide (two nucleotides joined by bonding between their phosphates). NAD^+ accepts two electrons (e^-) plus a hydrogen ion (H^+) and NADH + H^+ result. When NADH passes the electrons to another substrate or carrier, NAD^+ is formed.

NAD^+ is called a coenzyme of oxidation-reduction because it can oxidize a metabolite by accepting electrons and can reduce a metabolite by giving up electrons. Only a small amount of NAD^+ need be present in a cell, because each NAD^+ molecule is used over and over again. **FAD** is another coenzyme of oxidation-reduction which is sometimes used instead of NAD^+. FAD accepts two electrons and two hydrogen ions (H^+) to become $FADH_2$.

NAD^+ and FAD are two coenzymes of oxidation-reduction that are active during cellular respiration.

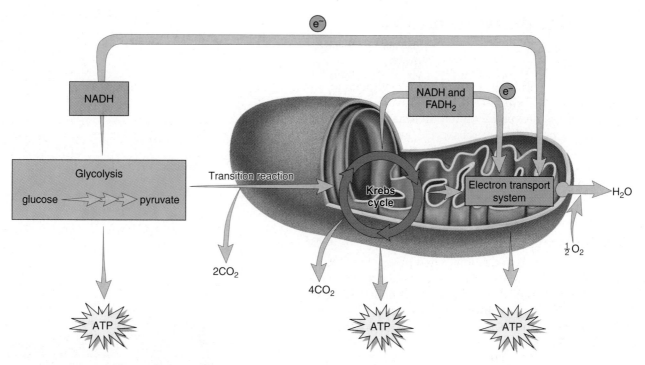

Figure 8.2 **The four phases of complete glucose breakdown.**
The complete breakdown of glucose consists of four phases. Glycolysis in the cytosol produces pyruvate which enters mitochondria if oxygen is available. The transition reaction and the Krebs cycle which follow occur inside the mitochondria. Also, inside mitochondria, the electron transport system receives the electrons that were removed from glucose breakdown products. The end result of glucose breakdown is 36 to 38 ATP depending on the particular cell.

Phases of Complete Glucose Breakdown

Glucose breakdown involves four phases: three metabolic pathways plus one individual reaction. These phases will be color coded throughout this chapter in the same manner as shown in Figure 8.2. Glycolysis takes place outside the mitochondria and does not utilize oxygen. The other phases of cellular respiration take place inside the mitochondria where oxygen is utilized.

- **Glycolysis** is the breakdown of glucose to two molecules of pyruvate. Enough energy is released for the immediate buildup of two ATP.
- During the **transition reaction,** pyruvate is oxidized to an acetyl group, and CO_2 is removed. Since glycolysis ends with two molecules of pyruvate, the transition reaction occurs twice per glucose molecule.
- The **Krebs cycle** is a cyclical series of reactions that release CO_2 and produce ATP. The Krebs cycle turns twice because two acetyl-CoA molecules enter the cycle per glucose molecule. Altogether, the Krebs cycle accounts for two immediate ATP molecules per glucose molecule.
- The **electron transport system** is a series of carriers that accept the electrons removed from glucose during

glycolysis, the transition reaction, and the Krebs cycle. Usually the coenzyme NAD^+ carries these electrons from these phases to the electron transport system. The system passes the electrons along from one carrier to the next until they are finally received by oxygen. As the electrons pass from a higher energy to a lower energy state, energy is released and stored for ATP buildup. The electron transport system accounts for 32 or 34 ATP, depending on the particular cell.

Pyruvate is a pivotal metabolite in cellular respiration. If oxygen is not available to the cell, **fermentation,** an anaerobic process, occurs in the cytosol. During fermentation, glucose is incompletely metabolized to lactate or to carbon dioxide and alcohol, depending on the organism. As we shall see on page 137, fermentation results in a net gain of only two ATP per glucose molecule.

The complete breakdown of glucose to carbon dioxide and water is aerobic and requires oxygen, which is utilized in mitochondria.

8.2 Outside the Mitochondria: Glycolysis

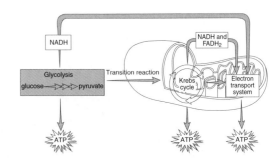

Glycolysis [Gk. *glykeros*, sweet, and *lyo*, loose, dissolve], which takes place within the cytosol outside mitochondria, is the breakdown of glucose to two pyruvate molecules. Since glycolysis is universally found in organisms, it most likely evolved before the Krebs cycle and the electron transport system. This may be why glycolysis occurs in the cytosol and does not require oxygen. Bacteria evolved before other organisms, and there are some bacteria today that are anaerobic; and indeed they die in the presence of oxygen.

Energy Investment Steps

As glycolysis begins, the addition of two phosphate groups activates glucose (C_6) to react. This requires two separate reactions and uses two ATP. The resulting C_6 molecule splits into two C_3 molecules, each of which carries a phosphate group. From this point on, each C_3 molecule undergoes the same series of reactions.

Energy Harvesting Steps

During glycolysis, oxidation occurs by the removal of electrons which are accepted by NAD^+. Each NAD^+ accepts two electrons and one hydrogen ion (H^+); altogether two NADH molecules result. Enough energy is released to generate four ATP molecules by **substrate-level phosphorylation** [Gk. *phos*, light, and *phoreus*, carrier]. During substrate-level phosphorylation, a phosphate is enzymatically transferred from a high-energy metabolite to ADP. For example, in Figure 8.3, the molecule designated as PGAP gives up a phosphate to ADP, and ATP results.

Subtracting the two ATP that were used to get started, there is a net gain of two ATP from glycolysis. Much chemical energy still remains in a glucose molecule and this energy becomes available when glycolysis is followed by the breakdown of pyruvate inside mitochondria. Pyruvate enters mitochondria if oxygen is available. If oxygen is not available, glycolysis becomes a part of fermentation (see page 137).

Figure 8.4 gives the main reactions of glycolysis. After glucose is split, each succeeding reaction occurs twice. Therefore, these reactions are preceded by a 2×. Altogether the inputs and outputs of glycolysis are as follows:

Glycolysis	
inputs	outputs
glucose	2 pyruvate
2 NAD$^+$	2 NADH
2 ATP	4 ATP (net 2 ATP)
2 ADP + 2 (P)	

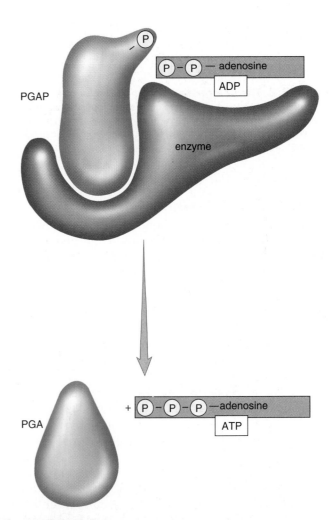

Figure 8.3 Substrate level phosphorylation.
During substrate level phosphorylation, a phosphate group is transferred from a high-energy substrate in a metabolic pathway to ADP. The result is an immediate gain of one ATP molecule. When PGAP, a substrate in the glycolytic pathway shown in Figure 8.4, transfers a phosphate group to ADP, it becomes PGA.

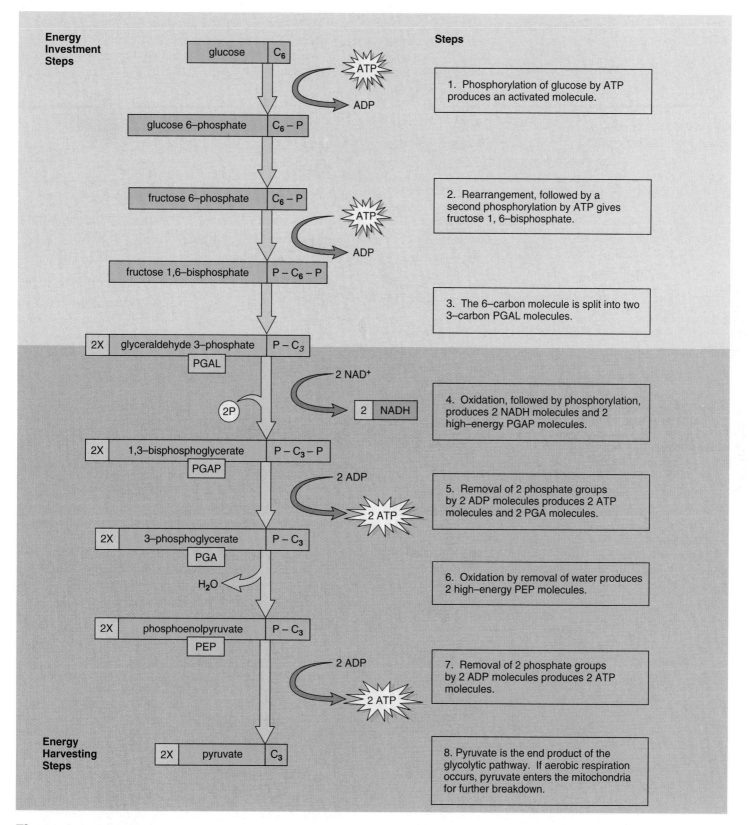

Figure 8.4 Glycolysis.
This metabolic pathway begins with glucose and ends with pyruvate. Net gain of two ATP molecules can be calculated by subtracting those expended during the energy investment steps from those produced during the energy harvesting steps. Text in boxes to the far right explains the reactions.

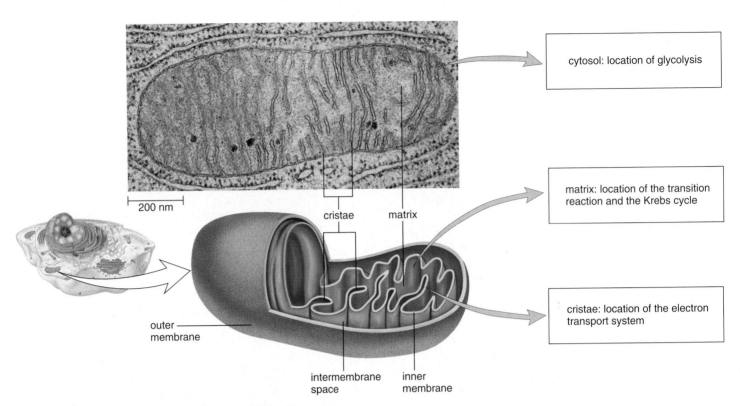

cytosol: location of glycolysis

matrix: location of the transition reaction and the Krebs cycle

cristae: location of the electron transport system

cristae   matrix

outer membrane

intermembrane space   inner membrane

Figure 8.5 **Mitochondrion structure and function.**
A mitochondrion is bounded by a double membrane with an intermembrane space. The inner membrane invaginates to form the shelf-like cristae. Glycolysis takes place in the cytosol outside mitochondria. The transition reaction and the Krebs cycle occur within the mitochondrial matrix. The electron transport system is located on the cristae of a mitochondrion.

8.3 Inside the Mitochondria

Glucose breakdown continues in mitochondria where the transition reaction, Krebs cycle, and the electron transport system are located (Fig. 8.5). Eventually, pyruvate from glycolysis is broken down completely to carbon dioxide and water.

A **mitochondrion** has a double membrane, with an intermembrane space (between the outer and inner membrane). Cristae are folds of inner membrane that jut out into the mitochondrial matrix, the innermost compartment, which is filled with a gel-like fluid. The transition reaction and the Krebs cycle enzymes are located in the matrix, and the electron transport system is located in the cristae. Most of the ATP produced during cellular respiration is produced in mitochondria; therefore, mitochondria are often called the powerhouses of the cell.

Transition Reaction

The transition reaction is so called because it connects glycolysis to the Krebs cycle. In this reaction, pyruvate is converted to a two-carbon acetyl group attached to coenzyme A, collectively termed **acetyl-CoA,** and carbon dioxide is given off. This is an redox reaction in which electrons are removed from pyruvate by an enzyme that uses NAD^+ as a coenzyme that receives the electrons. The reaction occurs twice for each original glucose molecule.

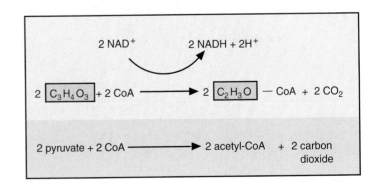

$$2\ NAD^+ \qquad 2\ NADH + 2H^+$$

$$2\ \boxed{C_3H_4O_3} + 2\ CoA \longrightarrow 2\ \boxed{C_2H_3O} - CoA + 2\ CO_2$$

2 pyruvate + 2 CoA ⟶ 2 acetyl-CoA + 2 carbon dioxide

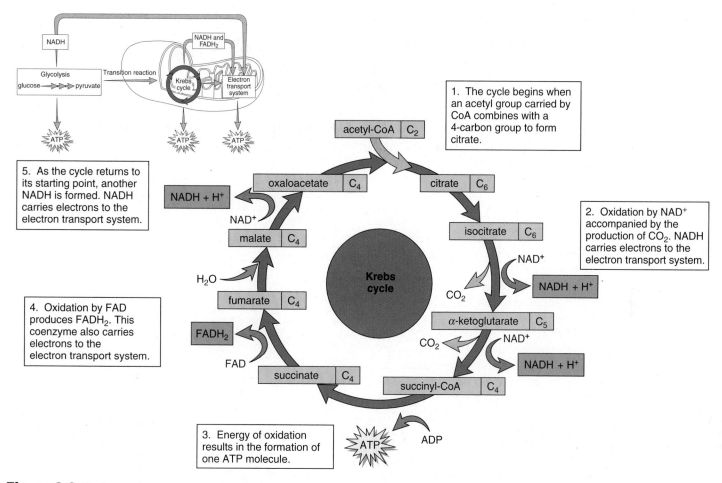

Figure 8.6 Krebs cycle.

The net result of this cycle is the removal of two molecules of carbon dioxide (CO_2) as oxidation occurs. There is a gain of one ATP during the cycle but much energy still resides in the electrons that were received by three molecules of NAD^+ and one molecule of FAD. NADH and $FADH_2$ take these electrons to the electron transport system. (Keep in mind that the Krebs cycle turns twice per glucose molecule.)

The Krebs Cycle

The Krebs cycle is a cyclical metabolic pathway located in the mitochondrial matrix. The Krebs cycle is named for Sir Hans Krebs, a German-born British scientist who received the Nobel Prize for his part in identifying these reactions in the 1930s.

At the start of the Krebs cycle, the C_2 acetyl group produced by the transition reaction joins with a C_4 molecule, forming citrate, a C_6 molecule. For this reason, the cycle is also known as the citric acid cycle (Fig. 8.6). As the substrates undergo oxidation by removal of electrons, two molecules of carbon dioxide (CO_2) form. (Carbon dioxide is one of the end products of the complete breakdown of glucose.)

During the oxidation process most of the electrons are accepted by NAD^+ and NADH then forms. But in one instance, electrons are taken by FAD, and $FADH_2$ forms. NADH and $FADH_2$ carry these electrons to the electron transport system. Some of the energy released when oxidation

occurs is used immediately to form ATP by substrate-level phosphorylation, as in glycolysis. A high-energy metabolite accepts a phosphate group and subsequently passes it on to ADP so that ATP forms.

The Krebs cycle turns twice for each original glucose molecule. Therefore, the input and output of the Krebs cycle per glucose molecule are as follows:

Krebs Cycle	
inputs	outputs
2 acetyl groups	4 CO_2
2 ADP + 2 Ⓟ	2 ATP
6 NAD^+	6 NADH
2 FAD	2 $FADH_2$

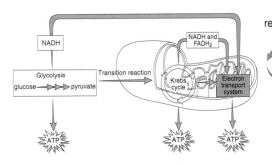

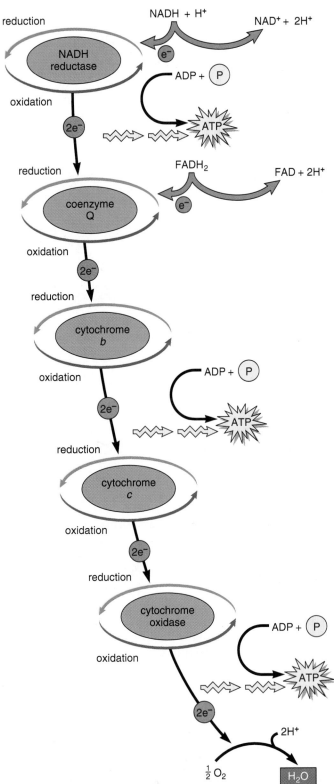

The Electron Transport System

The electron transport system located in the cristae of the mitochondria is a series of carriers that pass electrons from one to the other. Notice that some of the protein carriers of the system are cytochrome molecules.

The electrons that enter the electron transport system are carried by NADH and $FADH_2$. Figure 8.7 is arranged to show that high-energy electrons enter the system, and low-energy electrons leave the system. When NADH gives up its electrons, it becomes NAD^+ and the next carrier gains the electrons and is reduced. This oxidation-reduction reaction starts the process, and each of the carriers in turn becomes reduced and then oxidized as the electrons move down the system. As the pair of electrons is passed from carrier to carrier, energy is released and stored in the form a hydrogen ion (H^+) gradient. When these ions flow down their electrochemical gradient through an ATP synthase complex, ATP is formed (Fig. 8.8).

Oxygen receives the energy-spent electrons from the last of the carriers. After receiving electrons, oxygen combines with hydrogen ions and water forms. The term **oxidative phosphorylation** refers to the production of ATP as a result of energy released by the electron transport system.

When NADH delivers electrons to the first carrier of the electron transport system, enough energy is released by the time the electrons are received by O_2 to permit the production of three ATP molecules. When $FADH_2$ delivers electrons to the electron transport system, only two ATP are produced.

The cell needs only a limited supply of the coenzymes NAD^+ and FAD because they are constantly being recycled and reused. Therefore, once NADH has delivered electrons to the electron transport system, it is "free" to return and pick up more hydrogens. In the same manner, the components of ATP are recycled in cells. Energy is required to join ADP + ℗, and then when ATP is used to do cellular work, ADP and ℗ are made available once more. The recycling of coenzymes and ADP increases cellular efficiency since it does away with the necessity to synthesize large quantities of NAD^+, FAD, and ADP anew.

As electrons pass down the electron transport system, energy is released and ATP is produced.

Figure 8.7 The electron transport system.
NADH and $FADH_2$ bring electrons to the electron transport system. As the electrons move down the system, energy is released and used to form ATP. For every pair of electrons that enters by way of NADH, three ATP result. For every pair of electrons that enters by way of $FADH_2$, two ATP result. Oxygen, the final acceptor of the electrons, becomes a part of water.

The Cristae of a Mitochondrion

The carriers of the electron transport system and the proteins concerned with ATP synthesis are spatially arranged in a particular manner in the cristae of mitochondria. Essentially the electron transport system consists of three protein complexes and two protein mobile carriers. The mobile carriers transport electrons between the complexes (Fig. 8.8).

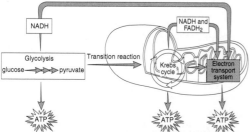

The carriers of the electron transport system accept electrons, which they pass from one to the other. What happens to the hydrogen ions (H^+) carried by NADH and $FADH_2$? The carriers of the electron transport system use the released energy to pump these hydrogen ions from the matrix into the intermembrane space of a mitochondrion. The vertical arrows in Figure 8.8 show that the NADH dehydrogenase complex, the cytochrome *b-c* complex, and the cytochrome oxidase complex all pump H^+ into the intermembrane space. This establishes a strong electrochemical gradient; there are about ten times as many hydrogen ions in the intermembrane space than there are in the matrix.

ATP Production The cristae contain an ATP synthase complex through which hydrogen ions flow down a gradient from the intermembrane space into the matrix. As hydrogen ions flow from high to low concentration, the enzyme ATP synthase synthesizes ATP from ADP + ℗. Just how H^+ flow drives ATP synthesis is not known; perhaps the hydrogen ions participate in the reaction, or perhaps they cause a change in the shape of ATP synthase and this brings about ATP synthesis. Mitochondria produce ATP by **chemiosmosis,** so called because ATP production is tied to an electrochemical gradient that is an H^+ gradient.

The finding of respiratory poisons has lent support to the chemiosmotic model of ATP synthesis. When one poison inhibits ATP synthesis, the H^+ gradient becomes larger than usual, and when another type makes the membrane leaky to H^+, no ATP is made.

Once formed, ATP molecules diffuse out of the mitochondrial matrix by way of a channel protein.

> Mitochondria synthesize ATP by chemiosmosis. ATP production is dependent upon an electrochemical gradient established by the pumping of H^+ into the intermembrane space.

Figure 8.8 Organization of cristae.
The electron transport system is located in the cristae. As electrons move from one complex to the other, hydrogen ions (H^+) are pumped from the matrix into the intermembrane space. As hydrogen ions flow down a concentration gradient from the intermembrane space into the mitochondrial matrix, ATP is synthesized by the enzyme ATP synthase, which is a part of the ATP synthase complex. ATP leaves the matrix by way of a channel protein.

Energy Yield from Glucose Breakdown

Figure 8.9 calculates the ATP yield for the complete breakdown of glucose to CO_2 and H_2O in eukaryotes. The diagram includes the number of ATP produced by substrate phosphorylation and the number that is produced by oxidative phosphorylation as a result of electrons passing down the electron transport system.

Substrate-Level Phosphorylation

Per glucose molecule, there is a net gain of two ATP from glycolysis in the cytosol and two more from the Krebs cycle in the matrix of mitochondria. Altogether, four ATP are formed outside the electron transport system.

Oxidative Phosphorylation

Most of the ATP produced by cellular respiration is due to oxidative phosphorylation and energy released by the electron transport system. Per glucose molecule, ten NADH and two $FADH_2$ take electrons to the electron transport system. For each NADH formed *inside* the mitochondria by the Krebs cycle, three ATP result, but for each $FADH_2$, only two ATP are produced. Figure 8.7 explains the reason for this difference: $FADH_2$ delivers its electrons to the transport system after NADH and therefore these electrons cannot account for as much ATP production.

What about the ATP yield of NADH generated *outside* the mitochondria by the glycolytic pathway? NADH cannot cross mitochondrial membranes, but there is a "shuttle" mechanism that allows its electrons to be delivered to the electron transport system inside the mitochondria. The shuttle consists of an organic molecule, which can cross the outer membrane, accept the electrons, and in most cells, deliver them to a FAD molecule in the inner membrane. If FAD is utilized, only two ATP result.

Heart and liver cells, which have high metabolic rates, are exceptions; in these cells cytoplasmic NADH results in the production of three ATP. Also, since prokaryotes (bacteria) do not have mitochondria, each NADH produces three ATP for a total of 38 ATP.

Efficiency of Complete Glucose Breakdown

It is interesting to calculate how much of the energy in a glucose molecule eventually becomes available to the cell. The difference in energy content between the reactants (glucose and O_2) and the products (CO_2 and H_2O) is 686 kcal. An ATP phosphate bond has an energy content of 7.3 kcal, and 36 to 38 of these are usually produced during glucose breakdown. Taking the lower number, 36 phosphates are equivalent to a total of 263 kcal. Therefore, at least 263 kcal/686 kcal × 100, or about 39% of the available energy is transferred from glucose to ATP as a result of glucose breakdown.

Figure 8.9 Energy yield per glucose molecule.
Substrate-level phosphorylation during glycolysis and the Krebs cycle results in the production of four ATP molecules per glucose molecule. Oxidative phosphorylation accounts for 32 or 34 ATP, and the grand total of ATP is therefore 36 or 38 ATP. The delivery of electrons from NADH generated outside the mitochondrion explains this variation. If the electrons from NADH are delivered by a shuttle mechanism at the start of the electron transport system, six ATP result per NADH; otherwise, four ATP result.

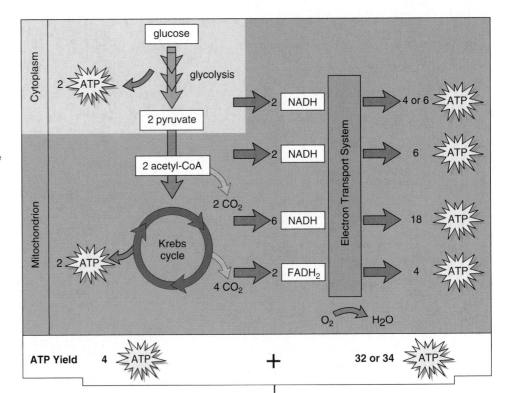

8.4 Fermentation

Cellular respiration also includes fermentation. **Fermentation** consists of glycolysis followed by the reduction of pyruvate by NADH to either lactate or alcohol and CO_2 (Fig. 8.10). The pathway operates anaerobically because after NADH transfers its electrons to pyruvate, it is "free" to return and pick up more electrons during the earlier reactions of glycolysis.

Certain anaerobic bacteria such as lactic-acid bacteria, which help us manufacture cheese, consistently produce lactate in this manner. Other bacteria produce chemicals of industrial importance anaerobically: isopropanol, butyric acid, propionic acid, and acetic acid. Yeasts are good examples of organisms that generate alcohol and CO_2. Yeast is used to leaven bread; the CO_2 produced makes bread rise. On the other hand, yeast is used to ferment sugar when wine is made; in that case, it is the ethyl alcohol that is desired. Eventually yeasts are killed by the very alcohol they produce.

Animal, including human, cells are similar to lactic-acid bacteria in that pyruvate, when produced faster than it can be oxidized through the Krebs cycle, is reduced to lactate.

Advantages and Disadvantages of Fermentation

Despite its low yield, fermentation is essential to humans because it can provide a rapid burst of ATP; muscle cells more than other cells are apt to carry on fermentation. When our muscles are working vigorously over a short period of time, fermentation is a way to produce ATP even though oxygen is temporarily in limited supply.

Lactate, however, is toxic to cells. At first, blood carries away all the lactate formed in muscles. Eventually, however, lactate begins to build up, changing the pH and causing the muscles to fatigue so that they no longer contract. When we stop running, our bodies are in **oxygen debt**, a term that refers to the amount of oxygen needed to restore ATP to its former level and rid the body of lactate. Oxygen debt is signified by the fact that we continue to breathe very heavily for a time. Recovery involves transporting lactate to the liver, where it is converted back to pyruvate. Some of the pyruvate is respired completely, and the rest is converted back to glucose.

Efficiency of Fermentation?

The two ATP produced per glucose during fermentation is equivalent to 14.6 kcal. Complete glucose breakdown to CO_2 and H_2O represents a possible energy yield of 686 kcal per molecule. Therefore, the efficiency for fermentation is only 14.6 kcal/686 kcal $\times$ 100, or 2.1%. This is much less efficient

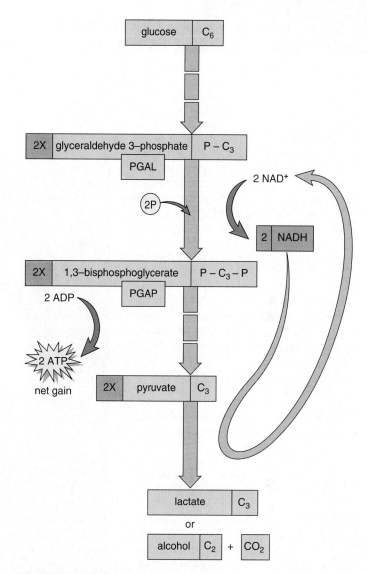

Figure 8.10 Fermentation.
Fermentation consists of glycolysis followed by a reduction of pyruvate. This "frees" NAD^+ and it returns to the glycolytic pathway to pick up more electrons.

than the complete breakdown of glucose. The inputs and outputs of fermentation are as shown next.

Fermentation	
inputs	outputs
glucose	2 lactate or
2 ATP	2 alcohol and 2 CO_2
2 ADP + 2 (P)	4 ATP (net 2 ATP)

Exercise: A Test of Homeostatic Control

Exercise is a dramatic test of the body's homeostatic control systems—there is a large increase in muscle oxygen (O_2) requirement, and a large amount of carbon dioxide (CO_2) is produced. These changes must be countered by increases in breathing and blood flow to increase oxygen delivery and removal of the metabolically produced carbon dioxide. Also, heavy exercise can produce a large amount of lactic acid due to the utilization of fermentation, an anaerobic process. Both the accumulation of carbon dioxide and lactic acid can lead to an increase in intracellular and extracellular acidity. Further, during heavy exercise, working muscles produce large amounts of heat that must be removed to prevent overheating. In a strict sense, the body rarely maintains true homeostasis while performing intense exercise or during prolonged exercise in a hot or humid environment. However, a better maintenance of homeostasis is observed in those who have had endurance training.

The number of mitochondria increases in the muscles of persons who train; and, therefore, there is greater reliance on the Krebs cycle and the electron transport system to generate energy. Muscle cells with few mitochondria must have a high ADP concentration to stimulate the limited number of mitochondria to start consuming oxygen. After an endurance training program, the large number of mitochondria start consuming oxygen as soon as the ADP concentration starts rising due to muscle contraction and subsequent breakdown of ATP. Therefore, a steady state of oxygen intake by mitochondria is achieved earlier in the athlete. This faster rise in oxygen uptake at the onset of work means that the oxygen deficit is less, and the formation of lactate due to fermentation is less. Further, any lactate that is produced is removed and processed more quickly.

Training also results in greater reliance on the Krebs cycle and increased fatty acid metabolism, because fatty acids are broken down to acetyl-CoA, which enters the Krebs cycle. This preserves plasma glucose concentration and also helps the body maintain homeostasis.

Source: *Scott K. Powers and Edward T. Howley, Exercise Physiology, 2d ed., 1994. McGraw-Hill Companies, Dubuque, IA.*

In athletes, there is:
- a smaller oxygen deficit due to a more rapid increase in oxygen uptake at the onset of work;
- an increase in fat metabolism that spares blood glucose;
- a reduction in lactate and hydrogen ion (H^+) formation;
- an increase in ability to remove and process lactate.

8.5 Metabolic Pool

Degradative reactions, collectively called **catabolism,** break down molecules and tend to be exergonic. Synthetic reactions, collectively called **anabolism,** tend to be endergonic. Is it correct to say then, that catabolism drives anabolism?

Catabolism

We already know that glucose is broken down during cellular respiration. However, other molecules can also undergo catabolism. When a fat molecule is used as an energy source, it breaks down to glycerol and three fatty acids. As Figure 8.11 indicates, glycerol is converted to PGAL, a metabolite in glycolysis. The fatty acids are converted to acetyl-CoA and the acetyl groups enter the Krebs cycle. An 18-carbon fatty acid results in nine acetyl-CoA molecules. In the human body, oxidation of these acetyl-CoA molecules can produce a total of 216 ATP molecules. For this reason,

fats are an efficient form of stored energy—there are, after all, three long fatty acid chains per fat molecule.

The carbon skeleton of amino acids can also be broken down. In humans, the carbon skeleton is produced in the liver when an amino acid undergoes **deamination,** or the removal of the amino group. The amino group becomes ammonia (NH_3), which enters the urea cycle and becomes part of urea, the primary excretory product of humans. Just where the carbon skeleton begins degradation is dependent on the length of the R group, since this determines the number of carbons left after deamination.

Anabolism

We have already mentioned that the ATP produced during catabolism drives anabolism. But there is another way catabolism is related to anabolism. The substrates making up the pathways in Figure 8.11 can be used as starting materials for synthetic reactions. In other words, compounds that enter the pathways are oxidized to substrates that can be used for biosynthesis. This is the cell's **metabolic pool** [Gk. *meta,* implying change] in which one type of molecule can be converted to another. In this way, carbohydrate intake can result in the formation of fat. PGAL can be converted to glycerol, and acetyl groups can be joined to form fatty acids. Fat synthesis follows. This explains why you gain weight from eating too much candy, ice cream, and cake.

Some metabolites of the Krebs cycle can be converted to amino acids through transamination, the transfer of an amino group to an organic acid, forming a different amino acid. Plants are able to synthesize all of the amino acids they need. Animals, however, lack some of the enzymes necessary for synthesis of all amino acids. Adult humans, for example, can synthesize eleven of the common amino acids, but they cannot synthesize the other nine. The amino acids that cannot be synthesized must be supplied by the diet; they are called the essential amino acids. The nonessential amino acids can be synthesized. It is quite possible for animals to suffer from protein deficiency if their diet does not contain adequate quantities of all the essential amino acids.

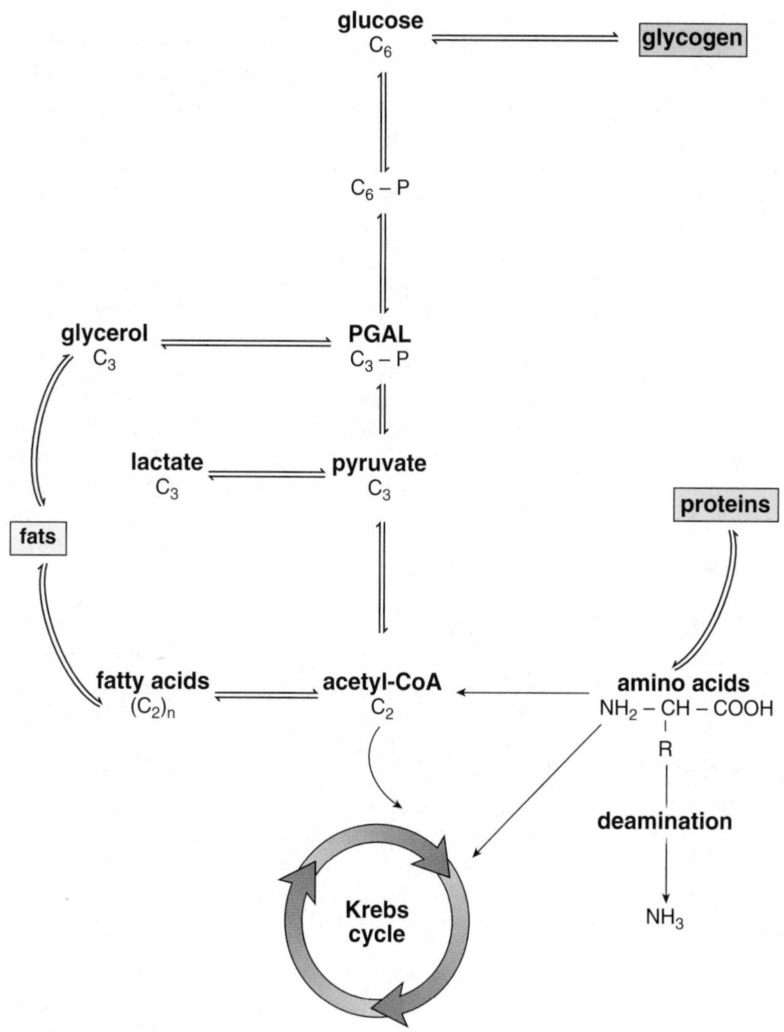

Figure 8.11 The metabolic pool concept.
When they are used as energy sources, carbohydrates, fats, and proteins enter degradative pathways at specific points. Catabolism produces metabolites that can also be used for anabolism of other compounds.

All the reactions involved in cellular respiration are a part of a metabolic pool; the metabolites from the pool can be used for catabolism or for anabolism.

Connecting Concepts

The organelles of eukaryotic cells have a structure that suits their function. Cells didn't arise until they had a membranous covering, and membrane is also absolutely essential to the organization of chloroplasts and mitochondria. In a chloroplast, membrane forms the grana, which are stacks of interconnected, flattened membranous sacs called thylakoids. The inner membrane of a mitochondrion invaginates to form the convoluted cristae.

The detailed structure of chloroplasts and mitochondria is different, but essentially they operate similarly: an assembly line of particles in the thylakoid membrane and cristae carry out functions necessary to photosynthesis and cellular respiration, respectively. In both organelles, electron transport system carriers pump hydrogen ions into an enclosed space, establishing an electrochemical gradient. When hydrogen ions flow down this gradient through ATP synthase complex, the energy released is used to produce ATP. In chloroplasts the electrons sent to the electron transport system are energized by the sun; in mitochondria energized electrons are removed from the substrates of the glycolytic and Krebs cycle.

In chloroplasts, the gel-like fluid of the stroma contains the enzymes of the Calvin cycle, which reduce carbon dioxide to a carbohydrate, and in mitochondria, the gel-like fluid of the matrix contains the enzymes of the Krebs cycle, which oxidize carbohydrate products received from the cytosol. In chloroplasts reduction of carbon dioxide requires ATP produced by chemiosmosis, while in mitochondria oxidation of substrates releases carbon dioxide; the ATP produced by chemiosmosis is made available to the cell.

According to the endosymbiotic hypothesis, chloroplasts and mitochondria were independent prokaryotic organisms at one time. Indeed, each contains genes (DNA) not found in the eukaryotic nucleus. Through evolution all organisms are related, and therefore these organelles may be related also. The similar organization of these organelles suggests that this is the case.

Summary

8.1 Cellular Respiration
The oxidation of glucose to CO_2 and H_2O is an exergonic reaction that drives ATP synthesis, an endergonic reaction. Four phases are required: glycolysis, the transition reaction, the Krebs cycle, and passage of electrons along the electron transport system. Oxidation of substrates involves the removal of hydrogen atoms ($H^+ + e^-$) from substrate molecules, usually by the coenzyme NAD^+, but in one case by FAD.

8.2 Outside the Mitochondria: Glycolysis
Glycolysis, the breakdown of glucose to two molecules of pyruvate, is a series of enzymatic reactions that occur in the cytosol. Breakdown releases enough energy to immediately give a net gain of two ATP by substrate-level phosphorylation. Two NADH are formed.

8.3 Inside the Mitochondria
When oxygen is available, pyruvate from glycolysis enters the mitochondrion, where the transition reaction takes place. During this reaction, oxidation occurs as CO_2 is removed from pyruvate. NAD^+ is reduced, and CoA receives the C_2 acetyl group that remains. Since the reaction must take place twice per glucose molecule, two NADH result.

The acetyl group enters the Krebs cycle, a cyclical series of reactions located in the mitochondrial matrix. Complete oxidation follows, as two CO_2 molecules, three NADH molecules, and one $FADH_2$ molecule are formed. The cycle also produces one ATP molecule. The entire cycle must turn twice per glucose molecule.

The final stage of glucose breakdown involves the electron transport system located in the cristae of the mitochondria. The electrons received from NADH and $FADH_2$ are passed down a chain of carriers until they are finally received by oxygen, which combines with H^+ to produce water. As the electrons pass down the system, energy is released and stored for ATP production. The term oxidative phosphorylation is sometimes used for ATP production associated with the electron transport system.

The cristae of mitochondria contain protein complexes of the electron transport system that pass electrons from one to the other and pump H^+ into the intermembrane space, setting up an electrochemical gradient. When H^+ flows down this gradient through an ATP synthase complex, energy is released and used to form ATP molecules from ADP and Ⓟ. This is ATP synthesis by chemiosmosis.

Of the 36 to 38 ATP formed by complete glucose breakdown, four are the result of substrate-level phosphorylation and the rest are produced by oxidative phosphorylation. The energy for the latter comes from the electron transport system. For most NADH molecules that donate electrons to the electron transport system, three ATP molecules are produced. In some cells each NADH formed in the cytosol, however, results in only two ATP molecules. This occurs when the hydrogen atoms are shuttled across the mitochondrial membrane by a carrier that passes them to FAD. $FADH_2$ results in the formation of only two ATP because its electrons enter the electron transport system at a lower energy level.

8.4 Fermentation
Fermentation involves glycolysis followed by the reduction of pyruvate by NADH either to lactate or to alcohol and carbon dioxide (CO_2). The reduction process "frees" NAD^+ so that it can accept more hydrogen atoms from glycolysis.

Although fermentation results in only two ATP molecules, it still serves a purpose. In vertebrates, it provides a quick burst of ATP energy for short-term, strenuous muscular activity. The accumulation of lactate puts the individual in oxygen debt because oxygen is needed when lactate is completely metabolized to CO_2 and H_2O.

8.5 Metabolic Pool
Carbohydrate, protein, and fat can be catabolized by entering the degradative pathways at different locations. These pathways also provide metabolites needed for the anabolism of various important substances. Catabolism and anabolism, therefore, both utilize the same pools of metabolites.

Reviewing the Chapter

1. What is the overall chemical equation for the complete breakdown of glucose to CO_2 and H_2O? Explain how this is an oxidation-reduction reaction. Why is the reaction able to drive ATP buildup? 128
2. What are NAD^+ and FAD? What are their functions? 128
3. What are the three pathways involved in the complete breakdown of glucose to carbon dioxide (CO_2) and water (H_2O)? What reaction is needed to join two of these pathways? 129
4. What are the main events of glycolysis? How is ATP formed? 130
5. Give the substrates and products of the transition reaction. Where does it take place? 132
6. What are the main events during the Krebs cycle? 133
7. What is the electron transport system, and what are its functions? 134
8. Describe the organization of protein complexes within the cristae. Explain how the complexes are involved in ATP production. 135
9. Calculate the energy yield of glycolysis and complete glucose breakdown. Distinguish between substrate-level phosphorylation and oxidative phosphorylation. 136
10. What is fermentation and how does it differ from glycolysis? Mention the benefit of pyruvate reduction during fermentation. What types of organisms carry out lactate fermentation, and what types carry out alcoholic fermentation? 137
11. Give examples to support the concept of the metabolic pool. 139

Testing Yourself

Choose the best answer for each question. For questions 1–8, identify the pathway involved by matching them to the terms in the key.

Key:

     a. glycolysis
     b. Krebs cycle
     c. electron transport system

1. carbon dioxide (CO_2) given off
2. water (H_2O) formed
3. PGAL
4. NADH becomes NAD^+
5. oxidative phosphorylation
6. cytochrome carriers
7. pyruvate
8. FAD becomes $FADH_2$
9. The transition reaction

     a. connects glycolysis to the Krebs cycle.
     b. gives off CO_2.
     c. utilizes NAD^+.
     d. results in an acetyl group.
     e. All of these are correct.

10. The greatest contributor of electrons to the electron transport system is
     a. oxygen.
     b. glycolysis.
     c. the Krebs cycle.
     d. the transition reaction.
     e. fermentation.
11. Substrate-level phosphorylation takes place in
     a. glycolysis and the Krebs cycle.
     b. the electron transport system and the transition reaction.
     c. glycolysis and the electron transport system.
     d. the Krebs cycle and the transition reaction.
     e. Both b and d are correct.
12. Which of these is not true of fermentation?
     a. net gain of only two ATP
     b. occurs in cytosol
     c. NADH donates electrons to electron transport system
     d. begins with glucose
     e. carried on by yeast
13. Fatty acids are broken down to
     a. pyruvate molecules, which take electrons to the electron transport system.
     b. acetyl groups, which enter the Krebs cycle.
     c. amino acids, which excrete ammonia.
     d. glycerol, which is found in fats.
     e. All of these are correct.
14. Label this diagram of a mitochondrion and state a function for each portion named.

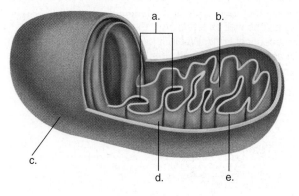

Thinking Scientifically

1. In mitochondria, NADH supplies electrons to the electron transport system. Molecular oxygen (with the highest affinity for electrons) is the final receiver. In photosynthesis, however, the oxygen in water (H_2O) is the source of electrons and the final receiver is $NADP^+$. How can oxygen act as both a donor and receiver of electrons?

2. You are working with pyruvate molecules that contain radioactive carbon. They are incubated with all the components of the Krebs cycle long enough for one turn of the cycle. Carbon dioxide is produced, but only one third of it is radioactive. How can this observation be explained?

Bioethical Issue

Feeling tired and run-down? Want to jump start your mitochondria? If you seem to have no specific ailment, you might be tempted to turn to what is now called alternative medicine. Alternative medicine includes such nonconventional therapies as herbal supplements, acupuncture, chiropractic therapy, homeopathy, osteopathy, and therapeutic touch (e.g., laying on of hands).

In 1992, Congress established what is now called the National Center for Complementary and Alternative Medicine (NCCAM), whose budget has grown from $2 million to $50 million for 1999. In 1994, the Dietary Supplement Health and Education Act allowed the marketing of vitamins, minerals, and herbs without the requirement that they be approved by the Food and Drug Administration (FDA).

Many scientists feel that alternative medicine should be subjected to the same rigorous clinical testing as traditional medicine. They approve of a control study that is now testing the efficacy of the herb Saint-John's-wort. The results are expected to tell whether Saint-John's-wort, a relatively inexpensive remedy, works just as well as a relatively expensive drug produced by pharmaceutical firms. Would it be satisfactory to you if alternative medical practices succeed simply for psychological reasons rather than for their physical benefit?

Understanding the Terms

acetyl-CoA 132	Krebs cycle 129
anabolism 139	metabolic pool 139
catabolism 139	mitochondrion 132
cellular respiration 128	NAD^+ 128
chemiosmosis 135	oxidative
deamination 139	phosphorylation 134
electron transport	oxygen debt 137
system 129	pyruvate 129
FAD 128	substrate-level
fermentation 129, 137	phosphorylation 130
glycolysis 129, 130	transition reaction 129

Match the terms to these definitions:

a. _____ Anaerobic breakdown of glucose that results in a gain of two ATP and end products such as alcohol and lactate.

b. _____ Cycle of reactions in mitochondria that begins with citric acid; it produces CO_2, ATP, NADH, and $FADH_2$; also called the citric acid cycle.

c. _____ Metabolites that are the products of and/or the substrates for key reactions in cells allowing one type of molecule to be changed into another type, such as the conversion of carbohydrates to fats.

d. _____ Molecule made up of a two-carbon group attached to coenzyme A. During cellular respiration, the two-carbon group enters the Krebs cycle for further breakdown.

e. _____ Series of membrane-bounded carrier molecules that pass electrons from one to the other, releasing energy that is used for the synthesis of ATP.

Web Connections

Exploring the Internet

http://www.mhhe.com/biosci/genbio/mader
(click on *Biology 7/e*)

The *Biology 7/e* Online Learning Center provides many resources for studying the material in this chapter including links to the following sites:

Learn more about the basics of cell carbohydrate metabolism in Basic Concepts of Metabolism: The Totality of Chemical Reactions of Living Matter. At this site, the user can find information about catabolism and anabolism, autotrophic and heterotrophic pathways, and redox reactions.

http://www.blc.arizona.edu/interactive/metabolism2.95/metabolism.html

Lipid Metabolism. This site describes in great detail the pathways by which lipids are metabolized in the body.

http://web.indstate.edu/thcme/mwking/lipsynth.html

Glycolysis and the Krebs Cycle. This MIT hypertextbook has terrific graphics and text describing these processes.

http://esg-www.mit.edu:8001/esgbio/glycolysis/dir.html

Fermentations: Changing the Course of Human History. An interesting description of fermentation processes used by humans.

http://www.accessexcellence.org/TSN/SS/ferm_background.html

Selected References on Fermentation, including intriguing publications and links, including "How to Brew Your First Beer."

http://www.accessexcellence.org/TSN/SS/ferm_references.html

Cellular Reproduction and the Cell Cycle

c h a p t e r

From one cell, two cells.

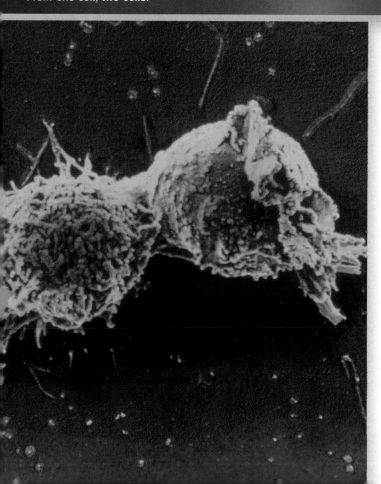

Consider the development of a human being. We begin life as one cell—an egg fertilized by a sperm. Yet in nine short months, we become complex organisms consisting of trillions of cells. How is such a feat possible? Cell division enables a single cell to produce many cells, allowing an organism to grow in size and to replace worn-out tissues.

The instructions for cell division lie in the genes. During the first part of an organism's life, the genes instruct all cells to divide. When adulthood is reached, however, only specific cells—human blood and skin cells, for example—continue to divide daily. Other tissues, such as nervous tissue, no longer routinely produce new cells.

Why don't all types of adult cells reproduce routinely? They contain the full complement of genetic material in their nuclei. Such questions are being intensely studied. Cell biologists have recently discovered that specific enzymes regulate the cell cycle, the period that extends from the time a new cell is produced until it too completes division. Proper function of these enzymes ensures that cells divide normally. Cancer may result when the enzymes regulating the cell cycle go awry.

9.1 How Prokaryotic Cells Divide

In all organisms, the genes consist of DNA located in one or more chromosomes. The reproduction of cells usually consists of duplicating the chromosome(s) and distributing a complete set to the daughter cells. In this way the daughter cells are genetically identical to the parent cell.

Bacteria and protists, such as amoeboids and paramecia, are unicellular. Cell division in unicellular organisms produces two new individuals. This is **asexual reproduction** because one parent has produced identical offspring.

Plants and animals are multicellular. Cell division in multicellular organisms is part of a lifelong developmental process. Growth occurs as the multicellular form develops into the adult organism and it occurs during renewal and repair.

Cell division allows unicellular organisms to reproduce and is necessary to the growth and repair of multicellular organisms.

The Prokaryotic Chromosome

Prokaryotes (unicellular bacteria and archaea) lack a nucleus and other membranous organelles found in eukaryotic cells. They do have a **chromosome** which is composed of DNA associated with proteins. Prokaryotes have a single chromosome that contains just a few proteins. A eukaryotic chromosome has many more proteins than a prokaryotic chromosome.

In electron micrographs the bacterial chromosome appears as an electron-dense, irregularly shaped region called the **nucleoid** [L. *nucleus,* nucleus, kernel, and Gk. *-eides,* like], which is not enclosed by a membrane. When stretched out, the chromosome is seen to be a circular loop attached to the inside of the plasma membrane. Its length is up to about 1,000 times the length of the cell, which is why it needs to be folded inside the cell.

The prokaryotic chromosome is largely a single loop of DNA that is tightly folded into a region called the nucleoid.

Binary Fission

Prokaryotes reproduce asexually by binary fission. The process is termed **binary fission** because division (fission) produces two (binary) daughter cells that are identical to the original parent cell. Before division takes place, DNA is

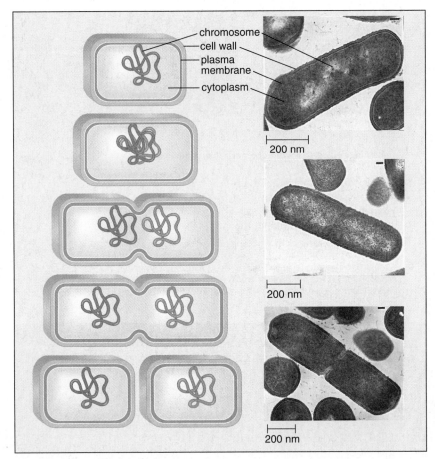

Figure 9.1 Binary fission.
In electron micrographs, it is possible to observe a bacterium dividing to become two bacteria. The diagrams depict chromosomal duplication and distribution. First DNA replicates, and as the plasma membrane lengthens, the two chromosomes separate. Upon fission, each bacterium has its own chromosome.

replicated so that there are two chromosomes attached to the inside of the plasma membrane. Following replication, the two chromosomes separate by an elongation of the cell that pulls the chromosomes apart. When the cell is approximately twice its original length, the plasma membrane grows inward and the new cell wall forms, dividing the cell into two approximately equal portions (Fig. 9.1).

Escherichia coli, which lives in our intestines, has a generation time (time it takes the cell to divide) of about 20 minutes under favorable conditions. In about seven hours a single cell can increase to over one million cells! Most bacteria, however, have a generation time of from one to three hours and others may require even more than 24 hours.

Asexual reproduction in prokaryotes is by binary fission. DNA replicates and the two resulting chromosomes separate as the cell elongates.

9.2 How Eukaryotic Cells Divide 🔊

Some eukaryotes are unicellular but most are multicellular. In multicellular forms cell division is necessary to growth and repair of tissues.

Eukaryotic Chromosomes

The DNA in the chromosomes of eukaryotes is associated with various proteins including *histone proteins* that are especially involved in organizing chromosomes. When a eukaryotic cell is not undergoing division, the DNA (and associated proteins) within a nucleus is a tangled mass of thin threads called **chromatin** [Gk. *chroma,* color, and *teino,* stretch]. At the time of division, chromatin becomes highly coiled and condensed, and it is easy to see the individual chromosomes.

When the chromosomes are visible it is possible to photograph and count them. Each species has a characteristic chromosome number (Table 9.1); for instance, human cells contain 46 chromosomes, corn has 20 chromosomes, and a crayfish has 200! This is called the full or **diploid (2n) number** [Gk. *diplos,* twofold, and *-eides,* like] of chromosomes that is found in all cells of the body. The diploid number includes two chromosomes of each kind. Half the diploid number, called the **haploid (n) number** [Gk. *haplos,* single, and *-eides,* like] of chromosomes, contains only one of each kind of chromosome. In the life cycle of many animals, only sperm and eggs have the haploid number of chromosomes.

Cell division in eukaryotes involves nuclear division (karyokinesis) and **cytokinesis,** which is division of the cytoplasm. The nuclei of somatic, or body, cells undergo **mitosis**—nuclear division in which the chromosome number stays constant. A 2n nucleus divides to produce daughter nuclei that are also 2n. Before nuclear division takes place, DNA replicates, duplicating the chromosomes. Each chromosome now has two identical parts called **sister chromatids** (Fig. 9.2). Sister chromatids are genetically identical; that is, they contain exactly the same genes. Sister chromatids are constricted and attached to each other at a region called the **centromere** [Gk. *centrum,* center, and *meros,* part]. During nuclear division the two sister chromatids separate at the centromeres, and in this way each duplicated chromosome gives rise to two daughter chromosomes. These chromosomes, which consist of only one chromatid, are distributed equally to the daughter cells. In this way, each daughter cell gets a copy of each chromosome.

Each type of eukaryote has a characteristic number of chromosomes in the nucleus of each cell. The chromosomes duplicate prior to mitosis, so that despite nuclear division the chromosome number stays constant.

Table 9.1

Diploid Chromosome Number of Some Eukaryotes

Type of Organism	Name of Organism	Chromosome Number
Fungi	*Aspergillus nidulans* (mold)	8
	Neurospora crassa (mold)	14
	Saccharomyces cerevisiae (yeast)	32
Plants	*Vicia faba* (broad bean)	12
	Zea mays (corn)	20
	Solanum tuberosum (potato)	48
	Nicotiana tabacum (tobacco)	48
Animals	*Musca domestica* (housefly)	12
	Rana pipiens (frog)	26
	Felis domesticus (cat)	38
	Homo sapiens (human)	46
	Pan troglodytes (chimp)	48
	Equus caballus (horse)	64
	Gallus gallus (chicken)	78
	Canis familiaris (dog)	78

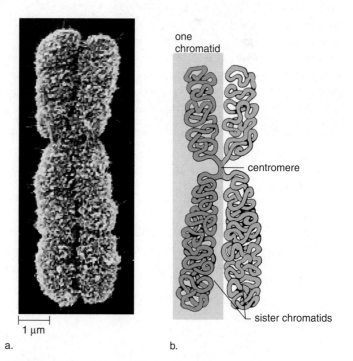

one chromatid

centromere

sister chromatids

1 μm

a.   b.

Figure 9.2 Duplicated chromosomes.

A duplicated chromosome contains two sister chromatids, each with copies of the same genes. **a.** Electron micrograph of a highly coiled and compacted chromosome, typical of a nucleus about to divide. **b.** Diagrammatic drawing of a compacted chromosome. One chromatid is screened in blue. The chromatids are held together at a region called the centromere.

The Mitotic Spindle

The **centrosome** [Gk. *centrum*, center, and *soma*, body], the main microtubule organizing center of the cell, divides before mitosis begins. Centrosomes are believed to be responsible for organizing the spindle, a structure that brings about chromosome movement during cell division. Each centrosome contains a pair of barrel-shaped organelles called **centrioles;** however, the fact that plant cells lack centrioles suggests that centrioles are not required for spindle formation.

The **spindle** contains many fibers, each composed of a bundle of microtubules. Microtubules are hollow cylinders found in the cytoplasm and other structures such as flagella and centrioles. Microtubules are made up of the protein tubulin. They assemble when tubulin subunits join and disassemble when tubulin subunits become free once more. The cytoskeleton, which is a network of interconnected filaments and tubules, begins to disassemble when spindle fibers begin forming. Most likely, the cytoskeleton provides material for spindle formation.

Mitosis in Animal Cells

Mitosis is a continuous process that is arbitrarily divided into five phases for convenience of description (Fig. 9.3).

Prophase

It is apparent during *prophase* that nuclear division is about to occur because chromatin has condensed and the chromosomes are now visible. As the chromosomes continue to compact, the nucleolus disappears and the nuclear envelope fragments.

The already duplicated chromosomes are composed of two sister chromatids held together at a centromere. Counting the number of centromeres in diagrammatic drawings gives the number of chromosomes for the cell depicted. During prophase, the chromosomes have no apparent orientation within the cell. However, specialized protein complexes called *kinetochores* develop on either side of each centromere, and these are important to future chromosome orientation.

The spindle begins to assemble as pairs of centrosomes migrate away from one another. Short microtubules radiate out in a starlike **aster** [Gk. *aster,* star] from the pair of centrioles located in each centrosome.

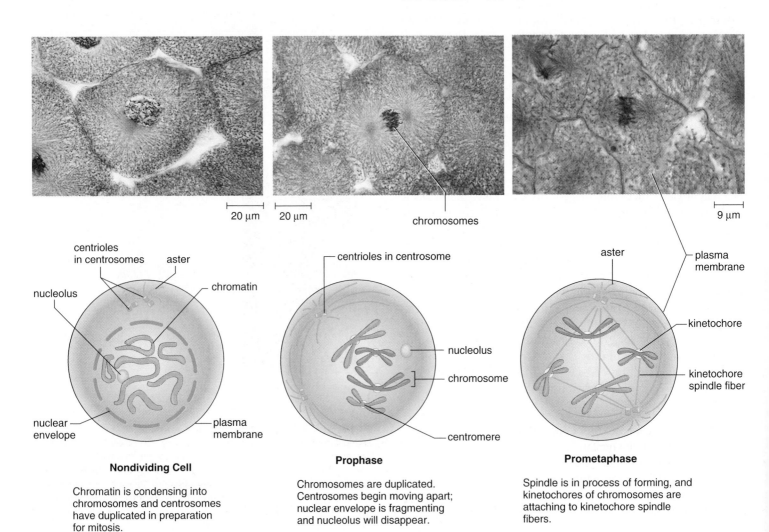

20 μm   20 μm

chromosomes

9 μm

Nondividing Cell

Chromatin is condensing into chromosomes and centrosomes have duplicated in preparation for mitosis.

Prophase

Chromosomes are duplicated. Centrosomes begin moving apart; nuclear envelope is fragmenting and nucleolus will disappear.

Prometaphase

Spindle is in process of forming, and kinetochores of chromosomes are attaching to kinetochore spindle fibers.

Figure 9.3 Phases of mitosis in animal cells.

Prometaphase

As *prometaphase* begins, the spindle consists of poles, asters, and fibers, which are bundles of parallel microtubules. An important event during prometaphase is the attachment of the chromosomes to the spindle and their movement as they align at the metaphase plate (equator) of the spindle. The kinetochores of sister chromatids capture spindle fibers coming from opposite poles. Such spindle fibers are called *kinetochore spindle fibers.* In response to attachment by first one kinetochore and then the other, a chromosome moves first toward one pole and then toward the other until the chromosome is aligned at the metaphase plate of the spindle.

Metaphase

During *metaphase,* the chromosomes, attached to kinetochore fibers, are aligned at the metaphase plate. There are many nonattached spindle fibers called *polar spindle fibers,* some of which reach beyond the metaphase plate and overlap.

Anaphase

At the start of *anaphase,* the two sister chromatids of each duplicated chromosome separate at the centromere, giving rise to two daughter chromosomes. Daughter chromosomes, each with a centromere and single chromatid, begin to move toward opposite poles. What accounts for the movement of the daughter chromosomes? First, the polar spindle fibers lengthen as they slide past one another. Second, the kinetochore spindle fibers disassemble at the region of the kinetochores, and this pulls the daughter chromosomes to the poles.

Telophase

During *telophase,* the spindle disappears as new nuclear envelopes form around the daughter chromosomes. Each daughter nucleus contains the same number and kinds of chromosomes as the original parent cell. Remnants of the polar spindle fibers are still visible between the two nuclei.

The chromosomes become more diffuse chromatin once again, and a nucleolus appears in each daughter nucleus. Cytokinesis is nearly complete, and soon there will be two individual daughter cells, each with a nucleus that contains the diploid number of chromosomes.

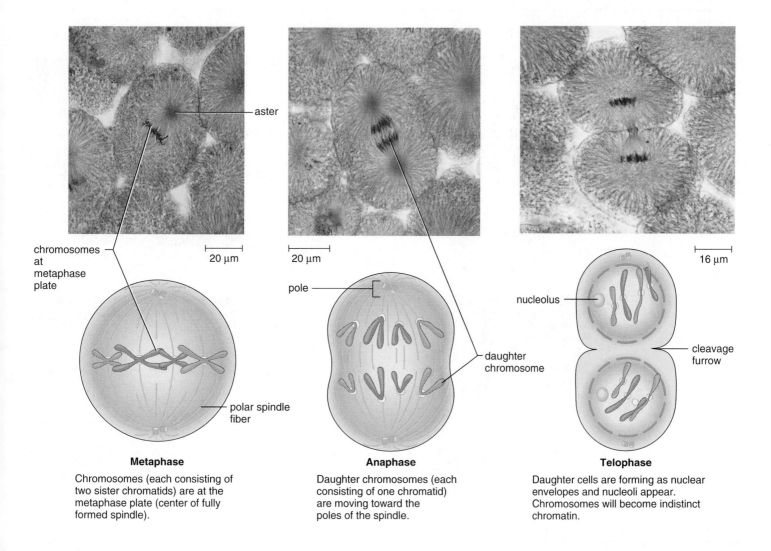

aster

chromosomes at metaphase plate

20 μm

20 μm

16 μm

pole

nucleolus

polar spindle fiber

daughter chromosome

cleavage furrow

Metaphase

Chromosomes (each consisting of two sister chromatids) are at the metaphase plate (center of fully formed spindle).

Anaphase

Daughter chromosomes (each consisting of one chromatid) are moving toward the poles of the spindle.

Telophase

Daughter cells are forming as nuclear envelopes and nucleoli appear. Chromosomes will become indistinct chromatin.

Mitosis in Plant Cells

As with animal cells, mitosis in plant cells permits growth and repair. A certain type of plant tissue, called meristematic tissue, retains the ability to divide throughout the life of a plant. Root tip and shoot tip meristematic tissue allows these structures to increase in length. Lateral meristem accounts for the ability of trees to widen their girth.

　　Figure 9.4 illustrates mitosis in plant cells. Note that there are exactly the same stages in plant cells as in animal cells. During prophase, the chromatin condenses into scattered previously duplicated chromosomes and the spindle forms; during prometaphase (not illustrated), chromosomes attach to spindle fibers; during metaphase, the chromosomes are at the metaphase plate of the spindle; during anaphase, the daughter chromosomes move to the poles of the spindle; and during telophase, cytokinesis begins. Although plant cells have a centrosome and spindle, there are no centrioles nor asters during cell division.

Mitosis in plant and animal cells ensures the daughter cells receive the same number and kinds of chromosomes as the parent cell.

Cytokinesis in Plant and Animal Cells

Cytokinesis, or cytoplasmic cleavage, usually accompanies mitosis. By the end of mitosis each newly forming cell has received a share of the cytoplasmic organelles which duplicated during interphase. Division of the cytoplasm begins in anaphase, continues in telophase, but does not reach completion until the following interphase begins.

Cytokinesis in Plant Cells

Cytokinesis in plant cells occurs by a process different from that seen in animal cells (Fig. 9.5). The rigid cell wall that surrounds plant cells does not permit cytokinesis by furrowing. Instead, the Golgi apparatus, a membranous organelle in cells, produces membranous sacs called vesicles, which move along microtubules to the midpoint between the two daughter nuclei. These vesicles fuse, forming a **cell plate.** Their membrane completes the plasma membrane for both cells. They also release molecules that signal the formation of plant cell walls, which are strengthened by the addition of cellulose fibrils.

A spindle forms during mitosis in plant cells, but there are no centrioles or asters. Cytokinesis in plant cells involves the formation of a cell plate.

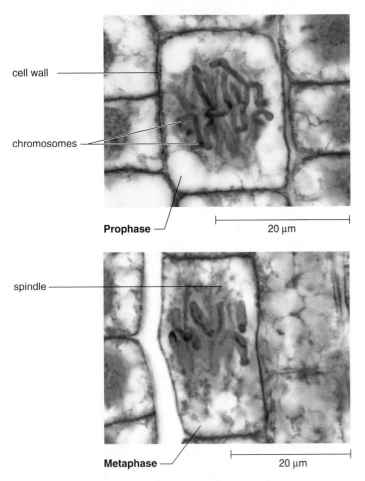

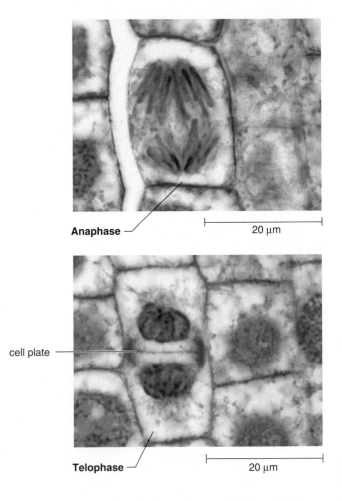

Figure 9.4 **Phases of mitosis in plant cells.**
Note the absence of centrioles and asters and the presence of the cell wall. In telophase, a cell plate develops between the two daughter cells. The cell plate marks the boundary of the new daughter cells, where new plasma membrane and a new cell wall will form for each cell.

Cytokinesis in Animal Cells

In animal cells, a cleavage furrow, which is an indentation of the membrane between the two daughter nuclei, begins as anaphase draws to a close. The cleavage furrow deepens when a band of actin filaments, called the contractile ring, slowly forms a constriction between the two daughter cells. The action of the contractile ring can be likened to pulling a drawstring ever tighter about the middle of a balloon. As the drawstring is pulled tight, the balloon constricts in the middle.

A narrow bridge between the two cells can be seen during telophase, and then the contractile ring continues to separate the cytoplasm until there are two independent daughter cells (Fig. 9.6).

Cytokinesis in animal cells is accomplished by a furrowing process.

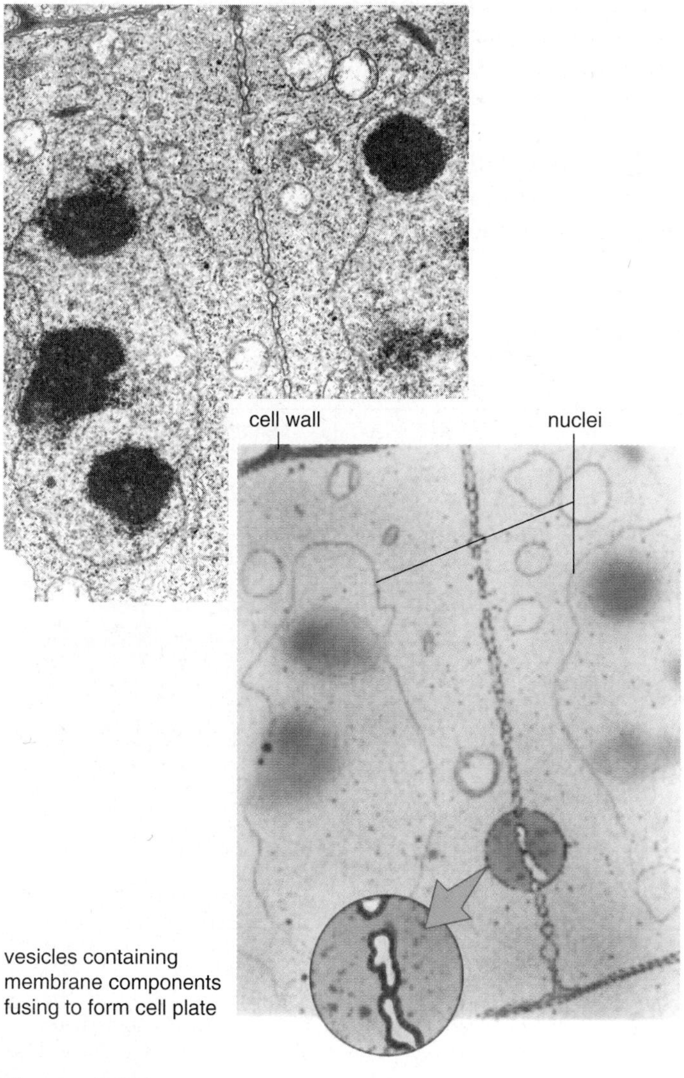

Cell Division in Other Eukaryotic Organisms

Protists and fungi also undergo mitosis and cytokinesis. In fungi and some groups of protists the nuclear envelope does not fragment. It's possible that the first role of microtubules was to support the nuclear envelope during mitosis, and only later did microtubules become attached to the chromosomes themselves. When mitosis is complete in these protists and fungi, the nuclear envelope divides and one nucleus goes to each daughter cell.

In plants and animals, as we have seen, the nuclear envelope fragments and plays no role in mitosis and cytokinesis.

The cells of all organisms divide and new cells only come from preexisting cells. This is a tenet of the cell theory.

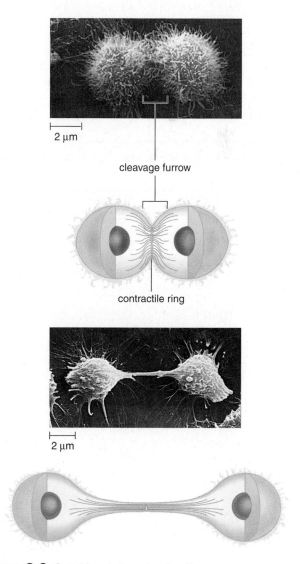

Figure 9.6 Cytokinesis in animal cells.
A single cell becomes two cells by a furrowing process. A contractile ring composed of actin filaments gradually gets smaller, and the cleavage furrow pinches the cell into two cells.

Figure 9.5 Cytokinesis in plant cells.
During cytokinesis in a plant cell, a cell plate forms midway between two daughter nuclei and extends to the plasma membrane.

9.3 How Eukaryotic Cells Cycle

By the 1870s, microscopy could provide detailed and accurate descriptions of chromosomal movements during mitosis, but there was no knowledge of cellular events between divisions. Because there was little visible activity between divisions, this period of time was dismissed as a resting state termed **interphase** [L. *inter*, between, and Gk. *phasis*, appearance]. When it was discovered in the 1950s that DNA replication occurs during interphase, the **cell cycle** concept was proposed.

Cells grow and divide during a cycle that has four stages (Fig. 9.7). The entire cell division stage, including both mitosis and cytokinesis, is termed the *M stage* (M = mitosis). The period of DNA synthesis when replication occurs is termed the *S stage* (S = synthesis) of the cycle. The proteins associated with DNA in eukaryotic chromosomes are also synthesized during this stage. There are two other stages of the cycle. The period of time prior to the S stage is termed the *G₁ stage*, and the period of time prior to the M stage is termed the *G₂ stage*. At first, not much was known about these stages, and they were thought of as G = gap stages. Now we know that during the G_1 stage, the cell grows in size and the cellular organelles increase in number. During the G_2 stage, various metabolic events occur in preparation for mitosis. Some biologists today prefer the designation G = growth for these two G stages. In any case, interphase consists of G_1, S, and G_2 stages.

Cells undergo a cycle that includes the G_1, S, G_2, and M stages.

The Cell-Cycle Clock

Some cells, such as skin cells, divide continuously throughout the life of the organism. Other cells, such as skeletal muscle cells and nerve cells, are arrested in the G_1 stage. If the nucleus from one of these cells is placed in the cytoplasm of an S-stage cell, it finishes the cell cycle. Cardiac muscle cells are arrested in the G_2 stage. If an arrested cell is fused with a cell undergoing mitosis, it too starts to undergo mitosis. It appears, then, that there are stimulatory substances that cause the cell to proceed through two critical checkpoints:

$$G_1 \text{ stage} \rightarrow S \text{ stage}$$
$$G_2 \text{ stage} \rightarrow M \text{ stage}$$

Over the past few years biologists have made remarkable progress in identifying the proteins that cause a cell to move from the G_1 stage to the S stage and the proteins that cause a cell to move from the G_2 stage to the M stage. Some of these biologists worked with frog eggs, others with yeast cells, and still others used cell cultures as their experimental material. The researchers identified two types of proteins of interest—kinases and cyclins. A **kinase** is an enzyme that removes a phosphate group from ATP (the form of chemical energy used by cells) and adds it to a protein. Activation by a kinase is a common way for cells to turn on a cellular process, but it turned out that the kinases involved in the cell cycle are themselves activated when they combine with a protein called cyclin. **Cyclins** are so named because their quantity is not constant in the cell.

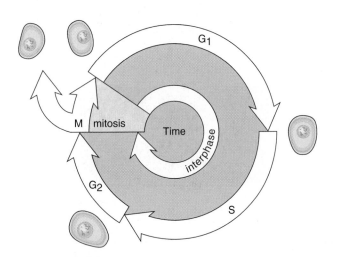

Stage	Main Events	Length of time (hours)	
		Vicia faba	*Homo sapiens* (cultured fibroblasts)
G_1	Organelles begin to double in number	4.9	6.3
S	Replication of DNA	7.5	7.0
G_2	Synthesis of proteins	4.9	2.0
M	Mitosis	2.0	0.7
	Total:	19.3	16.0

Figure 9.7 The cell cycle.
Cells go through a cycle that consists of four stages (G_1, S for synthesis, G_2, and M for mitosis). The length of the different stages varies both among species and among different cell types in the same individual. The approximate lengths of the phases for the broad bean (*Vicia faba*) and humans (*Homo sapiens*) are given.

Figure 9.8 is an illustration that shows the process in a clockwise diagram. After S-kinase combines with S-cyclin, the kinase phosphorylates a protein that causes the cell to move from the G_1 stage to the S stage when DNA is synthesized (replicated). Then, S-cyclin is destroyed, and S-kinase is no longer active.

Similarly, after M-kinase combines with M-cyclin, the kinase phosphorylates a protein that causes the cell to move from the G_2 stage to the M stage when mitosis occurs. Three things occur: (1) chromosomes condense, (2) the nuclear envelope disassembles, and (3) the spindle forms. Now M-cyclin is destroyed.

Until recently, the mechanics of the cell cycle and the causes of cancer were thought to be distantly related. Now they are known to be intimately related. For example, oncogenes are cancer-causing genes, and it is possible that they control genes that code for cyclins that no longer function as they should. Growth factors are molecules that attach to plasma membrane receptors and thereby bring about cell growth. Ordinarily, a cyclin might combine with its kinase only when a growth factor is present. But a cyclin that has gone awry might combine with its kinase even when a growth factor is not present. The result would be uncontrolled cell growth as seen in cancer. On the other hand, tumor-suppressor genes usually function to prevent cancer from occurring. It has been shown that the product of one major tumor-suppressor gene (*p53*) brings about the production of a protein that can combine with a cyclin so that a kinase never attaches to it. In this way *p53* is instrumental in stopping the cell cycle. The next section discusses in greater detail the role of *p53* in preventing the development of cancer.

Kinases activated by combination with a cyclin at two critical checkpoints in the cell cycle phosphorylate a protein, and this triggers the beginning of the S stage and the M stage.

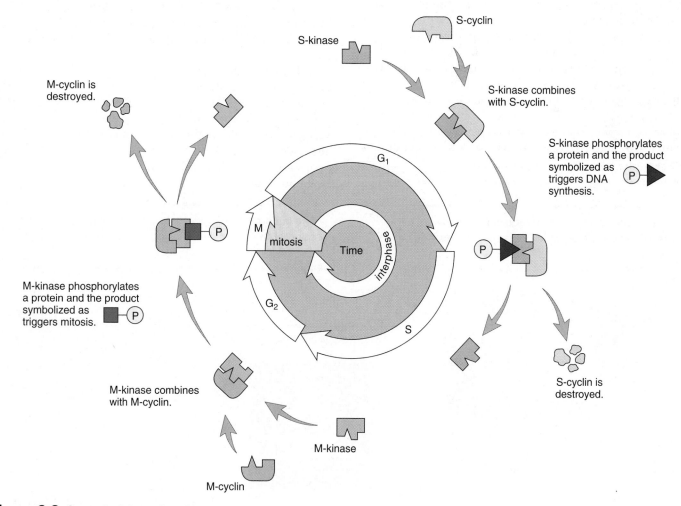

Figure 9.8 Control of the cell cycle.
At two critical checkpoints a kinase combines with a cyclin, and this moves the cell cycle forward. When the kinases phosphorylate proteins, the proteins are activated and produce effects appropriate to the particular stage. At the start of the S stage, S-kinase combines with S-cyclin, then synthesis (replication) of DNA takes place. At the start of the M stage, M-kinase combines with M-cyclin. Then mitosis occurs.

152

9.4 How Cancer Develops

Carcinogenesis is the development of cancer. **Cancer** is a genetic disease requiring a series of mutations, each propelling cells toward the development of a **tumor** [L. *tumor*, swelling], an abnormal mass of cells. The presence of a tumor indicates a failure in cell division control—a failure that is quite often due to a faulty *p53* gene. The *p53* **gene** ordinarily halts the cell cycle when DNA mutates and is in need of repair (Fig. 9.9). Why might DNA be in need of repair? DNA molecules are constantly acted on by physical and chemical agents that can cause mutations that lead to cancer. The best known mutagenic carcinogens are radiation, organic chemicals, and certain viruses. Radiation includes ultraviolet light, radon gas, X rays, and accidental emissions from nuclear power plants. Organic chemicals in tobacco smoke, certain foods, and pesticides and herbicides also bring about harmful changes in DNA molecules. A cell constantly monitors its DNA and if any agent has caused changes, repair enzymes set to work to correct the harm done. The p53 protein (the product of the *p53* gene) is involved in mobilizing repair enzymes and stopping the cell cycle while repair is going on. Only if repair is possible does the cell cycle start up again. If repair of DNA is not possible, the p53 protein promotes cell suicide, also called apoptosis. While ordinarily we think of cell death as a bad thing, it is obviously the best solution if cancer will develop otherwise.

The pivotal role of the *p53* gene is substantiated first by the observation that many different types of human cancers contain no or a faulty *p53* gene. Also, scientists have added the p53 protein to rapidly dividing cancer cells in a petri dish. The cells stopped dividing and died.

Apoptosis [Gk. *apo*, off, and *ptosis*, fall], defined as programmed cell death, is a set sequence of cellular changes involving shattering the nucleus, chopping up the chromosomes, digesting the cytoskeleton, and packaging the cellular remains into membrane-enclosed vesicles (apoptotic bodies) that can be engulfed by macrophages. The appearance of membrane blisters is a tip-off that a cell is undergoing apoptosis (Fig. 9.9).

A remarkable finding of the past few years is that cells routinely harbor the enzymes, now called caspases, that bring about apoptosis. The enzymes are ordinarily held in check by inhibitors but they can be unleashed in two ways. During human development, exterior signals cause certain cells to die, allowing paddles to be converted into fingers and toes, for example. In adults, cells that have DNA damaged beyond repair usually go ahead and kill themselves.

There are two sets of caspases. The first set are the "initiators" that receive the message to activate the "executioners," which then activate the enzymes that dismantle the cell. For example, there is an executioner that frees an endonuclease to enter the nucleus and start chopping DNA. Initiators, executioners, and dismantling enzymes all begin to work when they are clipped to make them shorter and ready for action.

Knowledge about apoptosis can possibly lead to new therapy regimens. Tumor cells, but not normal adult cells, contain high levels of a protein called survivin, which blocks apoptosis. If researchers can find a way to inactivate survivin, cancer cells might be more susceptible to radiation and chemotherapy. In Parkinson's disease and stroke, excess apoptosis may kill off brain cells. If so, inhibitors of apoptosis could be administered to keep brain cells alive.

The two cellular responses to activation of *p53* are either arrest of the cell cycle while DNA repair is going on or apoptosis.

The occurrence of apoptosis is usually essential for the good of the organism. A lack of apoptosis allows cancer to develop.

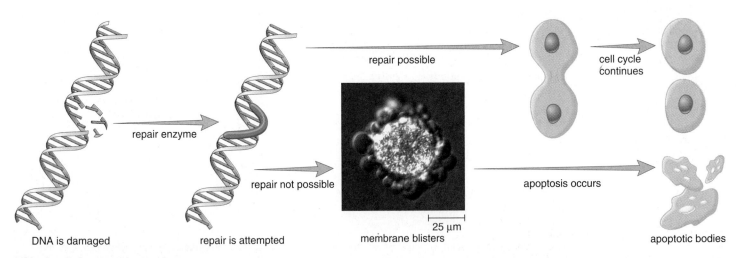

repair possible

cell cycle continues

repair enzyme

repair not possible

25 μm
membrane blisters

apoptosis occurs

DNA is damaged

repair is attempted

apoptotic bodies

Figure 9.9 Functions of *p53*.
If DNA is damaged by a mutagen, *p53* is instrumental in stopping the cell cycle and activating repair enzymes. If repair is impossible, the p53 protein promotes apoptosis.

Characteristics of Cancer Cells

Cancer cells exhibit characteristics that indicate they have experienced a severe failure in regulating the cell cycle.

Cancer Cells Lack Differentiation

Most cells are specialized; they have a specific form and function that suits them to the role they play in the body. Cancer cells are nonspecialized and do not contribute to the functioning of a body part. A cancer cell does not look like a differentiated muscle, nervous, or connective tissue cell and instead has a shape and form that is distinctly abnormal (Fig. 9.10). Normal cells can enter the cell cycle for about 50 times, and then they die. Cancer cells can enter the cell cycle repeatedly, and in this way they are immortal. In cell tissue culture, they die only because they run out of nutrients or are killed by their own toxic waste products.

Cancer Cells Have Abnormal Nuclei

The nuclei of cancer cells are enlarged, and there may be an abnormal number of chromosomes. The chromosomes have mutated; some parts may be duplicated and some may be deleted. In addition, gene amplification (extra copies of specific genes) is seen much more frequently than in normal cells.

Cancer Cells Form Tumors

Normal cells anchor themselves to a substratum or adhere to their neighbors. They exhibit contact inhibition—when they come in contact with a neighbor, they stop dividing. In culture, normal cells form a single layer that covers the bottom of a petri dish. Cancer cells have lost all restraint; they pile on top of one another and grow in multiple layers. They have a reduced need for the growth factors that are needed by normal cells.

In the body, a cancer cell divides to produce a tumor which invades and destroys neighboring tissue. This new growth, termed neoplasia, is made of cells that are disorganized, a condition termed anaplasia. A benign tumor is a disorganized, usually encapsulated, mass that does not invade adjacent tissue.

Cancer Cells Undergo Angiogenesis and Metastasis

Angiogenesis, the formation of new blood vessels, is required to bring nutrients and oxygen to a cancerous tumor whose growth is not contained within a capsule. Cancer cells release a growth factor that causes neighboring blood vessels to branch into the cancerous tissue. Some modes of cancer treatment are aimed at preventing angiogenesis from occurring.

Cancer in situ is found in its place of origin without any invasion of normal tissue. Malignancy is present when **metastasis** [Gk. *meta*, between, and L. *stasis*, standing, a position] establishes new tumors that are distant from the primary tumor. To accomplish metastasis, cancer cells must first make their way across the extracellular matrix (substances including fibers secreted by the cell) and into a blood vessel or lymphatic vessel. It has been discovered that cancer cells have receptors that allow them to adhere to a component of the extracellular matrix; they also produce enzymes that degrade the matrix and allow them to invade underlying tissues. Cancer cells tend to be motile, have a disorganized internal cytoskeleton, and lack intact actin filament bundles. After traveling through the blood or lymph, cancer cells may then start tumors elsewhere in the body.

The patient's prognosis (probable outcome) is dependent on the degree to which the cancer has progressed: (1) whether the tumor has invaded surrounding tissues, (2) if so, whether there is any lymph node involvement, and (3) whether there are metastatic tumors in distant parts of the body. With each progressive step of the cancerous condition, the prognosis becomes less favorable.

Cancer cells are nonspecialized, have abnormal chromosomes, and divide uncontrollably. Because they are not constrained by their neighbors, they form a tumor. Then they metastasize, forming new tumors wherever they relocate.

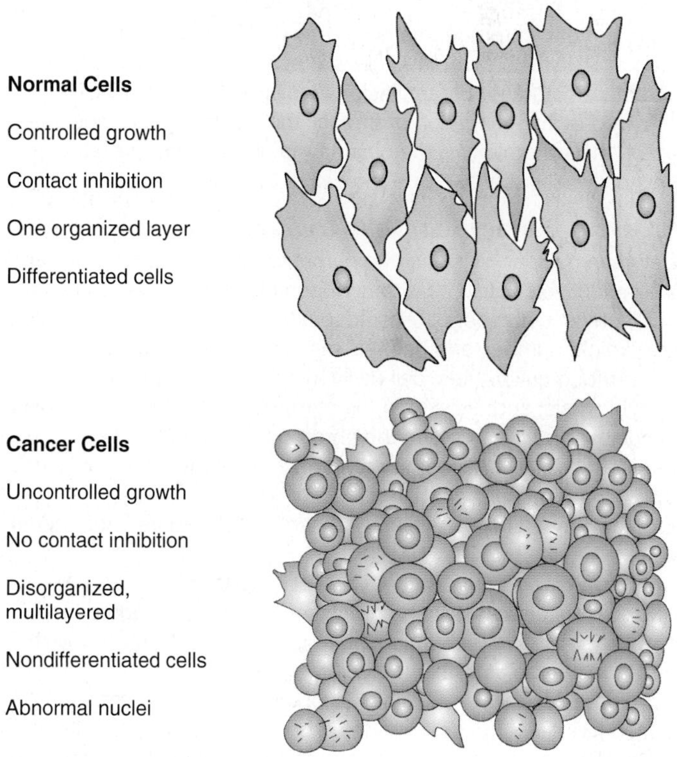

Normal Cells

Controlled growth

Contact inhibition

One organized layer

Differentiated cells

Cancer Cells

Uncontrolled growth

No contact inhibition

Disorganized, multilayered

Nondifferentiated cells

Abnormal nuclei

Figure 9.10 Cancer cells.
Cancer cells differ from normal cells in the ways noted.

Prevention of Cancer

As mentioned, certain environmental agents, such as radiation and certain organic chemicals and certain viruses are known to be carcinogenic. Prevention of cancer includes avoiding these agents whenever possible. Early detection is also important. For women, routine screening tests for cancer include: Pap smear, mammogram, and breast self-exam.

Men should do a self-exam for testicular cancer. For colon cancer detection, there is a stool blood test that can be initiated at home and a physician can examine the colon for growths in his or her office.

Of interest to most is the discovery that diet can protect us from developing cancer. Fresh fruits and vegetables in the cabbage family have been found to be especially protective.

Connecting Concepts

Cells have an elaborate internal structure that is not revealed by use of the light microscope and complex enzymatic pathways that can only be discovered by biochemical analyses. Similarly, the process of cell division is more complicated than it first appears. We now know that cell division is a part of a tightly regulated cell cycle and there are negative consequences if the cell cycle should come out of sync. In humans, overproduction of skin cells due to an overstimulated cell cycle produces a chronic inflammatory condition known as psoriasis. In a rare condition

called progeria, the reproductive capacity of all the body's cells is severely diminished and young people grow old and die at an early age. Many different types of cancer can result when the signals that keep the cell cycle in check are not transmitted or received properly. The hope is that if we learn to control the cell cycle, these conditions will be curable one day.

The newfound ability to clone farm animals from single adult cells shows that we are now able to initiate and control the process of cell division even in mammals.

Tissue engineering during which organs are formed in the laboratory, as discussed in chapter 17, is an even better example that we can now manipulate the cell cycle.

The end product of ordinary cell division (i.e., mitosis) is two new cells, each with the same number and kinds of chromosomes as the parent cell. But what about the special type of cell division (i.e., meiosis) that produces the sex cells—sperm and egg? As we'll see in the next chapter, following meiosis, the sex cells have only half the chromosome number.

Summary

9.1 How Prokaryotic Cells Divide

A prokaryotic chromosome has a few proteins and a single, long loop of DNA. The chromosome is attached to the inside of the plasma membrane. Binary fission involves replication of DNA, followed by an elongation of the cell that pulls the chromosomes apart. Inward growth of the plasma membrane and formation of new cell wall material divide the cell in two.

9.2 How Eukaryotic Cells Divide

Between nuclear divisions, the chromosomes are not distinct and are collectively called chromatin. Each eukaryotic species has a characteristic number of chromosomes. The total number is called the diploid number, and half this number is the haploid number.

Among eukaryotes, cell division involves nuclear division (karyokinesis) and division of the cytoplasm (cytokinesis). Mitosis is nuclear division in which the chromosome number stays constant because each chromosome is duplicated and gives rise to two daughter chromosomes.

Mitosis has five phases, which are described here for animal cells.

Prophase—duplicated chromosomes are distinct, the nucleolus is disappearing, the nuclear envelope is fragmenting, and the spindle is forming between centrosomes. Asters radiate from the centrioles within the centrosomes.

Prometaphase—the kinetochores of sister chromatids attach to kinetochore spindle fibers extending from opposite poles. The chromosomes move back and forth until they are aligned at the metaphase plate.

Metaphase—the spindle is fully formed and the duplicated chromosomes are aligned at the metaphase plate. The spindle consists of polar spindle fibers that overlap at the metaphase plate and kinetochore spindle fibers that are attached to chromosomes.

Anaphase—daughter chromosomes move toward the poles. The polar spindle fibers slide past one another and the kinetochore spindle fibers disassemble. Cytokinesis by furrowing begins.

Telophase—nuclear envelopes re-form, chromosomes begin changing back to chromatin, the nucleoli reappear, and the spindle disappears.

Plant cells lack centrioles and, therefore, asters. Even so, the mitotic spindle forms and the same five mitotic phases are observed.

Cytokinesis in plant cells involves the formation of a cell plate from which the plasma membrane and cell wall are completed. Cytokinesis in animal cells is a furrowing process that divides the cytoplasm.

9.3 How Eukaryotic Cells Cycle

The cell cycle has four stages. During the G_1 stage the organelles increase in number; during the S stage, DNA replication occurs; during the G_2 stage, various proteins are synthesized; and during the M stage, mitosis occurs. Interphase consists of G_1, S, and G_2 stages.

Biologists have made great strides in understanding how the cell cycle is controlled. Kinases activated when they combine with cyclins phosphorylate proteins that trigger passage from the G_1 to the S stage, and the passage from the G_2 stage to the M stage.

9.4 How Cancer Develops

The gene *p53* ordinarily stops the cell cycle whenever DNA repair is needed to prevent harmful mutations. If repair is impossible, *p53* directs apoptosis, programmed cell death, to occur. Quite often when cancer occurs, *p53* is absent or nonfunctional.

The cell routinely contains the enzymes, called caspases, which bring about apoptosis. The initiator caspases are usually held in check by inhibitors, but when set in motion they activate executioner caspases which activate the cellular enzymes that destroy the cell. These enzymes shatter the nucleus, chop up the chromosomes, digest the cytoskeleton, cause membrane blisters, and package the cell in vesicles for absorption by macrophages.

Cancer cells are nondifferentiated, divide repeatedly, have abnormal nuclei, do not require growth factors, and are not constrained by their neighbors. After forming a tumor, cancer cells metastasize and start new tumors elsewhere in the body. Certain behaviors such as avoiding unnecessary radiation (e.g., solar radiation), exposure to certain organic chemicals (e.g., tobacco smoke), and adopting a diet rich in fruits and vegetables is protective against the development of cancer.

Reviewing the Chapter

1. Describe the prokaryotic chromosome and the process of binary fission.   144
2. Describe the eukaryotic chromosome and the significance of the duplicated chromosome.   145
3. Define the following words: chromosome, chromatin, chromatid, centriole, cytokinesis, centromere, and kinetochore.   144–46
4. Describe the events that occur during the phases of mitosis.   146–47
5. How does plant cell mitosis differ from animal cell mitosis?   148
6. Contrast cytokinesis in plant cells and animal cells.   148–49
7. Describe the cell cycle, including a description of interphase.   150
8. How are the two critical checkpoints in the cell cycle controlled?   150
9. What role does the *p53* gene play in the development of cancer?   152
10. Describe the process of apoptosis and how it is controlled. 152
11. List and discuss four characteristics of cancer cells that distinguish them from normal cells.   153

Testing Yourself

Choose the best answer for each question.

1. What feature in prokaryotes substitutes for the spindle action in eukaryotes?
   a. centrioles with asters
   b. fission instead of cytokinesis
   c. elongation of plasma membrane
   d. looped DNA
   e. presence of one chromosome
2. How does a prokaryotic chromosome differ from a eukaryotic chromosome? A prokaryotic chromosome
   a. is shorter and fatter.
   b. has a single loop of DNA.
   c. never replicates.
   d. contains many histones.
   e. All of these are correct.
3. The diploid number of chromosomes
   a. is the 2n number.
   b. is in a parent cell and therefore in the two daughter cells following mitosis.
   c. varies according to the particular organism.
   d. is in every somatic cell.
   e. All of these are correct.

For questions 4–6, match the descriptions that follow to the terms in the key.

Key:
   a. centriole
   b. chromatid
   c. chromosome
   d. centromere
   e. cyclin

4. point of attachment for sister chromatids
5. found at a pole in the center of an aster
6. coiled and condensed chromatin
7. If a parent cell has fourteen chromosomes prior to mitosis, how many chromosomes will each daughter cell have?
   a. twenty-eight because each chromatid is a chromosome
   b. fourteen because the chromatids separate
   c. seven only after mitosis is finished
   d. any number between seven and twenty-eight
   e. seven in the nucleus and seven in the cytoplasm, for a total of fourteen
8. In which phase of mitosis are the chromosomes moving toward the poles?
   a. prophase
   b prometaphase
   c. metaphase
   d. anaphase
   e. telophase
9. Interphase
   a. is the same as prophase, metaphase, anaphase, and telophase.
   b. includes stages G_1, S, and G_2.
   c. requires the use of polar spindle fibers and kinetochore spindle fibers.
   d. is a stage in the cell cycle.
   e. Both b and d are correct.
10. Cytokinesis
   a. is mitosis in plants.
   b. requires the formation of a cell plate in plant cells.
   c. is the longest part of the cell cycle.
   d. is half a chromosome.
   e. is a form of apoptosis.
11. When cancer occurs,
   a. mutations have occurred.
   b. the gene *p53* is operational.
   c. apoptosis has occurred.
   d. the cells can no longer enter the cell cycle.
   e. All of these are correct.
12. Label this diagram of a cell in prophase of mitosis.

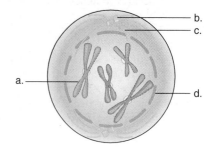

Thinking Scientifically

1. After DNA is duplicated in eukaryotes it must be bound to histone proteins. This requires the synthesis of hundreds of millions of new protein molecules, a process that the cell most likely regulates. With reference to Figure 9.8, when in the cell cycle would histones be made? At what point might histone synthesis be switched on and off?

2. When animal cells are grown in dishes in the laboratory most divide a few dozen times and then die. It would seem likely that the cell cycle is suddenly not functioning properly. With the help of Figure 9.8, hypothesize what could be wrong with the regulation of the cell cycle to turn it off.

Bioethical Issue

Turn on the television news or talk shows, or read a paper, and you're bound to hear about the latest research on breast cancer. Long overlooked as a disease, breast cancer is now winning national attention as a major factor in women's health. That, undoubtedly, is good. But attention tends to focus on one thing, at the expense of others. Some people suggest breast cancer has stolen the spotlight, leaving out prostate, liver, or stomach cancer, which also are deadly forms of cancer.

How should the nation prioritize cancer research? Is it fair that one form of the disease tends to dominate the news? Should attention focus on diseases that affect the highest number of people—or diseases that are most deadly? And how should research funding be allocated among cancers that affect only women or only men?

Understanding the Terms

apoptosis 152	cytokinesis 145
asexual reproduction 144	diploid (2n) number 145
aster 146	haploid (n) number 145
binary fission 144	interphase 150
cancer 152	kinase 150
cell cycle 150	metastasis 153
cell plate 148	mitosis 145
centriole 146	nucleoid 144
centromere 145	*p53* gene 152
centrosome 144, 146	sister chromatid 145
chromatin 145	spindle 146
chromosome 144	tumor 152
cyclin 150	

Match the terms to these definitions:

a. _____ Central microtubule organizing center of cells consisting of granular material. In animal cells, it contains two centrioles.

b. _____ Constriction where sister chromatids of a chromosome are held together.

c. _____ Microtubule structure that brings about chromosome movement during nuclear division.

d. _____ One of two genetically identical chromosome units that are the result of DNA replication.

e. _____ Programmed cell death that is carried out by enzymes routinely present in the cell.

Web Connections

Exploring the Internet

http://www.mhhe.com/biosci/genbio/mader
(click on *Biology 7/e*)

The *Biology 7/e* Online Learning Center provides many resources for studying the material in this chapter including links to the following sites:

Cell Division: Binary Fission and Mitosis contains an excellent review of these topics, including color diagrams of the cell cycle, prokaryotic and eukaryotic modes of cell division, and the phases of mitosis. Great links to other sites.

http://gened.emc.maricopa.edu/bio/bio181/BIOBK/BioBookmito.html

The McGill University Mitosis Page is another great site that describes mitosis and includes full color micrographs and downloadable video and diagrams.

http://www.mcgill.ca/nrs/mitosis.htm

Mitosis. Photomicrographs and text description of mitosis in an animal cell.

http://clab.cecil.cc.md.us/faculty/biology1/mitosis.htm

Onion Root Tip Mitosis

http://biog-101-104.bio.cornell.edu/BioG101_104/tutorials/
cell_division/onion_review.html

and

Whitefish Blastula Mitosis; nice photomicrographs of all phases of mitosis.

http://biog-101-104.bio.cornell.edu/BioG101_104/tutorials/
cell_division/wf_review.html

And for a fun review of the subject:

Mitosis and Meiosis; an interactive review. Click on a cell and identify the phase of mitosis seen.

http://www.mssc.edu/biology/B101/biolab6.htm

and

Word Search Puzzle: find terms related to mitosis in the puzzle, and unscramble other words.

http://copland.udel.edu/~april/mitosis.html

Further Readings Part I

Alberts, B., et al. 1998. *Essential cell biology.* New York: Garland Publishing, Inc. This is an introductory molecular biology text.

Armbruster, P., and Hessberger, F. P. September 1998. Making new elements. *Scientific American* 279(3):72. The process of creating new artificial elements is examined.

Bayley, H. September 1997. Building doors into cells. *Scientific American* 277(3):62. Protein engineers are designing artificial pores for drug delivery.

Braun, V. December 18, 1998. Pumping iron through cell membranes. *Science* 282(5397):2202. Gated protein channels allow ions and small molecules to flow across a cell membrane in a regulated way.

Caret, R. L., et al. 1997. *Principles and applications of organic and biological chemistry.* 2d ed. Dubuque, Ia.: Wm. C. Brown Publishers. For undergraduates, this text emphasizes material unique to health-related studies.

Chang, R. 1998. *Chemistry.* 6th ed. Dubuque, Ia.: McGraw-Hill. This general chemistry text provides a foundation in chemical concepts and principles, and presents topics clearly.

Chapman, C. 1999. *Basic chemistry for biology.* 2d ed. Dubuque, Ia.: WCB/McGraw-Hill. The goal of this workbook is to provide a review of basic principles for biology students.

Cooper, G. M. 1997. *The cell: A molecular approach.* Sunderland, Mass.: Sinauer Associates, Inc. This text is for those beginning coursework in cell and molecular biology.

Ferber, D. January 8, 1999. Immortalized cells seem cancer-free so far. *Science* 283(5399):154. The gene for telomerase has been added to cells to make them "immortal"; perhaps these immortal cells might be used for cell replacement.

Flannery, M. February 1999. Proteins: The unfolding- and folding-picture. *American Biology Teacher* 61(2):150. Various proteins and protein-folding are discussed in depth.

Ford, B. J. April 1998. The earliest views. *Scientific American* 278(4):50. Presents experiments of early microscopists.

Foyer, C., and Noctor, G. April 23, 1999. Leaves in the dark see light. *Science* 284(5414):599. Excess light may be dangerous to plants because it can cause persistent decreases in rates of photosynthesis.

Frank, J. September/October 1998. How the ribosome works. *American Scientist* 86(5):428. New imaging techniques using cryo-electron microscopy allows researchers to study a three-dimensional map of the ribosome.

Gerstein, M., and Levitt, M. November 1998. Simulating water and the molecules of life. *Scientific American* 279(5):100. Computer models show how water affects the structure and movement of proteins and other biological molecules.

Gibson, A. November 1998. Photosynthetic organs of desert plants. *BioScience* 48(11):911. The structure of nonsucculent desert plants casts doubt on the view that saving water is their key strategy.

Ingber, D. E. January 1998. The architecture of life. *Scientific American* 278(1):48. Simple mechanical rules may govern cell movements, tissue organization, and organ development.

Krauskopf, S. January 1999. Doing the meiosis shuffle. *American Biology Teacher* 61(1):60. A playing card demonstration walks students through the stages of meiosis.

Lang, F., and Waldegger, S. September/October 1997. Regulating cell volume. *American Scientist* 85(5):456. Changes in cell volume may threaten organ or tissue function.

Nemecek, S. October 1997. Gotta know when to fold 'em. *Scientific American* 277(4):28. Details about how proteins fold are discussed.

Nurse, P., et al. October 1998. Understanding the cell cycle. *Nature Medicine* 4(1):1103. Article discusses the relevance of cell-cycle research.

Ojcius, D. M., et al. January/February 1998. Pore-forming proteins. *Science & Medicine* 5(1):44. Peptide molecules that cause pore formation in membranes are similar in structure and function.

Palazzo, R. E. March/April 1999. The centrosome. *Science & Medicine* 6(2):32. Article discusses centrosomal research.

Pennisi, E. February 5, 1999. Trigger for centrosome replication found. *Science* 283(5403):770. An enzyme called Cdk2 helps tell the dividing cell to copy its centrosome.

Pennisi, E. May 21, 1999. Nuclear transport protein does double duty in mitosis. *Science* 284(5418):1260. A protein called Ran, which plays a key role in nuclear transport, also triggers cell division.

Ross, F. C. 1997. *Foundation of allied health sciences: An introduction to chemistry and cell biology.* Dubuque, Ia.: Wm. C. Brown Publishers. This introductory text provides the background necessary for students in allied health sciences.

Scerri, E. R. November/December 1997. The periodic table and the electron. *American Scientist* 85(6):546. Electron configurations may only give an approximate explanation of the periodic table.

Scerri, E. R. September 1998. The evolution of the periodic system. *Scientific American* 279(3):78. Article discusses the history and evolution of the periodic table.

Schwartz, A. T., et al. 1997. *Chemistry in context: Applying chemistry to society.* 2d ed. Dubuque, Ia.: Wm. C. Brown Publishers. This introductory text is designed for students in the allied health fields.

Science 283(5407):1475. March 5, 1999. An entire section is devoted to topics involving mitochondria.

Sperelakis, N., editor. 1998. *Cell physiology source book.* 2d ed. San Diego: Academic Press. For advanced biology students, this is a comprehensive and authoritative text covering topics in cell physiology written by experts in the field.

Szalai, V. A., and Bridvig, G. W. November/December 1998. How plants produce dioxygen. *American Scientist* 86(6):542. Oxygen production through photosynthesis occurs in a manganese-containing complex in chloroplast membranes.

Zubay, G. L. 1998. *Biochemistry.* 4th ed. Dubuque, Ia.: Wm. C. Brown Publishers. This text for chemistry majors relates biochemistry to cell biology, physiology, and genetics.

part

ii Genetic Basis of Life

Hereditary information is stored in DNA, molecules that compose the genes located within chromosomes. A special form of cell division causes sex cells to have half the usual number of chromosomes. Fertilization gives the zygote the full number of chromosomes.

Principles of inheritance include those that allow us to predict the chances that an offspring will inherit a particular characteristic from one of the parents. These principles have been applied to the breeding of plants and animals and the study of human genetic disorders. But to go further, and to control an organism's characteristics, it is necessary to understand how DNA and RNA function in protein synthesis. The human endeavor known as biotechnology is based on our newfound knowledge of nucleic acid structure and function.

The principles of inheritance are central to understanding many other topics in biology—from the evolution and diversity of life to the reproduction and development of organisms.

Meiosis and Sexual Reproduction

chapter

One sperm out of many fertilizes an egg.

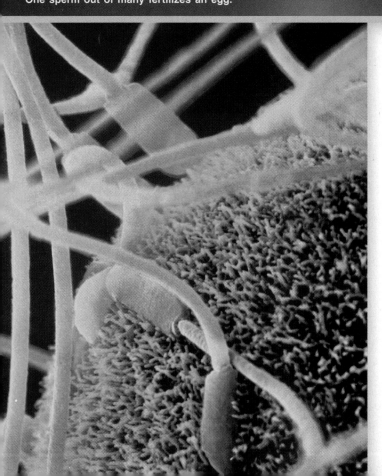

Think about what the sex act accomplishes—a sperm fertilizes an egg and a new individual begins life. The egg and sperm have to have half the number of chromosomes or else the chromosome number would double with each new generation. The production of reproductive cells also ensures that the next generation is populated with offspring that are genetically different from their parents and from each other.

During meiosis, the type of nuclear division involved in reproductive cell production, chromosome pairs come together. They often swap segments with each other producing different combination of genes on the chromosomes. Then, the reproductive cells receive only one of each kind of chromosome in all possible combinations. Finally, the sperm and egg that join during fertilization are usually from two different individuals and, if so, genetic recombination is bound to occur.

While asexual reproduction produces offspring that are identical to the single parent; sexual reproduction introduces genetic variability. In this way, sexual reproduction contributes to the process of evolution, especially if the environment is changing.

chapter 10

10.1 Halving the Chromosome Number

In sexually reproducing organisms, **meiosis** [Gk. *mio*, less, and *-sis*, act or process of] is the type of nuclear division that reduces the chromosome number from the diploid (2n) number [Gk. *diplos*, twofold, and *-eides*, like] to the haploid (n) number. The **haploid (n) number** [Gk. *haplos*, single, and *-eides*, like] of chromosomes is half the diploid number. **Gametes** (reproductive cells, often the sperm and egg) always have the haploid number of chromosomes. Gamete formation and then fusion of gametes to form a cell called a zygote are integral parts of **sexual reproduction.** A **zygote** always has the full or **diploid (2n) number** of chromosomes. In animals the zygote undergoes development to become the adult animal.

Obviously, if the gametes contained the same number of chromosomes as the body cells, the number of chromosomes would double with each new generation. Within a few generations, the cells of an animal would be nothing but chromosomes! The early cytologists (biologists who study cells) realized this, and Pierre-Joseph van Beneden, a Belgian, was gratified to find in 1883 that the sperm and the egg of the worm *Ascaris* each contained only two chromosomes, while the zygote and subsequent embryonic cells always have four chromosomes.

Homologous Pairs of Chromosomes

In diploid body cells, the chromosomes occur in pairs. Notice in Figure 10.1*a*, a pictorial display of human chromosomes, the chromosomes have been arranged according to pairs. The members of each pair are called **homologous chromosomes** or **homologues** [Gk. *homologos*, agreeing, cor-responding]. The homologues look alike; they have the same length and centromere position. When stained, homologues have a similar banding pattern because they contain genes for the same traits. Although homologous chromosomes may have genes for the same traits such as finger length; the gene on one homologue may be for short fingers and the gene at the same location on the other homologue may be for long fingers.

The chromosomes in Figure 10.1*a* are duplicated as they would be just before nuclear division. Recall that during the S stage of the cell cycle, DNA replicates and the chromosomes become duplicated. The results of the duplication process are depicted in Figure 10.1*b*. When duplicated, a chromosome is composed of two identical parts called sister chromatids. The sister chromatids are held together at a region called the centromere.

Why does the zygote have two chromosomes of each kind? One member of a homologous pair was inherited from the male parent and the other was inherited from the female parent by way of the gametes. In Figure 10.1*b*, and throughout the chapter, the paternal chromosome is colored blue and the maternal chromosome is colored red. *Therefore, you should use size and centromere location to recognize homologues and not color.* We will see that while body cells contain two chromosomes of each kind, the gametes contain only one chromosome of each kind—derived from either the paternal or maternal homologue.

The zygote, which is always diploid, contains homologous chromosomes. Gametes are haploid due to meiosis, the type of cell division that reduces the chromosome number.

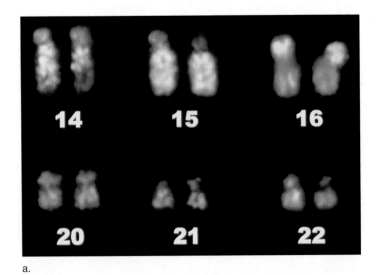

a.

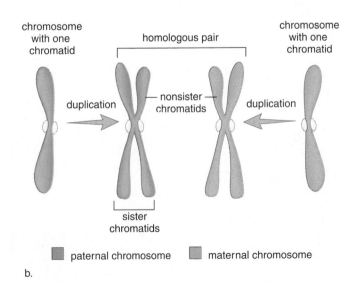

b.

Figure 10.1 Homologous chromosomes.
In a diploid body cell, the chromosomes occur in pairs called homologous chromosomes. **a.** In this micrograph of stained chromosomes from a human cell, the pairs have been numbered. **b.** These chromosomes are duplicated and each one is composed of two chromatids. The sister chromatids contain the exact same genes; the nonsister chromatids contain only genes for the same traits, like type of hair, color of eyes.

Overview of Meiosis

Meiosis requires two nuclear divisions and produces four haploid daughter cells, each having one of each kind of chromosome. Therefore, the daughter cells have half the total number of chromosomes present in the diploid parent nucleus. In this and other ways to be discussed, meiosis

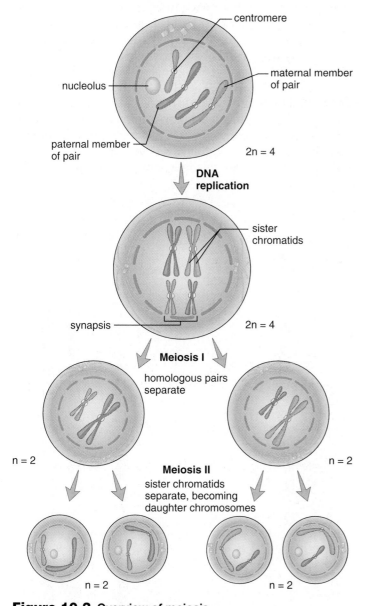

Figure 10.2 Overview of meiosis.
Following DNA replication, each chromosome is duplicated and consists of two chromatids. During meiosis I, the chromosome pairs separate, and during meiosis II, the sister chromatids of each duplicated chromosome separate. At the completion of meiosis, there are four haploid daughter cells.

ensures that offspring will have a different combination of chromosomes and genes than either parent.

Figure 10.2 presents an overview of meiosis, indicating the two cell divisions, meiosis I and meiosis II. Prior to meiosis I, DNA (deoxyribonucleic acid) replication has occurred; therefore, each chromosome has two sister chromatids. During meiosis I, something new happens that does not occur in mitosis. The homologous chromosomes come together and line up side by side due to a means of attraction still unknown. This so-called **synapsis** [Gk. *synaptos*, united, joined together] results in a **bivalent** [L. *bis*, two, and *valens*, strength]—that is, two homologous chromosomes that stay in close association during the first two phases of meiosis I. Sometimes the term tetrad [Gk. *tetra*, four] is used instead of bivalent because, as you can see, a bivalent contains four chromatids.

Following synapsis, the members of a homologous pair separate. This separation means that only one duplicated chromosome from each homologous pair reaches a daughter nucleus. It is important for daughter nuclei to have a member from each pair of homologous chromosomes because only in that way can there be a copy of each kind of chromosome in the daughter nuclei. The members of the homologous pairs separate in such a way that any particular kind of chromosome can be with any other kind in the daughter nuclei. Therefore, all possible combinations of chromosomes can occur within the gametes that result after meiosis is complete.

During meiosis I, homologous chromosomes separate and the daughter cells have one copy of each kind of chromosome.

No replication of DNA is needed between meiosis I and meiosis II because the chromosomes are already duplicated; they already have two sister chromatids. During meiosis II, the daughter chromosomes derived from sister chromatids move to opposite poles. Therefore, the chromosomes in the four daughter cells have only one chromatid. You can count the number of centromeres to verify that the parent cell has the diploid number of chromosomes and each daughter cell has the haploid number.

Following meiosis II, there are four haploid daughter cells and each chromosome consists of one chromatid.

In the animal life cycle, the daughter cells mature into gametes that fuse during fertilization. Fertilization restores the diploid number of chromosomes so that the body cells of an animal contains the diploid number of chromosomes.

10.2 Genetic Recombination

We have seen that meiosis provides a way to keep the chromosome number constant generation after generation. Without meiosis, the chromosome number of the next generation would continually increase. Meiosis also helps ensure that genetic recombination occurs with each generation. Due to genetic recombination, offspring have a different combination of genes than their parents. Asexually reproducing organisms, like prokaryotes, depend primarily on mutations to generate variation among offspring. This is sufficient because they produce great numbers of offspring within a limited amount of time. Mutation also occurs among sexually reproducing organisms, but the shuffling of genetic material during the process of reproduction contributes greatly to the possibility of offspring that may be better adapted to the environment. Meiosis brings about genetic recombination in two key ways: crossing-over and independent assortment of homologous chromosomes.

Crossing-Over of Nonsister Chromatids

It's often said that we inherit half our chromosomes from our mother and half from our father, but this is not strictly correct, because of crossing-over. **Crossing-over** is an exchange of genetic material between nonsister chromatids of a bivalent during meiosis I. At synapsis, homologues line up side by side, and a nucleoprotein lattice (called the synaptonemal complex) appears between them (Fig. 10.3). This lattice holds the bivalent together in such a way that the DNA of the nonsister chromatids is aligned. Now crossing-over may occur. As the lattice breaks down, homologues are temporarily held together by *chiasmata* (sing., chiasma), regions where the nonsister chromatids are attached due to crossing-over (Fig. 10.4). Then homologues separate and are distributed to different daughter cells.

In order to appreciate the significance of crossing-over, it is necessary to remember that the members of a homologous pair can carry slightly different instructions for the same genetic traits. For example, one homologue may carry

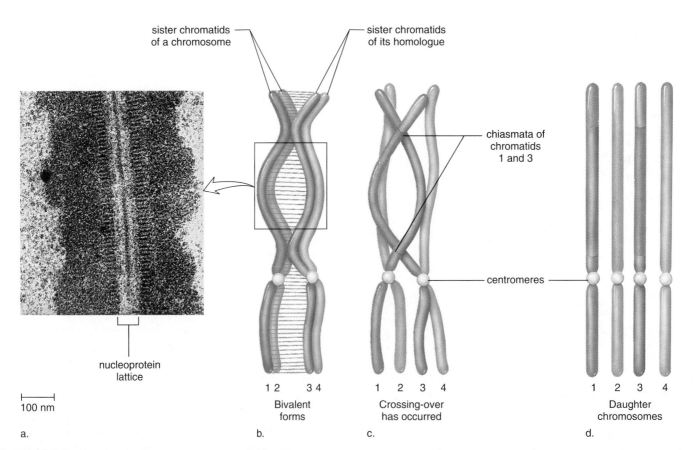

Figure 10.3 Crossing-over occurs during meiosis I.
a. The homologous chromosomes pair up, and a nucleoprotein lattice, called the synaptonemal complex, develops between them. This is an electron micrograph of the complex, which zippers the members of the bivalent together so that corresponding genes are in alignment. **b.** This diagrammatic representation shows only two places where nonsister chromatids 1 and 3 have come into contact. Actually, the other two nonsister chromatids most likely are also crossing over. **c.** Chiasmata indicate where crossing-over has occurred. The exchange of color represents the exchange of genetic material. **d.** Following meiosis II, daughter chromosomes have a new combination of genetic material due to crossing-over, which occurred between nonsister chromatids during meiosis I.

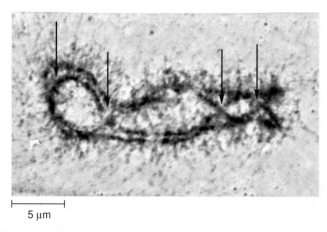

Figure 10.4 Chiasmata

Chiasmata (arrows) of a chromosome bivalent, from a testis cell of a grasshopper. The chiasmata mark the places where crossing-over between nonsister chromosomes of the bivalent has occurred. The chiasmata hold the members of the bivalent together until separation of homologues occurs.

instructions for brown eyes while the corresponding homologue may carry instructions for blue eyes. The same is true for all the genes carried on all the homologues. In the end, crossing-over means that the genetic instructions from a mother and father are mixed and the chromatids held together by a centromere are no longer identical. Therefore, when the chromatids separate during meiosis I, the daughter cells receive chromosomes with recombined genes.

Independent Assortment of Homologous Chromosomes

Due to **independent assortment** the homologous chromosomes separate independently or in a random manner. When homologues align at the metaphase plate, the maternal or paternal homologue may be orientated toward either pole. Figure 10.5 shows four possible orientations for a cell

that contains only three pairs of chromosomes. Each orientation results in gametes that have a different combination of maternal and paternal chromosomes. Once all possible orientations are considered, the result will be 2^3 or eight combinations of maternal and paternal chromosomes in the resulting gametes from this cell.

In humans, where there are 23 pairs of chromosomes, the possible chromosomal combinations in the gametes is a staggering 2^{23}, or 8,388,608. And this does not even consider the genetic variations that are introduced due to crossing-over.

Fertilization

The variation that results from meiosis is enhanced by fertilization. Each person has genes for the same traits, but again, each gene's specific instructions can vary. Therefore, the gametes produced by one person are expected to be genetically different from the gametes produced by another person. When *the gametes fuse at fertilization*, the chromosomes donated by the parents are combined, and in humans, this means that $(2^{23})^2$, or 70,368,744,000,000, chromosomally different zygotes are possible, even assuming no crossing-over. If crossing-over occurs once, then $(4^{23})^2$, or 4,951,760,200,000,000,000,000,000,000, genetically different zygotes are possible for every couple.

There are three ways by which genetic recombination comes about during sexual reproduction:

1. Independent alignment of bivalents at the metaphase plate means that gametes have different combinations of chromosomes.

2. Crossing-over means that the chromosomes in one gamete have a different combination of genes than chromosomes in another gamete.

3. Upon fertilization, combining of chromosomes from genetically different gametes occurs.

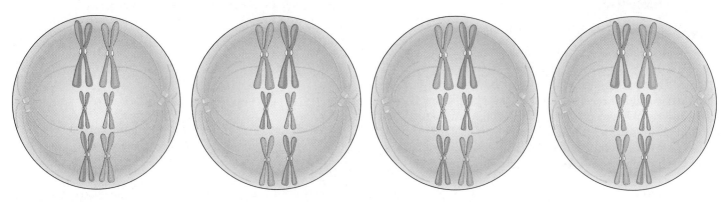

Figure 10.5 Independent assortment.

Four possible orientations of homologue pairs at the metaphase plate are shown. Each of these will result in daughter nuclei with a different combination of parental chromosomes. When a cell has three pairs of homologous chromosomes, there are 23 possible combinations of parental chromosomes in the daughter nuclei.

10.3 The Phases of Meiosis

Both meiosis I and meiosis II have these phases: prophase, metaphase (preceded by prometaphase), anaphase, and telophase.

Prophase I

It is apparent during prophase I that nuclear division is about to occur because a spindle forms as the centrosomes migrate away from one another. The nuclear envelope fragments, and the nucleolus disappears.

The homologous chromosomes, each having two sister chromatids, undergo synapsis to form bivalents. As depicted in Figure 10.3 by the exchange of color, crossing-over between the nonsister chromatids may occur at this time. After crossing-over, the sister chromatids of a duplicated chromosome are no longer identical.

Throughout prophase I, the chromosomes have been condensing so that by now they have the appearance of metaphase chromosomes.

Metaphase I

During prometaphase I, the bivalents held together by chiasmata (see Fig. 10.4) have moved toward the metaphase plate (equator of the spindle). Metaphase I is characterized by a fully formed spindle and alignment of the bivalents at the metaphase plate. *Kinetochores*, protein complexes just outside the centromeres, are seen, and these are attached to spindle fibers called kinetochore spindle fibers.

Bivalents independently align themselves at the metaphase plate of the spindle. The maternal homologue of each bivalent may be orientated toward either pole, and the paternal homologue of each bivalent may be aligned toward either pole. This means that all possible combinations of chromosomes can occur in the daughter cells.

Anaphase I

During anaphase I, the homologues of each bivalent separate and move to opposite poles. Notice that each chromosome still has two chromatids.

Telophase I

In some species, there is a telophase I stage at the end of meiosis I. If so, the nuclear envelopes re-form and nucleoli appear. This phase may or may not be accompanied by cytokinesis, which is separation of the cytoplasm. Figure 10.6 shows only two of the four possible combinations of haploid chromosomes when the parent cell has two homologous pairs of chromosomes. Can you determine what the other two possible combinations of chromosomes are?

Interkinesis

Interkinesis is similar to interphase between mitotic divisions except that DNA replication does not occur—the chromosomes are already duplicated.

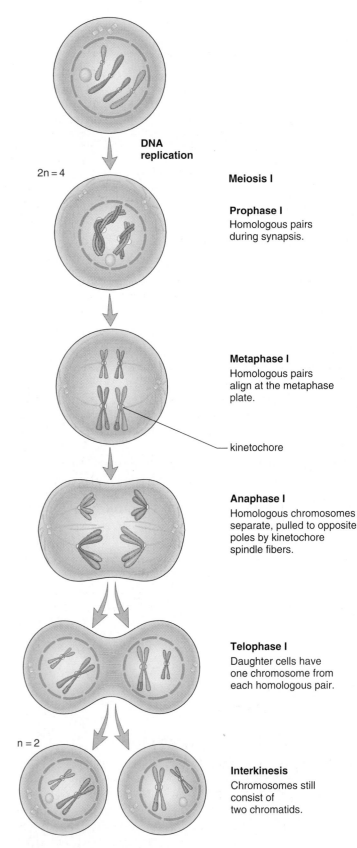

DNA replication

2n = 4

Meiosis I

Prophase I
Homologous pairs during synapsis.

Metaphase I
Homologous pairs align at the metaphase plate.

— kinetochore

Anaphase I
Homologous chromosomes separate, pulled to opposite poles by kinetochore spindle fibers.

Telophase I
Daughter cells have one chromosome from each homologous pair.

n = 2

Interkinesis
Chromosomes still consist of two chromatids.

Figure 10.6 Meiosis I.
The exchange of color between nonsister chromatids represents crossing-over.

Figure 10.7 Meiosis II.
During meiosis II, daughter chromosomes consisting of one chromatid each move to the poles. Following meiosis II, there are four haploid daughter cells. Comparing the number of centromeres in the daughter cells with the number in the parental cell at the start of meiosis I verifies that the daughter cells are haploid.

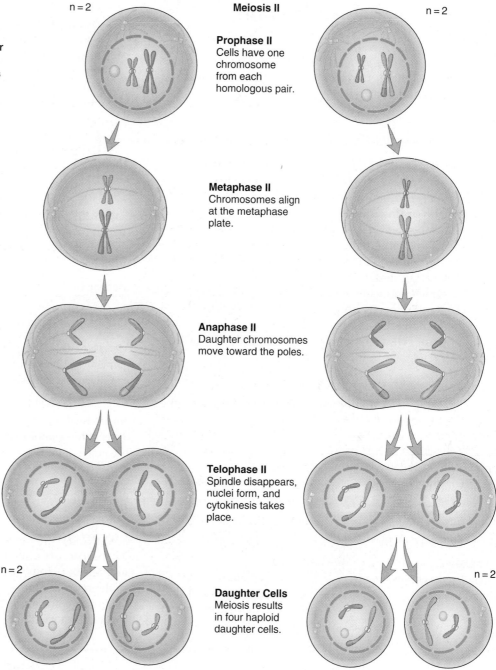

n = 2

Meiosis II

Prophase II
Cells have one chromosome from each homologous pair.

n = 2

Metaphase II
Chromosomes align at the metaphase plate.

Anaphase II
Daughter chromosomes move toward the poles.

Telophase II
Spindle disappears, nuclei form, and cytokinesis takes place.

n = 2

Daughter Cells
Meiosis results in four haploid daughter cells.

n = 2

Meiosis II

During metaphase II, the haploid number of chromosomes, which are still duplicated, align at the metaphase plate (Fig. 10.7). During anaphase II, the two sister chromatids separate at the centromere, giving rise to two daughter chromosomes. These daughter chromosomes move toward the poles. At the end of telophase II and cytokinesis, there are four haploid cells. Due to crossing-over of chromatids, each gamete will most likely contain chromosomes with varied genes.

Following meiosis II, the haploid cells mature and become gametes in animals. In plants, they become spores that divide to produce a haploid adult generation. This haploid generation produces gametes that fuse to become the diploid generation. Thus, plants have both a haploid and diploid generation in their life cycle. In some fungi and some algae, the zygote that results from gamete fusion immediately undergoes meiosis, and therefore the adult is always haploid.

10.4 Comparison of Meiosis with Mitosis

Figure 10.8 compares mitosis to meiosis. The differences between these cellular divisions can be categorized according to process and occurrence.

Process

The following are differences between meiosis and mitosis:

1. DNA replication takes place only once during both meiosis and mitosis; but there are two nuclear divisions during meiosis and only one nuclear division during mitosis.
2. Four daughter cells are produced by meiosis; mitosis results in two daughter cells.
3. The four daughter cells formed by meiosis are haploid; the daughter cells produced by mitosis have the same chromosome number as the parental cell.
4. The daughter cells from meiosis are not genetically identical to each other or to the parental cell. The daughter cells from mitosis are genetically identical to each other and to the parental cell.

Comparison of Meiosis I to Mitosis

The following are distinctive differences between the processes of meiosis I and mitosis:

Meiosis I	Mitosis
Prophase I	Prophase
Pairing of chromosomes	No pairing of chromosomes
Metaphase I	Metaphase
Homologous chromosomes at metaphase plate	Duplicated chromosomes at metaphase plate
Anaphase I	Anaphase
Homologous chromosomes separate	Sister chromatids separate, becoming daughter chromosomes that move to the poles
Telophase I	Telophase
Daughter cells are haploid	Daughter cells are diploid

These events distinguish meiosis I from mitosis:

1. During prophase I of meiosis, homologous chromosomes pair and undergo crossing-over but this does not occur during mitosis.

2. During metaphase I of meiosis, paired homologous chromosomes align independently at the metaphase plate; during metaphase of mitosis, individual (duplicated) chromosomes align at the metaphase plate.
3. During anaphase I in meiosis, homologous chromosomes (with centromeres intact) separate and move to opposite poles; during anaphase of mitosis, sister chromatids separate, becoming daughter chromosomes that move to opposite poles.

Comparison of Meiosis II to Mitosis

The events of meiosis II are just like those of mitosis except that in meiosis II, the nuclei contain the haploid number of chromosomes. The following listing compares meiosis II to mitosis:

Meiosis II	Mitosis
Prophase II	Prophase
No pairing of chromosomes	No pairing of chromosomes
Metaphase II	Metaphase
Haploid number of duplicated chromosomes at metaphase plate	Diploid number of duplicated chromosomes at metaphase plate
Anaphase II	Anaphase
Sister chromatids separate, becoming daughter chromosomes that move to the poles	Sister chromatids separate, becoming daughter chromosomes that move to the poles
Telophase II	Telophase
Four daughter cells	Two daughter cells

Occurrence

Meiosis occurs only at certain times in the life cycle of sexually reproducing organisms. In humans, meiosis occurs only in the reproductive organs and produces the gametes. Mitosis is more common because it occurs in all tissues during growth and repair.

Meiosis is a specialized process that reduces the chromosome number and occurs only during the production of gametes. Mitosis is a process that occurs during growth and repair of all tissues.

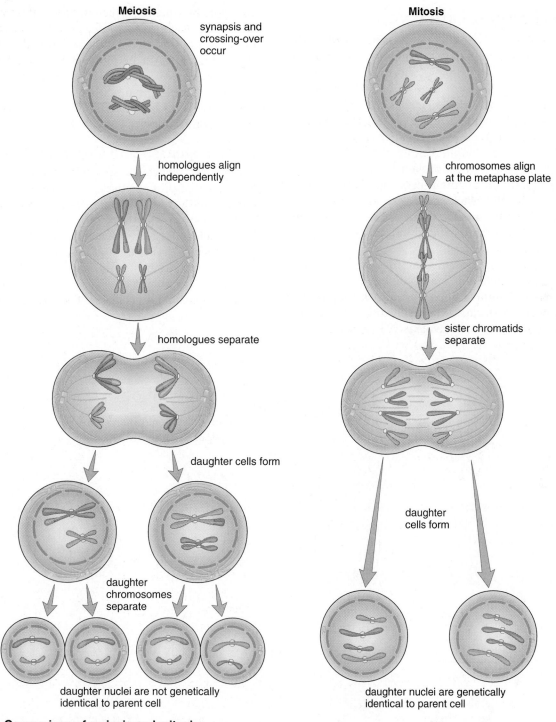

Meiosis

synapsis and crossing-over occur

homologues align independently

homologues separate

daughter cells form

daughter chromosomes separate

daughter nuclei are not genetically identical to parent cell

Mitosis

chromosomes align at the metaphase plate

sister chromatids separate

daughter cells form

daughter nuclei are genetically identical to parent cell

Figure 10.8 Comparison of meiosis and mitosis.
Why does meiosis produce haploid daughter cells while mitosis produces diploid daughter cells? Compare metaphase I of meiosis to metaphase of mitosis. Only in metaphase I are the homologous chromosomes paired at the metaphase plate. Members of the homologous chromosomes separate during anaphase I and therefore the daughter cells are haploid. The exchange of color between nonsister chromatids represents the crossing-over that occurred during meiosis I.

10.5 The Human Life Cycle

The term **life cycle** refers to all the reproductive events that occur from one generation to the next similar generation. In animals, the adult is always diploid and meiosis produces the gametes, the only haploid stage of the life cycle. In plants, there are two adult stages, one is diploid and the other is haploid. The haploid stage may be larger or smaller than the diploid stage depending on the species. The mosses growing on bare rock are haploid most of their life cycle while oak trees are diploid most of their life cycle. In fungi (and some algae) only the zygote is ever diploid and it undergoes meiosis. So the black mold you sometimes see growing on bread and the green coating you see growing on a pond are haploid. It is these haploid individuals that produce gamete nuclei.

In animals, such as humans, meiosis occurs during the production of gametes. In males, meiosis is a part of **spermatogenesis** [Gk. *sperma*, seed, and L. *genitus*, producing], which occurs in the testes and produces sperm. In females, meiosis is a part of **oogenesis** [Gk. *oon*, egg, and

L. *genitus*, producing], which occurs in the ovaries and produces eggs. A sperm and egg join at fertilization and the resulting zygote undergoes mitosis during development of the fetus, which is the stage of development before birth. After birth, mitosis is involved in the continued growth of the child and repair of tissues at any time (Fig. 10.9). As a result of mitosis, each somatic cell in the body has the same number of chromosomes.

Spermatogenesis and Oogenesis in Humans

Figure 10.10 contrasts spermatogenesis with oogenesis, processes that produce the gametes in mammals, including humans. In the testes of males, primary spermatocytes with 46 chromosomes divide to form two secondary spermatocytes, each with 23 duplicated chromosomes. Secondary spermatocytes divide to produce four spermatids, also with 23 daughter chromosomes. Spermatids then differentiate into sperm (spermatozoa). The process of meiosis in males always results in four cells that become sperm.

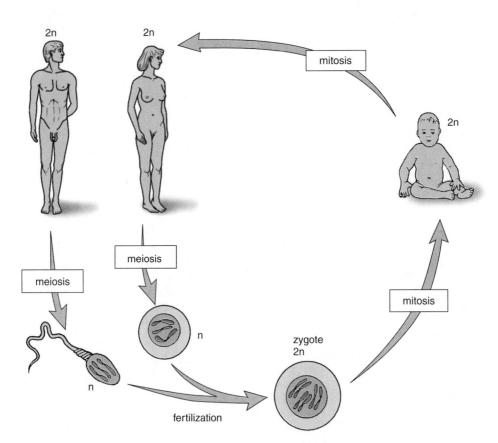

Figure 10.9 Life cycle of humans.
Meiosis in males is a part of sperm production, and meiosis in females is a part of egg production. When a haploid sperm fertilizes a haploid egg, the zygote is diploid. The zygote undergoes mitosis as it develops into a newborn child. Mitosis continues after birth until the individual reaches maturity; then the life cycle begins again.

In the ovaries of females, a primary oocyte has 46 chromosomes and divides meiotically into two cells, each having 23 chromosomes. One of these cells, termed the **secondary oocyte** [Gk. *oon*, egg, and *kytos*, cell], receives almost all the cytoplasm (Fig. 10.10). The other is a **polar body** that may disintegrate or may divide again. The secondary oocyte begins meiosis II and then stops at metaphase II. Then at ovulation, it leaves the ovary and enters an oviduct where it may be approached by a sperm. If a sperm does enter the oocyte, the oocyte is activated to continue meiosis II to completion. Therefore meiosis does not go to completion in females unless fertilization occurs. The mature egg has 23

chromosomes. Meiosis in human females produces only one egg and two polar bodies. The polar bodies are a way to discard unnecessary chromosomes while retaining much of the cytoplasm in the egg. The cytoplasm serves as a source of nutrients for the developing embryo.

In the animal life cycle, such as the human life cycle, the diploid adult produces the gametes by meiosis. Some other organisms are haploid as adults and meiosis occurs at some other juncture in the life cycle.

Spermatogenesis

Oogenesis

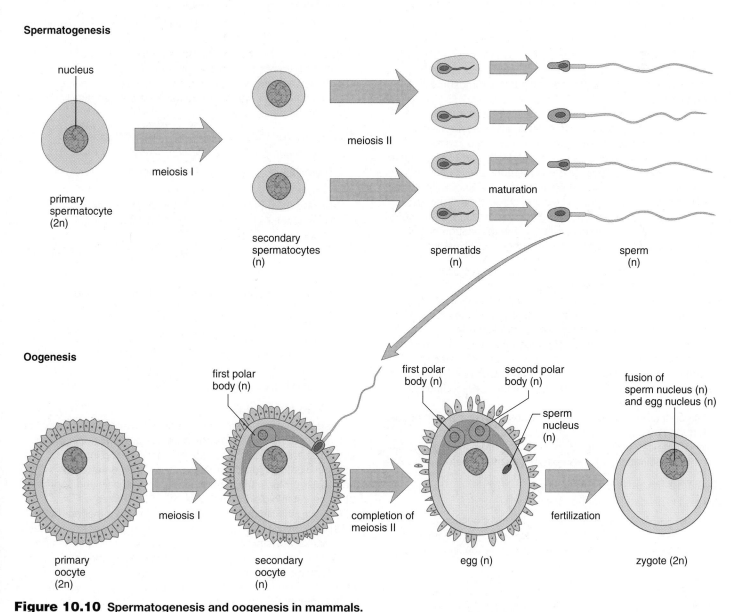

Figure 10.10 **Spermatogenesis and oogenesis in mammals.**
Spermatogenesis produces four viable sperm, whereas oogenesis produces one egg and at least two polar bodies. In humans, both sperm and egg have 23 chromosomes each; therefore, following fertilization, the zygote has 46 chromosomes.

Connecting Concepts

Meiosis is similar to the process of mitosis except that meiosis is a more elaborate process. During meiosis, controlling mechanisms ensure that homologous chromosomes first pair and then separate during the first division and that sister chromatids do not separate until the second division. In addition, signaling molecules ensure that only certain types of cells undergo meiosis during a restricted period of an organism's life span.

There is an evolutionary cost to sexual reproduction: the increased number of genes controlling the process can lead to an increased chance of mutations and the possibility of faulty or inviable gametes. But there is also an evolutionary advantage: sexually reproducing species have a greater likelihood of genetic diversity among offspring than do asexually reproducing species.

Understanding the behavior of chromosomes during meiosis is critical to understanding the manner in which genes segregate during gamete formation. The next chapter reviews the fundamental laws of genetics established by Gregor Mendel. Although Mendel had no knowledge of chromosome behavior, modern students have the advantage of applying their knowledge of meiosis to increase their understanding of Mendel's laws.

Summary

10.1 Halving the Chromosome Number

Meiosis ensures that the chromosome number in offspring stays constant generation after generation. The nucleus contains pairs of chromosomes, called homologous chromosomes (homologues).

Meiosis requires two cell divisions and results in four daughter cells. Replication of DNA takes place before meiosis begins. During meiosis I, the homologues undergo synapsis (resulting in a bivalent) and align independently at the metaphase plate. The daughter cells receive one member of each pair of homologous chromosomes. There is no replication of DNA during interkinesis. During meiosis II, the sister chromatids separate at the centromeres, giving rise to daughter chromosomes that move to opposite poles as they do in mitosis. The four daughter cells contain the haploid number of chromosomes and only one of each kind.

10.2 Genetic Recombination

Sexual reproduction ensures that the offspring have a different genetic makeup than the parents. Meiosis contributes to genetic variability in two ways: crossing-over and independent assortment of the homologous chromosomes. When homologous chromosomes lie side by side during synapsis, nonsister chromatids may exchange genetic material. Due to crossing-over the chromatids that separate during meiosis II have a different combination of genes.

When the homologous chromosomes align at the metaphase plate during metaphase I either the maternal or the paternal chromosome can be facing either pole. Therefore there will be all possible combinations of chromosomes in the gametes.

10.3 The Phases of sMeiosis

Meiosis I is divided into four phases:

Prophase I—Bivalents form, and crossing-over occurs as chromosomes condense; the nuclear envelope fragments.
Metaphase I—Bivalents independently align at the metaphase plate.
Anaphase I—Homologous chromosomes separate.
Telophase I—Nuclei become haploid, having received one duplicated chromosome from each homologous pair.

Meiosis II is divided into four phases:

Prophase II—Chromosomes condense and the nuclear envelope fragments.
Metaphase II—The haploid number of still duplicated chromosomes align at the metaphase plate.
Anaphase II—Daughter chromosomes move to the poles.
Telophase II—Four haploid daughter cells are genetically different from the parent cell.

10.4 Comparison of Meiosis with Mitosis

Mitosis and meiosis can be compared in this manner:

Meiosis I	Mitosis
Prophase	
Pairing of homologous chromosomes	No pairing of chromosomes
Metaphase	
Bivalents at metaphase plate	Duplicated chromosomes at metaphase plate
Anaphase	
Homologous chromosomes separate	Sister chromatids separate
Telophase	
Daughter nuclei are always haploid number	Daughter nuclei have the parent cell chromosome number

Meiosis II is like mitosis except the nuclei are haploid.

10.5 The Human Life Cycle

Meiosis occurs in any life cycle that involves sexual reproduction. In the animal life cycle, only the gametes are haploid; in plants and fungi, meiosis produces spores that develop into a multicellular haploid adult that produces the gametes. In unicellular protists, the zygote undergoes meiosis and spores become a haploid adult that gives rise to gametes.

During the life cycle of humans, and many other animals, meiosis is involved in spermatogenesis and oogenesis. Whereas spermatogenesis produces four sperm per meiosis, oogenesis produces one egg and two nonfunctional polar bodies. Spermatogenesis occurs in males and oogenesis occurs in females. When a sperm fertilizes an egg, the zygote has the diploid number of chromosomes.

Reviewing the Chapter

1. Why did early investigators predict that there must be a reduction division in the sexual reproduction process? 160
2. What are homologous chromosomes? Contrast the genetic makeup of sister chromatids with nonsister chromatids. 160
3. What is synapsis? Contrast in general meiosis I with meiosis II. 161
4. Draw and explain a diagram that illustrates synapsis and another that shows the significance of independent assortment of homologous pairs. How do these events ensure genetic variability of the gametes? 161–62
5. Draw and explain a series of diagrams that illustrate the stages of meiosis I. 164
6. Draw and explain a series of diagrams that illustrate the stages of meiosis II. 165
7. Construct a chart to describe the many differences between meiosis and mitosis. 166
8. What accounts for (1) the genetic similarity between daughter cells and the parent cell following mitosis and (2) the genetic dissimilarity between daughter cells and the parent cell following meiosis? 166
9. Explain the human (animal) life cycle and compare it to that of protists and plants. 168
10. Compare spermatogenesis of males to oogenesis in females. 168–69

Testing Yourself

Choose the best answer for each question.

1. A bivalent (tetrad) is
   a. a homologous chromosome.
   b. the paired homologous chromosomes.
   c. a duplicated chromosome composed of sister chromatids.
   d. the two daughter cells after meiosis I.
   e. the two centrioles in a centrosome.
2. If a parent cell has twelve chromosomes, then each of the daughter cells following meiosis will have
   a. forty-eight chromosomes.
   b. twenty-four chromosomes.
   c. twelve chromosomes.
   d. six chromosomes.
   e. Any one of these could be correct.
3. At the metaphase plate during metaphase I of meiosis, there are
   a. chromosomes consisting of one chromatid.
   b. unpaired duplicated chromosomes.
   c. bivalents (tetrads).
   d. homologous pairs of chromosomes.
   e. Both c and d are correct.

4. At the metaphase plate during metaphase II of meiosis, there are
   a. chromosomes consisting of one chromatid.
   b. unpaired duplicated chromosomes.
   c. bivalents (tetrads).
   d. homologous pairs of chromosomes.
   e. Both c and d are correct.
5. Gametes contain one of each kind of chromosome because
   a. the homologous chromosomes separate during meiosis.
   b. the chromatids separate during meiosis.
   c. only one replication of DNA occurs during meiosis.
   d. crossing-over occurs during prophase I.
   e. the parental cell contains only one of each kind of chromosome.
6. Crossing-over occurs between
   a. sister chromatids of the same chromosome.
   b. two different kinds of bivalents.
   c. two different kinds of chromosomes.
   d. nonsister chromatids of a bivalent.
   e. two daughter nuclei.
7. During which phase of meiosis do homologous chromosomes separate?
   a. prophase II
   b. telophase I
   c. metaphase I
   d. anaphase I
   e. anaphase II
8. Fertilization
   a. is a source of variation during sexual reproduction.
   b. is fusion of the gametes.
   c. occurs in both animal and plant life cycles.
   d. restores the diploid number of chromosomes.
   e. All of these are correct.
9. Which of these is not a difference between spermatogenesis and oogenesis in humans?

	Spermatogenesis	Oogenesis
a.	occurs in males	occurs in females
b.	produces four sperm per meiosis	produces one egg per meiosis
c.	produces haploid cells	produces diploid cells
d.	always goes to completion	does not always go to completion

10. Which of these drawings represents metaphase I? How do you know?

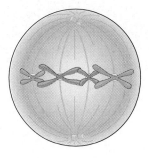

Thinking Scientifically

1. A population of lizards does not appear to contain any males, yet young are being born. If analysis shows that the offspring are diploid and have the same genetic traits as their mothers, what is the most likely source of maternal DNA to fertilize the eggs? How would you test this hypothesis?

2. During anaphase I of meiosis, spindle fibers pull the homologues of a bivalent in opposite directions. Explain with reference to attachment of spindle fibers to kinetochores. (see Figure 10.6)

Bioethical Issue

Cloning is making exact multiple copies of DNA or a cell or an organism. The first two procedures have been around for some time. Through biotechnology, bacteria produce cloned copies of human DNA. When a single bacterium reproduces asexually in a petri dish, a colony results. Each member of the colony is a clone of the original cell. Now, for the first time in our history, it is possible to produce a clone of an organism. No sperm and egg are required. The DNA of an adult cell is placed in an enucleated egg and the egg undergoes development to become an exact copy of the organism that donated the DNA. Some people fear that billionaires and celebrities will hasten to make multiple copies of themselves. Others feel that this is unlikely. Rather, they fear a different type of cloning.

Suppose it were possible to use the DNA of a burn victim to produce embryonic cells that are cajoled into becoming skin cells. These cells could be used to provide grafts of brand new skin. Would this be a proper use of cloning in humans?

Or suppose parents want to produce a child free of a genetic disease. Scientists produce a zygote through in vitro fertilization, and then they clone the zygote to produce any number of cells. Genetic engineering to correct the defect doesn't work on all the cells—only a few. They implant just those few in the uterus where development continues to term. Would this be a proper use of cloning in humans?

Well, what if science progressed to producing children with increased intelligence or athletic prowess in the same way? Would this be an acceptable use of cloning in humans? Presently, research in the cloning of humans is banned. Should it be? Why or why not?

Understanding the Terms

bivalent 161	life cycle 168
crossing-over 162	meiosis 160
diploid (2n) number 160	oogenesis 168
gamete 160	polar body 169
haploid (n) number 160	secondary oocyte 169
homologous	sexual reproduction 160
chromosome 160	spermatogenesis 168
homologue 160	synapsis 161
independent assortment 163	zygote 160

Match the terms to these definitions:

a. _____ Production of sperm in males by the process of meiosis and maturation.

b. _____ Pair of homologous chromosomes at the metaphase plate during meiosis I.

c. _____ A nonfunctional product of oogenesis.

d. _____ The functional product of meiosis I in oogenesis becomes the egg.

e. _____ Member of a pair of chromosomes that carry genes for the same traits.

Web Connections

Exploring the Internet

http://www.mhhe.com/biosci/genbio/mader
(click on *Biology 7/e*)

The *Biology 7/e* Online Learning Center provides many resources for studying the material in this chapter including links to the following sites:

Meiosis and Genetic Recombination. This site is a section from the Mendelian genetics chapter of the MIT hypertextbook. Good discussion of crossing-over and recombination during meiosis.

http://esg-www.mit.edu:8001/esgbio/mg/meiosis.html

Meiosis Tutorial. This exercise shows the events of meiosis with both text and illustrations.

http://www.biology.arizona.edu/cell_bio/tutorials/meiosis/main.html

Meiosis—an Access Excellence short review of meiosis.

http://www.accessexcellence.org/AB/GG/meiosis.html

Meiosis. The first part of this laboratory exercise has a number of questions on meiosis that would serve as a good review.

http://www.hiline.net/~siremba/worksheets/meiosis.html

Lillium Meiosis. Labeled photomicrographs of the stages of meiosis in a lily.

http://www.dmacc.cc.ia.us/instructors/lillium.htm

Mendelian Patterns of Inheritance

Like begets like.

The science of genetics explains why young giraffes resemble and have a combination of their parents' characteristics. An understanding of genetics has been acquired from studying a varied collection of organisms—peas, fruit flies, bread molds, bacteria, and humans.

Gregor Mendel, the father of genetics, chose the garden pea as his experimental material. He proposed that each parent donates particulate hereditary factors to offspring. Mendel worked in the nineteenth century, and his work was largely ignored until the twentieth century, when genetics took a modern turn. It wasn't until then that the term "gene" was coined and it was reasoned that the genes are on the chromosomes.

But what do genes do? Red bread mold experiments allowed Beadle and Tatum to conclude that genes in some way control the synthesis of enzymes. Not until the early 1950s did scientists know that genes are composed of DNA, and it was 1958 before Watson and Crick deduced the structure of DNA. From then on, work with the bacterium *Escherichia coli* brought us into the era of modern genetics and the ability to transform the genes of all organisms.

11.1 Gregor Mendel

Zebras always produce zebras, never bluebirds, and poppies always produce seeds for poppies, never dandelions. Almost everyone who observes such phenomena reasons that parents must pass hereditary information to their offspring. Many also observe, however, that offspring rarely resemble either parent exactly. After all, black-coated mice occasionally produce white-coated mice. The laws of heredity must explain not only the stability but also the variation that is observed between generations of organisms.

Gregor Mendel was an Austrian monk who formulated two fundamental laws of heredity in the early 1860s (Fig. 11.1). Previously, he had studied science and mathematics at the University of Vienna, and at the time of his genetic research he was a substitute natural science teacher at a local technical high school. Various hypotheses about heredity had been proposed before Mendel began his experiments. In particular, investigators were trying to support a blending concept of inheritance at this time.

Blending Concept of Inheritance

When Mendel began his work, most plant and animal breeders acknowledged that both sexes contribute equally to a new individual. They felt that parents of contrasting appearance always produce offspring of intermediate appearance. Therefore, according to this concept, a cross between plants with red flowers and plants with white flowers would yield only plants with pink flowers. When red and white flowers reappeared in future generations, the breeders mistakenly attributed this to an instability in the genetic material.

A blending concept of inheritance offered little help to Charles Darwin, the father of evolution who wanted to give his ideas a genetic basis. If populations contained only intermediate individuals and normally lacked variations, how could diverse forms evolve? Only a particulate theory of inheritance, as proposed by Mendel, can account for the presence of discrete variations (differences) among the members of a population generation after generation. Although Darwin was a contemporary of Mendel, Darwin never learned of Mendel's work because it went unrecognized until 1900. Therefore, Darwin was never able to make use of the particulate theory of inheritance to support his theory of evolution.

At the time Mendel began his study of heredity, the blending concept of inheritance was popular.

Mendel's Experimental Procedure

Most likely his background in mathematics prompted Mendel to give a statistical basis to his breeding experiments. He prepared for his experiments carefully and conducted preliminary studies with various animals and plants. He then chose to work with the garden pea, *Pisum sativum* (Fig. 11.2a).

Figure 11.1 Mendel working in his garden.
Mendel grew and tended the pea plants he used for his experiments. For each experiment, he observed as many offspring as possible. For a cross that required him to count the number of round seeds to wrinkled seeds, he observed and counted a total of 7,324 peas!

The garden pea was a good choice. The plants were easy to cultivate and had a short generation time. And although peas normally self-pollinate (pollen only goes to the same flower), they could be cross-pollinated by hand. Many varieties of peas were available, and Mendel chose twenty-two for his experiments. When these varieties self-pollinated, they were *true-breeding*—the offspring were like the parent plants and like each other. In contrast to his predecessors, Mendel studied the inheritance of relatively simple and distinguishable traits—seed shape, seed color, and flower color (Fig. 11.2b).

As Mendel followed the inheritance of individual traits, he kept careful records of the numbers of offspring that expressed each characteristic. And he used his understanding of the mathematical laws of probability to interpret the results. In other words, Mendel simply observed facts objectively, and if he had personal beliefs, he set them aside for the sake of the experiment. This is one of the qualities that make his experiments as applicable today as they were in 1860.

Mendel carefully designed his experiments and gathered mathematical data.

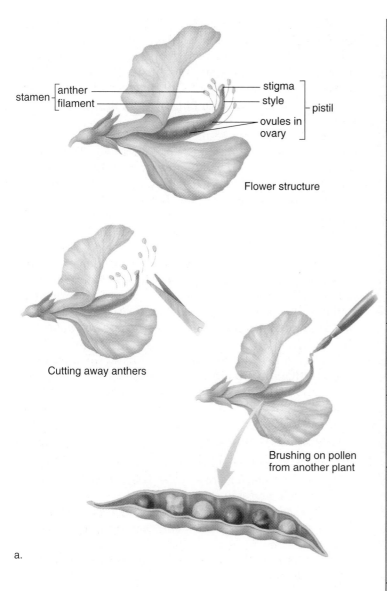

Trait	Characteristics		F₂ Results*	
			Dominant	**Recessive**
Stem length	Tall	Short	787	277
Pod shape	Inflated	Constricted	882	299
Seed shape	Round	Wrinkled	5,474	1,850
Seed color	Yellow	Green	7,022	2,001
Flower position	Axial	Terminal	651	207
Flower color	Purple	White	705	224
Pod color	Green	Yellow	428	152

*All of these produce approximately a 3:1 ratio. For example,

$$\frac{787}{277} \approx \frac{3}{1}$$

b.

Figure 11.2 Garden pea anatomy and traits.

a. In the garden pea, *Pisum sativum,* pollen grains produced in the anther contain sperm, and ovules in the ovary contain eggs. When Mendel did crosses he brushed pollen from one plant on the stigma of another plant. After sperm fertilized eggs, the ovules developed into seeds (peas). The open pod shows the results of a cross between plants with round, yellow seeds and plants with wrinkled, green seeds. b. Mendel selected these traits for study. He made sure his parental (P generation) plants bred true and then he cross-pollinated the plants. The offspring called F₁ (first filial) generation always resembled the parent with the dominant characteristic on the left. Mendel then allowed the F₁ plants to self-pollinate. In the F₂ (second filial) generation he always achieved a 3:1 (dominant to recessive) ratio. The text explains how Mendel went on to interpret these results.

11.2 Monohybrid Inheritance

After ensuring that his pea plants were true-breeding, Mendel was then ready to perform a cross-pollination experiment between two strains. For these initial experiments, Mendel chose varieties that differed in only one trait. Crosses that involve only one trait are called monohybrid crosses. If the blending theory of inheritance were correct, then the cross should yield offspring with an intermediate appearance compared to the parents. For example, the offspring of a cross between a tall plant and short plant should be intermediate in height.

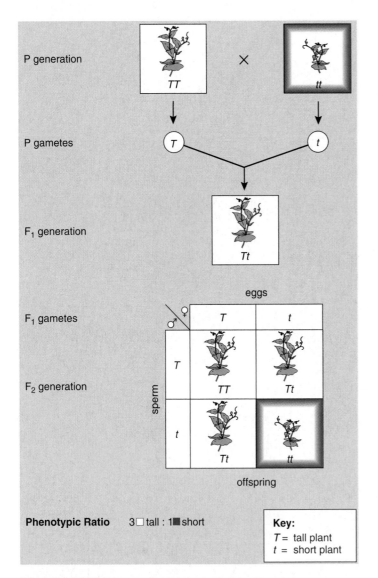

Phenotypic Ratio   3□ tall : 1■ short

Key:
T = tall plant
t = short plant

Figure 11.3 Monohybrid cross done by Mendel.
The P generation plants differ in one regard—length of the stem. The F₁ generation are all tall, but the factor for short has not disappeared because ¼ of the F₂ generation are short. The 3:1 ratio allowed Mendel to deduce that individuals have two discrete and separate genetic factors for each trait.

Mendel called the original parents the *P generation* and the first-generation offspring the *F₁* (for filial) *generation* (Fig. 11.3). He performed *reciprocal crosses:* first he dusted the pollen of tall plants on the stigmas of short plants, and then he dusted the pollen of short plants on the stigmas of tall plants. In both cases, all F₁ offspring resembled the tall parent.

Certainly, these results were contrary to those predicted by the blending theory of inheritance. Rather than being intermediate, the F₁ offspring were tall and resembled only one parent. Did these results mean that the other characteristic (i.e., shortness) had disappeared permanently? Apparently not, because when Mendel allowed the F₁ plants to self-pollinate, ¾ of the *F₂ generation* were tall and ¼ were short, a 3:1 ratio (Fig. 11.3).

Mendel counted many plants. For this particular cross, he counted a total of 1,064 plants, of which 787 were tall and 277 were short. In all crosses that he performed, he found a 3:1 ratio in the F₂ generation. The characteristic that had disappeared in the F₁ generation reappeared in ¼ of the F₂ offspring.

His mathematical approach led Mendel to interpret his results differently from previous breeders. He knew that the same ratio was obtained among the F₂ generation time and time again for the same type cross despite the particular trait, and he sought an explanation. A 3:1 ratio among the F₂ offspring was possible if:

1. the F₁ parents contained two separate copies of each hereditary factor, one of these being dominant and one being recessive;
2. the factors separated when the gametes were formed, and each gamete carried only one copy of each factor; and
3. random fusion of all possible gametes occurred upon fertilization.

In this way, Mendel arrived at the first of his laws of inheritance—the law of segregation.

Mendel's law of segregation:
Each organism contains two factors for each trait, and the factors segregate during the formation of gametes so that each gamete contains only one factor for each trait.

Mendel's law of segregation is in keeping with a particulate theory of inheritance because many individual factors are passed on from generation to generation. It is the reshuffling of these factors that explains how variations come about and why offspring differ from their parents.

As Viewed by Modern Genetics

Figure 11.3 also shows how we now interpret the results of Mendel's experiments on inheritance of stem length in peas. Each trait in a pea plant is controlled by two **alleles** [Gk. *allelon,* reciprocal, parallel], alternate forms of a gene that in this case control the length of the stem. In genetic notation, the alleles are identified by letters, the **dominant allele** (so named because of its ability to mask the expression of the other allele) with an uppercase (capital) letter and the **recessive allele** with the same but lowercase (small) letter. With reference to the cross being discussed, there is an allele for tallness (*T*) and an allele for shortness (*t*). Alleles occur on a homologous pair of chromosomes at a particular location that is called the **gene locus** (Fig. 11.4).

During meiosis, the type of cell division that reduces the chromosome number, the homologous chromosomes of a bivalent separate during meiosis I. Therefore, the process of meiosis gives an explanation for Mendel's law of segregation and for the reason there is only one allele for each trait in the gametes.

In Mendel's cross, the original parents (P generation) were true-breeding; therefore, the tall plants had two alleles for tallness (*TT*) and the short plants had two alleles for shortness (*tt*). When an organism has two identical alleles, as these had, we say it is **homozygous** [Gk. *homo,* same, and *zygos,* balance, yoke]. Because the parents were homozygous, all gametes produced by the tall plant contained the allele for tallness (*T*), and all gametes produced by the short plant contained an allele for shortness (*t*).

After cross-pollination, all the individuals of the resulting F₁ generation had one allele for tallness and one for shortness (*Tt*). When an organism has two different alleles at a gene locus, we say that it is **heterozygous** [Gk. *hetero,* different, and *zygos,* balance, yoke]. Although the plants of the F₁ generation had one of each type of allele, they were all tall. The allele that is expressed in a heterozygous individual is the dominant allele. The allele that is not expressed in a heterozygote is a recessive allele.

Genotype Versus Phenotype

It is obvious from our discussion that two organisms with different allelic combinations for a trait can have the same outward appearance (*TT* and *Tt* pea plants are both tall). For this reason, it is necessary to distinguish between the alleles present in an organism and the appearance of that organism.

The word **genotype** [Gk. *genos,* birth, origin, race, and *typos,* image, shape] refers to the alleles an individual receives at fertilization. Genotype may be indicated by letters or by short, descriptive phrases. Genotype *TT* is called homo-

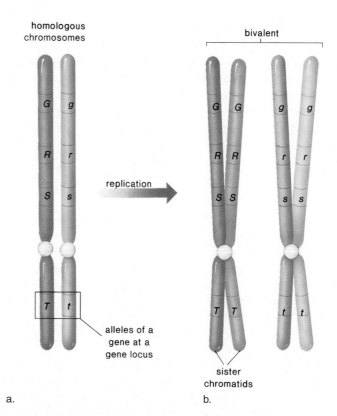

Figure 11.4 Homologous chromosomes.
a. The letters represent alleles; that is, alternate forms of a gene. Each allelic pair, such as *Gg* or *Tt,* is located on homologous chromosomes at a particular gene locus. **b.** Following DNA replication, each sister chromatid carries the same alleles in the same order.

Table 11.1		
Genotype Versus Phenotype		
Genotype	**Genotype**	**Phenotype**
TT	Homozygous dominant	Tall plant
Tt	Heterozygous	Tall plant
tt	Homozygous recessive	Short plant

zygous dominant, and genotype *tt* is called homozygous recessive. Genotype *Tt* is called heterozygous.

The word **phenotype** [Gk. *phaino,* appear, and *typos,* image, shape] refers to the physical appearance of the individual. The homozygous dominant individual and the heterozygous individual both show the dominant phenotype and are tall, while the homozygous recessive individual shows the recessive phenotype and is short (Table 11.1).

Monohybrid Genetics Problems

When solving genetics problems, it is first necessary to know which characteristic is dominant. For example, the following key indicates that unattached earlobes are dominant over attached earlobes:

> **Key**: *E* = unattached earlobes
> *e* = attached earlobes

If a man, homozygous for unattached earlobes, reproduces with a woman who has attached earlobes, what type of earlobe will the child have? In row 1, P represents the parental generation, and the letters in this row are the genotypes of the parents. Row 2 shows that the gametes of each parent have only one type of allele for earlobes; therefore, the child (F generation) will have a heterozygous genotype and unattached earlobes:

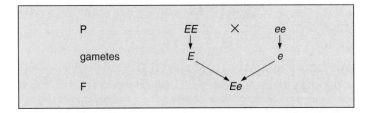

If two heterozygotes reproduce with one another, will the child have unattached or attached earlobes? In the P generation there was only one possible type of gamete for each parent because they were homozygous. Heterozygotes, however, can produce two types of gametes; ½ of the gametes will contain an *E*, and ½ will contain an *e*.

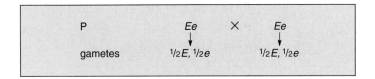

When determining the gametes, it is necessary to keep in mind that although an individual is diploid—that is, has two alleles for each trait—*each gamete is haploid—that is, has only one allele for each trait*. This is true of single-trait crosses as well as multiple-trait crosses.

When doing genetics problems, first decide on the appropriate key, and then determine the genotype of both parents and the various types of gametes for both parents.

Practice Problems 1 will help you learn to designate the gametes.

> ### Practice Problems 1*
>
> 1. For each of the following genotypes, give all genetically different gametes, noting the proportion of each for the individual.
>   a. *WW*
>   b. *Ww*
>   c. *Tt*
>   d. *TT*
> 2. For each of the following, state whether a genotype (genetic makeup of an organism) or a type of gamete is represented.
>   a. *D*
>   b. *GG*
>   c. *P*
>
> * Answers to Practice Problems appear in Appendix A.

Laws of Probability

When we calculate the expected results of the cross under consideration, or any genetic cross, we utilize the laws of probability. Imagine flipping a coin; *each time* you flip the coin there is a 50% chance of heads and a 50% chance of tails. In like manner, if the parent has the genotype *Ee*, what is the chance of any child inheriting either an *E* or *e* from that parent?

> The chance of $E = \frac{1}{2}$
> The chance of $e = \frac{1}{2}$

But in the cross *Ee* × *Ee*, a child will inherit an allele from both parents. The multiplicative law of probability states that *the chance, or probability, of two or more independent events occurring together is the product (multiplication) of their chance of occurring separately.* Therefore, the probability of receiving these genotypes is as follows:

1. The chance of $EE = \frac{1}{2} \times \frac{1}{2} = \frac{1}{4}$
2. The chance of $Ee = \frac{1}{2} \times \frac{1}{2} = \frac{1}{4}$
3. The chance of $eE = \frac{1}{2} \times \frac{1}{2} = \frac{1}{4}$
4. The chance of $ee = \frac{1}{2} \times \frac{1}{2} = \frac{1}{4}$

Now we have to consider the additive law of probability: *the chance of an event that can occur in two or more independent ways is the sum (addition) of the individual chances.* Therefore,

The chance of a child with unattached earlobes (*EE*, *Ee*, or *eE*) is ¾ (add **1, 2,** and **3**), or 75%.
The chance of a child with attached earlobes (*ee*) is ¼ (only **4**), or 25%.

The Punnett Square

The **Punnett square** was introduced by a prominent poultry geneticist, R. C. Punnett, in the early 1900s as a simple method to figure the probable results of a genetic cross. Figure 11.5 shows how the results of the cross under consideration (*Ee* × *Ee*) can be determined using a Punnett square. In a Punnett square all possible types of sperm are lined up vertically and all possible types of eggs are lined up horizontally (or vice versa), and every possible combination of alleles is placed within the squares. In our cross each parent has two possible types of gametes (*E* or *e*), so these two types of gametes are lined up vertically and horizontally.

The results of the Punnett square calculations show that the expected genotypes of offspring are ¼ *EE*, ½ *Ee*, and ¼ *ee*, giving a 1:2:1 genotypic ratio. Since ¾ have unattached earlobes and ¼ have attached earlobes, this is a 3:1 phenotypic ratio.

The gametes combine at random, and in practice it is usually necessary to observe a very large number of offspring before a 3:1 ratio can be verified. Only if many offspring are counted can it be assured that all genetically different sperm have had a chance to fertilize all genetically different eggs. If a number of heterozygotes produced 200 offspring, approximately 150 of these would have unattached earlobes and approximately 50 would have attached earlobes (a 3:1 ratio). In terms of genotypes, approximately 50 would be *EE*, about 100 would be *Ee*, and the remaining 50 would be *ee*.

We cannot arrange crosses between humans in order to count a large number of offspring. Therefore, in humans the phenotypic ratio is used to estimate the chances any child has for a particular characteristic. In the cross under consideration, each child has a ¾ (or 75%) chance of having unattached earlobes and ¼ (or 25%) chance of having attached earlobes. And we must remember that *chance has no memory:* if two heterozygous parents already have a child with attached earlobes, the next child still has a 25% chance of having attached earlobes.

You will note that the Punnett square makes use of the laws of probability we mentioned in the previous section. First, we recognize there is a ½ chance of a child getting the *E* allele or the *e* allele from a parent. In this way we are able to designate the possible gametes. What operation is in keeping with the multiplicative law of probability? The operation of combining the alleles and placing them in the squares. What operation is in keeping with the additive law of probability? The operation of adding the results, and arriving at the phenotypic ratio.

Mendel was quite familiar with the laws of probability and was able to make use of them to see that inheritance of traits depended upon the passage of discrete factors from generation to generation.

The laws of probability allow one to calculate the probable results of one-trait genetic crosses.

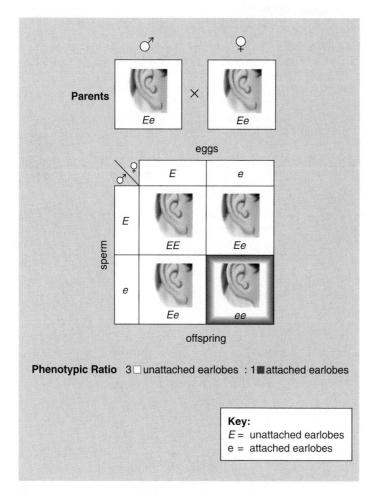

Phenotypic Ratio   3 ☐ unattached earlobes : 1 ■ attached earlobes

Key:
E = unattached earlobes
e = attached earlobes

Figure 11.5 Genetic inheritance in humans.
When the parents are heterozygous, each child has a 75% chance of having the dominant phenotype and a 25% chance of having the recessive phenotype.

Practice Problems 2*

1. In rabbits, if *B* = dominant black allele and *b* = recessive white allele, which of these genotypes (*Bb, BB, bb*) could a white rabbit have?

2. In pea plants, yellow seed color is dominant over green seed color. When two heterozygote plants are crossed, what percentage of plants would have yellow seeds? green seeds?

3. In humans, freckles is dominant over no freckles. A man with freckles reproduces with a woman with freckles, but the children have no freckles. What chance did each child have for freckles?

4. In horses, trotter (*T*) is dominant over pacer (*t*). A trotter is mated to a pacer, and the offspring is a pacer. Give the genotype of all horses.

* Answers to Practice Problems appear in Appendix A.

One-Trait Testcross

To test his idea about the segregation of alleles—in modern terms, that the F_1 was heterozygous—Mendel crossed his F_1 generation tall plants with true-breeding, short (homozygous recessive) plants. He reasoned that half the offspring should be tall and half should be short, producing a 1:1 phenotypic ratio (Fig. 11.6*a*). He obtained these results; therefore, his hypothesis that alleles segregate when gametes are formed was supported. It was Mendel's experimental use of simple dominant and recessive traits that allowed him to formulate and to test the law of segregation.

In Figure 11.6, the homozygous recessive parent can produce only one type of gamete—*t*—and so the same results would be obtained if the Punnett square had only one column. This is logical because the *t* means all the gametes that carry a *t*.

Today, a monohybrid **testcross** is used to determine if an individual with the dominant phenotype is homozygous dominant or heterozygous for a particular trait. Since both of these genotypes produce the dominant phenotype, it is not possible to determine the genotype by inspection. Figure 11.6*b* shows that if the F_1 in Mendel's cross had been homozygous dominant, then all the offspring would have been tall.

> The results of a testcross indicate whether an individual with the dominant phenotype is heterozygous or homozygous dominant.

Practice Problems 3*

1. In horses, *B* = black coat and *b* = brown coat. What type of cross should be done to best determine whether a black-coated horse is homozygous dominant or heterozygous?

2. In fruit flies, *L* = long wings and *l* = short wings. The offspring exhibit a 1:1 ratio when a long-winged fly is crossed with a short-winged fly. What is the genotype of the parental flies?

3. In the garden pea, round seeds are dominant over wrinkled seeds. An investigator crosses a plant having round seeds with a plant having wrinkled seeds. He counts 400 offspring. How many of the offspring have wrinkled seeds if the plant having round seeds is a heterozygote?

* Answers to Practice Problems appear in Appendix A.

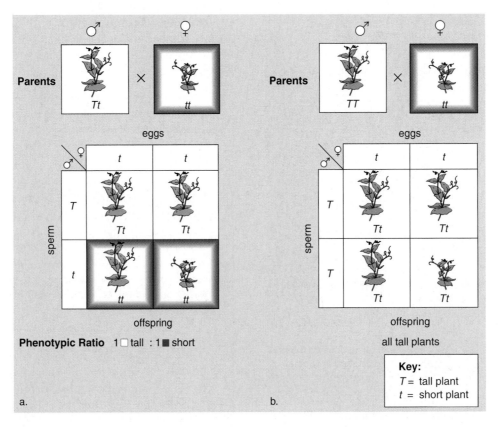

Phenotypic Ratio 1 □ tall : 1 ■ short

all tall plants

Key:
T = tall plant
t = short plant

a.   b.

Figure 11.6 Testcross.
Crossing an individual with the dominant phenotype with a recessive individual indicates the genotype. **a.** If a parent with the dominant phenotype is heterozygous, the phenotypic ratio among the offspring is 1:1. **b.** If a parent with the dominant phenotype is homozygous, all offspring have the dominant phenotype.

11.3 Dihybrid Inheritance

Mendel performed a second series of crosses in which he crossed true-breeding plants that differed in two traits; such crosses are appropriately called dihybrid crosses. For example, he crossed tall plants having green pods with short plants having yellow pods (Fig. 11.7). The F_1 plants showed both dominant characteristics. As before, Mendel then allowed the F_1 plants to self-pollinate. Two possible results could occur in the F_2 generation:

1. If the dominant factors (*TG*) always segregate into the F_1 gametes together, and the recessive factors (*tg*) always stay together, then there would be two phenotypes among the F_2 plants—tall plants with green pods and short plants with yellow pods.
2. If the four factors segregate into the F_1 gametes independently, then there would be four phenotypes among the F_2 plants— tall plants with green pods, tall plants with yellow pods, short plants with green pods, and short plants with yellow pods.

Figure 11.7 shows that Mendel observed four phenotypes among the F_2 plants, supporting the second hypothesis. Therefore, Mendel formulated his second law of heredity—the law of independent assortment.

Mendel's law of independent assortment: Members of one pair of factors separate (assort) independently of members of another pair of factors. Therefore, all possible combinations of factors can occur in the gametes.

Practice Problems 4*

1. For each of the following genotypes, give all possible gametes, noting the proportion of each gamete for the individual.
   a. *TtGG*
   b. *TtGg*
   c. *TTGg*
2. For each of the following, state whether a genotype (genetic makeup of an organism) or a type of gamete is represented.
   a. *Tg*
   b. *WwCC*
   c. *TW*

* Answers to Practice Problems appear in Appendix A.

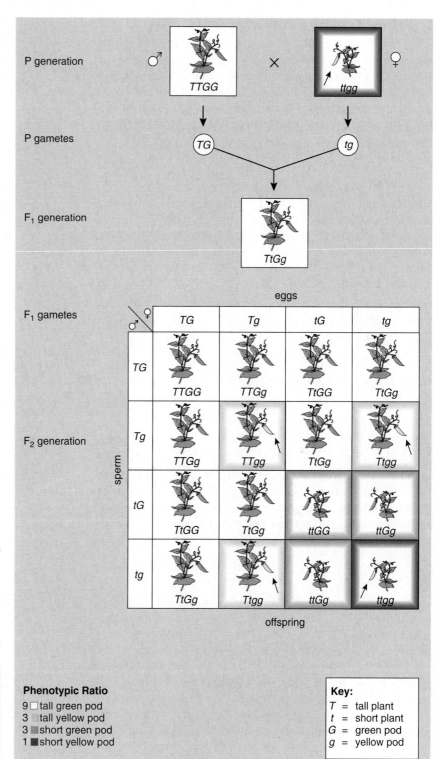

Phenotypic Ratio

9 ☐ tall green pod
3 ▨ tall yellow pod
3 ▦ short green pod
1 ■ short yellow pod

Key:

T = tall plant
t = short plant
G = green pod
g = yellow pod

Figure 11.7 Dihybrid cross done by Mendel.
P generation plants differ in two regards—length of the stem and color of the pod. The F_1 generation shows only the dominant traits, but all possible phenotypes appear among the F_2 generation. The 9:3:3:1 ratio allowed Mendel to deduce that factors segregate into gametes independently of other factors.

Dihybrid Genetics Problems

The fruit fly, *Drosophila melanogaster*, less than one-fifth the size of a housefly, is a favorite subject for genetic research because it has mutant characteristics that are easily determined. A "wild-type" fly has long wings and a gray body. There are mutant flies with short (vestigial) wings and black (ebony) bodies. The key for a cross involving these traits is L = long wing, l = short wing, G = gray body, and g = black body.

Laws of Probability

If two flies heterozygous for both traits are crossed, what are the probable results? Since each characteristic is inherited separately from any other, it is possible to apply again the laws of probability mentioned on page 178. For example, we know the F_2 results for two separate monohybrid crosses are as listed here:

1. The chance of long wings = ¾
   The chance of short wings = ¼
2. The chance of gray body = ¾
   The chance of black body = ¼

Using the multiplicative law, we know that:

The chance of long wings and gray body = ¾ × ¾ = ⁹⁄₁₆
The chance of long wings and black body = ¾ × ¼ = ³⁄₁₆
The chance of short wings and gray body = ¼ × ¾ = ³⁄₁₆
The chance of short wings and black body = ¼ × ¼ = ¹⁄₁₆

Using the additive law, we conclude that the phenotypic ratio is 9:3:3:1. Again, since all genetically different male gametes must have an equal opportunity to fertilize all genetically different female gametes to even approximately achieve these results, a large number of offspring must be counted.

The Punnett Square

In Figure 11.8, the flies of the P generation have only one possible type of gamete because they are homozygous dominant for both traits. All the F_1 flies are heterozygous (*LlGg*) and have the same phenotype (long wings, gray body).

The Punnett square in Figure 11.8 shows the expected results when the F_1 flies are crossed, assuming that all genetically different sperm have an equal opportunity to fertilize all genetically different eggs. Notice that ⁹⁄₁₆ of the offspring have long wings and a gray body, ³⁄₁₆ have long wings and a black body, ³⁄₁₆ have short wings and a gray body, and ¹⁄₁₆ have short wings and a black body. This phenotypic ratio of 9:3:3:1 is expected whenever a heterozygote for two traits is crossed with another heterozygote for two traits and simple dominance is present in both genes.

A Punnett square can also be used to predict the chances of an offspring having a particular phenotype. What are the chances of an offspring with long wings and gray body? The

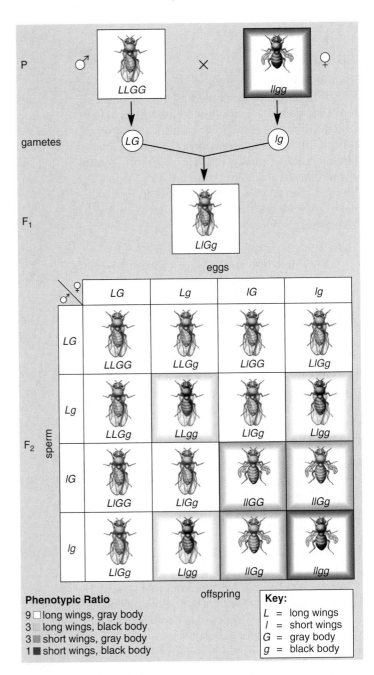

Phenotypic Ratio

9 ☐ long wings, gray body
3 ▨ long wings, black body
3 ▦ short wings, gray body
1 ■ short wings, black body

Key:
L = long wings
l = short wings
G = gray body
g = black body

Figure 11.8 Inheritance in fruit flies.
Each F_1 fly (*LlGg*) produces four types of gametes because all possible combinations of alleles can occur in the gametes. Therefore, all possible phenotypes appear among the F_2 offspring.

chances are ⁹⁄₁₆. What are the chances of an offspring with short wings and gray body? The chances are ³⁄₁₆, and so forth.

Today, we know that these results are obtained and the law of independent assortment holds because of the events of meiosis. The gametes contain one allele for each trait and in all possible combinations because homologues separate independently during meiosis I.

Two-Trait Testcross

A dihybrid testcross is used to determine if an individual is homozygous dominant or heterozygous for either of the two traits. Since it is not possible to determine the genotype of a long-winged, gray-bodied fly by inspection, the genotype may be represented as $L\_\_^1\ G\_\_$.

When doing a dihybrid testcross, an individual with the dominant phenotype is crossed with an individual with the recessive phenotype. For example, a long-winged, gray-bodied fly is crossed with a short-winged, black-bodied fly. A long-winged, gray-bodied fly heterozygous for both traits will form four different types of gametes. The homozygous fly with short wings and a black body can form only one kind of gamete:

P	$LlGg$	$\times$	$llgg$
	↓		↓
gametes	LG		lg
	Lg		
	lG		
	lg		

Figure 11.9 shows that ¼ of the expected offspring have long wings and a gray body; ¼ have long wings and a black body; ¼ have short wings and a gray body; and ¼ have short wings and a black body. This is a 1:1:1:1 phenotypic ratio. The presence of offspring with short wings and a black body shows that the $L\_\_G\_\_$ fly is heterozygous for both traits and has the genotype $LlGg$.

If the $L\_\_G\_\_$ fly is homozygous for both traits, then no offspring will have short wings or a black body when this fly is crossed with one that has the recessive phenotype for both traits. If the $L\_\_G\_\_$ fly is heterozygous for one trait but not the other, what is the expected phenotypic ratio among the offspring when this fly is crossed with one that has the recessive phenotype for both traits?

In dihybrid genetics problems, the individual has four alleles, two for each trait.

---

¹ The blank means that a dominant or recessive allele can be present.

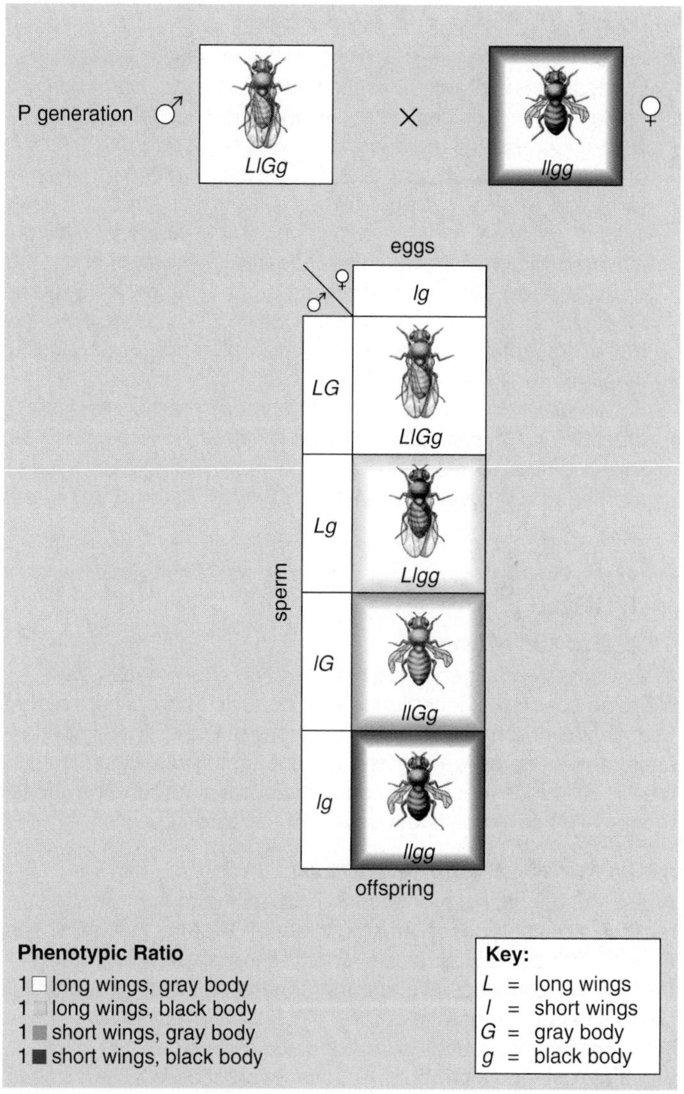

Phenotypic Ratio

1 ☐ long wings, gray body
1   long wings, black body
1 ▨ short wings, gray body
1 ■ short wings, black body

Key:
L = long wings
l = short wings
G = gray body
g = black body

Figure 11.9 Testcross.
Testcross to determine if a fly is heterozygous for both traits. If a fly heterozygous for both traits is crossed with a fly that is recessive for both traits, the expected ratio of phenotypes is 1:1:1:1. What would the result be if the test individual were homozygous dominant for both traits? homozygous dominant for one trait but heterozygous for the other?

Practice Problems 5*

1. In horses, B = black coat, b = brown coat, T = trotter, and t = pacer. A black pacer mated to a brown trotter produces a black trotter offspring. Give all possible genotypes for this offspring.

2. In fruit flies, long wings (L) is dominant over short wings (l), and gray body (G) is dominant over black body (g). In each instance, what are the most likely genotypes of the previous generation if a student gets the following phenotypic results?

   a. 1:1:1:1 (all possible combinations in equal number)

   b. 9:3:3:1 (9 dominant; 3 mixed; 3 mixed; 1 recessive)

3. In humans, short fingers and widow's peak are dominant over long fingers and straight hairline. A heterozygote in both regards reproduces with a similar heterozygote. What is the chance of any one child having the same phenotype as the parents?

* Answers to Practice Problems appear in Appendix A.

Connecting Concepts

Humans have practiced selective plant and animal breeding since agriculture and animal domestication began thousands of years ago. Many early breeders came to realize that their programs were successful because they were manipulating inherited factors for particular characteristics. A good experimental design and a bit of luck allowed Mendel, and not one of these breeders, to work out his rules of inheritance.

The use of a large number of pea crosses and a statistical analysis of the large number of resulting offspring contributed to the success of Mendel's work.

Although humans do not usually produce a large number of offspring it has been possible to come to the conclusion that Mendel's laws do apply to humans in many instances. Inheritance in large families that keep good historical records, such as Mormon families, has allowed researchers to show that a number of human genetic disorders are indeed controlled by a single allelic pair. Such disorders include cystic fibrosis, sickle-cell disease, albinism, achondroplasia (a form of dwarfism), neurofibromatosis, and Huntington disease.

Mendel was lucky in that he chose to study an organism, namely the garden pea, whose observable traits are often determined by a single allelic pair. In the common garden bean on the other hand, plant height, for example, is determined by several genes. Therefore, crosses of tall and short plants result in F_1 plants of intermediate height rather than all tall plants. This type of inheritance pattern, called polygenic, controls *many* important traits in farm animals, such as weight and milk production in cattle. You will learn more about polygenic and other types of inheritance patterns that differ from simple Mendelian inheritance in chapter 12.

Summary

11.1 Gregor Mendel

At the time Mendel began his hybridization experiments, the blending concept of inheritance was popular. This concept stated that whenever the parents were distinctly different, the offspring are intermediate between them. In contrast to preceding plant breeders, Mendel decided to do a statistical study, and he chose to study just seven distinctive traits of the garden pea.

11.2 Monohybrid Inheritance

When Mendel did his monohybrid crosses, he found that the recessive phenotype reappeared in about ¼ of the F_2 plants. This allowed Mendel to deduce his law of segregation, which states that the individual has two factors for each trait and the factors segregate into the gametes.

The laws of probability can be used to calculate the expected phenotypic ratio of a cross. In practice, a large number of offspring must be counted in order to observe the expected results, because only in that way can it be ensured that all possible types of sperm have fertilized all possible types of eggs.

Because humans do not produce a large number of offspring, it is best to use a predicted ratio as a means of estimating the chances of an individual inheriting a particular characteristic.

Mendel also crossed the F_1 plants having the dominant phenotype with homozygous recessive plants. The results indicated that the recessive factor was present in these F_1 plants (i.e., that they were heterozygous). Today, we call this a testcross, because it is used to test whether an individual showing the dominant characteristic is homozygous dominant or heterozygous.

11.3 Dihybrid Inheritance

Mendel did dihybrid crosses, in which the F_1 individuals showed both dominant characteristics, but there were four phenotypes among the F_2 offspring. This allowed Mendel to deduce the law of independent assortment, which states that the members of one pair of factors separate independently of those from another pair. Therefore, all possible combinations of factors can occur in the gametes.

With regard to Mendel's dihybrid crosses, the laws of probability show that 9/16 of the F_2 offspring have the two dominant traits, 3/16 have one dominant trait with one recessive trait, 3/16 have the other dominant trait with the other recessive trait, and 1/16 have both recessive traits, for a 9:3:3:1 ratio.

The dihybrid testcross allows an investigator to test whether an individual showing two dominant characteristics is homozygous dominant for both traits or for one trait only, or is heterozygous for both traits.

Table 11.2 lists the most typical crosses and the expected results. Learning these saves the trouble of working out the results repeatedly for each of these crosses.

Table 11.2

Common Crosses Involving Simple Dominance

Examples	Phenotypic Ratios
$Tt \times Tt$	3:1 (dominant to recessive)
$Tt \times tt$	1:1 (dominant to recessive)
$TtYy \times TtYy$	9:3:3:1 (9 dominant; 3 mixed; 3 mixed; 1 recessive)
$TtYy \times ttyy$	1:1:1:1 (all possible combinations in equal number)

Reviewing the Chapter

1. How did Mendel's procedure differ from that of his predecessors? What mechanism did he use to set aside any personal beliefs he may have had?   174
2. How did the monohybrid crosses performed by Mendel refute the blending concept of inheritance?   174
3. Using Mendel's monohybrid cross as an example, trace his reasoning to arrive at the law of segregation.   176
4. Define these terms: allele, dominant allele, recessive allele, genotype, homozygous, heterozygous, and phenotype.   177
5. Use a Punnett square and the laws of probability to show the results of a cross between two individuals who are heterozygous for one trait. What are the chances of an offspring having the dominant phenotype? the recessive phenotype?   179
6. In what way does a monohybrid testcross support Mendel's law of segregation?   180
7. How is a monohybrid testcross used today?   180
8. Using Mendel's dihybrid cross as an example, trace his reasoning to arrive at the law of independent assortment.   181

9. Use a Punnett square and the laws of probability to show the results of a cross between two individuals who are heterozygous for two traits. What are the chances of an offspring having the dominant phenotype for both traits? having the recessive phenotype for both traits?   182
10. What would be the results of a dihybrid testcross if an individual was heterozygous for two traits? heterozygous for one trait and homozygous dominant for the other? homozygous dominant for both traits?   183

Testing Yourself

Choose the best answer for each question. For questions 1–4, match the cross with the results in the key:

Key:

a. 3:1
b. 9:3:3:1
c. 1:1
d. 1:1:1:1
e. 3:1:3:1

1. *TtYy* × *TtYy*
2. *Tt* × *Tt*
3. *Tt* × *tt*
4. *TtYy* × *ttyy*
5. Which of these could be a normal gamete?
   a. *GgRr*
   b. *GRr*
   c. *Gr*
   d. *GgR*
   e. None of these are correct.
6. Which of these properly describes a cross between an individual who is homozygous dominant for hairline but heterozygous for finger length and an individual who is recessive for both characteristics? (*W* = widow's peak, *w* = straight hairline, *S* = short fingers, *s* = long fingers)
   a. *WwSs* × *WwSs*
   b. *WWSs* × *wwSs*
   c. *Ws* × *ws*
   d. *WWSs* × *wwss*
7. In peas, yellow seed (*Y*) is dominant over green seed (*y*). In the F$_2$ generation of a monohybrid cross that begins when a dominant homozygote is crossed with a recessive homozygote, you would expect
   a. plants that produce three yellow seeds to every green seed.
   b. plants with one yellow seed for every green seed.
   c. only plants with the genotype *Yy*.
   d. only plants that produce yellow seeds.
   e. Both c and d are correct.
8. In humans, pointed eyebrows (*B*) are dominant over smooth eyebrows (*b*). Mary's father has pointed eyebrows, but she and her mother have smooth. What is the genotype of the father?
   a. *BB*
   b. *Bb*
   c. *bb*
   d. *BbBb*
   e. Any one of these is correct.

9. In guinea pigs, smooth coat (*S*) is dominant over rough coat (*s*) and black coat (*B*) is dominant over white coat (*b*). In the cross *SsBb* × *SsBb*, how many of the offspring will have a smooth black coat on average?
   a. 9 only
   b. about 9/16
   c. 1/16
   d. 6/16
   e. 2/6
10. In horses, *B* = black coat, *b* = brown coat, *T* = trotter, and *t* = pacer. A black trotter that has a brown pacer offspring is
    a. *BT.*
    b. *BbTt.*
    c. *bbtt.*
    d. *BBtt.*
    e. *BBTT.*
11. In tomatoes, red fruit (*R*) is dominant over yellow fruit (*r*) and tallness (*T*) is dominant over shortness (*t*). A plant that is *RrTT* is crossed with a plant that is *rrTt*. What are the chances of an offspring being heterozygous for both traits?
    a. none
    b. 1/2
    c. 1/4
    d. 9/16
    e. 1/3
12. In the cross *RrTt* × *rrtt,*
    a. all the offspring will be tall with red fruit.
    b. 75% (3/4) will be tall with red fruit.
    c. 50% (1/2) will be tall with red fruit.
    d. 25% (1/4) will be tall with red fruit.

Additional Genetics Problems*

1. If a man homozygous for widow's peak (dominant) reproduces with a woman homozygous for straight hairline (recessive), what are the chances of their children having a widow's peak? a straight hairline?
2. John has unattached earlobes (recessive) like his father, but his mother has attached earlobes (dominant). What is John's genotype?
3. In humans, the allele for short fingers is dominant over that for long fingers. If a person with short fingers who had one parent with long fingers reproduces with a person having long fingers, what are the chances of each child having short fingers?
4. In a fruit fly experiment (see key on page 182), two gray-bodied fruit flies produce mostly gray-bodied offspring, but some offspring have black bodies. If there are 280 offspring, how many do you predict will have gray bodies and how many will have black bodies? How many of the 280 offspring do you predict will be heterozygous? If you wanted to test whether a particular gray-bodied fly was homozygous dominant or heterozygous, what cross would you do?
5. Using the term 2n in which n = the number of heterozygous gene pairs, determine the number of possible gametes for the genotypes *BBHH, BbHh,* and *BBHh.*

6. In rabbits, black color (*B*) is dominant over brown (*b*) and short hair (*S*) is dominant over long (*s*). In a cross between a homozygous black, long-haired rabbit and a brown, homozygous short-haired one, what would the F_1 generation look like? the F_2 generation? If one of the F_1 rabbits reproduced with a brown, long-haired rabbit, what phenotypes and in what ratio would you expect?

7. In horses, black coat (*B*) is dominant over brown coat (*b*) and being a trotter (*T*) is dominant over being a pacer (*t*). A black pacer is crossed with a brown trotter. The offspring is a brown pacer. Give the genotypes of all these horses.

8. The complete genotype of a long-winged, gray-bodied fruit fly is unknown (see key on page 182). When this fly is crossed with a short-winged, black-bodied fruit fly, the offspring all have a gray body but about half of them have short wings. What is the genotype of the long-winged, gray-bodied fly?

9. In humans, widow's peak hairline is dominant over straight hairline, and short fingers are dominant over long fingers. If an individual who is heterozygous for both traits reproduces with an individual who is recessive for both traits, what are the chances of their child also being recessive for both traits?

Thinking Scientifically

1. *Drosophila* that are homozygous recessive for the apterous (*apt*) mutation have no wings. Flies that are homozygous recessive for the vestigial (*vg*) mutation have small, nonfunctional wings. If these traits are alternative alleles of the same gene, what phenotype would you predict in the offspring from a cross between vestigial and apterous flies? If instead you obtain all flies with normal wings, what would you hypothesize about the number of genes that control wing development?

2. Mendel's paper reporting his results and conclusions included very detailed records of all of the crosses and offspring. The first parts of his paper show that the ratios he measured were not exactly 3:1 or 9:3:3:1. However, the data he shows for the last section is almost exactly what he had predicted. What would be a possible interpretation for this curious phenomenon?

Understanding the Terms

allele 177	homozygous 177
dominant allele 177	phenotype 177
gene locus 177	Punnett square 179
genotype 177	recessive allele 177
heterozygous 177	testcross 180

Match the terms to these definitions:

a. _____ Allele that exerts its phenotypic effect only in the homozygote; its expression is masked by a dominant allele.

b. _____ Alternative forms of a gene—which occur at the same locus on homologous chromosomes.

c. _____ Allele that exerts its phenotypic effect in the heterozygote; it masks the expression of the recessive allele.

d. _____ Cross between an individual with the dominant phenotype and an individual with the recessive phenotype to see if the individual with the dominant phenotype is homozygous or heterozygous.

e. _____ Genes of an organism for a particular trait or traits; for example, *BB* or *Aa*.

Web Connections

Exploring the Internet

http://www.mhhe.com/biosci/genbio/mader
(click on *Biology 7/e*)

The *Biology 7/e* Online Learning Center provides many resources for studying the material in this chapter including links to the following sites:

Mendelian Genetics explores Mendel's First and Second Laws of Genetics, and independent assortment along with a number of more advanced topics (i.e., gene interactions, modifier genes, and variation in gene expression). An excellent site with a wealth of information.

http://www.cc.ndsu.nodak.edu/instruct/mcclean/plsc431/mendel/

Genetics Virtual Library is a website catalog of hundreds of genetics sites. Here you can find sites discussing every organism from bacteria to cattle to slime molds to mosquitoes. Transgenic and genome resource sites are also listed.

http://www.ornl.gov/TechResources/Human_Genome/vl.html

Online Mendelian Inheritance in Man. This site supported by the National Center for Biotechnology Information includes a catalog of human genes and genetic disorders. It provides text, images, references, and a map of human chromosomes.

http://www3.ncbi.nlm.nih.gov/Omim/

The Human Transcript Map. The genes of the human genome, circa 1996 with a link to the GeneMap'98. Text material describes disease conditions associated with individual genes. Clickable by chromosome number.

http://www.ncbi.nlm.nih.gov/SCIENCE96/

Mendel Web. This site is a resource for teachers and students interested in classical genetics, data analysis, and the history and literature of science. It includes Mendel's original paper (written in German) and an English translation of the paper.

http://www.netspace.org/MendelWeb/

Chromosomes and Genes

A human chromosome

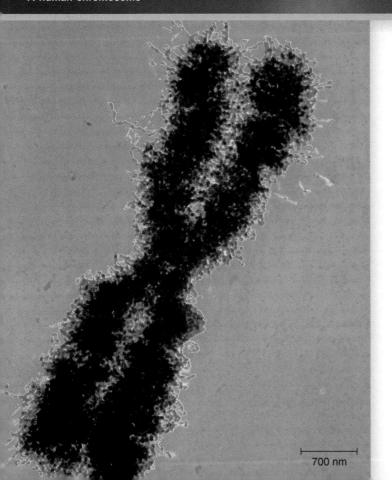

700 nm

Considering that Mendel knew nothing about chromosomes, genes, or DNA, it is astounding that his laws about the transfer of genetic information from parent to offspring do apply to all organisms and complex patterns of inheritance. As brilliant and groundbreaking as Mendel's work was, it was only the first step toward a more thorough understanding of how the genotype functions.

Researchers did not know until the early 1900s that the genes are on the chromosomes, and the behavior of chromosomes explains Mendel's law of segregation and independent assortment as long as the genes are on separate chromosomes. Mendel would not have been able to formulate his two laws if he had been working with genes on the same chromosome! Determining the sequence of genes on the chromosomes began with *Drosophila*. Now researchers are sequencing the genes for all sorts of organisms, including humans. Chromosomes can undergo mutations, permanent changes in number and structure, and you can well imagine that such alterations would have a profound effect on the phenotype.

12.1 Mendelism and the Genotype

Since Mendel's day, variations in the dominant/recessive relationship he described have been discovered. These variations make it clear that the concept of the genotype should be expanded to include all the genes. The idea of just two alleles per trait, one dominant and one recessive, is too restrictive because various genes work together to bring about a phenotype which is also influenced by the environment.

Incomplete Dominance and Codominance

Incomplete dominance describes a situation in which a dominant allele is unable to make up for the presence of a recessive allele. In a cross between a true-breeding, red-flowered four-o'clock strain and a true-breeding, white-flowered strain, the offspring have pink flowers (Fig. 12.1). While this may appear to be an example of the blending theory of inheritance, it is not, because if these F_1 plants self-pollinate, the F_2 generation has a phenotypic ratio of 1 red-flowered : 2 pink-flowered : 1 white-flowered plant. The reappearance of the parental phenotypes in the F_2 generation makes it clear we are still dealing with an example of particulate inheritance of the type described by Mendel.

When doing an incomplete dominance problem, use the same letter to indicate the alleles but do not use a capital and lowercase letter because one allele is not completely dominant over the other. Therefore, Figure 12.1 uses the notations R_1 and R_2 for the alleles. The genotype R_1R_2 for the pink-flowered F_1 plant makes it clear that R_1 is not dominant over R_2. There is a biochemical explanation for incomplete dominance. The pink-flowered plants are producing one-half the amount of pigment as the red-flowered plants. The white-flowered plants lack pigment.

Similarly, in many instances of simple dominance the dominant allele is coding for a product (e.g., enzyme), while the recessive allele is not coding for a product. But in a case of simple dominance, the F_1 appears to have the same phenotype as the homozygous dominant parent. In the case of incomplete dominance, it is apparent to the most casual observer that the F_1 does not have the appearance of the parent with the dominant phenotype.

In **codominance,** another example that differs from Mendel's findings, both alleles are fully expressed. When an individual has blood type A, A type of glycoprotein appears on the red blood cells. When an individual has blood type B, B type of glycoprotein appears on the red blood cells. But when an individual has the blood type AB, both A and B types of glycoproteins appear on the red blood cells. The two different capital letters signify that both alleles are coding for an effective product.

In incomplete dominance, the F_1 does not resemble either parent because one functioning allele is unable to produce the dominant phenotype. In codominance, both alleles are functioning and coding for a product.

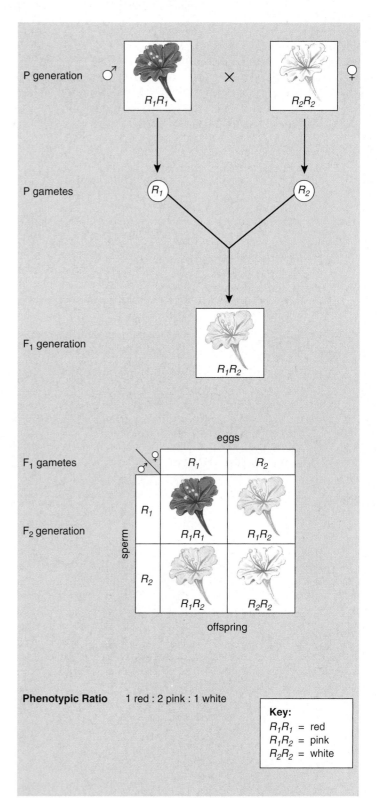

Figure 12.1 Incomplete dominance.
Incomplete dominance is illustrated by a cross between red- and white-flowered four-o'clocks. The F_1 plants are pink, a phenotype intermediate between those of the P generation; however, the F_2 results show that neither the red nor the white allele has disappeared. Therefore, this is still an example of particulate inheritance, though the heterozygote R_1R_2 is pink.

Epistasis

In **epistasis** [Gk. *epi*, on, and *stasis*, a standing], a gene at one locus interferes with the phenotypic expression of a gene at a different locus. In most instances, a recessive pair of alleles at one locus prevents the expression of a dominant allele at another locus. Both loci must have a functioning gene for the dominant phenotype to appear.

By studying the results of crosses in sweet peas, it has been deduced that there are two genes affecting pigmentation and that being homozygous recessive in either gene results in a lack of color. If the two varieties of white-flowered plants are crossed, the F_1 have purple flowers instead of the white flowers as expected. Among the F_2, following self-pollination of the F_1 plants, 9/16 of the plants have purple flowers and 7/16 have white flowers. Since the ratio is in sixteenths, the F_1 plants must have been heterozygous for both genes as shown in Figure 12.2*a*. Why do the F_1 plants have purple flowers? Because they have both a dominant *A* allele and a dominant *B* allele. Why is there a 9:7 ratio instead of a 9:3:3:1 ratio among the F_2 generation of plants? Whenever a plant is homozygous recessive for one of the genes, no pigment is produced. Both loci need at least one dominant allele to produce the dominant phenotype.

Although the exact details of pigmentation synthesis are known, the metabolic pathway shown in Figure 12.2*b* is hypothesized. If the *A* allele codes for the first enzyme and the *B* allele codes for the second enzyme, then being homozygous recessive for either gene would result in white instead of purple flowers.

A similar situation occurs in mammalian animals. If individuals inherit any one of several defects in the metabolic pathway for the synthesis of melanin, the individual is an albino.

In epistasis, genes at two different loci interact to control a single trait.

Pleiotropy

The term **pleiotropy** [Gk. *pleion*, more, and *tropos*, turning] is used to describe a gene that affects more than one characteristic of the individual. Individuals with Marfan syndrome tend to be tall and thin with long legs, arms, and fingers. They are nearsighted, and the wall of the aorta is weak, causing it to enlarge and, eventually, to split. All of these effects are caused by an inability to produce a normal extracellular matrix protein called fibrillin. Fibrillin strengthens elastic fibers and allows extracellular components to adhere to one another.

There are some who suggest that Abraham Lincoln had Marfan syndrome. Certainly it would account for his lanky frame and the symptoms he described for posterity. If he had not been shot, it's possible he still would have died shortly thereafter from circulatory failure.

In pleiotropy, a single gene affects more than one trait.

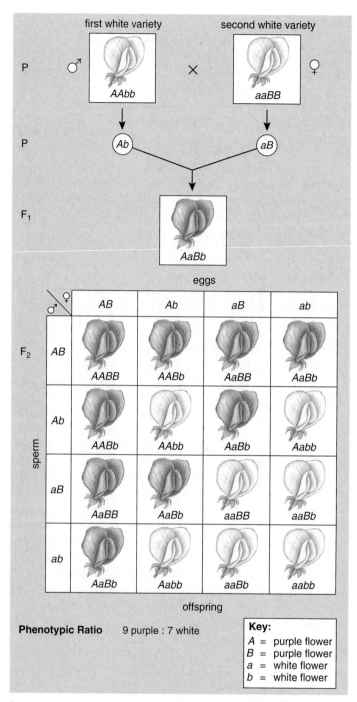

Phenotypic Ratio   9 purple : 7 white

Key:
A = purple flower
B = purple flower
a = white flower
b = white flower

a.

genotype *AA* or *Aa*   genotype *BB* or *Ba*

enzyme   enzyme

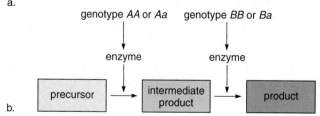

b.

Figure 12.2 Epistasis.
a. Two pairs of genes are believed to be involved in color production in sweet peas. Being homozygous recessive for either gene results in lack of color. **b.** It is hypothesized that each gene codes for an enzyme in a metabolic pathway that results in pigmentation. If either enzyme is lacking, an absence of color results.

Multiple Alleles

In **multiple alleles**, one gene has several possible alleles for its chromosomal locus. Each individual has only two of possible alleles. Three different peppered moth phenotypes are believed to be the result of three possible alleles: typical (*m*) is recessive to the other two; and mottled insularia (*M'*) is recessive to nearly black melanic allele (*M*). Therefore, there are three possible phenotypes: melanic (*M—*), insularia (*M'M'* or *M'm*) and typical (*mm*).

Inheritance by multiple alleles often results in more than two possible phenotypes for a particular trait. Blood type in humans is controlled by three alleles (*A, B,* and *O*) and there are four possible phenotypes: A, B, AB, and O types of blood (see page 210).

When inheritance is by multiple alleles, there are more than two alleles for a single gene locus and there are more than two possible phenotypes among the offspring.

Polygenic Inheritance

Polygenic inheritance [Gk. *polys*, many, and L. *genitus*, producing] occurs when one trait is governed by several genes occupying different loci on the same homologous pair of chromosomes or on different homologous pairs of chromosomes. Each gene has two alleles. The contributing allele is represented by a capital letter, and the noncontributing allele is represented by a small letter. Each contributing allele has a quantitative effect on the phenotype, and therefore the allelic effects of all contributing alleles are additive.

For example, H. Nilsson-Ehle studied the inheritance of seed color in wheat. Genes at three different loci determine seed color. After he crossed plants that produced white and dark-red seeds, the F_1 plants were allowed to self-pollinate. Each of the F_2 plants produced seeds having one of seven degrees of color (Fig. 12.3). The alleles responsible for the color of the seeds are represented by dots in the squares. The number of capitals (contributing allele) is represented by coloring in the dots. Since each contributing allele has a small but equal quantitative effect, there is a range of F_2 phenotypes. The proportions of the various phenotypes can be graphed and these proportions can be connected to form a bell-shaped curve.

In chapter 10, we learned that sexual reproduction contributes to evolution by increasing variation among the offspring. Similarly, polygenic inheritance also increases the chances that sexually reproducing organisms will produce a phenotype more suited to the environment than the previous generation, particularly if the environment is changing. Polygenic inheritance which results in a range of phenotypes is observed quite often in complex organisms. If we were observing the phenotypes in nature, we would probably arrive directly at a bell-shaped curve because environmental

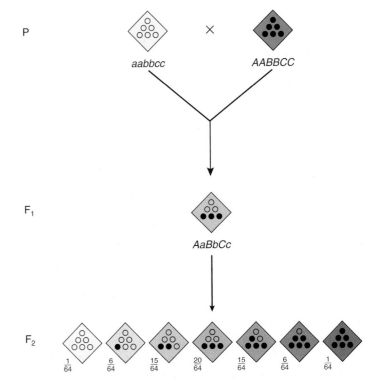

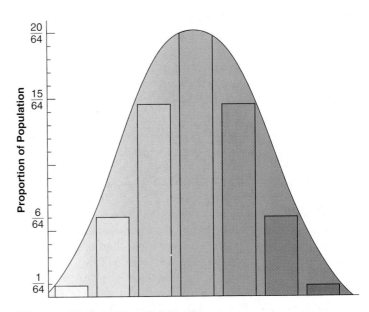

Figure 12.3 Polygenic inheritance.
In this example, a trait is controlled by three genes; only the alleles represented by a capital letter are contributing alleles. When two intermediate phenotypes are crossed, seven phenotypes are seen among the F_2 generation. The phenotype proportions are graphed. If environmental effects are considered, a bell-shaped curve results because of many intervening phenotypes.

effects cause many intervening phenotypes. Consider the inheritance of skin color or height in humans, which are believed to be examples of polygenic inheritance. In the first instance, exposure to sun can affect skin color and increase the number of phenotypic variations. In the second instance, nutrition can affect height, resulting in many more phenotypes than those expected.

> In polygenic inheritance, each contributing allele adds to the phenotype. A bell-shaped curve of phenotypic variations is due to the number of alleles involved and is also due to environmental effects.

The Environment and the Phenotype

There is no doubt that both the genotype and the environment affect the phenotype. The relative importance of genetic and environmental influences on the phenotype can vary, but in some instances the environment seems to have an extreme effect. In the water buttercup, *Ranunculus peltatus,* the submerged part of the plant has a different appearance from the part above water. Apparently, the presence or absence of an aquatic environment dramatically influences the phenotype.

Temperature can also have a dramatic effect on the phenotypes of plants. Primroses have white flowers when grown above 32 °C and red flowers when grown at 24 °C. The coats of Siamese cats and Himalayan rabbits are darker in color at the ears, nose, paws, and tail. Himalayan rabbits are known to be homozygous for the allele *ch,* which is involved in production of melanin. Experimental evidence suggests that the enzyme encoded by this gene is active only at a low temperature and that, therefore, black fur only occurs at the extremities where body heat is lost to the environment (Fig. 12.4). When the animal is placed in a warmer environment, new fur on these body parts is light in color.

So, we come to the conclusion that matters are a little more complex than Mendel had envisioned. Not only do gene interactions contribute to the phenotype so does the environment.

> An organism's environmental history in addition to the genotype can influence the phenotype.

a.

b.

c.

Figure 12.4 Coat color in Himalayan rabbits.
a. A Himalayan rabbit which has black extremities is usually homozygous recessive for the allele *ch,* which codes for an enzyme involved in the production of melanin. **b.** The influence of the environment on the phenotype has been demonstrated by plucking out the fur from one area and applying an ice pack. **c.** The new fur which grew in was black instead of white, showing that the enzyme is active only at low temperatures.

Practice Problems 1*

1. What genotypes and phenotypes are possible among the offspring if a moth with the genotype *Mm* is mated to a moth with the genotype *M'm*?

2. What are the results of a testcross involving incomplete dominance when pink-flowered four-o'clocks are crossed with white-flowered ones?

* Answers to Practice Problems appear in Appendix A.

3. Breeders of dogs note various colors among offspring that range from white to black. If the coat color is controlled by three pairs of alleles, how many different shades are possible if all dominant genes have the same quantitative effect?

4. Investigators note that albino tigers usually have crossed eyes. What two inheritance patterns can account for a phenotype such as this?

12.2 Mendelism and the Chromosomes

The behavior of chromosomes during mitosis was described by 1875, and for meiosis in the 1890s. By 1902, both Theodor Boveri, a German, and Walter S. Sutton, an American, had independently noted the parallel behavior of genes and chromosomes and had proposed the **chromosomal theory of inheritance,** which states that the genes are located on the chromosomes. This theory is supported by the following observations:

1. Both chromosomes and factors (now called alleles) are paired in diploid cells.
2. In keeping with Mendel's law of segregation, both homologous chromosomes and alleles of each pair separate during meiosis so that the gametes have one-half the total number.
3. In keeping with Mendel's law of independent assortment, both homologous chromosomes and alleles of each pair separate independently so that the gametes contain all possible combinations.
4. Fertilization restores both the diploid chromosome number and the paired condition for alleles in the zygote.

The genes are on the chromosomes; therefore, they behave similarly during meiosis and fertilization.

Sex Chromosomes

In animal species, the **autosomes,** or nonsex chromosomes, are the same between the sexes. One special pair of chromosomes is called the **sex chromosomes** because this pair determines the sex of the individual. The sex chromosomes in the human female are XX and those in the male are XY. Because human males can produce two different types of gametes—those that contain an X and those that contain a Y—normally males determine the sex of the new individual.

	X	Y
X	XX	XY

In addition to genes that determine sex, the sex chromosomes carry genes for traits that have nothing to do with the sex of the individual. By tradition, the term sex-linked or **X-linked** is used for genes carried on the X chromosome. The Y chromosome does not carry these genes and indeed carries very few genes.

X-Linked Alleles

The hypothesis that genes are on the chromosomes was substantiated by experiments performed by a Columbia University group of *Drosophila* geneticists, headed by Thomas Hunt Morgan. Fruit flies are even better subjects for genetic studies than garden peas: they can be easily and inexpensively raised in simple laboratory glassware; females mate only once and then lay hundreds of eggs during their lifetimes; and the generation time is short, taking only about ten days when conditions are favorable (Fig. 12.5).

Drosophila flies have the same sex chromosome pattern as humans, and this facilitates our understanding of a cross performed by Morgan. Morgan took a newly discovered mutant male with white eyes and crossed it with a red-eyed female:

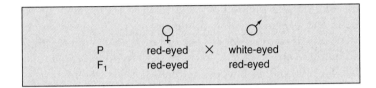

From these results, he knew that red eyes are dominant over white eyes. He then crossed the F_1 flies. In the F_2 generation, there was the expected 3 red-eyed : 1 white-eyed ratio, but it struck him as odd that all of the white-eyed flies were males:

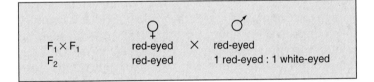

Obviously, a major difference between the male flies and the female flies was their sex chromosomes. Could it be possible that an allele for eye color was on the Y chromosome but not on the X? This idea could be quickly discarded because normal females have red eyes, and they have no Y chromosome. Perhaps an allele for eye color was on the X, but not on the Y, chromosome. Figure 12.5*b* indicates that this explanation would match the results obtained in the experiment. These results support the chromosomal theory of inheritance by showing that the behavior of a specific allele corresponds exactly with that of a specific chromosome—the X chromosome in *Drosophila.*

As discussed next, genes that are X-linked have a different pattern of inheritance than genes that are on the autosomes because the Y chromosome is blank for these genes and cannot offset the inheritance of a recessive allele

X-linked alleles are on the X chromosome, and the Y chromosome is blank for these alleles.

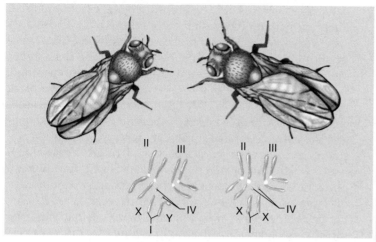

Figure 12.5 X-linked inheritance.
a. Both males and females have eight chromosomes, three pairs of autosomes (II–IV), and one pair of sex chromosomes (I). Males are XY and females are XX. **b.** Once researchers deduced that the alleles for red/white eye color are on the X chromosome in *Drosophila*, they were able to explain their experimental results. Males with white eyes in the F_2 inherited the recessive allele only from the female parent; they receive a blank Y from the male parent.

X-Linked Problems

Recall that when solving autosomal genetics problems, the key and genotypes are represented as follows:

Key: **Genotypes:**

L = long wing LL, Ll, ll
l = short wings

As noted in Figure 12.5, however, the key for an X-linked gene shows an allele attached to the X:

Key:

X^R = red eyes
X^r = white eyes

The possible genotypes in both males and females are as follows:

$X^R X^R$ = red-eyed female
$X^R X^r$ = red-eyed female
$X^r X^r$ = white-eyed female
$X^R Y$ = red-eyed male
$X^r Y$ = white-eyed male

Notice that there are three possible genotypes for females, but only two for males. Females can be heterozygous $X^R X^r$, in which case they are carriers. Carriers usually do not show a recessive abnormality, but they are capable of passing on a recessive allele for an abnormality. Males cannot be carriers; if the dominant allele is on the single X chromosome, they have the dominant phenotype, and if the recessive allele is on the single X chromosome, they show the recessive phenotype.

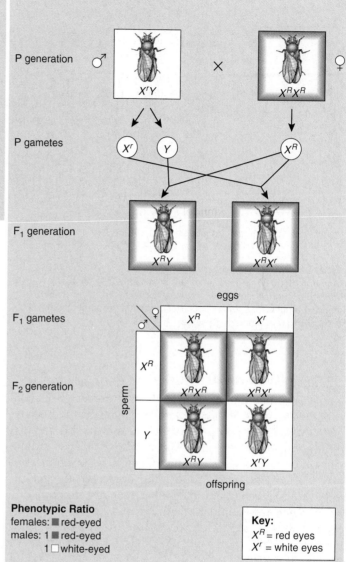

Phenotypic Ratio
females: ■ red-eyed
males: 1 ■ red-eyed
       1 □ white-eyed

Key:
X^R = red eyes
X^r = white eyes

b.

Practice Problems 2*

1. Using the key X^B = bar eyes and X^b = normal eyes, give a. three possible genotypes for females and b. two possible genotypes for males. Also give the possible gametes for these males.

2. a. Which *Drosophila* cross would produce white-eyed males: (1) $X^R X^R \times X^r Y$ or (2) $X^R X^r \times X^R Y$? b. In what ratio?

3. A woman is color blind (X-linked recessive). a. What are the chances of her sons being color blind if she reproduces with a man having normal vision? b. What are the chances of her daughters being color blind? c. Being carriers?

* *Answers to Practice Problems appear in Appendix A.*

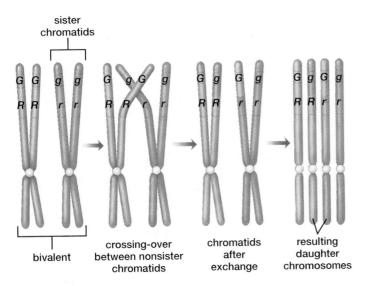

Figure 12.6 Crossing-over.
When homologous chromosomes are in synapsis, the nonsister chromatids exchange genetic material. Following crossing-over, recombinant chromosomes occur. Recombinant chromosomes contribute to recombinant gametes.

Linkage Groups

Drosophila probably has thousands of different genes controlling all aspects of its structure, biochemistry, and behavior. Yet it has only four pairs of chromosomes. This paradox led investigators like Sutton to conclude that each chromosome must carry a large number of genes. For example, it is now known that genes controlling eye color, wing type, body color, leg length, and antennae type are all located on the chromosomes numbered II in Figure 12.5. The alleles for these genes are said to form a **linkage group** because they are found on the same chromosome and they tend to be inherited together.

Crossing-over, you recall, occurs between nonsister chromatids when homologous pairs of chromosomes pair prior to separation during meiosis. During crossing-over the nonsister chromatids exchange genetic material and therefore genes. If crossing-over occurs between the two linked alleles of interest, a dihybrid produces four types of gametes instead of two (Fig. 12.6). Recombinant means a new combination of alleles. The recombinant gametes occur in reduced number because crossing-over is infrequent. Still, all possible phenotypes will occur among the offspring.

To take an actual example, suppose you are doing a cross between a gray-bodied, red-eyed heterozygote and a black-bodied, purple-eyed fly. Since the alleles governing these traits are both on chromosome II, you predict that the results will be 1:1 instead of 1:1:1:1, as is the case for unlinked genes. The reason, of course, is that linked alleles tend to stay together and do not separate independently, as predicted by Mendel's laws. Under these circumstances, the heterozygote forms only two types of gametes and produces offspring with only two phenotypes (Fig. 12.7a).

When you do the cross, however, you find that a very small number of offspring show recombinant phenotypes (i.e., those that are different from the original parents). Specifically, you find that 47% of the offspring have black bodies and purple eyes, 47% have gray bodies and red eyes, 3% have black bodies and red eyes, and 3% have gray bodies and purple eyes (Fig. 12.7b). What happened? In this instance, crossing-over led to a very small number of recombinant gametes, and when these were fertilized, recombinant phenotypes were observed in the offspring. An examination of chromosome II shows that these two sets of alleles are very close together. Doesn't it stand to reason that the closer together two genes are, the less likely they are to cross over? This is exactly what various crosses have repeatedly shown.

All the genes on one chromosome form a linkage group that tends to stay together, except when crossing-over occurs.

Chromosome Mapping

You can use the percentage of recombinant phenotypes to map the chromosomes, because there is a direct relationship between the frequency of crossing-over and the percentage of recombinant phenotypes. In our example (Fig. 12.7), a total of 6% of the offspring are recombinants, and for the sake of mapping the chromosomes, it is assumed that 1% of crossing-over equals one map unit. Therefore, the allele for black body and the allele for purple eyes are six map units apart.

Suppose you want to determine the order of any three genes on the chromosomes. To do so, you can perform crosses that tell you the map distance between all three pairs of alleles. If you know, for instance, that:

1. the distance between the black-body and purple-eye alleles = 6 map units,
2. the distance between the purple-eye and vestigial-wing alleles = 12.5 units, and
3. the distance between the black-body and vestigial-wing alleles = 18.5 units, then the order of the alleles must be as shown here:

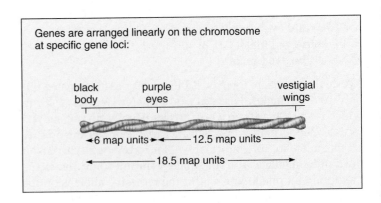

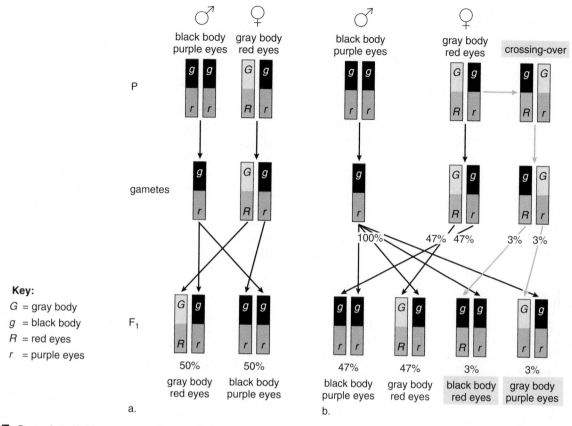

Key:
G = gray body
g = black body
R = red eyes
r = purple eyes

Figure 12.7 Complete linkage versus incomplete linkage.
a. Hypothetical cross in which genes for body and eye color on chromosome II of *Drosophila* are completely linked. Instead of the expected 1:1:1:1 ratio among the offspring, there would be a 1:1 ratio. b. Crossing-over occurs, and 6% of the offspring show recombinant phenotypes. The percentage of recombinant phenotypes is used to map the chromosomes (1% = 1 map unit).

Of the three possible orders (any one of the three genes can be in the middle), only the order given shows the proper distance between all three allelic pairs. Because it is possible to map the chromosomes, we conclude that genes are indeed located on chromosomes, they have a definite location, and they occur in a definite order.

Linkage data have been used to map the chromosomes of *Drosophila*, but the possibility of using linkage data to map human chromosomes is limited because we can only work with matings that have occurred by chance. This, coupled with the fact that humans tend not to have numerous offspring, means that additional methods are used to sequence the genes on human chromosomes. Today, it is customary to also rely on biochemical methods to map the human chromosomes.

The frequency of recombinant gametes that occurs due to the process of crossing-over has been used to map the chromosomes.

Practice Problems 3*

1. When *AaBb* individuals are allowed to self-breed, the phenotypic ratio is just about 3:1. a. What ratio was expected? b. What may have caused the observed ratio?

2. In two sweet pea strains, *B* = blue flowers, *b* = red flowers, *L* = long pollen grains, and *l* = round pollen grains. In a cross between a heterozygous plant with blue flowers and long pollen grains and a plant with red flowers and round pollen grains, 44% of offspring are blue, long; 44% are red, round; 6% are blue, round; and 6% are red, long. How many map units separate these two sets of alleles?

3. Investigators performed crosses that indicated bar-eye and garnet-eye alleles are 13 map units apart, scallop-wing and bar-eye alleles are 6 units apart, and garnet-eye and scallop-wing alleles are 7 units apart. What is the order of these alleles on the chromosome?

* *Answers to Practice Problems appear in Appendix A.*

12.3 Chromosomal Mutations

Mutations [L. *mutatus*, change] are permanent changes in genes or chromosomes that can be passed to offspring if they occur in cells that become gametes. Like crossing-over, recombination of chromosomes during meiosis, and gamete fusion during fertilization, mutations increase the amount of variation among offspring. Chromosomal mutations include changes in chromosome number and changes in chromosomal structure.

Changes in the Chromosome Number

Changes in the chromosome number include monosomies, trisomies, and polyploidy.

Monosomy and Trisomy

Monosomy occurs when an individual has only one of a particular type of chromosome ($2n - 1$), and *trisomy* occurs when an individual has three of a particular type of chromosome ($2n + 1$). The usual cause of monosomy and trisomy is nondisjunction during meiosis. *Nondisjunction* can occur during meiosis I if members of a homologous pair fail to separate, and during meiosis II if the daughter chromosomes go into the same daughter cell (see page 203). Although nondisjunction can also occur during mitosis, it is more common during meiosis.

Monosomy and trisomy occur in both plants and animals. In animals, autosomal monosomies and trisomies are generally lethal, although a trisomic individual is more likely to survive than a monosomic one. The survivors are characterized by a distinctive set of physical and mental abnormalities called a syndrome. In humans, Turner syndrome is a monosomy involving the sex chromosomes—the individual inherits a single X chromosome. The most common trisomy among humans is Down syndrome, which involves chromosome 21. Individuals with Turner syndrome are expected to live a full life span, and although those with Down syndrome are subject to various medical conditions, they generally do well also.

Polyploidy

Some mutant eukaryotes have more than two sets of chromosomes. They are called **polyploids** [Gk. *polys*, many, and *plo*, fold]. Polyploid organisms are named according to the number of sets of chromosomes they have. Triploids ($3n$) have three of each kind of chromosome, tetraploids ($4n$) have four sets, pentaploids ($5n$) have five sets, and so on.

Polyploidy is not seen in animals most likely because judging from trisomies, multiple copies of chromosomes would be lethal. Polyploidy is a major evolutionary mechanism in plants. It is estimated that 47% of all flowering plants are polyploids. Among these are many of our most important crops, such as wheat, corn, cotton, sugarcane, and fruits such as watermelons, bananas, and apples (Fig. 12.8). Also many attractive flowers, such as chrysanthemums and daylilies, are polyploids.

Polyploidy generally arises following hybridization. When two different species reproduce, the resulting organism, called a hybrid, may have an odd number of chromosomes. If so, the chromosomes cannot pair evenly during meiosis, and the organism will not be fertile. (Hybridization in animals can also lead to sterility—as when a horse and donkey produce a mule, which is unable to produce offspring.) In plants, hybridization, followed by doubling of the chromosome number, will result in an even number of chromosomes, and the chromosomes will be able to undergo synapsis during meiosis.

	Species	Hybrid	chromosome number doubles	Polyploid
	$AA \times BB$	AB		$AABB$
chromosome number	(24) (30)	(27) sterile		(54) fertile

Monosomies ($2n - 1$) and trisomies ($2n + 1$) cause abnormalities. In plants, hybridization followed by polyploidy is a positive force for change.

Figure 12.8 Polyploid plants.
Many food sources are specially developed polyploid plants.
a, b. Among these are seedless watermelons and bananas. They are infertile (seeds poorly developed) triploids, but they can be propagated by asexual means. **c.** Polyploidy makes plants and their fruits larger, such as these jumbo McIntosh apples.

a.

b.

c.

Changes in Chromosomal Structure

Some changes in chromosomal structure can be detected microscopically, and some cannot be detected. Various agents in the environment, such as radiation, certain organic chemicals, or even viruses, can cause chromosomes to break. Ordinarily, when breaks occur in chromosomes, the two broken ends reunite to give the same sequence of genes. Sometimes, however, the broken ends of one or more chromosomes do not rejoin in the same pattern as before, and the result is various types of **chromosomal mutations.** An inversion, a translocation, a deletion, and a duplication of chromosome segments are illustrated in Figure 12.9.

An *inversion* occurs when a segment of a chromosome is turned around 180°. You might think this is not a problem because the same genes are present, but the reversed sequence of genes can lead to altered gene activity.

A *translocation* is the movement of a chromosome segment from one chromosome to another, nonhomologous chromosome. In 5% of cases, a translocation that occurred in a previous generation between chromosomes 21 and 14 is the cause of Down syndrome. In these cases, Down syndrome is not related to the age of the mother, but instead tends to run in the family of either the father or the mother.

A *deletion* occurs when an end of a chromosome breaks off or when two simultaneous breaks lead to the loss of an internal segment. Even when only one member of a pair of chromosomes is affected, a deletion often causes abnormalities. An example is cri du chat (cat's cry) syndrome. The affected individual has a small head, is mentally retarded, and has facial abnormalities. Abnormal development of the glottis and larynx results in the most characteristic symptom—the infant's cry resembles that of a cat.

A *duplication* is the presence of a chromosomal segment more than once in the same chromosome. There are several ways a duplication can occur. A broken segment from one chromosome can simply attach to its homologue, or unequal crossing-over may occur, leading to a duplication and a deletion:

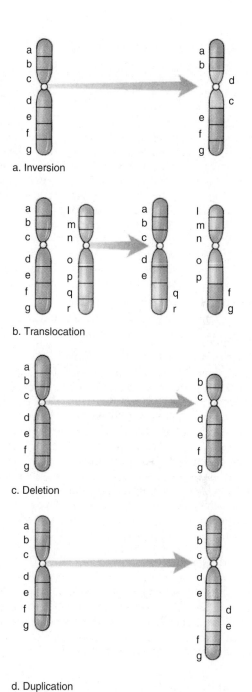

a. Inversion

b. Translocation

c. Deletion

d. Duplication

Figure 12.9 Types of chromosomal mutations.
a. Inversion occurs when a piece of chromosome breaks loose and then rejoins in the reversed direction. **b.** Translocation is the exchange of chromosome pieces between nonhomologous pairs. **c.** Deletion is the loss of a chromosome piece. **d.** Duplication occurs when the same piece is repeated within the chromosome.

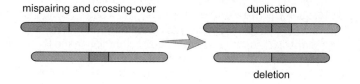

mispairing and crossing-over

duplication

deletion

Multiple copies of genes can mutate differently and thereby provide additional genetic variation for the species. For example, there are several closely linked genes for human globin (globin is a part of hemoglobin, which is present in red blood cells and carries oxygen). This may have arisen by a process of duplication followed by different mutations in each gene.

Chromosomal mutations include observable changes in chromosome structure. Often chromosomal mutations lead to abnormal gametes and offspring. In rare instances, the increase in variation among offspring is beneficial to the species.

Connecting Concepts

By analyzing the outcome of his crosses, Mendel deduced that inheritable factors (now called alleles) contributed by each parent segregate from one another during the production of gametes. Early cytogeneticists (scientists who microscopically observe and study chromosomes) knew nothing of Mendel's work but they saw how homologous chromosome pairs separate during meiosis. Boveri and Sutton were the first to realize that Mendel's work and the work of cytogeneticists must be interrelated—in other words, the genes are on the chromosomes! The development of the chromosomal theory of inheritance is a fine example of how different avenues of research can result in a major scientific breakthrough. It also exemplifies why communication between scientists through publications and scientific conferences is so important.

Once it was understood that genes are carried on chromosomes, previously confusing phenomena such as linked genes, sex-linkage, and the consequences of chromosomal abnormalities became much easier to interpret correctly. The ability to map genes along chromosomes was an important step toward understanding the nature of genomes. It is no accident that the first eukaryotic genomes to be completely base sequenced are those of model organisms such as the yeast *Saccharomyces cerevisiae* and the worm *Caenorhabditis elegans* which already had excellent genetic maps. By contrast, constructing a base sequence map of the human genome was hampered by the lack of a conventional genetic map based on recombination distances. Humans cannot be asked to procreate in order to construct a genetic map! Chapter 17 discusses how new laboratory techniques now permit the mapping and sequencing of the human genome.

Summary

12.1 Mendelism and the Genotype

There are patterns of inheritance discovered since Mendel's original contribution that make it clear that the genotype should be thought of as involving all the genes. For example, different degrees of dominance have been observed. With incomplete dominance, the F_1 individuals are intermediate between the parental types; this does not support the blending theory because the parental phenotypes reappear in F_2. In epistasis, genes interact as when homozygous recessive alleles at one locus mask the effect of a dominant allele at another locus. In pleiotropy, a dominant allele has an effect that drastically alters the phenotype in many regards. Some genes have multiple alleles, although each individual organism has only two alleles. Coat color in rabbits is controlled by multiple alleles, and four different type coats are possible.

Polygenic traits are controlled by genes that have an additive effect on the phenotype, resulting in quantitative variations. A bell-shaped curve is seen because environmental influences bring about many intervening phenotypes. The relative influence of the genotype and the environment on the phenotype can vary—there are examples of extreme environmental influence.

12.2 Mendelism and the Chromosomes

The chromosomal theory of inheritance says that Mendel's factors (the genes) are located on the chromosomes, which accounts for the similarity of their behavior during meiosis and fertilization.

Sex determination in animals is dependent upon the chromosomes. Usually females are XX and males are XY. Solid experimental support for the chromosomal theory of inheritance came when Morgan and his group were able to determine that the white-eye allele in *Drosophila* is on the X chromosome.

Alleles on the X chromosome are called X-linked alleles. Therefore, when doing X-linked genetics problems, it is the custom to indicate the sexes by using sex chromosomes and to indicate the alleles by superscripts attached to the X. The Y is blank because it does not carry these genes.

All the alleles on a chromosome form a linkage group. Linked alleles do not obey Mendel's laws because they tend to go into the same gamete together. Crossing-over can cause recombinant gametes and recombinant phenotypes to occur. The percentage of recombinant phenotypes is used to measure the distance between genes and to map the chromosomes.

12.3 Chromosomal Mutations

Chromosomal mutations fall into two categories: changes in chromosome number and changes in chromosomal structure.

Monosomy occurs when an individual has only one of a particular type of chromosome ($2n - 1$); trisomy occurs when an individual has three of a particular type of chromosome ($2n + 1$). Polyploidy occurs when the eukaryotic individual has more than two complete sets of chromosomes.

Changes in chromosomal structure include inversions, translocations, deletions, and duplications.

Reviewing the Chapter

1. Compare the F_2 phenotypic ratio for a cross involving a dominant allele, an incompletely dominant allele, and codominant alleles.   188
2. Show that if a dihybrid cross between two heterozygotes involves an epistatic gene, you do not get a ratio of 9:3:3:1.   189
3. If you were studying a particular population of organisms, how would you recognize that several traits are being affected by a pleiotropic gene?   189
4. Explain inheritance by multiple alleles. List the human blood types and give the possible genotypes for each.   190
5. Explain why traits controlled by polygenes show continuous variation that can be measured quantitatively, have many intermediate forms, and produce a distribution in the F_2 generation that follows a bell-shaped curve.   190
6. Give examples to show that the environment can have an extreme effect on the phenotype despite the genotype.   191
7. What is the chromosomal theory of inheritance? List the ways in which genes and chromosomes behave similarly during meiosis and fertilization.   192
8. How is sex determined in humans? Which sex determines the sex of the offspring?   192
9. How did a *Drosophila* cross involving an X-linked gene help investigators show that certain genes are carried on certain chromosomes?   192

10. Show that a dihybrid cross between a heterozygote and a recessive homozygote involving linked genes does not produce the expected 1:1:1:1 ratio. What is the significance of the small percentage of recombinants that occurs among the offspring? 194–95
11. What are the two types of chromosomal mutations? What is a monosomy? A trisomy? Why would you expect a monosomy to be more lethal than a trisomy? Why is polyploidy not generally found in animals? In what way may polyploidy have assisted plant evolution? 196
12. What four types of changes in chromosomal structure were discussed? How might it be possible for a duplication and a deletion to occur at the same time? 197

Testing Yourself

Choose the best answer for each question. For questions 1–4, match the statements that follow to the items in the key.

Key:

   a. multiple alleles
   b. incomplete dominance
   c. polygenes
   d. epistatic gene
   e. pleiotropic gene

1. A cross between oblong and round squash produced oval squash.
2. Although most people have an IQ of about 100, IQ generally ranges from about 50 to 150.
3. Investigators noted that whenever a particular species of plant had narrow instead of broad leaves, it was also short and yellow, instead of tall and green.
4. In humans, there are three alleles possible at the chromosomal locus that determine blood type.
5. When a white-eyed *Drosophila* female occurs,
   a. both parents could have red eyes.
   b. the female parent could have red eyes, but the male parent has to have white eyes.
   c. both parents must have white eyes.
   d. the female also has a gray body.
   e. Both a and b are correct.
6. Investigators found that a cross involving the mutant genes *a* and *b* produced 30% recombinants, a cross involving *a* and *c* produced 5% recombinants, and a cross involving *c* and *b* produced 25% recombinants. Which is the correct order of the genes?
   a. *a, b, c*
   b. *a, c, b*
   c. *b, a, c*
   d. Both a and b are correct.
   e. Both b and c are correct.
7. A boy is color blind (X-linked recessive) and has a straight hairline (autosomal recessive). Which could be the genotype of his mother?
   a. *bbww*
   b. X^bYWw
   c. bbX^wX^w
   d. X^BX^bWw
   e. X^WX^wBb

8. Which two of these chromosomal mutations are most likely to occur when homologous chromosomes are undergoing synapsis?
   a. inversion and translocation
   b. deletion and duplication
   c. deletion and inversion
   d. duplication and translocation
   e. inversion and duplication
9. Investigators do a dihybrid cross between two heterozygotes and get about a 3:1 ratio among the offspring. The reason must be due to
   a. polygenes.
   b. pleiotropic genes.
   c. linked genes.
   d. epistatic genes.
   e. multiple alleles.
10. In snakes, the recessive genotype *cc* causes the animal to be albino despite the inheritance of the dominant allele (*B* = black). What would be the results of a cross between two snakes with the genotype *CcBB*?
   a. all black snakes
   b. all white snakes
   c. 9:3:3:1
   d. 3 black : 1 albino
   e. 1 black : 1 albino

Additional Genetics Problems*

1. Chickens that are homozygous for the frizzled trait have feathers that are weak and stringy. When raised at low temperatures, the birds have circulatory, digestive, and hormonal problems. What inheritance pattern explains these results?
2. In radish plants, the shape of the radish may be long *(LL)*, round *(ll)*, or oval *(LI)*. If oval is crossed with oval, what proportion of offspring will also be oval?
3. If blood type in cats were controlled by three codominant and multiple alleles, how many genotypes and phenotypes would occur? Could the cross *AC* × *BC* produce a cat with *AB* blood type?
4. In *Drosophila, S* = normal, *s* = sable body; *W* = normal, *w* = miniature wing. In a cross between a heterozygous normal fly and a sable-bodied, miniature-winged fly, the results were 99 normal flies, 99 with a sable body and miniature wings, 11 with a normal body and miniature wings, and 11 with a sable body and normal wings. What inheritance pattern explains these results? How many map units separate the genes for sable body and miniature wing?
5. In *Drosophila,* the gene that controls red eye color (dominant) versus white eye color is on the X chromosome. What are the expected phenotypic results if a heterozygous female is crossed with a white-eyed male?
6. Bar eyes in *Drosophila* is dominant and X-linked. What phenotypic ratio is expected for reciprocal crosses between true-breeding flies?
7. In *Drosophila,* a male with bar eyes and miniature wings is crossed with a female who has normal eyes and normal wings. Half the female offspring have bar eyes and miniature wings and half have bar eyes and normal wings. What is the genotype of the female parent?

---

* Answers to Additional Genetics Problems appear in Appendix A.

Thinking Scientifically

1. A man known to be a carrier of a genetic disease affecting a lysosomal enzyme has no symptoms of the disease. However, when the enzyme activity is actually measured, it is seen that the man's cells have half the activity as those from someone who is homozygous dominant. Can this allele be considered to be completely dominant? What would such a situation suggest for the treatment of patients with this genetic disease?

2. A flowering shrub grown in a large garden has produced offspring identical to the parent for several generations. When the owner of the garden sends seeds to a friend in another county, the friend reports a very different flower color in the plant. Two hypotheses are possible: a new mutation has occurred; or there is an environmental effect on flower color. How would you test these two hypotheses?

Bioethical Issue

Do you approve of choosing a baby's gender even before it is conceived? As you know, the sex of a child is dependent upon whether an X-bearing sperm or a Y-bearing sperm enters the egg. A new technique has been developed that can separate X-bearing sperm from Y-bearing sperm. First, the sperm are dosed with a DNA-staining chemical. Because the X chromosome has slightly more DNA than the Y chromosome, it takes up more dye. When a laser beam shines on the sperm, the X-bearing sperm shine a little more brightly than the Y-bearing sperm. A machine sorts the sperm into two groups on this basis. The results are not perfect. Following artificial insemination, there's about an 85% success rate for a girl and about a 65% success rate for a boy.

Some might argue that it goes against nature to choose gender. But what if the mother is a carrier of an X-linked genetic disorder such as hemophilia or Duchenne muscular dystrophy? Is it acceptable to bring a child into the world with a genetic disorder that may cause an early death? Wouldn't it be better to select sperm for a girl, who at worst would be a carrier like her mother? Some authorities do not find gender selection acceptable even for this reason. Once you separate reproduction from the sex act, they say, it opens the door to children that have been genetically designed in every way. As a society, should we accept certain ways of interfering with nature and not accept other ways? Why or why not?

Understanding the Terms

autosome 192
chromosomal mutation 197
chromosomal theory of
    inheritance 192
codominance 188
epistasis 189
incomplete dominance 188
linkage group 194
multiple allele 190
mutation 196
pleiotropy 189
polygenic inheritance 190
polyploid (polyploidy) 196
sex chromosome 192
X-linked 192

Match the terms to these definitions:

a. _____ Any chromosome other than a sex chromosome.
b. _____ Condition in which an organism has more than two complete sets of chromosomes.
c. _____ Allele located on the X chromosomes that controls a trait unrelated to sex.
d. _____ Pattern of inheritance in which a trait is controlled by several allelic pairs; each dominant allele contributes in an additive and like manner.
e. _____ Condition in which an organism has more than two complete sets of chromosomes.

Web Connections

Exploring the Internet

http://www.mhhe.com/biosci/genbio/mader
(click on *Biology 7/e*)

The *Biology 7/e* Online Learning Center provides many resources for studying the material in this chapter including links to the following sites:

Genetic Linkage describes how linked genes yield distorted ratios in experimental crosses. This site is a thorough treatment of the subject, and includes how to determine the distance between linked genes, and detecting gene linkages in humans.

http://www.cc.ndsu.nodak.edu/instruct/mcclean/plsc431/linkage/

Variation in Chromosome Structure explores variations in chromosome number in plants and animals, including how variations in structure are related to human disorders.

http://www.cc.ndsu.nodak.edu/instruct/mcclean/plsc431/chromstruct/

and

Variation in Chromosome Number explores variations in chromosome number in plants and animals, including how variations in number are related to human disorders.

http://www.cc.ndsu.nodak.edu/instruct/mcclean/plsc431/chromnumber/

Pedigrees. A lengthy example of how pedigrees are used to determine patterns of inheritance in humans, from the MIT hypertextbook.

http://esg-www.mit.edu:8001/esgbio/mg/pedigrees.html

The Turner Center. A site with many links to other sources of information on aneuploidies.

http://www.aaa.dk/turner/engelsk/Download.htm#orientation

Self Quiz. This site has a number of questions in a quiz directly related to this chapter.

http://brooks.pvt.k12.ma.us/~bheun/apsq13.html

Human Genetics

Is thrill-seeking behavior genetic?

Scarcely a week goes by without a newspaper or television report of another discovery in the exploding field of human genetics. Some researchers believe they have found genes which predispose a person toward alcoholism or a need for thrill-seeking behavior. While genes undoubtedly play a role in almost all human behavior, they act in conjunction *with* the environment. Few aspects of human behavior are controlled only by genes or only by environment. The question of nature versus nurture—what percentage of the distribution of a trait is controlled by genes and what percentage is controlled by environment—cannot now and may never be answered for most traits; both are important.

Genetic counseling is more extensive today because of the availability of so many prenatal tests to detect chromosomal and gene mutations. Amniocentesis followed by karyotyping can indicate whether a developing child has Down syndrome or one of the other chromosomal abnormalities. Specific chromosomes can be tested for the presence of a mutant allele for cystic fibrosis, neurofibromatosis, and sickle-cell disease, among others.

13.1 Inheritance of Chromosomes

Somatic (body) cells in humans have 46 chromosomes. To view the chromosomes, a cell can be photographed just prior to division so that a picture of the chromosomes is obtained. The picture may be entered into a computer and the chromosomes electronically arranged by pairs (Fig. 13.1). The members of a pair have the same size, shape, and constriction (location of the centromere), and they also have the same characteristic banding pattern upon staining. The resulting display of pairs of chromosomes is called a **karyotype.** Both males and females normally have 23 pairs of chromosomes, but one of these pairs is of unequal length in males. The larger chromosome of this pair is the **X chromosome** and the smaller is the **Y chromosome.** These are called the **sex chromosomes** because they contain the genes that determine

sex. The other chromosomes, known as **autosomes,** include all the pairs of chromosomes except the X and Y chromosomes. In a karyotype, autosomes are usually ordered by size and numbered from the largest to smallest; the sex chromosomes are identified separately.

Sometimes there are medical reasons for doing a karyotype on an unborn child. As discussed on page 212 chorionic villi sampling and amniocentesis allow a physician to obtain a sample of cells in order to do prenatal testing including a karyotype. The chorionic villi project from an extraembryonic membrane in the region of the placenta where maternal blood exchange materials with embryonic blood. During **chorionic villi sampling,** a suction tube is used to remove a sample of chorionic villi cells for diagnostic purposes. The amniotic cavity contains amniotic fluid that protects the embryo from drying out and from mechanical

1. Blood is centrifuged to separate out blood cells.

2. Only white blood cells are transferred and treated to stop cell division.

3. Sample is fixed, stained, and spread on a microscope slide.

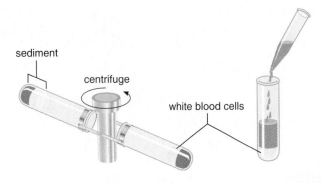

sediment

centrifuge

white blood cells

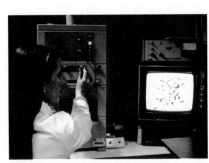

4. Slide is examined microscopically, and the chromosomes are photographed. Computer arranges the chromosomes into pairs.

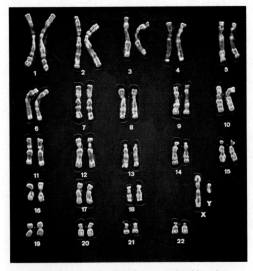

5. Karyotype: Chromosomes are paired by size, centromere location, and banding patterns.

Figure 13.1 Human karyotype preparation.

A karyotype displays the chromosomes of an individual from the largest to the smallest autosomal pairs. The sex chromosomes are either XX (females) or XY (males). As illustrated here, the stain used on the chromosomes can result in a banded appearance. The bands help researchers identify and analyze the chromosomes.

shock. During **amniocentesis,** a long needle is inserted into the amniotic cavity and a small sample of fluid and sloughed-off fetal cells are removed. The chromosomes of these cells can be karyotyped to see if the unborn child has a normal karyotype.

Nondisjunction during oogenesis or spermatogenesis can lead to the birth of a child with an abnormal chromosome number.

Nondisjunction

Gamete formation in humans involves meiosis, the type of cell division that reduces the chromosome number by one-half. **Nondisjunction** is the failure of homologous chromosomes to separate during meiosis I or daughter chromosomes to separate during meiosis II (Fig. 13.2*a*). Nondisjunction leads to gametes that have too few or too many chromosomes.

When these abnormal gametes fuse with normal gametes at fertilization, a monosomy or a trisomy can result. In a monosomy, instead of a pair of some particular chromosome, there is only one of that kind. In a trisomy there are three of a particular kind of chromosome instead of just two. Figure 13.2*b* lists various syndromes due to the inheritance of abnormal chromosome numbers. A *syndrome* is a group of symptoms that appear together when there is a particular medical condition.

The karyotype of a human being usually has 22 pairs of autosomes and one pair of sex chromosomes. Nondisjunction during meiosis leads to the inheritance of an abnormal chromosome number.

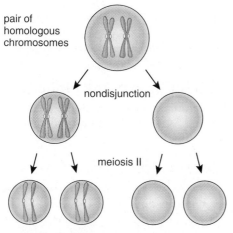

Abnormal gametes:
two gametes have one extra and two gametes have one less chromosome than normal.

a.

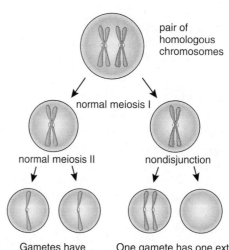

Gametes have usual number of chromosomes.

One gamete has one extra and the other has one less chromosome.

Syndrome	Description	Chromosomes	Incidences (newborns)
Down	Mental retardation; wide, flat face with upper eyelid fold, short stature; abnormal palm creases	Trisomy 21	1/800
Patau	Malformed internal organs, face, and head; extra digits; mental retardation	Trisomy 13	1/15,000
Edward	Malformed internal organs, face, and head; extreme muscle tone	Trisomy 18	1/6,000
Turner	Short stature; webbed neck; broad chest; no sexual maturity	XO	1/6,000
Klinefelter	Breast development possible; testes underdeveloped; no facial hair	XXY (or XXXY)	1/1,500
Triplo-X	Tall and thin with menstrual irregularities	XXX (or XXXX)	1/1,500
Jacob	Taller than average; persistent acne; speech and learning problems possible	XYY	1/1,000

b.   From Robert F. Weaver and Philip W. Hedrick, *Genetics,* 2d ed. Copyright 1992 WCB.

Figure 13.2 Nondisjunction of autosomes during meiosis.
a. Nondisjunction can occur during meiosis I if homologous chromosomes fail to separate, and during meiosis II if the daughter chromosome fails to separate. In either case, abnormal gametes carry an extra chromosome or lack a chromosome. **b.** Frequency of syndromes caused by abnormal chromosomal numbers.

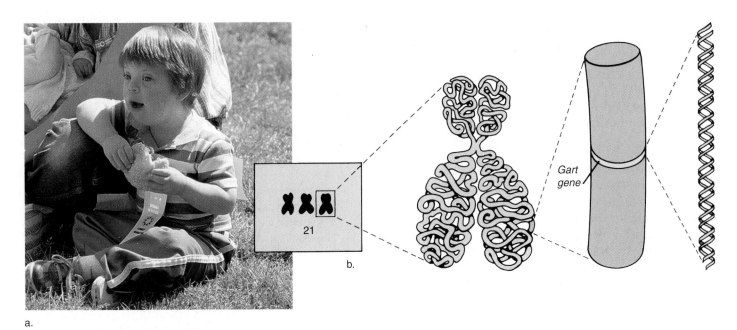

Figure 13.3 Down syndrome.
a. Characteristics of Down syndrome include a wide, flat face and narrow, slanting eyelids. **b.** The karyotype of an individual with Down syndrome often shows an extra chromosome 21. An extra *Gart* gene may account for the mental retardation that often accompanies the disorder.

Down Syndrome

Persons with Down syndrome, described in Figures 13.2*b* and 13.3, usually have three copies of chromosome 21 in their karyotype because the egg had two copies instead of one. The chances of a woman having a Down syndrome child increase rapidly with age, starting at about age 40, and the reasons for this are still being determined. In 23% of the cases of Down syndrome studied, the sperm, rather than the egg, had the extra chromosome 21. In about 5% of cases in either the sperm or the egg, the extra chromosome is attached to another chromosome, often chromosome 14. This abnormal chromosome arose because a translocation occurred between chromosomes 14 and 21 in one of the parents or even in a relative who lived generations earlier. Therefore, when Down syndrome is due to a translocation, it is not age related and instead tends to run in the family of either the father or the mother.

It is known that the genes that cause Down syndrome are located on the bottom third of chromosome 21 (Fig. 13.3*b*), and extensive investigative work has focused on discovering the specific genes responsible for the characteristics of the syndrome. Thus far, investigators have discovered several genes that may account for various conditions seen in persons with Down syndrome. For example, they have located genes most likely responsible for the increased tendency toward leukemia, cataracts, accelerated rate of aging, and mental retardation. The gene for mental retardation, dubbed the *Gart* gene, causes an increased level of purines in blood, a finding associated with mental retardation. It is hoped that someday it will be possible to control the expression of the *Gart* gene even before birth so that at least this symptom of Down syndrome can be suppressed.

Abnormal Sex Chromosomal Inheritance

Abnormal sex chromosomal inheritance can be due to receiving an abnormal number of sex chromosomes or an abnormal X chromosome.

Abnormal Number Syndromes

From birth, an XO individual with *Turner syndrome* has only one sex chromosome, an X; the O signifies the absence of a second sex chromosome. Turner females are short, have a broad chest, and folds of skin on the back of the neck. Even so, there is little reason to suspect a chromosomal abnormality until puberty. Turner females do not undergo puberty or menstruate, and there is a lack of breast development (Fig. 13.4*a*). The ovaries, oviducts, and uterus are very small and nonfunctional. They are usually of normal intelligence and can lead fairly normal lives, but they are also infertile even if they receive hormone supplements.

A male with *Klinefelter syndrome* has two or more X chromosomes in addition to a Y chromosome and is sterile. The testes and prostate gland are underdeveloped, and there is no facial hair. There may be some breast development (Fig. 13.4*b*). Affected individuals have large hands and feet and very long arms and legs. They are usually slow to learn but not mentally retarded unless they inherit more than two X chromosomes.

A *triplo-X* individual has more than two X chromosomes. It might be supposed that the XXX female is especially feminine, but this is not the case. Although in some cases there is a tendency toward learning disabilities, most triplo-X females have no apparent physical abnormalities except there may be menstrual irregularities, including

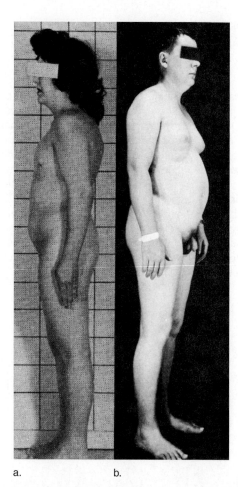

a.   b.

Figure 13.4 Abnormal sex chromosome inheritance.
a. A female with Turner syndrome (XO) is distinguished by a thick neck, short stature, and immature sexual features. **b.** A male with Klinefelter syndrome (XXY) has immature sex organs and shows breast development.

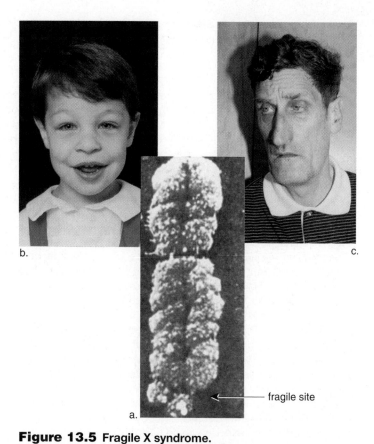

b.

c.

— fragile site

a.

Figure 13.5 Fragile X syndrome.
a. An arrow points out the fragile site of this fragile X chromosome. **b.** A young person with the syndrome appears normal but **(c)** with age, the elongated face has a prominent jaw, and the ears noticeably protrude.

early onset of menopause. Triplo-X individuals have an increased risk of having daughters who are also triplo-X or XXY sons.

XYY males with Jacob syndrome result from nondisjunction during meiosis II (see Fig. 13.2*a*). Affected males usually are taller than average, suffer from persistent acne, and tend to have speech and reading problems. At one time it was suggested that these men were likely to be criminally aggressive, but it has since been shown that the incidence of such behavior among them may be no greater than among XY males.

Fragile X Syndrome

Males outnumber females by about 25% in institutions for the mentally retarded. In some of these males, the X chromosome is nearly broken, leaving the tip hanging by a flimsy thread. These males are said to have fragile X syndrome (Fig. 13.5).

As children, fragile X syndrome individuals may be hyperactive or autistic; their speech is delayed in development and often repetitive in nature. As adults, they have large

testes and big, usually protruding ears. They are short in stature, but the jaw is prominent and the face is long and narrow. Stubby hands, lax joints, and a heart defect may also occur. Fragile X chromosomes also occurs in females, but when symptoms do appear in females, they tend to be less severe.

Fragile X syndrome is inherited in an unusual pattern; it passes from symptomless male carrier to a severely affected grandson, as discussed in the reading on page 206. The DNA sequence at the fragile site was isolated and found to have trinucleotide repeats. The base triplet CGG (cytosine, guanine, guanine) was repeated over and over again. There are about 6 to 50 copies of this repeat in normal persons but over 230 copies in persons with fragile X syndrome.

The most common autosomal chromosome abnormality is trisomy 21 (Down syndrome). Individuals also sometimes inherit an abnormal number of sex chromosomes or an abnormal X chromosome, as in fragile X syndrome.

Fragile X Syndrome

Fragile X syndrome is one of the most common genetic causes of mental retardation, second only to Down syndrome. It affects about one in 1,500 males and one in 2,500 females and is seen in all ethnic groups. It is called fragile X syndrome because its diagnosis used to be dependent upon observing an X chromosome whose tip is attached to the rest of the chromosome by a thin thread.

The inheritance pattern of fragile X syndrome is not like any other pattern we have studied (Fig. 13A). The chance of being affected increases in successive generations almost as if the pattern of inheritance switches from being a recessive one to a dominant one. Then, too, an unaffected grandfather can have grandchildren with the disorder; in other words, he is a carrier for an X-linked disease. This is contrary to what occurs with other mutant alleles on the X chromosome; in those cases, the male always shows the disorder.

In 1991, the DNA sequence at the fragile site was isolated and found to have trinucleotide repeats. The base triplet, CGG, was repeated over and over again. There are about 6 to 50 copies of this repeat in normal persons but over 230 copies in persons with fragile X syndrome. Carrier males have what is now termed a premutation; they have between 50 and 230 copies of the repeat and no symptoms. Both daughters and sons receive the premutation but only the daughters pass on the full mutation—that is, over 230 copies of the repeat. Any male, even those with fragile X syndrome and over 230 repeats, passes on at most the premutation number of repeats. It is unknown what causes the difference between males and females.

This type of mutation—called by some a dynamic mutation, because it changes, and by others an expanded trinucleotide repeat, because the number of triplet copies increases—is now known to characterize other conditions, such as certain forms of dystrophy, spinocerebellar ataxia type 1, and Huntington disease. With Huntington disease, the age of onset of the disorder is roughly correlated with the number of repeats, and the disorder is more likely to have been inherited from the father. For autosomal conditions, we would expect the sex of the parent to play no role in inheritance. The present exceptions have led

to the genomic imprinting hypothesis— that the sperm and egg carry chromosomes that have been "imprinted" differently. Imprinting is believed to occur during gamete formation, and thereafter, the genes are expressed one way if donated by the father and another way if donated by the mother. Perhaps when we discover why more repeats are passed on by one parent than the other, we will discover the cause of so-called genomic imprinting.

What might cause repeats to occur in the first place? Something must go wrong

during DNA replication prior to cell division. The difficulty that causes triplet repeats is not known. But when DNA codes for cellular proteins, the presence of repeats undoubtedly leads to nonfunctioning or malfunctioning proteins.

Scientists have developed a new technique that can identify repeats in DNA, and they expect that this technique will help them find the genes for other human disorders. They expect expanded trinucleotide repeats to be a very common mutation indeed.

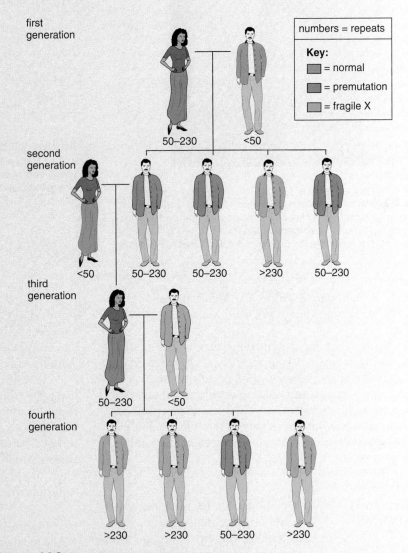

Figure 13A Fragile X syndrome.
Fragile X syndrome is a disorder caused by the presence of triplet repeats at a particular locus. Affected persons have over 230 repeats, a premutation is 50–230 repeats, and normal persons have fewer than 50 repeats. In each successive generation there are more affected individuals, usually males. The mutation is passed on by women with only a premutation number of repeats; men, even if affected, do not pass on the mutation.

13.2 Autosomal Genetic Disorders

Genetic disorders are medical conditions caused by alleles inherited from the parents. Some of these conditions are controlled by autosomal dominant or recessive alleles.

When a genetic disorder is a simple autosomal dominant, an individual with the alleles *AA* or *Aa* will have the disorder. When a genetic disorder is a simple autosomal recessive, only individuals with the alleles *aa* will have the disorder. Genetic counselors often construct pedigree charts to determine whether a condition is dominant or recessive. A **pedigree chart** shows the pattern of inheritance for a particular condition. Consider these two possible patterns of inheritance:

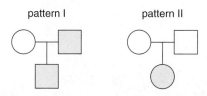

In both patterns, males are designated by squares and females by circles. Shaded circles and squares are affected individuals. A line between a square and a circle represents a union. A vertical line going downward leads, in these patterns, to a single child. (If there are more children, they are placed off a horizontal line.) Which pattern of inheritance do you suppose represents an autosomal dominant characteristic, and which represents an autosomal recessive characteristic?

In pattern I, the child is affected, as is one of the parents. When a disorder is dominant, an affected child usually has at least one affected parent. Of the two patterns, this one shows a dominant pattern of inheritance. Figure 13.6 shows a typical pedigree chart for an autosomal dominant disorder. Other ways to recognize an autosomal dominant pattern of inheritance are also given.

In pattern II, the child is affected but neither parent is; this can happen if the condition is recessive and the parents are *Aa*. Notice that the parents are **carriers** because they appear to be normal but are capable of having a child with a genetic disorder. Figure 13.7 shows a typical pedigree chart for an autosomal recessive genetic disorder. Other ways to recognize a recessive pattern of inheritance are also given in the figure.

It is important to realize that "chance has no memory," therefore, each child born to heterozygous parents has a 25% chance of having the disorder. In other words, it is possible that if a heterozygous couple has four children, each child might have the condition.

Dominant and recessive alleles have different patterns of inheritance.

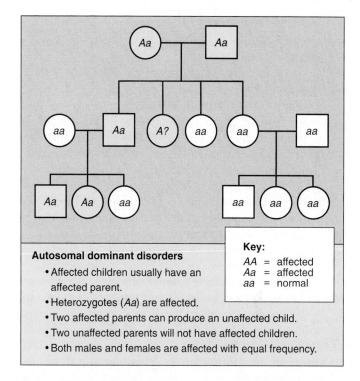

Autosomal dominant disorders
- Affected children usually have an affected parent.
- Heterozygotes (*Aa*) are affected.
- Two affected parents can produce an unaffected child.
- Two unaffected parents will not have affected children.
- Both males and females are affected with equal frequency.

Key:
AA = affected
Aa = affected
aa = normal

Figure 13.6 Autosomal dominant pedigree chart.
The list gives ways to recognize an autosomal dominant disorder.

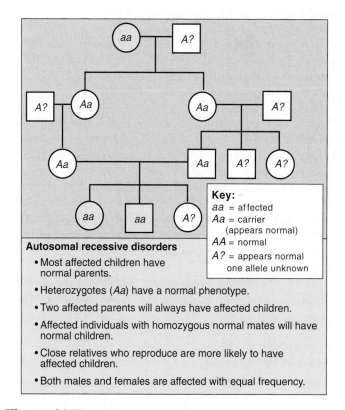

Autosomal recessive disorders
- Most affected children have normal parents.
- Heterozygotes (*Aa*) have a normal phenotype.
- Two affected parents will always have affected children.
- Affected individuals with homozygous normal mates will have normal children.
- Close relatives who reproduce are more likely to have affected children.
- Both males and females are affected with equal frequency.

Key:
aa = affected
Aa = carrier (appears normal)
AA = normal
A? = appears normal one allele unknown

Figure 13.7 Autosomal recessive pedigree chart.
The list gives ways to recognize an autosomal recessive disorder. Only those affected with the recessive genetic disorder are shaded.

Autosomal Dominant Disorders

Of the many autosomal dominant disorders, we will discuss only two.

Neurofibromatosis

Neurofibromatosis,[1] sometimes mistakenly called von Recklinghausen disease, is one of the most common genetic disorders. It affects roughly one in 3,000 people, including an estimated 100,000 in the United States. It is seen equally in every racial and ethnic group throughout the world.

At birth or later, the affected individual may have six or more large, tan spots (known as cafe-au-lait) on the skin. Such spots may increase in size and number and may get darker. Small benign tumors (lumps) called neurofibromas may occur under the skin or in various organs. Neurofibromas are made up of nerve cells and other cell types.

This genetic disorder shows *variable expressivity.* In most cases, symptoms are mild and patients live a normal life. In some cases, however, the effects are severe. Skeletal deformities, including a large head, are seen, and eye and ear tumors can lead to blindness and hearing loss. Many children with neurofibromatosis have learning disabilities and are hyperactive.

In 1990, researchers isolated the gene for neurofibromatosis, which was known to be on chromosome 17. By analyzing the DNA (deoxyribonucleic acid), they determined that the gene was huge and actually included three smaller genes. This was only the second time that nested genes have been found in humans. The gene for neurofibromatosis is a tumor-suppressor gene active in controlling cell division. When it mutates, a benign tumor develops.

Huntington Disease

One in 20,000 persons in the United States has *Huntington disease,* a neurological disorder that leads to progressive degeneration of brain cells, which in turn causes severe muscle spasms and personality disorders (Fig. 13.8). Most people appear normal until they are of middle age and have already had children who might also be stricken. Occasionally, the first signs of the disease are seen in these children when they are teenagers or even younger. There is no effective treatment, and death comes ten to 15 years after the onset of symptoms.

Several years ago, researchers found that the gene for Huntington disease was located on chromosome 4. A test was developed for the presence of the gene, but few want to know if they have inherited the gene because as yet there is no treatment for Huntington disease. After the gene was isolated in 1993, an analysis revealed that it contains many

Figure 13.8 Huntington disease.
Persons with this condition gradually lose psychomotor control of the body. At first there are only minor disturbances, but the symptoms become worse over time. Unfortunately there is no known cure for Huntington disease.

repeats of the base triplet CAG (cytosine, adenine, and guanine). Normal persons have 11 to 34 copies of the triplet, but affected persons tend to have 42 to more than 120 copies. The more repeats present, the earlier the onset of Huntington disease and the more severe the symptoms. It also appears that persons most at risk have inherited the disorder from their fathers. The latter observation is consistent with a new hypothesis called **genomic imprinting.** The genes are imprinted differently during formation of sperm and egg, and therefore the sex of the parent passing on the disorder becomes important.

It is now known that there are a number of other genetic diseases whose severity and time of onset vary according to the number of triplet repeats present within the gene. Moreover, the genes for these disorders are also subject to genomic imprinting.

There are many autosomal dominant disorders in humans. Among these are neurofibromatosis and Huntington disease, as listed in Table 13A on page 213.

---

[1] Although neurofibromatosis is commonly associated with Joseph Merrick, the severely deformed nineteenth-century Londoner depicted in *The Elephant Man,* researchers today believe Merrick actually suffered from a much rarer disorder called Proteus syndrome.

Autosomal Recessive Disorders

Of the many autosomal recessive disorders, we will discuss only three.

Cystic Fibrosis

Cystic fibrosis is the most common lethal genetic disease among Caucasians in the United States. About one in 20 Caucasians is a carrier, and about one in 2,500 children born to this group has the disorder. In these children, the mucus in the bronchial tubes and pancreatic ducts is particularly thick and viscous, interfering with the function of the lungs and pancreas. To ease breathing, the thick mucus in the lungs has to be manually loosened periodically, but still the lungs become infected frequently. The clogged pancreatic ducts prevent digestive enzymes from reaching the small intestine, and to improve digestion patients take digestive enzymes mixed with applesauce before every meal.

In the past few years, much progress has been made in our understanding of cystic fibrosis, and new treatments have raised the average life expectancy to 17 to 28 years of age (Fig. 13.9). Research has demonstrated that chloride ions (Cl^-) fail to pass through plasma membrane channel proteins in these patients. Ordinarily, after chloride ions have passed through the membrane, water follows. It is believed that lack of water is the cause of abnormally thick mucus in bronchial tubes and pancreatic ducts. The cystic fibrosis gene, which is located on chromosome 7, has been isolated, and placed in a nasal spray. The spray restores about 25% of the ability of chloride ions to cross the membrane. Researchers are hopeful that gene therapy will one day be a realistic approach to curing the disease.

Genetic testing for the gene in adult carriers and in fetuses is possible; if a disease-causing gene is present, couples have to consider that gene therapy may be possible some day.

Tay-Sachs Disease

Tay-Sachs disease is a well-known genetic disease that usually occurs among Jews in the United States, most of whom are of central and eastern European descent. At first, it is not apparent that a baby has Tay-Sachs disease. However, development begins to slow down between four months and eight months of age, and neurological impairment and psychomotor difficulties then become apparent. The child gradually becomes blind and helpless, develops uncontrollable seizures, and eventually becomes paralyzed. There is no treatment or cure for Tay-Sachs disease, and most affected individuals die by the age of three or four.

Tay-Sachs disease results from a lack of the enzyme hexosaminidase A (Hex A) and the subsequent storage of its substrate, a fatty substance known as glycosphingolipid, in lysosomes. Although more and more lysosomes build up in

Figure 13.9 Cystic fibrosis therapy.
Antibiotic therapy is used to control lung infections of cystic fibrosis patients. The antibiotic tobramycin can be aerosolized and administered using a nebulizer. It is inhaled twice daily for about fifteen minutes.

many body cells, the primary sites of storage are the cells of the brain, which accounts for the onset, and the progressive deterioration of psychomotor functions.

Carriers of Tay-Sachs have about half the level of Hex A activity found in normal individuals. Prenatal diagnosis of the disease also is possible following either amniocentesis or chorionic villi sampling.

Phenylketonuria (PKU)

Phenylketonuria (PKU) occurs once in 5,000 births, so it is not as frequent as the disorders previously discussed. However, it is the most commonly inherited metabolic disorder to affect nervous system development. First cousins who marry are more apt to have a PKU child.

Affected individuals lack an enzyme that is needed for the normal metabolism of the amino acid phenylalanine, and an abnormal breakdown product, a phenylketone, accumulates in the urine. The PKU gene is located on chromosome 12, and there is a prenatal DNA test for the presence of this allele. Years ago, the urine of newborns was tested at home for phenylketone in order to detect PKU. Presently, newborns are routinely tested in the hospital for elevated levels of phenylalanine in the blood. If necessary, newborns are placed on a diet low in phenylalanine, which must be continued until the brain is fully developed, around age 7, or else severe mental retardation develops.

There are many autosomal recessive disorders in humans. Among these are Tay-Sachs disease, cystic fibrosis, and phenylketonuria (PKU) (see Table 13A, page 213).

Beyond Simple Mendelian Inheritance

There are patterns of inheritance other than simple dominant and recessive traits.

Polygenic Inheritance

Polygenic inheritance occurs when one trait is governed by two or more loci. Each dominant allele has a quantitative effect on the phenotype, and these effects are additive. The result is a continuous variation of phenotypes, resulting in a distribution of these phenotypes that resembles a bell-shaped curve. The more genes involved, the more continuous the variation and the distribution of the phenotypes. Also, environmental effects cause many intervening phenotypes; in the case of height, differences in nutrition ensure a bell-shaped curve.

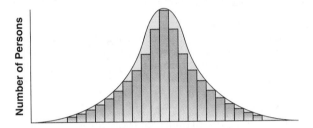

Just how many pairs of alleles control skin color is not known, but a range in colors can be explained on the basis of two pairs. When a very dark person reproduces with a very light person, the children have medium brown skin; and when two people with medium brown skin reproduce with one another, the children range in skin color from very dark to very light. This can be explained by assuming that skin color is controlled by two pairs of alleles and that each capital letter contributes to the color of the skin:

Phenotype	Genotypes
Very dark	*AABB*
Dark	*AABb* or *AaBB*
Medium brown	*AaBb* or *AAbb* or *aaBB*
Light	*Aabb* or *aaBb*
Very light	*aabb*

Notice again that there is a range in phenotypes and that there are several possible phenotypes in between the two extremes. Therefore, the distribution of these phenotypes is expected to follow a bell-shaped curve—few people have the extreme phenotypes, and most people have the phenotype that lies in the middle between the extremes.

Many human disorders, such as cleft lip and/or palate, clubfoot, congenital dislocations of the hip, hypertension, diabetes, schizophrenia, and even allergies and cancers, are most likely controlled by polygenes and subject to environmental influences. Therefore, many investigators are in the process of considering the nature versus nurture question; that is, what percentage of the distribution of the trait is controlled by genes and what percentage is controlled by the environment? Thus far, it has not been possible to come to precise, generally accepted percentages for any particular trait.

In recent years, reports have surfaced that all sorts of behavioral traits such as alcoholism, homosexuality, phobias, and even suicide can be associated with particular genes. No doubt behavioral traits are to a degree controlled by genes, but again, it is impossible at this time to determine to what degree.

> Many human traits most likely controlled by polygenes are subject to environmental influences. The frequency of the phenotypes of such traits follows a bell-shaped curve.

Multiple Alleles

Some traits are controlled by **multiple alleles;** that is, more than two alleles. However, each person inherits only two of the total possible number of alleles. Three alleles for the same gene control the inheritance of ABO blood types: *A* = A antigen on red blood cells; *B* = B antigen on red blood cells; *O* = no antigens on red blood cells. Both *A* and *B* are dominant over *O;* therefore, there are two possible genotypes for type A blood and two possible genotypes for type B blood. If a person inherits one of each of these alleles, the blood type will be AB. Type O can only result from the inheritance of two *O* alleles:

Phenotype	Possible Genotype
A	*AA, AO*
B	*BB, BO*
AB	*AB*
O	*OO*

An examination of possible matings between different blood types sometimes produces surprising results. For example, if the cross is *AO × BO*, the possible genotypes of children are *AB, OO, AO,* and *BO.*

Blood typing can sometimes aid in paternity suits. A man with type A blood (having genotype *AO*) could possibly be the father of a child with type O blood. On the other hand, a man with type AB blood cannot possibly be the father of a child with type O blood. Therefore, blood tests are legally used only to exclude a man from possible paternity.

The Rh factor is inherited separately from A, B, AB, or O blood types. In each instance, it is possible to be Rh positive (Rh$^+$) or Rh negative (Rh$^-$). It can be assumed that the inheritance of this antigen on red blood cells is controlled by a single allelic pair in which simple dominance prevails: the Rh-positive allele is dominant over the Rh-negative allele.

> Inheritance by multiple alleles occurs when a gene exists in more than two allelic forms. However, each individual usually inherits only two alleles for these genes.

Degrees of Dominance

The field of human genetics also has examples of codominance and incomplete dominance. *Codominance* occurs when alleles are equally expressed in a heterozygote. We have already mentioned that the multiple alleles controlling blood type are codominant. An individual with the genotype *AB* has type AB blood.

Sickle-Cell Disease   Sickle-cell disease is an example of a human disorder that is controlled by incompletely dominant alleles. Individuals with the $Hb^A Hb^A$ genotype are normal, those with the $Hb^S Hb^S$ genotype have sickle-cell disease, and those with the $Hb^A Hb^S$ genotype have the sickle-cell trait. Two individuals with sickle-cell trait can produce children with all three phenotypes, as indicated in Figure 13.10.

In persons with sickle-cell disease, the red blood cells aren't biconcave disks like normal red blood cells; they are irregular. In fact, many are sickle shaped. The defect is caused by an abnormal hemoglobin that accumulates inside the cells. Because the sickle-shaped cells can't pass along narrow capillary passageways like disk-shaped cells, they clog the vessels and break down. This is why persons with sickle-cell disease suffer from poor circulation, anemia, and poor resistance to infection. Internal hemorrhaging leads to further complications, such as jaundice, episodic pain of the abdomen and joints, and damage to internal organs.

Persons with sickle-cell trait do not usually have any sickle-shaped cells unless they experience dehydration or mild oxygen deprivation. Although a recent study found that army recruits with sickle-cell trait are more likely to die when subjected to extreme exercise, previous studies of athletes do not substantiate these findings. At present, most investigators believe that no restrictions on physical activity are needed for persons with the sickle-cell trait.

Among regions of malaria-infested Africa, infants with sickle-cell disease die, but infants with sickle-cell trait have a better chance of survival than the normal homozygote. When the parasite infects their red blood cells, the cells become sickle shaped and thereafter the cells lose potassium. This causes the parasite to die. The protection afforded by the sickle-cell trait keeps the allele for sickle-cell prevalent in populations exposed to malaria. As many as 60% of the population in malaria-infected regions of Africa have the allele. In the United States, about 10% of the African-American population carries the allele.

In a recent study, 22 children around the world with sickle-cell disease were given bone marrow transplants from healthy siblings and 16 were completely cured of the disease. Optimism over these results is dampened by the knowledge that only 6% of patients met the medical criteria for receiving treatment and the drugs used in the procedure result in infertility. Also, if unsuccessful, health could worsen instead of improve and there is a 10% risk of death from the treatment.

Innovative therapies are still being explored. For example, persons with sickle-cell disease produce normal fetal hemoglobin during development, and drugs that turn on the genes for fetal hemoglobin in adults are being developed. Mice have been genetically engineered to produce sickled red blood cells in order to test new antisickling drugs and various genetic therapies.

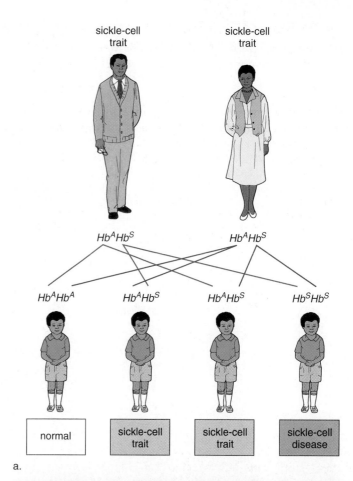

a.

b.

Figure 13.10 Inheritance of sickle-cell disease.
a. In this example, both parents have the sickle-cell trait. Therefore, each child has a 25% chance of having sickle-cell disease, a 25% chance of being perfectly normal and a 50% chance of having the sickle-cell trait. **b.** Sickled cells. Individuals with sickle-cell disease have sickled red blood cells that tend to clump, as illustrated here.

Sickle-cell disease is an inherited lifelong disorder that is being investigated on many fronts.

Genetic Counseling

Now that prospective parents are becoming aware that many illnesses are caused by faulty genes, more couples are seeking genetic counseling. The counselor studies the background of the couple and constructs a pedigree chart for the family. As much as possible, laboratory tests are performed on all persons involved. Blood tests can identify carriers of thalassemia and sickle-cell disease. By measuring enzyme levels in blood, ears, or skin cells, carriers of alleles coding for faulty enzymes can also be identified for certain inborn metabolic errors, such as Tay-Sachs disease. From this information, the counselor can sometimes predict the chances of a couple having a child with a genetic disorder.

If the woman is pregnant, chorionic villi sampling can be done early, and amniocentesis can be done later in the pregnancy. Women are only encouraged to undergo such procedures when there is reason for concern because the risk of complications resulting from these tests can sometimes be greater than the risk of having a child with a disorder. These procedures which are illustrated in Figure 13B, allow the testing of embryonic and fetal cells, respectively, to determine if the unborn child has a genetic disorder. Chromosomal tests are available for cystic fibrosis, neurofibromatosis, and Huntington disease. Appropriate biochemical tests identify other types of genetic disorders (Table 13A).

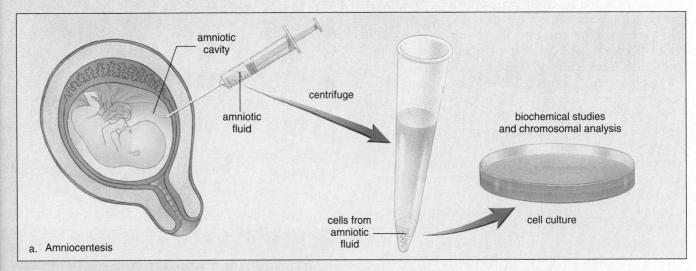

a. Amniocentesis

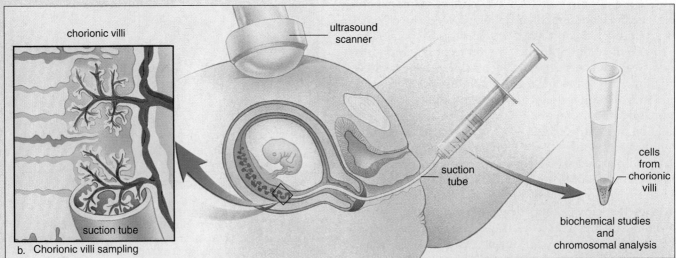

b. Chorionic villi sampling

Figure 13B **Genetic defect testing before birth.**
a. Amniocentesis is usually performed from the fifteenth to the seventeenth week of pregnancy. A long needle is passed through the abdominal wall to withdraw a small amount of amniotic fluid, along with fetal cells. Since there are only a few cells in the amniotic fluid, testing may be delayed as long as four weeks until cell culture produces enough cells for testing purposes. About 40 tests are available for different defects.
b. Chorionic villi sampling can be done as early as the fifth week of pregnancy. The doctor inserts a long, thin tube through the vagina into the uterus. With the help of ultrasound, which gives a picture of the uterine contents, the tube is placed between the lining of the uterus and the chorion. Then a sampling of the chorionic villi cells is obtained by suction. Chromosome analysis and biochemical tests for genetic defects can be done immediately on these cells.

Traditionally, it might take four weeks following chorionic villi sampling and amniocentesis for the cells to grow and multiply in cell culture in adequate number for test purposes. This is a distinct disadvantage to those who may wish the option to abort the pregnancy if an abnormality is found. There is a new technique, however, that can be used to detect many chromosomal abnormalities just one or two days after cells are obtained. Fluorescent probes specific for certain regions of chromosomes can be applied to amniotic cells and they will bind to and light up those regions. For example, a probe for the X chromosome can tell how many X chromosomes the child inherited.

Every year more and more tests become available for genetic mutations associated with disorders ranging from psychological conditions to colon cancers. Maybe genetic testing shouldn't be done if the presence of a mutation only indicates a possible risk of developing a condition. As a society we have not yet decided how many and what types of genetic tests should be done and how to interpret some of the results once they are done. As an example, suppose one prenatal twin is XY and the other is XYY—do you think the parents should be informed? It might cause them to treat the XYY child differently when actually many XYY individuals live a normal life.

Table 13A

Test and Treatment for Some Human Genetic Disorders

Name	Description	Chromosome	Incidence (Newborns)	Status
Autosomal Dominant Disorders				
Neurofibromatosis	Benign tumors occur under the skin or deeper.	17	One in 3,000	Allele located; chromosome test now available*
Huntington disease	Minor disturbances in balance and coordination develop in middle age and progress towards severe neurological disturbances leading to death.	4	One in 20,000	Allele located; chromosome test now available*
Autosomal Recessive Disorders				
Cystic fibrosis	Mucus in the lungs and digestive tract is thick and viscous, making breathing and digestion difficult.	7	One in 2,500 Caucasians	Allele located; chromosome test now available;* treatment being investigated
Tay-Sachs disease	Neurological impairment and psychomotor difficulties develop early, followed by blindness and uncontrollable seizures before death occurs, usually before age 5.	15	One in 3,600 eastern European Jews	Biochemical test now available*
Phenylketonuria	Inability to metabolize phenylalanine, and if a special diet is not begun, mental retardation develops.	12	One in 5,000	Biochemical test now available; treatment available
Incomplete Dominance				
Sickle-cell disease	Poor circulation, anemia, internal hemorrhaging, due to sickle-shaped red blood cells.	11	One in 500 African Americans	Chromosome test now available*
X-Linked Recessive				
Duchenne muscular dystrophy	Muscle weakness develops early and progressively intensifies until death occurs, usually before age 20.	X	One in 5,000 male births	Allele located; biochemical tests of muscle tissue available; treatment being investigated
Hemophilia A	Propensity for bleeding, often internally, due to the lack of a blood clotting factor.	X	One in 15,000 male births	Treatment available

Prenatal testing is done.

13.3 Sex-Linked Genetic Disorders

The alleles for **sex-linked** genetic disorders are on the sex chromosomes. Most of these alleles are on the X chromosome, and therefore are said to be **X-linked.** Sex-linked alleles code for characteristics that have nothing to do with the sex of the individual.

X-Linked Recessive Disorders

Figure 13.11 gives a pedigree chart for an X-linked recessive condition. It also lists ways to recognize this pattern of inheritance. X-linked conditions can be dominant or recessive, but most known are recessive. More males than females have the trait because recessive alleles on the X chromosome are always expressed in males since the Y chromosome does not have a corresponding allele. If a male has an X-linked recessive condition, his daughters are often carriers; therefore, the condition passes from grandfather to grandson. Females who have the condition inherited the allele from both their mother and their father; and all the sons of such a female will have the condition.

Three well-known X-linked recessive disorders are color blindness, muscular dystrophy, and hemophilia.

Color Blindness

In humans, there are three different classes of cone cells, the receptors for color vision in the retina of the eyes. Only one pigment protein is present in each type of cone cell; there are blue-sensitive, red-sensitive, and green-sensitive cone cells. The gene for the blue-sensitive protein is autosomal, but the genes for the red- and green-sensitive proteins are on the X chromosome. About 8% of Caucasian men have red/green color blindness. Most of these see brighter greens as tans, olive greens as browns, and reds as reddish-browns. A few cannot tell reds from greens at all. They see only yellows, blues, blacks, whites, and grays. Opticians have special charts by which they detect those who are color blind.

Duchenne Muscular Dystrophy

Muscular dystrophy, as the name implies, is characterized by a wasting away of the muscles. The most common form, *Duchenne muscular dystrophy,* is X-linked and occurs in about one out of every 3,600 male births. Symptoms, such as waddling gait, toe walking, frequent falls, and difficulty in rising, may appear as soon as the child starts to walk. Muscle weakness intensifies until the individual is confined to a wheelchair. Death usually occurs by age 20; therefore, affected males are rarely fathers. The recessive allele remains in the population by passage from carrier mother to carrier daughter.

Once the gene for muscular dystrophy was isolated, it was discovered that the absence of a protein called dystrophin is the cause of the disorder. Much investigative work determined that dystrophin is involved in the release of calcium from the calcium-storage sites in muscle fibers. The lack of dystrophin causes calcium to leak into the cell, which promotes the action of an enzyme that dissolves muscle fibers. When the body attempts to repair the tissue, fibrous tissue forms, and this cuts off the blood supply so that more and more cells die.

A test is now available to detect carriers for Duchenne muscular dystrophy. Also, various treatments are being attempted. Immature muscle cells can be injected into muscles, and for every 100,000 cells injected, dystrophin production occurs in 30–40% of the patient's muscle fibers. The gene for dystrophin has been inserted into the thigh muscle cells of mice, and about 1% of these cells then produced dystrophin.

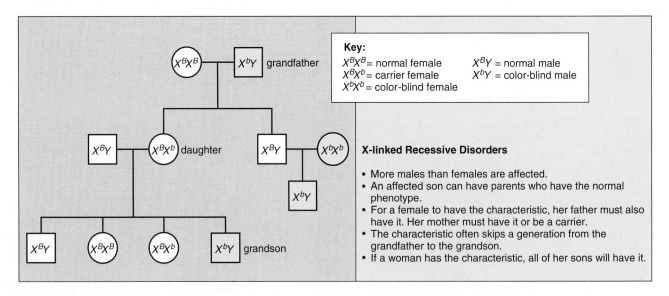

Figure 13.11 X-linked recessive pedigree chart.
The list gives ways of recognizing an X-linked recessive disorder. Only those affected with the recessive genetic disorder are shaded.

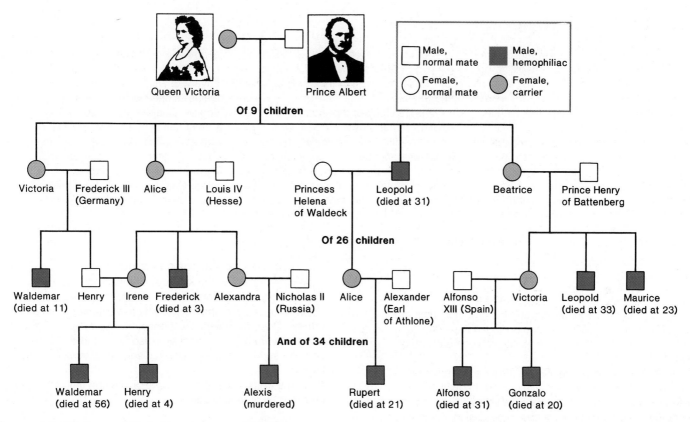

Figure 13.12 Hemophilia in European royal families.
Because Queen Victoria was a carrier, each of her sons had a 50% chance of having the disease and each of her daughters had a 50% chance of being a carrier. This pedigree shows only the affected individuals. Many others are unaffected, such as the members of the present British royal family.

Hemophilia

About one in 10,000 males is a hemophiliac. There are two common types of hemophilia: hemophilia A is due to the absence or minimal presence of a clotting factor known as factor IX, and hemophilia B is due to the absence of clotting factor VIII.

Hemophilia is called the bleeder's disease because the affected person's blood does not clot. Although hemophiliacs bleed externally after an injury, they also suffer from internal bleeding, particularly around joints. Hemorrhages can be checked with transfusions of fresh blood (or plasma) or concentrates of the clotting protein. Unfortunately, some hemophiliacs have contracted AIDS after receiving blood or using a blood concentrate, but donors are now screened more closely, and donated blood is now tested for HIV. Also, factor VIII is now available as a genetic engineering product.

At the turn of the century, hemophilia was prevalent among the royal families of Europe, and all of the affected males could trace their ancestry to Queen Victoria of England (Fig. 13.12). Of Queen Victoria's 26 grandchildren, five grandsons had hemophilia and four granddaughters were

carriers. Because none of Queen Victoria's forebears or relatives was affected, it seems that the faulty allele she carried arose by mutation either in Victoria or in one of her parents. Her carrier daughters, Alice and Beatrice, introduced the gene into the ruling houses of Europe. Alexis, the last heir to the Russian throne before the Russian Revolution, was a hemophiliac. There are no hemophiliacs in the present British royal family because Victoria's eldest son, King Edward VII, did not receive the gene and therefore could not pass it on to any of his descendants.

Certain genetic disorders are caused by X-linked recessive alleles (see Table 13A, page 213). Males have only one X chromosome, and therefore X-linked recessive alleles are always expressed.

Certain traits common in males, like pattern baldness, are controlled by an autosomal allele that acts as if it were dominant in males but recessive in females. Most likely the activity of such genes is influenced by the sex hormones. Therefore they are called **sex-influenced traits.**

Connecting Concepts

It is apparent from a study of this chapter that Mendel's laws are applicable to human genetics: some conditions, such as cystic fibrosis, have a recessive inheritance pattern while others like Huntington disease have a simple Mendelian inheritance pattern. We also now know that sex linkage, incomplete dominance, and polygenic inheritance explain other types of human inheritance patterns. Therefore, the principles of inheritance determined by doing specific crosses with peas, fruit flies, or other model organisms (as described in Chapters 11 and 12) are relevant to the study of inherited traits in humans.

From a study of this chapter, it is also apparent that human conditions such as cystic fibrosis, muscular dystrophy, sickle-cell anemia, and color blindness, are due to alleles that code for abnormal forms of proteins. In other words, we began to look at the molecular basis for genetic inheritance. We will continue this examination in the next few chapters. Chapter 14 traces the history of the discovery of DNA, the genetic material, explains its chemistry and how it is normally copied. Chapter 15 tells how the expression of genes (the genotype) results in the characteristics (phenotype) of the organism. Chapter 16 discusses the many ways in which gene expression is regulated. Chapter 17 tells how the genes of all organisms can be manipulated.

Summary

13.1 Inheritance of Chromosomes

It is possible to treat and photograph the chromosomes of a cell so that they can be sorted and arranged in pairs. The resulting karyotype can be used to diagnose chromosomal abnormalities.

Down syndrome (trisomy 21) is the most common autosomal abnormality. The occurrence of this syndrome, which is often related to the mother's age, can be detected by amniocentesis. Most often, Down syndrome is due to nondisjunction during gamete formation, but in a small percentage of cases, there has been a translocation between chromosomes 14 and 21, in which chromosome 21 is attached to chromosome 14.

Turner syndrome (XO) is a monosomy for the X chromosome. There are several trisomies: Klinefelter syndrome, which is XXY; triplo-X, which is XXX; and Jacob syndrome. Fragile X syndrome, which has an unusual pattern of inheritance, is due to the presence of an abnormal X chromosome.

13.2 Autosomal Genetic Disorders

When studying human genes, biologists often construct pedigree charts to show the pattern of inheritance of a characteristic within a family. The particular pattern indicates the manner in which a characteristic is inherited.

Certain genetic disorders are inherited in a simple Mendelian manner. Neurofibromatosis is an autosomal dominant disorder that is inherited in this manner. We now know that Huntington disease, long classified as an autosomal dominant disease, is due to expanded trinucleotide repeats, and the greater the number of repeats, the earlier the onset of the disease. Also, the disease is more likely to have been inherited from the father for reasons that are still being explored. Cystic fibrosis, Tay-Sachs disease, and PKU are autosomal recessive disorders that have been studied in detail.

Polygenic traits are controlled by more than one gene loci and the individual inherits an allelic pair for each loci. Skin color illustrates polygenic inheritance. Traits controlled by polygenes are subject to environmental effects and show continuous variations whose frequency distribution forms a bell-shaped curve.

ABO blood type is an example of a human trait controlled by multiple alleles. Sickle-cell disease is a human disorder that is controlled by incompletely dominant alleles.

13.3 Sex-Linked Genetic Disorders

X-linked genes are on the X chromosome. Since the Y chromosome is blank for X-linked alleles, males are more apt to exhibit the recessive phenotype, which is inherited from their mothers. Color blindness, Duchenne muscular dystrophy, and hemophilia are X-linked recessive disorders. Table 13A on page 213 summarizes the genetic disorders discussed in this chapter.

Some traits, like pattern baldness, are sex-influenced traits controlled by autosomal alleles.

Reviewing the Chapter

1. What does the normal human karyotype look like?   202
2. Diagram how nondisjunction can occur during meiosis I and meiosis II.   203
3. What are the characteristics of Down syndrome? What is the most frequent cause of this condition?   204
4. What is the only known sex chromosome monosomy in humans? Name and describe three sex chromosome trisomies.   204–5
5. How might you distinguish an autosomal dominant trait from an autosomal recessive trait when viewing a pedigree chart?   207
6. Describe the symptoms of neurofibromatosis and Huntington disease. How does neurofibromatosis illustrate variable expressivity? For most autosomal dominant disorders, what are the chances of a heterozygote and a normal individual having an affected child?   208
7. Describe the symptoms of cystic fibrosis, Tay-Sachs disease, and PKU. For any one of these, what are the chances of two carriers having an affected child? 209
8. What observational data would allow you to hypothesize that a human trait is controlled by polygenes?   210
9. Why is ABO blood type an example of inheritance by multiple alleles?   210
10. Explain how sickle-cell disease is inherited. What are the symptoms of sickle-cell trait and sickle-cell disease? If two persons with the sickle-cell trait reproduce, what are the chances of having a child with the sickle-cell trait? with sickle-cell disease? What ethnic group is more likely to have this condition? Why?   211

11. Explain how color blindness, Duchenne muscular dystrophy, and hemophilia are inherited. What are the symptoms of these conditions? What are the chances of having an affected male offspring if the mother is a carrier and the father is normal? 214–15
12. How does the mode of inheritance for a sex-influenced trait differ from that of an X-linked recessive trait? 215

Testing Yourself

Choose the best answer for each question. For questions 1–3, match the conditions in the key with the descriptions below:

Key:

a. Down syndrome
b. Turner syndrome
c. Klinefelter syndrome
d. XYY
e. triplo-X individual

1. male with underdeveloped testes and some breast development
2. trisomy 21
3. XO female
4. Down syndrome
   a. is always caused by nondisjunction of chromosome 21.
   b. occurs less frequently today because nutrition is better now.
   c. is more often seen in children of mothers past the age of thirty-five.
   d. can be cured by removing one of the X chromosomes from the cells of a fetus.
   e. All of these are correct.
5. A person has a genetic disorder. Which of these is inconsistent with autosomal recessive inheritance?
   a. Both parents have the disorder.
   b. Both parents do not have the disorder.
   c. All the children (males and females) have the disorder.
   d. All of these are consistent.
   e. All of these are inconsistent.
6. A male has a genetic disorder. Which one of these is inconsistent with X-linked recessive inheritance?
   a. Both parents do not have the disorder.
   b. Only males in a pedigree chart have the disorder.
   c. Only females in previous generations have the disorder.
   d. The sons of a female with the disorder will all have the disorder.
   e. Both a and c are inconsistent.

For questions 7–10, match the conditions in the key with the following descriptions:

Key:

a. cystic fibrosis
b. Huntington disease
c. hemophilia
d. Tay-Sachs disease
e. sickle-cell disease

7. autosomal dominant
8. most often seen among eastern European Jews
9. X-linked recessive
10. thick mucus in lungs and pancreatic ducts
11. Determine if the characteristic possessed by the shaded squares (males) and circles (females) below is an autosomal dominant, an autosomal recessive, or an X-linked recessive disorder.

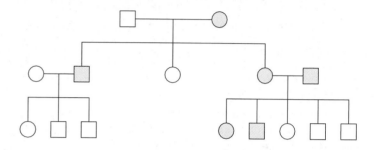

Additional Genetics Problems*

1. A hemophilic (X-linked recessive) man reproduces with a homozygous normal woman. What are the chances that their sons will be hemophiliacs? that their daughters will be hemophiliacs? that their daughters will be carriers?
2. A son with cystic fibrosis (autosomal recessive) is born to a couple who appear to be normal. What are the chances that any child born to this couple will have cystic fibrosis?
3. A man has type AB blood. What is his genotype? Could this man be the father of a child with type B blood? If so, what blood types could the child's mother have?
4. What is the genotype of a man who is color blind (X-linked recessive) and has a continuous hairline (autosomal recessive)? If this man has children by a woman who is homozygous dominant for normal color vision and widow's peak, what will be the genotype and phenotype of the children?
5. Determine if the characteristic possessed by the shaded squares (males) is dominant, recessive, or X-linked recessive. Write in the genotypes for the starred individual.

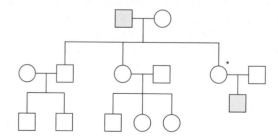

Thinking Scientifically

1. Not all individuals with Down syndrome have equally severe mental retardation or other physical abnormalities. Explain on the basis of a difference in the expression of alleles.

2. The particular recessive allele that causes cystic fibrosis (CF) can vary. Seventy percent of patients with CF are homozygous recessive for any number of different alleles that also cause CF. The screening test for heterozygotes detects only the most common allele for CF. If a person with CF relatives tests negative for the common allele, how might s/he determine that s/he need not worry about the possibility of having a rarer form of the CF allele?

Bioethical Issue

Sickle-cell disease is a prevalent type of debilitating anemia in the African-American community because African Americans are more likely to have sickle-cell trait. They are not sick, but if two persons with sickle-cell trait reproduce with one another, each child has a 25% chance of having sickle-cell disease, which can lead to an early death.

In the 1970s, the federal government funded a screening program to detect those with sickle-cell trait because they thought prospective parents might want to have this information. The procedure is inexpensive and requires the testing of just one drop of blood. At first, members of the black community were in favor of testing; ministers conducted tests on their congregations and the black Panthers offered the test door-to-door in black communities.

Due to a lack of understanding, however, the results of testing were not treated as expected. The government, employers, and those with sickle-cell trait themselves thought they were sick. The Massachusetts legislature required that schools, for health reasons, identify all those with sickle-cell trait as well as students with sickle-cell disease. Some insurance companies began to deny coverage to those with sickle-cell trait on the grounds that they had a preexisting medical condition. The U.S. Air Force Academy rejected black applicants who had sickle-cell trait. Some commercial airlines refused to hire those with sickle-cell trait, thinking that they might faint at high altitudes. Some prominent scientists suggested that those with sickle-cell trait should forego having children.

Although this example suggests that genetic testing has many drawbacks, do you feel there are some benefits to testing if the rights of the individual are safeguarded?

Understanding the Terms

amniocentesis   203
autosome   202
carrier   207
chorionic villi sampling   212
genetic disorder   207
genomic imprinting   208
karyotype   202
multiple allele   210
nondisjunction   203
pedigree chart   207
sex chromosome   202
sex-influenced trait   215
sex-linked   214
X chromosome   202
Y chromosome   202
X-linked   214

Match the terms to these definitions:

a. _____ Any chromosome other than a sex chromosome.

b. _____ Autosomal phenotype controlled by an allele that is expressed differently in the two sexes; for example, the possibility of pattern baldness is increased by the presence of testosterone in males.

c. _____ Chromosomes arranged by pairs according to their size, shape, and general appearance in mitotic metaphase.

d. _____ Failure of homologous chromosomes or daughter chromosomes to separate during meiosis I and meiosis II, respectively.

e. _____ Heterozygous individual who has no apparent abnormality but can pass on an allele for a recessively inherited genetic disorder.

Web Connections

Exploring the Internet

http://www.mhhe.com/biosci/genbio/mader
(click on *Biology 7/e*)

The *Biology 7/e* Online Learning Center provides many resources for studying the material in this chapter including links to the following sites:

Online Mendelian Inheritance in Man is a database of human genes and genetic disorders. It is a site designed for professionals, but can also be used by advanced students or those interested in taking a peek further into the field of genetics.

http://www3.ncbi.nlm.nih.gov/Omim/

Mendelian Genetics Chapter. A hypertextbook from MIT on genetics, including problems in linkage and pedigrees.

http://esg-www.mit.edu:8001/esgbio/mg/mgdir.html

Genomes Guide: Homo sapiens. *Clickable chromosomes, learn about diseases associated with particular chromosomes.*

http://www.ncbi.nlm.nih.gov/genome/guide/

Genes and Disease. A nifty site to look for a variety of genetically linked diseases.

http://www.ncbi.nlm.nih.gov/disease/

What is Fragile X? A site maintained by the Fragile X Association describes this condition.

http://www.fraxsocal.org/

DNA Structure and Functions

c h a p t e r   c o n c e p t s

Test tube containing DNA whose structure resembles a spiral staircase (digital composite).

One of the most exciting periods of scientific activity in history occurred during the thirty short years between the 1930s and 1960s. Geneticists knew that chromosomes contain protein and DNA (deoxyribonucleic acid). Of these two organic molecules, proteins are seemingly more complicated; they consist of countless sequences of 20 amino acids, which can coil and fold into complex shapes. DNA, on the other hand, contains only four different nucleotides. Surely, the diversity of life-forms on earth must be the result of the endless varieties of proteins.

   Due to several elegantly executed experiments, by the mid-1950s researchers realized that DNA, not protein, is the genetic material. But this finding only led to another fundamental question—*what exactly is the structure of DNA?* The biological community at the time knew that whoever determined the structure of DNA would get a Nobel Prize, and would go down in history. Consequently, researchers were racing against time and each other. The story of the discovery of DNA resembles a mystery, with each clue adding to the total picture until the breathtaking design of DNA—a double helix—was finally unraveled.

14.1 The Genetic Material

Even though previous investigators were able to confirm that the genes are on the chromosomes and were even able to map the *Drosophila* chromosomes, they still didn't know just what genes consisted of. You can well imagine, then, that the search for the genetic material was of utmost importance to biologists at the beginning of the twentieth century. They knew that this material must be:

1. able to *store information* that pertains to both the development and the metabolic activities of the cell or organism;
2. stable so that it *can be replicated* with high fidelity during cell division and be transmitted from generation to generation;
3. able to *undergo rare changes* called mutations [L. *muta*, change] that provide the genetic variability required for evolution to occur.

The genetic material must be able to store information, be replicated, and undergo mutations.

Knowledge about the chemistry of DNA was absolutely essential in order to come to the conclusion that DNA is the genetic material. In 1869, the Swiss chemist Friedrich Miescher removed nuclei from pus cells (these cells have little cytoplasm) and found that they contained a chemical he called *nuclein*. Nuclein, he said, was rich in phosphorus and had no sulfur, properties that distinguished it from protein. Later, other chemists did further work with nuclein and said that it contained an acidic substance they called **nucleic acid.** Soon it was realized that there are two types of nucleic acids: **DNA (deoxyribonucleic acid)** and **RNA (ribonucleic acid).**

Early in the twentieth century, it was discovered that nucleic acids contain only four types of **nucleotides,** molecules that are composed of a nitrogen-containing base, a phosphate, and a pentose (5-carbon sugar). Perhaps DNA was composed of repeating units, and each unit always had just one of each of the four different nucleotides. In that case, DNA could not vary between genes and could not be the genetic material! Everyone thought that the protein component of chromosomes must be the genetic material because proteins contain 20 different amino acids that can be sequenced in any particular way.

Transformation of Bacteria

In 1931, the bacteriologist Frederick Griffith performed an experiment with a bacterium (*Streptococcus pneumoniae*, or pneumococcus for short) that causes pneumonia in mammals. He noticed that when these bacteria are grown on culture plates, some, called S strain bacteria, produce shiny, smooth colonies and others, called R strain bacteria, produce colonies that have a rough appearance. Under the microscope, S strain bacteria have a capsule (mucous coat) but R strain bacteria do not. When Griffith injected mice with the S strain of bacteria, the mice died, and when he injected mice with the R strain, the mice did not die (Fig. 14.1). In an effort to determine if the capsule alone was responsible for the virulence (ability to kill) of the S strain bacteria, he injected mice with heat-killed S strain bacteria. The mice did not die.

Finally, Griffith injected the mice with a mixture of heat-killed S strain and live R strain bacteria. Most unexpectedly,

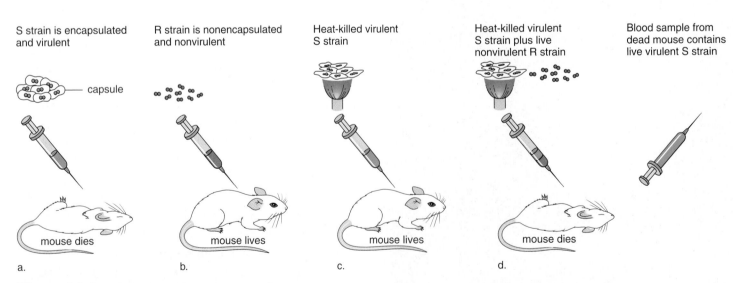

Figure 14.1 Griffith's transformation experiment.
a. Encapsulated S strain is virulent and kills the mouse. **b.** Nonencapsulated R strain is not virulent and does not kill the mouse. **c.** Heat-killed S strain bacteria do not kill the mouse. **d.** If heat-killed S strain and R strain are both injected into a mouse, it dies because the R strain bacteria have been transformed into the virulent S strain.

the mice died and living S strain bacteria were recovered from the bodies! Griffith concluded that some substance necessary to the synthesis of a capsule and, therefore, virulence must have passed from the dead S strain bacteria to the living R strain bacteria so that the R strain bacteria were *transformed* (Fig. 14.1*d*). This change in the phenotype of the R strain bacteria must be due to a change in their genotype. Indeed, couldn't the transforming substance that passed from S strain to R strain be genetic material? Reasoning such as this prompted investigators at the time to begin looking for the transforming substance to determine the chemical nature of the genetic material.

DNA: The Transforming Substance

Obviously, it is not convenient to look for the transforming substance in mice. It is not surprising, then, that the next group of investigators, led by Oswald Avery, isolated the genetic material in vitro (in laboratory glassware). After 16 years of research, this group published a paper demonstrating that the transforming substance is DNA. Their evidence included the following observations:

1. DNA from S strain bacteria causes R strain bacteria to be transformed.
2. Enzymes that degrade proteins cannot prevent transformation, nor did RNase, an enzyme that digests RNA.
3. Enzymatic digestion of the transforming substance with DNase, an enzyme that digests DNA, does prevent transformation.
4. The molecular weight of the transforming substance is so great that it must contain about 1,600 nucleotides! Certainly this is enough for some genetic variability.

These experiments certainly showed that DNA is the transforming substance. Some still remained skeptical that DNA was the genetic material, however. Perhaps, they said, DNA merely served to activate protein-based genes.

Transformation Experiments Today

Transformation experiments are often done today in various laboratories around the world from high schools to the most sophisticated research facilities. Transformation occurs when organisms receive foreign DNA and thereby acquire a new characteristic. One typical rudimentary experiment is to expose bacteria to DNA that allows them to grow in the presence of penicillin. Before they are transformed, the bacteria are unable to grow in the presence of penicillin but after they take up DNA from the medium they can grow in the presence of penicillin. The DNA contains a gene that makes bacteria resistant to penicillin!

Reproduction of Viruses

Soon after Avery published his results, many geneticists who were interested in determining the chemical nature of the genetic material began to work with bacteriophages [Gk. *bacterion*, rod, and *phagein,* to eat]. **Bacteriophages** are viruses that infect bacteria such as the bacterium *Escherichia coli* (*E. coli*), which normally lives within the human gut.

Viruses consist only of a protein coat called a capsid surrounding a nucleic acid core (Fig. 14.2). We now know that when a bacteriophage, or simply phage, latches onto a bacterium, only the nucleic acid (i.e., DNA) enters the cell and the capsid is left behind. Later the bacterium releases many hundreds of new viruses. Why? Because phage DNA contains the genetic information necessary to cause the bacterium to produce new phages. But we are getting ahead of our story. Back

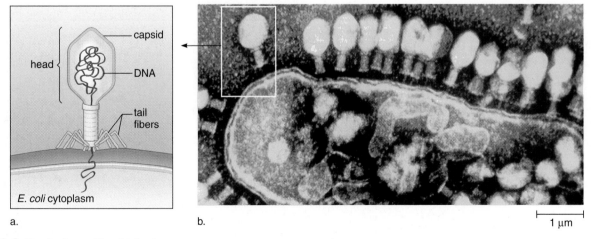

Figure 14.2 Bacteria and bacteriophages.
a. A T virus consists of a capsid (protein coat) surrounding a DNA core. When a T virus attacks a bacterium, only DNA enters the cell and later many fully formed viruses emerge from the cell. **b.** T viruses are pictured attacking an *E. coli* cell.

in the 1950s, biologists were still performing experiments to determine which one—DNA or protein—enters a virus. Whichever one does this has to be the genetic material.

In 1952, two experimenters, Alfred D. Hershey and Martha Chase, chose a bacteriophage known as T2 to determine which of the phage components—protein or DNA—entered bacterial cells and directed reproduction of the virus. Hershey and Chase relied on a chemical difference between DNA and protein.

> Phosphorus (P) is present (but not sulfur) in DNA.
> Sulfur (S) is present (but not phosphorus) in protein.

They used radioactive ^{32}P to label the DNA core of the phage and radioactive ^{35}S to label the protein in the capsid of the phage. Recall that radioactive isotopes serve as labels (i.e., tracers) in biological experiments because it is possible to detect the presence of radioactivity by standard laboratory procedures.

Hershey and Chase did two separate experiments (Fig. 14.3). In the first experiment phage DNA was labeled with radioactive ^{32}P. The phages were allowed to attach to and inject their genetic material into *E. coli* cells. Then the culture was agitated in a kitchen blender to remove whatever remained of the phages on the outside of the bacterial cells. Finally, the

culture was centrifuged (spun at high speed) so that the bacterial cells collected as a pellet at the bottom of the centrifuge tube. In this experiment, as you would predict, they found most of the ^{32}P-labeled DNA in the cells and not in the liquid medium. Why? Because the DNA had entered the cells.

In the second experiment, phage protein in capsids was labeled with radioactive ^{35}S. The phages were allowed to attach to and inject their genetic material into *E. coli* bacterial cells. Then the culture was agitated in a kitchen blender to remove whatever remained of the phages on the outside of the bacterial cells. Finally the culture was centrifuged so that the bacterial cells collected as a pellet at the bottom of the centrifuge tube. In this experiment, as you would predict, they found ^{35}S-labeled protein in the liquid medium and not in the cells. Why? Because the radioactive capsids remained on the outside of the cells and were removed by the blender.

These results indicated that the DNA of a virus (and not protein) enters the host, where viral reproduction takes place. Therefore, DNA is the genetic material. It transmits all the necessary genetic information needed to produce new viruses.

The Hershey and Chase experiment showed that DNA and not protein is the genetic material.

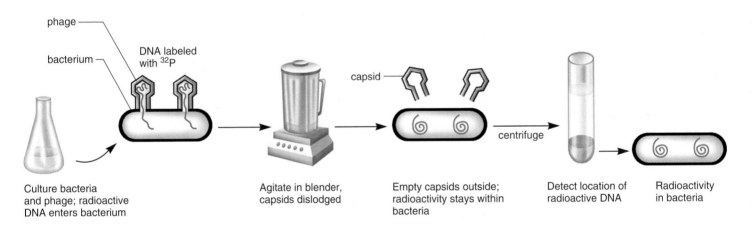

Culture bacteria and phage; radioactive DNA enters bacterium

Agitate in blender, capsids dislodged

Empty capsids outside; radioactivity stays within bacteria

Detect location of radioactive DNA

Radioactivity in bacteria

a. Viral DNA is labeled (red).

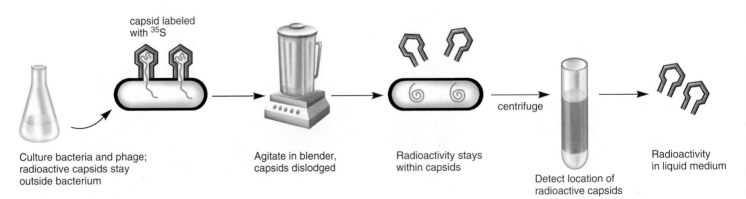

Culture bacteria and phage; radioactive capsids stay outside bacterium

Agitate in blender, capsids dislodged

Radioactivity stays within capsids

Detect location of radioactive capsids

Radioactivity in liquid medium

b. Viral capsid is labeled (red).

Figure 14.3 Hershey and Chase experiment.

14.2 The Structure of DNA

During the same period of time that biologists were using viruses to show that DNA is the genetic material, biochemists were busy trying to determine its structure. The structure of DNA shows how DNA stores information, as is required of the genetic material.

Nucleotide Data

With the development of new chemical techniques in the 1940s, it was possible for Erwin Chargaff to analyze in detail the base content of DNA. It was known that DNA contains four different types of nucleotides: two with **purine** bases, **adenine (A)** and **guanine (G),** which have a double ring, and two with **pyrimidine** bases, **thymine (T)** and **cytosine (C),** which have a single ring (Fig. 14.4*a* and *b*). Did each species contain 25% of each kind of nucleotide, or did the amounts vary?

A sample of Chargaff's data is seen in Figure 14.4*c*. You can see that while some species—*E. coli* and *Zea mays* (corn), for example—do have approximately 25% of each type of nucleotide, most do not. Further, the percentage of each type of nucleotide differs from species to species. Therefore, DNA does have the *variability* between species required of the genetic material.

Within each species, however, DNA has the *constancy* required of the genetic material. Further, the percentage of A equals the percentage of T, and the percentage of G equals the percentage of C. The percentage of A + G equals 50%, and the percentage of T + C equals 50%. These relationships are called Chargaff's rules.

Chargaff's rules:

1. The amount of A, T, G, and C in DNA varies from species to species.
2. In each species, the amount of A = T and the amount of G = C.

The so-called tetranucleotide hypothesis, which said that DNA has repeating units, each with one of the four bases, was not supported by these data. Each species had its own constant base composition.

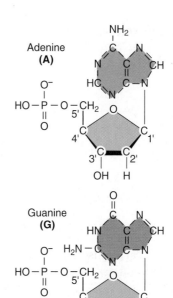

a. **Purine nucleotides**

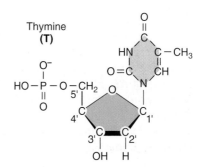

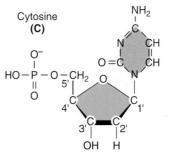

b. **Pyrimidine nucleotides**

Figure 14.4 Nucleotide composition of DNA.
All nucleotides contain phosphate, a five-carbon sugar, and a nitrogen-containing base. In DNA, the sugar is deoxyribose—there is an absence of oxygen in the 2′ position—and the nitrogen-containing bases are **(a)** the purines adenine and guanine, which have a double ring, or **(b)** the pyrimidines thymine and cytosine, which have a single ring. **c.** Chargaff's data show that the DNA of various species differs. For example, in humans the A and T percentages are about 31%, but in fruit flies these percentages are about 27%.

Chargaff's DNA Database Composition in Various Species (%)				
Species	**A**	**T**	**G**	**C**
Homo sapiens	31.0	31.5	19.1	18.4
Drosophila melanogaster	27.3	27.6	22.5	22.5
Zea mays	25.6	25.3	24.5	24.6
Neurospora crassa	23.0	23.3	27.1	26.6
Escherichia coli	24.6	24.3	25.5	25.6
Bacillus subtilis	28.4	29.0	21.0	21.6

c.

Variation in Base Sequence

Chargaff's data suggest that A is always paired with T and G is always paired with C. The paired bases occur in any order:

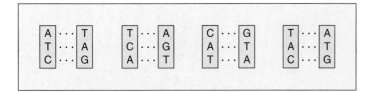

The variability that can be obtained is overwhelming. For example, it has been calculated that the human chromosome contains on the average about 140 million base pairs. Since any of the four possible nucleotides can be present at each nucleotide position, the total number of possible nucleotide sequences is $4^{140 \times 10^6}$ or $4^{140,000,000}$. No wonder each species has its own base percentages!

Diffraction Data

Rosalind Franklin, a student of M. H. F. Wilkins at King's College in London, studied the structure of DNA using X rays. She found that if a concentrated, viscous solution of DNA is made, it can be separated into fibers. Under the right conditions, the fibers are enough like a crystal (a solid substance whose atoms are arranged in a definite manner) that an X-ray pattern forms on a photographic film. Franklin's picture of DNA showed that DNA is a helix (Fig. 14.5). The helical shape is indicated by the crossed (X) pattern in the center of the photograph. The dark portions at the top and bottom of the photograph indicate that some portion of the helix is repeated.

The Watson and Crick Model

James Watson, an American, was on a postdoctoral fellowship at Cavendish Laboratories in Cambridge, England, and while there he began to work with the biophysicist Francis H. C. Crick. Using the data we have just presented, they constructed a model of DNA for which they received a Nobel Prize in 1962 (Fig. 14.6).

Watson and Crick knew, of course, that DNA is a polymer of nucleotides, but they did not know how the nucleotides were arranged within the molecule. This is what they hypothesized.

1. The Watson and Crick model shows that DNA is a double helix with sugar-phosphate backbones on the outside and paired bases on the inside. This arrangement fits the mathematical measurements provided by the X-ray diffraction data for the spacing between the base pairs (0.34 nm) and for a complete turn of the double helix (3.4 nm).

2. Chargaff's rules said that A = T and G = C. The model shows that A is hydrogen-bonded to T and G is hydrogen-bonded to C. This so-called **complementary base pairing** means that a purine is always bonded to a pyrimidine. Only in this way will the molecule have the width (2 nm) dictated by its X-ray diffraction pattern, since two pyrimidines together are too narrow and two purines together are too wide.

The double-helix model of DNA is like a twisted ladder; sugar-phosphate backbones make up the sides, and hydrogen-bonded bases make up the rungs, or steps, of the ladder.

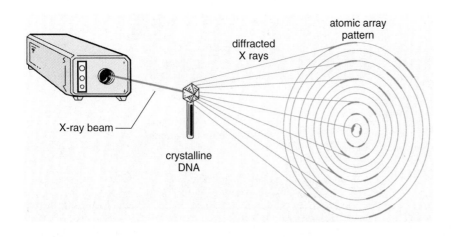

a.

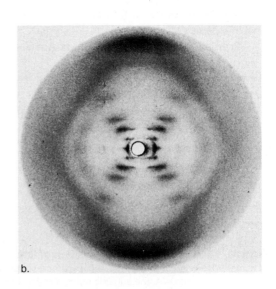

b.

Figure 14.5 X-ray diffraction of DNA.
a. When a crystal is X-rayed, the way in which the beam is diffracted reflects the pattern of the molecules in the crystal. The closer together two repeating structures are in the crystal, the farther from the center the beam is diffracted. b. The diffraction pattern of DNA produced by Rosalind Franklin. The crossed (X) pattern in the center told investigators that DNA is a helix, and the dark portions at the top and the bottom told them that some feature is repeated over and over. Watson and Crick determined that this feature was the hydrogen-bonded bases.

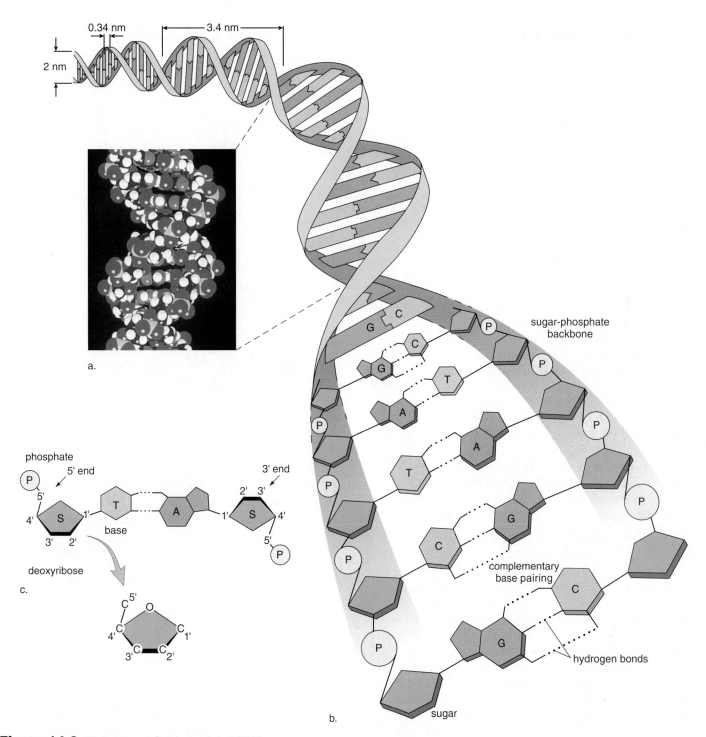

a.

c.

b.

Figure 14.6 Watson and Crick model of DNA.

a. A space-filling model of DNA. Notice the close stacking of the paired bases, as determined by the X-ray diffraction pattern of DNA. (Color code for atoms: yellow = phosphate, dark blue = carbon, red = oxygen, turquoise = nitrogen, and white = hydrogen.) **b.** Diagram of DNA double helix shows that the molecule resembles a twisted ladder. Sugar-phosphate backbones make up the sides of the ladder, and hydrogen-bonded bases make up the rungs of the ladder. Complementary base pairing dictates that A is bonded to T and G is bonded to C. **c.** The two strands of the molecule are antiparallel; that is, the sugar-phosphate groups are oriented in different directions: the 5′ end of one strand is opposite the 3′ end of the other strand.

14.3 Replication of DNA

The term **DNA replication** refers to the process of copying a DNA molecule. Following replication, there is usually an exact copy of the DNA double helix. As soon as Watson and Crick developed their double-helix model, they commented, "It has not escaped our notice that the specific pairing we have postulated immediately suggests a possible copying mechanism for the genetic material."

During DNA replication, each old DNA strand of the parent molecule serves as a template for a new strand in a daughter molecule (Fig. 14.7). A **template** is most often a mold used to produce a shape complementary to itself. DNA replication is termed **semiconservative replication** because one of the old strands is conserved, or present, in each daughter molecule.

Replication requires the following steps:

1. *Unwinding.* The old strands that make up the parent DNA molecule are unwound and "unzipped" (i.e., the weak hydrogen bonds between the paired bases are broken). There is a special enzyme called helicase that unwinds the molecule.
2. *Complementary base pairing.* New complementary nucleotides, always present in the nucleus, are positioned by the process of complementary base pairing.
3. *Joining.* The complementary nucleotides join to form new strands. Each daughter DNA molecule contains an old strand and a new strand.

Steps 2 and 3 are carried out by an enzyme complex called **DNA polymerase.**[1] DNA polymerase works in the test tube as well as in cells.

In Figure 14.7, the backbones of the parent molecule (original double strand) are bluish, and each base is given a particular color. Following replication, the daughter molecules each have a pinkish backbone (new strand) and a bluish backbone (old strand). A daughter DNA double helix has the same sequence of bases as the parent DNA double helix had originally. Although DNA replication can be explained easily in this manner, it is actually a complicated process. Some of the more precise molecular events are discussed in the reading on page 228.

DNA replication must occur before a cell can divide. Cancer, which is characterized by rapidly dividing cells, is sometimes treated with chemotherapeutic drugs that are analogs (have a similar, but not identical structure) to one of the four nucleotides in DNA. When these are mistakenly used by the cancer cells to synthesize DNA, replication stops and the cells die off.

During DNA replication, the parent DNA molecule unwinds and unzips. Then each old strand serves as a template for a new strand.

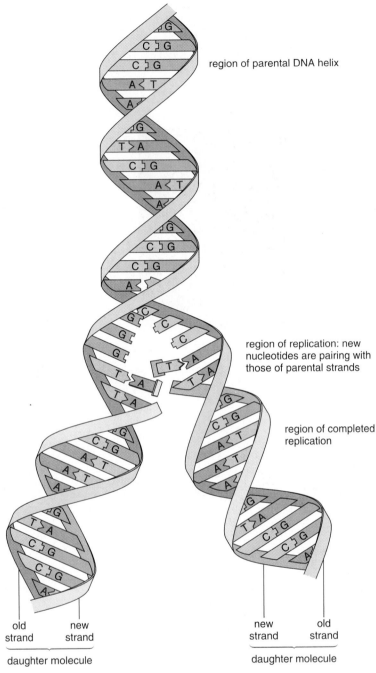

region of parental DNA helix

region of replication: new nucleotides are pairing with those of parental strands

region of completed replication

old strand   new strand   new strand   old strand

daughter molecule   daughter molecule

Figure 14.7 Semiconservative replication (simplified).
After the DNA molecule unwinds, each old strand serves as a template for the formation of the new strand. Complementary nucleotides available in the cell pair with those of the old strand and then are joined together to form a strand. After replication is complete, there are two daughter DNA molecules. Each is composed of an old strand and a new strand. Each daughter molecule has the same sequence of base pairs as the parent molecule had before unwinding occurred.

---

[1] The complex most likely contains a number of different DNA polymerases with specific functions.

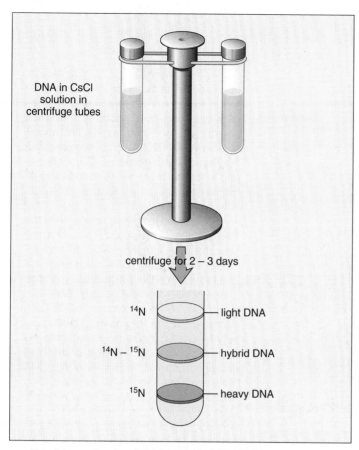

a. Possible results when DNA is centrifuged in CsCl

Figure 14.8 Meselson and Stahl's DNA replication experiment.
a. When DNA molecules are centrifuged in a CsCl density gradient, they separate on the basis of density. **b.** Cells grown in heavy nitrogen (^{15}N) have dense (heavy DNA) strands. After one division in light nitrogen (^{14}N), DNA molecules are hybrid and have intermediate density. After two divisions, DNA molecules separate into two bands—one for light DNA and one for hybrid DNA.

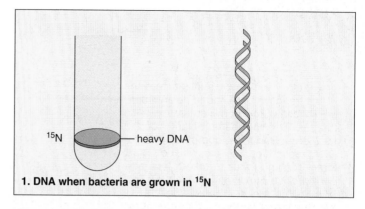

1. **DNA when bacteria are grown in ^{15}N**

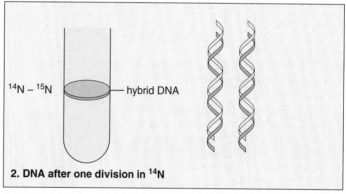

2. **DNA after one division in ^{14}N**

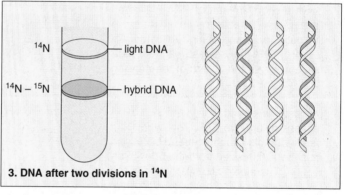

3. **DNA after two divisions in ^{14}N**

b. Steps in Meselson and Stahl experiment

Replication Is Semiconservative

DNA replication is termed semiconservative because each daughter double helix contains an old strand and a new strand. Semiconservative replication was experimentally confirmed by Matthew Meselson and Franklin Stahl in 1958.

Centrifuges spin tubes and in that way separate particles from the suspending fluid. Meselson and Stahl knew that it would be possible to centrifuge DNA molecules in a suspending fluid that would separate them on the basis of their different densities (Fig. 14.8a). A DNA molecule in which both strands contained heavy nitrogen (^{15}N, with an atomic weight of 15) is most dense. A DNA molecule in which both strands contained light nitrogen (^{14}N, with an atomic weight of 14) is least dense. A hybrid DNA molecule in which one strand is heavy and one is light has an intermediate density.

Meselson and Stahl first grew bacteria in a medium containing ^{15}N so that only heavy DNA molecules were extracted from the cells. Then they switched the bacteria to a medium containing ^{14}N. After one division, only hybrid DNA molecules were in the cells. After two divisions, half of the DNA molecules were light and half were hybrid. These were exactly the results to be expected if DNA replication is semiconservative.

DNA replication is semiconservative. Each new strand contains an old and a new strand.

Aspects of DNA Replication

Watson and Crick realized that the strands in DNA had to be antiparallel to allow for complementary base pairing. This opposite polarity of the strands introduces complications for DNA replication, as we will now see. First, it is important to take a look at a deoxyribose molecule in which the carbon atoms are numbered (Fig. 14Aa). Use the structure to see that one of the strands of DNA (Fig. 14Ab) runs from 3′ → 5′ in one direction and the other strand runs from 3′ → 5′ in the opposite direction.

During replication DNA polymerase has to synthesize the daughter strand in from 5′ → 3′. Why? Because DNA polymerase can only join a nucleotide to the free 3′ end of another nucleotide as shown in Figure 14Ab. This also means that *DNA polymerase cannot start the synthesis of a DNA chain.* Therefore, an RNA polymerase lays down a short amount of RNA, called an RNA primer, that is complementary to the parental strand being replicated. After that, DNA polymerase can join DNA nucleotides to the 3′ end of the growing daughter (new) strand.

As the helicase enzyme unwinds DNA, one parental strand runs in the 3′ → 5′ direction toward the fork. This works out perfect for this daughter strand because it must be synthesized from the 5′ → 3′ direction. Therefore, this so-called *leading strand* is synthesized continuously toward the region of the fork (Fig. 14Ac.) What about the situation for replication of the other parental strand which runs in the 3′ → 5′ direction away from the fork?

In this case the daughter strand must begin at the fork. Therefore, replication begins over and over again by new DNA polymerase molecules as the DNA molecule unwinds. Replication of this so-called *lagging strand* is therefore discontinuous and it results in segments called Okazaki fragments, after the Japanese scientist who discovered them.

Replication is only complete when the RNA primers are removed. This works out well for the lagging daughter strand. While proofreading, DNA polymerase removes the RNA primers and replaces them with complementary DNA nucleotides. Another enzyme, called DNA ligase, joins the fragments. There is no way for DNA polymerase to replicate the end of the leading strand after the RNA primer is removed. This means that DNA molecules get shorter as one replication follows another. The end of eukaryotic DNA molecules have a special nucleotide sequence called *telomeres.* Telomeres do not code for proteins and instead are repeats of a short nucleotide sequence like TTAGGG.

Mammalian cells grown in culture divide about 50 times and then they stop. After this number of divisions the continuous loss of telomeres apparently signals the cell to stop dividing. Ordinarily, telomeres are only added to chromosomes during gamete formation by an enzyme called telomerase. This enzyme unfortunately is often mistakenly turned on in cancer cells, an event that contributes to the ability of cancer cells to keep on dividing without limit.

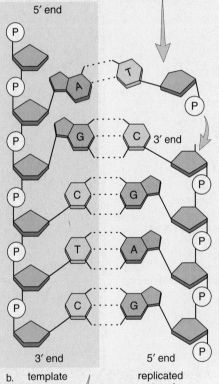

a.

DNA polymerase attaches new nucleotide to the 3′ carbon of previous nucleotide

b. template strand · replicated strand

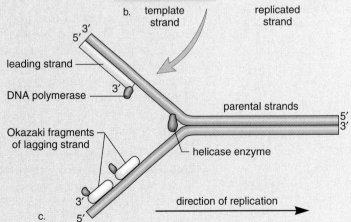

c.

Figure 14A DNA replication (in depth).

a. Structure of deoxyribose, showing where nitrogen base and phosphate groups are attached. b. Template strand and replicated strand, the latter of which always grows from the 5′ end toward the 3′ end. c. Both parental strands are templates for a daughter strand. Replication is a continuous process for one daughter strand and a discontinuous process for the other daughter strand. The enzymes are much larger than shown.

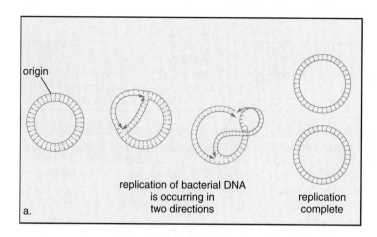

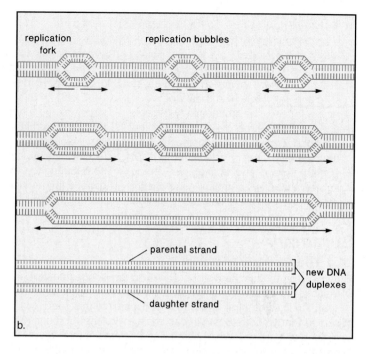

Figure 14.9 Prokaryotic versus eukaryotic replication.
a. In prokaryotes, replication can occur in two directions at once because the DNA molecule is circular. b. In eukaryotes, replication occurs at numerous replication forks. The bubbles thereby created spread out until they meet.

Prokaryotic Versus Eukaryotic Replication

Prokaryotes differ from eukaryotes in a number of ways, including how DNA replication takes place (Fig. 14.9).

Prokaryotic Replication

Bacteria have a single circular loop of DNA that must be replicated before the cell divides. In some circular DNA molecules, replication moves around the DNA molecule in one direction only. In others, as shown here, replication occurs in two directions. The process always occurs in the 5′ to 3′ direction.

Bacterial cells are able to replicate their DNA at a rate of about 10^6 base pairs per minute, and about 40 minutes are required to replicate the complete chromosome. Because bacterial cells are able to divide as often as once every 20 minutes, it is possible for a new round of DNA replication to begin even before the previous round is completed!

Eukaryotic Replication

In eukaryotes, DNA replication begins at numerous origins of replication along the length of the chromosome, and the so-called replication bubbles spread bidirectionally until they meet. Notice that there is a V shape wherever DNA is being replicated. This is called a **replication fork.**

Although eukaryotes replicate their DNA at a slower rate—500 to 5,000 base pairs per minute—there are many individual origins of replication. Therefore, eukaryotic cells complete the replication of the diploid amount of DNA (in humans over 6 billion base pairs) in a matter of hours!

Replication Errors

In molecular genetics, a gene is a section of DNA with a particular sequence of bases. A **genetic mutation** is a permanent change in this sequence of bases.

Some mutations are due to errors in DNA replication. During the replication process, DNA polymerase chooses complementary nucleotide triphosphates from the cellular pool. Then the nucleotide triphosphate is converted to a nucleotide monophosphate and aligned with the template nucleotide. A mismatched nucleotide slips through this selection process only once per 100,000 base pairs at most. The mismatched nucleotide causes a pause in replication, during which time it is excised from the daughter strand and replaced with the correct nucleotide. After this so-called **proofreading** has occurred, the error rate is only one mistake per one billion base pairs.

Some mutations are due to DNA damage. Many of these are caused by a variety of environmental factors. Antioxidants present in cells, the UV radiation in sunlight, organic chemicals in tobacco smoke, pesticides, and pollutants can all damage DNA. **DNA repair enzymes** are usually available and able to reverse most of these insults to DNA but some may escape notice.

The effect of a genetic mutation need not necessarily harm an organism. Some do a great deal of harm, as when they cause cancer in the individual and a genetic disease in offspring. Still, it is important to keep in mind that regardless of their effects, genetic variations are the raw material for the evolutionary process. Without changes in the genetic material, evolution would not be possible.

Mutations due to replication errors and environmental factors are rare due to the proofreading function of DNA polymerase and the presence of DNA repair enzymes in cells.

Connecting Concepts

Many of the Nobel Prizes in physiology, medicine, and chemistry between 1950 and 1990 were awarded to scientists studying the molecular basis of inheritance. Indeed, the biochemistry of genes and the basic structure of chromosomes did not become known until the middle of the twentieth century. The early studies of Griffith, Avery, and colleagues demonstrated that DNA contains genetic information; Watson and Crick later presented a model of its structure; and finally many researchers contributed to our knowledge of how DNA is copied.

Even to this date, details of DNA structure and function are still being clarified. Research in such fields as biochemistry, biophysics, bacteriology, and molecular biology, a new discipline, are still contributing to our understanding of how genetic information is stored and usually faithfully copied for the next generation.

This chapter reviews how DNA fulfills the requirements for the genetic material listed at the start of the chapter. The genetic material must be: (1) able to store information, (2) stable and capable of replication, and (3) able occasionally to undergo change. In the next chapter we will investigate how the sequence of bases in DNA specifies the blueprint for building a cell and an organism through the processes of transcription and translation.

Summary

14.1 The Genetic Material

Early work on the biochemistry of DNA wrongly suggested that DNA lacks the variability necessary for the genetic material.

Griffith injected strains of pneumococcus into mice and observed that smooth (S) strain bacteria are virulent but rough (R) strain bacteria are not. When heat-killed S strain bacteria were injected along with live R strain bacteria, however, virulent S strain bacteria were recovered from the dead mice. Griffith said that the R strain had been transformed by some substance passing from the dead S strain to the live R strain. Twenty years later, Avery and his colleagues reported that the transforming substance is DNA. Hershey and Chase turned to bacteriophage T2 as their experimental material. In two separate experiments, they labeled the protein coat with ^{35}S and the DNA with ^{32}P. They then showed that the radioactive P alone is largely taken up by the bacterial host and that reproduction of viruses proceeds normally. This convinced most researchers that DNA is the genetic material.

14.2 The Structure of DNA

Chargaff did a chemical analysis of DNA and found that A = T and G = C, and that the amount of purine equals the amount of pyrimidine. Franklin prepared an X-ray photograph of DNA that showed it is helical, has repeating structural features, and has certain dimensions. Watson and Crick built a model of DNA in which the sugar-phosphate molecules made up the sides of a twisted ladder and the complementary-paired bases were the rungs of the ladder.

14.3 Replication of DNA

The Watson and Crick model immediately suggested a method by which DNA could be replicated. The two strands unwind and unzip, and each parental strand acts as a template for a new (daughter) strand. In the end, each new duplex is like the other and like the parental duplex.

Meselson and Stahl demonstrated that replication is semiconservative by the following experiment: bacteria were grown in heavy nitrogen (^{15}N) and then switched to light nitrogen (^{14}N). The density of the DNA following replication was intermediate between these two, as measured by centrifugation of the molecules through a salt gradient.

The enzyme DNA polymerase joins the nucleotides together and proofreads them to make sure the bases have been paired correctly. Incorrect base pairs that survive the process are a mutation. Replication in prokaryotes proceeds from one point of origin until there are two copies of the circular chromosome. Replication in eukaryotes has many points of origin and many bubbles (places where the DNA strands are separating and replication is occurring). Replication occurs at the ends of the bubbles—at replication forks.

Reviewing the Chapter

1. List and discuss the requirements for genetic material.   220
2. Describe Griffith's experiments with pneumococcus, his surprising results, and his conclusion.   220–21
3. How did Avery and his colleagues demonstrate that the transforming substance is DNA?   221
4. Describe the experiment of Hershey and Chase, and explain how it shows that DNA is the genetic material.   222
5. What are Chargaff's rules?   223
6. Describe the Watson and Crick model of DNA structure. How did it fit the data provided by Chargaff and the X-ray diffraction pattern?   224–25
7. Explain how DNA replicates semiconservatively. What role does DNA polymerase play? What role does helicase play?   226–27
8. How did Meselson and Stahl demonstrate semiconservative replication?   227
9. List and discuss differences between prokaryotic and eukaryotic replication of DNA.   229
10. Explain why the replication process is a source of few mutations.   229

Testing Yourself

Choose the best answer for each question. For questions 1–4, match the names in the key to the statements below:

Key:

    a. Griffith   d. Hershey and Chase
    b. Chargaff   e. Avery
    c. Meselson and Stahl

1. A = T and G = C.
2. Only the DNA from T2 enters the bacteria.
3. R strain bacteria became an S strain through transformation.
4. DNA replication is semiconservative.
5. If 30% of an organism's DNA is thymine, then
    a. 70% is purine.   d. 70% is pyrimidine.
    b. 20% is guanine.   e. Both c and d are correct.
    c. 30% is adenine.
6. If you grew bacteria in heavy nitrogen and then switched them to light nitrogen, how many generations after switching would you have some light/light DNA?
    a. never, because replication is semiconservative
    b. the first generation
    c. the second generation
    d. only the third generation
    e. Both b and c are correct.
7. The double-helix model of DNA resembles a twisted ladder in which the rungs of the ladder are
    a. a purine paired with a pyrimidine.
    b. A paired with G and C paired with T.
    c. sugar-phosphate paired with sugar-phosphate.
    d. 5′ end paired with a 3′ end.
    e. Both a and b are correct.
8. Cell division requires that the genetic material be able to
    a. store information.
    b. undergo replication.
    c. undergo rare mutations.
    d. condense into spindle fibers.
    e. All of these are correct.
9. In a DNA molecule, the
    a. bases are covalently bonded to the sugars.
    b. sugars are covalently bonded to the phosphates.
    c. bases are hydrogen-bonded to one another.
    d. nucleotides are covalently bonded to one another.
    e. All of these are correct.
10. In the following diagram, blue stands for heavy DNA (contains ^{15}N) and pink stands for light DNA (does not contain ^{15}N). Label each strand of all three DNA molecules as heavy or light DNA, and explain why the diagram is in keeping with the semiconservative replication of DNA.

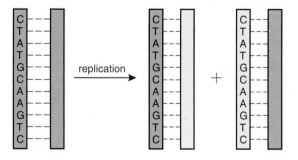

Thinking Scientifically

1. Replication of DNA in some viruses requires the use of proteins that have no enzymatic activity. Hypothesize how a protein might possibly act as a primer for DNA replication. What would be the advantage of using a protein rather than a RNA to get replication started? (See page 228.)
2. Skin cancer is much more common than brain cancer. Why might the frequency of cancer be related to rate of cell division in skin as opposed to rate of cell division in the brain? How might DNA sequencing help you test your hypothesis?

Bioethical Issue

If the results were absolutely private, would you want to know if your DNA harbors a genetic disease whose symptoms may not appear for several decades? If the disease were curable, it might be a good idea. Testing before symptoms appear encourages increased vigilance for the onset of breast and colon cancers. If gene therapy is the only way out, you might be first in line if such therapy is developed in the future.

Huntington disease is a particularly frightening genetic disorder, especially if you have seen a loved one suffer the mental and musculoskeletal deterioration that finally results in death. Although there is no cure for Huntington disease, you would be able to warn your children if you test positive, or it might help you decide whether to have a child. If you have this dominant allele, you will develop the condition and your children have a 50% chance of developing the condition. Children usually begin to have symptoms earlier than their parents exhibit symptoms.

Jason Brandt of the Johns Hopkins University School of Medicine has developed a program of pretest and posttest counseling for those who decide they want to be tested for Huntington disease. So far, about 200 have been tested, and almost twice that number have dropped out of pretest counseling, signifying no doubt they really didn't want to be tested.

Surprisingly, Brandt finds that people rarely make major life changes as a result of knowing they have the allele. Among 63 who tested positive, 10 got married to persons who knew they would come down with Huntington disease, and 10 others went on to have more children. One patient made a radical change after she knew she was negative for Huntington disease. She divorced her present husband, remarried, had another child and took up a career as a physical therapist.

Still, Brandt refuses to perform the test on persons he feels could not psychologically handle the results if they were positive. Do you think it is ever ethical to withhold medical information from patients?

Understanding the Terms

adenine (A) 223	nucleic acid 220
bacteriophage 221	nucleotide 220
complementary base	proofreading 229
pairing 224	purine 223
cytosine (C) 223	pyrimidine 223
DNA (deoxyribonucleic	replication fork 229
acid) 220	RNA (ribonucleic
DNA polymerase 226	acid) 220
DNA repair enzyme 229	semiconservative
DNA replication 226	replication 226
genetic mutation 229	template 226
guanine (G) 223	thymine (T) 223

Match the terms to these definitions:

a. _____ Permanent change in DNA base sequence.

b. _____ Bonding between particular purines and pyrimidines in DNA.

c. _____ During replication, an enzyme that joins the nucleotides complementary to a DNA template.

d. _____ Type of nitrogen-containing base, such as adenine and guanine, having a double-ring structure.

e. _____ Virus that infects bacteria.

Web Connections

Exploring the Internet

http://www.mhhe.com/biosci/genbio/mader
(click on *Biology 7/e*)

The *Biology 7/e* Online Learning Center provides many resources for studying the material in this chapter including links to the following sites:

Legacies–Transformation and DNA explores how genetic material can be transformed from one bacterium to another, as discovered during Griffith's experiments in the late 1920s. This website also describes the follow-up works of Avery, MacLeod, and MacCarthy that showed that DNA was the genetic material of all organisms.

http://www.accessexcellence.org/AB/BC/Transformation_and_DNA.html

The One Gene/One Enzyme Hypothesis discusses Beadle and Tatum's 1941 breakthrough in finding the connection between genes and enzymes. How understanding the genetic code will advance the field of biotechnology is also considered.

http://www.accessexcellence.org/AB/BC/One_Gene_One_Enzyme.html

In Experiments that Inspire, the Hershey-Chase experiments are described, along with information on when viruses were discovered, and why there was the need to know what was the genetic material.

http://www.accessexcellence.org/AB/BC/Experiments_that_Inspire.html

Genetics Society of America. This site provides links to genetics societies concerned with human and medical genetics. It also provides links to educational sites and sites describing careers in genetics.

http://www.faseb.org/genetics/

Amino Acids Section. 3-D models of all amino acids.

http://www.nyu.edu:80/pages/mathmol/library/life/life1.html

Gene Activity: How Genes Work

From four bases, many different organisms

Cytosine (C)

Thymine (T)

Adenine (A)

Guanine (G)

Nearly two million species have so far been discovered and named. Yet one gene differs from another only by the sequence of the nucleotide bases in DNA. How does a difference in base sequence cause the uniqueness of the species—that is, for example, whether you are a tiger or a human? For that matter, whether a human has blue, brown, or hazel eye pigments?

By studying the activity of genes in cells, geneticists have confirmed that proteins are the link between the genotype and the phenotype. Mendel's peas are smooth or wrinkled according to the presence or absence of a starch-forming enzyme. The allele *S* in peas dictates the presence of the starch-forming enzyme, whereas the allele *s* does not.

Through its ability to specify proteins, DNA brings about the development of the unique structures that make up a particular type of organism. It follows that you have blue or brown or hazel eye pigments because of the type of enzymes contained within your cells. When studying gene expression in this chapter, keep in mind this flow diagram: DNA's sequence of nucleotides → sequences of amino acids → specific enzymes → structures in organism.

15.1 The Function of Genes

In the early 1900s, the English physician Sir Archibald Garrod suggested that there is a relationship between inheritance and metabolic diseases. He introduced the phrase *inborn error of metabolism* to dramatize this relationship. Garrod observed that family members often had the same disorder, and he said this inherited defect could be caused by the lack of a particular enzyme in a metabolic pathway. Since it was known at the time that enzymes are proteins, Garrod was among the first to hypothesize a link between genes and proteins.

Genes Specify Enzymes

Many years later, in 1940, George Beadle and Edward Tatum performed a series of experiments on *Neurospora crassa*, the red bread mold fungus, which reproduces by means of spores. Normally, the spores become a mold capable of growing on minimal medium (containing only a sugar, mineral salts, and the vitamin biotin) because mold can produce all the enzymes it needs. In their experiments, Beadle and Tatum induced mutations in asexually produced haploid spores by the use of X-rays. Some of the X-rayed spores could no longer become a mold capable of growing on minimal medium; however, growth was possible on medium enriched by certain metabolites. In the example given in

Figure 15.1, a mold grows only when supplied with enriched medium that includes all metabolites or C and D alone. Since C and D are a part of this hypothetical pathway

$$A \xrightarrow{\;\;1\;\;} B \xrightarrow{\;\;2\;\;} C \xrightarrow{\;\;3\;\;} D$$

in which the numbers are enzymes and the letters are metabolites, it is concluded that the mold lacks enzyme 2. Beadle and Tatum further found that each of the mutant strains has only one defective gene leading to one defective enzyme and one additional growth requirement. Therefore, they proposed that each gene specifies the synthesis of one enzyme. This is called the *one gene–one enzyme hypothesis*.

Genes Specify a Polypeptide

The one gene–one enzyme hypothesis suggests that a genetic mutation causes a change in the structure of a protein. To test this idea, Linus Pauling and Harvey Itano decided to see if the hemoglobin in the red blood cells of persons with sickle-cell disease has a structure different from that of the red blood cells of normal individuals (Fig. 15.2). Recall that proteins are polymers of amino acids, some of which carry a charge. These investigators decided to see if there was a charge difference between normal hemoglobin (Hb^A) and

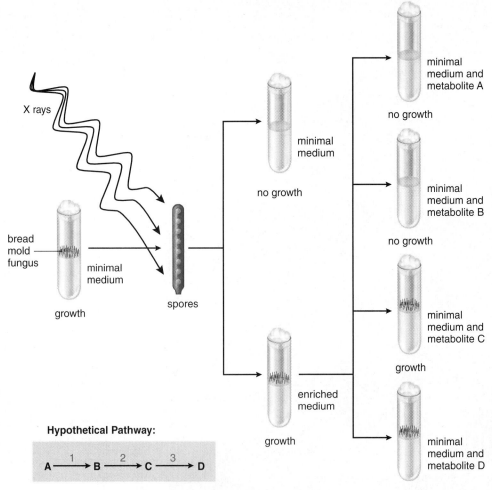

Figure 15.1 Beadle and Tatum experiment.
When haploid spores of *Neurospora crassa*, a bread mold fungus, are X-rayed, some are no longer able to germinate on minimal medium; however, they can germinate on enriched medium. In this example, the mycelia produced do not grow on minimal medium plus metabolite A or B, but they do grow on minimal medium plus metabolite C or D. This shows that enzyme 2 is missing from the hypothetical pathway.

Hypothetical Pathway:

$$A \xrightarrow{\;\;1\;\;} B \xrightarrow{\;\;2\;\;} C \xrightarrow{\;\;3\;\;} D$$

sickle-cell hemoglobin *(Hb^S)*. To determine this, they subjected hemoglobin collected from normal individuals, sickle-cell trait individuals, and sickle-cell disease individuals to electrophoresis, a procedure that separates molecules according to their size and charge, whether (+) or (−). Here is what they found:

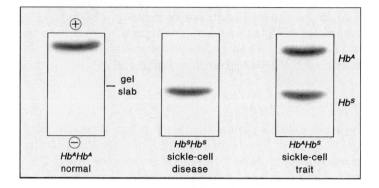

As you can see, there is a difference in migration rate toward the positive pole between normal hemoglobin and sickle-cell hemoglobin. Further, hemoglobin from those with sickle-cell trait separates into two distinct bands, one corresponding to that for *Hb^A* hemoglobin and the other

corresponding to that for *Hb^S* hemoglobin. Pauling and Itano therefore demonstrated that a mutation leads to a change in the structure of a protein.

Several years later, Vernon Ingram was able to determine the structural difference between *Hb^A* and *Hb^S*. Normal hemoglobin *Hb^A* contains negatively charged glutamate; in sickle-cell hemoglobin the glutamate is replaced by nonpolar valine (Fig. 15.2c). This causes *Hb^S* to be less soluble and to precipitate out of solution, especially when environmental oxygen is low. At these times, the *Hb^S* molecules stack up into long, semirigid rods that push against the plasma membrane and distort the red blood cell into the sickle shape.

Hemoglobin contains two types of polypeptide chains, designated α (alpha) and β (beta). Only the β chain is affected in persons with sickle-cell trait and sickle-cell disease; therefore, there must be a gene for each type of chain. A refinement of the one gene–one enzyme hypothesis was needed, and it was replaced by the *one gene–one polypeptide hypothesis*.

A gene is a segment of DNA that specifies the sequence of amino acids in a polypeptide of a protein.

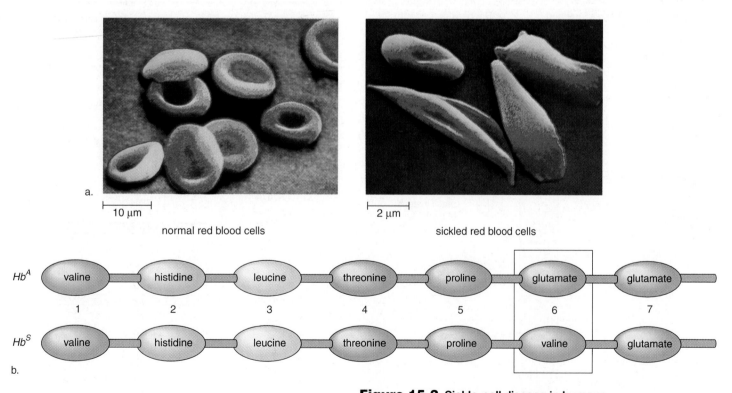

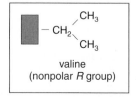

Figure 15.2 Sickle-cell disease in humans.
a. Scanning electron micrograph of normal *(left)* and sickled *(right)* red blood cells. b. Portion of the chain in normal hemoglobin *Hb^A* and in sickle-cell hemoglobin *Hb^S*. Although the chain is 146 amino acids long, the one change from glutamate to valine in the sixth position results in sickle-cell disease. c. Glutamate has a polar *R* group, while valine has a nonpolar *R* group, and this causes *Hb^S* to be less soluble and to precipitate out of solution, distorting the red blood cell into the sickle shape.

From DNA to RNA to Protein

Classical geneticists thought of a gene as a particle on a chromosome. To molecular geneticists, the complete definition of a gene is a sequence of DNA nucleotide bases that codes for a product. Therefore, a gene does not affect the phenotype directly; rather, the gene product affects the phenotype.

DNA specifies the production of proteins, even though in eukaryotes it is located in the nucleus, and proteins are synthesized at the ribosomes in the cytoplasm. **RNA (ribonucleic acid),** however, is not confined to the nucleus, it occurs in both the nucleus and the cytoplasm.

Types of RNA

Like DNA, RNA is a polymer of nucleotides. The nucleotides in RNA, however, contain the sugar ribose and the bases adenine (A), cytosine (C), guanine (G), and uracil (U).

Table 15.1

RNA Structure Compared to DNA Structure

	RNA	DNA
Sugar	Ribose	Deoxyribose
Bases	Adenine, guanine, uracil, cytosine	Adenine, guanine, thymine, cytosine
Strands	Single stranded	Double stranded with base pairing
Helix	No	Yes

In other words, the base **uracil** replaces thymine found in DNA. Finally, RNA is single stranded and does not form a double helix in the same manner as DNA (Table 15.1 and Fig. 15.3).

There are three major classes of RNA, each with specific functions in protein synthesis:

messenger RNA (mRNA): takes a message from DNA in the nucleus to the ribosomes in the cytoplasm.
ribosomal RNA (rRNA): along with proteins, makes up the ribosomes, where polypeptides are synthesized.
transfer RNA (tRNA): transfers amino acids to the ribosomes.

The Required Steps

A gene is expressed once there is a product. When the product is a protein, gene expression requires two steps. During **transcription** [L. *trans*, across, and *scriptio*, a writing] DNA serves as a template for RNA formation. Then RNA moves into the cytoplasm. There are micrographs showing radioactively labeled RNA moving from the nucleus to the cytoplasm, where protein synthesis occurs. During **translation** [L. *trans*, across, and *latus*, carry, bear] an mRNA transcript directs the sequence of amino acids in a polypeptide (Fig. 15.4).

During transcription, DNA serves as a template for the formation of RNA. During translation, mRNA is involved in polypeptide synthesis.

Figure 15.3 Structure of RNA.
Like DNA, RNA is a polymer of nucleotides. RNA, however, is single stranded, the pentose sugar is ribose, and uracil replaces thymine as one of the pyrimidine bases.

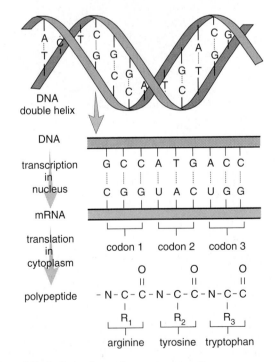

Figure 15.4 Overview of gene expression.
Transcription occurs in the nucleus when DNA acts as a template for mRNA synthesis. Translation occurs in the cytoplasm where the sequence of bases in mRNA determines the sequence of amino acids in a polypeptide.

15.2 The Genetic Code

The central dogma of molecular biology states that the sequence of nucleotides in DNA specifies (and a copy of this sequence in mRNA directs) the order of amino acids in a polypeptide. It would seem then that there must be a **genetic code** for each of the 20 amino acids found in proteins. But can four nucleotides provide enough combinations to code for 20 amino acids? If each code word, called a **codon**, were made up of two bases, such as AG, there could be only 16 codons (4 × 4)—not enough to code for 20 amino acids. But if each codon were made up of three bases, such as AGC, there would be 64 codons (4 × 4 × 4)—more than enough to code for 20 different amino acids:

Number of Bases in Genetic Code	Number of Different Amino Acids That Can Be Specified
1	4
2	16
3	64

It is expected, then, that the genetic code is a **triplet code** and that each codon, therefore, consists of three nucleotide bases.

Finding the Genetic Code

In 1961, Marshall Nirenberg and J. Heinrich Matthei performed an experiment that laid the groundwork for cracking the genetic code. First, they found a cellular enzyme could be used to construct a synthetic RNA (one that does not occur in cells), and then they found that the synthetic polymer could be translated in a cell-free system (a test tube that contains "freed" cytoplasmic contents of a cell). Their first synthetic RNA was composed only of uracil, and the protein that resulted was composed only of the amino acid phenylalanine. Therefore, the codon for phenylalanine was known to be UUU. Later, they were able to translate just three nucleotides at a time; in that way it was possible to assign an amino acid to each of the RNA codons (Fig. 15.5).

A number of important properties of the genetic code can be seen by careful inspection of Figure 15.5:

1. The genetic code is degenerate. This means that most amino acids have more than one codon; leucine, serine, and arginine have six different codons, for example. The degeneracy of the code is protective against potentially harmful effects of mutations.
2. The genetic code is unambiguous. Each triplet codon has only one meaning.
3. The code has start and stop signals. There is only one start signal but three stop signals.

First Base	Second Base				Third Base
	U	C	A	G	
U	UUU phenylalanine	UCU serine	UAU tyrosine	UGU cysteine	U
	UUC phenylalanine	UCC serine	UAC tyrosine	UGC cysteine	C
	UUA leucine	UCA serine	UAA *stop*	UGA *stop*	A
	UUG leucine	UCG serine	UAG *stop*	UGG tryptophan	G
C	CUU leucine	CCU proline	CAU histidine	CGU arginine	U
	CUC leucine	CCC proline	CAC histidine	CGC arginine	C
	CUA leucine	CCA proline	CAA glutamine	CGA arginine	A
	CUG leucine	CCG proline	CAG glutamine	CGG arginine	G
A	AUU isoleucine	ACU threonine	AAU asparagine	AGU serine	U
	AUC isoleucine	ACC threonine	AAC asparagine	AGC serine	C
	AUA isoleucine	ACA threonine	AAA lysine	AGA arginine	A
	AUG (*start*) methionine	ACG threonine	AAG lysine	AGG arginine	G
G	GUU valine	GCU alanine	GAU aspartate	GGU glycine	U
	GUC valine	GCC alanine	GAC aspartate	GGC glycine	C
	GUA valine	GCA alanine	GAA glutamate	GGA glycine	A
	GUG valine	GCG alanine	GAG glutamate	GGG glycine	G

Figure 15.5 Messenger RNA codons.
Notice that in this chart, each of the codons (in squares) is composed of three letters representing the first base, second base, and third base. For example, find the blue square where C for the first base and A for the second base intersect. You will see that U, C, A, or G can be the third base. The three bases CAU and CAC are codons for histidine; the three bases CAA and CAG are codons for glutamine.

The Code Is Universal

The genetic code in Figure 15.5 is just about universally used by living things. This suggests that the code dates back to the very first organisms on earth and that all living things are related. Once the code was established, changes in it would have been very disruptive, and we know that it has remained largely unchanged over eons.

The genetic code is a triplet code. Each codon consists of three DNA nucleotides. Except for the stop codons, all the codons code for amino acids.

15.3 The First Step: Transcription

Transcription, which takes place in the nucleus of eukaryotic cells, is the first step required for gene expression—the making of a gene product. The formation of mRNA leads to a polypeptide as the gene product. The molecules tRNA and rRNA are transcribed from DNA templates, and these are products in and of themselves. Enzymes called **RNA polymerases** are involved in transcription.

Messenger RNA Is Formed

During transcription, an mRNA molecule is formed that has a sequence of bases complementary to a portion of one DNA strand; wherever A, T, G, or C is present in the DNA template, U, A, C, or G, respectively, is incorporated into the mRNA molecule (Fig. 15.6). A segment of the DNA helix unwinds and unzips, and complementary RNA nucleotides pair with DNA nucleotides of the strand that is being transcribed. An RNA polymerase joins the nucleotides together in the $5' \rightarrow 3'$ direction. In other words, an RNA polymerase only adds a nucleotide to the 3' end of the polymer under construction.

Transcription begins when RNA polymerase attaches to a region of DNA called a promoter. A **promoter** defines the start of a gene, the direction of transcription, and the strand to be transcribed. The RNA-DNA association is not as stable as the DNA helix. Therefore, only the newest portion of an RNA molecule that is associated with RNA polymerase is bound to the DNA, and the rest dangles off to the side. Elongation of the mRNA molecule continues until RNA polymerase comes to a DNA sequence called a **terminator.** The terminator causes RNA polymerase to stop transcribing the DNA and to release the mRNA molecule, now called an **RNA transcript.**

Many RNA polymerase molecules can be working to produce mRNA transcripts at the same time (Fig. 15.7). This allows the cell to produce many thousands of copies of the same mRNA molecule and eventually many copies of the same protein within a shorter period of time than if the single copy of DNA were used to direct protein synthesis.

As a result of transcription, there will be many mRNA molecules directing protein synthesis. Many more copies of a protein are produced within a given time versus using DNA directly.

Figure 15.6 Transcription.
During transcription, complementary RNA is made from a DNA template. At the point of attachment of RNA polymerase, the DNA helix unwinds and unzips, and complementary RNA nucleotides are joined together. After RNA polymerase has passed by, the DNA strands rejoin and the RNA transcript dangles to the side.

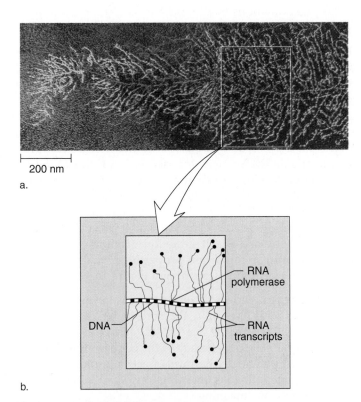

Figure 15.7 RNA polymerase.
a. Numerous RNA transcripts extend from a horizontal gene in an amphibian egg cell. b. The strands get progressively longer because transcription begins to the left. The dark dots along the DNA are RNA polymerase molecules. The dots at the end of the strands are spliceosomes involved in RNA processing (see Fig. 15.8).

Messenger RNA Is Processed

The newly formed mRNA molecule, called the primary *mRNA transcript*, is modified before it leaves the eukaryotic nucleus. First, the ends of the mRNA molecule are altered: a cap is put onto the 5' end and a poly-A tail is put onto the 3' end (Fig. 15.8). The "cap" is a modified guanine (G) nucleotide that helps tell a ribosome where to attach when translation begins. The "poly-A tail" consists of a chain of 150 to 200 adenine (A) nucleotides. The tail facilitates the transport of the mRNA out of the nucleus and also inhibits degradation of mRNA by hydrolytic enzymes.

Second, the primary mRNA transcript itself is changed. Most genes in plants and animals are interrupted by **introns,** segments of DNA that are never expressed. The introns occur between the **exons,** the segments of DNA that are expressed. During mRNA processing the introns are removed during an mRNA processing event called mRNA splicing (Fig. 15.8). The mRNA that has now been processed and leaves the nucleus is called mature mRNA.

How is mRNA processing carried out? And what is the function of introns in the first place? In most cases mRNA splicing is often done by *spliceosomes,* a complex that contains several kinds of ribonucleoproteins. A spliceosome cuts the primary mRNA and then rejoins the adjacent exons. There has been much speculation about the possible role of introns in the eukaryotic genome. It's possible that introns divide a gene into regions that can be joined in different combinations to produce various products in different cells. For instance, it's been shown that the thyroid gland and pituitary gland process the same primary mRNA transcript differently and therefore produce related but different hormones.

Some researchers are trying to determine whether introns exist in all organisms. They have found that the more simple the eukaryote, the less the likelihood of introns in the genes. An intron has been discovered in the gene for a tRNA molecule in *Anabaena,* a cyanobacterium. This particular intron is of interest because it is "self-splicing," that is, it has the capability of splicing itself out of an RNA transcript. RNAs with an enzymatic function are called **ribozymes.** Ribozymes are restricted in their function since each one cleaves RNA only at specific locations. Still, the discovery of ribozymes in prokaryotes supports the belief that RNA could have served as both the genetic material and as the first enzymes in the earliest living organisms.

Particularly in eukaryotes, the primary mRNA transcript is processed before it becomes a mature mRNA transcript.

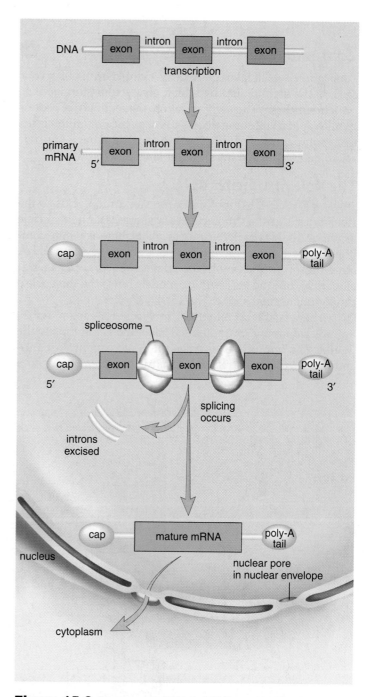

Figure 15.8 Messenger RNA (mRNA) processing in eukaryotes.
DNA contains both exons (coding sequences) and introns (noncoding sequences). Both of these are transcribed and are present in primary mRNA. During processing, a cap and a poly-A tail (a series of adenine nucleotides) are added to the molecule. Also, there is excision of the introns and a splicing together of the exons. This is accomplished by complexes called spliceosomes. Then the mature mRNA molecule is ready to leave the nucleus.

15.4 The Second Step: Translation

Translation, which takes place in the cytoplasm of eukaryotic cells, is the second step by which gene expression leads to protein synthesis. During translation, the sequence of codons in mRNA at a ribosome directs the sequence of amino acids in a polypeptide. In other words, one language (nucleic acids) gets translated into another language (protein).

The Role of Transfer RNA

Transfer RNA (tRNA) molecules transfer amino acids to the ribosomes. A tRNA molecule is a single-stranded nucleic acid that doubles back on itself to create regions where complementary bases are hydrogen-bonded to one another. The structure of a tRNA molecule is generally drawn as a flat cloverleaf, but the space-filling model shows the molecule's three-dimensional shape (Fig. 15.9).

There is at least one tRNA molecule for each of the 20 amino acids found in proteins. The amino acid binds to the 3′ end. The opposite end of the molecule contains an **anticodon,** a group of three bases that is complementary to a specific codon of mRNA. For example, a tRNA that has the anticodon GAA binds to the codon CUU and carries the amino acid leucine. (There are fewer tRNAs than there are codons because some tRNAs can pair with more than one codon. If the anticodon contains a U in the third position, it will pair with either an A or G in the third position of a codon. This is called the *wobble effect.*)

How does the correct amino acid become attached to the correct tRNA molecule? This task is carried out by amino acid-activating enzymes, called tRNA synthetases. Just as a key fits a lock, each enzyme has a recognition site for the amino acid to be joined to a particular tRNA. This is an energy-requiring process that utilizes ATP. Once the amino acid–tRNA complex is formed, it travels through the cytoplasm to a ribosome, where protein synthesis is occurring.

Transfer RNA (tRNA) molecules bind with one particular amino acid, and they bear an anticodon that is complementary to a particular codon—the codon for that amino acid.

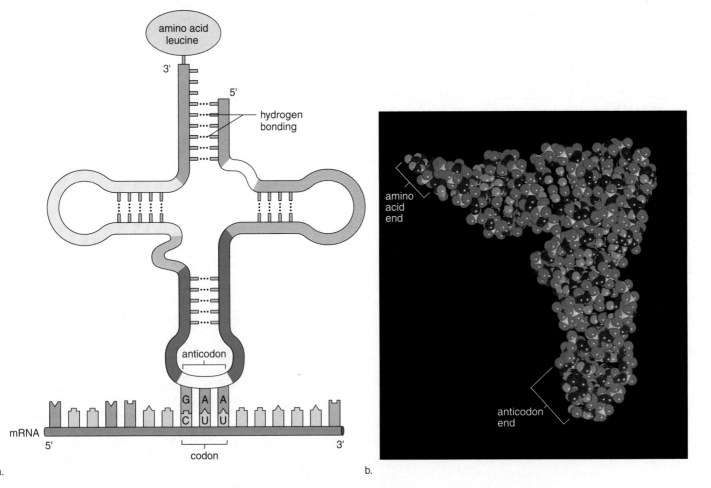

Figure 15.9 Structure of a transfer RNA (tRNA) molecule.
a. Complementary base pairing indicated by hydrogen bonding occurs between nucleotides of the molecule, and this causes it to form its characteristic loops. The anticodon that base-pairs with a particular messenger RNA (mRNA) codon occurs at one end of the folded molecule; the other two loops help hold the molecule at the ribosome. An appropriate amino acid is attached at the 3′ end of the molecule. For this mRNA codon and tRNA anticodon, the appropriate amino acid is leucine. **b.** Space-filling model of tRNA molecule.

The Role of Ribosomal RNA

Ribosomal RNA (rRNA) is produced off a DNA template in the nucleolus of a nucleus. Then the rRNA is packaged with a variety of proteins into ribosomal subunits, one of which is larger than the other. The subunits move separately through nuclear envelope pores into the cytoplasm where they combine when translation begins. Ribosomes can remain in the cytosol or they can become attached to endoplasmic reticulum.

Prokaryotic cells contain about 10,000 ribosomes, but eukaryotic cells contain many times that number. Ribosomes play a significant role in protein synthesis (Fig. 15.10). Ribosomes have a binding site for mRNA and binding sites for two transfer RNA (tRNA) molecules at a time. These binding sites facilitate complementary base pairing between tRNA anticodons and mRNA codons. Ribosomal RNA (i.e., a ribozyme) is also believed to join amino acids together, in a manner to be described, so that a polypeptide results. As the ribosome moves down the mRNA molecule, new tRNAs arrive; amino acids are joined, and the polypeptide forms and grows longer. Translation terminates once the polypeptide is fully formed; the ribosome dissociates into its two subunits and falls off the mRNA molecule.

As soon as the initial portion of mRNA has been translated by one ribosome, and the ribosome has begun to move down the mRNA, another ribosome attaches to the mRNA. Therefore, several ribosomes are often attached to and translating the same mRNA. The entire complex is called a **polyribosome** (Fig. 15.10).

What determines whether a ribosome remains in the cytosol or binds to endoplasmic reticulum (ER)? All ribosomes are at first free within the cytosol. But once synthesis begins, some polypeptides have a series of amino acids called a signal sequence, which enables a ribosome to bind to rough endoplasmic reticulum (rough ER). Then the polypeptide enters the rough ER lumen and is eventually secreted from the cell. Nearly all polypeptides have a signal sequence that targets them for their final location in the cell.

Ribosomal RNA (rRNA) is found in the ribosomes, structures that facilitate complementary base pairing between mRNA and tRNAs and join amino acids together.

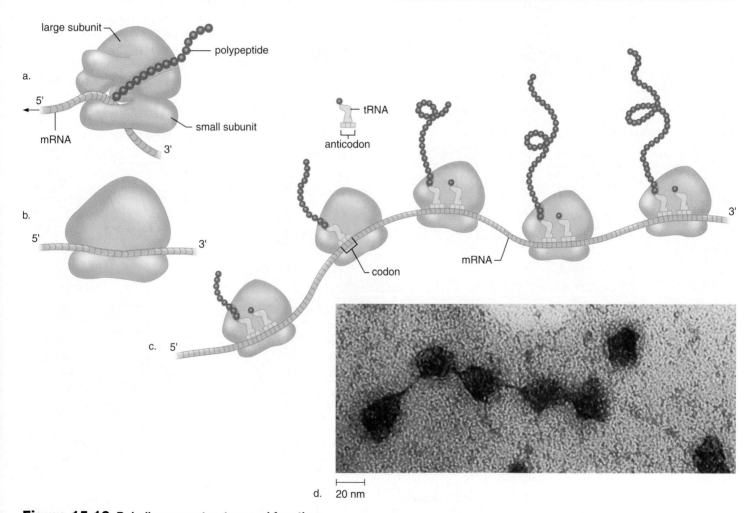

Figure 15.10 Polyribosome structure and function.
a. Side view of ribosome shows positioning of mRNA and growing polypeptide. **b.** A frontal view of a ribosome. **c.** Several ribosomes, collectively called a polyribosome, move along an mRNA at one time. Therefore, several polypeptides can be made at the same time. **d.** Electron micrograph of a polyribosome.

Translation Requires Three Steps

During translation, the codons of an mRNA base-pair with the anticodons of tRNA molecules carrying specific amino acids. The order of the codons determines the order of the tRNA molecules and the sequence of amino acids in a polypeptide. The process of translation must be extremely orderly so that the amino acids of a polypeptide are sequenced correctly.

Protein synthesis involves three steps: chain initiation, chain elongation, and chain termination. It should be kept in mind that enzymes are required for each of the steps to occur, and energy is needed for the first two steps also.

1. Chain initiation: In prokaryotes, a small ribosomal subunit attaches to the mRNA in the vicinity of the *start codon* (AUG). The first or initiator tRNA pairs

with this codon. Then a large ribosomal subunit joins to the small subunit (Fig. 15.11*a*).

Notice that a ribosome has two binding sites for tRNAs. One of these is called the P (for peptide) site, and the other is called the A (for amino acid) site. The initiator tRNA that is capable of binding to the P site carries the amino acid, methionine. The A site is for the next tRNA.

Proteins called initiation factors are required to bring the necessary translation components (small ribosomal subunit, mRNA, initiator tRNA, and large ribosomal subunit) together. Energy is also expended.

Following chain initiation, mRNA and the first tRNA are now at a ribosome.

---

2. Chain elongation: During elongation, a tRNA with an attached peptide is already at the P site, and a tRNA carrying its appropriate amino acid is just arriving at the A site. Proteins called elongation factors facilitate complementary base pairing between the tRNA anticodon and the mRNA codon (Fig. 15.11*b*).

The polypeptide is transferred and attached by peptide bond formation to the newly arrived amino acid. A ribozyme, which is a part of the larger ribosomal subunit, and energy are needed to bring about this transfer. Now the tRNA molecule at the P site leaves.

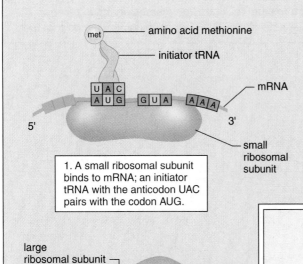

1. A small ribosomal subunit binds to mRNA; an initiator tRNA with the anticodon UAC pairs with the codon AUG.

2. The large ribosomal subunit completes the ribosome. Initiator tRNA occupies the P site. The A site is ready for the next tRNA.

a. Initiation

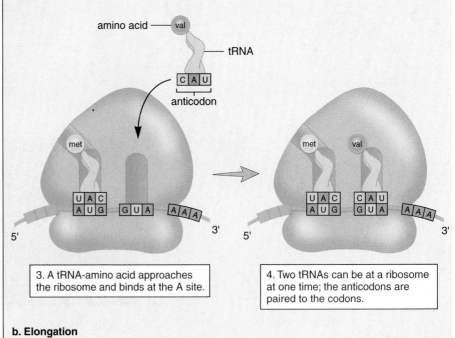

3. A tRNA-amino acid approaches the ribosome and binds at the A site.

4. Two tRNAs can be at a ribosome at one time; the anticodons are paired to the codons.

b. Elongation

Figure 15.11 Protein synthesis.

Next *translocation* occurs: the mRNA, along with the peptide-bearing tRNA, moves from the A site to the empty P site. Since the ribosome has moved forward three nucleotides, there is a new codon now located at the empty A site.

The complete cycle—complementary base pairing of new tRNA, transfer of peptide chain, translocation—is repeated at a rapid rate (about 15 times each second in *Escherichia coli*).

During chain elongation, amino acids are added one at a time to the growing polypeptide.

---

3. Chain termination: Termination of polypeptide synthesis occurs at a stop codon, which does not code for an amino acid (Fig. 15.11*c*). The polypeptide is enzymatically cleaved from the last tRNA by a release factor. The tRNA and polypeptide leave the ribosome, which dissociates into its two subunits (see also Fig. 15.10).

During chain termination, the ribosome separates into its two subunits and the polypeptide is released.

A newly synthesized polypeptide may function alone or it may become a part of a protein that has more than one polypeptide. Proteins play a role in the anatomy and physiology of cells, as discussed earlier in this text. The plasma membrane of all cells contains proteins that carry out various functions and many proteins are enzymes that participate in cellular metabolism. The tissues of multicellular animals are distinguished by the uniqueness of their proteins. Properly functioning proteins are of paramount importance to the cell and to the organism. Organisms inherit genes that code for their own particular mix of proteins in their cells. If an organism inherits a mutated gene, the result can be a genetic disorder or a propensity toward cancer, in which proteins are not fulfilling their usual functions. This topic is explored further in chapter 16.

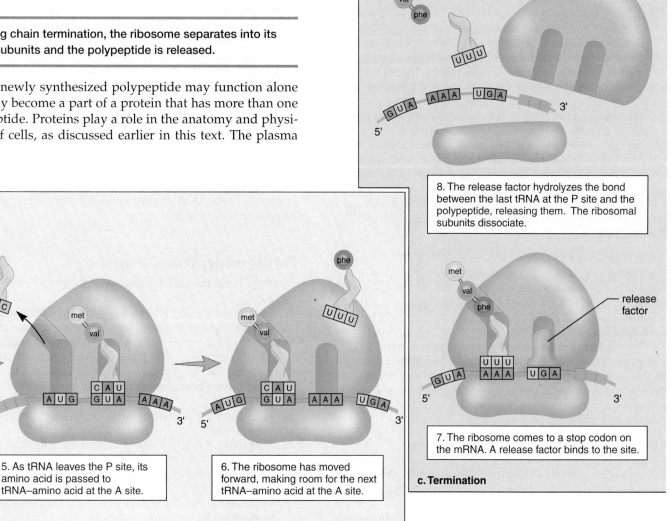

8. The release factor hydrolyzes the bond between the last tRNA at the P site and the polypeptide, releasing them. The ribosomal subunits dissociate.

release factor

7. The ribosome comes to a stop codon on the mRNA. A release factor binds to the site.

c. Termination

5. As tRNA leaves the P site, its amino acid is passed to tRNA–amino acid at the A site.

6. The ribosome has moved forward, making room for the next tRNA–amino acid at the A site.

Figure 15.11 (cont.)

Connecting Concepts

Early geneticists were amazed to discover that a single nucleotide change in a huge DNA molecule can have profound phenotypic consequences. A well-known example in humans is the single nucleotide change that leads to an amino acid change at one position of the ß chain of hemoglobin. The result is the often fatal condition known as sickle-cell disease because the red blood cells are sickle-shaped.

The genetic information stored by DNA is realized through the steps of transcription and translation. During transcription, DNA is used as a template for the production of a mRNA molecule. The actions of RNA polymerase, the enzyme that carries out transcription of DNA and DNA polymerase, the enzyme required for DNA replication, are similar enough to suggest that both enzymes evolved from a common ancestral enzyme. If RNA was the original genetic material, as has been proposed, then it must have specified the synthesis of an enzyme capable of replicating RNA. RNA replicase enzymes are present in RNA viruses still today. Such an enzyme could have been the common ancestor of the DNA and RNA polymerases known today.

Both RNA molecules and proteins are needed for the translation. During translation, protein synthesis is carried out according to the genetic information now borne by mRNA. Since a single gene can be transcribed many times and an mRNA molecule may be repeatedly translated, many copies of a protein may result. In the next chapter we will examine the ways cells can regulate the quantity of protein produced per gene.

Summary

15.1 The Function of Genes

Several investigators contributed to our knowledge of what genes do. Garrod is associated with the phrase "inborn error of metabolism" because he suggested that some of his patients had inherited an inability to carry out certain enzymatic reactions.

Beadle and Tatum X-rayed spores of *Neurospora crassa* and found that some of the subsequent cultures lacked a particular enzyme needed for growth on minimal medium. Since they found that the mutation of one gene results in the lack of a single enzyme, they suggested the one gene–one enzyme hypothesis.

Pauling and Itano found that the chemical properties of the β chain of sickle-cell hemoglobin differ from those of normal hemoglobin, and therefore the one gene–one polypeptide hypothesis was formulated instead. Later, Ingram showed that the biochemical change is due to the substitution of the amino acid valine (nonpolar) for glutamate (polar).

RNA differs from DNA in these ways: (1) the pentose sugar is ribose, not deoxyribose; (2) the base uracil replaces thymine; (3) RNA is single stranded.

15.2 The Genetic Code

The central dogma of molecular biology says that (1) DNA is a template for its own replication and also for RNA formation during transcription, and (2) the complementary sequence of nucleotides in mRNA directs the correct sequence of amino acids of a polypeptide during translation.

The sequence of bases in DNA specifies the proper sequence of amino acids in a polypeptide. The genetic code is a triplet code, and each codon (code word) consists of three bases. The code is degenerate; that is, more than one codon exists for most amino acids. There are also one start and three stop codons. The genetic code is just about universal.

15.3 The First Step: Transcription

Figure 15.12 provides a summary of transcription and translation. Transcription begins when RNA polymerase attaches to a promoter. Elongation occurs until RNA polymerase reaches a terminator.

Messenger RNA (mRNA) is processed following transcription, a cap is put onto the 5′ end and a poly-A tail is put onto the 3′ end; introns are removed in eukaryotes by spliceosomes.

15.4 The Second Step: Translation

Translation requires mRNA, ribosomal RNA (rRNA), and transfer RNA (tRNA). Each tRNA has an anticodon at one end and an amino acid at the other; there are amino acid-activating enzymes that ensure that the correct amino acid is attached to the correct tRNA. When tRNAs bind with their codon at a ribosome, the amino acids are correctly sequenced in a polypeptide according to the order predetermined by DNA.

Many ribosomes move along the same mRNA at a time. Collectively, these are called a polyribosome.

Translation requires these steps. During initiation, mRNA, the first (initiator) tRNA, and the ribosome all come together in the proper orientation at a start codon. During elongation, as the tRNAs bind to their codons, the growing peptide chain is transferred by peptide bonding to the next amino acid in the chain. During termination at a stop codon, the polypeptide is cleaved from the last tRNA. The ribosome now dissociates.

Polypeptides are a part of protein molecules with various functions in cells. Mutated genes code for proteins that may not function as they should.

Reviewing the Chapter

1. What made Garrod think there were inborn errors of metabolism?   234
2. Explain Beadle and Tatum's experimental procedure.   234
3. How did Pauling and Itano know that the chemical properties of Hb^S differed from those of Hb^A? What change does a substitution of valine for glutamate cause in the chemical properties of Hb^S compared to Hb^A?   234–35
4. What are the biochemical differences between RNA and DNA?   236
5. What are the two steps required for the expression of a gene?   236
6. How did investigators reason that the code must be a triplet code, and in what manner was the code cracked? Why is it said that the code is degenerate, unambiguous, and almost universal?   237
7. What are the specific steps that occur during transcription of RNA off a DNA template?   238–39
8. How is messenger RNA (mRNA) processed before leaving the eukaryotic nucleus?   239

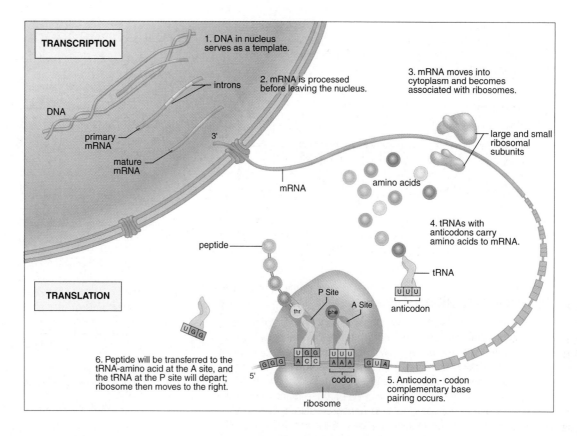

Figure 15.12 Summary of gene expression.

9. Compare the functions of mRNA, ribosomal RNA (rRNA), and transfer RNA (tRNA) during protein synthesis. What are the specific events of translation? 240–43
10. Genes specify the amino acid sequence in polypeptides. Explain with reference to Figure 15.12.

Testing Yourself

Choose the best answer for each question. For questions 1–4, match the investigator to the phrase in the key:

Key:

a. one gene–one enzyme hypothesis
b. inborn error of metabolism
c. one gene–one polypeptide hypothesis
d. one gene–one mRNA hypothesis

1. Sir Archibald Garrod
2. George Beadle and Edward Tatum
3. Linus Pauling and Harvey Itano
4. Considering the following pathway, if Beadle and Tatum found that *Neurospora* cannot grow if metabolite A is provided, but can grow if B, C, or D is provided, what molecule would be missing?

$$A \xrightarrow{\ 1\ } B \xrightarrow{\ 2\ } C \xrightarrow{\ 3\ } D$$

a. enzyme 1
b. enzyme 2
c. enzyme 3
d. the substrate in addition to the product
e. All of these are correct.

5. The central dogma of molecular biology
a. states that DNA is a template for all RNA production.
b. states that DNA is a template only for DNA replication.
c. states that translation precedes transcription.
d. pertains only to prokaryotes because humans are unique.
e. All of these are correct.
6. If the sequence of bases in DNA is TAGC, then the sequence of bases in RNA will be
a. ATCG.
b. TAGC.
c. AUCG.
d. GCTA.
e. Both a and b are correct.
7. RNA processing
a. is the same as transcription.
b. is an event that occurs after RNA is transcribed.
c. is the rejection of old, worn-out RNA.
d. pertains to function of transfer RNA during protein synthesis.
e. Both b and d are correct.
8. During protein synthesis, an anticodon on transfer RNA (tRNA) pairs with
a. DNA nucleotide bases.
b. ribosomal RNA (rRNA) nucleotide bases.
c. messenger RNA (mRNA) nucleotide bases.
d. other tRNA nucleotide bases.
e. Any one of these can occur.
9. Which statement regarding translation is out of order first?
a. Ribosomal subunits bind to mRNA.
b. The ribosome comes to a stop codon on the mRNA.
c. As a tRNA leaves the ribosome it passes its amino acid to the growing polypeptide.
d. A new tRNA-amino acid approaches the ribosome.
e. The messenger RNA codon binds to the tRNA anticodon.

10. This is a segment of a DNA molecule. (Remember that the template strand only is transcribed.) What are (a) the RNA codons, (b) the tRNA anticodons, and (c) the sequence of amino acids in a protein?

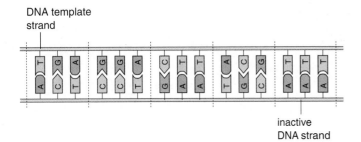

DNA template strand

inactive DNA strand

Thinking Scientifically

1. In one strain of bacteria you observe an x amount of some enzyme. In a mutant derived from that strain there is 1.5× the amount of the enzyme. A comparison of the sequence of the two strains shows that there is no change in the coding region of the gene. But there is a substitution of two A—T base pairs in the mutant for two G—C base pairs where DNA polymease attaches. What hypothesis would explain how such a mutation could produce this change in protein level? What change would be predicted in mRNA level?

2. Changes in DNA sequence, that is, mutations, account for evolutionary changes. Sometimes evolution seems to occur quite rapidly. What type of base change in DNA might bring about the greatest change in a protein and the greatest phenotypic change immediately?

Understanding the Terms

anticodon   240
codon   237
exon   239
genetic code   237
intron   239
messenger RNA (mRNA)   236
polyribosome   241
promoter   238
ribosomal RNA (rRNA)   236
ribozyme   239

RNA (ribonucleic acid)   236
RNA polymerase   238
RNA transcript   238
terminator   238
transcription   236
transfer RNA (tRNA)   236
translation   236
triplet code   237
uracil   236

Match the terms to these definitions:

a. _____ Enzyme that speeds the formation of mRNA from a DNA template.

b. _____ Noncoding segment of DNA that is transcribed but removed before mRNA leaves the nucleus.

c. _____ Process whereby the sequence of codons in mRNA determines (is translated into) the sequence of amino acids in a polypeptide.

d. _____ String of ribosomes, simultaneously translating different regions of the same mRNA strand during protein synthesis.

e. _____ Three nucleotides of DNA or mRNA; it codes for a particular amino acid or termination of translation.

Web Connections

Exploring the Internet

http://www.mhhe.com/biosci/genbio/mader
(click on *Biology 7/e*)

The *Biology 7/e* Online Learning Center provides many resources for studying the material in this chapter including links to the following sites:

DNA Structure, Replication and Eukaryotic Chromatin is an excellent, thorough treatment of DNA structure, DNA replication, and eukaryotic chromosome structure.

http://www.cc.ndsu.nodak.edu/instruct/mcclean//plsc431/
eukarychrom/index.htm

An easy-to-remember analogy for protein synthesis is presented in Protein Synthesis Activities. Although designed for a teacher, this site holds the key for understanding protein synthesis. Substantial background information on protein synthesis is also presented.

http://www.accessexcellence.org/AE/AEPC/WWC/1994/
protein_synthesis.html

Gene Cards: human genes, proteins, and diseases. A database of human genes—this is a very large database.

http://bioinformatics.weizmann.ac.il/cards/

National Organization for Rare Disorders, Inc. This site discusses and contains links to more information concerning the prevention, treatment, and cure of rare "orphan" diseases, such as phenylketonuria. Although rare, there are over 1,000 diseases in their databank.

http://www.rarediseases.org/

Central Dogma Chapter. This MIT hypertextbook chapter covers transcription, translation, and includes practice problems.

http://esg-www.mit.edu:8001/esgbio/dogma/dogmadir.html

Genome Organization and Regulation of Gene Activity

Cell division in these cancer cells is no longer regulated.

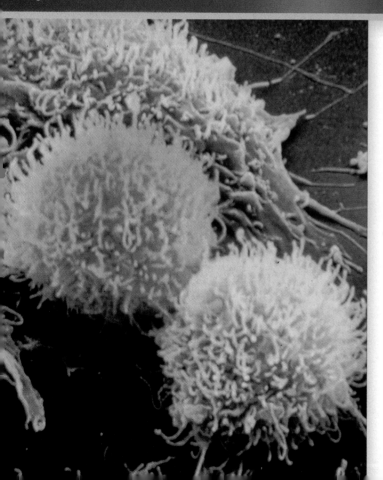

We all begin life as a one-celled zygote that has 46 chromosomes, and these same chromosomes are passed to all the daughter cells during mitosis. Yet cells become specialized in structure and function. The genes for digestive enzymes are expressed only in digestive tract cells and the genes for muscle proteins are expressed only in muscle cells. This shows it is possible to control transcription and translation of genes in each particular type of cell.

In this chapter we will see that regulation of gene activity extends from the nucleus (whether a gene is transcribed) to the cytoplasm (whether an enzyme is functioning). Complete knowledge of how gene expression is controlled has far-ranging applications. Only then will we understand how development progresses and what causes the occurrence of various disorders, including cancer. Cancer develops when genes that promote cell division are expressed and when genes that suppress cell division are not expressed. It has become increasingly apparent that the regulation of gene expression is of major importance to the health of all species, including human beings.

16.1 Prokaryotic Regulation

Bacteria don't need the same enzymes (and possibly other proteins) all the time. Suppose, for example, the available nutrients vary—wouldn't it be advantageous to produce just the enzymes needed to produce whatever metabolites are missing and/or break down whichever organic nutrients are present?

In 1961, French microbiologists François Jacob and Jacques Monod showed that *Escherichia coli* is capable of regulating the expression of its genes. They proposed what is called the **operon** [L. *opera,* works] model to explain gene regulation in prokaryotes and later received a Nobel Prize for their investigations. A **regulator gene,** located outside the operon, codes for a repressor that controls whether the operon is active or not.

An operon includes the following elements:

Promoter—a short sequence of DNA where RNA polymerase first attaches when a gene is to be transcribed.

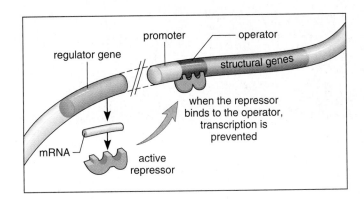

Operator—a short portion of DNA where an active repressor binds. When an active repressor is bound to the operator, RNA polymerase cannot attach to the promoter and transcription does not occur.

Structural genes—one to several genes coding for enzymes of a metabolic pathway that are transcribed as a unit.

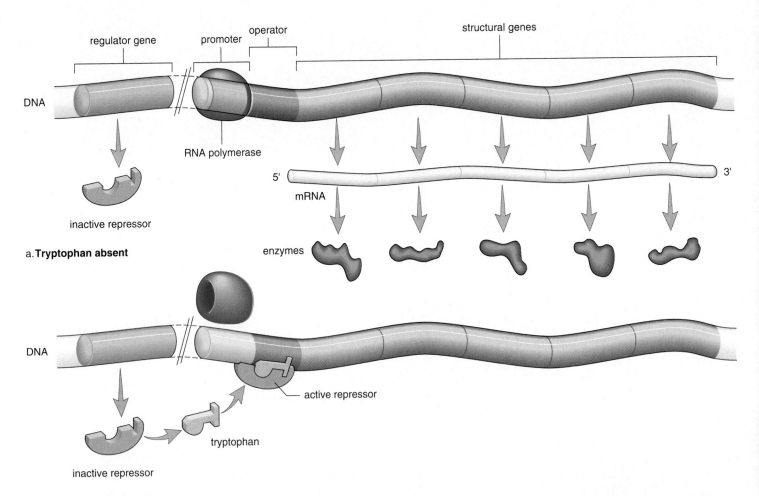

Figure 16.1 The *trp* operon.
a. The regulator gene codes for a repressor protein that is normally inactive. RNA polymerase attaches to the promoter and the structural genes are expressed. **b.** When the nutrient tryptophan is present, it binds to the repressor changing its shape. Now the repressor is active and can bind to the operator. RNA polymerase cannot attach to the promoter and the structural genes are not expressed.

The *trp* Operon

Jacob and Monod found that some operons in *E. coli* usually exist in the on rather than off condition. For example, in the *trp* operon, the regulator codes for a repressor that ordinarily is unable to attach to the operator. Therefore, RNA polymerase is able to bind to the promoter and the structural genes of the operon are ordinarily expressed (Fig. 16.1). Their products, five different enzymes, are a part of an anabolic pathway for the synthesis of the amino acid tryptophan.

If tryptophan happens to be already present in the medium, these enzymes are not needed by the cell and the operon is turned off by the following method. Tryptophan binds to the repressor. A change in shape now allows the repressor to bind to the operator and the structural genes are not expressed. The enzymes are said to be repressible, and the entire unit is called a **repressible operon.** Tryptophan is called the **corepressor.** Repressible operons are usually involved in anabolic pathways that synthesize a substance needed by the cell.

The *lac* Operon

When *E. coli* is denied glucose and is given the milk sugar lactose instead, it immediately begins to make the three enzymes needed for the metabolism of lactose. These enzymes are encoded by three genes: one gene is for an enzyme called β-galactosidase, which breaks down the disaccharide lactose to glucose and galactose; a second gene codes for a permease that facilitates the entry of lactose into the cell; and a third gene codes for an enzyme called transacetylase, which has an accessory function in lactose metabolism.

The three structural genes are adjacent to one another on the chromosome and are under the control of a single promoter and a single operator (Fig. 16.2). The regulator gene codes for a *lac* operon repressor that ordinarily binds to the operator and prevents transcription of the three genes. But when glucose is absent and lactose (or more correctly, allolactose, an isomer formed from lactose) is present, lactose binds to the **repressor,** and the repressor undergoes a change in shape that prevents it from binding to the operator.

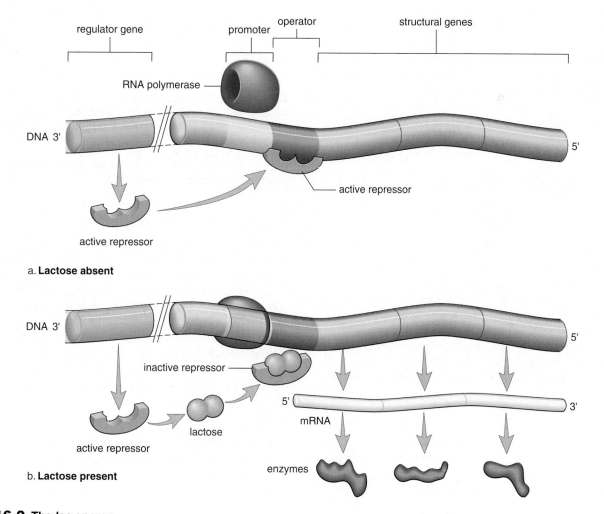

Figure 16.2 The *lac* operon.

a. The regulator gene codes for a repressor that is normally active. When it binds to the operator, RNA polymerase cannot attach to the promoter and structural genes are not expressed. **b.** When lactose is present, it joins to the repressor, changing its shape so that it is inactive and cannot bind to the operator. Now, RNA polymerase binds to the promoter and the structural genes are expressed.

Because the repressor is unable to bind to the operator, RNA polymerase is better able to bind to the promoter. After RNA polymerase carries out transcription, the three enzymes of lactose metabolism are synthesized.

Because the presence of lactose brings about expression of genes, it is called an **inducer** of the *lac* operon: the enzymes are said to be inducible enzymes, and the entire unit is called an **inducible operon.** Inducible operons are usually necessary to metabolic pathways that break down a nutrient. Why is that beneficial? Because these enzymes need only be active when the nutrient is present.

The *trp* operon is an example of a repressible operon because it is ordinarily turned on while the *lac* operon is an example of an inducible operon because it is ordinarily turned off.

Further Control of the lac *Operon*

E. coli preferentially breaks down glucose, and the bacterium has a way to ensure that the lactose operon is maximally turned on only when glucose is absent. When glucose is absent, a molecule called *cyclic AMP (cAMP)* accumulates. Cyclic AMP, which is derived from ATP, has only one phosphate group, which is attached to ribose at two locations.

Cyclic AMP
(cAMP)

Cyclic AMP binds to a molecule called a *catabolite activator protein (CAP)* and the complex attaches to a CAP binding site next to the *lac* promoter. When CAP binds to DNA, DNA bends exposing the promoter to RNA polymerase. RNA polymerase is now better able to bind to the promoter so that the *lac* operon structural genes are transcribed leading to their expression (Fig. 16.3).

When glucose is present there is little cAMP in the cell; CAP is inactive and the lactose operon does not function maximally. CAP affects other operons as well and takes its name for activating the catabolism of various other metabolites when glucose is absent. The cells' ability to encourage the metabolism of lactose and other metabolites when glucose is absent provides a backup system for survival when the preferred metabolite glucose is absent.

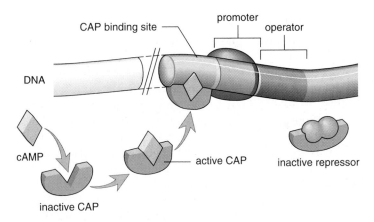

a. **Lactose present, glucose absent (cAMP level high)**

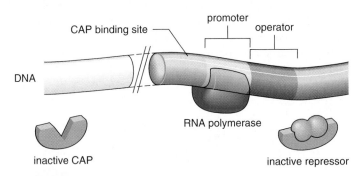

b. **Lactose present, glucose present (cAMP level low)**

Figure 16.3 Action of CAP.
When active CAP binds to its site on DNA, the RNA polymerase is better able to bind to the promoter so that the structural genes of the *lac* operon are expressed. **a.** CAP becomes active in the presence of cAMP, a molecule that is prevalent when glucose is absent. **b.** If glucose is present, CAP is inactive and RNA polymerase does not completely bind to the promoter.

Negative Versus Positive Control

Negative control of an operon is exemplified by the involvement of repressors. Why? Because active repressors shut down the activity of an operon. On the other hand, the CAP molecule is an example of positive control. Why? Because when this molecule is active it promotes the activity of an operon. The use of both a negative and a positive control mechanism to control an operon allows the cell to fine-tune its response. In the case of the *lac* operon, the operon is only maximally active when glucose is absent and lactose is present. If both glucose and lactose are present, the cell preferentially metabolizes glucose.

Bacterial DNA contains control regions whose sole purpose is to regulate the transcription of structural genes that code for enzymes or other products.

16.2 Eukaryotic Regulation

The **genome** is all of a cell's DNA including all of its genes that code for a protein product. As we have seen in prokaryotes, the genome is organized into regulators and operons that control the expression of structural genes. In eukaryotes, there is no universal regulatory mechanism that controls the activity of coding genes. Instead regulation is possible at any point in the pathway from gene to functional protein. These four levels of gene expression are commonly seen in eukaryotes (Fig. 16.4):

1. **Transcriptional control:** In the nucleus a number of mechanisms serve to control which structural genes are transcribed or the rate at which transcription of the genes occurs. These include the organization of chromatin and the use of transcription factors that initiate transcription, the first step in the process of gene expression.

2. **Posttranscriptional control:** Posttranscriptional control occurs in the nucleus after DNA is transcribed and primary mRNA is formed. Differential processing of preliminary mRNA before it leaves the nucleus, and also the speed with which mature mRNA leaves the nucleus, can affect the ultimate amount of gene product.

3. **Translational control:** Translational control occurs in the cytoplasm after mRNA leaves the nucleus and before there is a protein product. The life expectancy of mRNA molecules (how long they exist in the cytoplasm) can vary, as can their ability to bind ribosomes. It is also possible that some mRNAs may need additional changes before they are translated at all.

4. **Posttranslational control:** Posttranslational control, which also takes place in the cytoplasm, occurs after protein synthesis. The polypeptide product may have to undergo additional changes before it is biologically functional. Also, a functional enzyme is subject to feedback control—the binding of an end product can change the shape of an enzyme so that it is no longer able to carry out its reaction.

We will see that regulation of gene expression in eukaryotes means there is cellular control of the amount and activity of a gene product.

Control of gene expression occurs at four levels in eukaryotes. In the nucleus there is transcriptional and posttranscriptional control; in the cytoplasm there is translational and posttranslational control.

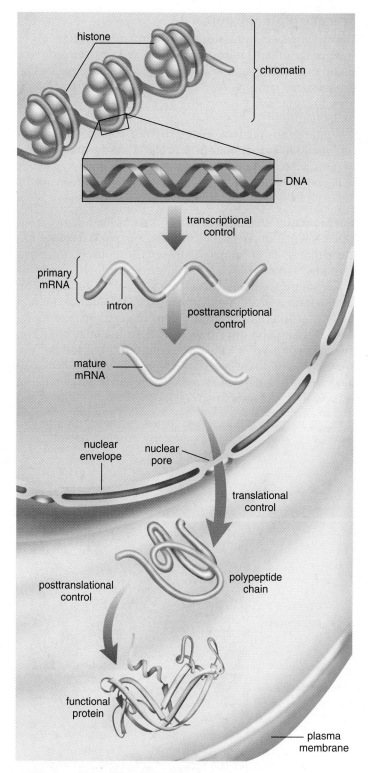

Figure 16.4 Levels of gene expression control in eukaryotic cells.
Transcriptional and posttranscriptional control occur in the nucleus. Translational and posttranslational control occur in the cytoplasm.

Transcriptional Control

We might expect transcriptional control in eukaryotes (1) to involve the organization of chromatin and (2) to include regulatory proteins such as those we have just observed in prokaryotes.

Organization of Chromatin

An interphase nucleus shows lightly stained chromatin regions called **euchromatin** and darkly stained chromatin regions called **heterochromatin** (Fig. 16.5). Euchromatin is believed to be genetically active, while heterochromatin is believed to be genetically inactive.

Euchromatin   A human cell contains at least 2 meters of DNA (Fig. 16.6*a*). Yet all of this DNA is packed into a nucleus that is about 5 μm in diameter. Chromosomes contain proteins, largely histones, in addition to DNA. The histones are responsible for packaging the DNA so that it can fit into such a small space. Usually the DNA double helix is wound at intervals around a core of eight histone molecules, giving the appearance of a string of beads (Fig. 16.6*b*). Each bead is called a nucleosome, and the nucleosomes are said to be joined by "linker" DNA that is associated with a histone known as H1. This level of organization is typical of euchromatin.

In nucleosomes, the DNA double helix is wound around a core of eight histone proteins (Fig. 16.7*a*). There are four primary types of histone molecules in a nucleosome designated H2A, H2B, H3, and H4. Remarkably, the amino acid sequences of H3 and H4 vary little between organisms. For example, the H4 of peas is only two amino acids different from the H4 of cattle. This similarity suggests that there have been few mutations in the histone proteins during the course of evolution and that the histones therefore have very important functions.

Euchromatin can readily become genetically active. When active the nucleosomes allow access to the DNA, so that a gene can be turned on and be expressed in the cell (Fig. 16.7*b*). The histone molecules labeled H2 to H4 may regulate this change in chromosomal structure. Recent studies seem to suggest that histones can both repress and activate genes.

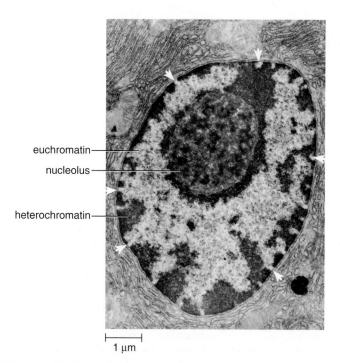

Figure 16.5 Eukaryotic nucleus.
The nucleus contains chromatin, DNA at two different levels of coiling and condensation. Euchromatin is at the level of coiled nucleosomes (30 nm), and heterochromatin is at the level of condensed chromatin (700 nm) in Figure 16.6. Arrows indicate nuclear pores.

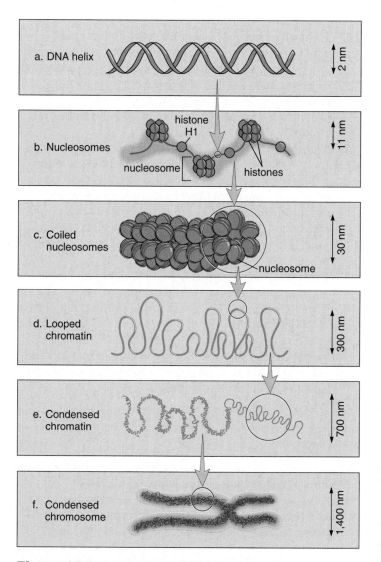

Figure 16.6 Levels of chromosomal structure.
Each drawing has a scale giving a measurement of length for that drawing. Notice that each measurement represents an ever-increasing length; therefore, it would take a much higher magnification to see the structure in **(a)** compared to that in **(f)**.

Heterochromatin   As you know, chromatin condenses to become compact chromosomes at the time of cell division. With the aid of histone H1, the beaded string is first coiled tightly into a fiber that has six nucleosomes per turn. This fiber is about 30 nm in thickness (Fig. 16.6*c*). Then the fiber loops back and forth (Fig. 16.6*d*) and can condense still further to produce a highly compacted form (Fig. 16.6*e* and *f*) characteristic of metaphase chromosomes.

Though heterochromatin in an interphase nucleus does not achieve the same degree of compacting as a metaphase chromosome, there are similarities. In heterochromatin, the beaded string is compacted into a 30 nm fiber that is folded into looped regions attached to the inside of the nuclear envelope.

Heterochromatin Is Inactive   To demonstrate that heterochromatin is genetically inactive, we can refer to the **Barr body,** a highly condensed structure. In mammalian females, one of the X chromosomes is found in the Barr body; chance alone determines which of the X chromosomes is condensed. For a given gene, if a female is heterozygous, 50% of her cells have Barr bodies containing one allele and the other 50% have the other allele. This causes the body of heterozygous females to be mosaic, with patches of genetically different cells (Fig. 16.8). The mosaic is exhibited in various ways: some females show columns of both normal and abnormal dental enamel; some have patches of pigmented and nonpigmented cells at the back of the eye; some have patches of normal muscle tissue and degenerative muscle tissue.

Barr bodies are not found in the cells of the female gonads, where the genes of both X chromosomes appear to be needed for maturation of the egg. But one X chromosome is inactive in the female zygote, lowering the amount of gene product during development to that seen in males. Most likely, development has become adjusted to this lower dosage, and a higher dosage would bring about abnormalities. We certainly know that, in regard to other chromosomes, any imbalance causes a greatly altered phenotype.

It appears that transcription is not occurring when chromatin is in the heterochromatin state.

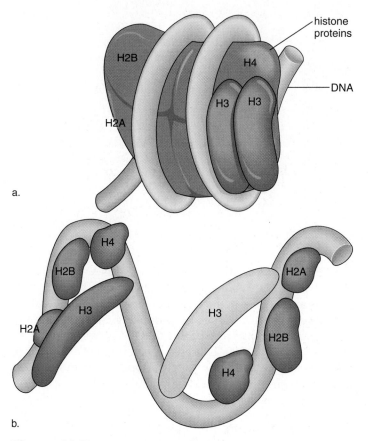

Figure 16.7 Nucleosome structure.
a. In a nucleosome, the DNA double helix winds twice around a group of histone proteins. Such tight packing is characteristic of heterochromatin. **b.** This model shows how it would be possible for the histones to loosen up, allowing transformation from heterochromatin to euchromatin as necessary for transcription to occur.

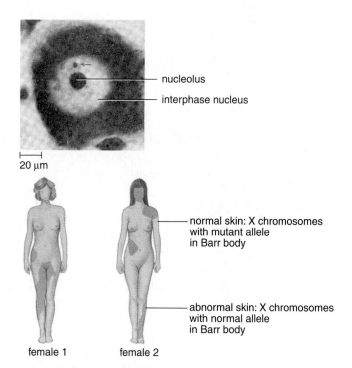

Figure 16.8 Barr body.
In the body of females, the nucleus of each cell contains a Barr body (at arrow) which is a condensed, inactive X chromosome. Chance alone dictates which of the two X chromosomes becomes a Barr body.

Figure 16.9 Lampbrush chromosomes.

These chromosomes are present in maturing amphibian egg cells and give evidence that when mRNA is being synthesized, chromosomes most likely decondense. Each chromosome has many loops extended from its axis (white). Many mRNA transcripts are being made off of these DNA loops (red).

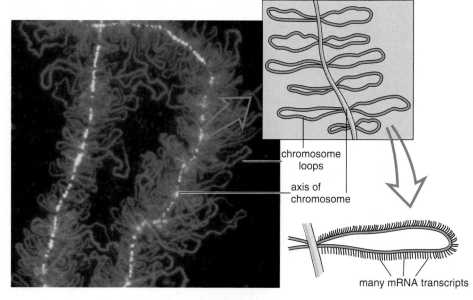

chromosome loops

axis of chromosome

many mRNA transcripts

Figure 16.10 Polytene chromosome.

Polytene chromosomes, such as this one from an insect, *Trichosia pubescens,* have about 1,000 parallel chromatids. As development occurs, puffs appear at specific sites, perhaps indicating where DNA is being transcribed. When ecdysone, a hormone that stimulates molting, is added, a pattern of puffs characteristic of natural molting appears.

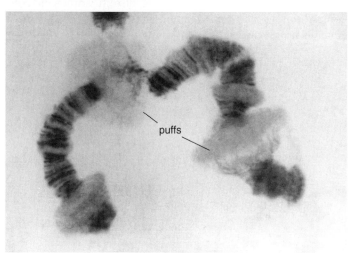

puffs

10 μm

Euchromatin Is Active   In contrast to heterochromatin, euchromatin is likely to be genetically active—it can be transcribed. The chromosomes within the developing egg cells of many vertebrates are called lampbrush chromosomes because they have many loops that appear to be bristles (Fig. 16.9). Here mRNA is being synthesized in great quantity as development proceeds.

In the salivary glands and other tissues of larval flies, the chromosomes duplicate and reduplicate many times without dividing mitotically. The homologues, each consisting of about 1,000 sister chromatids, synapse together to form giant chromosomes called polytene chromosomes [Gk. *poly,* many, and L. *taenia,* band, ribbon]. It is observed that as a larva develops, first one and then another of the chromosomal regions bulge out, forming chromosomal puffs (Fig. 16.10). The use of radioactive uridine, a label specific for RNA, indicates that DNA is being actively transcribed at these chromosomal puffs. It appears that the chromosome is decondensing at the puffs, allowing RNA polymerase to attach to a section of DNA.

Varying the amount of chromatin as in polytene chromosomes is another form of transcriptional control. When the gene product is either transfer RNA (tRNA) or ribosomal RNA (rRNA), only an increased amount of transcription permits an increase in the amount of gene product. In *Xenopus* (a frog) germ cells that are producing eggs, the number of nucleoli, and therefore copies of RNA genes, actually increases to nearly 1,000. This ensures an immense number of ribosomes in the egg cytoplasm to support protein synthesis during the early stages of development. This form of control is called *gene amplification.*

Transcription Factors

Although no operons like those of prokaryotic cells have been found in eukaryotic cells, transcription is controlled by DNA-binding proteins called **transcription factors.** Every cell contains many different types of transcription factors, and a different combination is believed to regulate the activity of any particular gene. A group of transcription factors binds to a promoter adjacent to a gene and then the complex

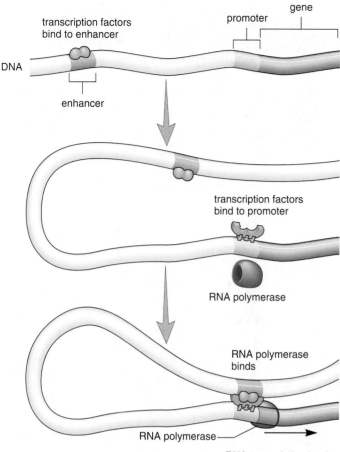

Figure 16.11 Transcription factors.
In this model of how transcription factors in eukaryotic cells work, transcription begins after transcription factors bind to a promoter and to an enhancer. The enhancer is far from the promoter, but physical contact is possible when the DNA loops bringing all factors into contact. Only then does transcription begin.

attracts and binds RNA polymerase, but transcription may still not begin. Quite often, enhancers are also involved in promoting transcription. Enhancers are regions where factors that help regulate transcription of the gene can also bind. *Enhancers* can be quite a distance from the promoter, but a hairpin loop in the DNA can bring the transcription factors attached to the enhancer into contact with the transcription factors at the promoter. Now RNA polymerase begins the transcription process (Fig. 16.11).

Transcription factors are always present in a cell and most likely they have to be activated in some way before they will bind to DNA. Activation probably occurs when they are phosphorylated by a kinase. Kinases, which add a phosphate group to molecules, and phosphatases, which remove a phosphate group, are known to be signaling proteins involved in a growth regulatory network that reaches from receptors in the plasma membrane to the nucleus. The growth regulatory network is discussed in more detail later in this chapter.

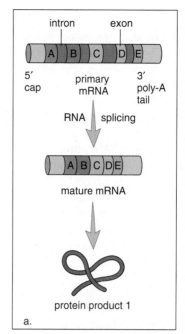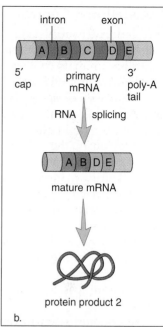

Figure 16.12 Processing of mRNA transcripts.
Because the primary mRNAs are processed differently in these two cells (**a** and **b**), distinct proteins result.

Posttranscriptional Control

Posttranscriptional control begins once there is an mRNA transcript. In eukaryotes, genes have both exons (coding regions) and introns (noncoding regions). Messenger RNA (mRNA) molecules (and other RNAs) are processed before they leave the nucleus and pass into the cytoplasm. Differential excision of introns and splicing of mRNA can vary the type of mRNA that leaves the nucleus. For example, both the hypothalamus and the thyroid gland produce a hormone called calcitonin, but the mRNA that leaves the nucleus is not the same in both types of cells. Radioactive labeling studies show that they vary because of a difference in mRNA splicing (Fig. 16.12). Evidence of different patterns of mRNA splicing is found in other cells, such as those that produce neurotransmitters, muscle regulatory proteins, and antibodies.

The speed of transport of mRNA from the nucleus into the cytoplasm can ultimately affect the amount of gene product realized per unit time following transcription. There is evidence that there is a difference in the length of time it takes various mRNA molecules to pass through a nuclear pore.

Transcriptional control in eukaryotes involves organization of chromatin and use of transcription factors. Posttranscriptional involves differential mRNA processing and factors that affect the length of time it takes mRNA to travel to the cytoplasm.

Translational Control

Translational control begins when the processed mRNA molecule reaches the cytoplasm. The eggs of frogs and certain other animals contain mRNA molecules that are not translated at all until fertilization occurs. The cell is unable to recognize these *masked messengers* as available for translation. As soon as fertilization occurs, unmasking takes place, and there is a rapid burst of specific gene product synthesis.

Obviously, the longer an active mRNA molecule remains in the cytoplasm, the more product there will eventually be. During maturation, mammalian red blood cells eject their nucleus, and yet they continue to synthesize hemoglobin for several months thereafter. This means that the necessary mRNAs are able to persist all this time. Differences in the guanine nucleotide cap at the 5' end and the poly-A tail at the 3' end of a mature mRNA transcript (see Fig. 15.8) might determine how long a particular transcript remains active before it is destroyed by a ribonuclease associated with ribosomes.

Hormones seem to cause the stabilization of certain mRNA transcripts. For example, the hormone prolactin promotes milk production in mammary glands by primarily affecting the length of time the mRNA for casein, a major protein in milk, persists and is translated. Similarly, an mRNA for phosphoprotein, called vitellin, persists for three weeks instead of 16 hours in amphibian cells if they are treated with estrogen. This hormone apparently interferes with the action of ribonuclease.

Posttranslational Control

Posttranslational control begins once a protein has been synthesized. Some proteins are not active immediately after synthesis. For example, bovine proinsulin is at first biologically inactive. After the single, long polypeptide folds into a three-dimensional structure, a sequence of about 30 amino acids is enzymatically removed from the middle of the molecule. This leaves two polypeptide chains that are bonded together by disulfide (S—S) bonds and results in an active protein.

Finally, most metabolic pathways are regulated by feedback inhibition (Fig. 16.13). When the end product of the pathway is present and binds at an allosteric site on the first enzyme of the pathway, the enzyme changes shape. Now the first reactant of the pathway cannot bind to the active site and the pathway is shut down.

Translational control determines the degree to which an mRNA is translated into a protein product. Posttranslational control affects the activity of a protein product, whether or not it is functional, and the length of time it is functional.

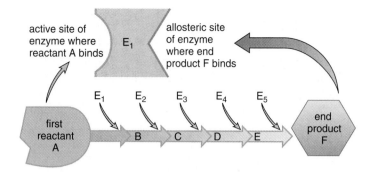

Overall view of pathway

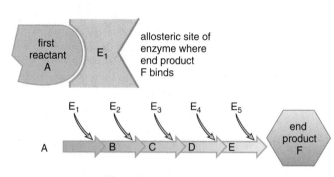

View of active pathway

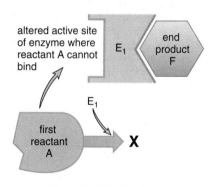

View of inhibited pathway

Figure 16.13 Feedback inhibition.
This hypothetical metabolic pathway is regulated by feedback inhibition. When reactant A binds to the active site of E_1, the pathway is active and the end product is produced. Once there is sufficient end product, some bind to the allosteric site of E_1. A change of shape prevents reactant A from binding to the active site of E_1 and the end product is no longer produced.

Barbara McClintock and the Discovery of Jumping Genes

When Barbara McClintock (Fig. 16A) first began studying inheritance in corn (maize) plants, geneticists believed that each gene had a fixed locus on a chromosome. Thomas Morgan and his colleagues at Columbia University were busy mapping the chromosomes of *Drosophila,* but McClintock preferred to work with corn. In the course of her studies, she came to the conclusion that "controlling elements" could move from one location to another on the chromosome. If a controlling element landed in the middle of a gene, it prevented the expression of that gene. Today, McClintock's controlling elements are called moveable genetic elements, transposons, or (in slang), "jumping genes."

Based on her experiments with maize, McClintock showed that because transposons are capable of suppressing gene expression, they could account for the pigment pattern of the corn strain popularly known as Indian corn. A colorless corn kernel results when cells are unable to produce a purple pigment due to the presence of a transposon within a particular gene needed to synthesize the pigment. While mutations are usually stable, a transposition is very unstable. When the transposon jumps to another chromosomal location, some cells regain the ability to produce the purple pigment and the result is a corn kernel with a speckled pattern (Fig. 16B).

When McClintock first published her results in the 1950s, the scientific community ignored them. Years later, when molecular genetics was well established, transposons were also discovered in bacteria, yeasts, plants, flies, and humans.

Geneticists now believe that transposons:

1. can cause localized mutations; that is, mutations that occur in certain cells and not others.
2. can carry a copy of certain host genes with them when they jump. Therefore, they can be a source of chromosome mutations such as translocations, deletions, and inversions.
3. can leave copies of themselves and certain host genes before jumping. Therefore, they can be a source of a duplication, another type of chromosome mutation.
4. can contain one or more genes that make a bacterium resistant to antibiotics.

Considering that transposition has a powerful effect on genotype and phenotype (Fig. 16C), it most likely has played an important role in evolution. For her discovery of transposons, McClintock was, in 1983, finally awarded the Nobel Prize in Physiology or Medicine. In her Nobel Prize acceptance speech, the eighty-one-year-old scientist proclaimed that "it might seem unfair to reward a person for having so much pleasure over the years, asking the maize plant to solve specific problems and then watching its responses."

Figure 16A Barbara McClintock.

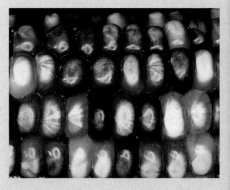

Figure 16B Corn kernels.
Some kernels are purple, some colorless, and some speckled.

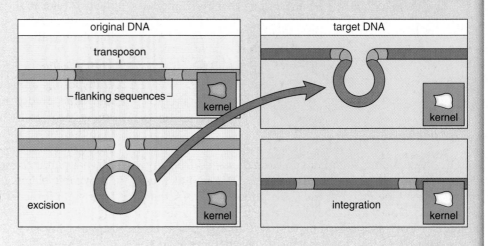

Figure 16C Transposon.
In its original location, a transposon is interrupting a gene (brown) that is not involved in kernel pigmentation. When the transposon moves to another chromosome position, it blocks the action of a gene (blue) required for synthesis of a purple pigment, and the kernel is now colorless.

16.3 Genetic Mutations

A **genetic mutation** is a permanent change in the sequence of bases in DNA. Genetic mutations vary in their phenotypic consequences depending on how protein activity is affected. Germ-line mutations are passed onto offspring while somatic mutations are not passed from one generation to the next. Germ-line mutations are the raw material for evolution; they produce the genetic variations that recombine to give novel genetic makeups. If one of these results in an adaptive phenotype, the individual will have more offspring than others of its kind. In this way certain genes and not others are preserved for future generations. Germ-line mutations coupled with genetic recombinations have resulted in the many species we see about us.

Cause of Mutations

Some mutations are spontaneous. They just happen for no apparent reason while others are due to environmental mutagens. Spontaneous mutations due to DNA replication errors are very rare. DNA polymerase, the enzyme that carries out replication, proofreads the new strand against the old strand and detects any mismatched nucleotides, and each is usually replaced with a correct nucleotide. In the end, there is only about one mistake for every one billion nucleotide pairs replicated.

Environmental Mutagens

A mutagen is an environmental agent that increases the chances of a mutation. Among the best-known mutagens are radiation and organic chemicals. **Cancer** is a genetic disorder caused by a failure in regulation of gene activity. Mutagens that increase the chances of cancer are called **carcinogens.**

Certain forms of radiation such as X rays and gamma rays are called ionizing radiation because they create free radicals, ionized atoms with unpaired electrons. Free radicals react with and alter the structure of other molecules, including DNA. Ultraviolet (UV) radiation is easily absorbed by the pyrimidines in DNA. Wherever there are two thymine molecules next to one another, ultraviolet radiation may cause them to bond together, forming thymine dimers.

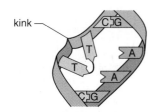

Usually, these dimers are removed from damaged DNA by repair enzymes which constantly monitor DNA and fix any irregularities. One enzyme excises a portion of DNA that contains the dimer; another makes a new section by using the other strand as a template; and still another seals the new section in place. The importance of repair enzymes is exemplified by individuals with the condition known as

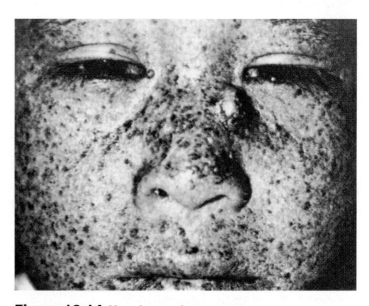

Figure 16.14 **Xeroderma pigmentosum.**
Deficient DNA repair enzymes leave the skin cells vulnerable to the mutagenic effects of ultraviolet light, and hundreds of skin cancers (small dark spots) appear on the skin exposed to the sun. This individual also has a tumor on the bridge of the nose.

xeroderma pigmentosum. They lack some of the repair enzymes, and as a consequence these individuals have a high incidence of skin cancer (Fig. 16.14).

Some organic chemicals act directly on DNA. The chemical 5-bromouracil pairs with thymine but then rearranges to a form that pairs with cytosine the next time DNA is replicated. What was once an A—T pair becomes a G—C pair. Chemicals that add hydrocarbon groups or remove amino groups from DNA bases cause mispairings. Tobacco smoke contains a number or organic chemicals that are known carcinogens, and it is estimated that one-third of all cancer deaths can be attributed to smoking. Lung cancer is the most frequent lethal cancer in the United States, and smoking is also implicated in the development of cancers of the mouth, larynx, bladder, kidney, and pancreas. The greater the number of cigarettes smoked per day, the earlier the habit starts, and the higher the tar content, the greater the possibility of cancer. When smoking is combined with drinking alcohol, the risk of these cancers increases even more.

Transposons

Transposons are specific DNA sequences that have the remarkable ability to move within and between chromosomes. As discussed in the reading on page 257, their movement to a new location sometimes alters neighboring genes, particularly increasing or decreasing their expression. This can happen if the transposon is a regulator gene. Although "moveable elements" in corn were described 40 years ago, their significance was only realized recently. So-called *jumping genes* now have been discovered in bacteria, fruit flies, humans, and many other organisms.

The white-eye mutant in *Drosophila*, first observed by Morgan, is due to a transposon located within a gene coding for a pigment-producing enzyme. In a rare human neurological disorder, called Charcot-Marie-Tooth disease, the muscles and nerves of the legs and feet gradually wither away. This syndrome is due to a transposon called Mariner, which is also found in *Drosophila!*

Effect on Protein Activity

The effect of a DNA base sequence change on protein activity can range from no effect to complete inactivity. To substantiate this statement we will consider point mutations and frameshift mutations.

 Point mutations involve a change in a single DNA nucleotide, and therefore a change in a specific codon. Figure 16.15 gives an example in which a single base change could have no effect or a drastic effect, depending on the particular base change that occurs. You already know that sickle-cell disease is due to a single base change in DNA. Because the β chain of hemoglobin now contains valine instead of glutamate at one location, hemoglobin molecules form semirigid rods. The resulting sickle-shaped cells clog blood vessels and die off more quickly than normal-shaped cells.

 The term *reading frame* applies to the sequence of codons because they are read from some specific starting point as in this sentence: THE CAT ATE THE RAT. If the letter C is deleted from this sentence and the reading frame is shifted, we read THE ATA TET HER AT—something that doesn't make sense. **Frameshift mutations** occur most often because one or more nucleotides are either inserted or deleted from DNA. The result of a frameshift mutation can be a completely new sequence of codons and nonfunctional proteins.

Nonfunctional Proteins

A single nonfunctioning protein can have a dramatic effect on the phenotype. For example, one particular metabolic pathway in cells is as follows:

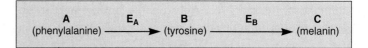

 If a faulty code for enzyme E_A is inherited, a person is unable to convert the molecule A to B. Phenylalanine builds up in the system and the excess causes mental retardation and the other symptoms of the genetic disorder called phenylketonuria (PKU). In the same pathway, if a person inherits a faulty code for enzyme E_B, then B cannot be converted to C and the individual is an albino. The human transposon called *Alu* is responsible for hemophilia when *Alu* inserts into the gene for clotting factor IX and places a premature stop codon there.

 Recall that cystic fibrosis is due to the inheritance of a faulty code for a chloride channel protein in the plasma membrane. A rare condition called androgen insensitivity is due to a faulty receptor for male sex hormones androgens, such as testosterone. Although there is plenty of testosterone in the blood, the cells are unable to respond to it. Female instead of male external genitals form and female instead of male secondary sexual characteristics occur. The individual who appears to be a normal female may be prompted to seek medical advice when menstruation never occurs. The karyotype is that of a male and not a female and the individual does not have the internal sexual organs of a female (Fig. 16.16).

No mutation   **Point mutations**

ATG	ATA	ATC	GTG
UAC	UAU	UAG	CAC
tyrosine (normal protein)	tyrosine (normal protein)	stop (incomplete protein)	histidine (faulty protein)

Figure 16.15 Point mutation.
The effect of a DNA base alteration can vary. Starting at the left, if after the base change the DNA codes for the same amino acid, there is no noticeable effect; if it now codes for a stop codon, the resulting protein will be incomplete; and if it now codes for a different amino acid, a faulty protein is possible.

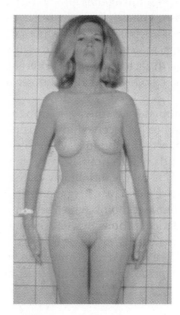

Figure 16.16 Androgen insensitivity.
This individual has a female appearance but the karyotype of a male, and there are testes instead of ovaries and a uterus in the abdominal cavity. Her cells are unable to respond to the male sex hormones because of a mutation that makes the androgen receptor ineffective.

Carcinogens

Factors that contribute to carcinogenesis (the origination of cancer) are listed in Figure 16.17. It's possible to inherit a gene that tends to cause cancer. The recently isolated *BRCA1* and *BRCA2* genes seem to account for about 20% of premenopausal breast cancer that runs in families and a substantial proportion of such ovarian cancers as well.

Tobacco is well known to cause lung and other cancers because it contains carcinogenic organic chemicals. Similarly, UV radiation is associated with skin cancer, and papillomavirus is implicated in cancer of the cervix. Even our diet influences whether we eventually develop cancer or not. Obesity is associated with uterine, postmenopausal breast cancer, as well as cancers of the colon, kidney, and gallbladder.

Regulation of the Cell Cycle

Carcinogens promote mutations in genes that control the cell cycle. An irregular mass of cells called a **tumor** is derived from an ancestral cell whose genes have undergone a series of mutations. These mutations cause the cell to repeatedly enter the cell cycle.

The cell cycle is a series of stages that occur in this sequence: G_1 stage—organelles begin to double in number; S stage—replication of DNA occurs and duplication of chromosomes occurs; G_2 stage—synthesis of proteins occurs that prepares the cell for mitosis; M stage—mitosis occurs. The passage of a cell from G_1 to the S stage is tightly regulated, as is the passage of a cell from G_2 to mitosis.

Two classes of genes known as proto-oncogenes and tumor-suppressor genes control the passage of cells through the cell cycle. **Proto-oncogenes** promote the cell cycle and **tumor-suppressor genes** inhibit the cell cycle. Each class of genes is a part of a regulatory pathway that involves extracellular signaling molecules called **growth factors,** plasma membrane growth factor receptors, internal signaling proteins within the cytoplasm, and a number of genes within the nucleus.

In the stimulatory pathway, a growth factor released by a neighboring cell is received by a plasma membrane receptor, and this sets in motion a whole series of enzymatic reactions that ends when stimulatory proteins enter the nucleus (Fig. 16.17). In the inhibitory pathway, a growth-inhibitory factor released by a neighboring cell is received by a plasma membrane receptor, which sets in motion a whole series of enzymatic reactions that ends when inhibitory proteins enter the nucleus. The balance between stimulatory signals and inhibitory signals determines whether proto-oncogenes are active or tumor-suppressor genes are active.

Oncogenes

Proto-oncogenes are so called because a mutation can cause them to become **oncogenes** (cancer-causing genes). An oncogene may code for a faulty receptor in the stimulatory pathway. A faulty receptor may be able to start the stimulatory process even when no growth factor is present! Or an oncogene may produce an abnormal protein product or else abnormally high levels of a normal product that stimulates the cell cycle to begin or go to completion. In either case, uncontrolled growth threatens.

Researchers have identified perhaps one hundred oncogenes that can cause increased growth and lead to tumors. The oncogenes most frequently involved in human cancers belong to the *ras* gene family. An alteration of only a single nucleotide pair is sufficient to convert a normally functioning *ras* proto-oncogene to an oncogene. The *ras*K oncogene is found in about 25% of lung cancers, 50% of colon cancers, and 90% of pancreatic cancers. The *ras*N oncogene is associated with leukemias (cancer of blood-forming cells) and lymphomas (cancers of lymphoid tissue), and both *ras* oncogenes are frequently found in thyroid cancers.

Tumor-Suppressor Genes

When a tumor-suppressor gene undergoes a mutation, the regulatory balance shifts in favor of cell cycle stimulation. Researchers have identified about a half-dozen tumor-suppressor genes. The *RB* tumor-suppressor gene was discovered when the inherited condition retinoblastoma was being studied. If a child receives only one normal *RB* gene and that gene mutates, eye tumors develop in the retina by the age of three. The *RB* gene has now been found to malfunction in cancers of the breast, prostate, and bladder, among others. Loss of the *RB* gene through chromosome deletion is particularly frequent in a type of lung cancer called small cell lung carcinoma. How the RB protein fits into the inhibitory pathway is known. When a particular growth-inhibitory factor attaches to a receptor, the RB protein is activated. An active RB protein turns off the expression of a proto-oncogene, whose product stimulates the cell cycle.

Another major tumor-suppressor gene is called *p53*, a gene that is more frequently mutated in human cancers than any other known gene. It has been found that the p53 protein acts as a transcription factor and as such is involved in turning on the expression of genes whose products are cell cycle inhibitors. The p53 protein can also stimulate **apoptosis**, programmed cell death. If DNA is damaged in any way, the p53 protein inhibits the cell cycle, and this gives cellular enzymes the opportunity to repair the damage. But if DNA damage should persist, the *p53* gene goes on to bring about apoptosis of the cell. No wonder many types of tumors contain cells that lack an active *p53* gene. Some cancer cells have a *p53* gene but make a large amount of bcl-2, a protein which binds to and inactivates the p53 protein.

Each cell contains regulatory pathways involving proto-oncogenes and tumor-suppressor genes that code for components active in the pathways.

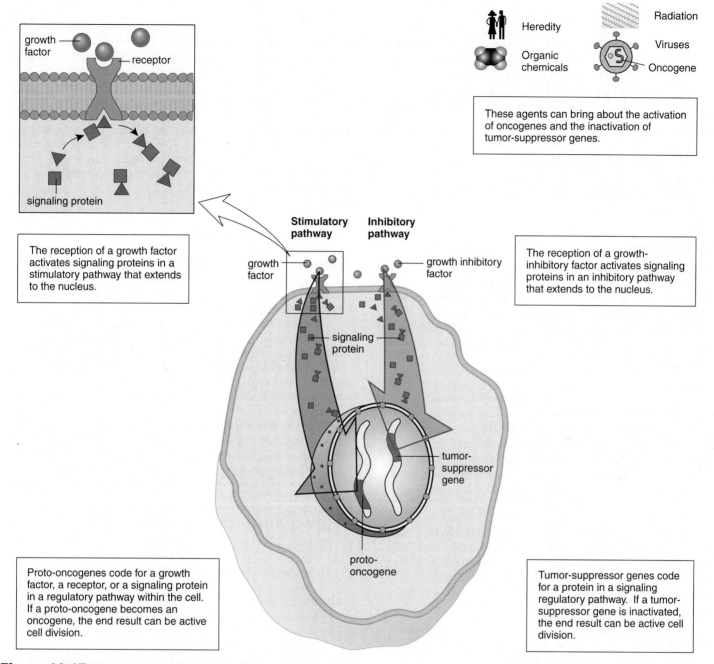

growth
factor
receptor

signaling protein

The reception of a growth factor activates signaling proteins in a stimulatory pathway that extends to the nucleus.

Heredity

Organic chemicals

Radiation

Viruses

Oncogene

These agents can bring about the activation of oncogenes and the inactivation of tumor-suppressor genes.

Stimulatory pathway   **Inhibitory pathway**

growth factor

growth inhibitory factor

signaling protein

The reception of a growth-inhibitory factor activates signaling proteins in an inhibitory pathway that extends to the nucleus.

tumor-suppressor gene

proto-oncogene

Proto-oncogenes code for a growth factor, a receptor, or a signaling protein in a regulatory pathway within the cell. If a proto-oncogene becomes an oncogene, the end result can be active cell division.

Tumor-suppressor genes code for a protein in a signaling regulatory pathway. If a tumor-suppressor gene is inactivated, the end result can be active cell division.

Figure 16.17 Causes of cancer.
Two types of regulatory pathways extend from the plasma membrane to the nucleus. In the stimulatory pathway, plasma membrane receptors receive growth-stimulatory factors. Then, proteins within the cytoplasm and proto-oncogenes within the nucleus stimulate the cell cycle. In the inhibitory pathway, plasma membrane receptors receive growth-inhibitory factors. Then, proteins within the cytoplasm and tumor-suppressor genes within the nucleus inhibit the cell cycle from occurring. Whether cell division occurs or not depends on the balance of stimulatory and inhibitory signals received. Hereditary and environmental factors cause mutations of proto-oncogenes and tumor-suppressor genes. These mutations can cause uncontrolled growth and a tumor.

Connecting Concepts

The basic mechanisms by which genetic information in DNA is converted first to an mRNA transcript and then to a protein by means of translation were explained in the previous chapter. These processes occur in all cells but not all genes are expressed in all cells of a multicellular organism. Gene regulation determines whether genes are expressed and/or the degree to which a gene is expressed. In differentiated cells like nerve cells, muscle fibers, reproductive cells, and so forth,

only certain genes are actively expressed. The collective work of many researchers was required to determine that the regulation of genes can occur at several different stages during the processes of transcription and translation.

Mutations of regulatory genes may cause structural genes to be abnormally turned off or on, or expressed in abnormal quantity. Such mutations can seriously affect a developing embryo or, as we saw in this chapter, can lead to development of

cancer. Cancers can arise when proto-oncogenes, which are normally not expressed, become oncogenes that are expressed. On the other hand cancers can also arise when tumor-suppressor genes fail to be adequately expressed.

In the next chapter, you will see how the basic knowledge of DNA structure, replication, and expression have contributed to a biotechnology revolution.

Summary

16.1 Prokaryotic Regulation

Regulation in prokaryotes usually occurs at the level of transcription. The operon model developed by Jacob and Monod says that a regulator gene codes for a repressor, which sometimes binds to the operator. When it does, RNA polymerase is unable to bind to the promoter, and transcription of structural genes cannot take place.

The *trp* operon is an example of a repressible operon because when tryptophan, the corepressor, is present, it binds to the repressor. The repressor is then able to bind to the operator, and transcription of structural genes does not take place.

The *lac* operon is an example of an inducible operon because when lactose, the inducer, is present, it binds to the repressor. The repressor is unable to bind to the operator, and transcription of structural genes takes place if glucose is absent.

These are two examples of negative control because a repressor is involved. There are also examples of positive control. The structural genes in the *lac* operon are not maximally expressed unless glucose is absent in addition to lactose being present. At that time cAMP attaches to a molecule called CAP and then CAP binds to a site next to the promoter. Now RNA polymerase is better able to bind to the promoter and transcription occurs.

16.2 Eukaryotic Regulation

The genome is all the DNA in a cell, including all coding genes. The following levels of control of gene expression are possible in eukaryotes: transcriptional control, posttranscriptional control, translational control, and posttranslational control.

Chromatin organization helps regulate transcription. Highly compacted heterochromatin is genetically inactive, as exemplified by Barr bodies. Less compacted euchromatin is genetically active, as exemplified by lampbrush chromosomes in vertebrates and polytene chromosomal puffs in insects. Gene amplification is the replication of a gene such that there are more copies than were originally present in the zygotic nucleus. Regulatory proteins called transcription factors, as well as DNA sequences called enhancers, play a role in controlling transcription in eukaryotes.

Posttranscriptional control refers to variations in messenger RNA (mRNA) processing and the speed with which a particular mRNA molecule leaves the nucleus.

Translational control affects mRNA translation and the length of time it is translated. Posttranslational control affects whether or not an enzyme is active and how long it is active.

16.3 Genetic Mutations

In molecular terms, a gene is a sequence of DNA nucleotide bases and a genetic mutation is a change in this sequence. Mutations can be spontaneous or due to an environmental mutagen. Carcinogens are mutagens like radiation and organic chemicals that cause cancer.

Point mutations can range in effect depending on the particular codon change. Frameshift mutations result when a base is added or deleted, and the result is usually a nonfunctional protein. Nonfunctional proteins can affect the phenotype drastically as in albinism, which is due to a single faulty enzyme, and androgen insensitivity, which is due to a faulty receptor for testosterone.

Cancer is due to an accumulation of genetic mutations among regulatory genes that control a pathway that reaches from the plasma membrane to the nucleus. In particular, the cell cycle occurs inappropriately when proto-oncogenes become oncogenes and tumor-suppressor genes are no longer effective.

Reviewing the Chapter

1. Name and state the function of the three components of operons.   248
2. Explain the operation of the *trp* operon, and note why it is considered a repressible operon.   249
3. Explain the operation of the *lac* operon, and note why it is considered an inducible operon.   249–50
4. What are the four levels of genetic regulatory control in eukaryotes?   251
5. Relate euchromatin and heterochromatin to levels of chromosome organization.   252
6. With regard to transcriptional control in eukaryotes, explain how Barr bodies show that heterochromatin is genetically inactive.   253
7. Explain how lampbrush chromosomes in vertebrates and giant (polytene) chromosomal puffs in insects show that euchromatin is genetically active.   254
8. What do transcription factors do in eukaryotic cells? What are enhancers?   255
9. Give examples of posttranscriptional, translational, and posttranslational control in eukaryotes.   255–56
10. What are oncogenes and tumor-suppressor genes? What role do they play in a regulatory network that controls cell division and involves plasma membrane receptors and signaling proteins?   260

Testing Yourself

Choose the best answer for each question.

1. Which type of prokaryotic cell would be more successful as judged by its growth potential?
   a. One that is able to express all its genes all the time.
   b. One that is unable to express any of its genes any of the time.
   c. One that expresses some of its genes some of the time.
   d. One that limits its growth regardless of the richness of the culture medium.
   e. Both a and d are correct.
2. When lactose is present, and glucose is absent
   a. the repressor is able to bind to the operator.
   b. the repressor is unable to bind to the operator.
   c. transcription of structural genes occurs.
   d. transcription of the structural genes, operator, and promoter occur.
   e. Both b and c are correct.
3. When tryptophan is present
   a. the repressor is able to bind to the operator.
   b. the repressor is unable to bind to the operator.
   c. transcription of structural genes occurs.
   d. transcription of the structural genes, operator, and promoter occur.
   e. Both b and c are correct.
4. Which of these is mismatched?
   a. posttranslational control—nucleus
   b. transcriptional control—nucleus
   c. translational control—cytoplasm
   d. posttranscriptional control—nucleus
   e. Both b and c are mismatched.
5. RNA processing varies in different cells. This is an example of _____ control of gene expression.
   a. transcriptional
   b. posttranscriptional
   c. translational
   d. posttranslational
   e. Both b and d are correct.
6. A scientist adds radioactive uridine (label for RNA) to a culture of cells and examines an autoradiograph. Which type of chromatin is apt to show the label?
   a. heterochromatin
   b. euchromatin
   c. the histones and not the DNA
   d. the DNA and not the histones
   e. Both a and d are correct.
7. Barr bodies are
   a. genetically active X chromosomes in males.
   b. genetically inactive X chromosomes in females.
   c. genetically active Y chromosomes in males.
   d. genetically inactive Y chromosomes in females.
   e. Both b and d are correct.

8. Which of these might cause a proto-oncogene to become an oncogene?
   a. exposure of cell to radiation
   b. exposure of cell to certain chemicals
   c. viral infection of the cell
   d. exposure of cell to pollutants
   e. All of these are correct.
9. A cell is cancerous. Where might you find an abnormality?
   a. only in the nucleus
   b. only in the plasma membrane receptors
   c. only in cytoplasmic reactions
   d. only in the cell cycle
   e. in any part of the cell concerned with growth and cell division
10. A tumor-suppressor gene
    a. inhibits cell division.
    b. opposes oncogenes.
    c. prevents cancer.
    d. is subject to mutations.
    e. All of these are correct.
11. Label this diagram of an operon.

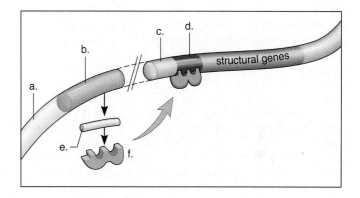

Thinking Scientifically

1. In patients with chronic myelogenous leukemia one sees an odd chromosome in all of the cancerous cells. A small piece of chromosome 9 is connected to chromosome 22. This 9:22 translocation has been termed the Philadelphia chromosome. How could a translocation cause genetic changes that result in cancer?
2. Interferon is a molecule that sets up an "alert" state in cells so that they can respond quickly to viral infection. This alert state actually causes the cell to self-destruct when a virus enters the cell. This is beneficial to the organism since the virus is prevented from producing progeny virus. For this system to work, the cell must be able to respond as rapidly as possible to the incoming virus. What hypothesis would explain how gene expression could produce the most rapid response? How could you use drugs that inhibit transcription to test the hypothesis?

Bioethical Issue

In the 1950s and 1960s, the U.S. government performed atomic bomb tests in Nevada. Radioactive iodine released into the air increased the risk of thyroid cancer for all U.S. citizens, and especially those who lived in Nevada, western states north of the test site, and states east of the site. People who were children then have an increased risk due to their small size at the time. Also, they probably drank milk from cows that fed on contaminated grass. It can take several decades for thyroid cancer to develop after exposure to radiation.

Physicians for Social Responsibility (PSR) are concerned because it took the government more than thirty years to decide that on the average people received 2 rads (radiation-absorbed doses) of radiation, and some children may have received levels above 120 rads. The Agency for Toxic Substances and Disease Registry sets a dose of 10 rads as the threshold for a need for a cancer monitoring program.

Still, the National Cancer Institute who released its report in two stages during 1997 and 1998, only after media pressure, does not believe that a monitoring program is necessary. Their argument is that there is no evidence that early detection of thyroid cancer will reduce mortality. Even so, the Physicians for Social Responsibility believe that monitoring should be offered, and further, a major research effort should begin on how to identify and treat people with thyroid cancer. A spokesperson for the group said, "Nuclear testing has exposed millions of American people to dangerous radioactivity without their knowledge or consent, and then the information about the exposure was withheld from them by federal officials. The Department of Health and Human Services should provide clear direction to citizens, physicians, and public health officials about [the] next steps [to be taken]." Should the U.S. government also be held responsible for cases of thyroid cancer that develop in the states mentioned? Why or why not?

Understanding the Terms

apoptosis   260
Barr body   253
cancer   258
carcinogen   258
corepressor   249
euchromatin   252
frameshift mutation   259
genetic mutation   258
genome   251
growth factor   260
heterochromatin   252
inducer   250
inducible operon   250
oncogene   260
operator   248
operon   248

point mutation   259
posttranscriptional control   251
posttranslational control   251
promoter   248
proto-oncogene   260
regulator gene   248
repressible operon   249
repressor   249
structural gene   248
transcription factor   254
transcriptional control   251
translational control   251
tumor   260
tumor-suppressor gene   260

Match the terms to these definitions:

a. _____ Cancer-causing gene.
b. _____ Abnormal growth derived from a single mutated cell that has repeatedly undergone cell division; may be benign or malignant.
c. _____ Dark-staining body in the nuclei of female mammals that contains a condensed, inactive X chromosome.
d. _____ Diffuse chromatin, which is being transcribed.
e. _____ Environmental agent that causes mutations leading to the development of cancer.

Web Connections

Exploring the Internet

http://www.mhhe.com/biosci/genbio/mader
(click on *Biology 7/e*)

The *Biology 7/e* Online Learning Center provides many resources for studying the material in this chapter including links to the following sites:

The website of the National Institutes of Health contains an information index that will help you to find the institution responsible for the subject of your choice. The Health Information Page will also supply you with a link to that institute's home page.

http://www.nih.gov/health/

National Cancer Institute. Has a list of centers testing experimental therapies, as well as fact sheets and updates, plus news about ongoing clinical trials. Also provides access to PDQ (Physician Data Query), the largest resource on treatments and centers specializing in cancer care.

http://cancernet.nci.nih.gov/

American Cancer Society. The best site for information on diagnoses, treatments, and emotional support, as well as links to useful web pages screened for accuracy and reliability.

http://www.cancer.org/

Eukaryotic Cell Cycle and Cancer. This site includes a thorough discussion of the cell cycle, oncogenes, tumor-suppressor genes, how oncogenes cause cancer, and where these genes are located within the human genome.

http://www.cc.ndsu.nodak.edu/instruct/mcclean/plsc431/cellcycle/

Prokaryotic Genetics and Gene Expression. This MIT hypertextbook chapter covers gene expression, and includes practice problems.

http://esg-www.mit.edu:8001/esgbio/pge/pgedir.html

Biotechnology

The tomatoes in the foreground were genetically engineered to be insect resistant.

S ince Mendel's work was rediscovered in 1900, geneticists have made startling advances which have led to a new era of DNA technology. Modern techniques enable genes to be removed from one organism and inserted into another in order to produce a desired substance, insulin for example. Not very long ago, people with insulin-dependent diabetes mellitus received the insulin they needed for survival from dead animals. Today, they receive human insulin, a product of biotechnology. Since the 1980s, biotechnology has produced drugs and vaccines to curb human illnesses, and nucleic acids for laboratory research.

Genetically engineered bacteria have been used to clean up environmental pollutants, increase the fertility of the soil, and kill insect pests. Biotechnology also extends beyond unicellular organisms; it is now possible to alter the genotype and subsequently the phenotype of plants and animals. Indeed, gene therapy in humans—attempting to repair a faulty gene—is already undergoing clinical trials. There are those who are opposed to manipulation of genes for any reason. Although there have been no ill effects as yet, they fear the possibility of health and ecological repercussions in the future.

17.1 Cloning of a Gene

The cloning of a gene produces many identical copies. Recombinant DNA technology is used when a very large quantity of the gene is required. The use of the polymerase chain reaction (PCR) creates a lesser number of copies within a laboratory test tube.

Recombinant DNA Technology

Recombinant DNA (rDNA) contains DNA from two different sources. To make rDNA, a technician often begins by selecting a **vector**, the means by which recombinant DNA is introduced into a host cell. One common type of vector is a plasmid. **Plasmids** are small accessory rings of DNA. The ring is not part of the bacterial chromosome and can be replicated independently. Plasmids were discovered by investigators studying the sex life of the intestinal bacterium *Escherichia coli*.

Two enzymes are needed to introduce foreign DNA into vector DNA (Fig. 17.1). The first enzyme, called a **restriction enzyme**, cleaves plasmid DNA, and the second, called **DNA ligase** [L. *ligo*, bind], seals foreign DNA into the opening created by the restriction enzyme.

Restriction enzymes occur naturally in bacteria, where they stop viral reproduction by cutting up viral DNA. They are called restriction enzymes because they *restrict* the growth of viruses. In 1970, Hamilton Smith, at Johns Hopkins University, isolated the first restriction enzyme; now hundreds of different restriction enzymes have been isolated and purified. Each one cuts DNA at a specific cleavage site. For example, the restriction enzyme called EcoRI always cuts double-stranded DNA when it has this sequence of bases at the cleavage site:

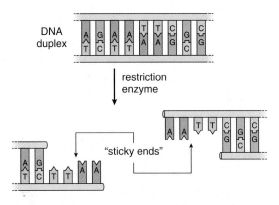

Notice there is now a gap into which a piece of foreign DNA can be placed if it ends in bases complementary to those exposed by the restriction enzyme. To assure this, it is only necessary to cleave the foreign DNA with the same type of restriction enzyme. The single-stranded but complementary ends of the two DNA molecules are called "sticky ends" because they can bind by complementary base pairing. They therefore facilitate the insertion of foreign DNA into vector DNA.

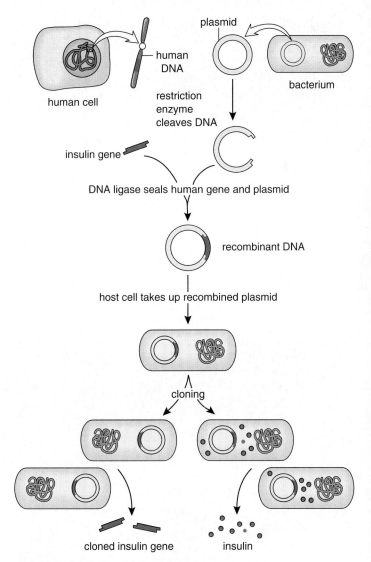

Figure 17.1 Cloning of a gene.
Human DNA and plasmid DNA are cleaved by the same type of restriction enzyme and spliced together by the enzyme DNA ligase. Gene cloning is achieved when a host cell takes up the recombined plasmid and the plasmid reproduces. Multiple copies of the gene are now available to an investigator. If the insulin gene functions normally as expected, the product (insulin) may also be retrieved.

The second enzyme needed for preparation of rDNA, DNA ligase, is a cellular enzyme that seals any breaks in a DNA molecule. Genetic engineers use this enzyme to seal the foreign piece of DNA into the vector. DNA splicing is now complete; an rDNA molecule has been prepared.

Plasmid Vector Compared to Viral Vector

A **clone** can be a large number of molecules (i.e., cloned genes) or cells (i.e., cloned bacteria) or organisms that are identical to an original specimen. Figure 17.2 compares the use of a plasmid and a virus to clone a gene. Bacterial cells take up recombined plasmids, especially if they are treated with calcium chloride to make them more permeable. Thereafter, as the host cell reproduces, a bacterial clone forms and each new cell contains at least one plasmid. Therefore, each of the bacteria contains the gene of interest which hopefully is expressing itself and producing a product. The investigator can recover either the cloned gene, or the protein product from this bacterial clone (see also Fig. 17.1).

Viruses that infect bacteria are called **bacteriophages.** In Figure 17.2*b*, the DNA of a bacteriophage called lambda is being used as a vector. After lambda attaches to a host bacterium, recombined DNA is released from the virus and enters the bacterium. Here, it will direct the reproduction of many more viruses. Each virus in the bacteriophage clone contains a copy of the gene being cloned.

Genomic Library

A **genome** is the full set of genes of an individual. A **genomic library** is a collection of bacterial or bacteriophage clones; each clone contains a particular segment of DNA from the source cell. When you make a genomic library, an organism's DNA is simply sliced up into pieces, and the pieces are put into vectors (i.e., plasmids or viruses) that are taken up by host bacteria. The entire collection of bacterial or bacteriophage clones that result contains all the genes of that organism.

In order for human gene expression to occur in a bacterium, the gene has to be accompanied by the proper regulatory regions. Also, the gene should not contain introns because bacterial cells do not have the necessary enzymes to process primary messenger RNA (mRNA). It's possible to make a human gene that lacks introns, however. The enzyme called reverse transcriptase can be used to make a DNA copy of all the mature mRNA molecules from a cell. This DNA molecule, called **complementary DNA (cDNA),** does not contain introns. Notice that a genomic library made from cDNA will contain only those genes that are being expressed in the source cell.

You can use a particular probe to search a genomic library for a certain gene. A **probe** is a single-stranded nucleotide sequence that will hybridize (pair) with a certain piece of DNA. Location of the probe is possible because the probe is either radioactive or fluorescent. Bacterial cells, each carrying a particular DNA fragment, can be plated onto agar in a petri dish. After the probe hybridizes with the gene of interest, the gene can be isolated from the fragment (Fig. 17.3). Now this particular fragment can be cloned further or even analyzed for its particular DNA sequence.

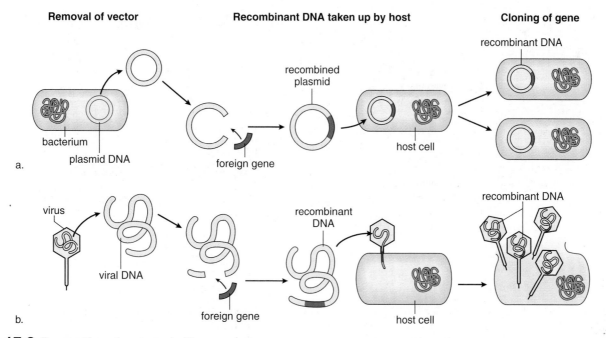

Figure 17.2 Preparation of a genomic library.
Each bacterial or viral clone in a genomic library contains a segment of DNA from a foreign cell. **a.** A plasmid is removed from a bacterium and is used to make recombinant DNA. After the recombined plasmid is taken up by a host cell, replication produces many copies. **b.** Viral DNA is removed from a bacteriophage such as lambda and is used to make recombinant DNA. The virus containing the recombinant DNA infects a host bacterium. Cloning is achieved when the virus reproduces and then leaves the host cell.

The Polymerase Chain Reaction

Kary B. Mullis developed the **polymerase chain reaction (PCR)** in 1983. Earlier methods of obtaining multiple copies of a specific sequence of DNA were time consuming and expensive. In contrast, PCR can create millions of copies of a single gene or any specific piece of DNA quickly in a test tube. PCR is very specific—the targeted DNA sequence can be less than one part in a million of the total DNA sample! This means that a single gene, or smaller piece of DNA, among all the human genes can be amplified (copied) using PCR.

PCR takes its name from DNA polymerase, the enzyme that carries out DNA replication in a cell. It is considered a chain reaction because DNA polymerase will carry out replication over and over again, until there are millions of copies of the desired DNA. PCR does not replace gene cloning, which is still used whenever a large quantity of gene or protein product is needed.

Before carrying out PCR, primers—sequences of about 20 bases that are complementary to the bases on either side of the "target DNA"—must be available. The primers are needed because DNA polymerase does not start the replication process; it only continues or extends the process. After the primers bind by complementary base pairing to the DNA strand, DNA polymerase copies the target DNA (Fig. 17.4).

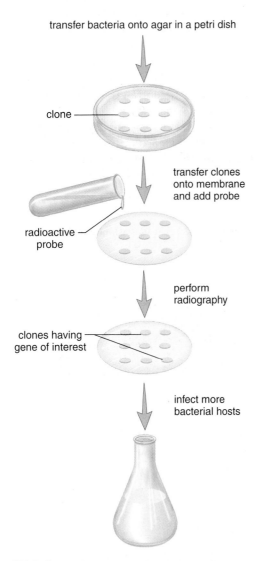

Figure 17.3 Identification of a cloned gene.
A probe, which may be single-stranded DNA or mRNA, hybridizes with the cloned DNA fragments containing the gene of interest. To see which clones (fragments) contain the gene, the probe has to be radioactive or fluorescent. Autoradiography is the use of a film that reveals the areas of radioactivity.

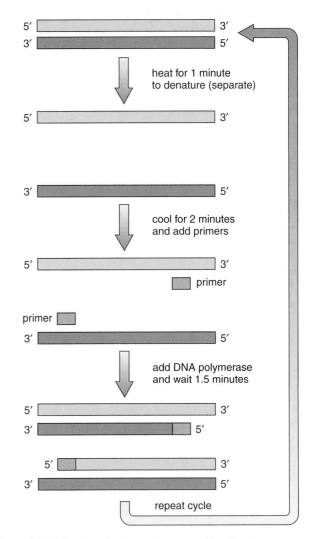

Figure 17.4 Polymerase chain reaction (PCR).
PCR is performed in laboratory test tubes. Primers (pink), which are DNA sequences complementary to the 3' end of the targeted DNA, are necessary for DNA polymerase to make a copy of the DNA strand.

PCR has been in use for several years, and now almost every laboratory has automated PCR machines to carry out the procedure. Automation became possible after a temperature-insensitive (thermostable) DNA polymerase was extracted from the bacterium *Thermus aquaticus,* which lives in hot springs. This enzyme can withstand the high temperature used to separate double-stranded DNA; therefore, replication need not be interrupted by the need to add more enzyme.

Analyzing DNA

The entire genome of an individual can be subjected to **DNA fingerprinting,** a process described in Figure 17.5. The genome is treated with restriction enzymes, which results in a unique collection of different-sized fragments. Therefore, **restriction fragment length polymorphisms (RFLPs)** exist between individuals. During a process called gel electrophoresis, the fragments can be separated according to their lengths, and the result is a number of bands that are so close together they appear as a smear. However, the use of probes for genetic markers produces a distinctive pattern that can be recorded on X-ray film.

The DNA from a single sperm is enough to identify a suspected rapist. Since DNA is inherited, its fingerprint resembles that of one's parents. DNA fingerprinting successfully identified the remains of a teenager who had been murdered eight years before because the skeletal DNA was similar to that of the parents' DNA. DNA fingerprinting has also been helpful to evolutionists. For example, it was used to determine that the quagga, an extinct zebralike animal, was a zebra rather than a horse. The only remains of the quagga consisted of dried skin.

Following PCR, DNA segments, as opposed to the full genome, can also be cut by restriction enzymes and subjected to gel electrophoresis. A probe is not needed because the restriction fragments will appear as distinctive bands. PCR amplification and analysis can be used (1) to diagnose viral infections, genetic disorders, and cancer; (2) in forensic laboratories to identify criminals; and (3) to determine the evolutionary relationships of various organisms. Sequencing mitochondrial DNA segments helped determine the evolutionary history of human populations. It has even been possible to sequence DNA taken from a 76,000-year-old mummified human brain and from a 17- to 20-million-year-old plant fossil following PCR amplification.

> Recombinant DNA technology and the polymerase chain reaction are two ways to clone a gene.

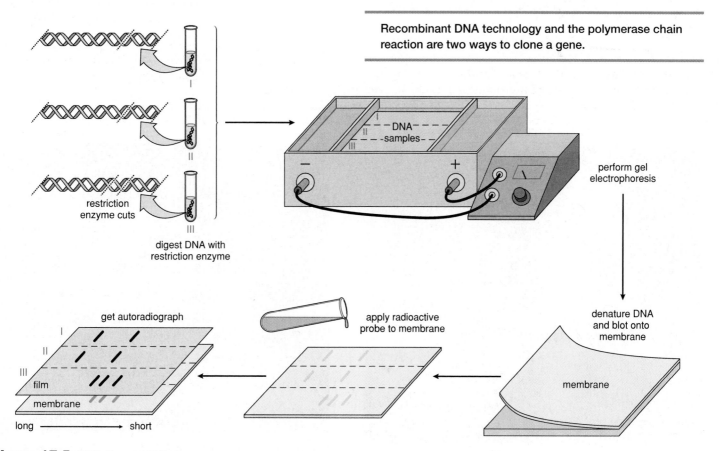

Figure 17.5 DNA fingerprinting.
DNA samples I and II are from the same individual. DNA sample III is from a different individual. Notice, therefore, that the restriction enzyme cuts are different for sample III. Gel electrophoresis separates the DNA fragments according to their length because shorter fragments migrate farther in an electrical field than do longer fragments. The fragments are denatured (separated) and transferred to a membrane where a radioactive probe can be applied. The resulting pattern (the DNA fingerprint) can then be detected by autoradiography. In a theoretical rape case, for example, sample I could be from the suspect's white blood cells, sample II could be from sperm in the victim's vagina, and sample III could be from the victim's white blood cells.

17.2 Biotechnology Products

Today, bacteria, plants, and animals are **genetically engineered** to produce biotechnology products. Organisms that have had a foreign gene inserted into them are called **transgenic organisms.** Organs for transplant from nonhuman sources, as discussed in the reading on page 271, are also considered biotechnology products.

Transgenic Bacteria

Recombinant DNA technology is used to produce bacteria that reproduce in large vats called bioreactors. If the foreign gene is replicated and actively expressed, a large amount of protein product can be obtained. Biotechnology products produced by bacteria, such as insulin, human growth hormone, t-PA (tissue plasminogen activator), and hepatitis B vaccine, are now on the market (Fig. 17.6).

Transgenic bacteria have been produced to promote the health of plants. For example, bacteria that normally live on plants and encourage the formation of ice crystals have been changed from frost-plus to frost-minus bacteria. Also, a bacterium that normally colonizes the roots of corn plants has now been endowed with genes (from another bacterium) that code for an insect toxin. The toxin protects the roots from insects.

Bacteria can be selected for their ability to degrade a particular substance, and then this ability can be enhanced by genetic engineering. For instance, naturally occurring bacteria that eat oil can be genetically engineered to do an even better job of cleaning up beaches after oil spills (Fig. 17.7).

Industry has found that bacteria can be used as biofilters to prevent airborne chemical pollutants from being vented into the air. They can also remove sulfur from coal before it is burned and help clean up toxic waste dumps. One such strain was given genes that allowed it to clean up levels of toxins that would have killed other strains. Further, these bacteria were given "suicide" genes that caused them to self-destruct when the job had been accomplished.

Organic chemicals are often synthesized by having catalysts act on precursor molecules or by using bacteria to carry out the synthesis. Today, it is possible to go one step further and to manipulate the genes that code for these enzymes. For instance, biochemists discovered a strain of bacteria that is especially good at producing phenylalanine, an organic chemical needed to make aspartame, the dipeptide sweetener better known as NutraSweet. They isolated, altered, and formed a vector for the appropriate genes so that various bacteria could be genetically engineered to produce phenylalanine.

Many major mining companies already use bacteria to obtain various metals. Genetic engineering may enhance the ability of bacteria to extract copper, uranium, and gold from low-grade sources. Some mining companies are testing genetically engineered organisms that have improved bioleaching capabilities.

Bacteria are being genetically altered to perform all sorts of tasks, not only in the factory, but also in the environment.

Figure 17.6 Biotechnology products.
Products like clotting factor VIII, which is administered to hemophiliacs, can be made by transgenic bacteria, plants, or animals. After being processed and packaged, it is sold as a commercial product.

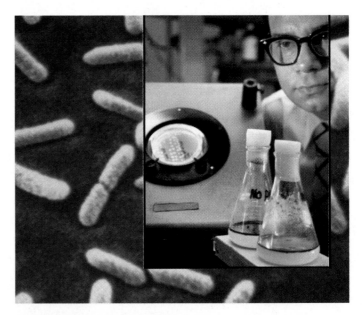

Figure 17.7 Bioremediation.
Bacteria capable of decomposing oil have been engineered and patented by the investigator Dr. Chakrabarty. In the inset, the flask toward the rear contains oil and no bacteria; the flask toward the front contains the bacteria and is almost clear of oil.

We now have the ability to transplant human kidneys, heart, liver, pancreas, lung, and other organs for two reasons. First, solutions have been developed that preserve donor organs for several hours, and second, rejection of transplanted organs can be prevented by immunosuppressive drugs. Unfortunately, however, there are not enough human donors to go round. Thousands of patients die each year while waiting for an organ.

It's no wonder, then, that scientists are suggesting that we should get organs from a source other than another human. **Xenotransplantation** is the use of animal organs instead of human organs in transplant patients. You might think that apes, such as the chimpanzee or the baboon, might be a scientifically suitable species for this purpose. But apes are slow breeders and probably cannot be counted on to supply all the organs needed. Also, many people might object to using apes for this purpose. In contrast, animal husbandry has long included the raising of pigs as a meat source, and pigs are prolific. A female pig can become pregnant at six months and can have two litters a year, each averaging about ten offspring.

Ordinarily, humans would violently reject transplanted pig organs. Genetic engineering, however, can make these organs less antigenic. Scientists have produced a strain of pigs whose organs would most likely, even today, survive for a few months in humans. They could be used to keep a patient alive until a human organ was available. The ultimate goal is to make pig organs as widely accepted by humans as type O blood. A person with type O blood is called a universal donor because the red blood cells carry no A nor B antigens.

As xenotransplantation draws near, other concerns have been raised. Some experts fear that animals might be infected with viruses, akin to Ebola virus or the virus that causes "mad cow" disease. After infecting a transplant patient, these viruses might spread into the general populace and begin an epidemic. Scientists believe that HIV was spread to humans from monkeys when humans ate monkey meat. Those in favor of using pigs for xenotransplantation point out that pigs have been around humans for centuries without infecting them with any serious diseases.

Just a few years ago, scientists believed that transplant organs had to come from humans or other animals. Now, however, **tissue engineering** is demonstrating that it is possible to make some bioartificial organs—hybrids created from a combination of living cells and biodegradable polymers. Presently, only lab-grown hybrid tissues are on the market. A product composed of skin cells growing on a polymer is used to temporarily cover the wounds of burn patients. Similarly, damaged cartilage can be replaced with a hybrid tissue produced after chondrocytes are harvested from a patient. Another connective tissue product made from fibroblasts and collagen is available to help heal deep wounds without scarring. Soon to come are a host of other products including replacement corneas, heart valves, bladder valves, and breast tissue.

Tissue engineers have also created implants—cells producing a useful product encapsulated within a narrow plastic tube or a capsule the size of a dime or quarter (Fig. 17A). The pores of the container are large enough to allow the product to diffuse out but are too small for immune cells to enter and destroy the cells. An implant whose cells secrete natural pain killers will survive for months in the spinal cord and it can be easily withdrawn when desired. A "bridge to a liver transplant" is a bedside vascular apparatus. The patient's blood passes through porous tubes surrounded by pig liver cells. These cells convert toxins in the blood to nonpoisonous substances.

The goal of tissue engineering is to produce fully functioning organs for transplant. After nine years, a Harvard Medical School team headed by Anthony Atala has produced a working urinary bladder in the laboratory. The right culture conditions and combination of growth factors was needed to build the bladder wall from cells genetically engineered to be nonantigenic. After testing the bladders in laboratory animals, the Harvard group is ready to test them in humans whose own bladders have been damaged by accident or disease, or will not function properly due to a congenital birth defect. Another group of scientists has been able to grow arterial blood vessels in the laboratory. Still to come, tissue engineers are hopeful they can one day produce larger internal organs like the liver and kidney. Such organs will be more challenging because they are much more complex than hollow structures like bladders and arteries.

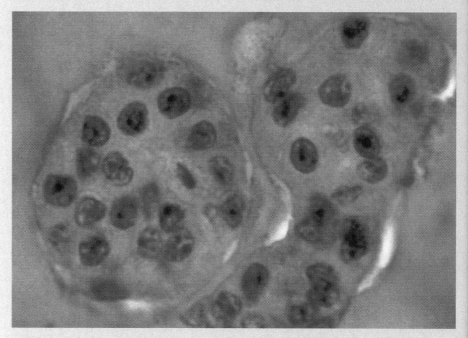

Figure 17A Microreactors.
Microreactors filled with insulin-producing pancreatic cells from pigs flourished for 10 weeks in a diabetic mouse without immune system-suppressing drugs.

Transgenic Plants

Techniques have been developed to introduce foreign genes into immature plant embryos, or into plant cells that have had the cell wall removed and are called protoplasts. It is possible to treat protoplasts with an electric current while they are suspended in a liquid containing foreign DNA. The electric current makes tiny, self-sealing holes in the plasma membrane through which genetic material can enter. Then a protoplast will develop into a complete plant.

Foreign genes transferred to cotton, corn, and potato strains have made these plants resistant to pests because their cells now produce an insect toxin. Similarly, soybeans have been made resistant to a common herbicide. Some corn and cotton plants are both pest and herbicide resistant. In 1999, these transgenic crops were planted on more than 70 million acres worldwide and the acreage is expected to triple in about five years. Improvements still to come are increased protein or starch content and modified oil or amino acid composition.

Agribusiness companies also are in the process of developing transgenic versions of wheat and rice in addition to corn. This is considered an absolute necessity if the 2020 global demand for rice, wheat, and corn is to be met. World grain harvests have continued to rise since the 1960s when special high-yield hybrid plants were developed during the so-called Green Revolution. But the per capita production has now flattened out because of continued population growth. The hope is that genetic engineering will allow farmers to surpass the yield barrier. Perhaps the stomates, the porelike openings in leaves, could be altered to boost carbon dioxide intake or cut down on water loss. Another possible goal is to increase the efficiency of the enzyme RuBP, which captures carbon dioxide in most plants. A team of Japanese scientists are attempting to introduce the C_4 cycle into rice. Plants that utilize the C_4 cycle avoid the inefficiency of carboxylase by using a different means of capturing carbon dioxide. Unlike the single gene transfers that have been done so far, these modifications would require a thorough re-engineering of plant cells.

Single gene transfers will cause plants to produce various products. A weed called mouse-eared cress has been engineered to produce a biodegradable plastic (polyhydroxybutyrate, or PHB) in cell granules. Plants are being engineered to produce human hormones, clotting factors, and antibodies, in their seeds. One type of antibody made by corn can deliver radioisotopes to tumor cells, and another made by soybeans can be used as treatment for genital herpes. Plant-made antibodies are inexpensive and there is little worry about contamination with pathogens that could infect people. Clinical trials have begun.

Farmers are now planting genetically altered crops. Medicines made by biotech plants will soon be used to treat cancer and other types of diseases.

Transgenic Animals

Techniques have been developed to insert genes into the eggs of animals. It is possible to microinject foreign genes into eggs by hand, but another method uses vortex mixing. The eggs are placed in an agitator with DNA and silicon-carbide needles, and the needles make tiny holes through which the DNA can enter. When these eggs are fertilized, the resulting offspring are transgenic animals. Using this technique, many types of animal eggs have taken up the gene for bovine growth hormone (bGH). The procedure has been used to produce larger fishes, cows, pigs, rabbits, and sheep. Genetically engineered fishes are now being kept in ponds that offer no escape to the wild because there is much concern that they will upset or destroy natural ecosystems.

Gene pharming, the use of transgenic farm animals to produce pharmaceuticals, is being pursued by a number of firms. Genes that code for therapeutic and diagnostic proteins are incorporated into the animal's DNA, and the proteins appear in the animal's milk. There are plans to produce drugs for the treatment of cystic fibrosis, cancer, blood diseases, and other disorders. Antithrombin III, for preventing blood clots during surgery, is currently being produced by a herd of goats, and clinical trials have begun. Figure 17.18*b* outlines the procedure for producing transgenic mammals: DNA containing the gene of interest is injected into donor eggs. Following in vitro fertilization, the zygotes are placed in host females where they develop. After female offspring mature, the product is secreted in their milk.

USDA scientists have been able to genetically engineer mice to produce human growth hormone in their urine instead of in milk. They expect to be able to use the same technique on larger animals. Urine is a preferable vehicle for a biotechnology product than milk because all animals in a herd urinate—only females produce milk; animals start to urinate at birth—females don't produce milk until maturity; and it's easier to extract proteins from urine than from milk.

Cloning of Transgenic Animals

Imagine that an animal has been genetically altered to produce a biotechnology product. What would be the best possible method of getting identical copies of the animal? Asexual reproduction through cloning the animal would be the preferred procedure to use. Cloning is a form of asexual reproduction because it requires only the genes of that one animal. For many years it was believed that adult vertebrate animals could not be cloned. Although each cell contains a copy of all the genes, certain genes are turned off in mature specialized cells. Different genes are expressed in muscle cells, which contract, compared to nerve cells, which conduct nerve impulses, and to glandular cells, which secrete. Cloning of an adult vertebrate requires that all genes of an adult cell be turned on again if development is to proceed normally. It had long been thought this would be impossible.

a.

Figure 17.8 Genetically engineered animals.
a. This goat is genetically engineered to produce antithrombin III, which is secreted in her milk. This researcher and many others are involved in the project.
b. The procedure to produce a transgenic animal.
c. The procedure to clone a transgenic animal.

In 1997, scientists at the Raslin Institute in Scotland announced that they achieved this feat and had produced a cloned sheep called Dolly. Since then calves and goats have also been cloned. Figure 17.8*c* shows that after enucleated eggs have been injected with 2n nuclei of adult cells, they can be coaxed to begin development. The offspring have the genotype and phenotype of the adult that donated the nuclei; therefore, the adult has been cloned. In the procedure that produced cloned mice, the 2n nuclei were taken from cumulus cells. Cumulus cells are those that cling to an egg after ovulation occurs. A specially prepared chemical bath was used to stimulate the eggs to divide and begin development. Now that scientists have a method to clone mammals, this procedure will undoubtedly be used routinely. In the United States, a presidential order prohibits the cloning of humans. But certain other countries are experimenting with the possibility.

Genetic engineering of animals has made much progress. Many firms are interested in gene pharming, the use of genetically engineered animals to produce pharmaceuticals in milk. Procedures have been developed to allow the cloning of these animals.

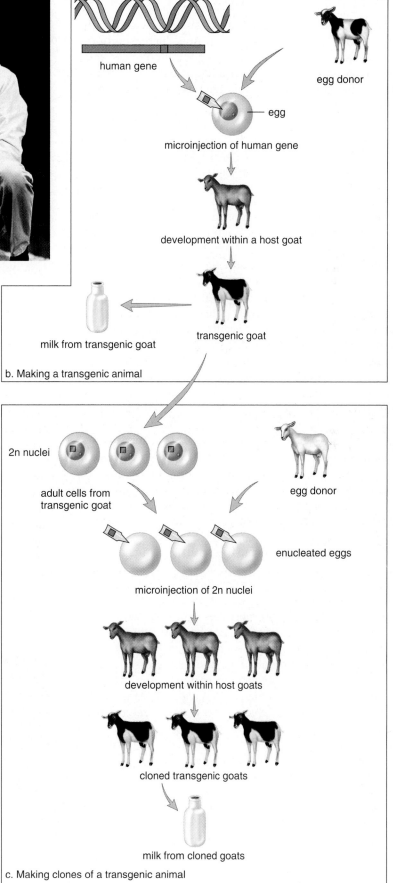

human gene

egg donor

egg

microinjection of human gene

development within a host goat

transgenic goat

milk from transgenic goat

b. Making a transgenic animal

2n nuclei

adult cells from transgenic goat

egg donor

enucleated eggs

microinjection of 2n nuclei

development within host goats

cloned transgenic goats

milk from cloned goats

c. Making clones of a transgenic animal

17.3 The Human Genome Project

The Human Genome Project is a massive effort originally funded by the U.S. government and now increasingly by U.S. pharmaceutical companies to map the human chromosomes. Many nonprofit and for profit biochemical laboratories about the world are now involved in the project which has two primary goals.

The first goal is to construct a genetic map of the human genome. The aim is to show the sequence of genes along the length of each type chromosome, such as depicted for the X chromosome in Figure 17.9. If the estimate of 1,000+ human genes is correct, each chromosome on average would contain about 50 alleles.

The map for each chromosome is presently incomplete, and in many instances scientists rely on the placement of RFLPs (see page 269). These sites eventually allow scientists to pinpoint disease-causing genes because a particular RFLP and a defective gene are often inherited together. For example, it is known that persons with Huntington disease have a unique site where a restriction enzyme cuts DNA. The test for Huntington disease relies on this difference from the normal.

The genetic map of a chromosome can be used not only to detect defective genes, but possibly also to tailor treatments to the individual. Only certain hypertension patients benefit from a low-salt diet, and it would be useful to know which patients these are. Myriad Genetics, a genome company, has developed a test for a mutant angiotensinogen gene because they want to see if patients with this mutation are the ones who benefit from a low-salt diet. Several other mutant genes have also been correlated with specific drug treatments (Table 17.1). One day the medicine you take might carry a label that it is effective only in persons with genotype #101!

The second goal is to construct a base sequence map. There are three billion base pairs in the human genome, and it's estimated it would take an encyclopedia of 200 volumes, each with 1,000 pages, to list all of these. Yet, this goal has been reached and all the chromosomes have been sequenced.

The methodology, thus far, has been to first chop up the genome into small pieces, each just 1,000 to 2,000 base pairs long. PCR instruments copy the pieces many times, and then an automatic DNA sequencer determines the order of the base pairs. You need many DNA copies because of the way the sequencer works. A computer program later strings the sequenced pieces together in the correct order by looking for base sequence overlaps between them. Instrumentation has gradually improved, and recently one scientist, J. Craig Venter, has founded a company which has now sequenced the entire genome.

Venter used what is called a whole-genome shotgun sequencing method. He worked with the entire human genome at once. Each overlapping fragment was about

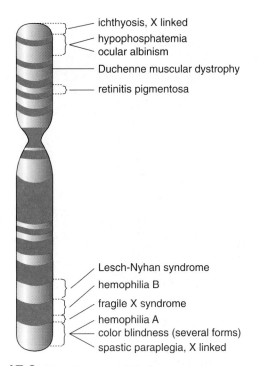

Figure 17.9 Genetic map of X chromosome.
The human X chromosome has been partially mapped, and this is the order of some of the genes now known to be on this chromosome.

5,000 bases long, and he sequenced the ends of each fragment using powerful new sequencing machines. Again, a computer program strung the fragments together by looking for overlapping regions. Why is Venter going off on his own, instead of participating in the worldwide effort by many laboratories and scientists to sequence the human genome? His backers expect to market the whole-genome database to subscribers, and to patent rare but pharmacologically interesting genes. Private enterprise is giving new impetus to the field now called genomics.

Knowing the base sequence of normal genes may make it possible one day to treat certain human ills by administering normal genes and/or their protein products to those who suffer from a genetic disease.

Table 17.1

Customizing Drug Treatments

Mutant Gene for	Disease	Treatment
Apolipoprotein E	Alzheimer	Experimental Glaxo Wellcome drug
Cytochrome P-450	Cancer	Amonafide
Chloride gate	Cystic fibrosis	Pulmozyme
Dopamine receptor D4	Schizophrenia	Clozapine
Angiotensinogen	Hypertension	Low-salt diet

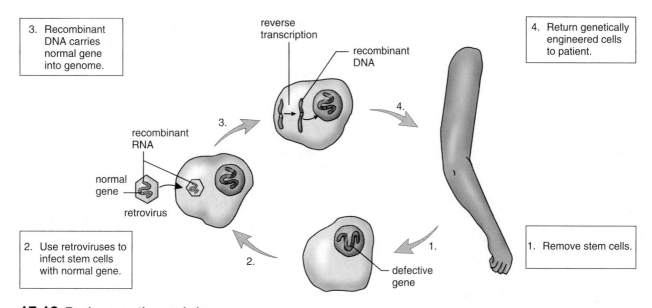

Figure 17.10 Ex vivo gene therapy in humans.
Bone marrow stem cells are withdrawn from the body, a virus is used to insert a normal gene into them, and they are returned to the body.

17.4 Gene Therapy

Gene therapy is the insertion of genetic material into human cells for the treatment of a disorder. It includes procedures that give a patient healthy genes to make up for faulty genes and also includes the use of genes to treat various other human illnesses such as cancer and cardiovascular disease. Currently there are approximately 1,000 patients enrolled in nearly 200 approved gene therapy trials in the United States. There are ex vivo (outside the body) and in vivo (inside the body) methods of gene therapy.

Genetic Disorders

As an example of an ex vivo method of gene therapy, consider Figure 17.10, which describes a methodology for the treatment of children with severe combined immunodeficiency syndrome (SCID). These children lack an enzyme called adenosine deaminase (ADA) that is involved in the maturation of T and B cells, and therefore they are subject to life-threatening infections. Bone marrow stem cells are removed from the blood and infected with a retrovirus (RNA virus) that carries a normal gene for the enzyme. Then the cells are returned to the patient. Bone marrow stem cells are preferred for this procedure because they divide to produce more cells with the same genes. With an ex vivo method of genetic therapy, it is possible to test and make sure gene transfer has occurred before the cells are returned to the patient. Patients who have undergone this procedure do have a significant improvement in their immune function that is associated with a sustained rise in the level of ADA enzyme activity in the blood.

Among the many gene therapy trials, one is for the treatment of familial hypercholesterolemia, a condition that develops when liver cells lack a receptor for removing cholesterol from the blood. The high levels of blood cholesterol make the patient subject to fatal heart attacks at a young age. In a newly developed procedure, a small portion of the liver is surgically excised and infected with a retrovirus containing a normal gene for the receptor. Several patients have experienced a lowering of serum cholesterol levels following this procedure.

Cystic fibrosis patients lack a gene that codes for transmembrane carrier of the chloride ion. Patients often die due to numerous infections of the respiratory tract. An in vivo method of treatment is being tried. Liposomes—microscopic vesicles that spontaneously form when lipoproteins are put into a solution—have been coated with the gene needed to cure cystic fibrosis. Then the solution is sprayed into patients' nostrils. Due to limited gene transfer this methodology has not as yet been successful.

In a recent and surprising move, some researchers are investigating the possibility of directly correcting the base sequence of patients with a genetic disorder. The exact procedure has not yet been published.

Cancer

Chemotherapy in cancer patients often kills off healthy cells as well as cancer cells. In clinical trials, researchers have given genes to cancer patients that either make healthy cells more tolerant of chemotherapy or make tumors more vulnerable to it. In one ex vivo clinical trial, bone marrow stem cells from about 30 women with late-stage ovarian cancer were infected with a virus carrying a gene to make them more tolerant of chemotherapy. Once the bone marrow stem cells were protected, it was possible to increase the level of chemotherapy to kill the cancer cells.

In a recent in vivo study, a retrovirus carrying a normal *p53* gene was injected directly into the tumor of lung cancer patients. This gene, which helps regulate the cell cycle and also brings about apoptosis in cells with damaged DNA, is often mutated in tumor cells. No cures were reported but the tumors shrank in three patients and stopped growing in three others. Expression of *p53* is only needed for a short time, and an elevated amount in normal cells seems to do them no harm.

Some investigators prefer the use of adenoviruses rather than retroviruses. Adenoviruses can be produced in much larger quantities, and they are active even when they are not dividing. (Retroviruses integrate DNA into the host chromosome where it is inactive unless replication occurs.) When adenoviruses infect a cell, they normally produce a protein that binds to *p53* and inactivates it. In a cleverly designed procedure, researchers genetically engineered adenoviruses to lack the gene that produces this protein. Therefore, the virus will kill tumor cells that lack *p53* but not healthy cells that have a *p53* gene. Clinical trials are underway, and it is expected that the virus will spread through the cancer, killing the cancer cells, and stopping when it reaches normal cells.

Other Illnesses

During coronary artery angioplasty, a balloon catheter is sometimes used to open up a closed artery. Unfortunately, the artery has a tendency to close up again. But investigators have come up with a new procedure. The balloon is coated with a plasmid that contains a gene for VEGF (vascular endothelial growth factor). The expression of the gene, which promotes the proliferation of blood vessels to bypass the obstructed area, has been observed in at least one patient.

Perhaps it will be possible also to use in vivo therapy to cure hemophilia, diabetes, Parkinson disease, or AIDS. To treat hemophilia, patients could get regular doses of cells that contain normal clotting-factor genes. Or such cells could be placed in organoids, artificial organs that can be implanted in the abdominal cavity. To cure Parkinson disease, dopamine-producing cells could be grafted directly into the brain.

The Human Genome Project produces information useful to gene therapists. Researchers are envisioning all sorts of ways to cure human genetic disorders as well as many other types of illnesses.

Connecting Concepts

Basic research into the nature and organization of genes in various organisms allowed geneticists to produce recombinant DNA molecules. A knowledge of transcription and translation made it possible for scientists to manipulate the expression of genes in foreign organisms. These breakthroughs have spurred a biotechnology revolution. One result is that bacteria and eukaryotic cells are now used to produce vaccines, hormones, and growth factors for use in humans. Today, plants and animals are also engineered to produce a product or have characteristics desired by humans. In addition, biotechnology offers the promise of treating and even someday curing human genetic disorders such as muscular dystrophy, cystic fibrosis, hemophilia, and many others. Mapping the human genome relies on both traditional linkage data and biotechnology techniques to discover the locus of many other genetic disorders. This is the first step toward the gene therapy that may result in a cure of various genetic disorders.

Some people are concerned that transgenic organisms may spread out of control and wreak ecological havoc, much as plants and animals new to an area sometimes do. Or they worry that transgenic plants may pass on their traits, such as resistance to pesticides or herbicides, to weeds that will then prosper as never before. Thus far a "superweed" has not occurred but that does not mean it could not happen in the future. The alteration of organisms as a result of genetic changes is one of the definitions of evolution, a topic that will be discussed in detail in the next section of the text.

Summary

17.1 Cloning of a Gene

Two methods are currently available for making copies of DNA. Recombinant DNA contains DNA from two different sources. A restriction enzyme is used to cleave plasmid DNA and to cleave foreign DNA. The "sticky ends" produced facilitate the insertion of foreign DNA into vector DNA. The foreign gene is sealed into the vector DNA by DNA ligase. Both bacterial plasmids and viruses can be used as vectors to carry foreign genes into bacterial host cells. A genomic library can be used as a source of genes to be cloned. A radioactive or fluorescent probe is used to identify the location of a single gene among the cloned fragments of an organism's DNA.

If just a portion of the genome is of interest or available, PCR uses the enzyme DNA polymerase to make multiple copies of target DNA. Analysis of DNA segments following PCR can involve gel electrophoresis to identify the DNA as belonging to a particular organism or can involve determining the base sequence of the DNA segment. The entire genome is used for fingerprinting. First, restriction enzymes are used to fragment DNA. Then the use of probes is necessary in order to see a pattern following gel electrophoresis.

17.2 Biotechnology Products

Transgenic organisms are ones that have had a foreign gene inserted into them. Genetically engineered bacteria, agricultural plants, and farm animals now produce commercial products of interest to humans, such as hormones and vaccines. Bacteria secrete the product. The seeds of plants and the milk of animals contain the product.

Transgenic bacteria have been produced to promote the health of plants, perform bioremediation, extract minerals, and produce chemicals. Transgenic agricultural plants which have been engineered to resist herbicides and pests are commercially available. Transgenic animals have been given various genes, in particular the one for bovine growth hormone (bGH). Cloning of animals is now possible.

17.3 The Human Genome Project

The Human Genome Project has two goals. The first goal is to construct a genetic map which will show the sequence of the genes on each chromosome. Although the known location of genes is expanding, the genetic map still contains many RFLPs (restriction fragment length polymorphisms) instead as the first step toward finding more genes. The second goal of the project is to sequence the bases on all the chromosomes. To do this researchers rely on PCR and automatic sequencing instruments. As the sequencers have improved so has the speed with which DNA is sequenced. The hope is that knowing the location and sequence of bases in a gene will promote the possibility of gene therapy.

17.4 Gene Therapy

Gene therapy is used to correct the genotype of humans and to cure various human ills. There are ex vivo and in vivo methods of gene therapy. Gene therapy has apparently helped children with SCID to lead a normal life; the treatment of cystic fibrosis has been less successful. A number of imaginative therapies are being employed in the war against cancer and other human illness such as cardiovascular disease.

Reviewing the Chapter

1. What is the methodology for producing recombinant DNA to be used in gene cloning?   266
2. Bacteria can be used to clone a gene or produce a product. Explain.   266–67
3. What is a genomic library, and how do you locate a gene of interest in the library?   267
4. What is the polymerase chain reaction (PCR), and how is it carried out to produce multiple copies of a DNA segment?   268
5. What is DNA fingerprinting, a process that utilizes the entire genome?   269
6. What are some practical applications of DNA segments analysis following PCR?   268–69
7. For what purposes have bacteria, plants, and animals been genetically altered?   270–73
8. Explain how and why transgenic animals that secrete a product are often cloned.   272–73
9. Explain the two primary goals of the Human Genome Project. What are the possible benefits of the project?   274
10. Explain and give examples of ex vivo and in vivo gene therapies in humans.   275

Testing Yourself

Choose the best answer for each question.

1. Which of these is a true statement?
   a. Both plasmids and viruses can serve as vectors.
   b. Plasmids can carry recombinant DNA but viruses cannot.
   c. Vectors carry only the foreign gene into the host cell.
   d. Only gene therapy uses vectors.
   e. Both a and d are correct.

2. Which of these is a benefit to having insulin produced by biotechnology?
   a. It is just as effective.   d. It is less expensive.
   b. It can be mass-produced.   e. All of these are
   c. It is nonallergenic.   correct.

3. Restriction fragment length polymorphisms (RFLPs)
   a. are achieved by using restriction enzymes.
   b. identify individuals genetically.
   c. are the basis for DNA fingerprints.
   d. can be subjected to gel electrophoresis.
   e. All of these are correct.

4. Which of these would you not expect to be a biotechnology product?
   a. vaccine   d. protein hormone
   b. modified enzyme   e. steroid hormone
   c. DNA probe

5. What is the benefit of using a retrovirus as a vector in gene therapy?
   a. It is not able to enter cells.
   b. It incorporates the foreign gene into the host chromosome.
   c. It eliminates a lot of unnecessary steps.
   d. It prevents infection by other viruses.
   e. Both b and c are correct.

6. Gel electrophoresis
   a. cannot be used on nucleotides.
   b. measures the size of plasmids.
   c. tells whether viruses are infectious.
   d. measures the charge and size of proteins and DNA fragments.
   e. All of these are correct.

7. Put these phrases in the correct order to form a plasmid carrying recombinant DNA.

   1 use restriction enzymes
   2 use DNA ligase
   3 remove plasmid from parent bacterium
   4 introduce plasmid into new host bacterium

   a. 1, 2, 3, 4
   b. 4, 3, 2, 1
   c. 3, 1, 2, 4
   d. 2, 3, 1, 4

8. Which of these is incorrectly matched?
   a. xenotransplantation—source of organs
   b. protoplast—plant cell engineering
   c. RFLPs—DNA fingerprinting
   d. DNA polymerase—PCR
   e. DNA ligase—mapping human chromosomes

9. The restriction enzyme called EcoRI has cut double-stranded DNA in this manner. The piece of foreign DNA to be inserted has what bases from left to the right?

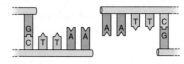

10. The following drawings pertain to gene therapy. Label the drawings, using these terms: retrovirus, recombinant RNA (twice), defective gene, recombinant DNA, reverse transcription, and human genome.

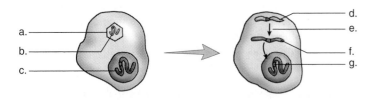

Thinking Scientifically

1. cDNA libraries contain only expressed DNA sequences. Therefore a cDNA library produced for a liver cell will contain genes unique to the cell. How could a CDNA library for a liver cell be used to acquire a complete copy of a liver-cell gene from a DNA library that contains the entire genome? A complete gene contains the promoter and introns.

2. There has been much popular interest in recreating extinct animals from DNA obtained from various types of fossils. However, such DNA is always badly degraded, consisting of extremely short pieces. Even if one hypothetically had 10 intact genes from a dinosaur, why might it still be impossible to create a dinosaur?

Bioethical Issue

Somatic gene therapy attempts to treat or prevent human illnesses. Some day, for example, it may be possible to give children who have cystic fibrosis, Huntington disease, or any other genetic disorder a normal gene to make up for the inheritance of a faulty gene. And gene therapy is even more likely for treatment of diseases like cancer, AIDS, and heart disease.

Germ-line gene therapy is the expression now being used to mean the use of gene therapy solely to improve the traits of an individual. It would be the genetic equivalent of procedures like body building, liposuction, or hair transplants. If genetic interference occurred early—that is, on the eggs, sperm, or embryo—it's possible that it would indeed affect the germ line—that is, all the future descendants of the individual.

How might germ-line gene therapy become routine? Consider this scenario. Presently, a gene for VEGF (vascular endothelial growth factor), a protein produced by cells to grow new blood vessels, is being used to treat atherosclerosis. Improved arterial circulation in the legs of some recent patients did away with the threat of possible amputation. This same gene is now being considered for the treatment of blocked coronary arteries. There may be instances, though, in which healthy people want to grow new blood vessels for enhancement purposes. Runners might want to improve their circulation in order to win races, and parents might think that increased circulation to the brain would increase the intelligence of their children. Bioethicist Eric Juengst of Case Western thinks that as a society, there is nothing we can now do to prevent us from crossing the line between the use of gene therapy for therapeutic purposes and its use for enhancement reasons. Do you have any concerns about gene therapy for enhancement reasons, such as its cost and general availability to everyone?

Understanding the Terms

bacteriophage 267	polymerase chain reaction
clone 266	(PCR) 268
complementary DNA	probe 267
(cDNA) 267	recombinant DNA (rDNA) 266
DNA fingerprinting 269	restriction enzyme 266
DNA ligase 266	restriction fragment length
gene therapy 275	polymorphism (RFLP) 269
genetic engineering 270	tissue engineering 271
genome 267	transgenic organism 270
genomic library 267	vector 266
plasmid 266	xenotransplantation 271

Match the terms to these definitions:

a. _____ Bacterial enzyme that stops viral reproduction by cleaving viral DNA; used to cut DNA at specific points during production of recombinant DNA.

b. _____ Free-living organisms in the environment that have had a foreign gene inserted into them.

c. _____ Known sequences of DNA that are used to find complementary DNA strands; can be used diagnostically to determine the presence of particular genes.

d. _____ Production of identical copies; in genetic engineering, the production of many identical copies of a gene.

e. _____ Self-duplicating ring of accessory DNA in the cytoplasm of bacteria.

Web Connections

Exploring the Internet

http://www.mhhe.com/biosci/genbio/mader
(click on *Biology 7/e*)

The *Biology 7/e* Online Learning Center provides many resources for studying the material in this chapter including links to the following sites:

The Howard Hughes Medical Institute's site, Blazing a Genetic Trail, focuses on the gene mutations that cause disease as they review recent genetic research and its applications.

http://www.hhmi.org/GeneticTrail/

The Human Genome Project describes the history of the project and progress made to date.

http://www.nhgri.nih.gov/HGP/

National Centre for Biotechnology Education. An overview of the origins and nature of biotechnology and enzymes used in food production can be found in Food Biotechnology: past, present, and future. This well-written, comprehensive website includes examples of current plant biotechnology, and plants that are currently undergoing field trials. Some of the concerns for environmental safety are explained.

http://www.ncbe.reading.ac.uk/

Biotechnology and Scientific Services Home Page. Information is found here on subjects ranging from GM (genetically modified) foods to regulation in the industry.

http://www.aphis.usda.gov/biotech/index.html

Recombinant DNA Chapter. This MIT hypertextbook chapter on immunology contains a wealth of information, particularly on the methodology involved in biotechnology.

http://esg-www.mit.edu:8001/esgbio/rdna/rdnadir.html

Further Readings for Part II

Ashley, M. January/February 1999. Molecular conservation genetics. *American Scientist* 87(1):28. Article discusses how knowing the structure of DNA in endangered species can help protect them.

Berns, M. W. April 1998. Laser scissors and tweezers. *Scientific American* 278(62):4. New laser techniques allow manipulation of chromosomes and other structures inside cells.

Borek, C. November/December 1997. Antioxidants and cancer. *Science & Medicine* 4(6):52. The importance of supplemental antioxidant vitamins depends on factors such as diet and lifestyle.

Curiel, T. September/October 1997. Gene therapy: AIDS-related malignancies. *Science & Medicine* 4(5):4. The field of AIDS-related gene therapies is advancing.

Galili, U. September/October 1998. Anti-Gal antibody prevents xenotransplantation. *Science & Medicine* 5(5):28. Prevention of interaction of the anti-Gal antibody with pig cells is necessary to the progress of xenotransplantation.

Garnick, M. B., and Fair, W. R. December 1998. Combating prostate cancer. *Scientific American* 279(6):74. Article details the recent developments in diagnosis and treatment of prostate cancer.

Glausiusz, J. May 1998. The great gene escape. *Discover* 19(5):90. Genes from genetically engineered plants can escape from crops into the wild, causing resistance in the wild plant.

Glausiusz, J. January 1999. The genes of 1998. *Discover* 20(1):33. Nine important human genes that were identified in 1998 through the Human Genome Project are examined.

Goldberg, J. April 1998. A head full of hope. *Discover* 19(4):70. A new gene therapy for killing brain cancer cells is presented.

Hawley, R. S., and Mori, C. A. 1999. *The human genome: A user's guide.* San Diego: Academic Press. This advanced text focuses on the genetics of human development, and covers other relevant genetic topics.

Jordan, V. C. October 1998. Designer estrogens. *Scientific American* 279(4):60. Selective estrogen receptor modulators may protect against breast and endometrial cancers, osteoporosis, and heart disease.

Kher, U. January 1998. A man-made chromosome. *Discover* 18(1):40. Researchers announce a promising new gene carrier, a human artificial chromosome, for use in gene therapy.

Miller, R. V. January 1998. Bacterial gene swapping in nature. *Scientific American* 278(1):66. The study of the process of DNA exchange between bacteria can help limit the risks of releasing genetically engineered microbes into the environment.

Moxon, E. R., and Wills, C. January 1999. DNA microsatellites: Agents of evolution? *Scientific American* 280(1):94. Repetitive DNA sequences may determine how an organism, such as a bacterium, adapts to its environment.

Nielson, P. E. September/October 1998. Peptide nucleic acids. *Science & Medicine* 5(5):48. Peptide nucleic acids mimic DNA and can substitute for DNA in gene therapy.

O'Brochta, D. A., and Atkinson, P. W. December 1998. Building a better bug. *Scientific American* 279(6):90. Transgenic insect technology could decrease pesticide use, and prevent certain infectious diseases. Article discusses the production of a transgenic insect.

Pennisi, E. 13 November 1998. Training viruses to attack cancers. *Science* 282(5392):1244. Certain viruses can replicate in and kill cancer cells, but leave normal tissue intact.

Plomerin, R., and DeFries, J. C. May 1998. The genetics of cognitive abilities and disabilities. *Scientific American* 278(5):62. The search is underway for the genes involved in cognitive abilities and disabilities, including dyslexia.

Pool, R. May 1998. Saviors. *Discover* 19(5):52. Genetic engineering may make animal organs compatible for human transplants.

Scientific American editors. 276(6):95. June 1997. Special report: Making gene therapy work. Obstacles must be overcome before gene therapy is ready for widespread use.

Scientific American 280(4):59–89. April 1999. The promise of tissue engineering. Much of the issue examines the hopes and challenges of tissue engineering for use in gene therapy and for the growth of new organs.

Scientific American Special Issue. 275(3). September 1996. What you need to know about cancer. The entire issue is devoted to the causes, prevention, and early detection of cancer, and cancer therapies—conventional and future.

Stix, G. October 1997. Growing a new field. *Scientific American* 277(4):15. Tissue engineers try to grow organs in the laboratory.

Stone, R. April 1999. Cloning the woolly mammoth. *Discover* 20(4):56. Researchers are searching for viable woolly mammoth sperm, with which they hope to impregnate an Asian elephant.

Van Noorden, C. J. F., et al. March/April 1998. Metastasis. *American Scientist* 86(2):130. The mechanisms by which cancer cells metastasize are discussed.

Velander, W. H., et al. January 1997. Transgenic livestock as drug factories. *Scientific American* 276(1):70. Farm animals can be bred to produce quantities of medicinal proteins in their milk.

Vogel, S. April 1999. Why we get fat. *Discover* 20(4):94. The genetic basis of obesity is examined.

Wills, C. January 1998. A sheep in sheep's clothing? *Discover* 18(1):22. Some pros and cons of cloning are discussed.

Wilmut, I. December 1998. Cloning for medicine. *Scientific American* 279(6):58. Cloning holds many benefits for the advancement of medical science and animal husbandry.

Winkonkal, N. M., and Brash, D. E. September/October 1998. Squamous cell carcinoma. *Science & Medicine* 5(5):18. Mutations of tumor-suppressor gene *p53* are commonly found in squamous cell carcinomas.

part iii

Evolution

Evolution refers to both descent with modification and adaptation to the environment. Descent from a common ancestor explains the unity of life—living things share a common chemistry and cellular structure because they are all descended from the same original source. Each type of living thing has a history that can be traced by way of the fossil record and discerned from a comparative study of other living things. Human evolution can also be understood by the application of these evolutionary principles.

Adaptation to a unique environment explains the diversity of life. Natural selection is a mechanism that results in adaptation to the environment. Individuals with variations that make them better adapted have more offspring than those who are not as well adapted. In that way certain characteristics become more common among a particular group of organisms. Each species has its own unique, evolved solutions to life's problems such as acquiring nutrients, finding a mate, and reproducing.

Darwin and Evolution

The modern horse, Equus, and its oligocene ancestor, Mesohippus.

M odern geologists believe the earth is more than 4 billion years old and that life began about 3.5 billion years ago. From simple, unicellular organisms, new life-forms arose and changed in response to environmental pressures, producing the past and present biodiversity. Prior to the 1800s, however, most people thought the earth was only a few thousand years old. They also believed that species were specially created and fixed in time. Change was explained by the notion of global catastrophes—mass extinctions and repopulations of species—had occurred periodically throughout history.

Into this prevailing climate came Charles Darwin, Alfred Wallace, and other innovative minds who changed the field of biology forever. On a five-year ocean voyage, Darwin observed many diverse life-forms, and he eventually concluded that species evolve in response to their environment. Further, all living things share common characteristics because they have a common ancestry. Because the concept of evolution challenged the widely accepted biblical account of creation, acceptance required an intellectual revolution of great magnitude.

18.1 History of the Theory of Evolution

Charles Darwin was only 22 in 1831 when he accepted the position of naturalist aboard the HMS *Beagle*, a British naval ship about to sail around the world (Fig. 18.1). Darwin's major mission was to expand the navy's knowledge of natural resources (e.g., water and food) in foreign lands. The captain was also hopeful that Darwin would find evidence of the biblical account of creation. The results of Darwin's observations were just the opposite, however, as we shall examine later in the chapter.

Table 18.1 tells us that prior to Darwin, people had an entirely different way of looking at the world. Their mind-set was determined by deep-seated beliefs held to be intractable truths. To turn from these beliefs and accept the

Figure 18.1 Voyage of the HMS *Beagle*.
a. Map shows the journey of the HMS *Beagle* around the world. Notice the encircled colors are keyed to the frames of the photographs, which show us what Charles Darwin may have observed. **b.** As Darwin traveled along the east coast of South America, he noted that a bird called a rhea looked like the African ostrich. **c.** The sparse vegetation of the Patagonian Desert is in the southern part of the continent. **d.** The Andes Mountains of the west coast, with strata containing fossilized animals. **e.** The lush vegetation of a rain forest. **f.** On the Galápagos Islands, marine iguanas have large claws to help them cling to rocks and blunt snouts for eating seaweed. **g.** Galápagos finches are specialized to feed on various foods.

Table 18.1

Contrast of Worldviews

Pre-Darwinian View	Post-Darwinian View
1. Earth is relatively young—age is measured in thousands of years.	1. Earth is relatively old—age is measured in billions of years.
2. Each species is specially created; species don't change, and the number of species remains the same.	2. Species are related by descent—it is possible to piece together a history of life on earth.
3. Adaptation to the environment is the work of a creator, who decided the structure and function of each type of organism. Any variations are imperfections.	3. Adaptation to the environment is the interplay of random variations and environmental conditions.
4. Observations are supposed to substantiate the prevailing worldview.	4. Observation and experimentation are used to test hypotheses, including hypotheses about evolution.

Darwinian view of the world required an intellectual revolution of great magnitude. This revolution was fostered by changes in both the scientific and the social realms. Here, we will only touch on a few of the scientific contributions that helped bring about the new worldview.

Although it is often believed that Darwin forged this change in worldview by himself, biologists during the preceding century had slowly begun to accept the idea of **evolution** [L. *evolutio,* an unrolling]; that is, that species change with time. Evolution explains the unity and diversity of life. Living things share common characteristics because they have a common ancestry. Living things are diverse because each species is adapted to its habitat and way of life. We will see that the history of evolutionary thought is a history of ideas about descent and adaptation. Darwin himself used the expression "descent with modification," by which he meant that as descent occurs through time so does diversification. He saw the process of adaptation as the means by which diversification comes about.

Mid-Eighteenth-Century Contributions

Taxonomy, the science of classifying organisms, was an important endeavor during the mid-eighteenth century. Chief among the taxonomists was Carolus Linnaeus (1707–78), who gave us the binomial system of nomenclature (a two-part name for species, such as *Homo sapiens*) and who developed a system of classification for all known plants. Linnaeus, like other taxonomists of his time, believed in the fixity of species. Each species had an "ideal" structure and function and also a place in the *scala naturae,* a sequential ladder of life. The simplest and most material of beings was on the lowest rung of the ladder, and the most complex and most spiritual of beings was on the highest rung. Human beings occupied the last rung of the ladder.

These ideas, which were consistent with Judeo-Christian teachings of special creation, can be traced to the works of the famous Greek philosophers Plato and

Figure 18.2 Linnaeus.
For the most part, Linnaeus believed that each species was created separately and that classification should reveal God's divine plan. Variations were imperfections of no real consequence.

Aristotle. Plato said that every object on earth was an imperfect copy of an ideal form, which can be deduced upon reflection and study. To Plato, individual variations were imperfections that only distract the observer. Aristotle saw that organisms were diverse, and some were more complex than others. His belief that all organisms could be arranged in order of increasing complexity became the scala naturae just described.

Linnaeus (Fig. 18.2) and other taxonomists wanted to describe the ideal characteristics of each species and also wanted to discover the proper place for each species in the scala naturae. Therefore, Linnaeus did not even consider the possibility of evolutionary change for most of his working life. There is evidence, however, that he did eventually perform hybridization experiments, which made him think that a species might change with time.

Georges-Louis Leclerc, better known by his title, Count Buffon (1707–88), was a French naturalist who devoted many years of his life to writing a 44-volume natural history that described all known plants and animals. He provided evidence of descent with modification, and he even speculated on various mechanisms such as environmental influences, migration, geographical isolation, and the struggle for existence. Buffon seemed to vacillate, however, as to whether or not he believed in evolutionary descent, and often he professed to believe in special creation and the fixity of species.

Erasmus Darwin (1731–1802), Charles Darwin's grandfather, was a physician and a naturalist. His writings on both botany and zoology contained many comments, although they were mostly in footnotes and asides, that suggested the possibility of common descent. He based his conclusions on changes undergone by animals during development, artificial selection by humans, and the presence of vestigial organs (organs that are believed to have been functional in an ancestor but are reduced and nonfunctional in a descendant). Like Buffon, Erasmus Darwin offered no mechanism by which evolutionary descent might occur.

Figure 18.3 A mastodon.
Although mastodons are known only from the fossil record, Cuvier reconstructed the structure of these animals when provided only with a single bone. He said these animals were shorter than modern elephants but had massive, pillarlike legs. The skull was lower and flatter and of generally simpler construction than in modern elephants.

Figure 18.4 Inheritance of acquired characteristics.
Jean-Baptiste de Lamarck is most famous for suggesting that the environment influences heritable traits. The long neck of the giraffe, he said, is due to continual stretching to reach food. Each generation of giraffes stretched a little farther, and this was passed to the next generation. With the advent of modern genetics, it became possible to explain why inheritance of acquired characteristics would not be possible.

Late Eighteenth-Century Contributions

Cuvier and Catastrophism

In addition to taxonomy, comparative anatomy was of interest to biologists prior to Darwin. Explorers and collectors traveled the world and brought back not only currently existing species to be classified but also fossils (remains of once-living organisms) to be studied. Georges Cuvier (1769–1832), a distinguished vertebrate (animals with backbones) zoologist, was the first to use comparative anatomy to develop a system of classifying animals. He also founded the science of **paleontology** [Gk. *palaios,* ancient, old, and *ontos,* having existed; -logy, study of, from *logikos,* rational, sensible], the study of fossils, and was quite skilled at using fossil bones to deduce the structure of an animal (Fig. 18.3).

Because Cuvier was a staunch advocate of special creation and fixity of species, he faced a real problem when a particular region showed a succession of life-forms in the earth's strata (layers). To explain these observations, he hypothesized that a series of local catastrophes or mass extinctions had occurred whenever a new stratum of that region showed a new mix of fossils. After each catastrophe, the region was repopulated by species from surrounding areas, and this accounted for the appearance of new fossils in the new stratum. The result of all these catastrophes was the appearance of change with time. Some of his followers even suggested that there had been worldwide catastrophes and that after each of these events, God created new sets of species. This explanation of the history of life came to be known as **catastrophism** [Gk. *katastrophe,* calamity, misfortune].

Lamarck's Theory of Evolution

Jean-Baptiste de Lamarck (1744–1829) was the first biologist to believe that evolution does occur and to link diversity with adaptation to the environment. Lamarck's ideas about descent were entirely different from those of Cuvier, perhaps because he was an invertebrate (animals without backbones) zoologist. Lamarck concluded, after studying the succession of life-forms in strata, that more complex organisms are descended from less complex organisms. He mistakenly said, however, that increasing complexity was the result of a natural force—a desire for perfection—that was inherent in all living things.

To explain the process of adaptation to the environment, Lamarck supported the idea of **inheritance of acquired characteristics**—that the environment can bring about inherited change. One example that he gave—and for which he is most famous—is that the long neck of a giraffe developed over time because animals stretched their necks to reach food high in trees and then passed on a long neck to their offspring (Fig. 18.4). The theory of the inheritance of acquired characteristics has never been substantiated by experimentation. The molecular mechanism of inheritance explains why. Phenotypic changes acquired during an organism's lifetime do not result in genetic changes that can be passed to subsequent generations.

Figure 18.5 Formation of sedimentary rock.
a. This diagram shows how water brings sediments into the sea; the sediments then become compacted to form sedimentary rock. Fossils are often trapped in this rock, and as a result of a later geological upheaval, the rock may be located on land.
b. Fossil remains of freshwater snails, *Turritella*, in sedimentary rocks.

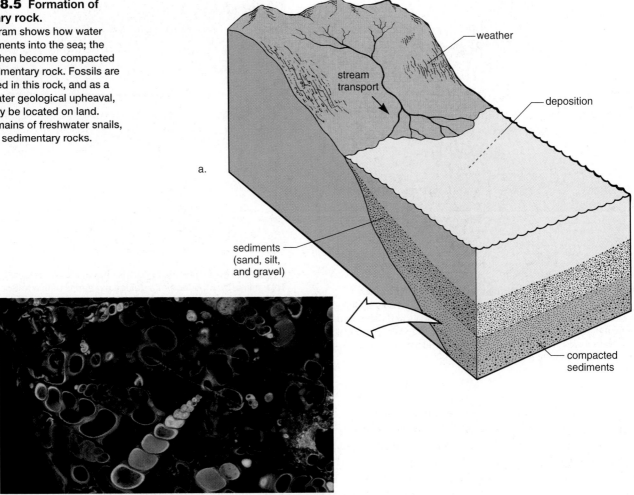

a.

weather

stream transport

deposition

sediments (sand, silt, and gravel)

compacted sediments

b.

18.2 Darwin's Theory of Evolution

When Darwin signed on as naturalist aboard the HMS *Beagle*, he had a suitable background for the position. He was an ardent student of nature and had long been a collector of insects. His sensitive nature prevented him from studying medicine, and he went to divinity school at Cambridge instead. Even so, he attended many lectures in both biology and geology, and he was also tutored in these subjects by a friend and teacher, the Reverend John Henslow. As a result of arrangements made by Henslow, Darwin spent the summer of 1831 doing fieldwork with Adam Sedgwick, a geologist at Cambridge, and it was Henslow who recommended Darwin for the post aboard the HMS *Beagle*. The trip was to take five years, and the ship was to traverse the Southern Hemisphere (see Fig. 18.1), where we now know that life is most abundant and varied. Along the way, Darwin encountered forms of life very different from those in his native England.

Occurrence of Descent

Although it was not his original intent, Darwin began to gather evidence that organisms are related through common descent and that adaptation to various environments results in diversity.

Geology and Fossils

Darwin took Charles Lyell's *Principles of Geology* on the voyage. This book presented arguments to support a theory of geological change proposed by James Hutton. In contrast to the catastrophists, Hutton believed the earth was subject to slow but continuous cycles of erosion and uplift. Weather causes erosion; thereafter dirt and rock debris are washed into the rivers and transported to oceans. These loose sediments are deposited in thick layers, which are converted eventually into sedimentary rocks (Fig. 18.5). Then sedimentary rocks, which often contain fossils, are uplifted from below sea level to form land. Hutton concluded that extreme geological changes can be accounted for by slow, natural processes, given enough time. Lyell went on to propose a theory of **uniformitarianism,** that these slow changes occurred at a uniform rate. Hutton's general ideas about slow and continual geological change are still accepted today, although modern geologists realize that rates of change have not always been uniform. Darwin was not taken by the idea of uniform change, but he was convinced, as was Lyell, that the earth's massive geological changes are the result of slow processes and that the earth, therefore, must be very old.

Figure 18.7 The Patagonian hare, *Dolichotis patagonium.*
This animal has the face of a guinea pig and is native to South America, which has no native rabbits. The Patagonian hare has long legs and other adaptations similar to those of rabbits.

Figure 18.6 Glyptodont compared to an armadillo.
a. A giant armadillo-like glyptodont, *Glyptodon,* known only by the study of its fossil remains. Darwin found such fossils and came to the conclusion that this extinct animal must be related to living armadillos. The glyptodont weighed 2,000 kilograms. **b.** A modern armadillo, *Dasypus,* weighs about 4.5 kilograms.

On his trip, Darwin observed massive geological changes firsthand. When he explored what is now Argentina, he saw raised beaches for great distances along the coast. When he got to the Andes, he was impressed by their great height. In Chile, he found marine shells inland, well above sea level, and witnessed the effects of an earthquake that caused the land to rise several feet. While Darwin was making geological observations, he also collected fossil specimens. For example, on the east coast of South America, he found the fossil remains of a giant ground sloth and an armadillo-like animal (Fig. 18.6). Once Darwin accepted the supposition that the earth must be very old, he began to think that there would have been enough time for descent with modification to occur. Therefore, living forms could be descended from extinct forms known only from the fossil record. It would seem that species were not fixed; instead they changed over time.

Darwin's geological observations were consistent with those of Hutton and Lyell. He began to think that the earth was very old, and there would have been enough time for descent with modification to occur.

Biogeography

Biogeography [Gk. *bios,* life, *geo,* earth, and *grapho,* writing] is the study of the geographic distribution of life-forms on earth. Darwin could not help but compare the animals of South America to those with which he was familiar. For example, instead of rabbits he found the Patagonian hare in

the grasslands of South America. The Patagonian hare has long legs and ears but the face of a guinea pig, a rodent native to South America (Fig. 18.7). Did the Patagonian hare resemble a rabbit because the two types of animals were adapted to the same type of environment? Both animals ate grass, hid in bushes, and moved rapidly using long hind legs. Did the Patagonian hare have the face of a guinea pig because of common descent with guinea pigs?

As he sailed southward along the eastern coast of the continent of South America, Darwin saw how similar species replaced each other. For example, the greater rhea (an ostrich-like bird) found in the north was replaced by the lesser rhea in the south. Therefore, Darwin reasoned that related species could be modified according to the environment. When he got to the Galápagos Islands, he found further evidence of this. The Galápagos Islands are a small group of volcanic islands off the western coast of South America. The few types of plants and animals found there were slightly different from species Darwin had observed on the mainland, and even more important, they also varied from island to island.

Tortoises   Each of the Galápagos Islands seemed to have its own type of tortoise, and Darwin began to wonder if this could be correlated with a difference in vegetation among islands (Fig. 18.8). Long-necked tortoises seemed to inhabit only dry areas, where food was scarce, most likely because the longer neck was helpful in reaching cacti. In moist regions with relatively abundant ground foliage, short-necked tortoises were found. Had an ancestral tortoise given rise to these different types, each adapted to a different environment?

a.   b.

Figure 18.8 Galápagos tortoises, *Testudo.*
Darwin wondered if all of the tortoises of the various islands were descended from a common ancestor. **a.** The tortoises with dome shells and short necks feed at ground level and are from well-watered islands where grass is available. **b.** Those with shells that flare up in front have long necks and are able to feed on tall treelike cacti. They are from arid islands where prickly pear cactus is the main food source. Only on these islands are the cacti treelike.

a. *Geospiza magnirostris*   b. *Certhidea olivacea*   c. *Cactornis scandens*

Figure 18.9 Galápagos finches.
Each of the present-day thirteen species of finches has a bill adapted to a particular way of life. **a.** For example, the heavy beak of the large ground-dwelling finch is suited to a diet of seeds. **b.** The beak of the warbler-finch is suited to feeding on insects found among ground vegetation or caught in the air. **c.** The long, somewhat decurved beak and the split tongue of the cactus-finch is suited to probing cactus flowers for nectar.

Finches   Although the finches on the Galápagos Islands seemed to Darwin like mainland finches, there are many more types (Fig. 18.9). Today, there are ground-dwelling finches with different-sized beaks, depending on the size of the seeds they feed on, and a cactus-eating finch with a more pointed beak. The beak size of the tree-dwelling finches also varies but according to the size of their insect prey. The most unusual of the finches is a woodpecker-type finch. This bird has a sharp beak to chisel through tree bark but lacks the woodpecker's long tongue which probes for insects. To make up for this, the bird carries a twig or cactus thorn in its beak and uses it to poke into crevices (see Fig. 18.1g). Once an insect emerges, the finch drops this tool and seizes the insect with its beak.

Later, Darwin speculated whether all the different species of finches he saw could have descended from a type of mainland finch. In other words, he wondered if a mainland finch was the common ancestor to all the types on the Galápagos Islands. Had speciation occurred because the islands allowed isolated populations of birds to evolve independently? Could the present-day species have resulted from accumulated changes occurring within each of these isolated populations?

Biogeography had a powerful influence on Darwin and made him think that adaptation to the environment accounts for diversification; one species can give rise to many species, each adapted differently.

Natural Selection and Adaptation

Once Darwin decided that adaptations develop over time (instead of being the instant work of a creator), he began to think about a mechanism by which adaptations might arise. Both Darwin and Alfred Russel Wallace, who is discussed in the reading on page 289, proposed **natural selection** as a mechanism for evolutionary change. Natural selection is a process in which preconditions (1–3) may result in certain consequences (4–5):

1. The members of a population have heritable variations.
2. In a population, many more individuals are produced each generation than the environment can support.
3. Some individuals have adaptive characteristics that enable them to survive and reproduce better than do other individuals.
4. An increasing proportion of individuals in succeeding generations have the adaptive characteristics.
5. The result of natural selection is a population adapted to its local environment.

Notice that because natural selection utilizes only variations that happen to be provided by genetic changes, it lacks any directedness or anticipation of future needs. Natural selection is an ongoing process because the environment of living things is constantly changing. Extinction (loss of a species) can occur when previous adaptations are no longer suitable to a changed environment.

Organisms Have Variations

Darwin emphasized that the members of a population vary in their functional, physical, and behavioral characteristics (Fig. 18.10). Before Darwin (see Table 18.1), variations were imperfections that should be ignored since they were not important to the description of a species. For Darwin, variations were essential to the natural selection process. Darwin suspected—but did not have the evidence we have today—that the occurrence of variations is completely random; they arise by accident and for no particular purpose. New variations are just as likely to be harmful as helpful to the organism.

The variations that make adaptation to the environment possible are those that are passed on from generation to generation. The science of genetics was not yet well established, so Darwin was never able to determine the cause of variations or how they are passed on. Today, we realize that genes determine the phenotype of an organism, and that mutations and recombination of alleles during sexual reproduction can cause new variations to arise.

Organisms Struggle to Exist

In Darwin's time, a socioeconomist, Thomas Malthus, stressed the reproductive potential of human beings. He proposed that death and famine were inevitable because the human population tends to increase faster than the supply of food. Darwin applied this concept to all organisms and

Figure 18.10 Variation in a population.
For Darwin, variations, such as those seen in a human population, were highly significant and were required for natural selection to result in adaptation to the environment.

saw that the available resources were not sufficient for all members of a population to survive. He calculated the reproductive potential of elephants. Assuming a life span of about 100 years and a breeding span of from 30 to 90 years, a single female probably bears no fewer than six young. If all these young survive and continue to reproduce at the same rate, after only 750 years, the descendants of a single pair of elephants will number about 19 million!

Each generation has the same reproductive potential as the previous generation. Therefore, there is a constant struggle for existence, and only certain members of a population survive and reproduce each generation.

Organisms Differ in Fitness

Fitness is the reproductive success of an individual relative to other members of a population. The most fit individuals are the ones that capture a disproportionate amount of resources, and that convert these resources into a larger number of viable offspring. Since organisms vary anatomically and physiologically and the challenges of local environments vary, what determines fitness varies for different populations. For example, among western diamondback rattlesnakes (*Crotalus atrox*) living on lava flows, the most fit are those that are black in color. But among those living on desert soil, the most fit are those with the typical light and dark brown coloring. Background matching helps an animal both capture prey and avoid being captured; therefore, it is expected to lead to survival and increased reproduction.

Alfred Russel Wallace (1823–1913) is best known as the English naturalist who independently proposed natural selection as a process to explain the origin of species (Fig. 18A). Like Darwin, Wallace was a collector at home and abroad. Even at age 14, while learning the trade of surveying, he became interested in botany and started collecting plants. While he was a schoolteacher at Leicester in 1844–45, he met Henry Walter Bates, an entomologist, who interested him in insects. Together they went on a collecting trip to the Amazon, which lasted for several years. Wallace's knowledge of the world's extensive flora and fauna was much expanded by a tour he made of the Malay Archipelago from 1854–62. After studying the animals of every important island, he divided the islands into a western group, with animals like those of the Orient, and an eastern group, with animals like those of Australia. The dividing line between the islands of the archipelago is a narrow but deep strait that is now known as the Wallace Line (Fig. 18B).

Like Darwin, Wallace was a writer of articles and books. As a result of his trip to the Amazon, he wrote two books, entitled *Travels on the Amazon and Rio Negro* and *Palm Trees of the Amazon.* In 1855, during his trip to Malay, he wrote an essay called "On the Law Which Has Regulated the Introduction of New Species." In the essay, he said that "every species has come into existence coincident both in time and space with a preexisting closely allied species." It's clear, then, that by this date he believed in the origin of new species rather than the fixity of species. Later, he said that he had pondered for many years about a mechanism to explain the origin of species. He, too, had read Malthus's treatise on human population increases and, in 1858, while suffering an attack of malaria, the idea of "survival of the fittest" came upon him. He quickly completed an essay discussing a natural selection process, which he chose to send to Darwin for comment. Darwin was stunned upon its receipt. Here before him was the

Figure 18A Alfred Russel Wallace.

hypothesis he had formulated as early as 1844 but had never dared to publish. In 1856 he had begun to work on a book that would supply copious data to support natural selection as a mechanism for evolutionary change. He told his friend and colleague Charles Lyell that Wallace's ideas were so similar to his own that even Wallace's "terms now stand as heads of my chapters."

Darwin suggested that Wallace's paper be published immediately, even though he as yet had nothing in print. Lyell and others who knew of Darwin's detailed work substantiating the process of natural selection suggested that a joint paper be read to the Linnean society. The title of Wallace's section was "On the Tendency of Varieties to Depart Indefinitely from the Original Type." Darwin presented an abstract of a paper he had written in 1844 and an abstract of his book *On the Origin of Species,* which was published in 1859.

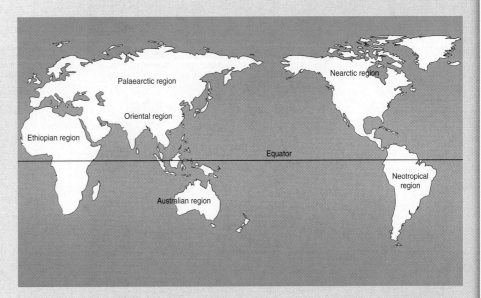

Figure 18B Biogeographical regions.
Aside from presenting a hypothesis that natural selection explains the origin of new species, Alfred Wallace is well known for another contribution. He said that the world can be divided into six biogeographical regions separated by impassable barriers. The deep waters between the Oriental and Australian regions are called the Wallace Line.

red chow

bloodhound

French bulldog

Boston terrier

Shetland sheepdog

dalmatian

Chihuahu

beagle

Figure 18.11 Artificial selection of animals.

All dogs, *Canis familiaris,* are descended from the wolf, *Canis lupus,* which began to be domesticated about 14,000 years ago. In evolutionary terms, the process of diversification has been exceptionally rapid. Several factors may have contributed: (1) the wolves under domestication were separated from other wolves because human settlements were separate, and (2) humans in each tribe selected for whatever traits appealed to them. Artificial selection of dogs continues even today.

Darwin noted that when humans help carry out *artificial selection,* the process by which a breeder chooses which traits to perpetuate, they select the animals that will reproduce. For example, prehistoric humans probably noted desirable variations among wolves and selected particular animals for breeding. Therefore, the desired traits increased in frequency in the next generation. This same process was repeated many times over. The result today is that there are many varieties of dogs all descended from the wolf (Fig. 18.11). In a similar way, several varieties of vegetables can be traced to a single ancestor. Chinese cabbage, brussels sprouts, and kohlrabi are all derived from a single species, *Brassica oleracea* (Fig. 18.12).

In nature, interactions with the environment determine which members of a population reproduce to a greater degree than other members. In contrast to artificial selection, the result of natural selection is not predesired. Natural selection occurs because certain members of a population happen to have a variation that allows them to survive and reproduce to a greater extent than other members. For example, any variation that increases the speed of a hoofed animal helps it escape predators and live longer; a variation that reduces water loss is beneficial to a desert plant; and one that increases the sense of smell helps a wild dog find its prey. Therefore, we expect organisms with these traits to have increased fitness.

Organisms Become Adapted

An **adaptation** [L. *ad,* toward, and *aptus,* fit, suitable] is a trait that helps an organism be more suited to its environment. We can especially recognize an adaptation when unrelated organisms, living in a particular environment, display similar characteristics. For example, manatees, penguins, and sea turtles all have flippers, which help them move through the water. Natural selection results in the adaptation of populations to their specific environments. Because of differential reproduction generation after generation, adaptive traits are increasingly represented in each succeeding generation. There are other processes of evolution aside from natural selection, but natural selection is the only process that results in adaptation to the environment.

On the Origin of Species by Darwin

After the HMS *Beagle* returned to England in 1836, Darwin waited more than 20 years to publish his ideas. During the intervening years, he used the scientific process to test his hypothesis that today's diverse life-forms arose by descent from a common ancestor and that natural selection is a mechanism by which species can change and even new species can arise. Darwin was prompted to publish his book after reading a similar hypothesis from Alfred Russel Wallace, as discussed in the reading on page 289.

Darwin became convinced that descent with modification explains the history of life. His theory of natural selection proposes a mechanism by which adaptation to the environment occurs.

a.   b.   c.

Figure 18.12 Artificial selection of plants.
All these vegetables are derived from a single species of *Brassica oleracea.* **a.** Chinese cabbage. **b.** Brussels sprouts. **c.** Kohlrabi. Darwin believed that artificial selection provided a model by which to understand natural selection. With natural selection, however, the environment provides the selective force.

18.3 Evidence for Evolution

Many different lines of evidence support the hypothesis that organisms are related through common descent. This is significant, because the more varied the evidence supporting a hypothesis, the more certain it becomes. Darwin cited much of the evidence we will discuss, except he had no knowledge, of course, of the biochemical data that became available after his time.

Fossil Evidence

The **fossil record** is the history of life recorded by remains from the past. Fossils are at least 10,000 years old and include such items as pieces of bone, impressions of plants pressed into shale, and even insects trapped in tree resin (which we know as amber). For the last two centuries, paleontologists have studied fossils in the earth's strata (layers) all over the world and have pieced together the story of past life.

The fossil record is rich in information. One of its most striking patterns is the succession of life-forms over time. Catastrophists offered an explanation for the extinction and subsequent replacement of one group of organisms by another group, but they never could explain successive changes that link groups of organisms historically. Particularly interesting are the fossils that serve as transitional links between groups. The amphibious fish *Eustheopteron*, the reptile-like amphibian *Seymouria*, and the mammal-like reptiles, or therapsids are well-known examples. Two newly found fossils from China, *Protarchaeopteryx* and *Caudipteryx* (Fig.

18.13), offer even more convincing evidence than the famous fossil, *Archaeopteryx*, that birds are descended from dinosaurs. Called by some, one of the most exciting discoveries of the century, if not the discovery of the century, these fossils are definitely recognized as dinosaurs that had feathers on their arms and tails. There is some evidence of body feathers as well. It is speculated that flapping their forelimbs while running may have given them added speed in chasing prey and escaping predators. Once lift-off occurred in a descendent, birds came into existence.

Sometimes the fossil record is complete enough to allow us to trace the history of an organism, such as the modern-day horse, *Equus* (Fig. 18.14). *Equus* evolved originally from *Hyracotherium*, which was about the size of a large dog (35 kg). This fossil animal had cusped, low-crowned molars, four toes on each front foot, and three toes on each hind foot. When grasslands replaced the forest home of *Hyracotherium*, the ancestors of *Equus* were subject to selective pressure for the development of strength, intelligence, speed, and durable grinding teeth. A larger size provided the strength needed for combat, a larger skull made room for a larger brain, elongated legs ending in hooves provided greater speed to escape enemies, and the durable grinding teeth enabled the animals to feed efficiently on grasses.

Figure 18.14 shows that the evolutionary history of *Equus* is like a tree, with multiple branchings and rebranchings from one source. A common ancestor is at each fork of the evolutionary tree, and we can trace the evolutionary history of *Equus* from common ancestor to common ances-

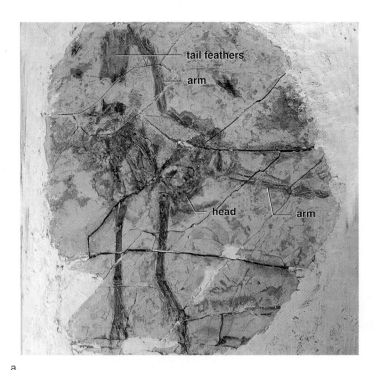

a.

b.

Figure 18.13 Transitional link.
a. *Caudipteryx*, discovered in 1998, is hailed by most paleontologists as unambiguous evidence of a dinosaur–bird link. Skeletal evidence that birds are descended from dinosaurs includes the similarity of their breastbones, three-toed feet, hollow bones, and swiveling wrist joints. b. Artist's representation of *Caudipteryx*.

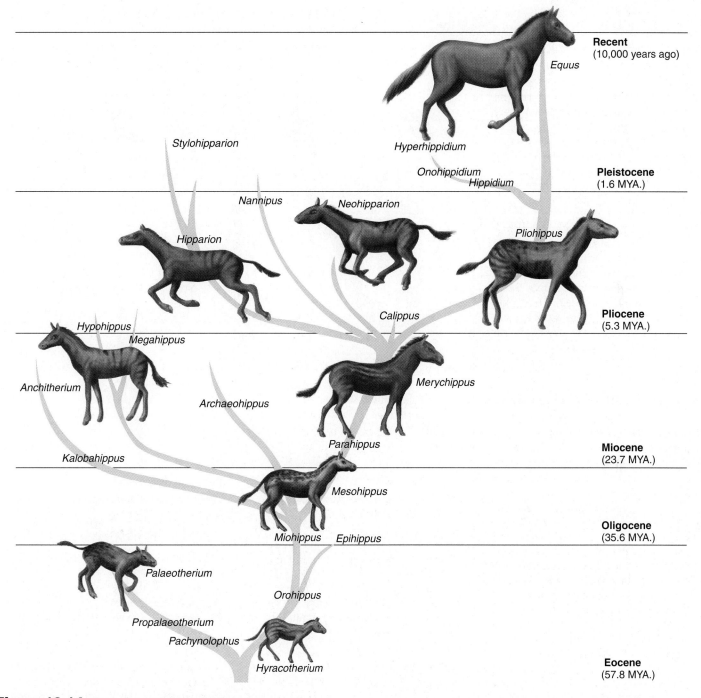

Figure 18.14 Evolutionary history of *Equus.*
The evolutionary tree of *Equus* is known to have included many branchings, several of which came to dead ends. By ignoring these, it is possible to trace the history of *Equus* back to *Hyracotherium.*

tor through time. When we do so, there appears to have been a gradual change in form from *Hyracotherium* to *Equus.* We can also observe that many of the side branches became **extinct,** that is, died out. The paleontologist George Gaylord Simpson estimated that 99.9% of all species eventually become extinct. We can hypothesize that environments are constantly changing and that the ability to adapt to a changing environment is a requirement for long-term survival of the species.

Living organisms closely resemble the most recent fossils in their line of descent. Fossils can be linked over time because there is a similarity in form, despite observed changes; therefore, the fossil record supports common descent.

The fossil record broadly traces the history of life and more specifically allows us to study the history of particular groups.

The Pace of Evolution

Evolutionists who support phyletic gradualism [Gk. *phyle,* tribe], as did Darwin, suggest that evolutionary change is rather slow and steady. In other words, fossils of the same species designation can show a trend over time, say a change in plumage color (Fig. 18C*a*). Further divergence, when a common ancestor gives rise to two separate lineages, is not necessarily dependent upon speciation—that is, the origination of a new species. Indeed, the fossil record, even if complete, is unlikely to indicate when speciation has occurred. Since evolution occurs gradually, transitional links (see Fig. 18.13) are expected and most likely more will eventually be found in the fossil record.

Is the phyletic gradualism model applicable to the evolutionary history of *Equus* (Fig. 18.14)? Is it possible, for example, to show overall trends such as an increase in size, an increase in the grinding surface of the molar teeth, and a reduction in the number of toes? Most agree that it is applicable only if we pick and choose among the many fossils available. Closer examination reveals that as *Hyracotherium* evolved into *Equus,* the evolution of every character varied greatly, and there were even times of reversal. If one of the ancestral animals had lived on and *Equus* had become extinct, we no doubt would be discussing a different set of "trends."

Considering such difficulties, other paleontologists—Stephen J. Gould, Nile Eldredge, and Steven Stanley in particular—have proposed a new model they call punctuated equilibrium (Fig. 18C*b*). They point out there are examples of organisms that are called *living fossils* because they are so similar to an ancestor known from the fossil record. A few years ago, investigators found exquisitely preserved specimens of cyanobacteria that have the same sizes, shapes, and organization as living forms. These findings suggest that the cyanobacteria of today have not changed at all in over 3 billion years. Among plants, the dawn redwood was thought to be extinct; then a living specimen was discovered in a small area of China. Horseshoe crabs, crocodiles, and coelacanth fish are animals that still resemble their earli-

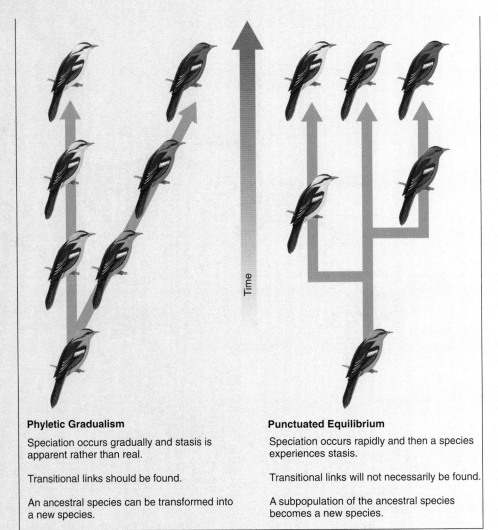

Phyletic Gradualism

Speciation occurs gradually and stasis is apparent rather than real.

Transitional links should be found.

An ancestral species can be transformed into a new species.

Punctuated Equilibrium

Speciation occurs rapidly and then a species experiences stasis.

Transitional links will not necessarily be found.

A subpopulation of the ancestral species becomes a new species.

Figure 18C Phyletic gradualism versus punctuated equilibrium.
The differences between phyletic gradualism and punctuated equilibrium are reflected in these patterns of time versus speciation.

est ancestors. A recently found scaly anteater fossil shows that these animals have changed minimally in 60 million years. A time of limited evolutionary change in a lineage is called *stasis.*

In most lineages, however, a period of equilibrium (stasis) is punctuated by evolutionary change—that is, speciation occurs. With reference to the length of the fossil record (about 3.5 billion years), speciation occurs relatively rapidly. Therefore, transitional links are less likely to become fossils, and to be found! Indeed, speciation most likely involves only an isolated population at one locale. Only when a new species evolves and displaces existing species, is it apt to show up in the fossil record.

Carlton Brett at the University of Rochester studied the sequence of fossil communities in the Devonian seas that covered the present state of New York 360 to 408 million years ago. He found that the mix of species in a community did not change as long as the sea level remained high. A low sea level disrupted the community and there was a change of species that maintained itself throughout the next interval of a high sea level. It would appear that gradual evolutionary processes are the norm but environmental disturbances promote rapid evolutionary change and the replacement of old species by new species.

Biogeographical Evidence

Biogeography is the study of the distribution of plants and animals throughout the world. Such distributions are consistent with the hypothesis that related forms evolved in one locale and then spread out into other accessible regions. As previously mentioned, Darwin noted that South America lacked rabbits, even though the environment was quite suitable to them. He concluded there are no rabbits in South America because rabbits originated somewhere else and they had no means to reach South America.

The islands of the world have many unique species of animals and plants found no place else, even when the soil and climate are the same as other places. Why are there so many species of finches on the Galápagos Islands when these same species are not on the mainland? The reasonable explanation is that the same ancestral finch originally inhabited the different islands. Geographic isolation allowed the ancestral finch to evolve into a different species on each island.

Physical factors, such as the location of continents, often determine where a population can spread. Both cacti and euphorbia are plants adapted similarly to a hot, dry environment—they both are succulent, spiny, flowering plants. Why do cacti grow in North American deserts and euphorbia grow in African deserts when each would do well on the other continent? It seems obvious that they just happened to evolve on their respective continents.

At one time in the history of the earth, South America, Antarctica, and Australia were all connected. Marsupials (pouched mammals) arose at this time, and today are found in both South America and Australia. When Australia separated and drifted away, the marsupials diversified into many different forms suited to various environments (Fig. 18.15). They were free to do so because there were few, if any, placental mammals in Australia. In other regions such as South America, where there are placental mammals, marsupials are not as diverse.

> The distribution of organisms on the earth is explainable by assuming that related forms evolved in one locale. They then diversified as they spread out into other accessible areas.

Coarse-haired wombat, *Vombatus*, nocturnal and living in burrows

Kangaroo, *Macropus*, a herbivore of plains and forests

Australian native cat, *Dasyurus*, a carnivore of forests

Sugar glider, *Petaurista*, a tree dweller

Tasmanian wolf, *Thylacinus*, a nocturnal carnivore of deserts and plains

Figure 18.15 Biogeography.
Each type of marsupial in Australia is adapted to a different way of life. All of the marsupials in Australia presumably evolved from a common ancestor that entered Australia some 60 million years ago.

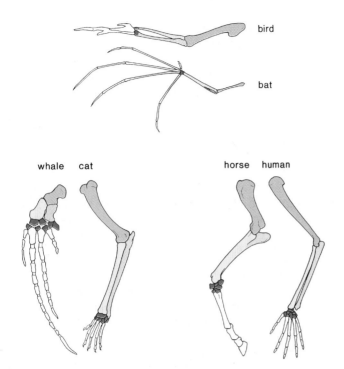

Figure 18.16 **Significance of structural similarities.**
Although the specific design details of vertebrate forelimbs are
different, the same bones are present (they are color-coded). This unity
of plan is evidence of a common ancestor.

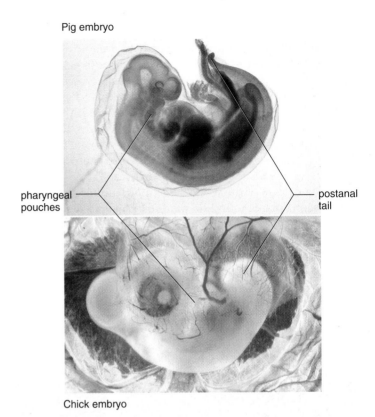

Figure 18.17 **Significance of developmental similarities.**
At this comparable developmental stage, a chick embryo and a pig
embryo have many features in common, which suggests they evolved
from a common ancestor.

Anatomical Evidence

Darwin was able to show that a common descent hypothesis
offers a plausible explanation for anatomical similarities
among organisms. Vertebrate forelimbs are used for flight
(birds and bats), orientation during swimming (whales and
seals), running (horses), climbing (arboreal lizards), or swing-
ing from tree branches (monkeys). Yet all vertebrate forelimbs contain the same sets of bones organized in similar
ways, despite their dissimilar functions (Fig. 18.16). The most
plausible explanation for this unity is that the basic forelimb
plan belonged to a common ancestor, and then the plan was
modified in the succeeding groups as each continued along
its own evolutionary pathway. Structures that are anatomically similar because they are inherited from a common
ancestor are called **homologous structures** [Gk. *homologos*,
agreeing, corresponding]. In contrast, **analogous structures**
serve the same function but they are not constructed similarly,
nor do they share a common ancestry. The wings of birds
and insects are analogous structures. The presence of homology, not analogy, is evidence that organisms are related.

Vestigial structures [L. *vestigium*, trace, footprint] are
anatomical features that are fully developed in one group of
organisms but are reduced and may have no function in
similar groups. Most birds, for example, have well-developed wings used for flight. Some bird species (e.g., ostrich),
however, have greatly reduced wings and do not fly. Similarly, snakes have no use for hindlimbs, and yet some have
remnants of a pelvic girdle and legs. Humans have a

tailbone but no tail. The presence of vestigial structures can
be explained by the common descent hypothesis. Vestigial
structures occur because organisms inherit their anatomy
from their ancestors; they are traces of an organism's evolutionary history.

The homology shared by vertebrates extends to their
embryological development (Fig. 18.17). At some time during development, all vertebrates have a postanal tail and exhibit paired pharyngeal pouches. In fishes and amphibian
larvae, these pouches develop into functioning gills. In humans, the first pair of pouches becomes the cavity of the
middle ear and the auditory tube. The second pair becomes
the tonsils, while the third and fourth pairs become the thymus and parathyroid glands. Why should terrestrial vertebrates develop and then modify structures like pharyngeal
pouches that have lost their original function? The most
likely explanation is that fishes are ancestral to other vertebrate groups.

Organisms that share homologous structures are closely
related and have a common ancestry. This is
substantiated by comparative anatomy and
embryological development.

Biochemical Evidence

Almost all living organisms use the same basic biochemical molecules, including DNA (deoxyribonucleic acid), ATP (adenosine triphosphate), and many identical or nearly identical enzymes. Further, organisms utilize the same DNA triplet code and the same 20 amino acids in their proteins. Organisms even share the same introns and type of repeats. There is obviously no functional reason why these elements need be so similar. But their similarity can be explained by descent from a common ancestor.

Also of interest, evo-devo researchers (evolutionary developmental biologists) have found that many developmental genes are shared in animals ranging from worms to humans. It appears that life's vast diversity has come about by only a slight difference in the same genes. The result has been widely divergent body plans. For example, a similar gene in arthropods and vertebrates determines the dorsal-ventral axis. But although the base sequences are similar, the genes have opposite effects. Therefore in arthropods, like fruit flies and crayfish, the neural tube is ventral, whereas in vertebrates, like chicks and humans, the neural tube is dorsal.

When the degree of similarity in DNA base sequences or the degree of similarity in amino acid sequences of proteins is examined, the data are as expected assuming common descent. Cytochrome *c* is a molecule that is used in the electron transport system of all the organisms appearing in Figure 18.18. Data regarding differences in the amino acid sequence of the cytochrome *c* show that in a human it differs from that in a monkey by only one amino acid, from that in a duck by 11, and from that in *Candida*, a yeast, by 51 amino acids. These data are consistent with other data regarding the anatomical similarities of these animals, and therefore their relatedness.

Darwin discovered that many lines of evidence support the hypothesis of common descent. Since his time, it has been found that biochemical evidence also supports the hypothesis. A hypothesis is strengthened when it is supported by many different lines of evidence.

Evolution is no longer considered a hypothesis. It is one of the great unifying theories of biology. In science, the word *theory* is reserved for those conceptual schemes that are supported by a large number of observations and have not yet been found lacking. The theory of evolution has the same status in biology that the germ theory of disease has in medicine.

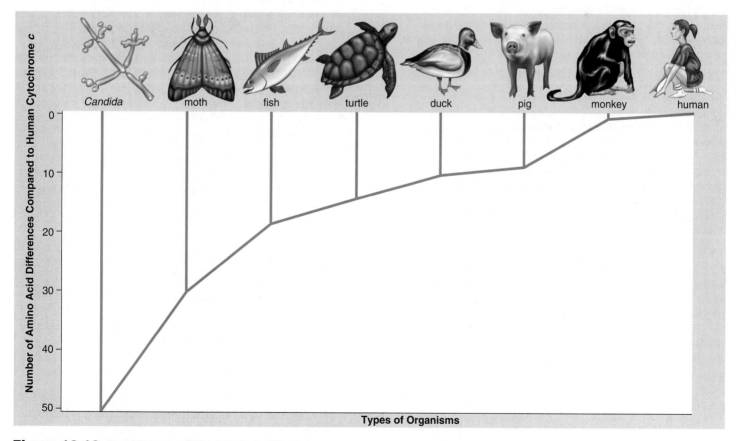

Figure 18.18 **Significance of biochemical differences.**
The branch points in this diagram tell the number of amino acids that differ between human cytochrome *c* and the organisms depicted. These biochemical data are consistent with that provided by a study of the fossil record and comparative anatomy.

Connecting Concepts

Before the 1800s, most people believed that the origin and diversity of life on earth was due to the work of a supernatural being who created each species at the beginning of the world, and modern organisms are essentially unchanged descendants of their ancestors. Scientists, however, seek natural, testable hypotheses to explain natural events rather than relying on religious dogma.

At the time Charles Darwin boarded the *Beagle,* he had studied writings of his grandfather Erasmus Darwin, James Hutton, Charles Lyell, Lamarck, Malthus, Linnaeus, and other original thinkers. He had ample time during his five-year voyage to reflect on the ideas of these authors, and collectively, they built a framework that helped support his theory of descent with modifications.

One aspect of scientific genius is the power of astute observation—to see what others miss or fail to appreciate. In this area, Darwin excelled. By the time he reached the Galápagos Islands, Darwin had already begun to hypothesize that species could be modified according to the environment. His observation of the finches on the isolated Galápagos Islands supported his hypothesis. He concluded that the finches on each island varied from each other and from mainland finches because each species had become adapted to a different habitat; therefore, one species had given rise to many. The fact that Alfred Wallace almost simultaneously proposed natural selection as an evolutionary mechanism suggests that the world was ready for a revised view of life on earth.

The theory of evolution has quite rightly been called the grand unifying theory (GUT) of biology. Fossils, comparative anatomy, biogeography, and biochemical data all indicate that living things share common ancestors. Evolutionary principles help us understand why organisms are different and alike, and why some species flourish and others die out. As the earth's habitats change over millions of years, those individuals with the traits best adapted to new environments survive and reproduce; thus populations change over time.

Summary

18.1 History of the Theory of Evolution

In general, the pre-Darwinian worldview was different from the post-Darwinian worldview (see Table 18.1). The scientific community, however, was ready for a new worldview, and it received widespread acceptance.

A century before Darwin's trip, classification of organisms had been a main concern of biology. Linnaeus thought that classification should describe the fixed features of species and reveal God's divine plan. Gradually, some naturalists, such as Count Buffon and Erasmus Darwin, began to put forth tentative suggestions that species do change over time.

Georges Cuvier and Jean-Baptiste de Lamarck, contemporaries of Darwin in the late eighteenth century, differed sharply on evolution. To explain the fossil record of a region, Cuvier proposed that a whole series of catastrophes (extinctions) and repopulations from other regions had occurred. Lamarck said that descent with modification does occur and that organisms do become adapted to their environments; however, he relied on commonly held beliefs (*scala naturae* and inheritance of acquired characteristics) to substantiate and provide a mechanism for evolutionary change.

18.2 Darwin's Theory of Evolution

Charles Darwin formulated hypotheses concerning evolution after taking a trip around the world as naturalist aboard the HMS *Beagle* (1831–36). His hypotheses were that common descent does occur and that natural selection results in adaptation to the environment.

Darwin's trip involved two primary types of observations. His study of geology and fossils caused him to concur with Lyell that the observed massive geological changes were caused by slow, continuous changes. Therefore, he concluded that the earth is old enough for descent with modification to occur.

Darwin's study of biogeography, including the animals of the Galápagos Islands, allowed him to conclude that adaptation to the environment can cause diversification, including the origin of new species.

Natural selection is the mechanism Darwin proposed for how adaptation comes about. Members of a population exhibit random but inherited variations. (In contrast to the previous worldview, variations are highly significant.) Relying on Malthus's ideas regarding overpopulation, Darwin stressed that there was a struggle for existence. The most fit organisms are those possessing characteristics that allow them to acquire more resources, survive, and reproduce more than the less fit. In this way, natural selection results in adaptation to a local environment.

18.3 Evidence for Evolution

The hypothesis that organisms share a common descent is supported by many lines of evidence. The fossil record, biogeography, comparative anatomy, and comparative biochemistry all support the hypothesis. The fossil record gives us the history of life in general and allows us to trace the descent of a particular group. Biogeography shows that the distribution of organisms on earth is explainable by assuming organisms evolved in one locale. Comparing the anatomy and the development of organisms reveals a unity of plan among those that are closely related. All organisms have certain biochemical molecules in common, and any differences indicate the degree of relatedness. A hypothesis is greatly strengthened when many different lines of evidence support it.

Today, the theory of evolution is one of the great unifying theories of biology because it has been supported by so many different lines of evidence.

Reviewing the Chapter

1. In general, contrast the pre-Darwinian worldview with the post-Darwinian worldview.   283
2. Cite naturalists who made contributions to biology in the mid-eighteenth century, and state their beliefs about evolutionary descent.   283
3. How did Cuvier explain the succession of life-forms in the earth's strata?   284
4. What is meant by the inheritance of acquired characteristics, a hypothesis that Lamarck used to explain adaptation to the environment?   284
5. What reading did Darwin do, and what observations did he make regarding geology?   285
6. What observations did Darwin make regarding biogeography? How did these influence his conclusions about the origin of new species?   286–87

7. What are the essential features of the process of natural selection as proposed by Darwin?   288
8. Distinguish between the concepts of fitness and adaptation to the environment.   288, 291
9. How do data from the fossil record support the concept that organisms are related through common descent? Explain why *Equus* is vastly different from its ancestor *Hyracotherium*, which lived in a forest.   292–93
10. How do data from biogeography support the concept of common descent? Explain why a diverse assemblage of marsupials evolved in Australia.   295
11. How do data from comparative anatomy support the concept of common descent? Explain why vertebrate forelimbs are similar despite different functions.   296
12. How do data from biochemical studies support the concept of common descent? Explain why the sequence of amino acids in cytochrome *c* differs between two organisms.   297

Testing Yourself

Choose the best answer for each question.

1. According to the theory of acquired inheritance,
   a. if a man loses his hand, then his children will also be missing a hand.
   b. changes in phenotype are passed on by way of the genotype to the next generation.
   c. organisms are able to bring about a change in their phenotype.
   d. evolution is striving toward particular traits.
   e. All of these are correct.
2. Why was it helpful to Darwin to learn that Lyell thought the earth was very old?
   a. An old earth has more fossils than a new earth.
   b. It meant there was enough time for evolution to have occurred slowly.
   c. There was enough time for the same species to spread out into all continents.
   d. Darwin said that artificial selection occurs slowly.
   e. All of these are correct.
3. All the finches on the Galápagos Islands
   a. are unrelated but descended from a common ancestor
   b. are descended from a common ancestor and therefore related.
   c. rarely compete for the same food source.
   d. Both a and c are correct.
   e. Both b and c are correct.
4. Organisms
   a. compete with other members of their species.
   b. differ in fitness.
   c. are adapted to their environment.
   d. are related by descent from common ancestors.
   e. All of these are correct.
5. DNA nucleotide differences between organisms
   a. indicate how closely related organisms are.
   b. indicate that evolution occurs.
   c. explain why there are phenotypic differences.
   d. are to be expected.
   e. All of these are correct.
6. If evolution occurs, we would expect different biogeographical regions with similar environments to
   a. all contain the same mix of plants and animals.
   b. each have its own specific mix of plants and animals.

c. have plants and animals with similar adaptations.
   d. have plants and animals with different adaptations.
   e. Both b and c are correct.
7. The fossil record offers direct evidence for common descent because you can
   a. see that the types of fossils change over time.
   b. sometimes find common ancestors.
   c. trace the ancestry of a particular group.
   d. trace the biological history of living things.
   e. All of these are correct.
8. Organisms such as whales and sea turtles which are adapted to an aquatic way of life
   a. will probably have homologous structures.
   b. will have similar adaptations but not necessarily homologous structures.
   c. may very well have analogous structures.
   d. will have the same degree of fitness.
   e. Both b and c are correct.

For questions 9–12, offer an explanation for each of these observations based on information in the section indicated. Write out your answer.

9. Fossils can be dated according to the strata in which they are located. See Fossil Evidence (p. 292).
10. Cacti and euphorbia exist on different continents, but both have spiny, water-storing, leafless stems. See Biogeographical Evidence (p. 295).
11. Amphibians, reptiles, birds, and mammals all have pharyngeal pouches at some time during development. See Anatomical Evidence (p. 296).
12. The base sequence of DNA differs from species to species. See Biochemical Evidence (p. 297).

Thinking Scientifically

1. Because viruses are rapidly replicated, it is possible to observe hundreds of generations in a single host (infected organism). Some viruses (such as influenza and HIV) evolve rapidly, and others (such as rabies virus and poliovirus) are relatively stable. Two selective forces that influence the speed of viral evolution are (1) the strength of the host immune response which works to destroy the virus and (2) host behavior in assisting transmission of the virus. How could these two selective forces influence the speed of viral evolution?
2. DNA evidence shows that the closest living relatives of elephants are manatees, aquatic mammals found in the Atlantic Ocean. Two possibilities exist: manatees evolved from elephants (or their immediate ancestors), or elephants evolved from manatees (or their immediate ancestors). A study of embryonic and adult anatomy of manatees and elephants might reveal structures that would help to more firmly establish the evolutionary relationship between these two animals. Hypothesize what kind of structures these might be.

Bioethical Issue

Evolution is a scientific theory. So is the cell theory, which says that all organisms are composed of cells, and so is the atomic theory that says all matter is composed of atoms. Yet, no one argues that schools should teach alternatives to the cell theory or the subatomic theory. Confusion reigns over the use of the expression, "the theory of evolution." But the term *theory* in science is reserved for those ideas that scientists have found to be all-encompassing because they are based on data collected in a number of different fields.

No wonder most scientists in our country are dismayed when state legislatures or school boards rule that teachers must put forward a variety of "theories" on the origin of life, including one that runs contrary to the mass of data that supports the theory of evolution. An institute in California called the Institute for Creation Research advocates that students be taught an "intelligent-design theory" which says that DNA could never have arisen without the involvement of an "intelligent agent," and that gaps in the fossil record mean that species arose fully developed with no antecedents.

Since our country forbids the mingling of church and state—no purely religious ideas can be taught in the schools—the advocates for an intelligent-design theory are careful to never mention the Bible or any ideas like "God created the world in seven days." Still, teachers who have a good scientific background do not feel comfortable teaching an intelligent-design theory because it does not meet the test of a scientific theory. Science is based on hypotheses that have been tested by observation and/or experimentation. A scientific theory has stood the test of time—no hypotheses have been supported by observation and/or experimentation that runs counter to the theory. Indeed, the theory of evolution is supported by data collected in such wide-ranging fields as development, anatomy, geology, biochemistry, and so forth.

The polls consistently show that nearly half of all Americans prefer to believe the Old Testament account of how God created the world in seven days. That, of course, is their right, but should schools be required to teach an intelligent-design theory that traces its roots back to the Old Testament, and is not supported by observation and experimentation?

Understanding the Terms

adaptation 291
analogous structure 296
biogeography 286
catastrophism 284
evolution 283
extinct 293
fitness 288
fossil record 292

homologous structure 296
inheritance of acquired
   characteristics 284
natural selection 288
paleontology 284
uniformitarianism 285
vestigial structure 296

Match the terms to these definitions:

a. _____ Study of the geographical distribution of organisms.
b. _____ Study of fossils that results in knowledge about the history of life.
c. _____ Poorly developed structure that was complete and functional in an ancestor but is no longer functional in a descendant.
d. _____ Organism's modification in structure, function, or behavior suitable to the environment.
e. _____ Lamarckian belief that organisms become adapted to their environment during their lifetime and pass on these adaptations to their offspring.

Web Connections

Exploring the Internet

http://www.mhhe.com/biosci/genbio/mader
(click on *Biology 7/e*)

The *Biology 7/e* Online Learning Center provides many resources for studying the material in this chapter including links to the following sites:

Darwin-Wallace 1858 Paper on Evolution. From this site you can search and read the seminal paper and related works.

http://www.inform.umd.edu/PBIO/darwin/darwindex.html

The Slow Death of Spontaneous Generation (1668–1859) describes the lengthy history of this belief and the major players who sought to refute this idea. Louis Pasteur finally laid this idea to rest, opening the door for ideas on evolution.

http://www.accessexcellence.org/AB/BC/Spontaneous_Generation.html

Enter Evolution: Theory and History is a well-written, thorough treatment of the founders of natural science, the great naturalists of the eighteenth century. The focus is on scientists who had ideas on evolution, and those who were proponents of natural selection.

http://www.ucmp.berkeley.edu/history/evolution.html

Evolution and Behavior. This site provides answers to FAQs related to many topics on evolution. It provides book reviews, information on evolutionary scientists, and perspectives on evolution and religion.

http://ccp.uchicago.edu/~jyin/evolution.html

The Talk Origins Archive. This site provides a discussion of Darwin's theory and traces the history of scientists' acceptance of evolution.

http://www.talkorigins.org/faqs/modern-synthesis.html

Process of Evolution

19

Antibiotics are selective agents for evolution.

W hen your grandparents were young, infectious diseases such as tuberculosis, pneumonia, and syphilis killed thousands of people every year. Then in the 1940s, penicillin and other antibiotics were developed, and public health officials believed infectious diseases were a thing of the past. Today, however, tuberculosis, pneumonia, and many other ailments are back with a vengeance. What happened? Natural selection occurred.

As Darwin and Wallace emphasized, there is variation among individuals in all populations or groups of organisms. Just as the cats in your neighborhood differ from one another, bacteria that cause a disease differ from one another. Some of the tubercular bacteria, for example, just happened to be resistant to drug treatment. The antibiotic didn't cause this resistance; the bacteria were already resistant (preadapted). So the antibiotic-resistant bacteria survived and reproduced. Now, 50 years later, several strains of "superbugs" that cause various illnesses cannot be killed by antibiotics. One type of bacteria actually feeds on the antibiotic vancomycin!

19.1 Evolution in a Genetic Context

Darwin stressed that the members of a population vary but he did not know how variations come about and how they are transmitted. It was not until the 1930s that population geneticists were able to apply the principles of genetics to populations and thereafter develop a way to recognize when evolution has occurred. A **population** is all the members of a single species occupying a particular area at the same time. Evolution that occurs within a population is called **microevolution.**

Microevolution

In **population genetics,** the various alleles at all the gene loci in all individuals make up the **gene pool** of the population. It is customary to describe the gene pool of a population in terms of gene frequencies. Suppose that in a *Drosophila* population, one-fourth of the flies are homozygous dominant for long wings, one-half are heterozygous, and one-fourth are homozygous recessive for short wings. Therefore, in a population of 100 individuals, we have

25 LL, 50 Ll, and 25 ll

What is the number of the allele L and the allele l in the population?

Number of L alleles:			Number of l alleles:		
LL $(2\,L \times 25)$	=	50	LL $(0\,l)$	=	0
Ll $(1\,L \times 50)$	=	50	Ll $(1\,l \times 50)$	=	50
ll $(0\,L)$	=	0	ll $(2\,l \times 25)$	=	50
		100 L			100 l

To determine the frequency of each allele, calculate its percentage from the total number of alleles in the population; in each case, $100/200 = 50\% = 0.5$. The sperm and eggs produced by this population will also contain these alleles in these frequencies. Assuming random mating (all possible gametes have an equal chance to combine with any other), we can calculate the ratio of genotypes in the next generation by using a Punnett square.

There is an important difference between a Punnett square used for a cross between individuals and the one below. Below the sperm and eggs are those produced by the members of a population—not those produced by a single male and female. As you can see, the results of the Punnett square indicate that the frequency for each allele in the next generation is still 0.5.

	sperm		Results:
	0.5 L	0.5 l	0.25LL + 0.5Ll + 0.25ll
eggs 0.5 L	0.25 LL	0.25 Ll	$(\frac{1}{4} LL + \frac{1}{2} Ll + \frac{1}{4} ll)$
0.5 l	0.25 Ll	0.25 ll	

Therefore, sexual reproduction alone cannot bring about a change in allele frequencies. Also, the dominant allele need not increase from one generation to the next. Dominance does not cause an allele to become a common allele. The potential constancy, or equilibrium state, of gene pool frequencies was independently recognized in 1908 by G. H. Hardy, an English mathematician, and W. Weinberg, a German physician. They used the binomial expression ($p^2 + 2pq + q^2$) to calculate the genotypic and allele frequencies of a population. Figure 19.1 shows you how this is done.

The **Hardy-Weinberg law** states that an equilibrium of allele frequencies in a gene pool, calculated by using the expression $p^2 + 2pq + q^2$, will remain in effect in each succeeding generation of a sexually reproducing population as long as five conditions are met:

$$p^2 + 2\,pq + q^2$$

p^2	= % homozygous dominant individuals
p	= frequency of dominant allele
q^2	= % homozygous recessive individuals
q	= frequency of recessive allele
$2\,pq$	= % heterozygous individuals

Realize that　　$p + q = 1$ (there are only 2 alleles)

$p^2 + 2\,pq + q^2 = 1$ (these are the only genotypes)

Example

An investigator has determined by inspection that 16% of a human population has a continuous hairline (recessive trait). Using this information, we can complete all the genotypic and allele frequencies for the population, provided the conditions for Hardy-Weinberg equilibrium are met.

Given:　　$q^2 = 16\% = 0.16$ are homozygous recessive individuals

Therefore,　　$q = \sqrt{0.16} = 0.4$ = frequency of recessive allele
$p = 1.0 - 0.4 = 0.6$ = frequency of dominant allele
$p^2 = (0.6)(0.6) = 0.36 = 36\%$ are homozygous dominant individuals
$2\,pq = 2(0.6)(0.4) = 0.48 = 48\%$ are heterozygous individuals

$\left.\begin{array}{c}\\ \\ \\ \\ \end{array}\right\}$ 84% have the dominant phenotype

or
$= 1.00 - 0.52 = 0.48$

Figure 19.1 Calculating gene pool frequencies using the Hardy-Weinberg equation.

1. No mutations: allelic changes do not occur, or changes in one direction are balanced by changes in the opposite direction.
2. No gene flow: migration of alleles into or out of the population does not occur.
3. Random mating: individuals pair by chance and not according to their genotypes or phenotypes.
4. No genetic drift: the population is very large, and changes in allele frequencies due to chance alone are insignificant.
5. No selection: no selective agent favors one genotype over another.

In real life, these conditions are rarely, if ever, met, and allele frequencies in the gene pool of a population do change from one generation to the next. Therefore, evolution has occurred. The significance of the Hardy-Weinberg law is that it tells us what factors cause evolution—those that violate the conditions listed. Evolution can be detected by noting any deviation from a Hardy-Weinberg equilibrium of allele frequencies in the gene pool of a population.

The accumulation of small changes in the gene pool over a relatively short period of two or more generations is called microevolution. Microevolution is involved in the origin of species to be discussed later in this chapter, as well as in the history of life recorded in the fossil record.

A change in allele frequencies results in a change in phenotype frequencies. Figure 19.2 illustrates a process called **industrial melanism.** Before soot is introduced into the air due to industry, the original peppered moth population has only 10% dark-colored moths. When dark-colored moths rest on light trunks, they are seen and eaten by predatory birds. With the advent of industry, the trunks of trees darken and it is the light-colored moths that stand out and are eaten. The birds are acting as a selective agent, and microevolution occurs; the last generation observed has 80% dark-colored moths.

A Hardy-Weinberg equilibrium provides a baseline by which to judge whether evolution has occurred. Any change of allele frequencies in the gene pool of a population signifies that evolution has occurred.

Practice Problems 1*

1. In a certain population, 21% are homozygous dominant, 49% are heterozygous, and 30% are homozygous recessive. What percentage of the next generation is predicted to be homozygous dominant, assuming a Hardy-Weinberg equilibrium?

2. Of the members of a population of pea plants, 9% are short (recessive). What are the frequencies of the recessive allele *t* and the dominant allele *T*? What are the genotypic frequencies in this population?

* Answers to Practice Problems appear in Appendix A.

Generation O   **Several generations later**

10% dark-colored phenotype   ⟶   80% dark-colored phenotype

Figure 19.2 Microevolution.
Microevolution has occurred when there is a change in gene pool frequencies—in this case, due to natural selection. On the far left, birds cannot see light moths on light tree trunks and, therefore, light moths are more frequent in the population. On the far right, birds cannot see dark moths on dark tree trunks, and dark moths are more frequent in the population. The percentage of the dark-colored phenotype has increased in the population because predatory birds can see light-colored moths against tree trunks that are now sooty due to pollution.

Causes of Microevolution

The list of conditions for allelic equilibrium implies that the opposite conditions can cause evolutionary change. The conditions that can cause a deviation from the Hardy-Weinberg equilibrium are mutation, gene flow, nonrandom mating, genetic drift, and natural selection. Only natural selection results in adaptation to the environment.

Genetic Mutations

Mutations are the raw material for evolutionary change; without mutations there could be no new variations among members of a population. Evidence of mutations in members of a *Drosophila pseudoobscura* population was gathered by R. C. Lewontin and J. L. Hubby in 1966. They extracted various enzymes and subjected them to electrophoresis, a process that separates proteins according to size and charge. These investigators concluded that a fly population has multiple alleles at no less than 30% of all its gene loci. Similar results have been found in studies on many species, demonstrating that high levels of allelic variation are the rule in natural populations.

Many mutations do not immediately affect the phenotype, and therefore they may not be detected. In a changing environment, even a seemingly harmful mutation can be a source of an adaptive variation. For example, the water flea *Daphnia* ordinarily thrives at temperatures around 20°C, but there is a mutation that requires *Daphnia* to live at temperatures between 25°C and 30°C. The adaptive value of this mutation is entirely dependent on environmental conditions.

Once alleles have mutated, certain combinations of several alleles might be more adaptive than others in a particular environment. The most favorable phenotype may not occur until just the right alleles are grouped by recombination.

> Mutations cause many alleles in a gene pool to have multiple alleles. Recombination of these alleles increases the possibility for favorable phenotypes.

Gene Flow

Gene flow, also called gene migration, is the movement of alleles between populations by migration of breeding individuals. There can be constant gene flow between adjacent animal populations due to the migration of organisms (Fig. 19.3). Gene flow can increase the variation within a population by introducing novel alleles that were produced by mutation in another population. Continued gene flow makes gene pools similar and reduces the possibility of allele frequency differences among populations due to natural selection and genetic drift. Indeed, gene flow among populations can prevent speciation from occurring.

> Gene flow tends to decrease the genetic diversity among populations, causing their gene pools to become more similar.

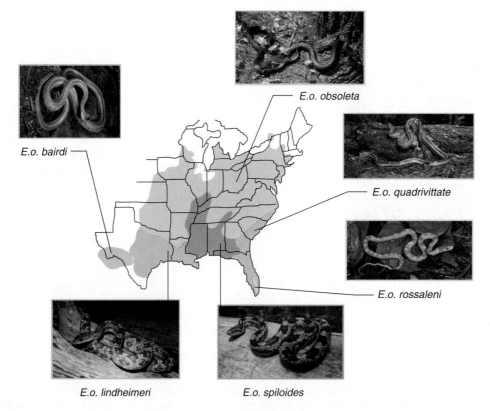

Figure 19.3 Gene flow.
Each rat snake represents a separate population of snakes. Because the populations are adjacent to one another, there is interbreeding and therefore gene flow among the populations. This keeps their gene pools somewhat similar, and each of these populations is a subspecies of the species *Elaphe obsoleta*. Therefore, each has a three-part name.

Nonrandom Mating

Random mating occurs when individuals pair by chance and not according to their genotypes or phenotypes. Inbreeding, or mating between relatives to a greater extent than by chance, is an example of **nonrandom mating.** Inbreeding does not change allele frequencies, but it does decrease the proportion of heterozygotes and increase the proportions of both homozygotes at all gene loci. In a human population, inbreeding increases the frequency of recessive abnormalities in the phenotype.

Assortative mating occurs when individuals tend to mate with those that have the same phenotype with respect to some characteristic. For example, in humans tall people seem to prefer to mate with each other. Assortative mating causes the population to subdivide into two phenotypic classes, between which there is reduced gene exchange. Homozygotes for the gene loci that control the trait in question increase in frequency, and heterozygotes for these loci decrease in frequency.

Sexual selection occurs when males compete for the right to reproduce and females choose to mate with males that have a particular phenotype. The elaborate tail of a peacock may have come about because peahens choose to mate with males with such tails.

Nonrandom mating involves inbreeding and assortative mating. The former results in increased frequency of homozygotes at all loci, and the latter results in increased frequency of homozygotes at only certain loci.

Genetic Drift

Genetic drift refers to changes in allele frequencies of a gene pool due to chance. Although genetic drift occurs in both large and small populations, a larger population is expected to suffer less of a sampling error than a smaller population. Suppose you had a large bag containing 1,000 green balls and 1,000 blue balls, and you randomly drew 10%, or 200, of the balls. Because there is a large number of balls of each color in the bag, you can reasonably expect to draw 100 green balls and 100 blue balls or at least a ratio close to this. But suppose you had a bag containing only 10 green balls and 10 blue balls and you drew 10%, or only 2 balls. The chances of drawing one green ball and one blue ball with a single trial are now considerably less.

When a population is small, there is a greater chance that some rare genotype might not participate at all in the production of the next generation. Suppose there is a small population of frogs in which certain frogs for one reason or another do not pass on their traits. Certainly, the next generation will have a change in allele frequencies. When genetic drift leads to a loss of one or more alleles, other alleles over time become *fixed* in the population (Fig. 19.4).

In an experiment with 107 *Drosophila* populations, each population was in its own culture bottle. Every bottle contained eight heterozygous flies of each sex. There were no

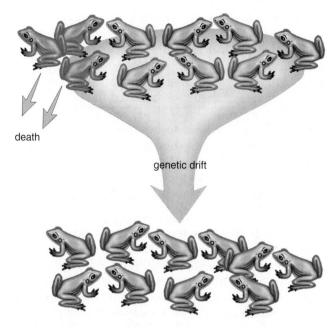

Figure 19.4 Genetic drift.
Genetic drift occurs when by chance only certain members of a population (in this case, green frogs) reproduce and pass on their genes to the next generation. The allele frequencies of the next generation's gene pool may be markedly different from that of the previous generation.

homozygous recessive or homozygous dominant flies. From the many offspring, the experimenter chose at random eight males and eight females. These were the parents for the next generation, and so forth for 19 generations. For the first few generations, most populations still contained many heterozygotes. But by the nineteenth generation, 25% of the populations contained only homozygous recessive flies and 25% contained only homozygous dominant flies for a brown-eyed allele.

Genetic drift is a random process, and therefore it is not likely to produce the same results in several populations. In California, there are a number of cypress groves, each a separate population. The phenotypes within each grove are more similar to one another than they are to the phenotypes in the other groves. Some groves have longitudinally shaped trees, and others have pyramidally shaped trees. The bark is rough in some colonies and smooth in others. The leaves are gray to bright green or bluish, and the cones are small or large. Because the environmental conditions are similar for all groves, and no correlation has been found between phenotype and environment across groves, it is hypothesized that these variations among populations are due to genetic drift.

Bottleneck Effect   Sometimes a species is subjected to near extinction because of a natural disaster (e.g., earthquake or fire) or because of overharvesting and habitat loss. It is as if most of the population has stayed behind and only a few survivors have passed through the neck of a bottle. The **bottleneck effect** prevents the majority of genotype types from participating in the production of the next generation.

The extreme genetic similarity found in cheetahs is believed to be due to a bottleneck. In a study of 47 different enzymes, each of which can come in several different forms, all the cheetahs had exactly the same form. This demonstrates that genetic drift can cause certain alleles to be lost from a population. Exactly what caused the cheetah bottleneck is not known. It is speculated that perhaps cheetahs were slaughtered by nineteenth-century cattle farmers protecting their herds, or were captured by Egyptians as pets 4,000 years ago, or were decimated by a mass extinction tens of thousands of years ago. Today, cheetahs suffer from relative infertility because of the intense inbreeding that occurred after the bottleneck.

Founder Effect   The **founder effect** is an example of genetic drift in which rare alleles, or combinations of alleles, occur at a higher frequency in a population isolated from the general population. After all, founding individuals contain only a fraction of the total genetic diversity of the original gene pool. Which particular alleles are carried by the founders is dictated by chance alone. The Amish of Lancaster County, Pennsylvania, are an isolated group that was begun by German founders. Today, as many as one in 14 individuals carries a recessive allele that causes an unusual form of dwarfism (affecting only lower arms and legs) and polydactylism (extra fingers) (Fig. 19.5). In the population at large, only one in 1,000 individuals has this allele.

Genetic drift is changes in gene pool frequencies due to chance.

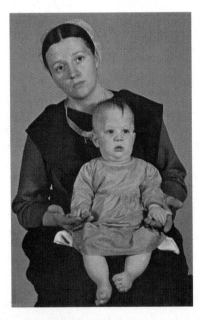

Figure 19.5 Founder effect.
A member of the founding population of Amish in Pennsylvania had a recessive allele for a rare kind of dwarfism linked with polydactylism. The percentage of the Amish population now carrying this allele is much higher compared to that of the general population.

19.2 Natural Selection

Natural selection is the process that results in adaptation of a population to the biotic and abiotic environments. The biotic environment includes organisms that seek resources through competition, predation, and parasitism. The abiotic environment includes weather conditions dependent chiefly upon temperatures and precipitation. In the previous century, Charles Darwin, the father of evolution, became convinced that species evolve (change) with time and suggested natural selection as the mechanism for adaptation to the environment. Here, we restate Darwin's hypothesis of natural selection in the context of modern evolutionary theory.

Evolution by natural selection requires:

1. variation. The members of a population differ from one another.

2. inheritance. Many of these differences are heritable genetic differences.

3. differential adaptedness. Some of these differences affect how well an organism is adapted to its environment.

4. differential reproduction. Individuals that are better adapted to their environment are more likely to reproduce, and their fertile offspring will make up a greater proportion of the next generation.

Differential reproduction is the measure of an individual's fitness. Population geneticists speak of **relative fitness**, that is the fitness of one phenotype compared to another.

Types of Selection

Most of the traits on which natural selection acts are polygenic and controlled by more than one pair of alleles located at different gene loci. Such traits have a range of phenotypes, the frequency distribution of which usually resembles a bell-shaped curve.

Three types of natural selection have been described for any particular trait. They are directional selection, stabilizing selection, and disruptive selection.

Directional Selection

Directional selection occurs when an extreme phenotype is favored and the distribution curve shifts in that direction. Such a shift can occur when a population is adapting to a changing environment.

Industrial melanism, discussed earlier and depicted in Figure 19.2, is an example of directional selection. As you may know, indiscriminate use of antibiotics and pesticides results in a wide distribution of bacteria and insects that are resistant to these chemicals. When an antibiotic is administered, some bacteria may survive because they are genetically resistant to the antibiotic. These are the bacteria that are

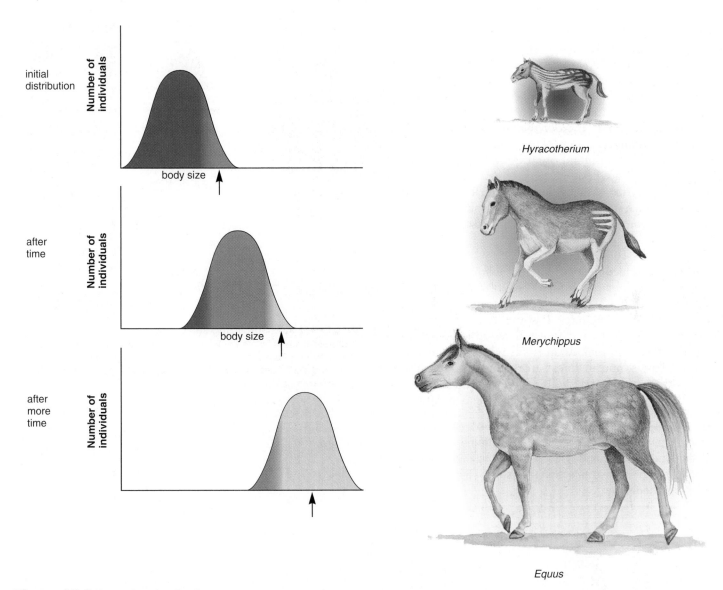

Figure 19.6 Directional selection.
Natural selection favors one extreme phenotype (see arrows), and there is a shift in the distribution curve. *Equus,* the modern-day horse, evolved from *Hyracotherium,* which was about the size of a dog. This small animal could have hidden among trees and had low-crowned teeth for browsing. When grasslands began to replace forest, the ancestors of *Equus* may have been subject to selective pressure for the development of strength, intelligence, speed, and durable grinding teeth. A larger size provided the strength needed for combat, a larger skull made room for a larger brain, elongated legs ending in hooves provided greater speed to escape enemies, and the durable grinding teeth enabled the animals to feed efficiently on grasses.

likely to pass on their genes to the next generation. As a result, the number of resistant bacteria ever increases. Drug-resistant strains of bacteria that cause tuberculosis have now become a serious threat to the health of people worldwide.

Another example of directional selection is the human struggle against malaria, a disease caused by an infection of the liver and the red blood cells. The *Anopheles* mosquito transmits the disease-causing protozoan *Plasmodium vivax* from person to person. In the early 1960s, international health authorities thought that malaria would soon be eradicated. A new drug, chloroquine, seemed effective against *Plasmodium,* and DDT (an insecticide) spraying had reduced

the mosquito population. But in the mid-1960s, *Plasmodium* was showing signs of chloroquine resistance and, worse yet, mosquitoes were becoming resistant to DDT. A few drug-resistant parasites and a few DDT-resistant mosquitoes had survived and multiplied, making the fight against malaria more difficult than ever.

The gradual increase in the size of the modern horse, *Equus,* is an example of directional selection that can be correlated with a change in the environment from forestlike conditions to grassland conditions (Fig. 19.6). Even so, as discussed previously, the evolution of the horse should not be viewed as a straight line of descent because we know of many side branches that became extinct.

Stabilizing Selection

Stabilizing selection occurs when an intermediate pheno-type is favored (Fig. 19.7). It can improve adaptation of the population to those aspects of the environment that remain constant. With stabilizing selection, extreme phenotypes are selected against, and individuals near the average are fa-vored. As an example, consider the birth weight of human infants, which ranges from 0.89 to 4.9 kg (2 to 10.8 lb). The death rate is higher for infants who are at these extremes and is lowest for babies who have an intermediate birth weight (about 3.2 kg or 7 lb). Most babies have a birth weight within this range, which gives the best chance of survival. Similar results have been found in other animals, also.

Disruptive Selection

In **disruptive selection,** two or more extreme phenotypes are favored over any intermediate phenotype (Fig. 19.8). For example, British land snails *(Cepaea nemoralis)* have a wide habitat range that includes low-vegetation areas (grass fields and hedgerows) and forest areas. In low-vegetation areas, thrushes feed mainly on snails with dark shells that lack light bands, and in forest areas, they feed mainly on snails with light-banded shells. Therefore, these two dis-tinctly different phenotypes are found in the population.

Directional selection favors one of the extreme phenotypes; stabilizing selection favors the intermediate phenotype; disruptive selection favors more than one extreme phenotype.

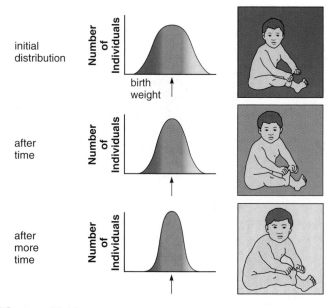

Figure 19.7 Stabilizing selection.
Natural selection favors the intermediate phenotype (see arrows) over the extremes. Today, it is observed that most human babies are of intermediate weight (about 3.2 kg, or 7 lb), and very few babies are either very small or very large.

Figure 19.8 Disruptive selection.
Natural selection favors two extreme phenotypes (see arrows). Today, it is observed that British land snails comprise mainly two different phenotypes, each adapted to a different habitat.

Maintenance of Variations

A population always shows some genotypic variation. The maintenance of variation is beneficial because populations with limited variation may not be able to adapt to new conditions and may become extinct. How can variation be maintained in spite of selection constantly working to reduce it?

First, we must remember that the forces that promote variation are still at work: mutation still creates new alleles, and recombination still recombines these alleles during gametogenesis and fertilization. Second, gene flow might still occur. If the receiving population is small and is mostly homozygous, gene flow can be a significant source of new alleles. Finally, we have seen that natural selection reduces, but does not eliminate, the range of phenotypes. And disruptive selection even promotes polymorphism in a population. There are also other ways variation is maintained.

Diploidy and the Heterozygote

Only alleles that are exposed (cause a phenotypic difference) are subject to natural selection. In diploid organisms, this makes the heterozygote a potential protector of recessive alleles that otherwise would be weeded out of the gene pool. Consider these gene pool frequency distributions:

Frequency of Allele *a* in Gene Pool	Genotypic Frequencies		
	AA	*Aa*	*aa*
0.9	0.01	0.18	0.81
0.1	0.81	0.18	0.01

Notice that even when selection reduces the recessive allele from a frequency of 0.9 to 0.1, the frequency of the heterozygote remains the same. The heterozygote remains a source of the recessive allele for future generations. In a changing environment, the recessive phenotype may then be favored by natural selection.

Sickle-Cell Disease

In certain regions of Africa, the importance of the heterozygote in maintaining variation is exemplified by sickle-cell disease. The relative fitness of the heterozygote and the two homozygotes will determine their percentages in the population. When the ratio of two or more phenotypes remains the same in each generation, it is called *balanced polymorphism*. The optimum ratio will be the one that correlates with the survival of the most offspring.

Individuals with sickle-cell disease have the genotype Hb^SHb^S and tend to die at an early age due to hemorrhaging and organ destruction. Those who are heterozygous and have sickle-cell trait (Hb^AHb^S) are better off; their red blood cells usually become sickle shaped only when the oxygen content of the environment is low. Geneticists studying the distribution of sickle-cell disease in Africa

Figure 19.9 Distribution of sickle-cell disease and malaria. The pink color shows the areas where malaria was prevalent in Africa, the Middle East, and southern Europe in 1920, before eradication programs began; the blue color shows the areas where sickle-cell disease most often occurred. The overlap of these two distributions (purple) suggested that there might be a causal connection.

have found that the recessive allele (Hb^S) has a higher frequency (0.2 to as high as 0.4 in a few areas) in regions with malaria (Fig. 19.9).

Malaria is caused by a parasite that lives in and destroys the red blood cells of the normal homozygote (Hb^AHb^A). The parasite is unable to live in the red blood cells of the heterozygote (Hb^AHb^S) because the infection causes the red blood cells to become sickle shape. Sickle-shaped red blood cells lose potassium and this causes the parasite to die. Therefore, the homozygote (Hb^SHb^S) is maintained at the same level in regions of Africa subject to malaria because the heterozygote is protected from both sickle-cell disease and from malaria.

Genotype	Phenotype	Result
Hb^AHb^A	Normal	Dies due to malarial infection
Hb^AHb^S	Sickle-cell trait	Lives due to protection from both
Hb^SHb^S	Sickle-cell disease	Dies due to sickle-cell disease

Even after populations become adapted to their environments, variation is promoted and maintained by various mechanisms. In diploid organisms, the heterozygote genotype can help maintain variation.

least flycatcher, *Empidonax minimus*

Acadian flycatcher, *Empidonax virescens*

Traill's flycatcher, *Empidonax trailli*

Figure 19.10 Biological definition of a species.
Although the three species are nearly identical, we would still expect to find some structural feature that distinguishes them. We know they are separate species because they are reproductively isolated—the members of each species reproduce only with one another. Each species has a characteristic song and its own particular habitat during the mating season as well.

19.3 Speciation

Speciation is the splitting of one species into two or more species or the transformation of one species into a new species over time. Speciation is the final result of changes in gene pool allele and genotypic frequencies.

What Is a Species?

Sometimes it is very difficult to tell one **species** [L. *species*, a kind] from another. Before we consider the origin of species, then, it is first necessary to define a species. For Linnaeus, the father of taxonomy, one species was separated from another by morphology; that is, their physical traits differed. Darwin saw that similar species, such as the three flycatcher species in Figure 19.10, are related by common descent. The field of population genetics has produced the *biological definition of a species:* the members of one species interbreed and have a shared gene pool, and each species is reproductively isolated from every other species. The flycatchers in Figure 19.10 are members of separate species because they do not interbreed in nature.

Gene flow occurs between the populations of a species but not between populations of different species. For example, the human species has many populations that certainly differ in physical appearance. We know, however, that all humans belong to one species because the members of these populations can produce fertile offspring. On the other hand, the red maple and the sugar maple are separate species. Each species is found over a wide geographical range in the eastern half of the United States and is made up of many populations. The members of each species' populations, however, rarely hybridize in nature. Therefore, these two plants are related but separate species.

With the advent of biochemical genetics, a new way has arisen to help distinguish species. The phylogenetic species concept suggests that DNA/DNA comparison techniques can indicate the relatedness of groups of organisms.

Reproductive Isolating Mechanisms

For two species to be separate, they must be reproductively isolated; that is, gene flow must not occur between them. A *reproductive isolating mechanism* is any structural, functional, or behavioral characteristic that prevents successful reproduction from occurring. Table 19.1 lists the mechanisms by which reproductive isolation is maintained.

Prezygotic isolating mechanisms are those that prevent reproduction attempts and make it unlikely that fertilization will be successful if mating is attempted. Habitat isolation, temporal isolation, behavioral isolation, and mechanical isolation make it highly unlikely that particular genotypes will contribute to the gene pool of a population.

Table 19.1

Reproductive Isolating Mechanisms

Isolating Mechanism	Example
Prezygotic	
Habitat isolation	Species at same locale occupy different habitats.
Temporal isolation	Species reproduce at different seasons or different times of day.
Behavioral isolation	In animals, courtship behavior differs or they respond to different songs, calls, pheromones, or other signals.
Mechanical isolation	Genitalia unsuitable for one another.
Postzygotic	
Gamete isolation	Sperm cannot reach or fertilize egg.
Zygote mortality	Fertilization occurs, but zygote does not survive.
Hybrid sterility	Hybrid survives but is sterile and cannot reproduce.
F_2 fitness	Hybrid is fertile but F_2 hybrid has reduced fitness.

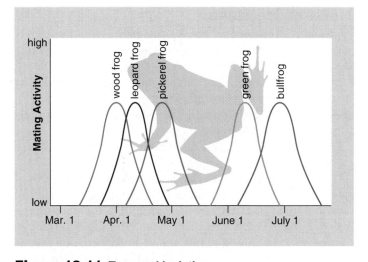

Figure 19.11 Temporal isolation.
Five species of frogs of the genus *Rana* are all found at Ithaca, New York. The species remain separate because the period of most active mating is different for each and because whenever there is an overlap, different breeding sites are used. For example, pickerel frogs are found in streams and ponds on high ground, leopard frogs in lowland swamps, and wood frogs in woodland ponds or shallow water.

Habitat isolation. When two species occupy different habitats, even within the same geographic range, they are less likely to meet and to attempt to reproduce. This is one of the reasons the flycatchers in Figure 19.10 do not mate, and the red maple and sugar maple already mentioned do not exchange pollen. In tropical rain forests, many animal species are restricted to a particular level of the forest canopy, and in this way they are isolated from similar species.

Temporal isolation. Two species can live in the same locale, but if each reproduces at a different time of year, they do not attempt to mate. For example, *Reticulitermes hageni* and *R. virginicus* are two species of termites. The former has mating flights in March through May, whereas the latter mates in the fall and winter months. Similarly, the frogs featured in Figure 19.11 have different periods of most active mating.

Behavioral isolation. Many animal species have courtship patterns that allow males and females to recognize one another. Male fireflies are recognized by females of their species by the pattern of their flashings; similarly, male crickets are recognized by females of their species by their chirping. Many males recognize females of their species by sensing chemical signals called pheromones. For example, female gypsy moths secrete chemicals from special abdominal glands. These chemicals are detected downwind by receptors on antennae of males.

Mechanical isolation. When animal genitalia or plant floral structures are incompatible, reproduction cannot occur. Inaccessibility of pollen to certain pollinators can prevent cross-fertilization in plants, and the sexes of many insect species have genitalia that do not

match or other characteristics that make mating impossible. For example, male dragonflies have claspers that are suitable for holding only the females of their own species.

Postzygotic isolating mechanisms prevent hybrid offspring from developing or breeding, even if reproduction attempts have been successful. Gamete isolation, zygote mortality, hybrid sterility, and reduced F_2 fitness all make it unlikely that particular genotypes will contribute to the gene pool of a population.

Gamete isolation. Even if the gametes of two different species meet, they may not fuse to become a zygote. In animals, the sperm of one species may not be able to survive in the reproductive tract of another species, or the egg may have receptors only for sperm of its species. In plants, the stigma controls which pollen grains can successfully complete pollination.

Zygote mortality, hybrid sterility, and F_2 fitness. If by chance two of the frog species in Figure 19.11 do form hybrid zygotes, the zygotes fail to complete development or else the offspring are frail. As is well known, a cross between a horse and a donkey produces a mule, which is usually sterile—it cannot reproduce. In some cases, mules are fertile, but the F_2 generation is not. This has also been observed in both evening primrose and cotton plants.

The members of a biological species are able to breed and produce fertile offspring only among themselves. There are several mechanisms that keep species reproductively isolated from one another.

Modes of Speciation

Whenever reproductive isolation develops, speciation has occurred. Ernst Mayr, at Harvard University, proposed one model of speciation after observing that when a population is geographically isolated from other populations, gene flow stops. Variations due to different mutations, genetic drift, and directional selection build up, causing first postzygotic and then prezygotic reproductive isolation to occur. Mayr called this model **allopatric speciation** [Gk. *allo*, different, and *patri*, fatherland] (Fig. 19.12*a*).

With **sympatric speciation** [Gk. *sym*, together, and *patri*, fatherland], a population develops into two or more reproductively isolated groups without prior geographic isolation (Fig. 19.12*b*). The best evidence for this type of speciation is found among plants, where it can occur by means of polyploidy. In this case, there would be a multiplication of the chromosome number in certain plants of a single species. Sympatric speciation can also occur due to hybridization between two species, followed by a doubling of the chromosome number. Polyploid plants are reproductively isolated by a postzygotic mechanism; they can reproduce successfully only with other like polyploids, and backcrosses with diploid parents are sterile.

Adaptive Radiation

Adaptive radiation is the rapid development from a single ancestral species of many new species, which have spread out and become adapted to various ways of life. The 13 species of finches that live on the Galápagos Islands are believed to be descended from a single type of ancestral finch from the mainland. The populations on the various islands were subjected to the founder effect and the process of natural selection. Because of natural selection, each population became adapted to a particular habitat on its island. In time, the various populations became so genotypically different that now, when by chance they reside on the same island, they do not interbreed and are therefore separate species. There is evidence that the finches use beak shape to recognize members of the same species during courtship. Rejection of suitors with the wrong type of beak is a behavioral type of prezygotic isolating mechanism.

Similarly, on the Hawaiian Islands, there is a wide variety of honeycreepers that are descended from a common goldfinch-like ancestor that arrived from Asia or North America about 5 million years ago. Today, honeycreepers have a range of beak sizes and shapes for feeding on various food sources, including seeds, fruits, flowers, and insects (Fig. 19.13). Adaptive radiation has also been observed in plants on the Hawaiian Islands, as discussed in the reading on pages 314–315.

> Allopatric speciation but not sympatric speciation is dependent on a geographic barrier. Adaptive radiation is a particular form of allopatric speciation.

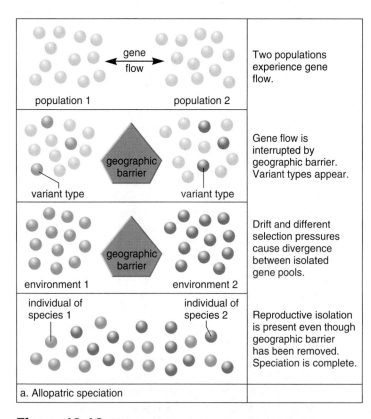

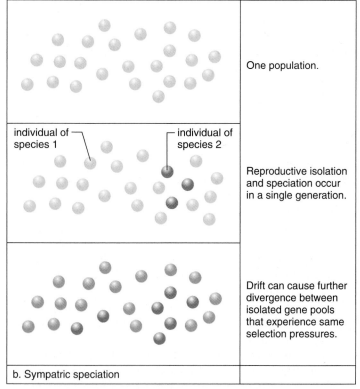

Figure 19.12 Allopatric versus sympatric speciation.
a. Allopatric speciation occurs after a geographic barrier prevents gene flow between populations that originally belonged to a single species.
b. Sympatric speciation occurs when members of a population achieve immediate reproductive isolation without any prior geographic barrier.

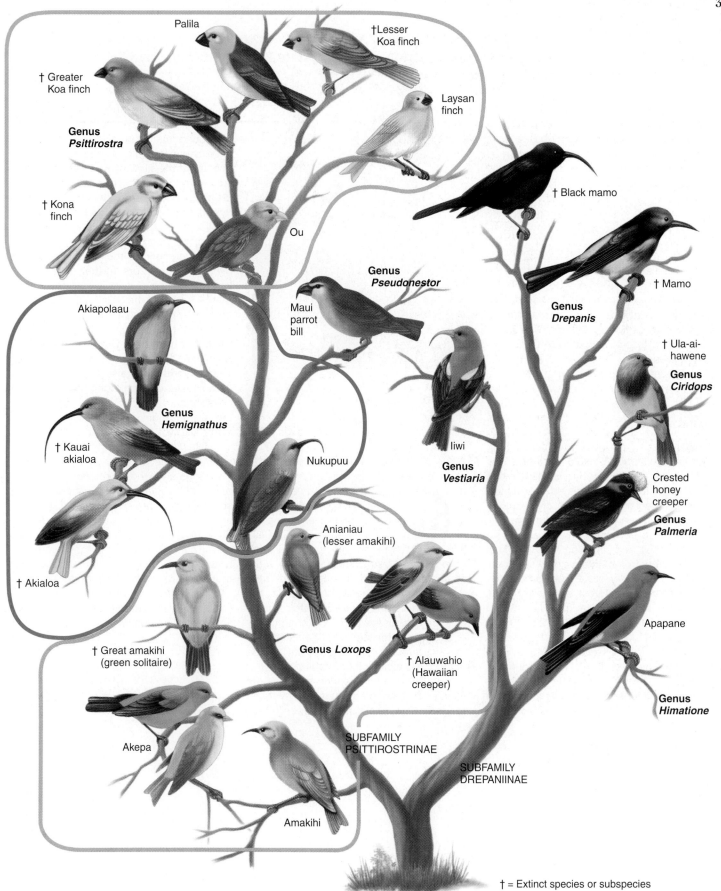

Figure 19.13 Adaptive radiation in Hawaiian honeycreepers.
More than 20 species evolved from a single species of a finch-like bird that colonized the Hawaiian Islands. The bills of honeycreepers are specialized for eating different types of foods.

Origin and Adaptive Radiation of the Hawaiian Silversword Alliance

When I was a graduate student at the University of California at Davis, I studied a genus of plants *(Calycadenia)* that belongs to a largely Californian group of plants called tarweeds. I knew that the tarweeds and plants belonging to the silversword alliance (an alliance is an assemblage of closely related species) are in the same large family of plants called Asteraceae (Compositae). But Sherwin Carlquist's anatomical research had suggested that the silversword plants and the tarweeds are even more closely related. The silverswords are found only in Hawaii, so when I took a faculty position at the University of Hawaii, I decided to gather evidence to possibly support Carlquist's interpretation.

There are 28 species of plants in the silversword alliance: five species of *Argyroxiphium,* two species of *Wilkesia,* and 21 species of *Dubautia*. This alliance constitutes one of the most spectacular examples of adaptive radiation among plants. Adaptive radiation characterizes many insular groups that have evolved in isolation away from related and nonrelated organisms. Members of the silversword alliance range in form from mat-like subshrubs and rosette shrubs to large trees and climbing vines (lianas). They grow in habitats as diverse as exposed lava, dry scrub, dry woodland, moist forest, wet forest, and bogs. These habitats have a range in elevation from 75 to 3,800 meters (250– 12,500 feet), and in annual precipitation from 38 to 1,230 cm (15–485 inches).

Members of the alliance found in moist to wet forest habitats typically exhibit modifications that are adaptive in competition for light, such as increased

Gerald D. Carr
University of Hawaii at Manoa

height, vining habit, and thin leaves with a comparatively large surface area (Fig. 19A). Members of the alliance from open, more arid sites typically show features associated with conservation of water, such as decreased height, thickened leaves with comparatively low surface area, and compact internal tissues (Fig. 19B). Species of *Argyroxiphium* have more or less succulent leaves with compact tissue and channels filled with a water-binding gelatinous matrix of pectin (Fig. 19C). These adaptations help this species survive under the conditions of extreme water stress in its habitats— i.e., largely in oxygen-deficient, acid bogs or dry alpine cinder habitats.

I have done cytogenetic analyses of meiotic chromosome pairing in hybrids to determine relationships among the

silversword plants and between these plants and the tarweeds. I have sought and found many natural interspecific and intergeneric hybrids among the diverse species of the silversword alliance. Many such hybrids also were produced artificially. Each newly discovered or created hybrid potentially provided information to fill in a missing piece of an intriguing and mysterious natural puzzle of evolution—or sometimes these findings complicated the picture further. Nearly 25 years later, the picture is still not complete. Perhaps the most exciting and personally gratifying result of my involvement with this group is the series of hybrids that have been produced between Hawaiian species and the tarweeds. These hybrids, and also a growing body of molecular data provided by one of my collaborators, Bruce Baldwin, clearly establish the origin of the Hawaiian silversword alliance from the tarweeds.

I like working with others who are innately curious about their natural surroundings and who do research for pure personal satisfaction. My scientific research helps provide insight into the mystery and meaning of the wonderful diversity of nature. An added element of excitement comes in sharing with others a discovery of one of nature's secrets that perhaps no other human has witnessed. Therefore, for me, teaching and research are naturally complementary and rewarding activities.

Readings and photographs courtesy of Gerald D. Carr, University of Hawaii at Manoa.

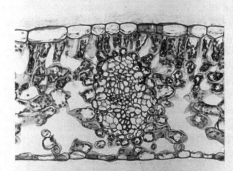

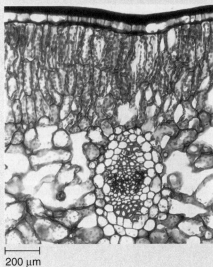

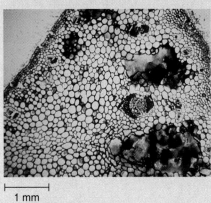

200 μm

200 μm

1 mm

Figure 19A *Dubautia knudsenii* is adapted to living in a moist habitat.
In the cross section of the leaf, note the loose organization of tissue and thin cuticle on the upper and lower epidermis.

Figure 19B *Dubautia menziesii* is adapted to living in open, more arid sites.
In cross section, note the thick leaf with compact organization of tissue and very highly developed cuticle on upper and lower epidermis (lower epidermis not shown).

Figure 19C *Argyroxiphium kauense* is adapted to living under conditions of water stress.
In cross section, note the compact tissue and large channels of water-binding extracellular pectin that alternate with the major vascular bundles.

Connecting Concepts

We have seen that there are variations among the individuals in any population, whether the population is tuberculosis-causing bacteria in a city, the dandelions on a hill, or the squirrels in your neighborhood. Individuals vary because of the presence of mutations and, in sexually reproducing species, because of the recombination of alleles and chromosomes due to the process of meiosis and fertilization.

The field of population genetics, which utilizes the Hardy-Weinberg law, shows us how the study of evolution can be objective rather than subjective. A change in gene pool allele frequencies defines and signifies that evolution has

occurred. There are various agents of evolutionary change, and natural selection is one of these.

Population genetics has also given us the biological definition of a species: the members of one species can successfully reproduce with each other but cannot successfully reproduce with members of another species. This criteria allows us to know when a new species has arisen. Species usually come into being after two populations have been geographically isolated. Suppose the present population of squirrels in your neighborhood was divided by a cavern following an earthquake. Then, there would be two genetically different populations of squirrels that

are geographically isolated from each other. Suppose also that the area west of the cavern is slightly drier than that to the east. Over time, each population would become adapted to its particular environment. Eventually, the two populations may become so genetically different that even if members of each population came into contact, they would not be able to produce fertile offspring. Since gene flow between the two populations would not be possible, the squirrels would be considered separate species. By the same process, multiple species can repeatedly arise, as when a common ancestor led to thirteen species of Darwin's finches.

Summary

19.1 Evolution in a Genetic Context

All the various genes of a population make up its gene pool. The Hardy-Weinberg equilibrium is a constancy of gene pool allele frequencies that remains from generation to generation if certain conditions are met. The conditions are no mutations, no gene flow, random mating, no genetic drift, and no selection. Since these conditions are rarely met, a change in gene pool frequencies is likely. When gene pool frequencies change, evolution has occurred. Deviations from a Hardy-Weinberg equilibrium allow us to determine when evolution has taken place.

Mutations are the raw material for evolutionary change. Recombinations help bring about adaptive genotypes. Mutations, gene flow, nonrandom mating, genetic drift, and natural selection all cause deviations from a Hardy-Weinberg equilibrium. Certain genotypic variations may be of evolutionary significance only should the environment change. Gene flow occurs when a breeding individual (animals) migrates to another population or when gametes and seeds (plants) are carried into another population. Constant gene flow between two populations causes their gene pools to become similar. Nonrandom mating occurs when relatives mate (inbreeding) and assortative mating occurs. Both of these cause an increase in homozygotes. Genetic drift occurs when allele frequencies are altered by chance—that is, by sampling error. Genetic drift can cause the gene pools of two isolated populations to become dissimilar as some alleles are lost and others are fixed. Genetic drift is particularly evident after a bottleneck, when severe inbreeding occurs, or when founders start a new population.

19.2 Natural Selection

The process of natural selection can now be restated in terms of population genetics. A change in gene pool frequencies results in adaptation to the environment.

Most of the traits of evolutionary significance are polygenic; the many variations in population result in a bell-shaped curve. Three types of selection occur: (1) directional—the curve shifts in one direction as when dark-colored peppered moths become prevalent in polluted areas; (2) stabilizing—the peak of the curve increases, as when most human babies have a birth weight near the optimum for survival; and (3) disruptive—the curve has two peaks, as when *Cepaea* snails vary because a wide geographic range causes selection to vary.

Despite constant natural selection, variation is maintained. Mutations and recombination still occur; gene flow among small populations can introduce new alleles; and natural selection itself sometimes results in variation. In sexually reproducing diploid organisms, the heterozygote acts as a repository for recessive alleles whose frequency is low. In regard to sickle-cell disease, the heterozygote is more fit in areas with malaria and, therefore, both homozygotes are maintained in the population.

19.3 Speciation

The biological definition of a species recognizes that populations of the same species breed only among themselves and are reproductively isolated from other species. Reproductive isolating mechanisms prevent gene flow among species. Prezygotic isolating mechanisms (habitat, temporal, behavioral, and mechanical isolation) prevent mating from being attempted. Postzygotic isolating mechanisms (gamete isolation, zygote mortality, hybrid sterility, and F_2 fitness) prevent hybrid offspring from surviving and/or reproducing.

Allopatric speciation requires geographic isolation before reproductive isolation occurs. Sympatric speciation does not require geographic isolation for reproductive isolation to develop. The occurrence of polyploidy in plants is an example of this other type of speciation.

Adaptive radiation, as exemplified by the Hawaiian honeycreepers, is a form of allopatric speciation. It occurs because the opportunity exists for new species to adapt to new habitats.

Reviewing the Chapter

1. What is the Hardy-Weinberg law?   302–3
2. Name and discuss the five conditions of evolutionary change.   304–6
3. What is a bottleneck, and what is the founder effect?   305–6
4. State the steps required for adaptation by natural selection in modern terms.   306
5. Distinguish among directional, stabilizing, and disruptive selection by giving examples.   306–8
6. State ways in which variation is maintained in a population.   309
7. What is the biological definition of a species?   310
8. What is a reproductive isolating mechanism? Give examples of both prezygotic and postzygotic isolating mechanisms.   310–11
9. How does allopatric speciation occur? sympatric speciation?   312
10. What is adaptive radiation and how is it exemplified by the Galápagos finches and the Hawaiian honeycreepers?   313

Testing Yourself

Choose the best answer for each question.

1. Assuming a Hardy-Weinberg equilibrium, 21% of a population is homozygous dominant, 50% is heterozygous, and 29% is homozygous recessive. What percentage of the next generation is predicted to be homozygous recessive?
   a. 21%
   b. 50%
   c. 29%
   d. 42%
   e. 58%
2. A human population has a higher-than-usual percentage of individuals with a genetic disorder. The most likely explanation is
   a. mutations and gene flow.
   b. mutations and natural selection.
   c. nonrandom mating and genetic drift.
   d. nonrandom mating and gene flow.
   e. All of these are correct.
3. The offspring of better-adapted individuals are expected to make up a larger proportion of the next generation. The most likely explanation is
   a. mutations and nonrandom mating.
   b. gene flow and genetic drift.
   c. mutations and natural selection.
   d. mutations and genetic drift.
4. The continued occurrence of sickle-cell disease in parts of Africa with malaria is due to
   a. continual mutation.
   b. gene flow between populations.
   c. relative fitness of the heterozygote.
   d. disruptive selection.
   e. protozoan resistance to DDT.

5. Which of these is/are necessary to natural selection?
   a. variations
   b. differential reproduction
   c. inheritance of differences
   d. differential adaptiveness
   e. All of these are correct.
6. When a population is small, there is a greater chance of
   a. gene flow.
   b. genetic drift.
   c. natural selection.
   d. mutations occurring.
   e. sexual selection.
7. The biological definition of a species is simply the
   a. anatomical and developmental differences between two groups of organisms.
   b. geographic distribution of two groups of organisms.
   c. differences in the adaptations of two groups of organisms.
   d. reproductive isolation of two groups of organisms.
   e. difference in mutations between two groups of organisms.
8. Which of these is a prezygotic isolating mechanism?
   a. habitat isolation
   b. temporal isolation
   c. hybrid sterility
   d. zygote mortality
   e. Both a and b are correct.
9. Male moths recognize females of their species by sensing chemical signals called pheromones. This is an example of
   a. gamete isolation.
   b. habitat isolation.
   c. behavioral isolation.
   d. mechanical isolation.
   e. temporal isolation.
10. Allopatric but not sympatric speciation requires
   a. reproductive isolation.
   b. geographic isolation.
   c. prior hybridization.
   d. spontaneous differences in males and females.
   e. changes in gene pool frequencies.
11. The many species of Galápagos finches were each adapted to eating different foods. This is the result of
   a. gene flow.
   b. adaptive radiation.
   c. sympatric speciation.
   d. genetic drift.
   e. All of these are correct.

12. The following diagrams represent a distribution of phenotypes in a population. Superimpose another diagram on (a) to show that disruptive selection has occurred, on (b) to show that stabilizing selection has occurred, and on (c) to show that directional selection has occurred.

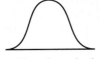
a. Disruptive selection

b. Stabilizing selection

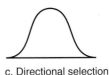
c. Directional selection

Additional Genetics Problems*

1. If $p^2 = 0.36$, what percentage of the population has the recessive phenotype, assuming a Hardy-Weinberg equilibrium?
2. If 1% of a human population has the recessive phenotype, what percentage has the dominant phenotype, assuming a Hardy-Weinberg equilibrium?
3. Four percent of the members of a population of pea plants are short (recessive characteristic). What are the frequencies of both the recessive allele and the dominant allele? What are the genotypic frequencies in this population, assuming a Hardy-Weinberg equilibrium?

Thinking Scientifically

1. You are observing a grouse population in which there are two feather phenotypes in males. One is relatively dark and blends into shadows well, and the other is relatively bright, and so is more obvious to predators. The females are uniformly dark-feathered. Observing the frequency of mating between females and the two types of males, you have recorded the following:

    matings with dark-feathered males: 13
    matings with bright-feathered males: 32

    Propose a hypothesis to explain why females apparently prefer bright-feathered males. What selective advantage might there be in choosing a male with alleles that make it more susceptible to predation? What data would help test the hypothesis?

2. A farmer uses a new pesticide. He applies the pesticide as directed by the manufacturer and loses about 15% of his crop to insects. A farmer in the next state learns of these results, uses three times as much pesticide and loses only 3% of her crop to insects. Each farmer follows this pattern for 5 years. At the end of 5 years, the first farmer is still losing about 15% of his crop to insects, but the second farmer is losing 40% of her crop to insects. How could these observations be interpreted on the basis of natural selection?

Understanding the Terms

adaptive radiation   312
allopatric speciation   312
assortative mating   305
bottleneck effect   305
directional selection   306
disruptive selection   308
founder effect   306
gene flow   304
gene pool   302
genetic drift   305
Hardy-Weinberg law   302
industrial melanism   303
microevolution   302
natural selection   306
nonrandom mating   305
population genetics   302
postzygotic isolating
 mechanism   311
prezygotic isolating
 mechanism   310
relative fitness   306
sexual selection   305
speciation   310
species   310
stabilizing selection   308
sympatric speciation   312

Match the terms to these definitions:

a. _____ Outcome of natural selection in which extreme phenotypes are eliminated and the average phenotype is conserved.
b. _____ Anatomical or physiological difference between two species that prevents successful reproduction after mating has taken place.
c. _____ Change in the genetic makeup of a population due to chance (random) events; important in small populations or when only a few individuals mate.
d. _____ Evolution of a large number of species from a common ancestor.
e. _____ Sharing of genes between two populations through interbreeding.

Web Connections

Exploring the Internet

http://www.mhhe.com/biosci/genbio/mader
(click on *Biology 7/e*)

The *Biology 7/e* Online Learning Center provides many resources for studying the material in this chapter including links to the following sites:

How convergent evolution led to flight in pterosaurs, birds, and bats is explored in Vertebrate Flight, and the pages linked to follow.

http://www.ucmp.berkeley.edu/vertebrates/flight/evolve.html

Punctuated Equilibrium. This site provides a history of the observations and ideas that led to the punctuated equilibrium model of evolution, as well as a detailed description of the model and the reasons why it is important, particularly to paleontologists.

http://www.talkorigins.org/faqs/punc-eq.html

_____
* Answers to Additional Genetics Problems appear in Appendix A.

Origin and History of Life

20.1 Origin of Life

- A chemical evolution proceeded from monomers to polymers to protocells.   320
- The primitive atmosphere contained no oxygen, and the first cell may have been an anaerobic fermenter.   322
- The first cell was bounded by a membrane and contained a replication system; that is, DNA, RNA, and proteins.   323

20.2 History of Life

- The fossil record allows us to trace the history of life, which is divided into the Precambrian, Paleozoic, Mesozoic, and Cenozoic eras.   324
- The first fossils are of prokaryotes dated about 3.5 BYA.[1] Prokaryotes diversified for about 2 billion years before the eukaryotic cell and then multicellular forms evolved during the Precambrian.   326

- Fossils of complex marine multicellular invertebrates and vertebrates appeared during the Cambrian period of the Paleozoic era. During the Carboniferous period, swamp forests on land contained nonseed vascular plants, insects, and amphibians.   329
- The Mesozoic era was the age of cycads and reptiles. Mammals and flowering plants evolved during the Cenozoic era.   331, 333

20.3 Factors That Influence Evolution

- The position of the continents changes over time because the earth's crust consists of moving plates.   338
- Continental drift and meteorite impacts have contributed to several episodes of mass extinctions during the history of life.   334

---

[1] BYA = billions of years ago

The earth was once devoid of life.

One of the most fascinating and frequently asked questions by laypeople and scientists alike is where did life come from? Although various answers have been proposed throughout history, today the most widely accepted hypothesis is that inorganic molecules in Earth's prebiotic oceans combined to produce organic molecules and eventually primitive cells arose. These earliest cells probably appeared around 3.5 billion years ago. About a billion years ago, oxygen-releasing photosynthesis began and an atmospheric ozone layer began to form. This shield protects the earth's surface from intense ultraviolet radiation, and consequently, life could move from water onto land. Shortly afterward (at least in geologic time), the number of multicellular life-forms increased dramatically.

If we could trace the lineages of all the millions of species ever to have evolved, the entire would resemble a dense bush. Some lines of descent are cut off close to the base; some continue in a straight line even to today; others have split, producing two or even several groups. The history of life on earth has many facets and twists and turns.

20.1 Origin of Life

Today we do not believe that life arises spontaneously from nonlife, and we say that "life comes only from life." But if this is so, how did the first form of life come about? Since it was the very first living thing, it had to come from nonliving chemicals. Could there have been an increase in the complexity of the chemicals—could a **chemical evolution** have produced the first cell(s) on the primitive earth?

The Primitive Earth

The sun and the planets, including Earth, probably formed over a 10-billion-year period from aggregates of dust particles and debris. At 4.6 billion years ago (BYA), the solar system was in place. Intense heat produced by gravitational energy and radioactivity caused the earth to become stratified into several layers. Heavier atoms of iron and nickel became the molten liquid core and dense silicate minerals became the semiliquid mantle. Upwellings of volcanic lava produced the first crust.

The mass of the earth is such that the gravitational field is strong enough to have an atmosphere. If the earth had less mass, atmospheric gases would escape into outer space. The earth's primitive atmosphere was not the same as today's atmosphere; it was produced primarily by outgassing from the interior, exemplified by volcanic eruptions. The primitive atmosphere most likely consisted mostly of water vapor (H_2O), nitrogen (N_2), and carbon dioxide (CO_2), with only small amounts of hydrogen (H_2) and carbon monoxide (CO). The primitive atmosphere, with little if any free oxygen, was a reducing atmosphere as opposed to the oxidizing atmosphere of today. This was fortuitous because oxygen (O_2) attaches to organic molecules, preventing them from joining to form larger molecules.

At first the earth was so hot that water was present only as a vapor that formed dense, thick clouds. Then as the earth cooled, water vapor condensed to liquid water, and rain began to fall. It rained in such enormous quantity over hundreds of millions of years that the oceans of the world were produced. The earth is an appropriate distance from the sun: any closer, water would have evaporated; any farther, water would have frozen.

It's also possible that the oceans were fed by celestial comets that entered Earth's gravitational field. In 1999, physicist Louis Frank presented images taken by cameras on NASA's Polar satellite to substantiate his claim that the earth is bombarded with 5 to 30 icy comets the size of a house every minute. The ice becomes water vapor that later comes down as rain, enough rain, says Frank, to raise the oceans' level by an inch in just 10,000 years.

Monomers Evolve

Other and larger comets, and pieces of them, called meteorites, frequently pelted the earth until about 3.8 BYA. Any one of these may have carried the first organic molecules to Earth. Others even suspect that bacterium-like cells evolved

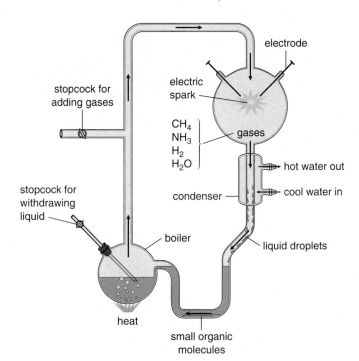

Figure 20.1 **Chemical evolution in the atmosphere.** Atmospheric gases were admitted to the apparatus, circulated past an energy source (electric spark), and cooled to produce a liquid that could be withdrawn. Upon chemical analysis, the liquid was found to contain various small organic molecules.

first on another planet and then were carried to Earth. A meteorite from Mars labeled ALH84001 landed on Earth some 13,000 years ago. When examined, experts found tiny rods similar in shape to fossilized bacteria.

As early as 1938, Aleksandr Oparin, a Soviet biochemist, suggested that the first organic molecules could have been produced on Earth from primitive atmospheric gases in the presence of strong energy sources. The energy sources on the primitive earth included heat from volcanoes and meteorites, radioactivity from isotopes in the earth's crust, powerful electric discharges in lightning, and solar radiation, especially ultraviolet radiation.

In 1953, Stanley Miller provided support for Oparin's hypothesis through an ingenious experiment (Fig. 20.1). Miller placed a mixture resembling a strongly reducing atmosphere—methane (CH_4), ammonia (NH_3), hydrogen (H_2), and water (H_2O)—in a closed system, heated the mixture, and circulated it past an electric spark (simulating lightning). After a week's run, Miller discovered that a variety of amino acids and organic acids had been produced. Since that time, other investigators have achieved similar results by utilizing other, less-reducing combinations of gases dissolved in water.

These experiments apparently lend support to the hypothesis that the earth's first atmospheric gases could have reacted with one another to produce small organic compounds. If so, neither oxidation (there was no free oxygen) nor decay (there were no bacteria) would have destroyed these molecules, and they would have accumulated in the oceans for hundreds of millions of years. With the accumulation of small organic molecules, the oceans would have become a thick, warm organic soup.

Other investigators are concerned that Miller used ammonia as one of the atmospheric gases. They point out that whereas inert nitrogen gas (N_2) would have been abundant in the primitive atmosphere, ammonia (NH_3) would have been scarce. Where might ammonia have been abundant? A team of researchers at the Carnegie Institution in Washington, D.C. believe they have found the answer: hydrothermal vents on the ocean floor. These vents line huge **ocean ridges,** where molten magma wells up and adds material to the ocean floor (Fig. 20.2). Cool water seeping through the vents is heated to a temperature as high as 350°C, and when it spews back out it contains various mixed iron-nickel sulfides that can act as catalysts to change N_2 to NH_3. A laboratory test of this theory worked perfectly. Under ventlike conditions, 70% of various nitrogen sources were converted to ammonia within 15 minutes. German organic chemists Gunter Wachtershaüser and Claudia Huber have gone one more step. They have managed to show that organic molecules will react and amino acids will form peptides in the presence of iron-nickel sulfides under ventlike conditions.

Comets from outer space, atmospheric reactions, and hydrothermal vents could be responsible for the first organic molecules on Earth.

Figure 20.2 Chemical evolution at hydrothermal vents. Minerals that form at deep-sea hydrothermal vents like this one can catalyze the formation of ammonia and even organic molecules.

Polymers Evolve

In cells, monomers join to form polymers in the presence of enzymes which, of course, are proteins. How did the first organic polymers form if there were no proteins yet? As mentioned above, Gunter Wachtershaüser and Claudia Huber have managed to achieve the formation of peptides utilizing iron-nickel sulfides as inorganic catalysts under ventlike conditions of high temperature and pressure. These minerals have a charged surface that attracts amino acids and provides electrons so they can bond together.

Sidney Fox has shown that amino acids polymerize abiotically when exposed to dry heat. He suggests that once amino acids were present in the oceans, they could have collected in shallow puddles along the rocky shore. Then the heat of the sun could have caused them to form **proteinoids,** small polypeptides that have some catalytic properties. When he simulates this scenario in the lab and returns proteinoids to water, they form **microspheres** [Gk. *mikros,* small, little, and *sphaera,* ball], structures composed only of protein that have many properties of a cell. It's possible that even newly formed polypeptides had enzymatic properties, and some proved to be more capable than others. Those that led to the first cell or cells had a selective advantage. Fox's **protein-first hypothesis** assumes that DNA genes came af-

ter protein enzymes arose. After all, it is protein enzymes that are needed for DNA replication.

Another hypothesis is put forth by Graham Cairns-Smith. He believes that clay was especially helpful in causing polymerization of both proteins and nucleic acids at the same time. Clay also attracts small organic molecules and contains iron and zinc, which may have served as inorganic catalysts for polypeptide formation. In addition, clay has a tendency to collect energy from radioactive decay and to discharge it when the temperature and/or humidity changes. This could have been a source of energy for polymerization to take place. Cairns-Smith suggests that RNA nucleotides and amino acids became associated in such a way that polypeptides were ordered by and helped synthesize RNA. It is clear that this hypothesis suggests that both polypeptides and RNA arose at the same time.

There is still another hypothesis concerning this stage in the origin of life. The **RNA-first hypothesis** suggests that only the macromolecule RNA (ribonucleic acid) was needed to progress toward formation of the first cell or cells. Thomas Cech and Sidney Altman shared a Nobel Prize in 1989 because they discovered that RNA can be both a substrate and an enzyme. Some viruses today have RNA genes;

therefore, the first genes could have been RNA. It would seem, then, that RNA could have carried out the processes of life commonly associated today with DNA (deoxyribonucleic acid, the genetic material) and proteins (enzymes). Those who support this hypothesis say that it was an "RNA world" some 4 billion years ago.

Polymerization of monomers to produce proteins and nucleotides is the next step toward the first cell.

A Protocell Evolves

Before the first true cell arose, there would have been a **protocell** [Gk. *protos,* first], a structure that has a lipid-protein membrane and carries on energy metabolism (Fig. 20.3). Fox has shown that if lipids are made available to microspheres, lipids tend to become associated with microspheres producing a lipid-protein membrane.

Oparin, who was mentioned previously, showed that under appropriate conditions of temperature, ionic composition, and pH, concentrated mixtures of macromolecules tend to give rise to complex units called **coacervate droplets.** Coacervate droplets have a tendency to absorb and incorporate various substances from the surrounding solution. Eventually, a semipermeable-type boundary may form about the droplet. In a liquid environment, phospholipid molecules automatically form droplets called **liposomes** [Gk. *lipos,* fat, and *soma,* body]. Perhaps the first membrane formed in this manner, and the protocell contained only RNA, which functioned as both genetic material and enzymes.

The protocell would have had to carry on nutrition so that it could grow. If organic molecules formed in the atmosphere and were carried by rain into the ocean, nutrition would have been no problem because simple organic molecules could have served as food. This hypothesis suggests that the protocell was a heterotroph [Gk. *hetero,* different, and *trophe,* food], an organism that takes in preformed food. On the other hand, if the protocell evolved at hydrothermal vents, it may have carried out chemosynthesis. Chemosynthetic bacteria are autotrophs. They obtain energy for synthesizing organic molecules by oxidizing inorganic compounds like hydrogen sulfide (H_2S), a molecule that is abundant at the vents. When hydrothermal vents were first discovered in the 1970s, investigators were surprised to discover complex vent ecosystems supported by organic molecules formed by chemosynthesis, a process that does not require the energy of the sun.

At first, the protocell may have used preformed ATP (adenosine triphosphate), but as this supply dwindled, natural selection favored any cells that could extract energy from carbohydrates in order to transform ADP (adenosine diphosphate) to ATP. Glycolysis is a common metabolic

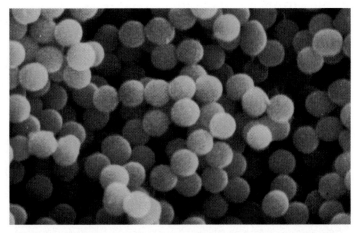

a.

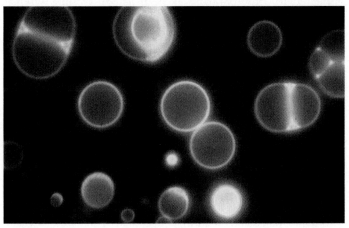

b.

Figure 20.3 Protocell anatomy.
a. Microspheres, which are composed only of protein, have a number of cellular characteristics and could have evolved into the protocell. **b.** Liposomes form automatically when phospholipid molecules are put into water. Plasma membranes may have evolved similarly.

pathway in living things, and this testifies to its early evolution in the history of life. Since there was no free oxygen, we can assume that the protocell carried on a form of fermentation. At first the protocell must have had limited ability to break down organic molecules and that it took millions of years for glycolysis to evolve completely. It is of interest that Fox has shown that microspheres from which protocells may have evolved have some catalytic ability and that Oparin found that coacervates do incorporate enzymes if they are available in the medium.

The protocell is hypothesized to have had a membrane boundary and to have been either a heterotroph or a chemoautotroph.

A Self-Replication System Evolves

Today's cell is able to carry on protein synthesis needed to produce the enzymes that allow DNA to replicate. The central dogma of genetics states that DNA directs protein synthesis and that there is a flow of information from DNA → RNA → protein. It is possible that this sequence developed in stages.

According to the RNA-first hypothesis, RNA would have been the first to evolve, and the first true cell would have had RNA genes. These genes would have directed and enzymatically carried out protein synthesis. As mentioned, ribozymes are composed of RNA and have enzymatic properties. Also, today we know there are viruses that have RNA genes. These viruses have a protein enzyme called reverse transcriptase that uses RNA as a template to form DNA. Perhaps with time, reverse transcription occurred within the protocell, and this is how DNA genes arose. If so, RNA was responsible for both DNA and protein formation. Once there were DNA genes, then protein synthesis would have been carried out in the manner dictated by the central dogma of genetics.

According to the protein-first hypothesis, proteins, or at least polypeptides, were the first of the three (i.e., DNA, RNA, and protein) to arise. Only after the protocell developed sophisticated enzymes did it have the ability to synthesize DNA and RNA from small molecules provided by the ocean. These researchers point out that a nucleic acid is a very complicated molecule, and they believe the likelihood that RNA arose *de novo* (on its own) is minimal. It seems more likely to them that enzymes were needed to guide the synthesis of nucleotides and then nucleic acids. Again, once there were DNA genes, protein synthesis would have been carried out in the manner dictated by the central dogma of genetics.

Cairns-Smith proposes that polypeptides and RNA evolved simultaneously. Therefore, the first true cell would have contained RNA genes that could have replicated because of the presence of proteins. This eliminates the baffling chicken-and-egg paradox: which came first, proteins or RNA? But it does mean, however, that two unlikely events would have to happen at the same time.

After DNA formed, the genetic code had to evolve before DNA could store genetic information. The present genetic code is subject to fewer errors than a million other possible codes. Also the present code is among the best at minimizing the effect of mutations. A single-base change in a present codon is likely to result in a substitution of a chemically similar amino acid, and therefore minimal changes in the final protein. This evidence suggests that the genetic code did undergo a natural selection process before finalizing into today's code.

Once there was a flow of information from DNA → RNA → protein, the protocell became a true cell, and biological evolution began.

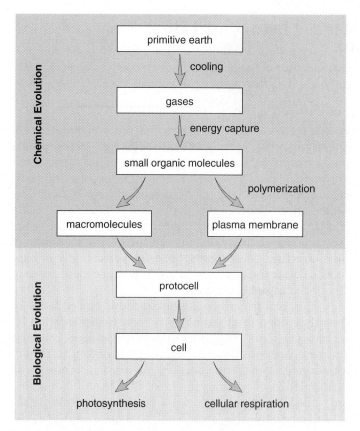

Figure 20.4 Origin of the first cell(s).
There was an increase in the complexity of macromolecules, leading to a self-replicating system (DNA → RNA → protein) enclosed by a plasma membrane. The protocell, a heterotrophic fermenter, underwent biological evolution, becoming a true cell, which then diversified.

Figure 20.4 reviews how most biologists believe life could have evolved on Earth:

1. There was an abiotic synthesis of small organic molecules such as amino acids and nucleotides either perhaps in the atmosphere or at hydrothermal vents.
2. These monomers joined together to form polymers either on land (warm seaside rocks or clay) or at the vents. The first polymers could have been proteins or RNA or they could have evolved together.
3. The aggregation of polymers inside a plasma membrane produced a protocell, which had some enzymatic properties such that it could grow. If the protocell developed in the ocean it was a heterotroph; if it developed at hydrothermal vents it was a chemoautotroph.
4. A true cell had evolved once the protocell contained DNA genes. The first genes may have been RNA molecules but later DNA became the information storage molecule of heredity. Biological evolution now began. The history of life began!

20.2 History of Life

In this chapter we will be tracing the events that encompass **macroevolution,** which is large-scale patterns of change taking place over very long time spans.

Fossils Tell a Story

Fossils [L. *fossilis,* dug up] are the remains and traces of past life or any other direct evidence of past life. Traces include trails, footprints, burrows, worm casts, or even preserved droppings. Usually when an organism dies, the soft parts are either consumed by scavengers or undergo bacterial decomposition. Occasionally, the organism is buried quickly and in such a way that decomposition is never completed or is completed so slowly that the soft parts leave an imprint of their structure. Most fossils, however, consist only of hard parts such as shells, bones, or teeth, because these are usually not consumed or destroyed.

The great majority of fossils are found embedded in or recently eroded from sedimentary rock. **Sedimentation** [L. *sedimentum,* a settling], a process that has been going on since the earth was formed, can take place on land or in bodies of water. Weathering and erosion of rocks produces an accumulation of particles that vary in size and nature and are called sediment. Sediment becomes a **stratum** (pl., strata), a recognizable layer in a stratigraphic sequence (Fig. 20.5). Any given stratum is older than the one above it and younger than the one immediately below it.

The fossils trapped in strata are the fossil record that tells us about the history of life (Fig. 20.6). **Paleontology** [Gk. *palaios,* ancient, old, and *ontos,* having existed; *-logy,* "study of" from *logikos,* rational, sensible] is the science of discovering and studying the fossil record and, from it, making decisions about the history of life.

Relative Dating of Fossils

In the early nineteenth century, even before the theory of evolution was formulated, geologists sought to correlate the strata worldwide. The problem was that strata change their character over great distances, and therefore a stratum in England might contain different sediments than one of the same age in Russia. Geologists discovered, however, that a stratum of the same age tended to contain the same fossil, and therefore the sequence of fossils comprises a **relative dating** method. For example, a particular species of fossil ammonite (an animal related to the chambered nautilus) has been found over a wide range and for a limited time period. Therefore, all strata around the world that contain this fossil must be of the same age.

This approach helped geologists determine the relative dates of the strata despite upheavals, but it was not particularly helpful to biologists who wanted to know the absolute age of fossils in years.

Absolute Dating of Fossils

An **absolute dating** method that relies on radioactive dating techniques assigns an actual date to a fossil. All radioactive isotopes have a particular half-life, the length of time it takes for half of the radioactive isotope to change into another stable element. If the fossil has organic matter, half of the carbon 14, ^{14}C, will have changed to nitrogen 14, ^{14}N, in 5,730 years. In order to know how much ^{14}C was in the organism to begin with, it is reasoned that organic matter always begins with the same amount of ^{14}C. (In reality, it is known that the ^{14}C levels in the air—and therefore the amount in organisms—can vary from time to time.) Now we need only compare the ^{14}C radioactivity of the fossil to that of a modern sample of organic matter. The amount of radiation left can be converted to the age of the fossil. After 50,000 years, however, the amount of ^{14}C radioactivity is so low it cannot be used to measure the age of a fossil accurately.

^{14}C is the only radioactive isotope contained within organic matter, but it is possible to use others to date rocks and from that infer the age of a fossil contained in the rock. For instance, the ratio of potassium 40 (^{40}K) to argon 40 trapped in rock is often used. If the ratio happens to be 1:1, then half of the ^{40}K has decayed and researchers know the rock is 1.3 billion years old.

Fossils, which can be dated relatively according to their location in strata and absolutely according to their content of radioactive isotopes, give us information about the history of life.

Figure 20.5 Strata.
The strata exposed by roadcuts is familiar to most travelers along major highways.

Figure 20.6 Fossils.
Fossils are the remains of past life. They can be impressions left in rocks, footprints, mineralized bones, shells, or any other evidences of life-forms that lived in the past.

petrified stone trees, 190 MYA

midge embedded in amber, 40 MYA

ammonites, 135 MYA

dinosaur track, 135 MYA

fern leaf, 245 MYA

The Precambrian

As a result of their study of fossils in strata, geologists have devised the **geological timescale** which divides the history of the earth into eras, then periods and epochs (Table 20.1). We will follow the biologist's tradition of first discussing the Precambrian, a period of time that encompasses the first two eras: the Archean era and the Proterozoic era.

The Precambrian is a very long period of time—it comprises about 87% of the geological timescale. It is during this period of time that life arose and the first cells came into existence. The first cells were probably prokaryotes. Prokaryotes do not have a nucleus or any membrane-bounded organelles. Of the living prokaryotes today, the archaea live in the most inhospitable of environments, such as hot springs,

Table 20.1

The Geological Timescale: Major Divisions of Geological Time with Some of the Major Evolutionary Events of Each Geological Period

Era	Period	Epoch	Millions of Years Ago	Plant Life	Animal Life
Cenozoic* (from the present to 66.4 million years ago)	Neogene	Holocene	0–0.01	Destruction of tropical rain forests by humans accelerates extinctions.	AGE OF HUMAN CIVILIZATION
			Significant Mammalian Extinction		
		Pleistocene	0.01–2	Herbaceous plants spread and diversify.	Modern humans appear.
		Pliocene	2–6	Herbaceous angiosperms flourish.	First hominids appear.
		Miocene	6–24	Grasslands spread as forests contract.	Apelike mammals and grazing mammals flourish; insects flourish.
	Paleogene	Oligocene	24–37	Many modern families of flowering plants evolve.	Browsing mammals and monkeylike primates appear.
		Eocene	37–58	Subtropical forests with heavy rainfall thrive.	All modern orders of mammals are represented.
		Paleocene	58–66	Angiosperms diversify.	Primitive primates, herbivores, carnivores, and insectivores appear.
Mesozoic (from 66.4 to 245 million years ago)			**Mass Extinction: Dinosaurs and Most Reptiles**		
	Cretaceous		66–144	Flowering plants spread; coniferous trees decline.	Placental mammals appear; modern insect groups appear.
	Jurassic		144–208	Cycads and other gymnosperms flourish.	Dinosaurs flourish; birds appear.
			Mass Extinction		
	Triassic		208–245	Cycads and ginkgoes appear; forests of gymnosperms and ferns dominate.	First mammals appear; first dinosaurs appear, corals and mollusks dominate seas.
Paleozoic (from 245 to 570 million years ago)			**Mass Extinction**		
	Permian		245–286	Conifers appear.	Reptiles diversify; amphibians decline.
	Carboniferous		286–360	Age of great coal-forming forests: club mosses, horsetails, and ferns flourish.	Amphibians diversify; first reptiles appear; first great radiation of insects.
			Mass Extinction		
	Devonian		360–408	First seed ferns appear.	Jawed fishes diversify and dominate the seas; first insects and first amphibians appear.
	Silurian		408–438	Low-lying vascular plants appear on land.	First jawed fishes appear.
			Mass Extinction		
	Ordovician		438–505	Marine algae flourish.	Invertebrates spread and diversify; jawless fishes, first vertebrates, appear.
	Cambrian		505–570	Marine algae flourish.	Invertebrates with skeletons are dominant.
Precambrian time (from 570 to 4,600 million years ago)			600 1,400–700 1,500 3,500 4,500	Oldest soft-bodied invertebrate fossils Protists evolve and diversify. Oldest eukaryotic fossils Oldest known fossils (prokaryotes) Earth forms.	

* Many authorities divide the Cenozoic era into the Tertiary period (contains Paleocene, Eocene, Oligocene, Miocene, and Pliocene) and the Quaternary period (contains Pleistocene and Holocene).

1.5 BYA	Oldest eukaryotic fossils
2.5 BYA	O₂ accumulates in atmosphere
3.5 BYA	Oldest known fossils
4.5 BYA	Formation of the earth

very salty lakes, and airless swamps—all of which may typify habitats on the primitive earth. The cell wall, plasma membrane, RNA polymerase, and ribosomes of archaea are more like those of eukaryotes than those of other bacteria.

The first identifiable fossils are those of complex prokaryotes. Sedimentary rocks from southwestern Greenland, dated at 3.8 BYA, contain chemical fingerprints of complex cells. And when paleobiologist J. William Schopf examined rock formations in northwestern Australia, he found 3.46 billion-year-old microfossils that resemble today's cyanobacteria, prokaryotes that carry on photosynthesis in the same manner as plants (Fig. 20.7*a*).

At this time only volcanic rocks jutted above the waves and there were as yet no continents. Strange looking boulders, called **stromatolites,** littered beaches and shallow waters (Fig. 20.7*b*). Living stromatolites can still be found today along Australia's southwestern coast. The outer surface of a stromatolite is alive with cyanobacteria that secrete a mucus. Grains of sand get caught in the mucus and bind with calcium carbonate from the water to form rock. To gain access

to sunlight, the photosynthetic organisms move outward toward the surface before they are cemented in. They leave behind a menagerie of aerobic and then anaerobic bacteria caught in the layers of the rock.

The cyanobacteria in ancient stromatolites added oxygen to the atmosphere. By 2 BYA, the presence of oxygen was such that most environments were no longer suitable for anaerobic prokaryotes, and they began to decline in importance. Photosynthetic cyanobacteria and aerobic bacteria proliferated as new metabolic pathways evolved. Due to the presence of oxygen, the atmosphere became an oxidizing one instead of a reducing one. Oxygen in the upper atmosphere forms ozone (O_3), which filters out the ultraviolet (UV) rays of the sun. Before the formation of the **ozone shield,** the amount of ultraviolet radiation reaching the earth could have helped create organic molecules, but it would have destroyed any land-dwelling organisms. Once the ozone shield was in place, it meant that living things would be sufficiently protected and would be able to live on land.

The evolution of photosynthesizing organisms caused oxygen to enter the atmosphere.

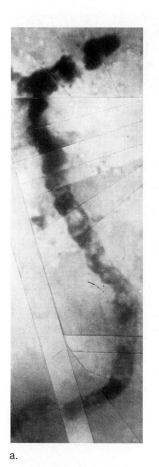
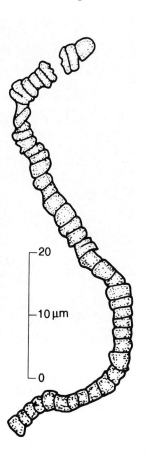

-20

-10 µm

-0

a.   b.

Figure 20.7 **Prokaryote fossil of the Precambrian.**
a. The prokaryotic microorganism, *Primaevifilum* (with interpretive drawing), was found in rocks dated 3.46 BYA. b. Stromatolites, also date back to this time. Living stromatolites are located in shallow waters off the shores of western Australia and also in other tropical seas.

540 MYA	Cambrian animals
600 MYA	Ediacaran animals
1.40 BYA	Protists evolve and diversify
1.50 BYA	Oldest eukaryotic fossils

Eukaryotic Cells Arise

The eukaryotic cell, which originated about 1.5 BYA, is nearly always aerobic and contains a nucleus as well as other membranous organelles. Most likely the eukaryotic cell acquired its organelles gradually. It may be that the nucleus developed by an invagination of the plasma membrane. The mitochondria of the eukaryotic cell probably were once free-living aerobic prokaryotes, and the chloroplasts probably were free-living photosynthetic prokaryotes. The **endosymbiotic hypothesis** says that a nucleated cell engulfed these prokaryotes, which then became organelles. It's been suggested that flagella (and cilia) also arose by endosymbiosis. First, slender undulating prokaryotes could have attached themselves to a host cell in order to take advantage of food leaking from the host's outer membrane. Eventually, these prokaryotes adhered to the host cell and became the flagella and cilia we know today. The first eukaryotes were unicellular, as are prokaryotes.

Multicellularity Arises

It is not known when multicellularity began, but the very first multicellular forms were most likely microscopic. It's possible that the first multicellular organisms practiced sexual reproduction. Among protists (eukaryotes classified in the kingdom Protista) today, we find colonial forms in which some cells are specialized to produce gametes needed for sexual reproduction. Separation of germ cells, which produce gametes from somatic cells, may have been an important first step toward the development of complex macroscopic animals that appeared about 600 MYA.

In 1947, fossils of soft-bodied invertebrates dated 600 MYA were found in the Ediacara Hills in South Australia. Since then, similar fossils have been discovered on a number of other continents. They represent a community of animals that most likely lived on mudflats in shallow marine waters. Large immobile bizarre creatures that resembled spoked wheels, corrugated ribbons, and lettuce-like fronds had no internal organs (Fig. 20.8a). Perhaps they could have absorbed nutrients from the sea. Fewer in number were mobile organisms that bear some resemblance to animals of today (Fig. 20.8b). All were soft-bodied and their fossils are like footprints—impressions made in the sandy seafloor before their bodies decayed away. Soft-bodied animals could flourish because there were no predators to eat them.

For two billion years of the Precambrian era only prokaryotic cells existed. After eukaryotic cells arose it was nearly another million years before multicellularity occurred.

a. *Charniodiscus*

b. *Dickinsonia*

Figure 20.8 Ediacaran fossils.
a. These large frondlike organisms looked somewhat like soft corals, known today as sea pens. b. These fossils are interpreted to be segmented worms.

The Paleozoic Era

The Paleozoic era lasted over 300 million years. Many events occurred during this time, even though the era was quite short compared to the length of the Precambrian. For one thing, there were three major mass extinctions (see Table 20.1). An **extinction** is the total disappearance of all the members of a species or higher taxonomic group. **Mass extinctions,** which are the disappearance of a large number of species or higher taxonomic group within an interval of just a few million years, are discussed later in the chapter.

Cambrian Fossils

Figure 20.9 shows that the seas teemed with invertebrate life during the Cambrian period. Invertebrates are animals without a vertebral column. All of today's groups of animals can trace their ancestry to this time and perhaps earlier according to new molecular clock data. A **molecular clock** is based on the principle that DNA differences in certain parts of the genome occur at a fixed rate and are not tied to natural selection. The number of DNA base pair differences tells how long two species have been evolving separately.

Even if certain animals had evolved earlier no fossil evidence occurs until the Cambrian period. Why are fossils easier to find at this time? Because the animals had protective outer skeletons, and skeletons are capable of surviving the forces that are apt to destroy fossils. For example, Cambrian seafloors were dominated by now-extinct trilobites, which had thick, jointed armor covering them from head to tail. Trilobites are classified as arthropods, a major phylum of animals today. (Some Cambrian species, with most unusual eating and locomotion appendages, have been classified in phyla that no longer exist today.)

Paleontologists have sought an explanation for why animals had skeletons during the Cambrian period but not before. By this time, not only cyanobacteria but also various algae, which are floating photosynthetic organisms, were pumping oxygen into the atmosphere at a rapid rate. Perhaps the oxygen supply became great enough to permit aquatic animals to acquire oxygen even though they had outer skeletons. The presence of a skeleton reduces possible access to oxygen in seawater. Steven Stanley of Johns Hopkins University suggests that predation may have played a role. Skeletons may have evolved during the Cambrian period because skeletons help protect animals from predators.

The fossil record is rich during the Cambrian period but the animals may have evolved earlier. The richness of the Cambrian period may be due to the evolution of outer skeletons.

a.   b.

0.5 cm

Figure 20.9 Sea life of the Cambrian period.
a. The animals depicted here are found as fossils in the Burgess Shale, a formation of the Rocky Mountains of British Columbia. Some lineages represented by these animals are still evolving today; others have become extinct. **b.** *Haplophrentis* has a tapering shell surrounded by an aperculum. The lateral appendages may have served as props.

Figure 20.10 Swamp forests of the Carboniferous period.
Vast swamp forests of treelike club mosses and horsetails dominated the land during the Carboniferous period (see Table 20.1). The air contained insects with wide wingspans, such as the dragonfly shown here, and amphibians lumbered from pool to pool.

Invasion of Land

Plants Sometime during the Paleozoic era, algae, which were common in the seas, most likely began to take up residence in bodies of fresh water; from there, they may have invaded damp areas on land. An association of plant roots with fungi called mycorrhizae is credited with allowing plants to live on bare rocks. The fungi are able to absorb minerals, which they pass to the plant, and the plant in turn passes carbohydrates, the product of photosynthesis, to the fungi.

Fossils of vascular plants with tissue for water transport date back to the Silurian period. They later flourished in the warm swamps of the Carboniferous period (Fig. 20.10). Club mosses, horsetails, and seed ferns were the trees of that time, and they grew to enormous size. A wide variety of smaller ferns and fernlike plants formed an underbrush.

Invertebrates The outer skeleton and jointed appendages of arthropods are adaptive for living on land. Various arthropods—spiders, centipedes, mites, and millipedes—all preceded the appearance of insects on land. Insects enter the fossil record in the Carboniferous period. The evolution of wings provided advantages that allowed insects to radiate into the most diverse and abundant group of animals today. Flying provides a way to escape enemies and find food.

Vertebrates Vertebrates are animals with a vertebral column. The vertebrate line of descent began in the early Ordovician period with the evolution of fishes. First there were jawless fishes and then fishes with jaws. Fishes are ectothermic (cold-blooded), aquatic vertebrates that have gills, scales, and fins. The cartilaginous and ray-finned fishes made their appearance in the Devonian period, which is called the Age of Fishes.

At this time the seas were filled with giant predatory fish covered with protective armor made of external bone. Sharks cruised up deep, wide rivers and the smaller lobe-finned fishes lived at the river's edge in waters too shallow for these large predators. Their fleshy fins helped them push aside debris or hold their place in strong currents. They may also have allowed these fishes to venture onto land and lay their eggs safe in inland pools. Lobe-finned fishes are believed to be ancestral to the amphibians.

Amphibians are thin-skinned vertebrates that are not fully adapted to life on land, particularly because they must return to water to reproduce. The Carboniferous swamp forests provided the water they needed and amphibians radiated into many different sizes and shapes. Some superficially resembled alligators and were covered with protective scales, others were small and snakelike, and a few were larger plant eaters. The largest measured 6 meters (20 feet) from snout to tail. The Carboniferous period is called the Age of the Amphibians.

There was a change of climate at the end of the Carboniferous period; cold and dry weather brought an end to the Age of the Amphibians and began the process that turned the great Carboniferous forests into the coal we use today to fuel our modern society.

Primitive vascular plants and amphibians were larger and more abundant during the Carboniferous period. Insects appeared and flourished to become the largest animal group today.

Figure 20.11 Dinosaurs of the Mesozoic era.

a. The dinosaurs of the Jurassic period included *Apatosaurus*, which fed on cycads and conifers. **b.** *Triceratops* (left) and *Tyrannosaurus rex* (right) were dinosaurs of the Cretaceous period, which ended with a mass extinction of dinosaurs.

The Mesozoic Era

Although there was a severe mass extinction at the end of the Paleozoic era, the evolution of certain types of plants and animals continued into the Triassic, the first period of the Mesozoic era. Nonflowering seed plants (collectively called gymnosperms), which had been present in the fossil record of the Permian period, became dominant. Among these largely cone-bearing plants were cycads and conifers. Cycads are short and stout with palmlike leaves; the female plant produces very large cones. Cycads were so prevalent during the Jurassic period that it is sometimes called the Age of the Cycads. Reptiles, too, can be traced back to the Permian period of the Paleozoic era. Unlike amphibians, reptiles can thrive in a dry climate because they have scaly skin and lay a shelled egg that hatches on land. Reptiles underwent an adaptive radiation during the Mesozoic era to produce forms that lived in the air, in the sea, and on the land. One group of reptiles, the therapsids, had several mammalian skeletal traits.

During the Jurassic period, large flying reptiles called pterosaurs ruled the air and giant marine reptiles with paddlelike limbs ate fishes in the sea, but on land it was the dinosaurs that prevented the evolving mammals from taking center stage. Some of the dinosaurs were of an enormous size. The gargantuan *Apatosaurus* (Fig. 20.11*a*) and the armored tractor-sized *Stegosaurus* fed on cycad seeds and conifer trees. One group of dinosaurs called theropods were bipedal and had an elongate, mobile S-shaped neck. The newly found fossil *Caudipteryx* (see Fig. 18.13) offers convincing evidence that birds are descended from dinosaurs. This fossil is a dinosaur with feathers on its arms and tail. The fossil record for birds begins with the famous fossil *Archaeopteryx*, which still retains some dinosaur-like features.

Up until 1999, Mesozoic mammal fossils largely consisted of teeth. This was changed by another fossil find from China, which has been dated at 120 MYA and named *Jeholodens*. The animal, identified as a mammal, apparently looked like a long-snouted rat. Surprisingly, *Jeholodens* still had the sprawling hindlimbs of a reptile but forelimbs under the belly like today's mammals. During the Cretaceous period, great herds of rhino-like dinosaurs, *Triceratops*, roamed the plains, as did the infamous *Tyrannosaurus rex*, which was carnivorous and played the same ecological role as lions do today (Fig. 20.11*b*). The size of a dinosaur such as *Apatosaurus* is hard for us to imagine. It was as tall as a four-story office building, and its weight was as much as that of a thousand people! How might dinosaurs have benefited from being so large? One theory is that being ectothermic (cold-blooded), the volume-to-surface ratio was favorable for retaining heat. Others believe dinosaurs were endothermic (warm-blooded) for reasons discussed in the reading on next page. At the end of the Cretaceous period, the dinosaurs became victims of a mass extinction, which will be discussed later.

During the Mesozoic era, the dinosaurs achieved an enormous size, while mammals remained small and insignificant.

Real Dinosaurs, Stand Up!

Today's paleontologists are setting the record straight about dinosaurs. Because dinosaurs are classified as reptiles, it is assumed that they must have had the characteristics of today's reptiles. They must have been ectothermic, slow-moving, and antisocial, right? Wrong!

First of all, not all dinosaurs were great lumbering beasts. Many dinosaurs were less than 1 meter (3 feet) long and their tracks indicate they moved "right along." These dinosaurs stood on two legs that were positioned directly under the body. Perhaps they were as agile as ostriches, which are famous for their great speed.

Dinosaurs may have been endothermic. Could they have competed successfully with the preevolving mammals otherwise? They must have been able to hunt prey and escape from predators as well as mammals, which are known to be active because of their high rate of metabolism. Some argue that, in contrast, ectothermic animals have little endurance and cannot keep up. They also believe that the bone structure of dinosaurs indicates they were endothermic.

Dinosaurs cared for their young much like birds do today. In Montana, paleontologist Jack Horner has studied fossilized nests complete with eggs, embryos, and nestlings (Fig. 20A). The nests are about 7.5 meters (24.6 feet) apart, the space needed for the length of an adult parent. About 20 eggs are laid in neatly arranged circles and may have been covered with decaying vegetation to keep them warm. Many contain the bones of juveniles as much as a meter long. It would seem then that baby dinosaurs remained in the nest to be fed by their parents. They must have obtained this size within a relatively short period of time, again indicating that dinosaurs were endothermic. Ectothermic animals grow slowly and take a long time to reach this size.

Dinosaurs were also social! An enormous herd of dinosaurs found by Horner and colleagues is estimated to have nearly 30 million bones, representing 10,000 animals in one area measuring about 1.6 square miles. Most likely, the herd kept on the move in order to be assured of an ad-

equate food supply, which consisted of flowering plants that could be stripped one season and grow back the next season. The fossilized herd is covered by volcanic ash, suggesting that the dinosaurs died following a volcanic eruption.

Some dinosaurs, such as the duck-billed dinosaurs and horned dinosaurs, have a skull crest. How might it have functioned? Perhaps it was a resonating chamber, used when dinosaurs communicated with one another. Or, as with modern horned animals that live in large groups, the males could have used the skull crest in combat to establish dominance.

If dinosaurs were endothermic, fast-moving, and social animals, should they be classified as reptiles? Some say no!

a.

b.

Figure 20A Behavior of dinosaurs.
a. Nest of fossil dinosaur eggs found in Montana, dating from the Cretaceous period.
b. Bones of a hatchling (about 50 cm [20 inches]) found in the nest. These dinosaurs have been named *Maiosaura*, which means "good mother lizard" in Greek.

Figure 20.12 Mammals of the Oligocene epoch.
The artist's representation of these mammals and their habitat vegetation is based on fossil remains.

The Cenozoic Era

A new system divides the Cenozoic era into a Paleogene period and a Neogene period. We are living in the Neogene period.

Mammalian Diversification

At the end of the Mesozoic era, mammals began an adaptive radiation into the many habitats now left vacant by the demise of the dinosaurs. Mammals are endothermic and they have hair, which helps keep body heat from escaping. Their name refers to the presence of mammary glands, which produce milk to feed their young. At the start of the Paleocene epoch, mammals were small and resembled a rat. By the end of the Eocene epoch, mammals had diversified to the point that most of the modern orders were in existence. Bats are mammals that have conquered the air. Whales, dolphins, and other marine mammals live in the sea where vertebrates began their evolution in the first place. Hoofed mammals populate forests and grasslands and are fed upon by diverse carnivores. Many of the types of herbivores and carnivores of the late Paleogene period, however, are extinct today (Fig. 20.12).

Evolution of Primates

Flowering plants (collectively called angiosperms) evolved at the end of the Mesozoic era and began their radiation in the Cenozoic era. Primates are a type of mammal adapted to living in flowering trees where there is protection from predators and where food in the form of fruit is plentiful. The first primates were small squirrel-like animals, but from them evolved the first monkeys and then the apes. Apes diversified during the Miocene epoch and gave rise to the first hominids, a group that includes humans. Many of the skeletal differences between apes and humans relate to the fact that humans walk upright. Exactly what caused humans to adopt bipedalism is still being debated.

Figure 20.13 Woolly mammoth of the Pleistocene epoch.
Woolly mammoths, *Mammuthus*, were magnificent animals, which lived along the borders of continental glaciers.

The world's climate was progressively cooler during the Neogene period, so much so that the latter two epochs are known as the Ice Age. During periods of glaciation, snow and ice covered about one-third of the land surface of the Earth. The Pleistocene epoch was an age of not only humans, but also giant ground sloths, beavers, wolves, bison, woolly rhinoceroses, mastodons, and mammoths (Fig. 20.13). Humans have survived, but what happened to the oversized mammals just mentioned? Some think that humans became such skilled hunters they are at least partially responsible for the extinction of these awe-inspiring animals.

The Cenozoic era is the present era. Only during this time did mammals diversify and human evolution (the subject of the next chapter) begin.

20.3 Factors That Influence Evolution

It used to be thought that the earth's crust was immobile, that the continents had always been in their present positions, and that the ocean floors were only a catch basin for the debris that washed off the land. In 1920 Alfred Wegener, a German meteorologist, presented data from a number of disciplines to support his hypothesis of **continental drift.**

Continental Drift

Continental drift was finally confirmed in the 1960s; the continents are not fixed; instead, their positions and the position of the oceans have changed over time (Fig. 20.14). About 225 MYA, the continents joined to form one supercontinent that Wegener called Pangaea. First, Pangaea divided into two large subcontinents, called Gondwanaland and Laurasia, and then these also split to form the continents of today. Presently, the continents are still drifting in relation to one another.

Continental drift explains why the coastlines of several continents are mirror images of each other—the outline of the west coast of Africa matches that of the east coast of South America. The same geological structures are also found in many of the areas where the continents touched. A single mountain range runs through South America, Antarctica, and Australia. Continental drift also explains the unique distribution patterns of several fossils. Fossils of the same species of seed fern *(Glossopteris)* have been found on all the southern continents. No suitable explanation was possible previously, but now it seems plausible that the plant evolved on one continent and spread to the others when they were joined as one. Similarly, the fossil reptile *Cynognathus* is found in Africa and South America and *Lystrosaurus,* a mammal-like reptile, has now been discovered in Antarctica, far from Africa and southeast Asia, where it also occurs. With mammalian fossils, the situation is different: Australia, South America, and Africa all have their own distinctive mammals because mammals evolved after the continents separated. The mammalian biological diversity of today's world is the result of isolated evolution on separate continents.

The relationship of the continents to one another has affected the biogeography of the earth.

Figure 20.14 Continental drift.
a. About 225 million years ago, all the continents were joined into a supercontinent called Pangaea. **b.** When the joined continents of Pangaea first began moving apart, there were two large continents called Laurasia and Gondwanaland. **c.** By 65 million years ago, all the continents had begun to separate. This process is continuing today. **d.** North America and Europe are presently drifting apart at a rate of about 2 cm per year.

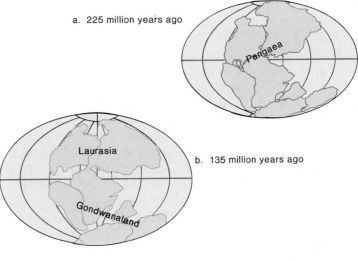

a. 225 million years ago

b. 135 million years ago

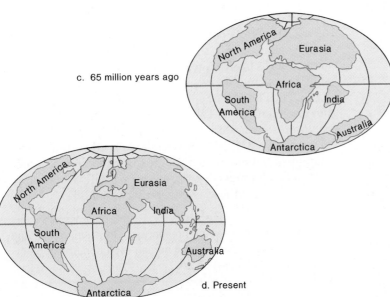

c. 65 million years ago

d. Present

Why do the continents drift? According to a branch of geology known as **plate tectonics** [Gk. *tektos*, fluid, molten, able to flow] (tectonics refers to movements of the earth's crust), the earth's crust is fragmented into slablike plates that float on a lower hot mantle layer. The continents and the ocean basins are a part of these rigid plates, which move like conveyor belts. At **ocean ridges,** seafloor spreading occurs as molten mantle rock rises and material is added to the ocean floor (Fig. 20.15*a*). Seafloor spreading causes the continents to move a few centimeters a year on the average. At *subduction zones,* the forward edge of a moving plate sinks into the mantle and is destroyed. When an ocean floor is at the leading edge of a plate, a deep trench forms that is bordered by volcanoes or volcanic island chains. When two continents collide, the result is often a mountain range; for example, the Himalayas resulted when India collided with Eurasia. Two plates meet along a *transform boundary* where two plates scrape past one another (Fig. 20.15*b*). The San Andreas *fault* in southern California is at a transform boundary, and the movement of the two plates is responsible for the many earthquakes in that region.

The earth's crust is divided into plates that move because of seafloor spreading at ocean ridges.

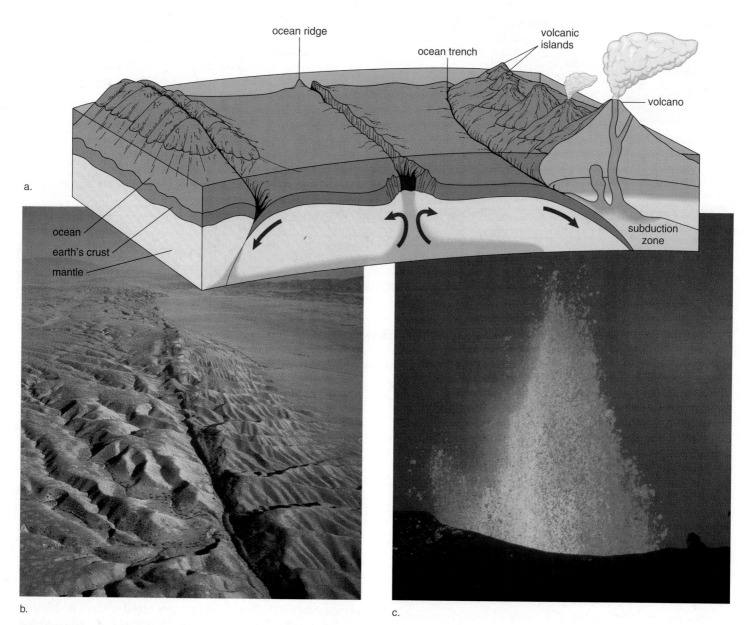

Figure 20.15 Plate tectonics.
a. Plates form and move away from ocean ridges toward subduction zones, where they are carried into the mantle and are destroyed. **b.** A transform boundary occurs where two plates scrape past each other. The San Andreas fault occurs at a transform boundary where earthquakes are apt to occur. **c.** Iceland is one of the few places in the world where an ocean ridge reaches the surface of the sea. The entire island is volcanic in origin.

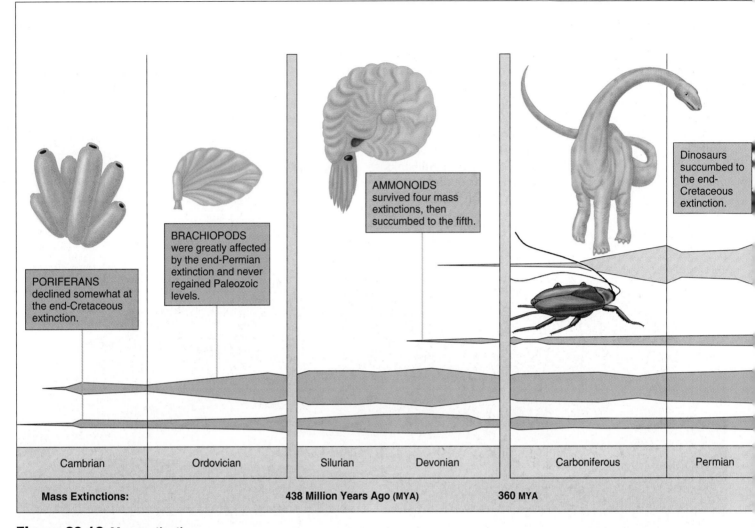

Figure 20.16 Mass extinctions.
Five significant mass extinctions and their effects on the abundance of certain forms of marine and terrestrial life. The width of the horizontal bars indicates the varying abundance of each life-form considered.

Source: Data supplied and illustration reviewed by J. John Sepkoski, Jr., Professor of Paleontology, University of Chicago.

Mass Extinctions

There have been at least five mass extinctions throughout history: at the ends of the Ordovician, Devonian, Permian, Triassic, and Cretaceous periods (Fig. 20.16). Is a mass extinction due to some cataclysmic event, or is it a more gradual process brought on by environmental changes including tectonic, oceanic, and climatic fluctuations? This question was brought to the fore when Walter and Luis Alvarez proposed in 1977 that the Cretaceous extinction was due to a bolide. A bolide is an asteroid (minor planet) that explodes, producing meteorites that fall to earth. They found that Cretaceous clay contains an abnormally high level of iridium, an element that is rare in the earth's crust but more common in asteroids and meteorites. The result of a large meteorite striking the earth could have been similar to that from a worldwide atomic bomb explosion: a cloud of dust would have mushroomed into the atmosphere, blocking out the sun and causing plants to freeze and die. A layer of soot has been identified in the strata alongside the iridium, and a

huge crater that could have been caused by a meteorite was found in the Caribbean–Gulf of Mexico region on the Yucatán peninsula.

In 1984, paleontologists David Raup and John Sepkoski suggested that the fossil record of marine animals shows that mass extinctions have occurred every 26 million years and, surprisingly, astronomers can offer an explanation. Our solar system is in a starry galaxy known as the Milky Way. Because of the vertical movement of our sun, our solar system approaches other members of the Milky Way every 26 to 33 million years, producing an unstable situation that could lead to the occurrence of a bolide.

Certainly continental drift contributed to the Ordovician extinction. This extinction occurred after Gondwanaland arrived at the south pole. Immense glaciers, which drew water from the oceans, chilled even the once-tropical land. Marine invertebrates and coral reefs, which were especially hard hit, didn't recover until Gondwanaland drifted away from the pole and warmth returned. The mass

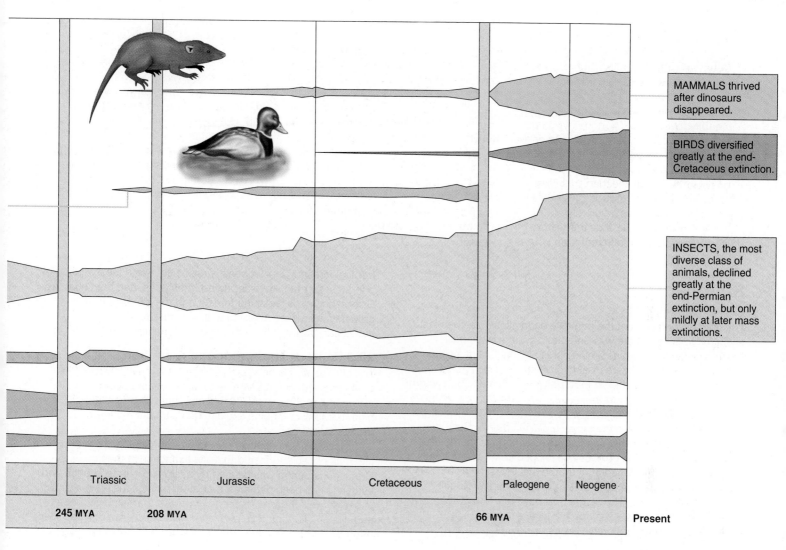

| Triassic | Jurassic | Cretaceous | Paleogene | Neogene |

245 MYA   208 MYA   66 MYA   **Present**

MAMMALS thrived after dinosaurs disappeared.

BIRDS diversified greatly at the end-Cretaceous extinction.

INSECTS, the most diverse class of animals, declined greatly at the end-Permian extinction, but only mildly at later mass extinctions.

extinction at the end of the Devonian period saw an end to 70% of marine invertebrates. Helmont Geldsetzer of Canada's Geological Survey notes that iridium has also been found in Devonian rocks in Australia, suggesting that a bolide event was involved in the Devonian extinction. Other scientists believe that this mass extinction could have been due to movement of Gondwanaland back to the south pole.

The extinction at the end of the Permian period was quite severe; 90% of species in the ocean and 70% on land disappeared. The latest hypothesis attributes the Permian extinction to excess carbon dioxide. When Pangaea formed, there were no polar ice caps to initiate ocean currents. The lack of ocean currents caused organic matter to stagnate at the bottom of the ocean. Then, as the continents drifted into a new configuration, ocean circulation switched back on. Now, the extra carbon on the seafloor was swept up to the surface where it became carbon dioxide, a deadly gas for sea life. The trilobites became extinct and the crinoids (sea lilies) barely hung on. Excess carbon dioxide on land led to a

global warming which altered the pattern of vegetation. Areas that were wet and rainy became dry and warm and vice versa. Burrowing animals that could escape land surface changes seemed to have had the best chance of survival.

The extinction at the end of the Triassic period is another that has been attributed to the environmental effects of a meteorite collision with Earth. Central Quebec has a crater half the size of Connecticut that some believe is the impact site. The dinosaurs may have benefited from this event because this is the time when the first of the gigantic dinosaurs took charge of the land. The second wave occurred in the Cretaceous period.

Mass extinctions seem to be due to climatic changes that occur after a meteorite collision and/or after the continents drift into a new and different configuration.

Connecting Concepts

Does the process of evolution always have to be the same? The traditional view of the evolutionary process proposes that speciation occurs gradually and steadily over time. A new hypothesis suggests that long periods of little or no evolutionary change are punctuated by periods of relatively rapid speciation. Is it possible that both mechanisms may be at work in different groups of organisms and at different times?

Is it also possible that the history of life could have been different from what it

was? The species alive today are the end product of the abiotic and biotic changes which occurred on Earth as life evolved. And what if the abiotic and biotic changes had been other than they were? For example, if the continents had not separated 65 million years ago, what types of mammals, if any, would be alive today? Given a different sequence of environments, another mix of plants and animals might very well have resulted than those with which we are familiar.

The history of life on earth, as we know it, is only one possible scenario. If we could rewind the "tape of life" and let history take its course anew, the end result might well be very different, depending on the geologic and biologic events which took place the second time around. As an analogy, consider that if you were born in another time period and in a different country, the end result of "you" might be very different than the "you" of today.

Summary

20.1 Origin of Life

The unique conditions of the primitive earth allowed a chemical evolution to occur. There was an abiotic synthesis of small organic molecules such as amino acids and nucleotides either perhaps in the atmosphere or at hydrothermal vents. These monomers joined together to form polymers either on land (warm seaside rocks or clay) or at the vents. The first polymers could have been proteins or RNA or they could have evolved together. The aggregation of polymers inside a plasma membrane produced a protocell which had some enzymatic properties such that it could grow. If the protocell developed in the ocean it was a heterotroph; if it developed at hydrothermal vents it was a chemoautotroph. A true cell had evolved once the protocell contained DNA genes. The first genes may have been RNA molecules but later DNA became the information storage molecule of heredity. Biological evolution now began.

20.2 History of Life

The fossil record allows us to trace the history of life. Prokaryotes evolved about 3.5 BYA during the Precambrian, and they were alone on earth for about 2 million years during which many metabolic pathways evolved. The oldest prokaryote fossils are cyanobacteria, which were the first organisms to add oxygen to the atmosphere. The eukaryotic cell evolved about 1.5 BYA but multicellularity is not found until 600 MYA.

A rich animal fossil record starts at the Cambrian period of the Paleozoic era. The occurrence of external skeletons, which seems to explain the increased number of fossils at this time, may have been due to the presence of plentiful oxygen in the atmosphere, or perhaps it was due to predation. The fishes are the first vertebrates to diversify and become dominant. Amphibians are descended from lobe-finned fishes.

Plants, and then insects, invaded land during the Silurian period. The swamp forests of the Carboniferous period contained primitive vascular plants, insects, and amphibians. This period is sometimes called the Age of Amphibians.

The Mesozoic era was the Age of Cycads and Reptiles. Twice during this era, dinosaurs of enormous size evolved. By the end of the Cretaceous period the dinosaurs were extinct. New fossil finds show that birds are descended from dinosaurs and that mammals arose during the Cretaceous period from reptilian ancestors.

The Cenozoic era is divided into the Paleogene period and the Neogene period. The Paleogene is associated with the evolution of mammals and flowering plants that formed vast tropical forests. The Neogene is associated with the evolution of primates; first monkeys appeared, then apes, and then humans. Grasslands were replacing forests and this put pressure on primates, who were adapted to living in trees. The result may have been the evolution of humans—primates who left the trees.

20.3 Factors That Influence Evolution

The continents are on massive plates that move, carrying the continents with them. Plate tectonics is the study of the movement of the plates. Continental drift has affected biogeography and helps explain the distribution pattern of today's land organisms.

Mass extinctions have played a dramatic role in the history of life. It has been suggested that the extinction at the end of the Cretaceous period was caused by a large meteorite impact, and evidence has been gathered that other extinctions have a similar cause as well. It has also been suggested that tectonic, oceanic, and climatic fluctuations, particularly due to continental drift, can bring about mass extinctions.

Reviewing the Chapter

1. List and describe the various hypotheses concerning the chemical evolution that produced macromolecules. 320–22
2. Trace in general the steps by which the protocell may have evolved from macromolecules. 322
3. List and describe the various hypotheses concerning the origin of a self-replication system. 323
4. Explain how the fossil record develops and how fossils are dated relatively and absolutely. 324
5. When did the prokaryote arise and what are stromatolites? 326–27
6. When and how might the eukaryotic cell have arisen? 328
7. Describe the first multicellular animals found in the Ediacara Hills in South Australia. 328
8. Why might there be so many fossils from the Cambrian period? 329
9. Which plants, invertebrates, and vertebrates were present on land during the Carboniferous period? 330
10. Which type vertebrate was dominant during the Mesozoic era? Which types began evolving at this time? 331
11. Which type vertebrate underwent an adaptive radiation in the Cenozoic era? 333
12. What is continental drift, and how is it related to plate tectonics? Give examples to show how biogeography supports the occurrence of continental drift. 334–35

13. Identify five significant mass extinctions during the history of the earth. What may have been the cause and what types of organisms were most affected by each extinction?   336–37

Testing Yourself

Choose the best answer for each question.

1. Which of these did Stanley Miller place in his experimental system to show that organic molecules could have arisen from inorganic molecules on the primitive earth?
   a. microspheres
   b. purines and pyrimidines
   c. primitive gases
   d. only RNA
   e. All of these are correct.
2. Which of these is not a place where polymers may have arisen?
   a. hydrothermal vents
   b. on rocks beside the sea
   c. in clay
   d. in the atmosphere
   e. Both b and c are correct.
3. Which of these is the chief reason the protocell was probably a fermenter?
   a. The protocell didn't have any enzymes.
   b. The atmosphere didn't have any oxygen.
   c. Fermentation provides the most amount of energy.
   d. There was not ATP yet.
   e. All of these are correct.
4. The significance of liposomes, phospholipid droplets, is they show that
   a. the first plasma membrane contained protein.
   b. a plasma membrane could have easily evolved.
   c. a biological evolution produced the first cell.
   d. there was water on the primitive earth.
   e. the protocell had organelles.
5. Evolution of the DNA → RNA → protein system was a milestone because the protocell could now
   a. be a heterotrophic fermenter.
   b. pass on genetic information.
   c. use energy to grow.
   d. take in preformed molecules.
   e. All of these are correct.
6. Which of these events did not occur during the Precambrian era?
   a. evolution of the prokaryotic cell
   b. evolution of the eukaryotic cell
   c. evolution of multicellularity
   d. evolution of the first animals
   e. All of these occurred during the Precambrian era.
7. The organisms with the longest evolutionary history are
   a. prokaryotes which left no fossil record.
   b. eukaryotes which left a fossil record.
   c. prokaryotes which are still evolving today.
   d. animals who had a shell.
8. Which of these is mismatched?
   a. Cenozoic era—mammalian diversification
   b. Paleozoic era—invasion of land
   c. Carboniferous period—swamps, insects, and amphibians
   d. Mesozoic era—dinosaur diversity, evolution of birds and mammals
   e. Precambrian era—plants but not animals present

9. Continental drift helps explain the occurrence of
   a. mass extinctions.
   b. distribution of fossils on earth.
   c. geological upheavals like earthquakes.
   d. climatic changes.
   e. All of these are correct.
10. Which of these is mismatched?
    a. Mesozoic—cycads and dinosaurs
    b. Cenozoic—grasses and humans
    c. Paleozoic—prokaryotes and unicellular eukaryotes arise
    d. Cambrian—marine organisms with external skeletons
    e. Precambrian—origin of the cell at hydrothermal vents
11. Complete the following listings using these phrases: *oldest eukaryotic fossils, O$_2$ accumulates in atmosphere, Ediacaran animals, oldest known fossils, Cambrian animals, protists evolve and diversify*

1.5 BYA	a. _____		540 MYA	d. _____
2.5 BYA	b. _____		600 MYA	e. _____
3.5 BYA	c. _____		1.40 BYA	f. _____
4.5 BYA	formation of the earth		1.50 BYA	oldest eukaryotic fossils

Thinking Scientifically

1. From a scientific standpoint, trying to devise an experimental system that mimics the conditions of the early Earth is an inherently frustrating endeavor. While one might make some interesting hypotheses and experimental observations, there is no way to know for sure if experimental conditions are anything like those that really existed billions of years ago. Why do scientists continue in this quest?
2. Many environmentalists are concerned about global warming and ozone depletion. How would we know if current changes in climate are man-made or just part of natural, long-term cycles? Even if they aren't, if life has survived changes in the past why shouldn't it survive these changes now?

Bioethical Issue

Dr. H. M. Morris, Director of the Institute for Creation Research, lists these contradictions between evolution research and creation research:[2]

Evolution Research	Creation Research
Fishes evolved before fruit trees.	Fruit trees were created before fishes.
Insects evolved before birds.	Birds were created before insects.
Sun was present before land plants.	Land vegetation was created before the sun.
Reptiles evolved before birds.	Birds were created before reptiles.
Reptiles evolved before whales.	Whales were created before reptiles.
Rain was present before man.	Man was created before rain.
Evolution is still continuing.	Creation has been completed.

Do we have an obligation to accept one list over the other? Why or why not? On what basis?

___

[2] Montagu, A. (Ed). 1984. *Science and Creationism.* New York: Oxford University Press, p. 246.

Understanding the Terms

absolute dating (of fossils) 324	molecular clock 329
chemical evolution 320	ocean ridge 321
coacervate droplets 322	ozone shield 327
continental drift 334	paleontology 324
endosymbiotic hypothesis 328	plate tectonics 335
	protein-first hypothesis 321
extinction 329	proteinoid 321
fossil 324	protocell 322
geological timescale 326	relative dating (of fossils) 324
liposome 322	RNA-first hypothesis 321
macroevolution 324	sedimentation 324
mass extinction 329	stratum 324
microsphere 321	stromatolite 327

Match the terms to these definitions:

a. _____ Concept that the rate at which mutational changes accumulate in certain types of genes is constant over time.

b. _____ Cell forerunner developed from cell-like microspheres.

c. _____ Droplet of phospholipid molecules formed in a liquid environment.

d. _____ A region where crust forms and from which it moves laterally in each direction.

e. _____ Formed from oxygen in the upper atmosphere, it protects the earth from ultraviolet radiation.

Web Connections

Exploring the Internet

http://www.mhhe.com/biosci/genbio/mader
(click on *Biology 7/e*)

The *Biology 7/e* Online Learning Center provides many resources for studying the material in this chapter including links to the following sites:

Learn more about the geologic timescale and rock strata in Geology and Geologic Time.

http://www.ucmp.berkeley.edu/exhibit/geology.html

Geological Timescale. Text and nice graphics illustrate geological timescales on Earth.

http://www.geo.ucalgary.ca/~macrae/timescale/timescale.html

History of Evolutionary Thought. This is a timeline of the major players who have contributed to our understanding of evolutionary thought.

http://www.ucmp.berkeley.edu/history/evotmline.html

Evolutionary Relationships of Archosaurs. View images and read more about the Archosaurs, Pterosaurs, and Dinosaurs.

http://www.ucmp.berkeley.edu/diapsids/archosy.html

Dinosaurs in Cyberspace: Dinolinks. University of California at Berkeley Museum of Paleontology. A list of dinosaur-oriented websites, scientific and otherwise. This site has pages and pages of links!

http://www.ucmp.berkeley.edu/diapsids/dinolinks.html#dinosites

Ecology of Populations

Social unit of female elephants *(Loxodonta africana)*

Elephants have a large size, are social, live a long time, and produce few offspring. Females live in social family units, and the much larger males visit them only during a breeding season. Females give birth about every five years to a single calf that is well cared for and has a good chance of meeting the challenges of its lifestyle. Normally, an elephant population exists at the carrying capacity of the environment.

A population ecologist studies the distribution and abundance of organisms and relates the hard, cold statistics to the species life history in order to determine what causes population growth or decline. Elephants are threatened because of human population growth, and also because males, in preference to females, are killed for their tusks. Males don't tend to breed until they have reached their largest size—the size that makes them prized by humans. By now, even a moratorium on killing males will not help much. So few breeding males are left that elephant populations are expected to continue to decline for quite some time. The study of population ecology is necessary to preservation of species.

23.1 Scope of Ecology

In 1866, the German zoologist Ernst Haeckel coined the word ecology from two Greek roots [Gk. *oikos*, home, house, and *-logy*, "study of" from *logikos*, rational, sensible]. He said that **ecology** is the study of the interactions of organisms with other organisms and with the physical environment. And he pointed out that ecology and evolution are intertwined because ecological interactions are selection pressures that result in evolutionary change and evolutionary change affects ecological interactions, and so forth.

Ecology, like so many biological disciplines, is wide-ranging. At one of its lowest levels, ecologists study how the individual organism is adapted to its environment. For example, they study why fishes in a coral reef live only in warm tropical waters and how the fishes feed within that **habitat** (the place where an organism lives) (Fig. 23.1). Most organisms do not exist singly; rather, they are part of a population, a functional unit that interacts with the environment. A **population** is defined as all the organisms within an area belonging to the same species. At this level of study, ecologists are interested in factors that affect the growth and regulation of population size.

A **community** consists of all the various populations interacting at a locale. In a coral reef, there are numerous populations of fishes, crustacea, corals, and so forth. At this level ecologists want to know how interactions like predation and competition affect the organization of a community.

An **ecosystem** contains a community of populations and also the abiotic environment. Energy flow and chemical cycling are significant aspects of understanding how an ecosystem functions. The **biosphere** is the zones of the earth's soil, water, and air in which living organisms are found.

Modern ecology is not just descriptive, it is predictive. It analyzes levels of organization and develops models and hypotheses that can be tested. A central goal of modern ecology is to develop models that explain and predict the distribution and abundance of organisms. Ultimately, ecology considers not one particular area, but the distribution and abundance of populations in the biosphere. What factors have brought about the mix of plants and animals in a tropical rain forest at one latitude and in a desert at another? While modern ecology is useful in and of itself, it also has almost unlimited application possibilities, such as the management of wildlife in order to prevent extinction, the maintenance of cultivated food sources, or even the ability to predict the course of an illness such as AIDS.

Ecology is the study of the interactions of organisms with other organisms and with the physical environment. These interactions determine the distribution and abundance of organisms at a particular locale and over the earth's surface.

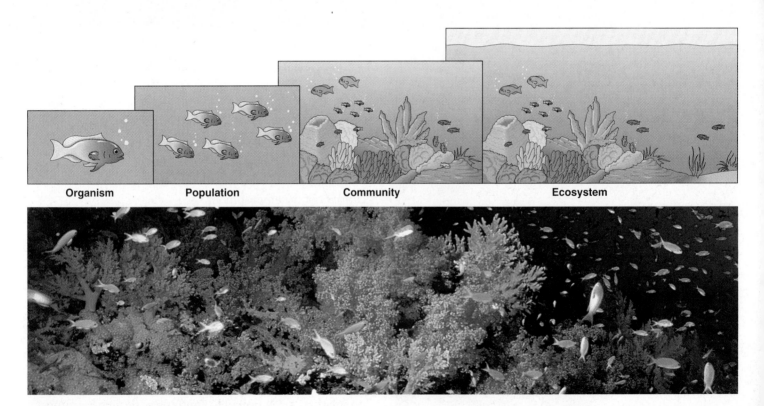

Organism   Population   Community   Ecosystem

Figure 23.1 Ecological levels.
The study of ecology encompasses levels of organization from the individual organism to the population, community, and finally an ecosystem.

Density and Distribution of Populations

Population density is the number of individuals per unit area or volume, while **population distribution** is the pattern of dispersal of individuals within the area of interest. Population density figures make it seem as if individuals are uniformly distributed but, actually, the members of a population are not usually distributed uniformly (Fig. 23.2*a*). In some populations, individuals are randomly distributed as in Figure 23.2*b*, but most are clumped as illustrated in Figure 23.2*c*.

As an example of the relationship between density and distribution, consider that we can calculate the average density of people in the United States, but we know full well that most people live in cities where the number of people per unit area is dramatically higher than in the country. And even within a city more people live in particular neighborhoods than others, and such distributions can change over time. Therefore, basing ecological models solely on population density, as has often been done in the past, can be misleading.

Today ecologists want to analyze and discover what causes the spatial and temporal "patchiness" of organisms. For example, as discussed on page 392, a study of the distribution of hard clams in a bay on the south shore of Long Island, New York, showed that clam abundance is associated with sediment shell content. Indeed, it might be possible to use this information to transform areas that have few clams to high abundance areas.

As with the clams, the distribution of organisms can be due to *abiotic* (nonliving) factors. Physical factors like the type of precipitation, and not just the average temperature, but also the daily and seasonal variations in temperature, and the type of soil can affect where a particular organism lives. In fact, moisture, temperature, or a particular nutrient can be a limiting factor for the distribution of an organism. **Limiting factors** are those factors that particularly determine whether an organism lives in an area. Trout live only in cool mountain streams where there is a high oxygen content, but carp and catfish are found in rivers near the coast because they can tolerate warm waters, which have a low concentration of oxygen. The timberline is the limit of tree growth in mountainous regions or in high latitudes. Trees cannot grow above the high timberline because of low temperature and the fact that water remains frozen most of the year. The distribution of organisms can also be due to a *biotic* (living) factor. In Australia, the red kangaroo does not live outside arid inland areas because it is adapted to feeding on the grasses that grow there.

Ecology as a science includes a study of the distribution of organisms: where and why organisms are located in a particular place at a particular time.

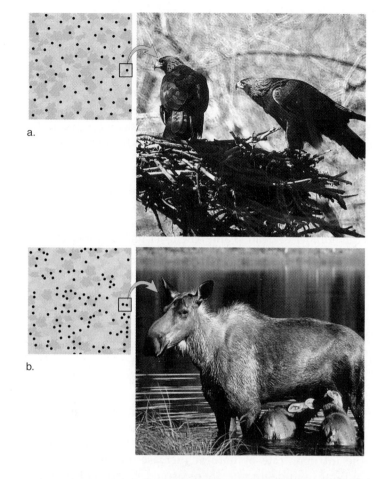

a.

b.

c.

Figure 23.2 Patterns of dispersion within a population. Members of a population may be distributed uniformly, randomly, or usually in clumps. **a.** Golden eagle pair distribution is uniform over a suitable habitat area due to the territoriality of the birds. **b.** The distribution of moose aggregates is random over a suitable habitat. **c.** Cedar trees tend to be clumped near the parent plant because of poor distribution of seeds.

23.2 Characteristics of Populations 🔊

At any one point in time, populations have a certain size. **Population size** is the number of individuals contributing to the population's gene pool. Simply counting the number of individuals present in a population is not usually an option; instead it is necessary to estimate the present population size. Methods of estimating population size depend on the kind of species being studied and the validity of the estimate varies according to the method used.

Assuming that we can determine the present size, what factors would determine the future size of a population? Just as you might suspect, populations increase in size whenever natality (the number of births) exceeds mortality (the number of deaths) and whenever immigration exceeds emigration.

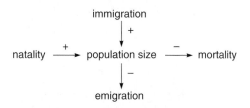

Usually it is possible to assume that immigration and emigration are about equal, and therefore it is only necessary to consider the birthrate and the death rate to arrive at the **intrinsic rate of natural increase,** or simply, *r*. Both birthrate and death rate are measured in terms of the individual; that is, per capita. For example, suppose a herd of elephants numbers 100. During the year, 10 births and 2 deaths occur; therefore, the birthrate is $10/100 = 0.10$ per elephant per year and the death rate is $2/100 = 0.02$ per elephant per year. We can combine both of these rates to arrive at $r = 0.08$ per capita per year. As we shall see, the intrinsic rate of natural increase allows us to calculate the growth and size of a population per any given unit of time.

Population Growth Models

We shall assume that there are two patterns of population growth. In the pattern called discrete breeding, the members of the population have only a single reproductive event in their lifetime. When this event draws near, the mature adults largely cease to grow, expend all their energy in reproduction, and then they die. Many insects and annual plants reproduce in this manner. They produce offspring or seeds that can survive dryness and/or cold and resume growth the next favorable season. In the pattern called continuous breeding, members experience many reproductive events throughout their lifetime. During their entire lives, they continue to invest energy in their future survival, increasing their chances of reproducing again. Most vertebrates, bushes, and trees have this pattern of reproduction.

Ecologists have developed mathematical models of population growth based on these two very different patterns of reproduction. Do these models have value even if the manner in which organisms reproduce does not always fit either of these two patterns, as exemplified in Figure 23.3? Although the mathematical models we will be describing are simplifications, they still may predict how best to control the distribution and abundance of organisms, or how to predict the responses of populations when their environment is altered in some way. Testing such predictions permit the development of new hypotheses that can then be tested.

a.

b.

Figure 23.3 Patterns of reproduction.
We shall assume that members of populations either have a single suicidal reproductive event or they reproduce repeatedly. But actually there are complications. **a.** Aphids reproduce repeatedly by asexual reproduction during the summer, and then reproduce sexually but once, right before winter comes on. Therefore, aphids utilize both patterns of reproduction. **b.** The offspring of annual plants can germinate several seasons later. Under these circumstances, population size could fluctuate according to environmental conditions.

Exponential Growth

As an example of discrete breeding, we will consider a population of insects in which females reproduce only once a year and then they die. Each female produces on the average 2.40 eggs per generation that will survive the winter and become offspring the next year. In the next generation, each female will again produce 2.40 eggs. In case of discrete breeding it is customary to replace r with R^1 = net reproductive rate. Why net reproductive rate? Because it is the observed reproductive rate after deaths have occurred.

Figure 23.4*a* shows how the population would grow year after year for ten years assuming that R stays constant from generation to generation. This growth is equal to the size of the population because all members of the previous generation have died. Figure 23.4*b* shows the growth curve for this population. This growth curve, which has a J shape, depicts exponential growth. With **exponential growth**, the number of individuals added each generation increases as the total number of females increases.

Notice that the curve has these phases:

lag phase: during this phase, growth is slow because the population is small.
exponential growth phase: during this phase, growth is accelerating.

Figure 23.4*c* gives the mathematical equation that allows you to calculate growth and size for any population that has discrete (nonoverlapping) generations. In other words, as discussed, all members of the previous generation die off before the new generation appears. In order to use this equation to determine future population size, it is necessary to know R, which is the net reproductive rate determined after gathering mathematical data regarding past population increases.

During exponential growth, a population is exhibiting its biotic potential. **Biotic potential** [Gk. *bios,* life] of a population is the maximum population growth that can possibly occur under ideal circumstances. These circumstances include plenty of room for each member of the population, unlimited resources, and no hindrances, such as predators or parasites. Resources include food, water, and a suitable place to exist. For exponential growth to occur, there must be no restrictions placed on growth. It is assumed that there is plenty of room, food, shelter, and any other requirements necessary to sustain unlimited growth. But in reality, exponential growth cannot continue for long because of environmental resistance. **Environmental resistance** is all those environmental conditions such as a limited supply of food, an accumulation of waste products, increased competition between members, or predation (if the population lives in the wild) that prevent populations from achieving their biotic potential.

Generation	Population size
0	10
1	24
2	57.6
3	138.2
4	331.7
5	796.1
6	1,910.6
7	4,585.4
8	11,005.0
9	26,412.0
10	63,388.8

a.

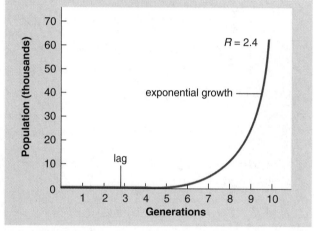

b.

To calculate population size from year to year, use this formula:

$$N_{t+1} = RN_t + N_t$$

N_t = number of females already present
R = net reproductive rate
N_{t+1} = population size the following year

c.

Figure 23.4 Model for exponential growth.
When the data for discrete reproduction in (a) is plotted, the exponential growth curve in (b) results. **c.** This formula produces the same results as (a) and generates the same graph.

Exponential growth produces a characteristic J-shaped curve. Because growth accelerates over time, the size of the population can increase dramatically.

___
[1] The change of r to R is simply customary in discrete breeding calculations; both coefficients deal with the same thing (birth minus death).

Growth of Yeast Cells in Laboratory Culture

Time (t) (hours)	Number of individuals (N)	Number of individuals added per 2-hour period $\left(\dfrac{\Delta N}{\Delta t}\right)$
0	9.6	0
2	29.0	19.4
4	71.1	42.1
6	174.6	103.5
8	350.7	176.1
10	513.3	162.6
12	594.4	81.1
14	640.8	46.4
16	655.9	15.1
18	661.8	5.9

a.

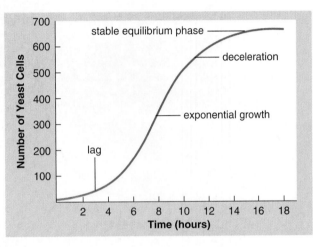

b.

To calculate population growth as time passes, use this formula:

$$\frac{dN}{dt} = rN\left(\frac{K-N}{K}\right)$$

N = population size

dN/dt = change in population size

r = intrinsic rate of natural increase

K = carrying capacity

$\dfrac{K-N}{K}$ = unutilized opportunity for population growth

c.

Figure 23.5 Model for logistic growth.
When the data for repeated reproduction (a) are plotted, the logistic growth curve in (b) results. c. This formula produces the same results as (a) and generates the same graph.

Logistic Growth

What type growth curve results when environmental resistance comes into play? In 1930 Raymond Pearl developed a method for estimating the number of yeast cells present every two hours in a laboratory culture vessel. His data are shown in Figure 23.5a. When the data are plotted, the growth curve has the appearance shown in Figure 23.5b. This type of growth curve is a sigmoidal (S) or S-shaped curve.

Notice that this so-called **logistic growth** has these phases:

lag phase: during this phase, growth is slow because the population is small.

exponential growth phase: during this phase, growth is accelerating.

deceleration phase: during this phase, the rate of population growth slows down.

stable equilibrium phase: during this phase, there is little if any growth because births and deaths are about equal.

Figure 23.5c gives you the mathematical equation that allows you to calculate logistic growth (so called because the exponential portion of the curve would produce a straight line if the log of N were plotted). The entire equation for logistic growth is:

$$\frac{dN}{dt} = rN\,\frac{(K-N)}{K}$$

but let's consider each portion of the equation separately.

Because the population has repeated reproductive events, we need to consider growth as a function of change in time (Δ):

$$\frac{\Delta N}{\Delta t} = rN$$

If the change in time is very small then we can turn to differential calculus, and the instantaneous population growth (d) is given by:

$$\frac{dN}{dt} = rN$$

This portion of the equation applies to the first two phases of growth—the lag phase and the exponential growth phase. During the exponential growth phase, the population is displaying its biotic potential. What would be the result if exponential growth was experienced by any population for any length of time? Apple trees produce many apples per season, and if each seed became an apple tree, we would soon see nothing but apple trees. Or, to take another example, it has been calculated that if a single female pig had her first litter at nine months and produced two litters a year, each of which contained an average of four females (which, in turn reproduced at the same rate), there would be 2,220 pigs by the end of three years (Fig. 23.6). Because of exponential growth, even species with a low biotic potential would soon

Figure 23.6 Biotic potential.
The ability of many populations like apple trees or pigs to reproduce exceeds by a wide margin the number necessary to replace those that die.

cover the face of the earth with their own kind. Even though elephants require 22 months to produce a single offspring, Charles Darwin calculated that a single pair of elephants could have over 19 million live descendants after 750 years.

Why did the growth curve level off for the yeast population and not for the insect population within the time span of the study? The yeast population, as you know, was grown in a vessel in which food could run short and waste products could accumulate. In other words, the pattern of growth was determined by the environmental resistance. As mentioned previously, environmental resistance opposes exponential growth when a population is displaying its biotic potential. Environmental resistance is all those factors such as a finite amount of resources and an accumulation of waste products that curtail unlimited population growth. Environmental resistance results in the *deceleration phase* and the *stable equilibrium phase* of the logistic growth curve (see Fig. 23.5). Now the population is at the carrying capacity of the environment.

Carrying Capacity

The **carrying capacity** of any environment is the maximum number of individuals of a given species the environment can support. The closer population size gets to the carrying capacity, the greater will be the environmental resistance—as resources become more scarce, the birthrate is expected to decline and the death rate is expected to increase. This will result in a decrease in population growth; eventually, the population stops growing and its size remains stable.

How does our mathematical model for logistic growth take this process into account? To our equation for growth under conditions of exponential growth we add the term

$$\frac{(K-N)}{K}$$

In this expression, K is the carrying capacity of the environment. The easiest way to understand the effects of this term is to consider two extreme possibilities. First, consider a time at which the population size is well below carrying capacity. Resources are relatively unlimited, and we expect rapid, nearly exponential growth to take place. Does the model predict this? Yes, it does. When N is very small relative to K, the term $(K-N)/K$ is very nearly $(K-0)/K$, or approximately 1. Therefore, $dN/dt =$ approximately rN.

Similarly, consider what happens when the population reaches carrying capacity. Here, we predict that growth will stop and the population will stabilize. What happens in the model? When $N=K$, the term $(K-N)/K$ declines from nearly 1 to 0, and the population growth slows to zero.

As mentioned, the model we have developed predicts that exponential growth will occur only when population size is much lower than the carrying capacity. So, as a practical matter, if we are using a fish population as a continuous food source, it would be best to maintain the population size in the exponential phase of the logistic growth curve. Biotic potential is having its full effect and the birthrate is the highest it can be during this phase. If we overfish, the population will sink into the lag phase, and it will be years before exponential growth recurs again. On the other hand, if we are trying to limit the growth of a pest, it is best, if possible, to reduce the carrying capacity rather than reduce the population size. Reducing the population size only encourages exponential growth to begin once again. Farmers can reduce the carrying capacity for a pest by alternating rows of different crops rather than growing one type of crop per the entire field.

Logistic growth curve produces a characteristic S-shaped curve. Population size stabilizes when the carrying capacity of the environment has been reached.

Table 23.1

A Life Table for a Bluegrass Cohort

Age (Months)	Number Observed Alive	Number Dying	Mortality Rate Per Capita	Avg. Number of Seeds/Individual
0–3	843	121	0.143	0
3–6	722	195	0.271	300
6–9	527	211	0.400	620
9–12	316	172	0.544	430
12–15	144	95	0.626	210
15–18	54	39	0.722	60
18–21	15	12	0.800	30
21–24	3	3	1.000	10
24	0	—	—	—

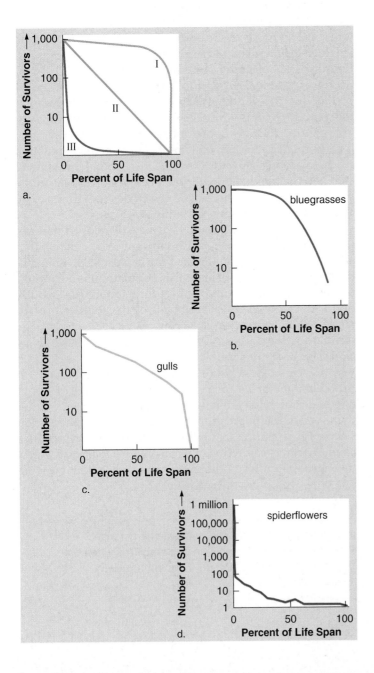

a.

b.

c.

d.

Mortality Patterns

Population growth patterns assume that populations are made up of identical individuals. Actually, the individuals are in different stages of their life span. Investigators studying population dynamics construct life tables that show how many members of an original group of individuals born at the same time, called a **cohort,** are still alive after certain intervals of time. For example, Table 23.1 is a life table for a bluegrass. The cohort contains 843 individuals. After three months, when 121 individuals have died, the mortality rate is 0.143 per capita. Another way to view this statistic, however, is to consider that 722 individuals are still alive—have survived—after three months. **Survivorship** is the probability of newborn individuals of a cohort surviving to particular ages. If we plot the number surviving, a survivorship curve is produced.

For the sake of discussion, three types of idealized survivorship curves are recognized (Fig. 23.7a). The type I curve is characteristic of a population in which most individuals survive well past the midpoint, and death does not come until near the end of the life span. On the other hand, the type III curve is typical of a population in which most individuals die very young. In the type II curve, survivorship decreases at a constant rate throughout the life span.

Figure 23.7 Survivorship curves.
Survivorship curves show the number of individuals of a cohort that are still living over time. **a.** Three generalized survivorship curves. **b.** The survivorship curve for bluegrasses seems to be a combination of the type I and type II curves. **c.** Survivorship curve for gulls fits the type II curve somewhat. **d.** The survivorship curve for spiderflowers is a type III curve.

The survivorship curves of natural populations don't fit these three idealized curves exactly. In the bluegrass cohort, for example, most individuals survive till six to nine months, and then the chances of survivorship diminish at an increasing rate. Statistics for a gull cohort are close enough to classify the survivorship curve in the type II category, while a spiderflower cohort has a type III curve (Fig. 23.7*d*).

There is much that can be learned about the life history of a species by studying its life table and survivorship curve. Would you predict that most or few members of a population with a type III survivorship curve are contributing offspring to the next generation? Obviously since death comes early for most members, only a few are living long enough to reproduce. What about the other two types of survivorship curves? Look again at bluegrass life table. It tells us that per capita seed production increases as plants mature. How does that compare to the human situation?

Populations have a pattern of mortality/survivorship that becomes apparent from studying the life table and survivorship curve of a cohort.

Age Distribution

When the individuals in a population reproduce repeatedly, several generations may be alive at any given time. From the perspective of population growth, there are three major age groups in a population: prereproductive, reproductive, and postreproductive. Populations differ by what proportion of the population falls in each age group. At least three **age structure diagrams** are possible (Fig. 23.8).

When the prereproductive group is the largest of the three groups, the birthrate is higher than the death rate, and a pyramid-shaped diagram is expected. Under such conditions, even if the growth for that year was matched by the deaths for that year, the population would continue to grow in the following years. Why? Because there are more individuals entering than leaving the reproductive years. Eventually, as the size of the reproductive group equals the size of the prereproductive group, a bell-shaped diagram will result. The postreproductive group will still be the smallest, however, because of mortality. If the birthrate falls below the death rate, the prereproductive group will become smaller than the reproductive group. The age structure diagram will then be urn-shaped because the postreproductive group is now the largest.

The age distribution reflects the past and future history of a population. Because a postwar baby boom occurred in the United States between 1946 and 1964, the postreproductive group will soon be the largest group.

Age distributions contribute to our understanding of the past and future history of a population's growth.

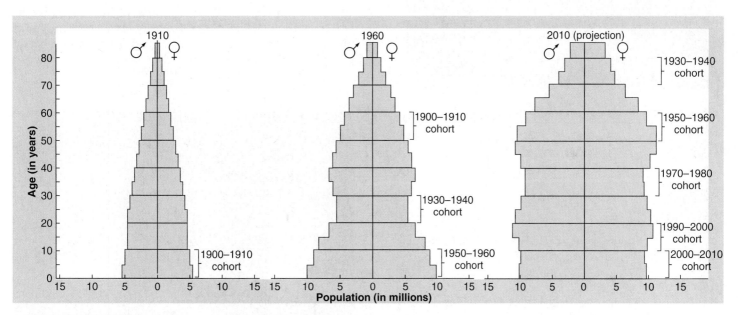

Figure 23.8 U.S. age distributions, 1910, 1960, and 2010 (projected).
In 1910, the distribution was shaped like a pyramid. In 1960, the distribution had shifted toward a bell shape, and in the year 2010, the age distribution is expected to be somewhat urn shaped. An unusually large number of offspring (called a baby-boom) were born following World War II. As the baby boomers grow older, there will be an unusually large number of persons in the postreproductive years.

23.3 Regulation of Population Size 🌐

We have developed two models of population growth: exponential growth with its J-shaped curve and logistic growth with its S-shaped curve. In a study of winter moth population dynamics, discussed in the reading on pages 388–389, it was discovered that a large proportion of eggs did not survive the winter and exponential growth never occurred. Perhaps the low number of individuals at the start of each season helps prevent the occurrence of exponential growth. This observation raises the question, "How well do the models for exponential and logistic growth predict population growth in natural populations?"

Is it possible, for example, that exponential growth may cause population size to rise above the carrying capacity of the environment, and as a consequence a population crash may occur? For example, in 1911, four male and 21 female reindeer (*Rangifer*) were released on St. Paul Island in the Bering Sea off Alaska. St. Paul Island had a completely undisturbed environment—there was little hunting pressure, and there were no predators. The herd grew exponentially to about 2,000 reindeer in 1938, overgrazed the habitat, and then abruptly declined to only eight animals in 1950 (Fig. 23.9).

Even though population growth may not follow our models exactly, we do find that environmental factors do regulate population size in natural environments. When ecologists first considered the question of environmental regulation, they emphasized that the environment contains abiotic (nonliving) and biotic (living) components. It seemed to them that both components could be involved in regulating population size. They suggested that abiotic factors, like weather and natural disasters, were **density-independent factors**. By this they meant that the number of organisms present did not influence the effect of the factor. The proportion of organisms killed by accidental fire, for example, is independent of density—fires don't necessarily kill a larger percentage of individuals in dense populations than they do in less dense populations (Fig. 23.10). On the other hand, biotic factors like parasitism, competition, and predation were designated as **density-dependent factors**. Predation increases when the prey population gets denser because it is easier for predators to find the prey they are looking for. Consider, for example, a population of crabs in which each crab needs a hole to hide in or else the crab is eaten by shorebirds. If there are only 100 holes, and 102 crabs inhabit the area, two will be without shelter. But since there are only two without shelter they may be hard to find. If neither crab is caught, then the predation rate is 0 captured/2 "available" = 0. However, if 200 crabs inhabit the area, 100 crabs will be without shelter. At this density, they are readily visible to birds and will probably attract a larger number of predators. If half of the exposed crabs are eaten, then the

a.

b.

Figure 23.9 Density-dependent effect.
a. A reindeer, *Rangifer.* b. On St. Paul Island, Alaska, reindeer grew exponentially for several seasons and then underwent a sharp decline as a result of overgrazing the available range.

Figure 23.10 Density-independent effect.
A fire can start and rage out of control regardless of how many organisms are present.

predation rate is 50 captured/100 "available" = 1/2. Thus, increasing the density has increased the proportion of individuals preyed upon.

Is it possible that other types of regulating factors sometimes keep the population size at just about the carrying capacity? Investigators have been collecting data on the population size of the bird called Great Tit *(Parus major)* for many years (Fig. 23.11*a*). Yearly counts during the breeding season for a population in Marley Wood, near Oxford, England, are given in Figure 23.11*b*. As you can see, the population size fluctuates above and below the carrying capacity. Clutch size (number of eggs produced per capita) does not seem to fluctuate from year to year, so other hypotheses are needed to explain why these fluctuations occur. Weather, resource abundance (food, shelter, etc.), and the presence and abundance of other animals (such as predators, pathogens, and parasites) are all clearly important—and all are extrinsic to the organism under investigation. Isn't it possible that intrinsic factors—those based on the anatomy, physiology, or behavior of the organisms—might have an effect on population size and growth rates?

Territoriality is apparent when spacing between members of a population is regular and more than seems necessary. Ninety to twenty meters are preferred by Great Tits, and the closer the nesting boxes the more likely some will go unoccupied. Therefore, territoriality is helping to regulate the Great Tit population size. Territoriality in birds and dominance hierarchies in mammals are behaviors that affect population size and growth rates. Recruitment, immigration,

and emigration are other social means by which the population size of more complex organisms are regulated by intrinsic means.

Do populations ever show extreme fluctuations in size and growth rates in spite of extrinsic and intrinsic regulating mechanisms? Yes, they do. Outside of any density-dependent and density-independent factors, it could be that populations have an innate instability. Ecologists have developed models that predict complex, erratic changes in even simple systems. For example, a computer model of Dungeness crab populations assumed that adults produce many larvae and then they die. Most of the larvae do not survive, and those that do stay close to home. Under these circumstances, the model predicted wild fluctuations in population size that are now termed *chaos*.

Density-independent and density-dependent factors can often explain the population dynamics of natural populations. Both types of factors are extrinsic to the organism; perhaps intrinsic factors like territoriality in birds also play a role.

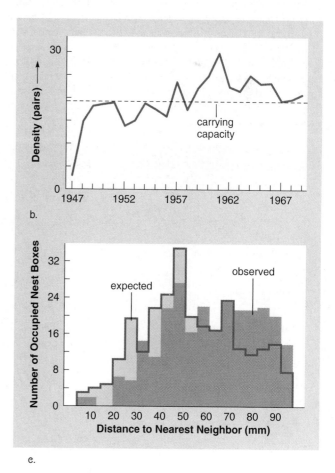

Figure 23.11 Great Tit, *Parus major.*
a. Photograph of Great Tit parents and offspring. b. Density dynamics of a breeding population in Marley Wood, near Oxford, England from 1947 to 1969. c. Great Tits are spaced out more than would be expected if distribution were random.

The Winter Moth: A Case Study

It would seem reasonable that many factors must be involved in regulating population size. When studies of population dynamics are done, investigators try to determine which are the key factors that determine mortality. For example, George Varley and George Gradwell studied the life cycle of the winter moth *Operophtera brumata* and several of its parasites and predators in order to determine which factor correlated best with observable fluctuations in population size.

Life Cycle of a Moth

Like other moths, winter moths have a life cycle that involves these stages: adult moths—larvae—pupae—adult moths. In the fall, adult females emerge from pupae in the soil litter and then climb (because they are wingless) the trunk of the nearest oak tree. After mating with a male (that has wings and can fly), each female lays about 150 eggs on twigs at the top of the tree. The eggs stay there all winter, and then in spring, they hatch when the buds on the tree open. The caterpillars feed on the growing leaves and then, when grown, they spin down to the ground on silk threads, crawl onto the lit-

ter, and pupate. In the fall the adults emerge once more (Fig. 23A).

The Parasites

The winter moth was accidently introduced from Europe into Nova Scotia sometime before 1949 and, within a few years, it was causing severe defoliation and beginning to spread westward. Two natural enemies of the moth were imported and became established. The adult female fly *Cyzenis albicans* deposits small resistant eggs on foliage, and these hatch only after they are eaten by the moth. Hatching occurs in the midgut of the moth, and the maggots bore from the gut into the blood cavity and then move to the salivary glands, where they feed slowly until the host pupates. After feeding some more, the maggots eventually form their puparia inside the moth's pupa. The adult flies emerge in the spring from these puparia.

The other parasite is a wasp, *Cratichneumon,* whose females lay an egg in each winter moth pupa they discover. The egg in turn hatches into a larva that consumes the winter moth pupa, and then pupates, later to emerge as an adult.

The Data

Varley and Gradwell counted the size of the population at each stage of the life cycle (Table 23A). They used sticky paper to capture and estimate the number of female moths climbing up the trees. They dissected several female moths to estimate the average number of eggs in each. They sampled the oak leaves to count the average number of caterpillars. They dissected larvae to see how many contained *Cyzenis* maggots. From this they knew that some larvae were killed by other parasites. They counted the number of moth pupae compared to how many *Cratichneumon* wasps emerged. From this they knew that some pupae were killed by predators.

The Conclusion

Varley and Gradwell used a mathematical formula that allowed them to assign a value (called a *k*-value in the table) to each environmental factor that caused moth mortality. Examine column three in Table 23A and note that most mortality was caused by winter disappearance due to inclement weather: females laid 658 eggs in the fall, but only 96.4 caterpillars (larvae) hatched

Table 23A

A Life Table for the Winter Moth

	Number Killed (per m²)	Number Alive (per m²)	*k*-value
Adult stage			
Females climbing trees, 1955	—	**4.39**	—
Egg stage			
Females × 150		658.0	—
Larval stage			
Winter disappearance	551.6	**96.4**	$0.84 = k_1$
Attacked by *Cyzenis*	**6.2**	90.2	$0.03 = k_2$
Attacked by other parasites	**2.6**	87.6	$0.01 = k_3$
Infected by protozoa	**4.6**	83.0	$0.02 = k_4$
Pupal stage			
Killed by predators	54.6	28.4	$0.47 = k_5$
Killed by *Cratichneumon*	**13.4**	15.0	$0.27 = k_6$
Adult stage			
Females climbing trees, 1956	—	7.5	—

Note: The figures in bold are those actually measured. The rest of the life table is derived from these.

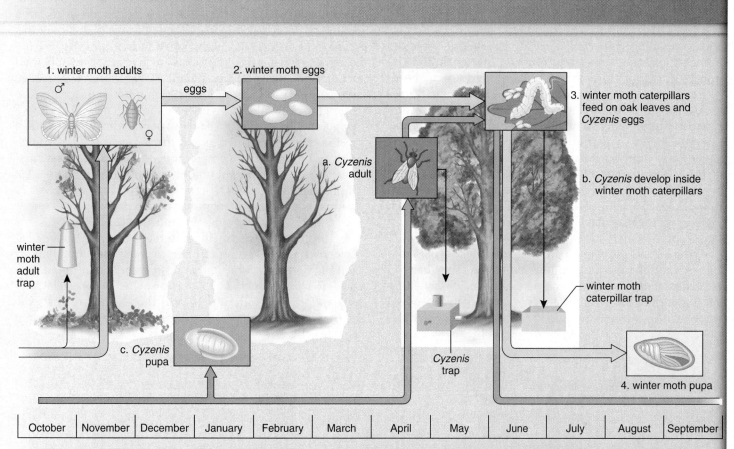

Figure 23A Life history of the winter moth *(Operophtera brumata)* and a parasitic fly *(Cyzenis)*.
Winter moth: (light blue) 1. In fall, females emerge from pupae and climb trees and mate. 2. Eggs are laid. 3. Caterpillars hatch in spring to eat oak leaves. 4. Caterpillars pupate. *Cyzenis* (orange): a. Flies emerge from pupa in spring and lay eggs on leaves. b. When eggs are eaten by winter moth caterpillars, they develop inside the caterpillars. c. *Cyzenis* pupates inside of winter moth pupa. The thin black arrows in the diagram indicates stages at which collections were made.

in the spring. The *k*-value for winter disappearance was 0.84, and the *k*-values for all other factors are much less. Mortality due to predators such as shrews and beetles has the second largest *k*-value.

The *k*-values for winter disappearance correlate best with a sum of all mortality *k*-values as shown in Figure 23B. None of the other *k*-values, including pupal predation k_5, correlated well. Still, Varley and Gradwell developed a mathematical model that predicted moth population size from year to year based on density-dependent factors such as parasitism and predation. Their reasoning was that winter disappearance was due to the weather and weather can never be predicted from year to year.

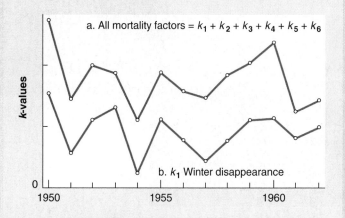

Figure 23B Key factor analysis of the winter moth.
Winter moth mortality, expressed as a *k*-value, due to (a) total mortality because of all factors, correlates well with winter moth mortality due to (b) winter disappearance. Therefore, winter disappearance largely accounts for population fluctuations in the adult population size.

23.4 Life History Patterns

We have already had an opportunity to point out that populations vary on such particulars as the number of births per reproduction, the age of reproduction, life span and the probability of living the entire life span. Such particulars are a part of a species' life history. Life histories contain characteristics that can be thought of as trade-offs. Each population is able to capture only so much of the available energy, and how this energy is distributed between its life span (short versus long), reproduction events (few versus many), care of offspring (little versus much), and so forth has evolved over the years. Natural selection shapes the final life history of individual species, and therefore it's not surprising that even related species may have different life history patterns, if they occupy different types of environments (Fig. 23.12).

The logistic population growth model has been used to suggest that members of some populations are subject to *r*-selection and some are subject to *K*-selection. In fluctuating and/or unpredictable environments, density-independent factors will keep populations in the lag or exponential phase of population growth. Population size is low relative to *K*, and **r-selection** favors *r*-strategists which produce large numbers of offspring when young. As a consequence of this pattern of energy allocation, small individuals that mature early and have a short life span are favored. They will tend to produce many relatively small offspring and to forego parental care in favor of a greater number of offspring. The more offspring, the more likely some of them will survive a population crash. Because of low population densities, most of the time density-dependent mechanisms such as predation and intraspecific competition are unlikely to play a major role in regulating population size and growth rates. Such organisms are often very good dispersers and colonizers of new habitats. Classic examples of such *opportunistic species* are many insects and annual plants (Fig. 23.13).

In contrast, we can imagine environments that are relatively stable and/or predictable, and in which populations tend to be near *K* with minimal fluctuations in population size. Resources such as food and shelter will be relatively scarce for these individuals, and those who are best able to compete will have the largest number of offspring.

strawberry arrow-poison frog, *Phyllobates lugubris*

Surinam toad, *Pipa pipa*

wood frog, *Rana sylvatica*

mouth-brooding frog, *Rhinoderma darwinii*

midwife toad, *Alyces obstetricans*

Figure 23.12 Parental care among frogs and toads.
Frogs and toads, which lay their eggs on land, as do wood frogs *(upper right)*, exhibit parental care that takes various forms. The midwife toad of Europe *(lower right)* carries strings of eggs entwined around his hind legs and takes them to water when they are ready to hatch. In mouth-brooding frogs of South America *(lower left)*, the male carries the larvae in a vocal pouch (brown area), which elongates the full length of his body before the froglets are released. In arrow-poison frogs of Costa Rica *(upper left)*, eggs are laid on land and after hatching, the tadpoles wiggle onto the parent's back and are then carried to water. Most amazing, in the Surinam toads of South America *(center)*, males fertilize the eggs during a somersaulting bout in which the eggs are placed on the female's back. Each egg develops in a separate pocket, where the tail of the tadpole acts as a placenta to take nourishment from the female's circulatory system.

K-selection favors *k*-strategists which allocate energy to their own growth and survival and to the growth and survival of their offspring. Therefore they are fairly large, are slow to mature, and have a fairly long life span. Because these organisms, termed *equilibrium species,* are strong competitors, they can become established and exclude opportunistic species. They are specialists rather than colonizers and tend to become extinct when their normal way of life is destroyed. The best possible examples of *K*-strategists are found among birds and mammals, such as bears (Fig. 23.13). The Florida panther is the largest of the animals in the Florida Everglades, requires a very large range, and produces few offspring that must be cared for. Currently, the Florida panther is unable to compensate for a reduction in its range, and is therefore on the verge of extinction.

Nature is actually more complex than these two possible life history patterns. It now appears that our description of *r*-strategist and *K*-strategist populations are at the ends of a continuum, and most populations lie somewhere in between these two extremes. For example, recall that plants have a two-generation life cycle, which includes a sporophyte and gametophyte generation. Ferns, which could be classified as *r*-strategists, distribute many spores and leave the gametophyte to fend for itself, but gymnosperms (e.g., pine trees) and angiosperms (e.g., oak trees), which could be classified as *K*-strategists, retain and protect the gametophyte. They produce seeds that contain the next sporophyte generation plus stored food. The added investment is significant, but these plants still release copious numbers of seeds.

A cod is a rather large fish weighing up to 25 pounds and measuring up to 6 feet in length—but the cod releases gametes in vast numbers, the zygotes form in the sea, and the parents make no further investment in developing offspring. Of the 6 to 7 million eggs released by a single female cod, only a few will become adult fish.

Differences in the environment result in different selection pressures and a range of life history characteristics.

Figure 23.13 Life history strategies. Are dandelions *r*-strategists with the characteristics noted, and are bears *K*-strategists with the characteristics noted? Most often the distinctions between these two possible life strategies are not as clear cut as they may seem.

r-strategists

Small individuals
Short life span
Fast to mature
Many offspring
Little or no care of offspring

K-strategists

Large individuals
Long life span
Slow to mature
Few offspring
Much care of offspring

Distribution of Hard Clams in the Great South Bay

The Great South Bay is a shallow bay located on the south shore of Long Island, New York, whose center is located about 1,010 kilometers east of New York City. The hard clam is a commercially harvested bivalve mollusc that is found throughout the Great South Bay. (It is eaten raw on the half shell, and is the key ingredient in baked clams as well as New England and Manhattan clam chowder.) The Great South Bay has often been referred to as a "hard clam factory" because in the 1970s, over half of the hard clams harvested in the United States came from its waters. For the past 20 years, I [Jeffrey Kassner] have been studying the distribution of hard clam abundance in the eastern third of the bay for the Town of Brookhaven which, by virtue of a 17th century grant from the King of England, owns 6,000 hectares of prime hard clam habitat.

Knowing the distribution and abundance of hard clams, as well as the responsible environmental factors, is important to Brookhaven because its ownership carries with it an obligation for managing a fishing industry for hard clams that has an annual value of $10 million and employs 300 fishermen. Of particular interest to Brookhaven is the possibility of using this information to develop projects, such as supplementing the natural hard clam production using aquaculture technology, that will increase hard clam abundance and hence the hard clam harvest and the economic benefits the hard clam resource provides to Brookhaven.

My study began with the censusing of the hard clam population. For several weeks during the summers, a barge-mounted crane with a 1 square meter clamshell bucket was used to take bottom grabs at 232 stations located throughout the study area. Each bottom sample was placed in a 1 square meter wire sieve and washed with a high pressure water hose to separate the hard clams from the sediment so that the hard clams could be counted and measured in order to calculate various demographic parameters of the hard clam population. The fieldwork was messy and physically hard, and by the end of the day, my field crew of students and biologists were tired, wet, and covered with mud. The results, however, have proven to be well worth the effort.

Working with Dr. Robert Cerrato of the State University of New York, I was able to draw up a composite census map showing the distribution of hard clam abundance. I was surprised to find that hard clams were not distributed uniformly throughout the study area, but occurred in distinct patches of high and low abundance. I termed the high abundance areas "beds" (a dense assemblage of clams is traditionally referred to as a "clam bed") and six such areas were identified.

When I overlaid the census map on a sediment map that I generated based on my field notes, nearly all of the beds coincided with areas of high shell content sediment associated with formerly productive oyster reefs, or what I call "relict" oyster reefs. This observation is of historical note as well as biological interest because up through the early years of this century, the Great South Bay was a major producer of oysters and was the source of the world famous "Blue Point Oyster." Although oysters are no longer found in the Great South Bay because of environmental changes, they left behind a legacy in the sediment that now supports high abundances of hard clams.

Having found that hard clam abundance was positively associated with relict oyster reefs, I wanted to find out what aspect of the sediment of the relict oyster reefs make them so productive, and conversely why low abundance areas have so few hard clams. This information would be useful to the Town of Brookhaven because it might lead to ways in which the sediment in low abundance areas can be transformed into high abundance areas. I therefore needed a sedimentary "portrait" of high and low abundance areas, and to develop one I borrowed techniques generally associated with other marine science disciplines: from shipwreck hunting, I used a side-scan sonar to map the topography of the bottom; from deep-sea research, an ROV (Remotely Operated Vehicle) to photograph the bottom; from commercial fishing, a fathometer to map the bathymetry; and from pollution studies, a sediment profile camera to photograph the sediment-water interface where hard clams live and feed.

I am now in the process of putting all these different information sources together on a single map (Fig. 23C). Because it will take time and perhaps more studies to develop the portrait, I am concurrently using my finding that hard clam abundance is strongly associated with sediment shell content to explore the feasibility of having shell placed on low abundance areas in order to create new relict oyster reefs. If this strategy works, it would be a tremendous boon to the shellfish industry because nearly three-quarters of the study area is low abundance.

My research project is not only scientifically interesting, but it is also personally rewarding. Over the years, I have become friends with many fishermen and I know that if I am successful, I will be helping them to continue in an occupation that in some cases goes back generations.

Figure 23C
Jeffrey Kassner is preparing a sedimentary "portrait" of high and low clam abundance areas in Great South Bay, Long Island, New York. This information will be used to increase the yield of clams for local fishermen.

23.5 Human Population Growth 🌐

The human population has an exponential pattern of growth and a J-shaped growth curve (Fig. 23.14). It is apparent from the position of 2000 on the growth curve in Figure 23.14 that growth is still quite rapid. The equivalent of a medium-sized city (200,000) is added to the world's population every day and 88 million (the equivalent of the combined populations of the United Kingdom, Norway, Ireland, Iceland, Finland, and Denmark) are added every year.

The present situation can be appreciated by considering the doubling time. The **doubling time**—the length of time it takes for the population size to double—is now estimated to be 47 years. Such an increase in population size will put extreme demands on our ability to produce and distribute resources. In 47 years, the world will need double the amount of food, jobs, water, energy, and so on just to maintain the present standard of living.

Many people are gravely concerned that the amount of time needed to add each additional billion persons to the world population has taken less and less time. The first billion didn't occur until 1800; the second billion arrived in 1930; the third billion in 1960, and today there are more than 6 billion. Only if the rate of natural increase declines can there be zero population growth when the birthrate equals the death rate and population size remains steady. The world's population may level off at 8, 10.5, or 14.2 billion, depending on the speed with which the net reproductive rate declines.

More-Developed Versus Less-Developed Countries

The countries of the world are divided into two groups. The **more-developed countries (MDCs)**, typified by countries in North America and Europe, are those in which population growth is low and the people enjoy a good standard of living. The **less-developed countries (LDCs)**, such as countries in Latin America, Africa, and Asia, are those in which population growth is expanding rapidly and the majority of people live in poverty. (Sometimes the term *third-world countries* is used to mean the less-developed countries. This term was introduced by those who thought of the United States and Europe as the first world and the former USSR as the second world.)

The more-developed countries (MDCs) doubled their populations between 1850 and 1950. This was largely due to a decline in the death rate, the development of modern medicine, and improved socioeconomic conditions. The decline in the death rate was followed shortly thereafter by a decline in the birthrate, so that populations in the MDCs experienced only modest growth between 1950 and 1975. This sequence of events (i.e., decreased death rate followed by decreased birthrate) is termed a **demographic transition.**

Yearly growth of the MDCs as a whole has now stabilized at about 0.1%. The populations of a few of the MDCs—Italy, Denmark, Hungary, Sweden—are not growing or are actually decreasing in size. In contrast, there is

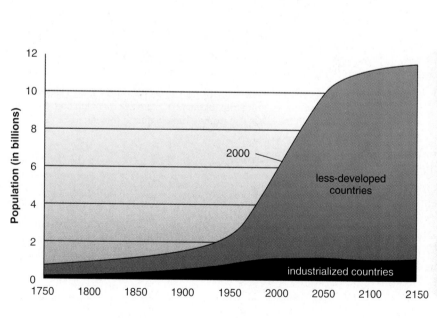

Figure 23.14 **World population growth, 1750–2150.**
The less-developed countries, with a minimal standard of living, will contribute most to world population growth. The more-developed or fully industrialized countries, with a high standard of living, will contribute least to world population growth.

no leveling off and no end in sight to U.S. population growth. Although yearly growth of the United States is only 0.6%, many people immigrate to the United States each year. In addition, there was an unusually large number of babies born between 1946 and 1964 (called a baby boom); therefore, a large number of women are still of reproductive age.

Although the death rate began to decline steeply in the LDCs following World War II with the importation of modern medicine from the MDCs, the birthrate remained high. The yearly growth of the LDCs peaked at 2.5% between 1960 and 1965. Since that time, a demographic transition has begun: the decline in the death rate has slowed and the birthrate has fallen. The yearly growth is now 1.7%. Still, the population of the LDCs may explode from 4.4 billion today to 10.2 billion in 2100 because of exponential growth. Most of this increase will occur in Africa, Asia, and Latin America. Ways to greatly reduce the expected increase have been suggested:

1. Establish and/or strengthen family planning programs. A decline in growth is seen in countries with good family planning programs supported by community leaders. Currently, 25% of women in sub-Saharan Africa say they would like to delay or stop childbearing, yet they are not practicing birth control; likewise, 15% of women in Asia and Latin America have an unmet need of birth control.
2. Use social progress to reduce the desire for large families. Many couples in the LDCs presently desire as many as four to six children. Providing education, raising the status of women, and reducing child mortality are desirable social improvements that seem to reduce the number of desired children.
3. Delay the onset of childbearing. A delay in the onset of childbearing and wider spacing of births could cause a temporary decline in the birthrate and reduce the present reproductive rate.

Comparing Age Distributions

The age-structure diagrams of the MDCs and LDCs in Figure 23.15 divide the population into three age groups: dependency, reproductive, and postreproductive. The LDCs are experiencing a population momentum because they have more women entering the reproductive years than there are older women leaving them.

Laypeople are sometimes under the impression that if each couple has two children, **zero population growth** (no increase in population size) will take place immediately. However, **replacement reproduction,** as it is called, will still cause most countries today to continue growing due to the age structure of the population. If there are more young women entering the reproductive years than there are older women leaving them, then replacement reproduction will still result in growth of the population.

Many MDCs have a stabilized age structure, but most

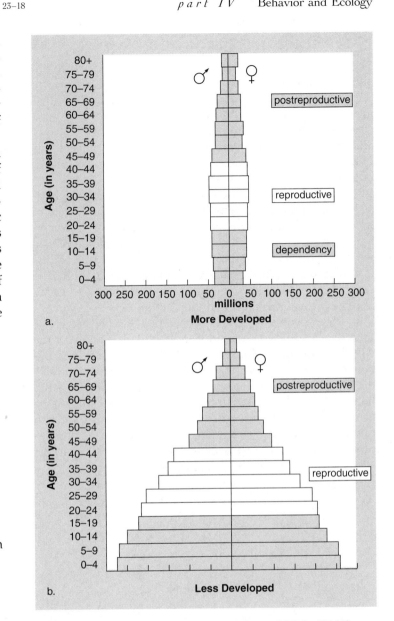

Figure 23.15 Age distributions for MDCs and LDCs (1989).
The diagrams illustrate that (a) the MDCs are approaching stabilization, whereas (b) the LDCs will expand rapidly due to their age distributions.

Source: Data from *World Population Profiles*, WP-89.

LDCs have a youthful profile—a large proportion of the population is younger than the age of 15. This means that their populations will still expand greatly, even after replacement reproduction is attained. The more quickly replacement reproduction is achieved, however, the sooner zero population growth will result.

Currently, the populations of Africa, Asia, and Latin America are expanding dramatically because of exponential growth.

A Sustainable World

While we are sometimes quick to realize that the growing populations of the LDCs are putting a strain on the environment, we should realize that the excessive resource consumption of the MDCs also stresses the environment. Environmental impact is measured not only in terms of population size, it is also measured in terms of resource consumption and the pollution caused by each person in the population. An average American family, in terms of per capita resource consumption and waste production, is the equivalent of 30 people in India (Fig. 23.16). It is time for us to realize that the carrying capacity of the earth is limited and only a certain number of people can be sustained at the standard of living in the developed countries.

Before the establishment of industrialized societies, people felt better connected to the plants and animals on which they depended, and they were better able to live in a sustainable way. After the Industrial Revolution, we especially began to think of ourselves as separate from nature and endowed with the right to exploit nature as much as possible. But our industrial society lives on *borrowed carrying capacity*—our cities not only borrow resources from the country, our entire population borrows from the past and future. The forests of the Carboniferous have become the fossil fuels that sustain our way of life today, and the environmental degradation we cause is going to be paid for by our children.

Overpopulation and overconsumption account for increased pollution and also for the mass extinction of wildlife that is going on. We are expected to lose one-third to two-thirds of the earth's species, any one of which could possibly have made a significant contribution to agriculture or medicine. It should never be said, "What use is this organism?" Aside from its contribution to the ecosystem in which it lives, one never knows how a particular organism might someday be useful to humans. Adult sea urchin skeletons are now used as molds for the production of small artificial blood vessels, and armadillos are used in leprosy research.

While it may seem like an either-or situation—either preservation of ecosystems or human survival—there is a growing recognition that this is not the case. Native peoples who harvest rubber from the trees of a tropical rain forest can have a sustainable income from the same trees year after year. One study calculated the market value of rubber and exotic produce that can be harvested continually from the Amazon rain forest. It concluded that selling these products would yield more than twice the income from either lumbering or cattle ranching, and the income would be sustainable.

It is clearly time for a new philosophy. We need to give up our desire for short-term personal gain and replace it with a reverence for the natural processes that make our lives possible. In a **sustainable world,** development will meet economic needs of all peoples while protecting the environment for future generations. Various organizations have singled out communities to serve as models of how to balance ecological and economic goals. For example, in Clinch Valley of southwest Virginia, the Nature Conservancy is helping to revive the traditional method of logging with draft horses. This technique, which allows the selective cutting of trees, preserves the forest and prevents soil erosion, which is so damaging to the environment. The United Nations has an established bioreserve system, a global network of sites that combine preservation with research on sustainable management for human welfare. More than 100 countries are now participants in the program. However, sustainability is more-than likely incompatible with the kinds of consumption/waste patterns currently practiced in more developed countries.

> All peoples can benefit from a sustainable world where economic development and environmental preservation are considered complementary, rather than opposing, processes.

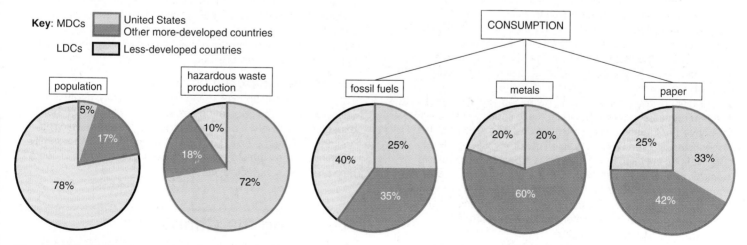

Figure 23.16 Resource consumption for MDCs and LDCs.
The populations of MDCs are smaller than LDCs, but MDCs produce most of the hazardous wastes because their consumption of fossil fuels, metals, and paper, for example, is much greater than the LDCs.

Connecting Concepts

Modern ecology began with descriptive studies by nineteenth century naturalists. In fact, an early definition of the field was "scientific natural history." However, modern ecology has grown to be much more than a simple descriptive field. Ecology is now very much an experimental, predictive science.

Much of the success in the development of ecology as a predictive science has come from studies of populations and the development of models that examine how populations change over time. The simplest models are based on population growth when there are unlimited resources. This results in exponential growth, a type of population growth that is only rarely seen in nature. Pest species may exhibit exponential growth until they

run out of resources. Because so few natural populations exhibit exponential growth, population ecologists realized they must incorporate resource limitation in their models. The simplest models that account for limited resources result in sigmoidal or logistic growth. Populations which exhibit logistic growth will cease growth when they reach the environmental carrying capacity.

Many modern ecological studies are concerned with identifying the factors that place limits on population growth and that set the environmental carrying capacity. A combination of careful descriptive studies, experiments done in nature, and sophisticated models has allowed ecologists to make good predictions about which factors have the

greatest influence on population growth. The example of the winter moth is a good case in point.

The next step in the development of modern ecology has been to try to understand how populations of different species affect each other. This is known as community ecology. Because each population in a community responds to environmental changes in slightly different ways, developing predictive models that explain how communities change has been challenging. However, ecologists are beginning to be able to predict how communities will change through time and to understand what factors influence community properties such as species number, abundance of individuals, and species interactions.

Summary

23.1 Scope of Ecology

Ecology is the study of the interactions of organisms with other organisms and with the physical environment. Ecology encompasses several levels of study: organism, population, community, ecosystem, and finally the biosphere. Ecologists are particularly interested in how interactions affect the distribution and abundance of organisms.

Population density is simply the number of individuals per unit area or volume. Distribution of these individuals can be uniform, random, or clumped. A population's distribution is often determined by limiting factors; that is, abiotic factors like water, temperature, and availability of nutrients.

23.2 Characteristics of Populations

Population size is dependent upon natality (number of births), mortality (number of deaths), immigration, and emigration. The number of births minus the number of deaths results in the net reproductive rate (symbolized as *r*) per capita per unit time.

One model for population growth assumes that the environment offers unlimited resources. In the example given, the members of the population have discrete reproductive events, and therefore the size of next year's population is given by the equation: $N_{t+1} = RN_t$. Under these conditions, exponential growth results in a J-shaped curve.

Most environments restrict growth, and exponential growth cannot continue indefinitely. Under these circumstances an S-shaped or logistic growth curve results. The growth of the population is given by the equation $dN/dt = rN(K-N)/K$ for populations in which individuals have repeated reproductive events. The term $(K-N)/K$ represents the unused portion of the carrying capacity (*K*). When the population reaches carrying capacity, the population stops growing because environmental resistance opposes biotic potential, the maximum net reproductive rate for a population.

Individuals are at different stages of their life span in a population. Mortality (deaths per capita) within a population can be recorded in a life table and illustrated by a survivorship curve. The pattern of population growth is reflected in the age distribution of a

population, which consists of prereproductive, reproductive, and postreproductive segments. Populations that are growing exponentially have a pyramid-shaped age distribution pattern.

23.3 Regulation of Population Size

Population growth is limited by density-independent factors (e.g., weather) and density-dependent factors (predation, competition, and resource availability). Do some populations have an intrinsic means of regulating population growth as opposed to density-independent and density-dependent factors, which are extrinsic means? Territoriality is given as an example of a possible intrinsic means of regulation.

23.4 Life History Patterns

The logistic growth model has been used to suggest that the environment promotes either *r*-selection or *K*-selection. So-called *r*-selection occurs in unpredictable environments where density-independent factors affect population size. Energy is allocated to producing as many small offspring as possible. Adults remain small and do not invest in parental care of offspring. *K*-selection occurs in environments that remain relatively stable, where density-dependent factors affect population size. Energy is allocated to survival and repeated reproductive events. The adults are large and invest in parental care of offspring. Actual life histories contain trade-offs between these two patterns.

23.5 Human Population Growth

The human population is expanding exponentially, and it is unknown when the population size will level off. Most of the expected increase will occur in certain LDCs (less-developed countries) of Africa, Asia, and Latin America. Support for family planning, human development, and delayed childbearing could help prevent an expected increase.

Reviewing the Chapter

1. What are the various levels of ecological study?   378
2. What is density, and why is it sometimes misleading to do studies based on the average number of organisms per unit area?   379

3. What four population attributes determine population dynamics? 380
4. What type growth curve indicates that exponential growth is occurring? What are the environmental conditions for exponential growth? 381
5. What type growth curve indicates that biotic potential is being opposed by environmental resistance? What environmental conditions are involved in environmental resistance? 382–383
6. What is the carrying capacity of an area? 383
7. What is a life table and the three general types of survivorship curves? 384
8. What will the age distribution tell you about the population under study? 385
9. Does population growth of natural populations fit either the exponential growth model or the logistic growth model? Explain why or why not. 386–387
10. Give support to the belief that intrinsic factors might regulate population size in some populations. 387
11. Why would you expect the life histories of natural populations to vary and contain some characteristics that are so-called *r*-selected and some that are so-called *K*-selected? 390–391
12. What type of growth curve presently describes the population growth of the human populations? In what types of countries is most of this growth occurring, and how might it be curtailed? 393–394

Testing Yourself

Choose the best answer for each question.

1. Which of these levels of ecological study involves both abiotic and biotic components?
   a. organisms
   b. populations
   c. communities
   d. ecosystem
   e. All of these are correct.
2. When phosphorus is made available to an aquatic community, the algal populations suddenly bloom. This indicates that phosphorus is a
   a. density-dependent regulating factor.
   b. reproductive factor.
   c. limiting factor.
   d. *r*-selection factor.
   e. All of these are correct.
3. A J-shaped growth curve should be associated with
   a. exponential growth.
   b. biotic potential.
   c. no environmental resistance.
   d. rapid population growth.
   e. All of these are correct.
4. An S-shaped growth curve
   a. occurs when there is no environmental resistance.
   b. includes an exponential growth phase.
   c. occurs in natural populations but not laboratory ones.
   d. is subject to a sharp decline.
   e. All of these are correct.
5. If a population has a type I survivorship curve (most live the entire life span), which of these would you also expect?
   a. a single reproductive event per adult
   b. overlapping generations

c. reproduction occurring near the end of the life span
d. a very low birthrate
e. None of these are correct.
6. A pyramid-shaped age distribution means that the
   a. prereproductive group is the largest group.
   b. population will grow for some time in the future.
   c. country is more likely an LDC rather than an MDC.
   d. fewer women are leaving the reproductive years than women entering them.
   e. All of these are correct.
7. Which of these is a population-independent regulating factor?
   a. competition
   b. predation
   c. weather
   d. resource availability
   e. the average age when child rearing begins
8. Fluctuations in population growth can correlate to changes in
   a. predation.
   b. weather.
   c. resource availability.
   d. parasitism.
   e. All of these are correct.
9. A species that has repeated reproductive events, lives a long time, but suffers a crash due to the weather is exemplifying
   a. *r*-selection.
   b. *K*-selection.
   c. a mixture of both.
   d. density-dependent and density-independent regulation.
   e. a pyramid-shaped age structure diagram.
10. The human population
    a. is undergoing exponential growth.
    b. is not subject to environmental resistance.
    c. fluctuates from year to year.
    d. only grows if emigration occurs.
    e. All of these are correct.

Thinking Scientifically

1. In the winter moth life cycle (p. 389) the two moth parasites were found to be a less important cause of mortality than mortality due to winter loss and predators. Give an evolutionary explanation for the inefficiency of parasites to control population size.
2. Many people enjoy backyard bird feeders and feel that they are helping preserve birds by providing them with food. Many more people unintentionally feed animals by leaving garbage cans and recycling bins where animals have access to the contents. This selects for what animal behaviors (and thus species with that behavior)? Which are selected against? How can feeding animals decrease diversity of local wildlife?

Bioethical Issue

The answer to how to curb the expected increase in the world's population lies in discovering how to curb the rapid population growth of the less-developed countries. In these countries, population experts have discovered what they call the "virtuous cycle." Family planning leads to healthier women, and healthier women have healthier children, and the cycle continues. Women no longer have to have many babies for a few to survive. More education is also helpful because better educated people are more interested in postponing childbearing and promoting women's rights. Women who have equal rights with men tend to have fewer children.

"There isn't any place where women have had the choice that they haven't chosen to have fewer children," says Beverly Winikoff at the Population Council in New York City. "Governments don't need to resort to force." Bangladesh is a case in point. Bangladesh is one of the densest and poorest countries in the world. In 1990 the birthrate was 4.9 children per woman and now it is 3.3. This achievement was due in part to the Dhaka-based Grameen Bank, which loans small amounts of money mostly to destitute women to start a business. The bank discovered that when women start making decisions about their lives, they also start making decisions about the size of their families. Family planning within Grameen families is twice as common as the national average; in fact, those women who get a loan promise to keep their families small! Also helpful has been the network of village clinics that counsel women who want to use contraceptives. The expression "contraceptives are the best contraceptives" refers to the fact that you don't have to wait for social changes to get people to use contraceptives—the two feed back on each other.

Recently, some of the less-developed countries, faced with economic crisis, have cut back on their family planning programs, and the more-developed countries have not taken up the slack. Indeed, some foreign donors have also cut back on aid—the U.S. by one-third. Are you in favor of foreign aid to help countries develop family planning programs. Why or why not?

Understanding the Terms

age structure diagram 385
biosphere 378
biotic potential 381
carrying capacity 383
cohort 384
community 378
demographic transition 393
density-dependent factor 386
density-independent
    factor 386
doubling time 393
ecology 378
ecosystem 378
environmental resistance 381
exponential growth 381
habitat 378
intrinsic rate of natural
    increase 380

K-selection 391
less-developed country
    (LDC) 393
limiting factor 379
logistic growth 382
more-developed country
    (MDC) 393
population 378
population density 379
population distribution 379
population size 380
replacement reproduction 394
r-selection 390
survivorship 384
sustainable world 395
zero population growth 394

Match the terms to these definitions:

a. _____ Due to industrialization, a decline in the birthrate following a reduction in the death rate so that the population growth rate is lowered.

b. _____ Group of organisms of the same species occupying a certain area and sharing a common gene pool.

c. _____ Growth, particularly of a population, in which the increase occurs in the same manner as compound interest.

d. _____ Largest number of organisms of a particular species that can be maintained indefinitely by a given environment.

e. _____ Maximum population growth rate under ideal conditions.

Web Connections

Exploring the Internet

http://www.mhhe.com/biosci/genbio/mader
(click on *Biology 7/e*)

The *Biology 7/e* Online Learning Center provides many resources for studying the material in this chapter including links to the following sites:

Population Ecology. This site provides online data, information from lecture courses, and the names of organizations, people, and journals involved in population ecology.

http://www.ento.vt.edu/~sharov/popechome/refernce.html#lectures

The Ecological Society of America Homepage. This large organization has a homepage that will link the user to hundreds of useful sites.

http://www.sdsc.edu/~ESA/

Zero Population Growth. This is the homepage for ZPG. Were you aware that the human population on earth surpassed 6 billion in October of 1999? Links and much information here.

http://www.zpg.org/

Biological Control: A Guide to Natural Enemies in Nature. Information on using insects as biological control agents.

http://www.nysaes.cornell.edu:80/ent/biocontrol/index.html

Constructing Life Tables for Homo sapiens. *A fun, yet provocative laboratory exercise in the construction of a life table and survivorship curve for humans using data from cemeteries. This lab can also be done using obituaries from the newspaper or the web.*

http://www.auburn.edu/~nolanpm/Steve'sPage/GraveLab.html

and

Life Tables. Probably more math than you wanted to know, but this includes the equations used by population biologists.

http://www.ets.uidaho.edu/wlf448/LifeTables.htm

Classification of
Living Things

Golden toad, *Bufo periglenses*, Costa Rican cloud forest.

Faced with the enormous number of living things on earth, scientists realized long ago that we need a way to classify and name individual species. Although the ancient Greek philosopher Aristotle devised a primitive classification system over two thousand years ago, it wasn't until the 1700s that a Swedish biologist, Carolus Linnaeus, developed a systematic method of naming species that is still used today. A species' name consists of two Latin words, as in *Homo sapiens* for humans. No two species have the same scientific name.

An organism is generally classified on the basis of its evolutionary relationship to other species. Suppose, for example, a new toad were found in a rain forest. The animal's anatomy, genetics, and reproductive behavior would all be examined and compared to similar known toads. Once the new toad's relationship to other toads was determined, it would be possible to decide on its name and classification. There are various schools of classification and some of these are quite new. The classification of organisms is not a static field of biology; it changes over time as new discoveries and ideas are developed.

Figure 28.1 Classifying organisms.
How would you name and classify these organisms? After naming them would you assign them to a particular group? Based on what principles? An artificial system would not take into account how they might be related through evolution, as would a natural system.

28.1 Taxonomy

Suppose you were asked to classify the living organisms you know about (Fig. 28.1). Most likely you would begin by making a list, and naturally this would require that you give each organism a name. Then you would start assigning the organisms on your list to particular groups. But what criteria would you use—color, size, how the organisms relate to you? Deciding on the number, types, and arrangement of the groups would not be easy, and periodically you might change your mind or even start over. Biologists, too, have not had an easy time deciding how living things should be classified, and changes have been made throughout the history of this field. These changes are often brought about by an increase in fossil, anatomical, or molecular data. Classification is usually based on our understanding about how organisms are related to one another through evolution. A natural system of classification as opposed to a artificial system reflects the evolutionary history of organisms.

Taxonomy [Gk. *tasso*, arrange, classify, and *nomos*, usage, law], the branch of biology concerned with identifying,

naming, and classifying organisms, began with the ancient Greeks and Romans. The famous ancient Greek philosopher Aristotle was interested in taxonomy, and he identified organisms as belonging to a particular group such as horses, birds, and oaks. In the middle ages these names were translated into Latin. The scientific names we use today are rendered in Latin. Much later, John Ray, a British naturalist of the seventeenth century, believed that each organism should have a set name. He said, "When men do not know the name and properties of natural objects—they cannot see and record accurately."

The Binomial System

The number of known types of organisms expanded greatly in the mid-eighteenth century due to European travel to distant parts of the world. It was during this time that Carolus Linnaeus developed the **binomial system** of naming species (Fig. 28.2). The name is a binomial because it has two parts. For example, *Lilium buibiferum* and *Lilium canadense* are two different species of lilies. The first word, *Lilium*, is the genus (pl., genera), a classification category

a.

b. *Lilium buibiferum*

c. *Lilium canadense*

Figure 28.2 Carolus Linnaeus.
a. Linnaeus was the father of taxonomy and gave us the binomial system of classifying organisms. He was particularly interested in classifying plants. Each of these two lilies (b) and (c) are species in the same genus, *Lilium.*

that can contain many species. The second word, the **specific epithet,** refers to one species within that genus. The specific epithet sometimes tells us something descriptive about the organism. Notice that the scientific name is in italics; the genus is capitalized while the specific epithet is not. The species is designated by the full binomial name; in this case either *Lilium buibiferum* or *Lilium canadense.* The specific epithet alone gives no clue as to species—just as the house number alone without the street name gives no clue as to which house is specified. The genus name can be used alone, however, to refer to a group of related species. Also, the genus can be abbreviated to a single letter if used with the specific epithet (e.g., *L. buibiferum*) and if the full name has been given previously.

Why do organisms need to have a scientific name in Latin? Why can't we just use common names for organisms? A common name will vary from country to country just because different countries use different languages. Hence the need for a universal language such as Latin, which not too long ago used to be well known by most scholars. Even those who speak the same language sometimes use different common names for the same organism. The Louisiana heron and the tricolored heron are the same

bird found in southern United States. Between countries, the same common name is sometimes given to different organisms. A "robin" in England is very different from a "robin" in the United States, for example. When scientists use the same scientific name, they know they are speaking of the same organism.

The job of identifying and naming the species of the world is a daunting task. Of the estimated 3 to 30 million species now living on earth, we have named a million species of animals and a half million species of plants and microorganisms. We are further along on some groups than others; it's possible we have just about finished the birds, but there may yet be hundreds of thousands of unnamed insects. International associations of taxonomists govern the principles for the naming of organisms and rule on the appropriateness of new names. The same binomial name for each organism is used throughout the world.

The scientific name of an organism consists of its genus and a specific epithet. The complete binomial name indicates the species.

Figure 28.3 Members of a species.
Identifying the members of a species can be difficult—especially when the male and female members do not look alike, as in these mallards, *Anas platyrhynchos.*

Figure 28.4 Hybridization between species.
Zebroids are horse-zebra hybrids. Like mules, zebroids are generally infertile, due to differences in the chromosomes of their parents.

Identification of a Species

There are several ways to distinguish species, and each way has its advantages and disadvantages. For Linnaeus, every species has its own distinctive structural characteristics that are not shared by members of a similar species. In birds, the structural differences can involve the shape, size, and color of the body, feet, bill, or wings. We know very well, however, that variations do occur among members of a species. Differences between males and females or between juveniles and adults may even make it difficult to tell when an organism belongs to a particular species (Fig. 28.3).

The biological definition of a species rests on the recognition that distinctive characteristics are passed on from parents to offspring. This definition, which states that members of a species interbreed and share the same gene pool, applies only to sexually reproducing organisms and cannot apply to asexually reproducing organisms. Sexually reproducing organisms are not always as reproductively isolated as we would expect. When a species has a wide geographic range, there may be variant types that tend to interbreed where their populations overlap (see Fig. 19.3). This observation has led to calling these populations subspecies, designated by a three-part name. For example, *Elaphe obsoleta bairdi* and *Elaphe obsoleta obsoleta* are two subspecies within the same snake species *Elaphe obsoleta*. It could be that these subspecies are actually distinct species. Even species that seem to be obviously distinct interbreed on occasion (Fig. 28.4). Therefore, the presence or absence of hybridization may not be informative as to what constitutes a species.

In the context of this chapter which concerns classification, we defined species as a taxonomic category below the rank of genus. A **taxon** (pl., taxa) is a group of organisms that fill a particular category of classification; *Rosa* and *Felis* are taxa at the genus level. Species in the same genus share a more recent common ancestor than do species from different genera. A **common ancestor** is one that produced at least two lines of descent; there is one ancestor for all types of roses, for example.

Classification Categories

Classification, which begins when an organism is named, includes taxonomy, since genus and species are two classification categories. Individuals we have so far mentioned were taxonomists who contributed to classification. Aristotle divided living things into 14 groups—mammals, birds, fish, and so on. Then he went on to subdivide the groups according to the size of the organisms. Ray used a more natural system, since he grouped animals and plants according to how he thought they were related; but Linnaeus simply used flower part differences to assign plants to these categories: species, genus, order, and class. His studies were published in a book called *Systema Naturae*.

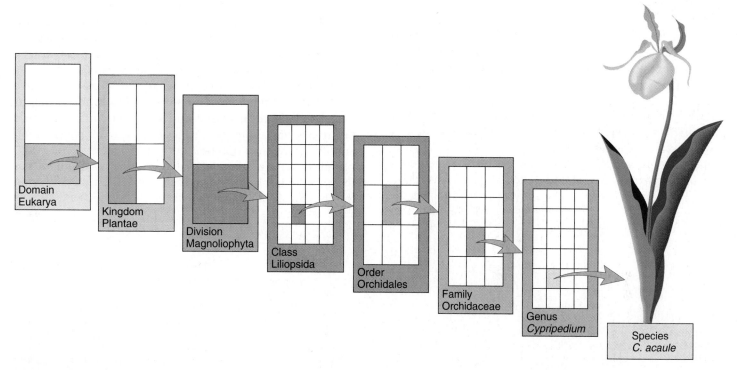

Figure 28.5 Taxonomy hierarchy.
A domain is the most inclusive of the classification categories. The plant kingdom is in the domain Eukarya. In the plant kingdom there are several divisions, each represented by a square in the first diagram. In the division Magnoliophyta, there are only two classes (the monocots and dicots). In the class Liliopsida, there are many orders. In the order Orchidales, there are many families, and in the family Orchidaceae, there are many genera, and in the genus *Cypripedium,* there are many species, for example, *Cypripedium acaule.*

Table 28.1

Hierarchy of the Taxa to Which Humans Are Assigned

Domain Eukarya	Organisms whose cells have a membrane-bounded nucleus
Kingdom Animalia	Usually motile, multicellular organisms, without cell walls or chlorophyll; usually, internal cavity for digestion of nutrients
Phylum Chordata	Organisms that at one time in their life history have a dorsal hollow nerve cord, a notochord, and pharyngeal pouches
Class Mammalia	Warm-blooded vertebrates possessing mammary glands; body more or less covered with hair; well-developed brain
Order Primates	Good brain development, opposable thumb and sometimes big toe; lacking claws, scales, horns, and hoofs
Family Hominidae	Limb anatomy suitable for upright stance and bipedal locomotion
Genus *Homo*	Maximum brain development, especially in regard to particular portions; hand anatomy suitable to the making of tools
Species *Homo sapiens**	Body proportions of modern humans; speech centers of brain well developed

* To specify an organism, you must use the full name, such as Homo sapiens.

Today, taxonomists make use of these categories of classification: **species, genus, family, order, class, phylum** and **kingdom.** (The plant kingdom uses the category *division* instead of phylum.) Recently, a higher taxonomic category, the **domain,** has been added to this list. There can be several species within a genus, several genera within a family, and so forth—the higher the category the more inclusive it is (Fig. 28.5). Therefore, there is a hierarchy of categories. The organisms that fill a particular classification category are distinguishable from other organisms by sharing a set of characteristics, or simply characters. A **character** is any structural, chromosomal, or molecular feature that distinguishes one group from another. Organisms in the same kingdom have general characters in common; those in the same species have quite specific characters in common. Table 28.1 lists some of the characters that help classify humans into major categories.

In most cases, categories of classification can be subdivided into three additional categories as in superorder, order, suborder, and infraorder. Considering this, there are more than 30 categories of classification.

28.2 Phylogenetic Trees

Taxonomy and classification are a part of the broader field of **systematics** [Gk. *systema,* an orderly arrangement], which is the study of the diversity of organisms at all levels of organization. One goal of systematics is to determine **phylogeny** [Gk. *phyle,* tribe, L. *genitus,* producing], or the evolutionary history of a group of organisms. Classification is a part of systematics because it lists the unique characters of each taxon and ideally is designed to reflect phylogeny. A species is most closely related to other species in the same genus, then to genera in the same family, and so forth, from order to class to phylum to kingdom. When we say that two species (or genera, families, etc.) are closely related, we mean they share a recent common ancestor.

Figure 28.6 shows how the classification of groups of organisms allows one to construct a **phylogenetic tree,** a diagram that indicates common ancestors and lines of descent (lineages). In order to classify organisms and to construct a phylogenetic tree, it is necessary to determine the characters of the various taxa. A **primitive character** is one that is present in the common ancestor and all members of a group. A **derived character** is one that is found only in a particular line of descent. Different lineages diverging from a common ancestor may have different derived characters. For example, all the animals in the family Cervidae have antlers, but they are highly branched in red deer and palmate (having the shape of a hand) in reindeer.

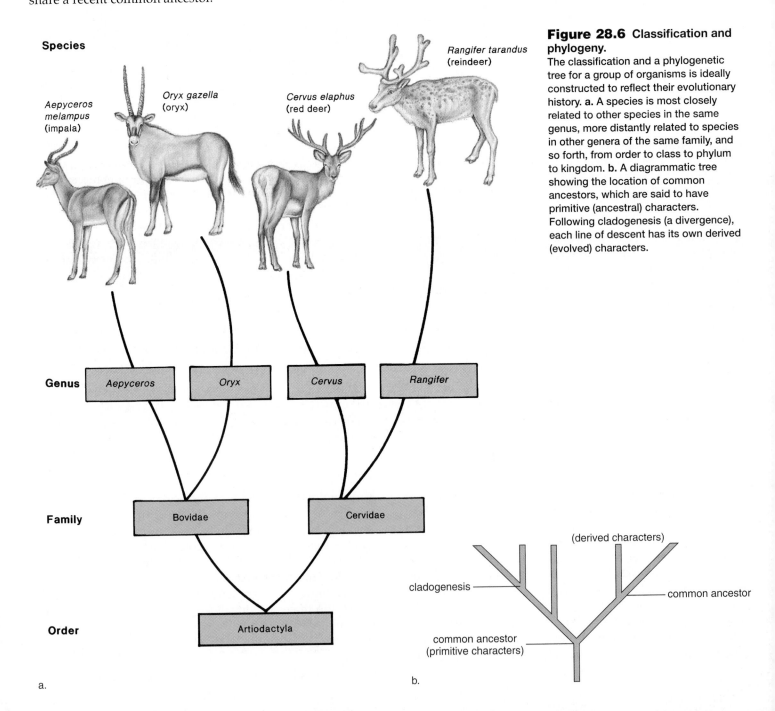

Figure 28.6 Classification and phylogeny.
The classification and a phylogenetic tree for a group of organisms is ideally constructed to reflect their evolutionary history. **a.** A species is most closely related to other species in the same genus, more distantly related to species in other genera of the same family, and so forth, from order to class to phylum to kingdom. **b.** A diagrammatic tree showing the location of common ancestors, which are said to have primitive (ancestral) characters. Following cladogenesis (a divergence), each line of descent has its own derived (evolved) characters.

Tracing Phylogeny

Systematists gather all sorts of data in order to discover the evolutionary relationship between species. They rely heavily on a combination of data from the fossil record, homology, and molecular data in order to determine the correct sequence of common ancestors in any particular group of organisms. If you can determine the common ancestors in the history of life then you know how evolution occurred and can classify organisms accordingly.

Fossil Record

As you know from a study of chapter 20, it is possible to use the fossil record to trace the history of life in broad terms, and sometimes to trace the history of lineages. One of the advantages of fossils is that they can be dated, but unfortunately it is not always possible to tell to which group, living or extinct, a fossil is related. For example, at the present, paleontologists are discussing whether fossil turtles indicate that turtles are distantly or closely related to crocodiles. On the basis of his interpretation of fossil turtles, Olivier C. Rieppel of the Field Museum of Natural History in Chicago is challenging the conventional interpretation that turtles are primitive (have traits seen in a common ancestor to all reptiles) and are not closely related to crocodiles, which evolved later. His interpretation is being supported by genetic analyses that shows turtles and crocodiles are closely related.

If the fossil record was more complete, there might be fewer controversies about the interpretation of fossils. One reason the fossil record is incomplete is that most fossils exist for only harder body parts, such as bones and teeth. Soft parts are usually eaten or decay before they have a chance to be buried. This may be one reason why it has been difficult to discover when angiosperms (flowering plants) first evolved. A Jurassic (see Geological Timescale, p. 326) fossil recently found, if accepted as an angiosperm by most botanists, may help pin down the date (Fig. 28.7).

Homology

Homology [Gk. *homologos*, agreeing, corresponding] is character similarity that stems from having a common ancestry. Comparative anatomy, including embryological evidence, provides information regarding homology. **Homologous structures** are related to each other through common descent, although they may now differ in their structure and function. The forelimbs of vertebrates are homologous because they contain the same bones organized in the same general way as in a common ancestor. For example, in a horse there is but a single digit and toe (the hoof) while in a bat, four lengthened digits provide support for the membranous wings.

Deciphering homology is sometimes difficult because of convergent evolution and parallel evolution. **Convergent evolution** is the acquisition of the same or similar characters in distantly related lines of descent. Similarity due to convergence is termed **analogy**. The wings of an insect and the wings of a bat are analogous. **Analogous structures** have the same function in different groups but do not have a common ancestry. Both spurges and cacti are adapted similarly to a hot, dry environment, and they both are succulent, spiny, flowering plants (Fig. 28.8). However, the details of their flower structure indicate that these plants are not closely related. **Parallel evolution** is the acquisition of the same or similar characters in two or more related lineages without it being present in a common ancestor. A similar banding pattern is found in several species of moths, for example. It is sometimes difficult to tell if features are primitive, derived, convergent, or parallel.

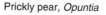

Prickly pear, *Opuntia*   Spurge, *Euphorbia*

Figure 28.7 Ancestral angiosperm.
A newly found fossil, named *Archaefructus liaoningensis*, dated from the Jurassic period may be the earliest angiosperm to be discovered. Without knowing the anatomy of the first flowering plant, it has been difficult to work out the correct classification of these plants.

Figure 28.8 Convergent evolution.
Cacti and spurges evolved on different continents, and yet they are both succulent flowering plants with spines. Cacti are adapted to living in American deserts, whereas spurges are adapted to living in tropical habitats of Africa. This is an example of convergent evolution.

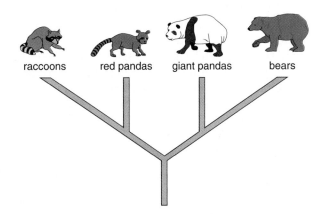

Molecular Data

Speciation occurs when mutations bring about changes in the base pair sequences of DNA. Systematists, therefore, assume that the more closely species are related, the fewer changes there will be in DNA base pair sequences. Since DNA codes for amino acid sequences in proteins, it also follows that the more closely species are related, the fewer differences there will be in the amino acid sequences within their proteins.

Because molecular data is straightforward and numerical, it can sometimes sort out relationships obscured by inconsequently anatomical variations or convergence. Software breakthroughs have made it possible to analyze nucleotide sequences or amino acid sequences quickly and accurately using a computer. Also, these analyses are available to anyone doing comparative studies through the Internet so each investigator doesn't have to start from scratch. The combination of accuracy and availability of past data has made molecular systematics a standard way today to study the relatedness of groups of organisms.

Protein Comparisons   Before amino acid sequencing became routine, immunological techniques were used to roughly judge the similarity of plasma membrane proteins. In one procedure, antibodies are produced by transfusing a rabbit with the cells of one species. Cells of the second species are exposed to these antibodies, and the degree of the reaction is observed. The stronger the reaction, the more similar the cells from the two species.

Later, it became customary to use amino acid sequencing to determine the number of amino acid differences in a particular protein. Cytochrome c is a protein that is found in all aerobic organisms and so its sequence has been determined for a number of different organisms. The amino acid difference in cytochrome c between chickens and ducks is only 3, but between chickens and humans there are 13 amino acid differences. From this data you can conclude that, as expected, chickens and ducks are more closely related than are chickens and humans. Since the number of proteins available for study in all living things at all times is limited, most new studies today study differences in RNA and DNA.

RNA and DNA Comparisons   All cells have ribosomes because they are essential for protein synthesis. Further, the genes that code for ribosomal RNA (rRNA) have changed very slowly during evolution in comparison to other genes. Therefore, it is believed that comparative rRNA sequencing provides a reliable indicator of the similarity between organisms. Ribosomal RNA sequencing helped investigators conclude that all living things can be divided into the three domains that will be discussed later in this chapter.

It is possible to determine DNA similarities by **DNA-DNA hybridization.** The DNA double helix of each species is separated into single strands. Then strands from both

Figure 28.9 Ancestry of giant pandas.
DNA hybridization studies suggest that giant pandas are more closely related to bears than to raccoons.

species are allowed to combine. The more closely related the two species, the better the two strands of DNA will stick together. Some long-standing questions in systematics have been resolved by doing DNA-DNA hybridization (Fig. 28.9). The giant panda, which lives in China, was at one time considered to be a bear, but its bones and teeth resemble those of a raccoon. The giant panda eats only bamboo and has a false thumb by which it grasps bamboo stalks. The red panda, which lives in the same area and has the same raccoonlike features, also feeds on bamboo but lacks the false thumb. The results of DNA hybridization studies suggest that after raccoons and bears diverged from a common lineage 50 million years ago, the giant panda diverged from the bear line and the red panda diverged from the raccoon line. Therefore, it can be seen that some of the characters of the giant panda and the red panda are primitive (present in a common ancestor), and some are due to parallel evolution.

Because hybridization studies do not provide numerical data, many researchers prefer to compare nucleotide sequences of a particular gene or genes. One study involving DNA differences produced the data shown in Figure 28.10. Although the data suggests that chimpanzees are more closely related to humans than they are to other apes, in most classifications, humans and chimpanzees are placed in different families; humans are in the family Hominidae and chimpanzees are in the family Pongidae. In contrast, the rhesus monkey and the green monkey, which have more numerous DNA differences, are placed in the same family (Cercopithecidae). To be consistent with the data, shouldn't humans and chimpanzees also be in the same family? Traditional systematists, in particular, believe that since humans are markedly different from chimpanzees because of adaptation to a different environment, it is justifiable to place humans in a separate family.

Mitochondrial DNA (mtDNA) changes ten times faster than nuclear DNA. Therefore, when determining the

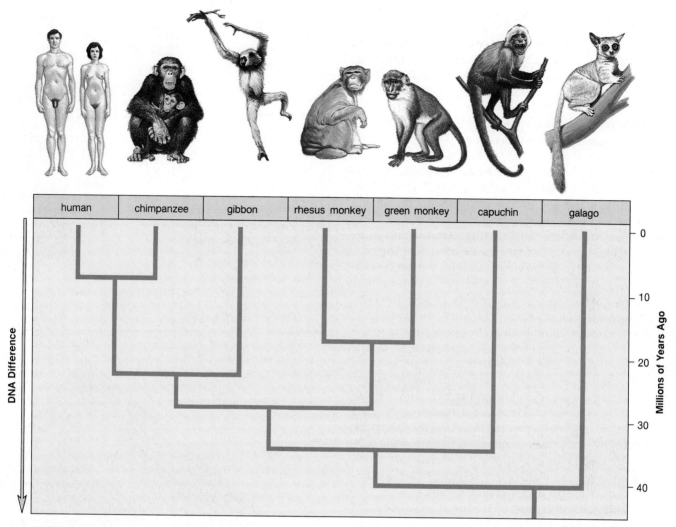

Figure 28.10 Genetic data.
The relationship of certain primate species based on a study of their genomes. The length of the branches indicates the relative number of nucleotide pair differences that were found between groups. This data along with knowledge of the fossil record for one divergence makes it possible to suggest a date for the other divergences in the tree.

phylogeny of closely related species, investigators often choose to sequence mtDNA instead of nuclear DNA. One such study concerned North American songbirds. It had long been suggested that these birds diverged into eastern and western subspecies due to retreating glaciers some 250,000 to 100,000 years ago. Sequencing of mtDNA allowed investigators to conclude that groups of North American songbirds diverged from one another an average of 2.5 MYA. Since the old hypothesis based on glaciation is flawed, a new hypothesis is required to explain why eastern and western subspecies arose among these songbirds.

Molecular Clocks When nucleic acid changes are neutral (not tied to adaptation) and accumulate at a fairly constant rate, these changes can be used as a kind of **molecular clock** to indicate relatedness and evolutionary time. The researchers doing comparative mtDNA sequencing used their data as a molecular clock when they equated a 5.1%

nucleic acid difference among songbird subspecies to 2.5 MYA. In Figure 28.10 the researchers used their DNA sequence data to suggest how long the different types of primates have been separate. The fossil record was used to calibrate the clock: when the fossil record for one divergence is known, it tells you how long it probably takes for each nucleotide pair difference to occur. Even so, the tree drawn from molecular data is usually used as a hypothesis until it is confirmed by the fossil record. When the fossil record and molecular clock data agree, researchers have more confidence that the proposed phylogenetic tree is correct.

The fossil record, homology, and molecular data help systematists decipher phylogeny and construct phylogenetic trees.

28.3 Systematics Today

There are three main schools of systematics: cladistics, phenetics, and traditional. We will begin by considering cladistics and then compare the other methodologies to this school.

Cladistic Systematics

Cladistic systematics, which is based on the work of Willi Hennig, uses shared derived characters to classify organisms and arrange taxa in a type of phylogenetic tree, called a **cladogram** [Gk. *klados,* branch, stem, *gramma,* picture]. A cladogram traces the evolutionary history of the group being studied. Let's see how it works.

The first step when constructing a cladogram is to draw up a table that summarizes the characters of the taxa being compared (Fig. 28.11*a*). At least one but preferably several species are studied as an outgroup; taxon (taxa) that is (are) not part of the study group. In this example, lancelets are the outgroup and selected vertebrates are the study group. Any character found both in the outgroup and study group is a shared primitive character (e.g., notochord in embryo) presumed to have been present in a common ancestor to both the outgroup and study group. Any character found in one or scattered taxa (e.g., long cylindrical body) is excluded from the cladogram. The other characters are shared derived characters, that is, they are homologies shared by certain taxa of the study group. In a cladogram, a **clade** [Gk. *klados,* branch, stem] is an evolutionary branch that includes a common ancestor, together with all its descendant species. A clade includes the taxa that share homologies.

The cladogram in Figure 28.11*b* has three clades that differ in size because the first includes the other two, and so forth. Notice that the common ancestor at the root of the tree had one primitive character: notochord in embryo. There follows common ancestors which have vertebrae, lungs and three-chambered heart, and finally amniotic egg and internal fertilization. Therefore, this is the sequence in which these characters evolved during the evolutionary history of vertebrates. These are also the homologies that show the clade species are closely related to one another. All the taxa in the study group belong to the first clade because they all have vertebrae; newts, snakes, and lizards are in the clade that has lungs and a three-chambered heart; and only snakes and lizards have an amniote egg and internal fertilization.

A cladogram is objective because it lists the characters that were used to construct the cladogram. Cladists typically make use of many more characters than appear in our simplified cladogram. They also feel that a cladogram is a hypothesis that can be tested and either corroborated or refuted on the basis of additional data. These are the reasons that cladistics, a relatively young discipline, has now become a respected way to decipher evolutionary history. The terms that you need to master in order to understand cladistics are given in Table 28.2.

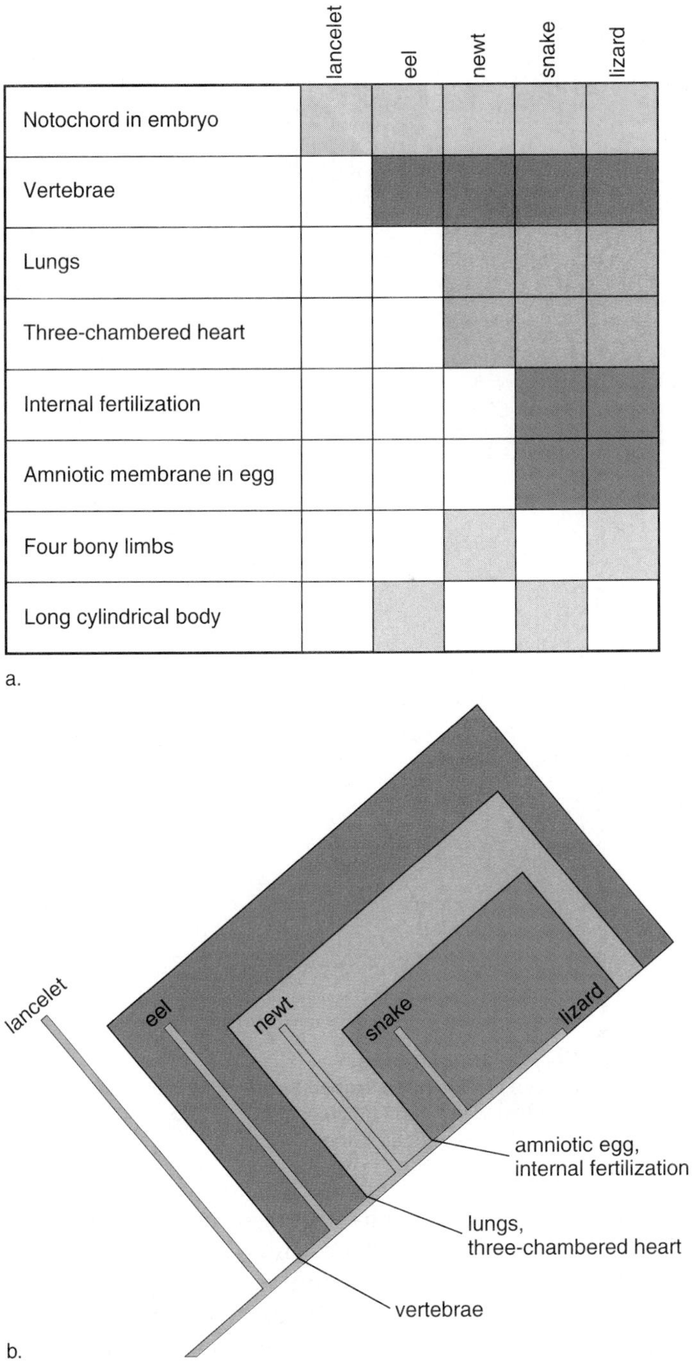

	lancelet	eel	newt	snake	lizard
Notochord in embryo					
Vertebrae					
Lungs					
Three-chambered heart					
Internal fertilization					
Amniotic membrane in egg					
Four bony limbs					
Long cylindrical body					

a.

b.

Figure 28.11 Constructing a cladogram.
a. First, a table is drawn up which lists characters for all the taxa. An examination of the table shows which characters are primitive (notochord) and which are derived (brown, orange, and green). The shared derived characters distinguish the taxa. **b.** In a cladogram, the shared derived characters are sequenced in the order they evolved and are used to define clades. A clade contains a common ancestor and all the species that share the same derived characters (homologies). Four bony limbs and long cylindrical body were not used in constructing the cladogram because they are in scattered taxa.

Table 28.2

Terms Used in Cladistics

Outgroup	Taxon (taxa) that define(s) the primitive characters of the study group
Study group	Taxa that will be placed into clades in a cladogram
Primitive characters	Structures that are present in the outgroup and also in study group
Clade	Evolutionary branch of a cladogram; a monophyletic taxon that contains a common ancestor and all its descendent species
Shared derived characters	Homologies that are present in a particular clade and not in the outgroup
Monophyletic taxon	Contains a single common ancestor and all its descendent species; no descendent species can be in any other taxon
Parsimony	Results in the simplest cladogram possible

Parsimony

Figure 28.12 shows a cladogram in which all three species represented by X, Y, and Z belong to the same monophyletic taxon, since they all trace their ancestry to same common ancestor which had the primitive characters designated by the first arrow. Species Y and Z are placed in the same clade because they share the derived characters designated by the second arrow. How do you know you have done the cladogram correctly, and that the other two patterns shown in Figure 28.12b and c are not likely? In the other two arrangements, the characters represented by the colored box would have had to evolve twice.

Cladists are always guided by the principle of *parsimony*—the minimum number of assumptions is the most logical. That is, they construct the cladogram that leaves the fewest number of shared derived characters unexplained or that minimizes the number of assumed evolutionary changes. However, cladists must be on the lookout for the possibility that convergent evolution has produced what appears to be common ancestry. Then, too, there is the realization that the reliability of a cladogram is dependent on the knowledge and skill of the particular investigator gathering the data and doing the character analysis.

Cladistics is based on the premise that shared derived characters (homologies) can be used to define monophyletic taxa and determine the sequence in which evolution occurred.

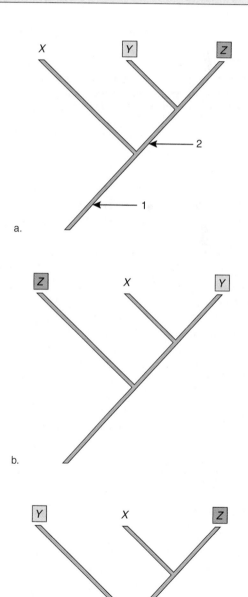

Figure 28.12 Alternate, simplified cladograms.
a. X, Y, Z share the same characters, designated by the first arrow, and are judged to form a monophyletic taxon. Y and Z are grouped together because they share the same derived character, designated by the second arrow and symbolized by the colored box. **b, c.** These cladograms are rejected because in each you would have to assume that the same character (colored boxes) evolved in different groups. Since this seems unlikely, the first branching pattern is chosen as the hypothesis.

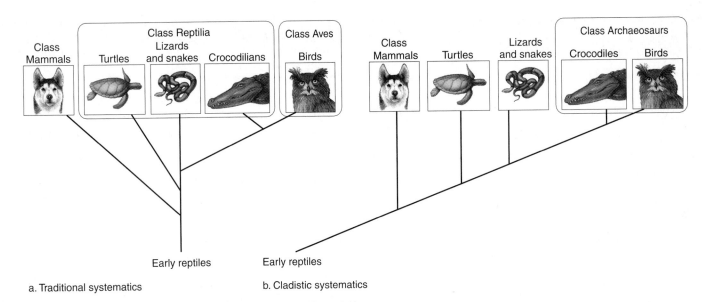

Figure 28.13 Traditional versus cladistic view of reptilian phylogeny.
a. According to traditionalists, mammals and birds are in separate classes. **b.** According to the cladists, crocodiles and birds all share a recent common ancestor and should be in the same subclass.

Phenetic Systematics

In **phenetic systematics,** species are classified according to the number of their similarities. Systematists of this school believe that since it is impossible to construct a classification that truly reflects phylogeny, it is better to rely on a method that does away with personal prejudices. They measure as many traits as possible, count the number the two species share, and then estimate the degree of relatedness. They simply ignore the possibility that some of the shared characters are probably the result of convergence or parallelism, or that some of the characters might depend on one another. For example, a large animal is bound to have larger parts. The results of their analysis are depicted in a phenogram. Figure 28.10 is an example of a phenogram that is based solely on the number of DNA differences among the species shown. (Phenograms have been known to vary for the same group of taxa, depending on how the data are collected and handled.)

Traditional Systematics

Soon after Darwin published his book, *The Origin of Species,* **traditional systematics** began and still continues today. These systematists mainly used anatomical data to classify organisms and construct phylogenetic trees based on evolutionary principles. Traditionalists differ from today's cladists largely by stressing both common ancestry *and* the degree of structural difference among divergent groups. Therefore, a group that has adapted to a new environment and shows a high degree of evolutionary change is not always classified with the common ancestor from which it evolved. In other words, traditionalists are not as strict as cladists are about making sure all taxa are monophyletic.

In the traditional phylogenetic tree shown in Figure 28.13*a,* birds and mammals are placed in different classes because it is quite obvious to the most casual observer that mammals (having hair and mammary glands) and birds (having feathers) are quite different in appearance from reptiles (having scaly skin). The traditionalist goes on to say that birds and mammals evolved from reptiles.

Cladists prefer the cladogram shown in Figure 28.13*b.* All the animals shown are in one clade because they all evolved from a common ancestor which laid eggs. Mammals can be placed in a class because they all have hair and mammary glands and three middle ear bones. Cladists doubt there should be a class Reptilia because the only thing that dinosaurs, crocodiles, snakes, lizards, and turtles have in common is that they are not birds or mammals. On the other hand, crocodiles and birds do share common derived characters not present in snakes and lizards. The fossil record indicates that snakes and lizards have a separate common ancestor from crocodiles and birds. Birds just seem different from crocodiles because each is adapted to a different way of life but actually they should be in a class called Archaeosaurs. Most biologists today are willing to admit to inconsistencies but still use the classes Aves and Reptilia for the sake of convenience.

Phenetics and traditionalists are not as strict as cladists about the use of only homologies and monophyletic groups to classify organisms and construct phylogenetic trees.

28.4 Classification Systems

From Aristotle's time to the middle of the twentieth century, biologists recognized only two kingdoms: kingdom Plantae (plants) and kingdom Animalia (animals). Plants were literally organisms that were planted and immobile, while animals were animated and moved about. After the light microscope was perfected in the late 1600s, unicellular organisms were revealed that didn't fit neatly into the plant or animal kingdoms. In the 1880s, a German scientist, Ernst Haeckel, proposed adding a third kingdom. The kingdom Protista (protists) included unicellular microscopic organisms and not multicellular, largely macroscopic, ones.

In 1969, R. H. Whittaker expanded the classification system to five kingdoms: Plantae, Animalia, Fungi, Protista, and Monera. Organisms were placed into these kingdoms based on type of cell (prokaryotic or eukaryotic), levels of organization (unicellular or multicellular), and type of nutrition.

The **five-kingdom system** of classification recognizes the fungi (yeast, mushrooms, and molds) as a separate kingdom. Fungi are eukaryotes that form spores, lack flagella, and have cell walls containing chitin. They also are saprotrophs, organisms that absorb nutrients from decaying organic matter. Whittaker pointed out that plants, animals, and fungi are all multicellular eukaryotes, but each has a distinctive nutritional mode: plants are autotrophic by photosynthesis, animals are heterotrophic by ingestion, and fungi are heterotrophic saprotrophs.

In Whittaker's system, the kingdom Protista contains a diverse group of organisms that are hard to classify and define. They are eukaryotes and mainly unicellular, but may be filaments, colonies, or multicellular sheets also. Protists do not have true tissues. They have ingestive, photosynthetic, or saprotrophic nutrition. There has been considerable debate over the classification of protists. In this text, the protists have been arranged in seven groups for the sake of discussion.

In the five-kingdom system, the Monera are distinguished by their structure—they are prokaryotic (lack a membrane-bounded nucleus)—whereas the organisms in the other kingdoms are eukaryotic (have a membrane-bounded nucleus). The only type of organism in kingdom Monera are called bacteria; therefore, all prokaryotes are called bacteria. As you can see in Figure 28.14, which depicts the five-kingdom system, monerans are at the base of the tree of life. It is suggested that protists evolved from the monerans, and the fungi, plants, and animals evolved from the protists via three separate lines of evolution.

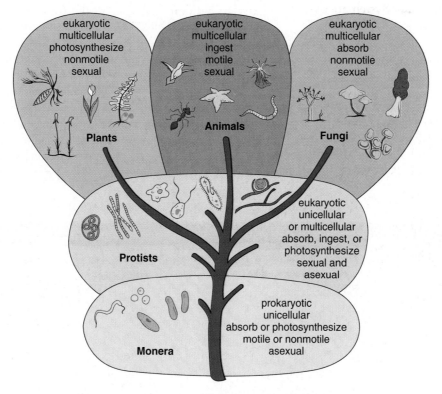

Figure 28.14 The traditional five-kingdom system of classification.
Representatives of each kingdom are depicted in the ovals, and the phylogenetic tree roughly indicates the lines of descent. In this system all prokaryotes are in the kingdom Monera. This text uses the three-domain system described in Figure 28.15.

Three-Domain System

Within the past ten years, new information has called into question the five-kingdom system of classification. Molecular data suggests that there are two groups of prokaryotes, the bacteria and archaea, and these groups are fundamentally different from each other—so different in fact that they should be assigned to separate domains, a category of classification that is higher than the kingdom category.

As mentioned previously, rRNA probably changes only slowly during evolution, and indeed may change only when there is a major evolutionary event. The sequencing of rRNA suggests that all organisms evolved from a common ancestor along three distinct lineages now called domain Bacteria, domain Archaea, and domain Eukarya. This is the **three-domain system** of classification (Table 28.3).

The bacteria diverged first in the tree of life, followed by the archaea and then the eukarya. The archaea and eukarya are more closely related to each other than either is to the bacteria:

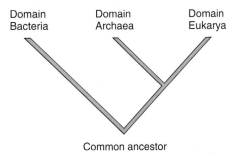

Common ancestor

Domain Bacteria and **domain Archaea** contain prokaryotic unicellular organisms that reproduce asexually. The two domains are distinguishable by a difference in their rRNA base sequences and also by differences in their plasma membrane and cell wall chemistry. Systematists are in the process of sorting out what kingdoms belong within the domains Bacteria versus Archaea. The archaea live in extreme environments thought to be similar to those of the primitive earth. For example, the methanogens live in anaerobic environments, such as swamps and marshes; the halophiles are salt lovers living in bodies of water like the Great Salt Lake in Utah, and the thermoacidophiles are both temperature and acid loving. These archaea live in extremely hot acidic environments, such as hot springs and geysers. At least some of the differences between bacteria and archaea can be attributed to the adaptations of archaea to harsh environments. The branched nature of diverse lipids in the archaea plasma membrane is thought to make it resistant to extreme conditions. Such conditions would disrupt the phospholipid bilayer of bacterial and eukaryotic membranes. The chemical nature of the archaeal cell wall is diverse and never the same as that of the bacterial cell. Most prokaryotes are bacteria, a group of organisms that are so diversified and plentiful that they are found in large numbers everywhere on earth. Most of next chapter will be devoted to discussing the bacteria.

Domain Eukarya contains unicellular to multicellular organisms whose cells have a membrane-bounded nucleus. Sexual reproduction is common and all various types of life cycles are seen. We will be studying the individual kingdoms that occur within the domain Eukarya. These kingdoms are differentiated as in the five-kingdom system (Figure 28.15 and Table 28.4). The protists are not a monophyletic taxon, and some suggest that the kingdom Protista should be divided into many different kingdoms. The other kingdoms are thought to be monophyletic at this time.

Recently, it has been suggested that there are three evolutionary domains: Bacteria, Archaea, and Eukarya. The domain Eukarya contains four kingdoms.

Table 28.3

Major Distinctions Between the Three Domains of Life

	Bacteria	Archaea	Eukarya
Unicellularity	Yes	Yes	Some, many multicellular
Membrane lipids	Phospholipids, unbranched	Varied branched lipids	Phospholipids, unbranched
Cell wall	Yes (contains peptidoglycan)	Yes (no peptidoglycan)	Some yes, some no
Nuclear envelope	No	No	Yes
Membrane-bounded organelles	No	No	Yes
Ribosomes	Yes	Yes	Yes
Introns	No	Some	Yes

Domain Eukarya, Kingdom Animalia
Grey wolf, *Canis*

Domain Eukarya, Kingdom Plantae
Black-eyed Susan, *Rudbeckia*

Domain Eukarya, Kingdom Protista
Paramecium, *Paramecium*

100 µm

400 nm

Domain Archaea,
Methanosarcina thermophila

Domain Bacteria
Escherichia coli

250 nm

Domain Eukarya, Kingdom Fungi
Mushroom, *Hygrocybe*

Figure 28.15 **The three domains of life.**
This is a pictorial representation of the domains Bacteria, Archaea, and Eukarya. There is an example for each of the four kingdoms in the domain Eukarya.

Table 28.4

Classification Criteria for Three Domains

	Domain Bacteria and Archaea	Domain Eukarya			
		Kingdom Protista	*Kingdom Fungi*	*Kingdom Plantae*	*Kingdom Animalia*
Type of cell	Prokaryotic	Eukaryotic	Eukaryotic	Eukaryotic	Eukaryotic
Complexity	Unicellular	Unicellular usual	Multicellular usual	Multicellular	Multicellular
Type of nutrition	Autotrophic or heterotrophic	Photosynthetic or heterotrophic by various	Heterotrophic saprotrophs	Photosynthetic	Heterotrophic by ingestion
Motility	Sometimes by flagella	Sometimes by flagella (or cilia)	Nonmotile	Nonmotile	Motile by contractile fibers
Life cycle*	Asexual usual	Various	Haplontic	Alternation of generations	Diplontic
Internal protection of zygote	No	No	No	Yes	Yes
Nervous system	None	Conduction of stimuli	None	None	Present

* See p. 532

Connecting Concepts

We have seen in this chapter that identifying, naming, and classifying living organisms is an ongoing process. Carolus Linnaeus' system of binomial nomenclature is still accepted by virtually all biologists—many species remain to be found and named (most in the rain forests). For several years now, Whittaker's five-kingdom concept of life on earth has been widely used. Now new findings suggest that there are three domains of life: Bacteria, Archaea, and Eukarya. The archaea are structurally similar to bacteria, but it has been found that their ribosomal subunits differ from those of bacteria and are instead similar to those of eukaryotes. Also, some archaeal genes are unique only to the archaea. Most likely, several kingdoms will eventually be recognized among the bacteria and archaea just as there are among the eukarya (protists, fungi, plants, and animals).

Most of today's systematists use evolutionary relationships among organisms for classification purposes. The traditional and cladistic schools differ as to how to determine such relationships. The traditionalist is willing to consider both structural similarities and obvious differences due to adaptations to new environments. The cladists believe that only similarities should be used to classify organisms. In the end, it may be the ability to quickly sequence genes that will do away with the need for any subjective analyses and make classification a purely objective science.

Summary

28.1 Taxonomy

Taxonomy deals with the naming of organisms; each species is given a binomial name consisting of the genus and specific epithet.

Distinguishing species on the basis of structure can be difficult because members of a species can vary in structure. Distinguishing species on the basis of reproductive isolation runs into problems because some species hybridize and because reproductive isolation is very difficult to observe. In this chapter, species is a taxon occurring below the level of genus. Species in the same genus share a more recent common ancestor than species in related genera, etc.

Classification involves the assignment of species to categories. When an organism is named, a species has been assigned to a particular genus. There are seven obligatory categories of classification: species, genus, family, order, class, phylum, and kingdom. Each higher category is more inclusive; species in the same kingdom share general characters, and species in the same genus share quite specific characters.

28.2 Phylogenetic Trees

Systematics, a very broad field, encompasses both taxonomy and classification. Classification should reflect phylogeny, and one goal of systematics is to create phylogenetic trees, based on primitive and derived characters.

The fossil record, homology, and molecular data are used to help decipher phylogenies. Because fossils can be dated, available fossils can establish the antiquity of a species. If the fossil record is complete enough, we can sometimes trace a lineage through time. Homology helps indicate when species belong to a monophyletic taxon (share a common ancestor); however, convergent evolution and parallel evolution sometimes make it difficult to distinguish homologous structures from analogous structures. Various molecular data are used to indicate relatedness, but DNA base sequence probably pertain more directly to phylogenetic characters.

28.3 Systematics Today

Today there are three main schools of systematics: the cladistic, the phenetic, and the traditional schools. The cladistic school analyzes primitive and derived characters and constructs cladograms on the basis of shared derived characters. A clade includes a common ancestor, and all the species derived from that common ancestor. Cladograms are diagrams based on homologies. The numerical phenetic school clusters species on the basis of the number of shared similarities regardless of whether they might be convergent, parallel, or depend on one another. The traditional school stresses common ancestry *and* the degree of structural difference among divergent groups in order to construct phylogenetic trees.

28.4 Classification Systems

The five-kingdom system of classification recognizes these kingdoms: Plantae, Animalia, Fungi, Protista, and Monera. On the basis of molecular data, it has been established that there are three evolutionary domains: Bacteria, Archaea, and Eukarya. The first two domains contain prokaryotes; the domain Eukarya contains the kingdoms Protista, Fungi, Plantae, and Animalia.

Reviewing the Chapter

1. Explain the binomial system of naming organisms. Why must species be designated by the complete name?   490–491
2. Why is it necessary to give organisms scientific names?   491
3. Discuss three ways to define a species. Which way relates to classification?   492
4. What are the seven obligatory classification categories? In what way are they a hierarchy?   493
5. How is it that taxonomy and classification are a part of systematics? What three types of data help systematists construct phylogenetic trees?   494–497
6. Discuss the principles of cladistics, and explain how to construct a cladogram.   498–499
7. In what ways do the cladistic school, the phenetic school, and the traditional school of systematics differ?   498–500
8. Compare the five-kingdom system of classification to the three-domain system.   501–502
9. Contrast the characteristics of archaea, the bacteria, and the eukarya.   502
10. Contrast the eukaryotic kingdoms: Protista, Fungi, Plantae, and Animalia.   503

Testing Yourself

Choose the best answer for each question.

1. Which is the scientific name of an organism?
   a. *Rosa rugosa*
   b. *Rosa*
   c. *rugosa*
   d. Rugosa rugosa
   e. Both a and d are correct.
2. Which of these best pertains to taxonomy? Species
   a. always have three-part names such as *Homo sapiens sapiens.*
   b. are always reproductively isolated from other species.
   c. always share the most recent common ancestor.
   d. always look exactly alike.
   e. Both c and d are correct.
3. The classification category below the level of family is
   a. class.
   b. species.
   c. phylum.
   d. genus.
   e. order.
4. Which kingdom is mismatched?
   a. Fungi—prokaryotic single cells
   b. Plantae—multicellular only
   c. Plantae—flowers and mosses
   d. Animalia—arthropods and humans
   e. Protista—unicellular eukaryotes
5. Which kingdom is mismatched?
   a. Fungi—usually saprotrophic
   b. Plantae—usually photosynthetic
   c. Animalia—rarely ingestive
   d. Protista—various modes of nutrition
   e. Both c and d are mismatched.
6. In a phylogenetic tree, which is incorrect?
   a. Dates of divergence are always given.
   b. Common ancestors occur at the notches.
   c. The more recently evolved are at the top of the tree.
   d. Ancestors have only primitive characters.
   e. All groups are the same level taxa.
7. Which is mismatched?
   a. homology—character similarity due to a common ancestor
   b. molecular data—DNA strands match
   c. fossil record—bones and teeth
   d. homology—functions always differ
   e. molecular data—molecular clock
8. One benefit of the fossil record is
   a. that hard parts are more likely to fossilize.
   b. fossils can be dated.
   c. its completeness.
   d. fossils congregate in one place.
   e. All of these are correct.

9. In cladistics
   a. a clade must contain the common ancestor plus all its descendants.
   b. derived characters help construct cladograms.
   c. data for the cladogram are presented.
   d. the species in a clade share homologous structures.
   e. All of these are correct.
10. In the traditional school of systematics, birds are assigned to a different group from reptiles because
    a. they evolved from reptiles and couldn't be a monophyletic taxon.
    b. they are adapted to a different way of life compared to reptiles.
    c. feathers came from scales and feet came before wings.
    d. all classes of vertebrates are only related by way of a common ancestor.
    e. All of these are correct.
11. Answer the following questions about this cladogram.
    a. This cladogram contains how many clades? How are they designated in the diagram?
    b. What character is shared by all taxa in the study group? What characters are shared by only snakes and lizards?
    c. Which taxa share a recent common ancestry? How do you know?

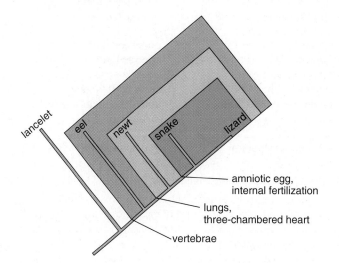

amniotic egg, internal fertilization

lungs, three-chambered heart

vertebrae

Thinking Scientifically

1. Recent DNA evidence suggests to some plant taxonomists that the traditional way of classifying flowering plants is not correct, and that flowering plants need to be completely reclassified. Other botanists disagree, saying it would be chaotic and unwise to disregard the historical classification groups. Argue for and against keeping traditional classification schemes.

2. Two populations of frogs apparently differ only in skin coloration. What data would you need to determine if both populations belong to the same species? If they are two different species, what data would you need to determine how closely related the two species are?

Understanding the Terms

analogous structure 495	homologous structure 495
analogy 495	homology 495
binomial system 490	kingdom 493
character 493	molecular clock 497
clade 498	order 493
cladogram 498	parallel evolution 495
class 493	phenetic systematics 500
cladistic systematics 498	phylogenetic tree 494
common ancestor 492	phylogeny 494
convergent evolution 495	phylum 493
derived character 494	primitive character 494
DNA-DNA hybridization 496	species 493
domain 493	specific epithet 491
domain Archaea 502	systematics 494
domain Bacteria 502	taxon (pl., taxa) 492
domain Eukarya 502	taxonomy 490
family 493	three-domain system 502
five-kingdom system 501	traditional systematics 500
genus 493	

Match the terms to these definitions:

a. _____ Branch of biology concerned with identifying, describing, and naming organisms.

b. _____ Diagram that indicates common ancestors and lines of descent.

c. _____ Group of organisms that fills a particular classification category.

d. _____ School of systematics that determines the degree of relatedness by analyzing primitive and derived characters and constructing cladograms.

e. _____ Similarity in structure due to having a common ancestor.

Web Connections

Exploring the Internet

http://www.mhhe.com/biosci/genbio/mader
(click on *Biology 7/e*)

The *Biology 7/e* Online Learning Center provides many resources for studying the material in this chapter including links to the following sites:

Journey into the World of Cladistics. This site discusses the introduction, methodology, implication, and the need for cladistics.

http://www.ucmp.berkeley.edu/clad/clad4.html

References About Phylogenetic Biology. A very long list of references (not links) on phylogenetic biology.

http://phylogeny.arizona.edu/tree/home.pages/references.html

BIOSIS. BIOSIS is a general but extensive Internet resource guide to animal taxa, animal diversity, various taxa, and mailing lists. Search for information by animal taxa or subject categories. This resource has an enormous number of links applicable for many zoological topics.

http://www.york.biosis.org/zrdocs/zoolinfo/grp_all.htm

NCBI (National Center for Biotechnology Information) Taxonomy Resources. This site provides information on systematics and molecular genetics.

http://www3.ncbi.nlm.nih.gov/Taxonomy/taxpage2.html

Taxonomic Resources and Expertise Directory (TRED). Find a new species in your backyard? This is the place to find information regarding how to classify it.

http://www.nbs.gov/cbi/programs/tred.html

Development

As development occurs, complexity increases.

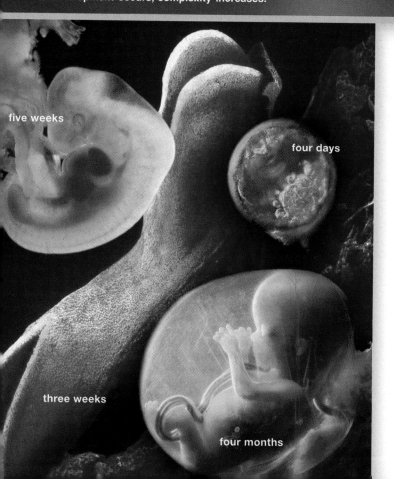

five weeks

four days

three weeks

four months

As development proceeds, specialization of cells becomes apparent. How does this occur, since all cells contain the same genes? Scientists do not have all the answers to this question, but they do know that specific molecules signal specific genes to become active at different times. In the end, nerve cells have axons and dendrites, not myofibrils like muscle cells, and bone cells deposit calcium salts, not skin pigment. And a baby has eyes and ears, fingers and toes in the right number and place.

The same processes observed during embryological development are also seen as a newborn matures, as lost parts regenerate, as a wound heals, and even as organisms age. Therefore, it has become increasingly clear that the study of development encompasses not only embryology but these other events as well.

The goal of developmental genetics is to discover which signaling molecules turn on which genes to make specialization come about. It's not possible to perform experiments on human embryos, but luckily scientists have discovered that concepts gained from studying frog, roundworm, and fly embryos apply to humans too.

51.1 Early Developmental Stages 💿

Fertilization [L. *fertilis*, fruitful], which results in a zygote, requires that the sperm and egg interact. Figure 51.1 shows the manner in which an egg is fertilized by a sperm in sea stars. The sperm has three distinct parts: a head, a middle piece, and a tail. The tail is a flagellum, which allows the sperm to swim toward the egg, and the middle piece contains ATP-producing mitochondria. The head contains a haploid nucleus capped by a membrane-bounded acrosome containing enzymes that allow the sperm to penetrate the egg.

Several mechanisms have evolved to assure that fertilization takes place and in a species-specific manner (Fig. 51.1). A male releases so many sperm that the egg is literally covered by them. The sea star egg has a plasma membrane, a glycoprotein layer called the vitelline envelope, and a jelly coat. The acrosome enzymes digest away the jelly coat as the acrosome extrudes a filament that attaches to a receptor located in the vitelline envelope. This is a lock-and-key reac-

tion that is species-specific. Then, the egg plasma membrane and sperm nuclear membrane fuse, allowing the sperm nucleus to enter. A zygote is present when the sperm nucleus fuses with the egg nucleus. Following fusion, the egg plasma membrane and the vitelline envelope undergo changes that prevent the entrance of any other sperm. The vitelline envelope is now called the fertilization envelope.

Embryonic Development

Development is all the changes that occur during the life cycle of an organism. During the first stages of development an organism is called an **embryo.** Most animals go through the same embryonic stages of zygote, morula, blastula, early gastrula, and late gastrula. As an example, we will consider the lancelet, an invertebrate chordate (see Fig. 35.2) whose egg has little yolk. **Yolk** is dense nutrient material.

Following fertilization, the zygote undergoes **cleavage,** which is cell division without growth (Fig. 51.2). DNA replication and mitotic cell division occur repeatedly, and the cells get smaller with each division. Because the lancelet has

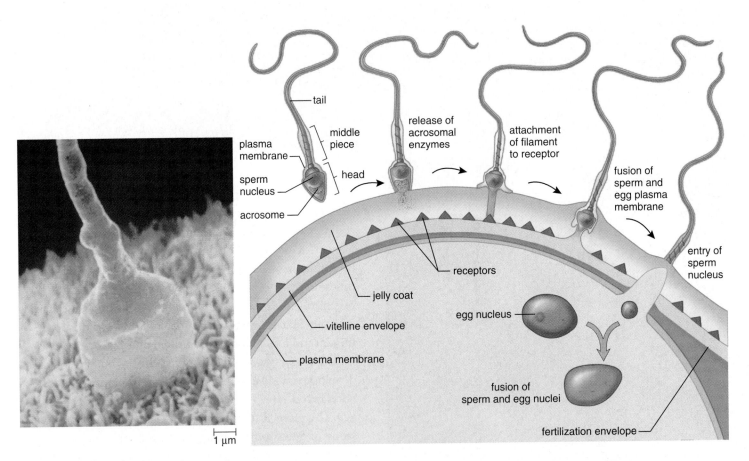

Figure 51.1 Fertilization of a sea star egg.
A head of a sperm has a membrane-bounded acrosome filled with enzymes. When released, these enzymes digest away the jelly coat around the egg, and the acrosome extrudes a filament that attaches to a receptor on the vitelline envelope. Now the sperm nucleus enters and fuses with the egg nucleus, and the resulting zygote begins to divide. The vitelline envelope becomes the fertilization envelope, which prohibits any more sperm from entering the egg.

little yolk, the cell divisions are equal, and the cells are of uniform size in the resulting **morula** [L. dim. of *morus*, mulberry]. Then a cavity called the **blastocoel** [Gk. *blastos*, bud, and *koiloma*, cavity] develops and a hollow ball of cells known as the **blastula** [Gk. dim. of *blastos*, bud, and L. *ula*, little] forms.

The **gastrula** [Gk. dim. of *gastros*, stomach] stage is evident in a lancelet when certain cells begin to push, or invaginate, into the blastocoel, creating a double layer of cells. The outer layer of cells is called the **ectoderm**, and the inner layer is called the **endoderm**. The space created by invagination will become the gut, but at this point it is termed either the archenteron or the primitive gut. The pore, or hole, created by invagination is the blastopore, and in a lancelet the blastopore eventually becomes the anus.

Gastrulation is not complete until three layers of cells are present. The third, or middle, layer of cells is called the **mesoderm**. In a lancelet, this layer begins as outpocketings from the primitive gut. These outpocketings grow in size until they meet and fuse. In effect then, two layers of mesoderm are formed, and the space between them is the coelom. The coelom is a body cavity that contains internal organs.

Ectoderm, mesoderm, and endoderm are called the embryonic **germ layers.** No matter how gastrulation takes place, the end result is the same: three germ layers are formed. It is possible to relate the development of future organs to these germ layers:

Embryonic Germ Layer	Vertebrate Adult Structures
Ectoderm (outer layer)	Epidermis of skin; epithelial lining of oral cavity and rectum; nervous system
Mesoderm (middle layer)	Skeleton; muscular system; dermis of skin; cardiovascular system; excretory system; reproductive system—including most epithelial linings; outer layers of respiratory and digestive systems
Endoderm (inner layer)	Epithelial lining of digestive tract and respiratory tract; associated glands of these systems; epithelial lining of urinary bladder

Karl E. Von Baer, the nineteenth-century embryologist, first related development to the formation of germ layers. This is called the germ layer theory.

The three embryonic germ layers arise during gastrulation, when cells invaginate into the blastocoel. The development of organs can be related to the three germ layers: ectoderm, mesoderm, and endoderm.

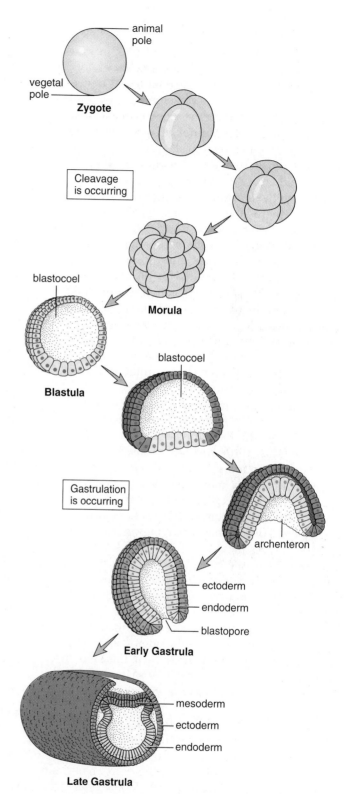

Figure 51.2 Lancelet early development.
A lancelet has little yolk, as an embryo, and it can be used to exemplify the early stages of development in such animals. Cleavage produces a number of cells that form a cavity. Invagination during gastrulation produces the germ layers ectoderm and endoderm. Mesoderm arises from pouches that pinch off from the endoderm.

The Effect of Yolk

Table 51.1 indicates the amount of yolk in four types of embryos and relates the amount of yolk to the environment in which the animal develops. The lancelet and frog develop in water, and they have less yolk than the chick because their development proceeds quickly to a swimming larval stage that can feed itself. The chick is representative of vertebrate animals that develop on land and lay a hard-shelled egg that contains plentiful yolk. Development continues in the shell until there is an offspring capable of land existence.

Early stages of human development resemble those of the chick embryo, yet this resemblance cannot be related to the amount of yolk because the human egg contains little yolk. But the evolutionary history of these two animals can provide an answer for this similarity. Both birds and mammals are related to reptiles. This explains why all three groups develop similarly, despite a difference in the amount of yolk in the eggs.

Figure 51.3 compares the appearance of early developmental stages in the lancelet, the frog, and the chick. In the frog embryo, cells at the animal pole have little yolk while those at the vegetal pole contain more yolk. The presence of yolk causes cells to cleave more slowly, and you can see that the cells of the animal pole are smaller than those of the vegetal pole. In the chick, cleavage is incomplete—only those cells lying on top of the yolk cleave. This means that although cleavage in the lancelet and the frog results in a morula, no such ball of cells is seen in the chick. Instead, during the morula stage the cells spread out on a portion of the yolk.

In the frog, the blastocoel is formed at the animal pole only. The heavily laden yolk cells of the vegetal pole do not participate in this step. In a chick, the blastocoel is created when the cells lift up from the yolk and leave a space between the cells and the yolk.

In the frog, the cells containing yolk do not participate in gastrulation and therefore they do not invaginate. Instead, a slitlike blastopore is formed when the animal pole cells begin to invaginate from above. Following this, other animal pole cells move down over the yolk, and the blastopore becomes rounded when these cells also invaginate from below. At this stage, there are some yolk cells temporarily left in the region of the blastopore; these are called the yolk plug. In the chick, there is so much yolk that endoderm formation does not occur by invagination. Instead, an upper layer of cells differentiates into ectoderm, and a lower layer differentiates into endoderm.

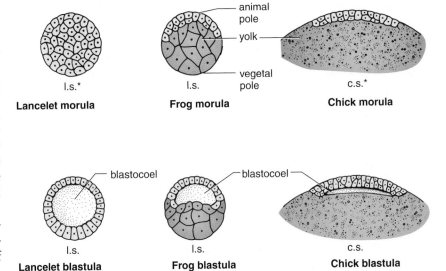

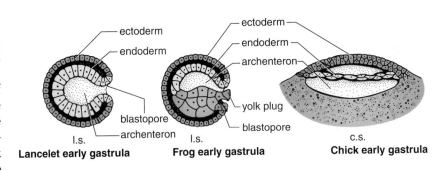

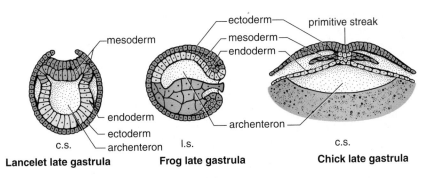

l.s. = longitudinal section; c.s. = cross section

Figure 51.3 Comparative animal development.

Table 51.1

Amount of Yolk in Eggs Versus Location of Development

Animal	Yolk	Location of Development
Lancelet	Little	External in water
Frog	Some	External in water
Chick	Much	Within hard shell
Human	Little	Inside mother

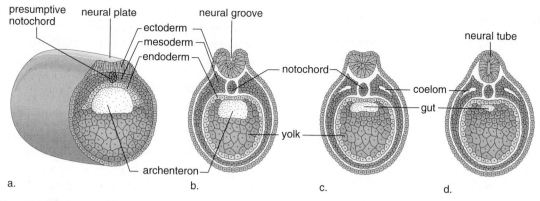

Figure 51.4 Development of neural tube and coelom in a frog embryo.
a. Ectoderm cells that lie above the future notochord (called presumptive notochord) thicken to form a neural plate. **b.** The neural groove and folds are noticeable as the neural tube begins to form. **c.** A splitting of the mesoderm produces a coelom, which is completely lined by mesoderm. **d.** A neural tube and a coelom have now developed.

In the frog, cells from the dorsal lip of the blastopore migrate between the ectoderm and endoderm, forming the mesoderm. Later, a splitting of the mesoderm creates the coelom. In the chick, the mesoderm layer arises by an invagination of cells along the edges of a longitudinal furrow in the midline of the embryo. Because of its appearance, this furrow is called the primitive streak. Later, the newly formed mesoderm will split to produce a coelomic cavity.

The amount of yolk typically affects the manner in which animals complete the first three stages of development.

Neurulation and the Nervous System

The newly formed mesoderm cells that lie along the main longitudinal axis of the animal coalesce to form a dorsal supporting rod called the **notochord** [Gk. *noto*, back, and *chord*, string]. The notochord persists in lancelets but in frogs, chicks, and humans, it is later replaced by the vertebral column. Therefore they are called vertebrates.

The nervous system develops from midline ectoderm located just above the notochord. At first, a thickening of cells called the **neural plate** is seen along the dorsal surface of the embryo. Then, neural folds develop on either side of a neural groove, which becomes the **neural tube** when these folds fuse. Figure 51.4 shows cross sections of frog development to illustrate the formation of the neural tube. At this point, the embryo is called a neurula. Later, the anterior end of the neural tube develops into the brain and the rest becomes the spinal cord.

Midline mesoderm cells that did not contribute to the formation of the notochord now become two longitudinal masses of tissue. These two masses become blocked off into the somites, which give rise to segmental muscles in all

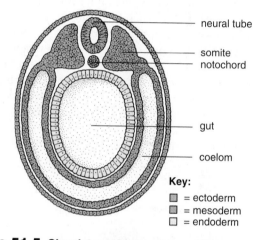

Figure 51.5 Chordate embryo, cross section.
At the neurula stage, each of the germ layers, indicated by color (see key), can be associated with the later development of particular parts. The somites give rise to the muscles of each segment and to the vertebrae, which replace the notochord in vertebrates.

chordates. In vertebrates, the somites also produce the vertebral bones.

The chordate embryo in Figure 51.5 shows the location of various parts. This figure and the chart on page 921 will help you relate the formation of chordate structures and organs to the three embryonic layers of cells: the ectoderm, the mesoderm, and the endoderm.

During neurulation, the neural tube develops just above the notochord. At the neurula stage of development, a cross section of all chordate embryos is similar in appearance.

51.2 Developmental Processes

Development requires (1) growth, (2) cellular differentiation, and (3) morphogenesis. **Cellular differentiation** occurs when cells become specialized in structure and function; a muscle cell looks different and acts differently than a nerve cell. **Morphogenesis** produces the shape and form of the body. One of the earliest indications of morphogenesis is cell movement as discussed in the reading on page 927. Later, morphogenesis includes **pattern formation** when tissues are organized into specific structures.

At one time investigators mistakenly believed that irreversible genetic changes must account for differentiation and morphogenesis. Perhaps the genes are parcelled out as development occurs and that's why cells of the body have a different structure and function. Our ability today to clone mammals such as sheep, goats, and mice from specialized adult cells shows that every cell in an organism's body contains a full complement of genes. It's said that cells in the adult body are **totipotent;** each one contains all the instructions needed by any other specialized cell in the body.

The answer to this puzzle becomes clear when we consider that only muscle cells produce the proteins myosin and actin; only red blood cells produce hemoglobin; and only skin cells produce keratin. In other words, we now know that specialization is not due to a parceling out of genes rather it is due to differential gene expression. Certain genes and not others are turned on in differentiated cells. In recent years, investigators have turned their attention to discovering the mechanisms that lead to differential gene expression. Two mechanisms—cytoplasmic segregation and induction—seem to be especially important.

Cytoplasmic Segregation

Differentiation must begin long before we can recognize specialized types of cells. Ectodermal, endoderm, and mesodermal cells in the gastrula look quite similar, but yet they must be different because they develop into different organs. The egg is now known to contain substances called maternal determinants because they influence the course of development. Cytoplasmic segregation is the parceling out of maternal determinants as mitosis occurs:

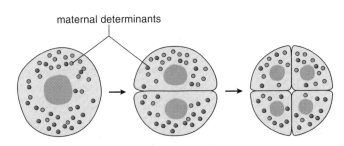

Ooplasmic Segregation

Cytoplasmic segregation helps determine how the various cells of the morula will develop.

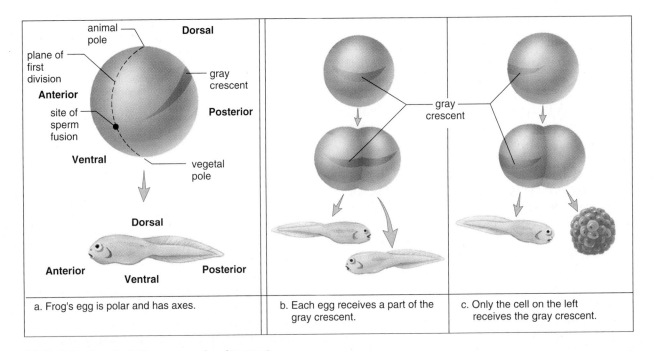

Figure 51.6 Cytoplasmic influence on development.
a. A frog's egg has anterior/posterior and dorsal/ventral axes that correlate with the position of the gray crescent. **b.** The first cleavage normally divides the gray crescent in half, and each daughter cell is capable of developing into a complete tadpole. **c.** But if only one daughter cell receives the gray crescent, then only that cell can become a complete embryo. This shows that maternal determinants are present in the cytoplasm of a frog's egg.

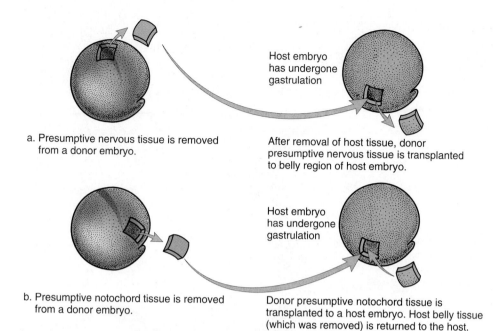

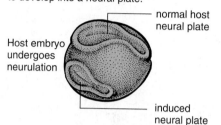

a. Presumptive nervous tissue is removed from a donor embryo.

Host embryo has undergone gastrulation

After removal of host tissue, donor presumptive nervous tissue is transplanted to belly region of host embryo.

Host embryo undergoes neurulation

normal host neural plate

tissue transplant

Due to normal induction process, a host neural plate develops. But donated tissue is not induced to develop into a neural plate.

b. Presumptive notochord tissue is removed from a donor embryo.

Host embryo has undergone gastrulation

Donor presumptive notochord tissue is transplanted to a host embryo. Host belly tissue (which was removed) is returned to the host.

Host embryo undergoes neurulation

normal host neural plate

induced neural plate

Host develops two neural plates – one induced by host notochord tissue, the second induced by transplanted notochord tissue.

Figure 51.7 Control of nervous system development.
a. In this experiment, the presumptive nervous system (blue) does not develop into the neural plate if moved from its normal location. **b.** In this experiment, the presumptive notochord (red) can cause even belly ectoderm to develop into the neural plate (blue). This shows that the notochord induces ectoderm to become a neural plate, most likely by sending out chemical signals.

An early experiment showed that the cytoplasm of a frog's egg is not uniform. It is polar and has both an anterior/posterior axis and a dorsal/ventral axis, which can be correlated with the **gray crescent,** a gray area that appears after the sperm fertilizes the egg (Fig. 51.6*a*). Hans Spemann, who received a Nobel Prize in 1935 for his extensive work in embryology, showed that if the gray crescent is divided equally by the first cleavage, each experimentally separated daughter cell develops into a complete embryo (Fig. 51.6*b*). If the egg divides so that only one daughter cell receives the gray crescent, however, only that cell becomes a complete embryo (Fig. 51.6*c*). This experiment allows us to speculate that the gray crescent must contain particular chemical signals that are needed for development to proceed normally.

Induction

As development proceeds, specialization of cells and formation of organs is influenced not only by maternal determinants but also by signals given off by neighboring cells. **Induction** [L. *in*, into, and *duco*, lead] is the ability of one embryonic tissue to influence the development of another tissue.

Spemann showed that a frog embryo's gray crescent becomes the dorsal lip of the blastopore, where gastrulation begins. Since this region is necessary for complete development, he called the dorsal lip of the blastopore the primary organizer. The cells closest to the Spemann's primary organizer become endoderm, those farther away

become mesoderm, and those farthest away become ectoderm. This suggests that there may be a molecular concentration gradient that acts as a chemical signal to induce germ layer differentiation.

The gray crescent of a frog's egg marks the dorsal side of the embryo where the mesoderm becomes notochord and ectoderm becomes nervous system. In a classic experiment Spemann and his colleague Hilde Mangold showed that presumptive (potential) notochord tissue induces the formation of the nervous system (Fig. 51.7). If presumptive nervous system tissue, located just above the presumptive notochord, is cut out and transplanted to the belly region of the embryo, it does not form a neural tube. On the other hand, if presumptive notochord tissue is cut out and transplanted beneath what would be belly ectoderm, this ectoderm differentiates into neural tissue. Still other examples of induction are now known. In 1905, Warren Lewis studied the formation of the eye in frog embryos. He found that an optic vesicle, which is a lateral outgrowth of developing brain tissue, induces overlying ectoderm to thicken and become a lens. The developing lens in turn induces an optic vesicle to form an optic cup, where the retina develops.

Cytoplasmic segregation and induction are two mechanisms that help explain the developmental processes of differentiation and morphogenesis.

Figure 51.8 Development of *C. elegans*, a nematode.
a. A fate map of the worm showing that as cells arise by cell division they are destined to become particular structures.
b. Apoptosis. When a cell-death signal is received, a master protein is inactive and no longer inhibits a cell-death cascade that ends with proteases and nucleases that destroy the cell.

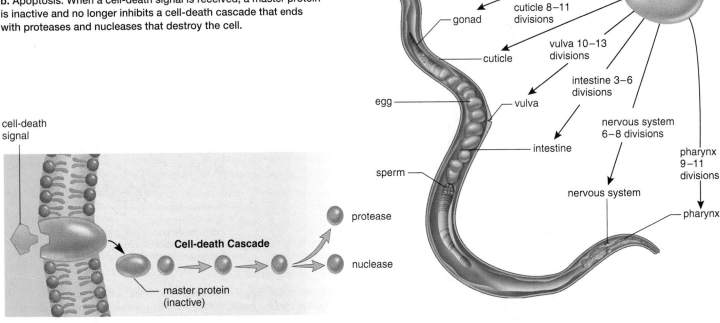

a. Fate map

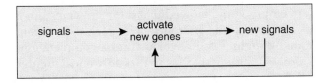

b. Apoptosis

Model Organisms

Developmental genetics has benefited from research utilizing the roundworm, *Caenorhabditis elegans,* the fruit fly, *Drosophila melanogaster,* and the mouse, *Mus musculus.* These organisms are referred to as model organisms because the study of their development produced concepts that help us understand development in general.

Caenorhabditis elegans

This tiny worm is only one millimeter long and vast numbers can be raised in the laboratory either in petri dishes or a liquid medium. The worm is hermaphroditic and self-fertilization is the rule. Therefore, even though induced mutations may be recessive, the next generation will yield individuals which are homozygous recessive and will show the mutation. Many modern genetic studies have been done. The entire genome has been sequenced. Individual genes have been altered, cloned, and their products injected into cells or extracellular fluid.

What have we learned? Development of *C. elegans* takes only three days and the adult worm contains only 959 cells. It's been possible for investigators to watch the process from beginning to end, especially since the worm is transparent. **Fate maps** have been developed that show the destiny of each cell as it arises following successive cell divisions (Fig. 51.8a). Some investigators have studied in detail the development of the vulva, a pore through which eggs are laid. A cell called the anchor cell induces the vulva to form. The cell closest to the anchor cell receives the most inducer and becomes the inner vulva. This cell in turn produces another inducer which acts on its two neighboring

cells and they become the outer vulva. The inducers are growthlike factors that alter the metabolism of the receiving cell and activate particular genes. Work with *C. elegans* has shown that induction requires the transcriptional regulation of genes in a particular sequence. This diagram shows how induction can occur sequentially:

```
signals ──────▶  activate   ──────▶ new signals
                 new genes
                     ▲
                     └─────────────────────┘
```

Apoptosis We have already discussed the importance of **apoptosis** (programmed cell death) in the normal day-to-day operation of the immune system and in preventing the occurrence of cancer. Apoptosis is also an important part of development in all organisms. In humans we know that apoptosis is necessary to the shaping of the hands and feet; if it does not occur, the child is born with webbing between fingers and toes.

The fate maps of *C. elegans* indicate that apoptosis occurs in 131 cells as development takes place. Researchers have been able to study the molecular basis for apoptosis in these cells. Certain proteins, called ced (for *cell death*) proteins, are part of a cell-death pathway always present in the cell. The cell-death pathway is ordinarily inhibited by a master protein present in the plasma membrane. But when a receptor protein binds to a cell-death signal, the master protein becomes inactive. Then, the cell-death cascade produces proteases and nucleases that slice up proteins and DNA in the cell (Fig. 51.8b).

Research with a Cellular Slime Mold Fruiting Body

We do not often think how remarkable it is that most of our cells and tissues are in the correct places and in the correct proportion to other tissues. Further, we do not always realize that there are mechanisms controlling these events—until one of these mechanisms fails. Only then is it obvious that control mechanisms play such important roles in our development. Some of the most exciting questions in developmental biology involve these fundamental processes of positioning and proportioning of different cell types. In large complex organisms such as ourselves, the controls are likely to be more complex than in more simple species. Thus, research into these questions often centers on comparatively simple organisms such as the cellular slime mold, *Dictyostelium*.

Much of my research has involved study of the proportions and movements of cells in *Dictyostelium*. I first became interested in these questions as a graduate student in John Bonner's laboratory at Princeton University. Although I certainly found *Dictyostelium's* apparently simple development intriguing, I think what initially attracted me (a wide-eyed, eager graduate student) was my first visit to Dr. Bonner's lab. After introducing me around the lab, he spent a few minutes talking with his technician about a particular experiment. Dr. Bonner concluded that the experiment had not been fruitful, yet he was reluctant to drop it because it had been "fun with slime molds." I had known that Dr. Bonner was an excellent scientist, and now I saw

that he found just doing experiments to be terrifically enjoyable. From that moment, I knew I wanted to join his lab; and since that time, I have also spent many pleasant years working with slime molds.

Dictyostelium exhibits a fascinating life cycle that includes a unicellular stage and several multicellular stages. In the unicellular stage, individual amoeboid cells feed on bacteria in the soil and grow and divide. When the food supply is diminished, the cells aggregate into a tiny multicellular mound. The mound forms a slug about a millimeter long that subsequently develops into a fruiting body. The fruiting body stands erect on the substrate and consists of a stalk holding aloft a small mass of spores. Each spore can germinate to produce a single amoeba to begin the life cycle again.

Recently my research has focused on one aspect of fruiting body formation. Stalk cells stack on top of one another as a fruiting body grows upward. Even so, the spores stay near the tip. How can they do that when they have lost their ability to move by amoeboid action? My hypothesis was that the cells nearest the spores, called anterior-like cells are involved in raising the spores to the tip of the fruiting body. To test the hypothesis I did experiments in which I removed the anterior-like cells. I found that when I removed the upper group of anterior-like cells, the spores were left along the middle of the fruiting body; they were not elevated to the tip. If undifferentiated stalk cells were trans-

planted in place of the upper anterior-like cells, the spores also remained along the middle of the fruiting body. This suggests that not just any motile cells can replace the function of the anterior-like cells. However, when I replaced the anterior-like cells with more anterior-like cells, the spores were again (although not 100% of the time) elevated to the tip. Altogether, these experiments indicate that the upper layer of anterior-like cells act as "elevator" cells, moving the spores to the top of the fruiting body (Fig. 51A).

When we learn about events and mechanisms in simple organisms, such as *Dictyostelium,* we are able to turn to more complex organisms, including ourselves, and ask if similar processes occur during our development. The type of research that undergraduates in my lab and I do holds a fascination for me and many others in biology. For me personally, I get enjoyment in performing the experiments and in the discovery of new facts about *Dictyostelium.* In addition, an investigator knows that while basic research may not be directed toward solving some immediate problem of humankind, it may eventually contribute to the betterment of our species, either directly or indirectly.

John Sternfeld

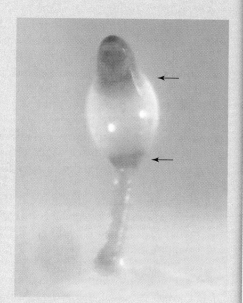

Figure 51A Cellular slime mold fruiting body.
The cells stained red (see arrows) are "elevator cells" which raise the spores (in the white area) to the top of the 0.6 mm high fruiting body.

John Sternfeld
State University of New York College at Cortland

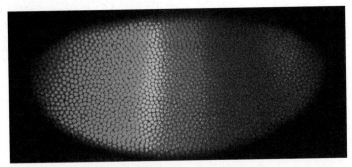

a. Protein products of *gap* genes

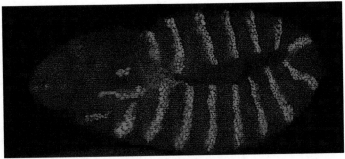

c. Protein product of a *segment-polarity* gene

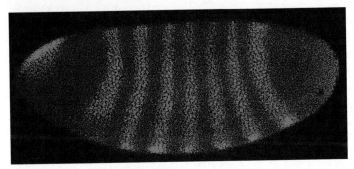

b. Protein product of *pair-rule* gene

Figure 51.9 Development in *Drosophila*, a fruit fly.
a. The different colors show that two different *gap* gene proteins are present from the anterior to the posterior end of an egg. **b.** The green stripes show that a *pair-rule* gene is being expressed as segmentation of the fly occurs. **c.** Now *segment-polarity* genes help bring about division of each segment into an anterior and posterior end.

Drosophilia melanogaster

Investigators studying morphogenesis in *Drosophila* (fruit fly) have discovered that there are some genes that determine the animal's anterior/posterior and dorsal/ventral axes, others that determine the fly's segmentation pattern, and still others, called homeotic genes, that determine the body parts on each segment.

The Anterior/Posterior Axes   One of the first events toward successful development is the establishment of the body axes: location of the head versus the tail and location of the back versus the belly. In the *Drosophila* egg there is a greater concentration of a protein called bicoid at one end. This end becomes the anterior region where the head develops. (*Bicoid* means "two tailed" and a *bicoid* gene mutation can cause the embryo to have only two posterior ends.) Researchers have cloned the *bicoid* gene and used it as a probe to establish that mRNA for the bicoid protein is present in a concentration gradient from the anterior end to the posterior end of the embryo.

Many other protein gradients in the *Drosophila* egg help determine the axes of the body. Proteins that influence morphogenesis are called **morphogens.** The bicoid gradient is a morphogen gradient. The bicoid gradient switches on the expression of segmentation genes in *Drosophila*. What is the advantage of a morphogen gradient? A morphogen gradient can have a range of effects depending on its concentration in a particular portion of the animal.

The Segmentation Pattern   The next event in the development of *Drosophila* is the establishment of its segments. The

bicoid gradient initiates a cascade in which a series of segmentation gene sets are turned on, one after the other.

Christiane Nusslein-Vollard and Eric Wieschaus received a Nobel Prize for their work in discovering the segmentation genes of *Drosophila*. They exposed the flies to mutagenic chemicals and then performed innumerable crosses to map the mutated genes that caused segmental abnormalities. They went on to clone many of these genes. The first set of segmental genes to be activated are called *gap* genes (Fig. 51.9a). (If one of these genes mutates there are *gaps*, that is, large blocks of segments are missing.) Then the *pair-rule* genes become active and the embryo has precisely 14 segments (Fig. 51.9b). If one of these mutates, the animal has half the number of segments. Next the *segment-polarity* genes are expressed and each segment has an anterior and posterior half (Fig. 51.9c).

Work with *Drosophila* has suggested how morphogenesis comes about. Sequential sets of master genes code for morphogen gradients that activate the next set of master genes in turn. How do morphogen gradients turn on genes? They are transcription factors which regulate which genes are active in which parts of the embryo in what order.

Homeotic Genes   **Homeotic genes** control pattern formation, the organization of differentiated cells into specific three-dimensional structures. During normal development of *Drosophila* the homeotic genes are activated after the segmentation genes. If a mutant is missing the set of homeotic genes called the *bithorax complex*, the fly still has the normal number of posterior segments.

a.

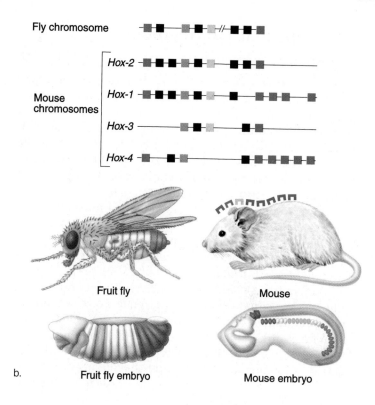

b.   Fruit fly embryo   Mouse embryo

Figure 51.10 Pattern formation in *Drosophila.*
Homeotic genes control pattern formation, an aspect of
morphogenesis. **a.** If homeotic genes are activated at inappropriate
times, abnormalities such as a fly with four wings occurs. **b.** The green,
blue, yellow, and red colors show that homologous homeotic genes
occur on a fly chromosome and four mouse chromosomes in the same
order. These genes are color coded to the region of the embryo and,
therefore, the adult, where they regulate pattern formation. The black
boxes are homeotic genes that are not identical between the two
animals. In mammals, homeotic genes are called *Hox* genes.

As early as the 1940s, Edward B. Lewis had discovered
the homeotic genes in *Drosophila*. He was able to determine
that certain genes controlled whether a particular segment
would bear antennae, legs, or wings. A homeotic mutation
caused these appendages to be misplaced—a mutant fly
could have extra legs where antennae should be or two pairs
of wings (Fig. 51.10*a*).

Homeotic genes have now been found in many other
organisms and, surprisingly, they all contain the same particular sequence of nucleotides, called a **homeobox.** (Because homeotic genes contain a homeobox in mammals they
are called *Hox* genes.) The homeobox codes for a particular
sequence of 60 amino acids called a homeodomain:

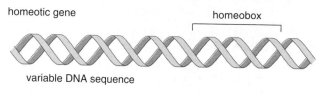

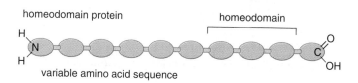

Homeotic genes, like many other developmental
genes, code for transcription factors. The homeodomain
protein is that part of a transcription factor that binds to

DNA but the other more variable sequences of a transcription factor determine which particular genes are turned on.
Researchers envision that a homeodomain protein produced
by one homeotic gene binds to and turns on the next
homeotic gene and so forth. This orderly process in the end
determines the morphology of particular segments.

Mice and humans have the same four clusters of
homeotic genes located on four different chromosomes. In
Drosophila, homeotic genes are located on a single chromosome. In all three types of animals, homeotic genes are expressed from anterior to posterior in the same order. The
first clusters determine the final development of anterior
segments of the animal, while those later in the sequence
determine the final development of posterior segments of
the embryo.

Since the homeotic genes of so many different organisms contain the same homeodomain, we know that this nucleotide sequence arose early in the history of life that has
been largely conserved as evolution occurred. In general it
has been very surprising to learn how similar developmental genetics is in organisms from yeasts to plants to a wide
variety of animals. Certainly, the genetic mechanisms of development appear to be quite similar in all animals.

There is a hierarchy of gene activity that causes
development to be orderly. Morphogen gradients contain
transcription factors that cause cells to produce yet other
morphogen gradients until finally specific structures are
formed.

51.3 Human Embryonic and Fetal Development

In humans, the length of the time from conception (fertilization followed by **implantation**) to birth (parturition) is approximately nine months. It is customary to calculate the time of birth by adding 280 days to the start of the last menstruation, because this date is usually known, whereas the day of fertilization is usually unknown. Because the time of birth is influenced by so many variables, only about 5% of babies actually arrive on the forecasted date.

Human development is often divided into embryonic development (months 1 and 2) and fetal development (months 3–9). The **embryonic period** consists of early formation of the major organs, and fetal development is the refinement of these structures.

Before we consider human development chronologically, we must understand the placement of **extraembryonic membranes** [L. *extra*, on the outside]. Extraembryonic membranes are best understood by considering their function in reptiles and birds. In reptiles, these membranes made development on land first possible. If an embryo develops in the water, the water supplies oxygen for the embryo and takes away waste products. The surrounding water prevents desiccation, or drying out, and provides a protective cushion. For an embryo that develops on land, all these functions are performed by the extraembryonic membranes.

In the chick, the extraembryonic membranes develop from extensions of the germ layers, which spread out over the yolk. Figure 51.11 shows the chick surrounded by the membranes. The **chorion** [Gk. *chorion*, membrane] lies next to the shell and carries on gas exchange. The **amnion** [Gk. *amnion*, membrane around fetus] contains the protective amniotic fluid, which bathes the developing embryo. The **allantois** [Gk. *allantos*, sausage] collects nitrogenous wastes, and the **yolk sac** surrounds the remaining yolk, which provides nourishment.

Humans (and other mammals) also have these extraembryonic membranes. The chorion develops into the fetal half of the placenta; the yolk sac, which lacks yolk, is the first site of blood cell formation; the allantoic blood vessels become the umbilical blood vessels; and the amnion contains fluid to cushion and protect the embryo, which develops into a fetus. Therefore, the function of the membranes in humans has been modified to suit internal development, but their very presence indicates our relationship to birds and to reptiles. It is interesting to note that all chordate animals develop in water, either in bodies of water or within amniotic fluid.

The presence of extraembryonic membranes in reptiles made development on land possible. Humans also have these membranes, but their function has been modified for internal development.

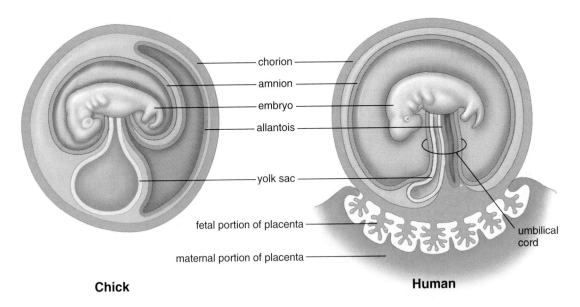

Figure 51.11 Extraembryonic membranes.
Extraembryonic membranes, which are not part of the embryo, are found during the development of chicks and humans, where each has a specific function.

Embryonic Development

Embryonic development includes the first two months of development.

The First Week

Fertilization occurs in the upper third of an oviduct (Fig. 51.12), and cleavage begins even as the embryo passes down this duct to the uterus. By the time the embryo reaches the uterus on the third day, it is a morula. The morula is not much larger than the zygote because, even though multiple cell divisions have occurred, there has been no growth of these newly formed cells. By about the fifth day, the morula is transformed into the blastocyst. The **blastocyst** has a fluid-filled cavity, a single layer of outer cells called the **trophoblast** [Gk. *trophe*, food, and *blastos*, bud], and an inner cell mass. Later, the trophoblast, reinforced by a layer of mesoderm, gives rise to the chorion, one of the extraembryonic membranes (Fig. 51.11). The inner cell mass eventually becomes the embryo, which develops into a fetus.

The Second Week

At the end of the first week, the embryo begins the process of implanting in the wall of the uterus. The trophoblast secretes enzymes to digest away some of the tissue and blood vessels of the endometrium of the uterus (Fig. 51.12). The embryo is now about the size of the period at the end

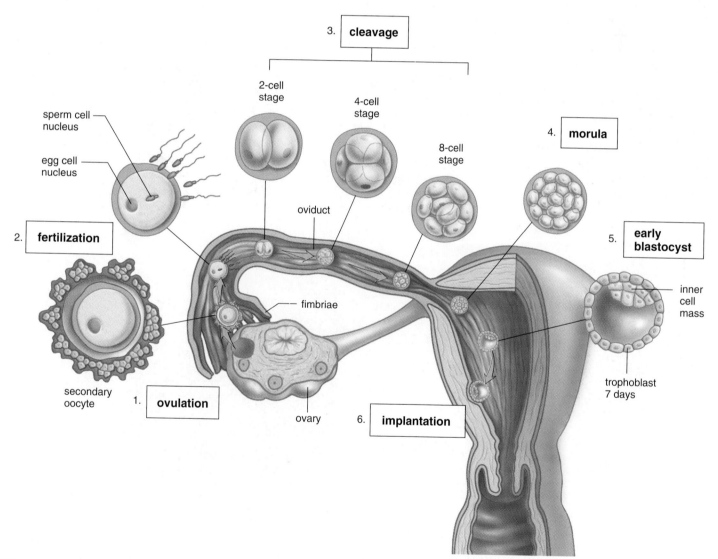

Figure 51.12 Human development before implantation.
Structures and events proceed counterclockwise. At ovulation (1), the secondary oocyte leaves the ovary. A single sperm nucleus enters the egg, and fertilization (2) occurs in the oviduct. As the zygote moves along the oviduct, it undergoes cleavage (3) to produce a morula (4). The blastocyst forms (5) and implants itself in the uterine lining (6).

of this sentence. The trophoblast begins to secrete **human chorionic gonadotropin (HCG),** the hormone that is the basis for the pregnancy test and that serves to maintain the corpus luteum past the time it normally disintegrates. Because of this, the endometrium is maintained and menstruation does not occur.

As the week progresses, the inner cell mass detaches itself from the trophoblast, and two more extraembryonic membranes form (Fig. 51.13*a*). The yolk sac, which forms below the embryonic disk, has no nutritive function as in chicks, but it is the first site of blood cell formation. However, the amnion and its cavity are where the embryo (and then the fetus) develops. In humans, amniotic fluid acts as an insulator against cold and heat and also absorbs shock, such as that caused by the mother exercising.

Gastrulation occurs during the second week. The inner cell mass now has flattened into the **embryonic disk,** composed of two layers of cells: ectoderm above and endoderm below. Once the embryonic disk elongates to form the primitive streak, the third germ layer, mesoderm, forms by invagination of cells along the streak. The trophoblast is reinforced by mesoderm and becomes the chorion (Fig. 51.13*b*).

It is possible to relate the development of future organs to these germ layers (see page 921).

The Third Week

Two important organ systems make their appearance during the third week. The nervous system is the first organ system to be visually evident. At first, a thickening appears along the entire dorsal length of the embryo, and then

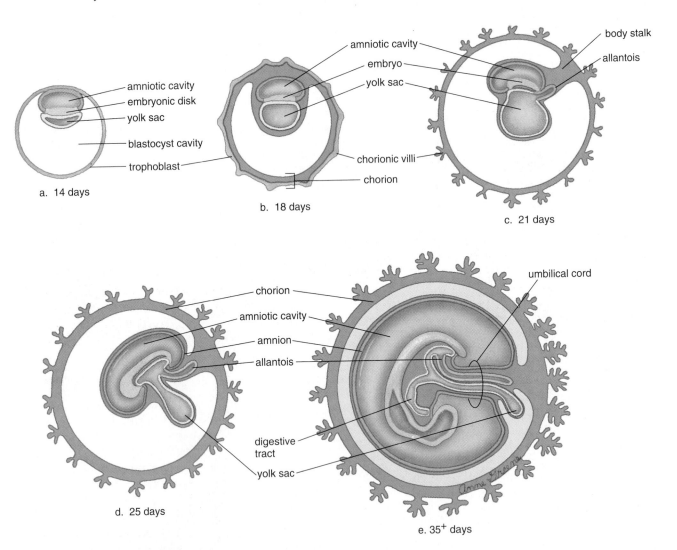

a. 14 days

b. 18 days

c. 21 days

d. 25 days

e. 35⁺ days

Figure 51.13 Human embryonic development.
a. At first there are no organs present in the embryo, only tissues. The amniotic cavity is above the embryo, and the yolk sac is below. **b.** The chorion is developing villi, so important to exchange between mother and child. **c.** The allantois and yolk sac are two more extraembryonic membranes. **d.** These extraembryonic membranes are positioned inside the body stalk as it becomes the umbilical cord. **e.** At 35+ days, the embryo has a head region and a tail region. The umbilical cord takes blood vessels between the embryo and the chorion (placenta).

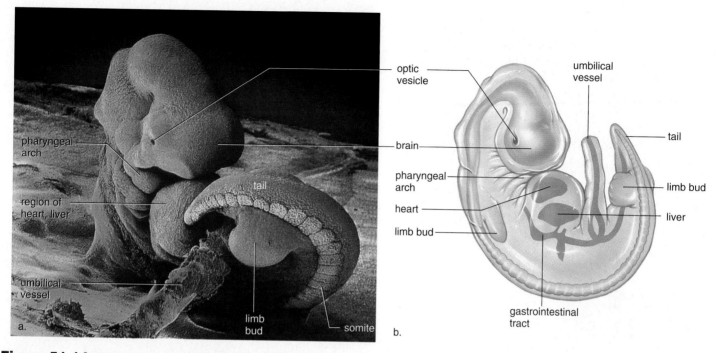

Figure 51.14 Human embryo at beginning of fifth week.
a. Scanning electron micrograph. b. The embryo is curled so that the head touches the heart, the two organs whose development is further along than the rest of the body. The organs of the gastrointestinal tract are forming, and the arms and the legs develop from the bulges that are called limb buds. The tail is an evolutionary remnant; its bones regress and become those of the coccyx (tailbone). The pharyngeal arches become functioning gills only in fishes and amphibian larvae; in humans, the first pair of pharyngeal pouches becomes the auditory tubes. The second pair becomes the tonsils, while the third and fourth become the thymus gland and the parathyroid glands.

invagination occurs as neural folds appear. When the neural folds meet at the midline, the neural tube, which later develops into the brain and the nerve cord, is formed (see Fig. 51.4). After the notochord is replaced by the vertebral column, the nerve cord is called the spinal cord.

Development of the heart begins in the third week and continues into the fourth week. At first, there are right and left heart tubes; when these fuse, the heart begins pumping blood, even though the chambers of the heart are not fully formed. The veins enter posteriorly and the arteries exit anteriorly from this largely tubular heart, but later the heart twists so that all major blood vessels are located anteriorly.

The Fourth and Fifth Weeks

At four weeks, the embryo is barely larger than the height of this print. A bridge of mesoderm called the body stalk connects the caudal (tail) end of the embryo with the chorion, which has treelike projections called **chorionic villi** [Gk. *chorion*, membrane, and L. *villus*, shaggy hair] (Fig. 51.13*c* and *d*). The fourth extraembryonic membrane, the allantois, is contained within this stalk, and its blood vessels become the umbilical blood vessels. The head and the tail then lift up, and the body stalk moves anteriorly by constriction. Once this process is complete, the **umbilical cord** [L. *umbilicus*,

navel], which connects the developing embryo to the placenta, is fully formed (Fig. 51.13*e*).

Little flippers called limb buds appear (Fig. 51.14); later, the arms and the legs develop from the limb buds, and even the hands and the feet become apparent. At the same time—during the fifth week—the head enlarges and the sense organs become more prominent. It is possible to make out the developing eyes, ears, and even nose.

The Sixth Through Eighth Weeks

There is a remarkable change in external appearance during the sixth through eighth weeks of development—a form that is difficult to recognize as a human becomes easily recognized as human. Concurrent with brain development, the head achieves its normal relationship with the body as a neck region develops. The nervous system is developed well enough to permit reflex actions, such as a startle response to touch. At the end of this period, the embryo is about 38 mm (1.5 inches) long and weighs no more than an aspirin tablet, even though all organ systems are established.

During the embryonic period of development, the extraembryonic membranes appear and serve important functions; the embryo acquires organ systems.

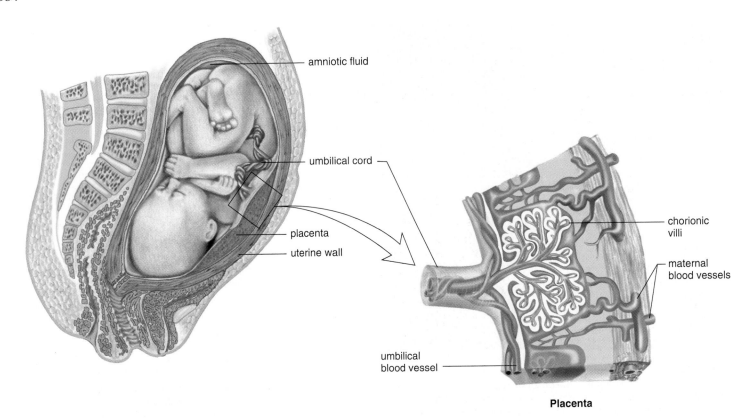

Figure 51.15 Anatomy of the placenta in a fetus at six to seven months.
The placenta is composed of both fetal and maternal tissues. Chorionic villi penetrate the uterine lining and are surrounded by maternal blood. Exchange of molecules between fetal and maternal blood takes place across the walls of the chorionic villi.

The Structure and Function of the Placenta

The **placenta** is a mammalian structure that functions in gas, nutrient, and waste exchange between embryonic (later fetal) and maternal circulatory systems. The placenta begins formation once the embryo is fully implanted. At first the entire chorion has chorionic villi that project into endometrium. Later, these disappear in all areas except where the placenta develops. By the tenth week, the placenta (Fig. 51.15) is fully formed and is producing progesterone and estrogen. These hormones have two effects: due to their negative feedback control of the hypothalamus and the anterior pituitary, they prevent any new follicles from maturing, and they maintain the lining of the uterus—now the corpus luteum is not needed. There is no menstruation during pregnancy.

The placenta has a fetal side contributed by the chorion and a maternal side consisting of uterine tissues. Notice in Figure 51.15 how the chorionic villi are surrounded by maternal blood; yet maternal and fetal blood never mix, since exchange always takes place across plasma membranes. Carbon dioxide and other wastes move from the fetal side to the maternal side, and nutrients and oxygen move from the maternal side to the fetal side of the placenta. The umbilical cord stretches between the placenta and the fetus. Although it may seem that the umbilical cord travels from the placenta to the intestine, actually the umbilical cord is simply taking fetal blood to and from the placenta. The umbilical cord is the lifeline of the fetus because it contains the umbilical arteries and vein, which transport waste molecules (carbon dioxide and urea) to the placenta for disposal and take oxygen and nutrient molecules from the placenta to the rest of the fetal circulatory system.

Harmful chemicals can also cross the placenta. This is of particular concern during the embryonic period, when various structures are first forming. Each organ or part seems to have a sensitive period during which a substance can alter its normal development. For example, if a woman takes the drug thalidomide, a tranquilizer, between days 27 and 40 of her pregnancy, the infant is likely to be born with deformed limbs. After day 40, however, the infant is born with normal limbs.

During mammalian development, the embryo and later the fetus are dependent on the placenta for gas exchange and also for acquiring nutrients and for ridding the body of wastes.

Fetal Development and Birth

Fetal development (months 3–9) is marked by an extreme increase in size. Weight multiplies 600 times, going from less than 28 grams to 3 kilograms. During this time, too, the fetus grows to about 50 cm in length. The genitalia appear in the third month, so it is possible to tell if the fetus is male or female.

Soon, hair, eyebrows, and eyelashes add finishing touches to the face and head. In the same way, fingernails and toenails complete the hands and feet. A fine, downy hair (lanugo) covers the limbs and trunk, only to later disappear. The fetus looks very old because the skin is growing so fast that it wrinkles. A waxy, almost cheeselike substance (vernix caseosa) [L. *vernix*, varnish, and *caseus*, cheese] protects the wrinkly skin from the watery amniotic fluid.

The fetus at first only flexes its limbs and nods its head, but later it can move its limbs vigorously to avoid discomfort. The mother feels these movements from about the fourth month on. The other systems of the body also begin to function. After 16 weeks, the fetal heartbeat is heard through a stethoscope. A fetus born at 24 weeks has a chance of surviving, although the lungs are still immature and often cannot capture oxygen adequately. Weight gain during the last couple of months increases the likelihood of survival.

The Stages of Birth

The latest findings suggest that when the fetal brain is sufficiently mature, the hypothalamus causes the pituitary to stimulate the adrenal cortex so that androgens are released into the bloodstream. The placenta utilizes androgens as a precursor for estrogens, hormones that stimulate the production of prostaglandin (a molecule produced by many cells that acts as a local hormone) and oxytocin. All three of these molecules cause the uterus to contract and expel the fetus.

The process of birth (parturition) includes three stages. During the first stage, the cervix dilates to allow passage of the baby's head and body. The amnion usually bursts along about this time. During the second stage, the baby is born and the umbilical cord is cut. During the third stage, the placenta is delivered (Fig. 51.16).

During the fetal period there is a refinement of organ systems and the fetus gains weight. Finally birth occurs.

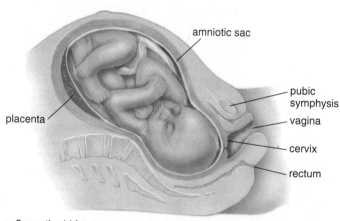

a. 9-month-old fetus

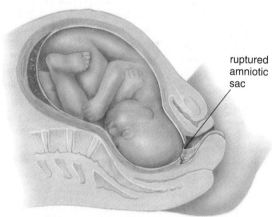

b. First stage of birth: cervix dilates

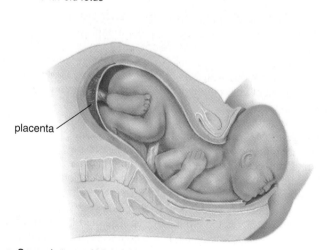

c. Second stage of birth: baby emerges

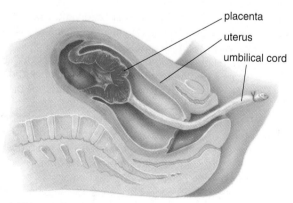

d. Third stage of birth: expelling afterbirth

Figure 51.16 Three stages of parturition.
a. Position of fetus just before birth begins. **b.** Dilation of cervix. **c.** Birth of baby. **d.** Expulsion of afterbirth.

Connecting Concepts

We have come full circle. We began our study of biology by considering the structure of the cell and its genetic machinery, including how the expression of genes is regulated. In this chapter, we have observed that animals go through the same early embryonic stages of morula, blastula, gastrula, and so forth. The set sequence of these stages is due to the expression of genes that bring about cellular changes. Therefore, once again, we are called upon to study organisms at the cellular level of organization.

We have seen that hormones are signals that affect cellular metabolism. Steroid hormones in animals, like gibberellins in plants, turn on the expression of genes. When a steroid hormone binds to a specific hormone receptor, a gene is transcribed, and then translation produces the corresponding protein. This same type of signal transduction pathway occurs during development. Transduction means that the signal has been transformed into an event that has an effect on the organism.

A set sequence of signaling molecules are produced as development occurs. Each new signal in the sequence turns on a specific gene, or more likely, a sequence of genes. Gene expression cascades are common during development. Homeotic genes are arranged in sets on the chromosomes, and a protein product from one set of genes acts as a transcription factor to turn on another set, and so forth. During the development of flies, it is possible to observe that first one region of a chromosome and then another puffs out, indicating that genes are transcribed in sequence as development occurs.

Developmental biology is now making a significant contribution to the field of evolution. Homeotic genes with the same homeoboxes (sequence of about 180 base pairs) have been discovered in many different types of organisms. This suggests that homeotic genes arose early in the history of life, and mutations in these genes could possibly account for macroevolution—the appearance of new species or even higher taxons.

Summary

51.1 Early Developmental Stages

Development occurs after fertilization. The acrosome of a sperm releases enzymes that digest away the jelly coat around the egg; the acrosome extrudes a filament that attaches to a receptor on the vitelline membrane. The sperm nucleus enters the egg and fuses with the egg nucleus. The resulting zygote begins to divide.

The early developmental stages in animals include the following events. During cleavage, division occurs, but there is no overall growth. The result is a morula, which becomes the blastula when an internal cavity (the blastocoel) appears. During the gastrula stage, invagination of cells into the blastocoel results in formation of the germ layers: ectoderm, mesoderm, and endoderm. Later development of organs can be related to these layers.

The development of three types of animals (lancelet, frog, and chick) is compared. The first three stages (cleavage, blastulation, and gastrulation) differ according to the amount of yolk in the egg.

During neurulation, the nervous system develops from midline ectoderm, just above the notochord. At this point, it is possible to draw a typical cross section of a chordate embryo (see Fig. 51.5).

51.2 Developmental Processes

Two important mechanisms—cytoplasmic segregation and induction—bring about cellular differentiation and morphogenesis as development occurs. The egg contains chemical signals called maternal determinants which are parceled out during cell division. After the first cleavage of a frog embryo, only a daughter cell that receives a portion of the gray crescent is able to develop into a complete embryo. This illustrates the importance of cytoplasmic segregation to early development of a frog.

Induction is the ability of one embryonic tissue to influence the development of another tissue. The notochord induces the formation of the neural tube in frog embryos. The reciprocal induction that occurs between the lens and the optic vesicle is another good example of induction. Induction occurs because the inducing cells give off chemical signals that influence their neighbors.

C. elegans and *Drosophila* are two model organisms that have contributed to our knowledge of developmental genetics. Fate maps and the development of vulva in *C. elegans* have shown that induction is an ongoing process in which one tissue after the other regulates the development of another through chemical signals coded for by particular genes. Apoptosis is necessary to development and the process has been studied on the cellular level in *C. elegans*.

Work with *Drosophila* has allowed researchers to identify genes that determine the axes of the body and segmentation genes that regulate the development of segments. An important concept has emerged: during development sequential sets of master genes code for morphogen gradients that activate the next set of master genes in turn. Morphogens are transcription factors that bind to DNA.

Homeotic genes control pattern formation such as the presence of antennae, wings, and limbs on the segments of *Drosophila*. Homeotic genes code for proteins that contain a homeodomain, a particular sequence of 60 amino acids. These proteins are also transcription factors and the homeodomain is the portion of the protein that binds to DNA. Homologous homeotic genes have been found in a wide variety of organisms and therefore they must have arisen early in the history of life and they have been conserved.

51.3 Human Embryonic and Fetal Development

Human development can be divided into embryonic development (months 1 and 2) and fetal development (months 3–9). The early stages in human development resemble those of the chick. The similarities are probably due to their evolutionary relationship, not the amount of yolk the eggs contain, because the human egg has little yolk.

The extraembryonic membranes appear early in human development. The trophoblast of the blastocyst is the first sign of the chorion, which goes on to become the fetal part of the placenta. Exchange occurs between fetal and maternal blood at the placenta. The amnion contains amniotic fluid, which cushions and protects the embryo. The yolk sac and allantois are also present.

Fertilization occurs in the oviduct, and cleavage occurs as the embryo moves toward the uterus. The morula becomes the blastocyst before implanting in the endometrium of the uterus. Organ development begins with neural tube and heart formation. There follows a steady progression of organ formation during embryonic development. During fetal development, refinement of features occurs, and the fetus adds weight. Birth occurs about 280 days after the start of the mother's last menstruation.

Reviewing the Chapter

1. Describe how fertilization of a sea star egg occurs. 920
2. State the germ layer theory, and tell which organs are derived from each of the germ layers. 921
3. Compare the process of cleavage and the formation of the blastula and gastrula in lancelets, frogs, and chicks. 922–23
4. Draw a cross section of a typical chordate embryo at the neurula stage, and label your drawing. 923
5. Describe two mechanisms that are known to be involved in the processes of cellular differentiation and morphogenesis. 924–25
6. Describe an experiment performed by Spemann suggesting that the notochord induces formation of the neural tube. Give another well-known example of induction between tissues. 925
7. With regard to *C. elegans,* what is a fate map? how does induction occur? and what causes apoptosis? 926
8. With regard to *Drosophila,* what is a morphogen gradient and what does such a gradient do? 928
9. What is the function of homeotic genes, and what is the significance of the homeobox within these genes? 929
10. List the human extraembryonic membranes, give a function for each, and compare their functions to those in the chick. 930
11. Tell where fertilization, cleavage, the morula stage, and the blastocyst stage occur in humans. What happens to the embryo in the uterus? 931
12. Describe the structure and the function of the placenta in humans. 932
13. List and describe the stages of birth. 935

Testing Yourself

Choose the best answer for each question.

1. Which of these stages is the first one out of sequence?
   a. cleavage
   b. blastula
   c. morula
   d. gastrula
   e. neurula
2. Which of these stages is mismatched?
   a. cleavage—cell division
   b. blastula—gut formation
   c. gastrula—three germ layers
   d. neurula—nervous system
   e. Both b and c are mismatched.
3. Which of the germ layers is best associated with development of the heart?
   a. ectoderm
   b. mesoderm
   c. endoderm
   d. neurula
   e. All of these are correct.
4. In many embryos, differentiation begins at what stage?
   a. cleavage
   b. blastula
   c. gastrula
   d. neurula
   e. after the completion of these stages
5. Morphogenesis is associated with
   a. protein gradients.
   b. induction.
   c. transcription factors.
   d. homeotic genes.
   e. All of these are correct.
6. In humans, the placenta develops from the chorion. This indicates that human development
   a. resembles that of the chick.
   b. is associated with extraembryonic membranes.
   c. cannot be compared to lower animals.
   d. begins only upon implantation.
   e. Both a and b are correct.
7. In humans, the fetus
   a. is surrounded by four extraembryonic membranes.
   b. has developed organs and is recognizably human.
   c. is dependent upon the placenta for excretion of wastes and acquisition of nutrients.
   d. is embedded in the endometrium of the uterus.
   e. Both b and c are correct.
8. Developmental changes
   a. require growth, differentiation, and morphogenesis.
   b. stop occurring when one is grown.
   c. are dependent upon a parceling out of genes into daughter cells.
   d. are dependent upon activation of master genes in an orderly sequence.
   e. Both a and d are correct.
9. Which of these is mismatched?
   a. brain—ectoderm
   b. gut—endoderm
   c. bone—mesoderm
   d. lens—endoderm
   e. heart—mesoderm
10. Label this diagram illustrating the placement of the extraembryonic membranes, and give a function for each membrane in humans:

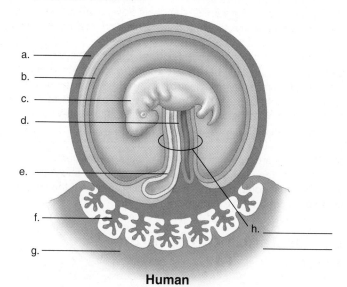

Human

Thinking Scientifically

1. A mutant gene is known to disrupt the earliest stages of development in sea urchins. Individuals with two copies of the mutant gene seem to develop normally. When normal males are crossed with mutant (normal-appearing) females, however, none of the offspring develop at all. How could this pattern of expression be explained?
2. Babies that were malnourished in utero are at a higher risk for many adult-onset diseases than those that were well-nourished. To determine how well babies were nourished in utero, physicians often determine the ratio of head circumference to abdominal circumference. If malnourished, the head circumference to abdominal circumference will be larger than usual because blood in the malnourished fetuses is preferentially directed toward the brain. Why is it better to use the circumference data rather than birth weight data to detect malnourished babies?

Bioethical Issue

The fetus is subject to harm by maternal use of medicines and drugs of abuse, including nicotine and alcohol. Also, various sexually transmitted diseases, notably an HIV infection, can be passed on to the fetus by way of the placenta. Women need to be aware of the need to protect their unborn child from harm. Indeed, their behavior should be protective if they are sexually active, even if they are using a recognized form of birth control. Harm can occur before a woman realizes she is pregnant!

Because we are now aware of the need for maternal responsibility before a child is born, there has been a growing acceptance of prosecuting women when a newborn has a condition such as fetal alcohol syndrome, a condition that can only be caused by the drinking habits of the mother. Employers have also become aware that they might be subject to prosecution. To protect themselves, Johnson Controls, a U.S. battery manufacturer, developed a fetal protection policy. No woman who could bear a child was offered a job that might expose her to toxins that could negatively affect the development of her baby. To get such a job, a woman had to show that she had been sterilized or was otherwise incapable of having children. In 1991, the U.S. Supreme Court declared this policy unconstitutional on the basis of sexual discrimination. The decision was hailed as a victory for women, but was it? The decision was written in such a way that women alone, and not an employer, are responsible for any harm done to the fetus by workplace toxins.

Some have noted that prosecuting women for causing prenatal harm can itself have a detrimental effect. The women may tend to avoid prenatal treatment, thereby increasing the risk to their children. Or they may opt for an abortion in order to avoid the possibility of prosecution. The women feel they are in a no-win situation. If they have a child that has been harmed due to their behavior, they feel they are bad mothers or if they abort, they feel they are also bad mothers. Should sexually active women who can bear a child be expected to avoid substances or situations that could possibly harm an unborn even if they are using birth control? Why or why not?

Understanding the Terms

allantois   930
amnion   930
apoptosis   926
blastocoel   921
blastocyst   931
blastula   921
cellular differentiation   924
chorion   930
chorionic villus   933
cleavage   920
ectoderm   921
embryo   920
embryonic disk   932
embryonic period   930
endoderm   921
extraembryonic
    membrane   930
fate map   926
fertilization   920
gastrula   921
gastrulation   921
germ layer   921

gray crescent   925
homeobox   929
homeotic genes   928
human chorionic gonadotropin
    (HCG)   932
implantation   930
induction   925
mesoderm   921
morphogen   928
morphogenesis   924
morula   921
neural plate   923
neural tube   923
notochord   923
pattern formation   924
placenta   934
totipotent   924
trophoblast   931
umbilical cord   933
yolk   920
yolk sac   930

Match the terms to these definitions:

a. _____ Ability of a chemical or a tissue to influence the development of another tissue.
b. _____ Primary tissue layer of a vertebrate embryo; namely ectoderm, mesoderm, or endoderm.
c. _____ Extraembryonic membrane of birds, reptiles, and mammals that forms an enclosing, fluid-filled sac.
d. _____ A 180-nucleotide sequence located in nearly all homeotic genes.
e. _____ Stage of early animal development during which the germ layers form, at least in part, by invagination.

Web Connections

 Exploring the Internet

http://www.mhhe.com/biosci/genbio/mader
(click on *Biology 7/e*)

The *Biology 7/e* Online Learning Center provides many resources for studying the material in this chapter including links to the following sites:

The Virtual Embryo. A guide to animal development.

http://www.ucalgary.ca/UofC/eduweb/virtualembryo/

The Visible Embryo. This site provides the user with a detailed look at the first few stages of embryonic development.

http://visembryo.ucsf.edu/

Embryo Development Overview. This site lets you view human development from conception to week 38.

http://www.med.upenn.edu/embryo_project/overview/overview.html

Society for Developmental Biology. This site includes many valuable websites of the members of the society.

http://sdb.bio.purdue.edu/index.html

Bill Wasserman's Developmental Biology Page. Many links are found in "web resources."

http://www.luc.edu/depts/biology/dev.htm

Further Readings for Part vii

Arakawa, T., and Langridge, W. R. H. May 1998. Plants are not just passive creatures! *Nature Medicine* 4(5):550. Plants are being used to produce foreign proteins for human immunity.

Barinaga, M. July 23, 1999. Mapping smells in the brain. *Science* 285(5427):508. An optical imaging technique detects neuron patterns that occur in response to particular odors—each smell activates a unique pattern, or code, for that smell.

Barkley, R. A. September 1998. Attention-deficit hyperactivity disorder. *Scientific American* 279(3):66. ADHD may result from neurological abnormalities with a genetic basis.

Beardsley, T. August 1997. The machinery of thought. *Scientific American* 277(2):78. Researchers have identified the area of the brain responsible for memory.

Belmonte, J. C. I. June 1999. How the body tells left from right. *Scientific American* 280(6):46. The precise orientation of our internal organs is controlled in part by proteins that are produced on one side of an embryo.

Blumenthal, M., et al. March 1999. Discoveries in allergy and asthma. *Discover* 20(3):S-1. This supplement examines advances in understanding and treating allergy and asthma.

Crooks, R., and Baur, K. 1998. *Our sexuality.* 7th ed. Redwood City, Calif.: Benjamin/Cummings Publishing. Introduction to the biological, psychosocial, behavioral, and cultural aspects of sexuality.

Crowley, L. 1997. *Introduction to human disease.* Boston, Mass.: Jones & Bartlett Publishers. This well-illustrated text for study in the allied health fields describes diseases, and their symptoms, diagnoses, and treatments.

Debinski, W. May/June 1998. Anti-brain tumor cytotoxins. *Science & Medicine* 5(3):36. Delivery of bacterial toxins to tumor cells is a new therapy for brain tumor treatment.

Deyo, R. A. August 1998. Low-back pain. *Scientific American* 279(2):48. Treatment options for low-back pain which don't involve bed rest or surgery are improving.

Dickman, S. July 1997. Mysteries of the heart. *Discover* 18(7):117. Article discusses why coronary arteries may still become blocked after treatment for atherosclerosis.

Gazzaniga, M. S. July 1998. The split brain revisited. *Scientific American* 279(1):50. Recent research on split brains has led to new insights into brain organization and consciousness.

Glausiusz, J. October 1997. The good bugs on our tongues. *Discover* 18(10):32. Without friendly bacteria that live on our tongues, we would be vulnerable to harmful bacteria such as *Salmonella.*

Glausiusz, J. September 1998. Infected hearts. *Discover* 19(9):30. Infectious bacteria may play a role in heart disease; antibiotics could prevent the need for heart surgery.

Halstead, L. S. April 1998. Post-polio syndrome. *Scientific American* 278(4):42. Recovered polio victims are experiencing fatigue, pain, and weakness, resulting from degeneration of motor neurons.

Hanson, L. A. November/December 1997. Breast-feeding stimulates the infant immune system. *Science & Medicine* 4(6):12. Long-lasting protection against some infectious diseases has been reported in breast-fed infants.

Harvard Health Letter. April 1998. A special report: Parkinson's disease. This overview presents the symptoms and diagnosis, and treatment of Parkinson's disease.

Jordan, V. C. October 1998. Designer estrogens. *Scientific American* 279(4):60. Selective estrogen receptor modulators may protect against breast and endometrial cancers, osteoporosis, and heart disease.

Julien, R. M. 1997. *A primer of drug action.* 8th ed. New York: W. H. Freeman and Company. A concise, nontechnical guide to the actions, uses, and side effects of psychoactive drugs.

Kempermann, G., and Gage, F. May 1999. New nerve cells for the adult brain. *Scientific American* 280(5):48. The knowledge that the human brain can produce new nerve cells in adulthood could lead to better treatments for neurological diseases.

Kooyman, G. L., and Ponganis, P. J. November/December 1997. The challenges of diving to depth. *American Scientist* 85(6):530. Marine animals do not experience problems associated with pressure at depth.

Kunzig, R. February 1999. What's a pinna for? *Discover* 20(2):24. Article examines the function of the folds of the outer ear.

MacDonald, P. C., and Casey, M. L. March/April 1996. Preterm birth. *Scientific American Science & Medicine* 3(2):42. Article discusses the role of oxytocin, prostaglandins, and infections in the initiation of human labor.

Mader, S. S. 1990. *Human reproductive biology.* 2d ed. Dubuque, Iowa: Wm. C. Brown Publishers. An introductory text covering human reproduction in a clear, easily understood manner.

Mader, S. S. 1998. *Human biology.* 6th ed. Dubuque, Iowa: WCB/McGraw-Hill, Inc. A student-friendly text that covers the principles of biology with emphasis on human anatomy and physiology.

Mader, S. S. 2000. *Understanding anatomy and physiology.* 4th ed. Dubuque, Iowa: Wm. C. Brown Publishers. A text that emphasizes the basics for beginning allied health students.

Mattson, M. P. March/April 1998. Experimental models of Alzheimer's disease. *Science & Medicine* 5(2):16. In Alzheimer's disease, mutations accelerate changes that occur during normal aging.

McDonald, J. W., et al. September 1999. Repairing the damaged spinal cord. *Scientific American* 281(3):64. New treatments being studied may minimize or reverse damage to the spinal cord, and give hope for some spinal cord restoration.

Moore, K., and Persaud, T. 1998. *Before we are born: Essentials of embryology and birth defects.* 5th ed. Philadelphia: W. B. Saunders and Co. For medical and associated health students, this text presents the essentials of normal and abnormal human embryological development.

Nature Medicine Vaccine Supplement. May 1998. Vol. 4, no. 5. The entire issue is devoted to the topic of vaccines, including history, recent developments and research in malaria, cancer, and HIV vaccines.

Newman, J. April 2000. How old is too old to have a baby? *Discover* 21(4):60. Article discusses advancements in reproductive technology that may make it possible for couples in their late forties to sixties to have children.

Nolte, J. 1998. *The human brain.* 4th ed. St. Louis: Mosby-Year Book, Inc. Beginners are guided through the basic aspects of brain structure and function.

Nucci, M. L., and Abuchowski, A. February 1998. The search for blood substitutes. *Scientific American* 278(2):72. Artificial blood substitutes based on hemoglobin are being developed from synthetic chemicals.

Osorio, D. July/August 1997. The evolution of arthropod nervous systems. *American Scientist* 85(3):244. Nervous systems of insects and crustaceans have common features.

Packer, C. July/August 1998. Why menopause? *Natural History* 107(6):24. Article addresses reasons why menopause occurs so early in life, compared to other aging processes.

Powledge, T. M. July 1999. Addiction and the brain. *BioScience* 49(7):513. Drug use changes the biochemistry and anatomy of neurons and alter the way they work.

Appendix A

ANSWER KEY

Chapter 1

Testing Yourself

1. d; **2.** c; **3.** b; **4.** e; **5.** c; **6.** b; **7.** c; **8.** b; **9.** c; **10.** d; **11. a.** After dye is spilled on culture plate, investigator notices that bacteria live despite exposure to sunlight; **b.** Dye protects bacteria against death by UV light; **c.** Expose all culture plates to UV light: one set of plates contains bacteria and dye, and the other set contains only bacteria. The bacteria in both sets die; **d.** Dye does not protect bacteria against death by UV light.

Understanding the Terms

a. metabolism; **b.** evolution; **c.** experimental variable; **d.** photosynthesis; **e.** control group

Chapter 2

Testing Yourself

1. c; **2.** e; **3.** e; **4.** d; **5.** e; **6.** d; **7.** b; **8.** c; **9.** a; **10.** 7p and 7n in nucleus; two electrons in first shell, and five electrons in outer shell. This means that nitrogen needs three more electrons in the outer shell to be stable; because each hydrogen contributes one electron, the formula for ammonia is NH_3.

Understanding the Terms

a. polar covalent bond; **b.** ion; **c.** acid; **d.** molecule; **e.** pH scale

Chapter 3

Testing Yourself

1. c; **2.** a; **3.** e; **4.** b; **5.** c; **6.** b; **7.** c; **8.** c; **9.** e; **10.** c; **11.** e; **12.** c; **13. a.** monomer; **b.** condensation; **c.** polymer; **d.** hydrolysis. The diagram shows the manner in which polymers are synthesized and degraded in cells.

Understanding the Terms

a. carbohydrate; **b.** lipid; **c.** polymer; **d.** isomer; **e.** peptide

Chapter 4

Testing Yourself

1. c; **2.** c; **3.** d; **4.** c; **5.** a; **6.** c; **7.** c; **8.** a; **9.** d; **10.** b; **11.** e; **12. a.** example; **b.** Mitochondria and chloroplasts are a pair because they are both membranous structures involved in energy metabolism; **c.** Centrioles and flagella are a pair because they both contain microtubules; centrioles give rise to the basal bodies of flagella; **d.** ER and ribosomes are a pair because together they are rough ER, which produces proteins. **13. a.** chromatin—DNA specifies the order of amino acids in proteins; **b.** nucleolus—forms ribosomal RNA, which participates in protein synthesis; **c.** smooth ER—forms transport vesicles; **d.** rough ER—produces proteins; **e.** Golgi apparatus—processes and packages proteins for distribution.

Understanding the Terms

a. Golgi apparatus; **b.** chromatin; **c.** nucleolus; **d.** cytoskeleton; **e.** lysosome

Chapter 5

Testing Yourself

1. a. hypertonic—cell shrinks due to loss of water; **b.** hypotonic—central vacuole expands due to gain of water; **2.** b; **3.** b; **4.** b; **5.** c; **6.** c; **7.** e; **8.** e; **9.** b; **10.** b

Understanding the Terms

a. differentially permeable; **b.** osmosis; **c.** hypertonic solution; **d.** osmotic pressure; **e.** cholesterol

Chapter 6

Testing Yourself

1. e; **2.** e; **3.** d; **4.** d; **5.** b; **6.** e; **7.** e; **8.** c; **9. a.** active site; **b.** substrates; **c.** product; **d.** enzyme; **e.** enzyme-substrate complex; **f.** enzyme. The shape of an enzyme is important to its activity because it allows an enzyme-substrate complex to form. **10. a.** high H^+ concentration; **b.** low H^+ concentration; **c.** H^+ pump in electron transport system; **d.** H^+; **e.** ATP synthase complex; **f.** ADP; **g.** P; **h.** ATP; **i.** energy from electron transfers. See also Figure 6.10, page 107.

Understanding the Terms

a. metabolism; **b.** potential energy; **c.** vitamin; **d.** entropy; **e.** coenzyme

Chapter 7

Testing Yourself

1. e; **2.** d; **3.** a; **4.** e; **5.** c; **6.** e; **7.** c; **8.** e; **9. a.** outer membrane; **b.** inner membrane; **c.** stroma; **d.** granum; **e.** thylakoid; **f.** thylakoid; **g.** stroma; **10. a.** water; **b.** oxygen; **c.** carbon dioxide; **d.** carbohydrate; **e.** ADP + $\textcircled{P}$ → ATP; **f.** $NADP^+$ → NADPH

Understanding the Terms

a. light-dependent reaction; **b.** photosystem; **c.** electron transport system; **d.** photosynthesis; **e.** Calvin cycle

Chapter 8

Testing Yourself

1. b; **2.** c; **3.** a; **4.** c; **5.** c; **6.** c; **7.** a; **8.** b; **9.** e; **10.** c; **11.** a; **12.** c; **13.** b; **14. a.** cristae, contains electron transport system and ATP synthase complex; **b.** matrix, location of transition reaction and Krebs cycle; **c.** outer membrane, defines the boundary of the mitochondrion; **d.** intermembrane space, accumulation of H^+; **e.** inner membrane, partitions the mitochondrion into the intermembrane space and the matrix.

Understanding the Terms

a. fermentation; **b.** Krebs cycle; **c.** metabolic pool; **d.** acetyl-CoA; **e.** electron transport system

Chapter 9

Testing Yourself

1. c; **2.** b; **3.** e; **4.** d; **5.** a; **6.** c; **7.** b; **8.** d; **9.** b; **10.** b; **11.** a; **12. a.** chromatid of chromosome; **b.** centriole; **c.** spindle fiber or aster; **d.** nuclear envelope (fragment)

Understanding the Terms

a. centrosome; **b.** centromere; **c.** spindle; **d.** sister chromatid; **e.** apoptosis

Chapter 10

Testing Yourself

1. b; **2.** d; **3.** e; **4.** b; **5.** a; **6.** d; **7.** d; **8.** e; **9.** c; **10.** The cell on the right represents metaphase I because bivalents are present at the metaphase plate.

Understanding the Terms

a. spermatogenesis; **b.** bivalent; **c.** polar body; **d.** secondary oocyte; **e.** homologue

Chapter 11

Practice Problems 1

1. a. all *W*; **b.** 1/2 *W*, 1/2 *w*; **c.** 1/2 *T*, 1/2 *t*; **d.** all *T*; **2. a.** gamete; **b.** genotype; **c.** gamete

Practice Problems 2

1. *bb*; **2.** 75% yellow; 25% green; **3.** 75%; **4.** *Tt* × *tt*, *tt*

Practice Problems 3

1. Testcross black-coated horse × brown-coated horse; **2.** *Ll* × *ll*; **3.** 200 have wrinkled seeds

Practice Problems 4

1. a. 1/2 *TG*, 1/2 *tG*; **b.** 1/4 *TG*, 1/4 *Tg*, 1/4 *tG*, 1/4 *tg*; **c.** 1/2 *TG*, 1/2 *Tg*; **2. a.** gamete; **b.** genotype; **c.** gamete

Practice Problems 5

1. *BbTt* only; **2. a.** *LlGg* × *llgg*; **b.** *LlGg* × *LlGg*; **3.** 9/16

Testing Yourself

1. b; **2.** a; **3.** c; **4.** d; **5.** c; **6.** d; **7.** a; **8.** b; **9.** b; **10.** b; **11.** c; **12.** d

Additional Genetics Problems

1. 100% chance for widow's peak and 0% chance for continuous hairline; **2.** *ee* (recessive); **3.** 50%; **4.** 210 gray bodies and 70 black bodies; 140 = heterozygous; cross fly with recessive (black body); **5.** *BBHH* = 2^0 = 1 possibility: *BH*; *BbHh* = 2^2 = 4

possibilities: *BH, Bh, bH, bh*; *BBHh* = 2^1 = 2 possibilities: *BH* and *Bh*; **6.** F$_1$ = all black with short hair; F$_2$ = 9 black, short: 3 black, long: 3 brown, short: 1 brown, long; offspring would be 1 brown long: 1 brown short : 1 black long : 1 black short; **7.** *Bbtt* × *bbTt* and *bbtt*; **8.** *GGLl*; **9.** 25%

Understanding the Terms

a. recessive allele; **b.** allele; **c.** dominant allele; **d.** testcross; **e.** genotype

Chapter 12

Practice Problems 1

1. *MM′*, *Mm* (both melanic), *M′m* (insularia), *mm* (typical); **2.** 1 pink: 1 white; or 50% pink, 50% white; **3.** 7; **4.** pleiotropy accounts for albinism and epistasis accounts for albinism and crossed eyes occurring together.

Practice Problems 2

1. a. $X^B X^B$, $X^B X^b$ (bar-eyed females), $X^b X^b$ (normal-eyed female); **b.** 2 possible genotypes for males are: $X^B Y$ (bar-eyed male has the gametes X^B, Y) and $X^b Y$ (normal-eyed male has the gametes X^b, Y); **2. a. (2)** b, ratio 1:1; **3. a.** 100%; **b.** none; **c.** 100%

Practice Problems 3

1. a. 9:3:3:1; **b.** linkage; **2.** 12 map units; **3.** bar eye, scalloped wings, garnet eye

Testing Yourself

1. b; **2.** c; **3.** e; **4.** a; **5.** b; **6.** b; **7.** d; **8.** b; **9.** c; **10.** d

Additional Genetics Problems

1. pleiotropy; **2.** 50%; **3.** 6, yes; **4.** linkage, 10 map units; **5.** Both males and females are 1:1; **6.** $X^B X^B$ × $X^b Y$ = all males and females are bar-eyed, $X^b X^b$ × $X^B Y$ = females are bar-eyed, males are all normal; **7.** $X^b X^b Ww$

Understanding the Terms

a. autosome; **b.** polyploid; **c.** X-linked gene; **d.** polygenic inheritance; **e.** polyploid

Chapter 13

Testing Yourself

1. c; **2.** a; **3.** b; **4.** c; **5.** d; **6.** c; **7.** b; **8.** d; **9.** c; **10.** a; **11.** autosomal dominant condition

Additional Genetics Problems

1. 0%, 0%, 100%; **2.** 25%; **3.** AB, yes, A, B, AB, or O; **4.** $X^c Yww$, $X^C X^C Ww$, $X^C YWw$,

both sexes have normal vision with widow's peak; **5.** sex-linked recessive, $X^A X^a$

Understanding the Terms

a. autosome; **b.** sex-influenced trait; **c.** karyotype; **d.** nondisjunction; **e.** carrier

Chapter 14

Testing Yourself

1. b; **2.** d; **3.** a; **4.** c; **5.** c; **6.** c; **7.** a; **8.** b; **9.** e; **10.** The parental helix is heavy-heavy, and each daughter helix is heavy-light. This shows that each daughter helix is composed of one old strand and one new strand, which is consistent with semiconservative replication.

Understanding the Terms

a. genetic mutation; **b.** complementary base pairing; **c.** DNA polymerase; **d.** purine; **e.** bacteriophage

Chapter 15

Testing Yourself

1. b; **2.** a; **3.** c; **4.** a; **5.** a; **6.** c; **7.** b; **8.** c; **9.** b; **10. a.** ACU CCU GAA UGC AAA; **b.** UGA GGA CUU ACG UUU; **c.** threonine-proline-glutamate-cysteine-lysine

Understanding the Terms

a. RNA polymerase; **b.** intron; **c.** translation; **d.** polyribosome; **e.** codon

Chapter 16

Testing Yourself

1. c; **2.** e; **3.** a; **4.** a; **5.** b; **6.** b; **7.** b; **8.** e; **9.** e; **10.** e; **11. a.** DNA; **b.** regulator gene; **c.** promoter; **d.** operator; **e.** mRNA; **f.** active repressor

Understanding the Terms

a. oncogene; **b.** tumor; **c.** Barr body; **d.** euchromatin; **e.** carcinogen

Chapter 17

Testing Yourself

1. a; **2.** e; **3.** e; **4.** e; **5.** b; **6.** d; **7.** c; **8.** e; **9.** AATTTTAA; **10. a.** retrovirus; **b.** recombinant RNA; **c.** human genome; **d.** recombinant RNA; **e.** reverse transcription; **f.** recombinant DNA; **g.** defective gene. See also Figure 17.10, page 275.

Understanding the Terms

a. restriction enzyme; **b.** transgenic organism; **c.** probe; **d.** clone; **e.** plasmid

Chapter 18

Testing Yourself

1. e; **2.** b; **3.** e; **4.** e; **5.** e; **6.** e; **7.** e; **8.** e; **9.** Life has a history, and it's possible to trace the history of individual organisms. **10.** Two different continents can have similar environments, and therefore unrelated organisms that are similarly adapted. **11.** All vertebrates share a common ancestor, who had pharyngeal pouches during development. **12.** Genetic differences account for speciation, and therefore evolution.

Understanding the Terms

a. biogeography; **b.** paleontology; **c.** vestigial structure; **d.** adaptation; **e.** inheritance of acquired characteristics

Chapter 19

Practice Problems 1

1. 21%; **2.** $t = q = 0.3$, $T = p = 0.7$; homozygous recessive $= q^2 = 9\%$; homozygous dominant $= p^2 = 49\%$; heterozygous $= 2pq = 42\%$

Testing Yourself

1. c; **2.** c; **3.** c; **4.** c; **5.** e; **6.** b; **7.** d; **8.** e; **9.** c; **10.** b; **11.** b; **12. a.** See Figure 19.8, page 308; **b.** See Figure 19.7, page 308; **c.** See Figure 19.6, page 307.

Additional Genetics Problems

1. 16%; **2.** 81%; **3.** recessive allele = 0.2, dominant allele = 0.8; homozygous recessive = 0.04, homozygous dominant = 0.64, heterozygous = 0.32

Understanding the Terms

a. stabilizing selection; **b.** postzygotic isolating mechanism; **c.** genetic drift; **d.** adaptive radiation; **e.** gene flow

Chapter 20

Testing Yourself

1. c; **2.** d; **3.** b; **4.** b; **5.** b; **6.** e; **7.** c; **8.** e; **9.** e; **10.** c; **11. a.** oldest eukaryotic fossils; **b.** O_2 accumulates; **c.** oldest known fossils; **d.** Cambrian animals; **e.** Ediacaran animals; **f.** protists evolve and diversify

Understanding the Terms

a. molecular clock; **b.** protocell; **c.** liposome; **d.** ocean ridge; **e.** ozone shield

Chapter 21

Testing Yourself

1. a; **2.** b; **3.** d; **4.** d; **5.** e; **6.** d; **7.** b; **8.** c; **9.** e;

10. c; **11. a.** Chordata; **b.** Vertebrata; **c.** Class; **d.** Order; **e.** Anthropoidea; **f.** Hominoidea; **g.** Hominidae; **h.** Genus; **i.** *Homo sapiens*

Understanding the Terms

a. anthropoid; **b.** Cro-Magnon; **c.** Neanderthal; **d.** *Homo ergaster*; **e.** hominoid

Chapter 22

Testing Yourself

1. b; **2.** c; **3.** a; **4.** e; **5.** c; **6.** c; **7.** c; **8.** b; **9.** c; **10.** b

Understanding the Terms

a. sexual selection; **b.** pheromone; **c.** inclusive fitness; **d.** imprinting; **e.** operant conditioning

Chapter 23

Testing Yourself

1. d; **2.** c; **3.** e; **4.** b; **5.** b; **6.** e; **7.** c; **8.** e; **9.** c; **10.** a

Understanding the Terms

a. demographic transition; **b.** population; **c.** exponential growth; **d.** carrying capacity; **e.** biotic potential

Chapter 24

Testing Yourself

1. b; **2.** e; **3.** d; **4.** e; **5.** b; **6.** e; **7.** c; **8.** e; **9.** e; **10.** e; **11. a.** population densities; **b.** environmental gradient. A community contains species with overlapping tolerances to environmental factors (see also Fig. 24.2, page 401).

Understanding the Terms

a. community; **b.** habitat; **c.** ecological succession; **d.** ecological niche; **e.** mutualism

Chapter 25

Testing Yourself

1. c; **2.** b; **3.** e; **4.** e; **5.** c; **6.** c; **7.** b; **8.** a; **9.** d; **10.** c; **11.** b; **12.** c; **13.** a; **14.** c; **15. a.** top carnivore, tertiary consumers; **b.** carnivore, secondary consumers; **c.** herbivore, primary consumers; **d.** producer, autotrophs; **e.** The numbers are the dry biomass weights of the organisms at each level.

Understanding the Terms

a. detritus; **b.** ozone shield; **c.** fossil fuel; **d.** nitrogen fixation; **e.** food web

Chapter 26

Testing Yourself

1. b; **2.** a; **3.** c; **4.** d; **5.** d; **6.** a; **7.** c; **8.** a; **9.** a; **10.** d; **11.** d; **12. a.** 4 + for both; **b.** 3 + for both; **c.** 2 + for both; **d.** 1 + for both

Understanding the Terms

a. estuary; **b.** benthic division; **c.** taiga; **d.** savanna; **e.** spring overturn

Chapter 27

Testing Yourself

1. e; **2.** a; **3.** b; **4.** d; **5.** e; **6.** e; **7.** d; **8.** b; **9.** e; **10.** e

Understanding the Terms

a. biodiversity hotspot; **b.** metapopulation; **c.** source population; **d.** population viability analysis; **e.** landscape

Chapter 28

Testing Yourself

1. a; **2.** c; **3.** d; **4.** a; **5.** c; **6.** b; **7.** d; **8.** b; **9.** c; **10.** b; **11. a.** three by color; **b.** all taxa: vertebra; only snakes and lizards: amniote egg and internal fertilization; **c.** the taxa in a clade; they share the same derived characters.

Understanding the Terms

a. taxonomy; **b.** phylogenetic tree; **c.** taxon; **d.** cladistics; **e.** homology

Chapter 29

Testing Yourself

1. a. attachment; **b.** bacterial chromosome; **c.** penetration; **d.** integration; **e.** prophage; **f.** maturation; **g.** release; See also Figure 29.3, page 511; **2.** d; **3.** c; **4.** c; **5.** c; **6.** c; **7.** a; **8.** e; **9.** e; **10.** a

Understanding the Terms

a. lysogenic; **b.** photoautotroph; **c.** saprotroph; **d.** symbiotic; **e.** archaea

Chapter 30

Testing Yourself

1. b; **2.** b; **3.** e; **4.** b; **5.** b; **6.** d; **7.** e; **8.** d; **9.** b; **10. a.** sexual reproduction; **b.** isogametes pairing; **c.** zygote (2n); **d.** zygospore (2n); **e.** asexual reproduction; **f.** zoospores (n); **g.** nucleus; **h.** chloroplast; **i.** starch granule; **j.** pyrenoid; **k.** flagellum; **l.** eyespot; **m.** gamete formation. See also Figure 30.3, page 526.

Understanding the Terms

a. pseudopod; **b.** euglenoid; **c.** diatom;
d. trypanosome; **e.** plankton

Chapter 31

Testing Yourself

1. b; **2.** c; **3.** e; **4.** a; **5.** c; **6.** a; **7.** d; **8.** a; **9.** d;
10. d; **11. a.** meiosis; **b.** basidiospores;
c. dikaryotic mycelium; **d.** fruiting body
(basidiocarp); **e.** stalk; **f.** gill; **g.** cap;
h. dikaryotic (n + n); **i.** diploid (2n);
j. zygote. See also Figure 31.6, page 550.

Understanding the Terms

a. basidium; **b.** mycelium; **c.** conidiospore;
d. fruiting body; **e.** mycorrhizae

Chapter 32

Testing Yourself

1. e; **2.** c; **3.** e; **4.** c; **5.** d; **6.** b; **7.** b; **8.** b; **9.** e;
10. a. sporophyte (2n); **b.** meiosis;
c. gametophyte (n); **d.** fertilization. See also
Figure 32.2, page 559.

Understanding the Terms

a. sporophyte; **b.** monocotyledon; **c.** pollen
grain; **d.** rhizoid; **e.** phloem

Chapter 33

Testing Yourself

1. d; **2.** e; **3.** e; **4.** d; **5.** b; **6.** e; **7.** a;
8. a. gastrovascular cavity; **b.** tentacle;
c. mouth; **d.** mesoglea; **9. a.** Cnidaria;
b. Nematoda; **c.** Cnidaria; **d.** Nematoda;
e. Platyhelminthes; **10. a.** tapeworm;
b. planarian; **c.** sponge; **d.** *Hydra*; **e.** rotifer

Understanding the Terms

a. gastrovascular cavity; **b.** coelom;
c. pseudocoelom; **d.** bilateral symmetry;
e. tube-within-a-tube body plan

Chapter 34

Testing Yourself

1. b; **2.** c; **3.** b; **4.** c; **5.** c; **6.** a; **7.** d; **8.** c; **9.** a;
10. a. all three; **b.** annelids, arthropods;
c. all three; **d.** all three; **e.** all three; **f.** all
three; **g.** arthropods; **h.** molluscs;
11. a. earthworms; **b.** clams; **c.** clams;
d. clams; **e.** earthworms; **f.** earthworms;
g. clams; **h.** clams; **i.** earthworms;
j. earthworms; **12. a.** head; **b.** antenna;
c. simple eye; **d.** compound eye; **e.** thorax;
f. tympanum; **g.** abdomen; **h.** forewing;
i. hindwing; **j.** ovipositor; **k.** spiracles; **l.** air
sac; **m.** spiracle; **n.** tracheae. See also Figure
34.14*a*, page 611.

Understanding the Terms

a. trachea; **b.** metamorphosis;
c. segmentation; **d.** nephridia; **e.** chitin

Chapter 35

Testing Yourself

1. b; **2.** b; **3.** e; **4.** b; **5.** c; **6.** e; **7.** a; **8.** c; **9.** e;
10. b; **11. a.** pharyngeal pouches; **b.** dorsal
tubular nerve cord; **c.** notochord;
d. postanal tail

Understanding the Terms

a. homeothermic; **b.** monotreme; **c.** reptile;
d. notochord; **e.** echinoderm

Chapter 36

Testing Yourself

1. c; **2.** b; **3.** c; **4.** c; **5.** b; **6.** b; **7.** b; **8.** c; **9.** c;
10. b; **11. a.** epidermis; **b.** cortex;
c. endodermis; **d.** phloem; **e.** xylem. See
also Figure 36.8, page 648; **12. a.** upper
epidermis; **b.** palisade mesophyll; **c.** leaf
vein; **d.** spongy mesophyll; **e.** lower
epidermis. See also Figure 36.18, page 658.

Understanding the Terms

a. mesophyll; **b.** vascular cambium;
c. cotyledon; **d.** stolon; **e.** phloem

Chapter 37

Testing Yourself

1. d; **2.** e; **3.** a; **4.** e; **5.** c; **6.** d; **7.** e; **8.** d; **9.** The
diagram shows that air pressure pushing
down on mercury in the pan can raise a
column of mercury only to 76 cm. When
water above the column is transpired, it
pulls on the mercury and raises it higher.
This suggests that transpiration would be
able to raise water to the top of trees.
10. See Figure 37.12, page 676. After K^+
enters guard cells, water follows by
osmosis and the stomate opens. **11.** There is
more solute in the left bulb than in the
right; therefore water enters the left bulb.
This creates a positive pressure that causes
water, along with solute, to flow toward the
right bulb. See also illustration, page 678.

Understanding the Terms

a. pressure-flow model; **b.** epiphyte;
c. transpiration; **d.** Casparian strip; **e.** guard
cell

Chapter 38

Testing Yourself

1. d; **2.** b; **3.** e; **4.** a; **5.** c; **6.** b; **7.** d; **8.** e;
9. e; **10.** e; **11.** e; **12. a.** epidermal cell;

b. guard cell. The hormone ABA in some
unknown manner causes K^+ to leave the
guard cell. Water follows the movement of
K^+ and the guard cell closes.

Understanding the Terms

a. circadian rhythm; **b.** gravitropism;
c. abscission; **d.** gibberellin;
e. photoperiodism

Chapter 39

Testing Yourself

1. d; **2.** a; **3.** b; **4.** a; **5.** a; **6.** e; **7.** a; **8.** e; **9.** c;
10. e; **11. a.** sporophyte; **b.** meiosis;
c. microspore; **d.** megaspore;
e. microgametophyte (pollen grain);
f. megagametophyte (embryo sac);
g. egg and sperm; **h.** fertilization;
i. zygote; **j.** seed. See also Figure 39.1,
page 700.

Understanding the Terms

a. pistil; **b.** fruit; **c.** megagametophyte;
d. seed; **e.** pollen grain

Chapter 40

Testing Yourself

1. c; **2.** b; **3.** a; **4.** e; **5.** e; **6.** e; **7.** b; **8.** e; **9.** e;
10. c; **11. a.** columnar epithelium, lining of
intestine (digestive tract), protection and
absorption; **b.** cardiac muscle, wall of heart,
pumps blood; **c.** compact bone, skeleton,
support and protection.

Understanding the Terms

a. ligament; **b.** epidermis; **c.** striated;
d. homeostasis; **e.** spongy bone

Chapter 41

Testing Yourself

1. b; **2.** b; **3.** a; **4.** d; **5.** d; **6.** c; **7.** b; **8.** b; **9.** e;
10. a. blood pressure; **b.** osmotic pressure;
c. blood pressure; **d.** osmotic pressure;
11. a. aorta; **b.** left pulmonary arteries;
c. pulmonary trunk; **d.** left pulmonary
veins; **e.** left atrium; **f.** semilunar valves;
g. atrioventricular (mitral) valve; **h.** left
ventricle; **i.** septum; **j.** inferior vena cava;
k. right ventricle; **l.** chordae tendineae;
m. atrioventricular (tricuspid) valve;
n. right atrium; **o.** right pulmonary veins;
p. right pulmonary arteries; **q.** superior
vena cava. See also Figure 41.6,
page 745.

Understanding the Terms

a. artery; **b.** platelet; **c.** plasma; **d.** vena
cavae; **e.** hemoglobin

Chapter 42

Testing Yourself

1. e; **2.** e; **3.** a; **4.** b; **5.** c; **6.** b; **7.** a; **8.** a; **9.** b; **10.** e; **11.** b; **12. a.** antigen-binding sites; **b.** light chain; **c.** heavy chain; **d.** variable region; **e.** constant region

Understanding the Terms

a. vaccine; **b.** lymph; **c.** antigen; **d.** apoptosis; **e.** T lymphocyte

Chapter 43

Testing Yourself

1. a; **2.** b; **3.** d; **4.** b; **5.** c; **6.** a; **7.** c; **8.** c; **9.** e; **10.** c; **11.** d; **12.** c; **13.** Test tube 1: no digestion—no enzyme and no HCl; Test tube 2: some digestion—no HCl; Test tube 3: no digestion—no enzyme; Test tube 4: digestion—both enzyme and HCl are present

Understanding the Terms

a. vitamins; **b.** lipase; **c.** lacteal; **d.** esophagus; **e.** gallbladder

Chapter 44

Testing Yourself

1. a; **2.** b; **3.** b; **4.** d; **5.** c; **6.** b; **7.** c; **8.** b; **9.** e; **10.** b; **11. a.** nasal cavity; **b.** nostril; **c.** pharynx; **d.** epiglottis; **e.** glottis; **f.** larynx; **g.** trachea; **h.** bronchus; **i.** bronchiole. See also Figure 44.6, page 802.

Understanding the Terms

a. pharynx; **b.** diaphragm; **c.** vocal cord; **d.** gill; **e.** expiration

Chapter 45

Testing Yourself

1. d; **2.** a; **3.** c; **4.** b; **5.** a; **6.** e; **7.** b; **8.** e; **9.** a; **10.** b; **11. a.** glomerulus; **b.** efferent arteriole; **c.** afferent arteriole; **d.** proximal convoluted tubule; **e.** loop of the nephron; **f.** descending limb; **g.** ascending limb; **h.** peritubular capillary network; **i.** distal convoluted tubule; **j.** renal vein; **k.** renal artery; **l.** collecting duct

Understanding the Terms

a. Malpighian tubule; **b.** glomerular capsule; **c.** distal convoluted tubule; **d.** aldosterone; **e.** uric acid

Chapter 46

Testing Yourself

1. b; **2.** b; **3.** e; **4.** c; **5.** a; **6.** a; **7.** c; **8.** d; **9.** b; **10.** b; **11. a.** central canal; **b.** gray matter; **c.** white matter; **d.** dorsal root ganglion; **e.** cell body of sensory neuron; **f.** axon of sensory neuron; **g.** cell body of motor neuron; **h.** axon of motor neuron; **i.** interneuron

Understanding the Terms

a. reflex; **b.** neurotransmitter; **c.** autonomic system; **d.** ganglion; **e.** acetylcholine

Chapter 47

Testing Yourself

1. e; **2.** c; **3.** c; **4.** e; **5.** d; **6.** c; **7.** c; **8.** b; **9.** c; **10. a.** retina—contains sensory receptors; **b.** choroid—absorbs stray light; **c.** sclera—protects and supports eyeball; **d.** optic nerve—transmits impulses to brain; **e.** fovea centralis—makes acute vision possible; **f.** muscle in ciliary body—holds lens in place, accommodation; **g.** lens—refracts and focuses light rays; **h.** iris—regulates light entrance; **i.** pupil—admits light; **j.** cornea—refracts light rays

Understanding the Terms

a. sensory receptor; **b.** retina; **c.** sclera; **d.** chemoreceptor; **e.** spiral organ

Chapter 48

Testing Yourself

1. b; **2.** f; **3.** c; **4.** e; **5.** e; **6.** b; **7.** b; **8.** e; **9.** a; **10.** e; **11. a.** T tubule; **b.** sarcoplasmic reticulum; **c.** myofibril; **d.** Z line; **e.** sarcomere; **f.** sarcolemma of muscle fiber

Understanding the Terms

a. osteoblast; **b.** sliding filament model; **c.** actin; **d.** appendicular skeleton; **e.** pectoral girdle

Chapter 49

Testing Yourself

1. a; **2.** e; **3.** f; **4.** b; **5.** c; **6.** a; **7.** e; **8.** e; **9.** c; **10.** e; **11.** b; **12.** e; **13.** d; **14. a.** inhibits; **b.** inhibits; **c.** releasing hormone; **d.** stimulating hormone; **e.** target gland hormone

Understanding the Terms

a. thyroid gland; **b.** hormone; **c.** pineal gland; **d.** peptide hormone; **e.** pheromone

Chapter 50

Testing Yourself

1. a. seminal vesicle; **b.** ejaculatory duct; **c.** prostate gland; **d.** bulbourethral gland; **e.** anus; **f.** vas deferens; **g.** epididymis; **h.** testis; **i.** scrotum; **j.** foreskin; **k.** glans penis; **l.** penis; **m.** urethra; **n.** vas deferens; **o.** urinary bladder. Path of sperm: testis, epididymis, vas deferens, urethra (in penis). See also Figure 50.3, page 904. **2.** b; **3.** e; **4.** c; **5.** e; **6.** c; **7.** c; **8.** c; **9.** c; **10.** a

Understanding the Terms

a. ovulation; **b.** parthenogenesis; **c.** progesterone; **d.** semen; **e.** gonad

Chapter 51

Testing Yourself

1. b; **2.** b; **3.** b; **4.** a; **5.** e; **6.** b; **7.** e; **8.** e; **9.** d; **10. a.** chorion (contributes to forming placenta where wastes are exchanged for nutrients and oxygen); **b.** amnion (protects and prevents desiccation); **c.** embryo; **d.** allantois (blood vessels become umbilical blood vessels); **e.** yolk sac (first site of blood cell formation); **f.** chorionic villi (embryonic portion of placenta); **g.** maternal portion of placenta; **h.** umbilical cord (connects developing embryo to the placenta). See also Figure 51.11, page 930.

Understanding the Terms

a. induction; **b.** germ layer; **c.** amnion; **d.** homeobox; **e.** gastrula

CLASSIFICATION OF ORGANISMS

Domain Archaea

Prokaryotic, unicellular organisms which lack a membrane-bounded nucleus and reproduce asexually. Many are autotrophic by chemosynthesis; some are heterotrophic by absorption. Most live in extreme or anaerobic environments. Archaea are distinguishable from bacteria by their unique rRNA base sequence; and their distinctive plasma membrane and cell wall chemistry. (519)

Domain Bacteria

Prokaryotic, unicellular organisms which lack a membrane-bounded nucleus and reproduce asexually. Metabolically diverse being heterotrophic by absorption; autotrophic by chemosynthesis or by photosynthesis. Motile forms move by flagella consisting of a single filament. (517)

Domain Eukarya

Eukaryotic, unicellular to multicellular organisms which have a membrane-bounded nucleus containing several chromosomes. Sexual reproduction is common. Phenotypes and nutrition are diverse; each kingdom has specializations that distinguish it from the other kingdoms. Flagella, if present, have a 9 + 2 organization.

Kingdom Protista

Eukaryotic, unicellular organisms and their immediate multicellular descendants. Asexual reproduction is common, but sexual reproduction as a part of various life cycles does occur. Phenotypically and nutritionally diverse, being either photosynthetic or heterotrophic by various means. Locomotion, if present, utilizes flagella, cilia, or pseudopods.

Algae*

    Phylum Chlorophyta: green algae (528)
    Phylum Rhodophyta: red algae (530)
    Phylum Phaeophyta: brown algae (531)

Diatoms

    Phylum Chrysophyta: golden-brown algae (533)

Flagellates

    Phylum Pyrrophyta: dinoflagellates (533)
    Phylum Euglenophyta: euglenoids (534)
    Phylum Zoomastigophora: zooflagellates (535)

Sarcodines

    Phylum Rhizopoda: amoeboids (536)
    Phylum Foraminifera: foraminiferans (536)
    Phylum Actinopoda: radiolarians (536)

Ciliates

    Phylum Ciliophora: ciliates (537)

Sporozoans

    Phylum Apicomplexa: sporozoans (538)

Slime Molds and Water Molds

    Phylum Myxomycota: plasmodial slime molds (539)
    Phylum Acrasiomycota: cellular slime molds (539)
    Phylum Oomycota: water molds (540)

* Not a classification category, but added for clarity

Kingdom Fungi

Multicellular eukaryotes which form nonmotile spores during both asexual and sexual reproduction as a part of the haplontic life cycle. The only multicellular forms of life to be heterotrophic by absorption. They lack flagella in all life cycle stages. Approximately 77,000 species

Division Zygomycota: zygospore fungi (546)
Division Ascomycota: sac fungi (549)
Division Basidiomycota: club fungi (551)
Division Deuteromycota: imperfect fungi (means of sexual reproduction is not known) (553)

Kingdom Plantae

Multicellular, primarily terrestrial, eukaryotes with well-developed tissues. Plants have an alternation of generations life cycle and are usually photosynthetic. Like green algae, they contain chlorophylls *a* and *b*, carotenoids; store starch in chloroplasts; and have a cell wall which contains cellulose. Approximately 270,000 species.

Nonvascular Plants

Division Hepatophyta: liverworts (560)
Division Bryophyta: mosses (560)
Division Anthocerotophyta: hornworts (560)

Seedless Vascular Plants

Division Psilotophyta: whisk ferns (564)
Division Lycopodophyta: club mosses, spike mosses, quillworts (565)
Division Equisetophyta: horsetails (565)
Division Pteridophyta: ferns (566)

Gymnosperms

Division Pinophyta: conifers, such as pines, firs, yews, redwoods, spruces (568)
Division Cycadophyta: cycads (570)
Division Ginkgophyta: maidenhair tree (570)
Division Gnetophyta: gnetophytes (572)

Angiosperms

Division Magnoliophyta: flowering plants (572)
Class Liliopsida: monocots
Class Magnoliopsida: dicots

Kingdom Animalia

Multicellular organisms with well-developed tissues that have the diplontic life cycle. Animals tend to be mobile and are heterotrophic by ingestion, generally in a digestive cavity. Complexity varies; the more complex forms have well-developed organ systems. More than a million species have been described.

Invertebrates

Phylum Porifera: sponges (582)
Phylum Cnidaria: hydras, jellyfishes (584)
Class Anthozoa: sea anemones, corals (585)
Class Hydrozoa: *Hydra, Obelia* (585–87)
Class Scyphozoa: *Aurelia* (585)
Phylum Ctenophora: comb jellies, sea walnuts (584)
Phylum Nemertea: ribbon worms (588)
Phylum Platyhelminthes: flatworms (588)
Class Turbellaria: planarians (588)
Class Trematoda: flukes (590)
Class Cestoda: tapeworms (591)
Phylum Nematoda: roundworms: *Ascaris* (593)
Phylum Rotifera: rotifers (594)
Phylum Mollusca: molluscs (600)
Class Polyplacophora: chitons (600)
Class Bivalvia: clams, scallops, oysters, mussels (600)
Class Cephalopoda: squids, chambered nautilus, octopus (602)
Class Gastropoda: snails, slugs, nudibranchs (603)
Phylum Annelida: annelids (604)
Class Polychaeta: clam worms, tube worms (604)
Class Oligochaeta: earthworms (605)
Class Hirudinea: leeches (606)
Phylum Arthropoda: arthropods (606)
Subphylum Trilobitomorpha: trilobites (606)
Subphylum Crustacea: crustaceans (608)
Subphylum Uniramia: millipedes, centipedes, insects (611)
Subphylum Chelicerata: spiders, scorpions, horseshoe crabs (613)
Phylum Echinodermata: echinoderms (618)
Class Crinoidea: sea lilies, feather stars (618)
Class Asteroidea: sea stars (618)
Class Ophiuroidea: brittle stars (618)
Class Echinoidea: sea urchins, sand dollars (618)
Class Holothuroidea: sea cucumbers (618)
Phylum Chordata: chordates (619)
Subphylum Cephalochordata: lancelets (620)
Subphylum Urochordata: tunicates (620)

Vertebrates

Subphylum Vertebrata (622)
Superclass Agnatha: jawless fishes (622)
Superclass Gnathostomata: jawed fishes, tetrapods (623)
Class Chondrichthyes: cartilaginous fishes (623)
Class Osteichthyes: bony fishes (624)
Class Amphibia: amphibians (625)
Class Reptilia: reptiles (628)
Class Aves: birds (632)
Class Mammalia
Monotremes (634)
Marsupials (634)
Placental mammals (635)

* Extinct

a

abscisic acid (ABA) Plant hormone that causes stomates to close and that initiates and maintains dormancy. 693

abscission Dropping of leaves, fruits, or flowers from a plant. 693

acetyl-CoA Molecule made up of a two-carbon acetyl group attached to coenzyme A. During cellular respiration, the acetyl group enters the Krebs cycle for further breakdown. 132

acetylcholine (ACh) Neurotransmitter active in both the peripheral and central nervous systems. 833

acetylcholinesterase (AChE) Enzyme that breaks down acetylcholine within a synapse. 833

acid Molecules tending to raise the hydrogen ion concentration in a solution and to lower its pH numerically. 28

acid deposition Return to earth as rain or snow of the sulfate or nitrate salts of acids produced by commercial and industrial activities. 433

actin Muscle protein making up the thin filaments in a sarcomere; its movement shortens the sarcomere, yielding muscle contraction. 875

action potential Electrochemical changes that take place across the axomembrane; the nerve impulse. 830

active site Region on the surface of an enzyme where the substrate binds and where the reaction occurs. 103

active transport Use of a plasma membrane carrier protein to move a molecule or ion from a region of lower to higher concentration; it opposes equilibrium and requires energy. 88

adaptation Organism's modification in structure, function, or behavior suitable to the environment. 4, 291

adaptive radiation Evolution of several species from a common ancestor into new ecological or geographical zones. 312

adenine (A) One of four nitrogen-containing bases in nucleotides composing the structure of DNA and RNA. 223

adenosine Portion of ATP and ADP that is composed of the base adenine and the sugar ribose. 50

adhesion junction Junction between cells in which the adjacent plasma membranes do not touch but are held together by intercellular filaments attached to buttonlike thickenings. 93

adipose tissue Connective tissue in which fat is stored. 726

ADP (adenosine diphosphate) Nucleotide with two phosphate groups that can accept another phosphate group and become ATP. 50, 101

adrenal cortex Outer portion of the adrenal gland; secretes hormones such as mineralocorticoid aldosterone and glucocorticoid cortisol. 891

adrenal medulla Inner portion of the adrenal gland; secretes the hormones epinephrine and norepinephrine. 891

adventitious root Fibrous roots which develop from stems or leaves, such as prop roots of corn or holdfast roots of ivy. 650

agglutination Clumping of red blood cells due to a reaction between antigens on red blood cell plasma membranes and antibodies in the plasma. 774

agnathan Vertebrates that lack jaws; includes only the jawless fishes; i.e., the lampreys and hagfishes. 622

aldosterone Hormone secreted by the adrenal cortex that regulates the sodium and potassium ion balance of the blood. 820

algae (sing., alga) Type of protist that carries on photosynthesis; unicellular forms are a part of phytoplankton and multicellular forms are called seaweed. 528

alien species Nonnative species that migrate or are introduced by humans into a new ecosystem; also called exotics. 477

allantois Extraembryonic membrane that accumulates nitrogenous wastes in birds and reptiles and contributes to the formation of umbilical blood vessels in mammals. 930

allele Alternative form of a gene—alleles occur at the same locus on homologous chromosomes. 177

allergen Foreign substance capable of stimulating an allergic response. 776

allopatric speciation Origin of new species between populations that are separated geographically. 312

allosteric site Regulatory binding site on an enzyme that controls the activity of that enzyme. 105

altruism Social interaction that has the potential to decrease the lifetime reproductive success of the member exhibiting the behavior. 372

alveolus In humans, terminal, microscopic, grapelike air sac found in lungs. 803

amino acid Organic molecule having an amino group and an acid group, that covalently bonds to produce peptide molecules. 45

amniocentesis Procedure for removing amniotic fluid surrounding the developing fetus for the testing of the fluid or cells within the fluid. 203

amnion Extraembryonic membrane of birds, reptiles, and mammals that forms an enclosing, fluid-filled sac. 930

amoeboid Cell that moves and engulfs debris with pseudopods. 536

amphibian Member of a class of vertebrates that includes frogs, toads, and salamanders; they are still tied to a watery environment for reproduction. 625

anabolism Metabolic process by which larger molecules are synthesized from smaller ones; anabolic metabolism. 139

analogous structure Structure that has a similar function in separate lineages but differs in anatomy and ancestry. 296, 495

angiosperm Flowering plant; the seeds are borne within a fruit. 572

annual ring Layer of wood (secondary xylem) usually produced during one growing season. 655

anther In flowering plants, pollen-bearing portion of stamen. 573, 701

antheridium Sperm-producing structure, as in the moss life cycle. 560

anthropoid Group of primates that includes monkeys, apes, and humans. 345

antibody Protein produced in response to the presence of an antigen; each antibody combines with a specific antigen. 753, 764

antibody-mediated immunity Specific mechanism of defense in which plasma cells derived from B cells produce antibodies that combine with antigens. 765

anticodon Three-base sequence in a transfer RNA molecule base that pairs with a complementary codon in mRNA. 240

antidiuretic hormone (ADH) Hormone secreted by the posterior pituitary that increases the permeability of the collecting ducts in a kidney. 820

antigen Foreign substance, usually a protein or a polysaccharide, that stimulates the immune system to react, such as to produce antibodies. 753, 764

anus Outlet of the digestive tube. 791

aorta In humans, the major systemic artery that takes blood from the heart to the tissues. 748

apical dominance Influence of a terminal bud in suppressing the growth of lateral buds. 685

apoptosis Programmed cell death involving a cascade of specific cellular events leading to death and destruction of the cell. 69, 152, 260, 765, 926

appendicular skeleton Part of the vertebrate skeleton forming the appendages, shoulder girdle, and hip girdle. 870

appendix In humans, small, tubular appendage that extends outward from the cecum of the large intestine. 791

aquifer Rock layers that contain water and will release it in appreciable quantities to wells or springs. 429

arboreal Living in trees. 342

Archaea One of the three domains of life containing prokaryotic cells that often live in extreme habitats and which have unique genetic, biochemical, and physiological characteristics. 502, 519

archegonium Egg-producing structure as in the moss life cycle. 560

arteriole Vessel that takes blood from an artery to capillaries. 742

artery Blood vessel that transports blood away from the heart. 742

ascus (pl., asci Fingerlike sac in which nuclear fusion, meiosis, and ascospore production occur during sexual reproduction of sac fungi. 549

asexual reproduction Reproduction that requires only one parent and does not involve gametes. 144

aster Short, radiating fibers produced by the centrosomes in animal cells. 146

asymmetry Body plan having no particular symmetry. 580

atom Smallest particle of an element that displays the properties of the element. 18

atomic mass Mass of an atom equal to the number of protons plus the number of neutrons within the nucleus. 19

atomic number Number of protons within the nucleus of an atom. 19

ATP (adenosine triphosphate) Nucleotide with three phosphate groups. The breakdown of ATP into ADP + Ⓟ makes energy available for energy-requiring processes in cells. 48, 50, 101

ATP synthase Enzyme that is part of an ATP synthase complex and functions in the production of ATP in chloroplasts and mitochondria. 107, 118

atrial natriuretic hormone (ANH) Hormone secreted by the heart that increases sodium excretion. 821

atrioventricular valve Heart valve located between an atrium and a ventricle. 744

atrium (pl., atria) Chamber; particularly an upper chamber of the heart lying above a ventricle. 744

australopithecine Any of the first evolved hominids; classified into several species of *Australopithecus*. 348

autoimmune disease Disease that results when the immune system mistakenly attacks the body's own tissues. 776

autonomic system Portion of the peripheral nervous system that regulates internal organs. 831

autosome Any chromosome other than the sex-determining pair. 192, 202

autotroph Organism that can capture energy and synthesize organic molecules from inorganic nutrients. 423

auxin Plant hormone regulating growth, particularly cell elongation; also called indoleacetic acid (IAA). 688

axial skeleton Part of the vertebrate skeleton forming the vertical support or axis, including the skull, the rib cage, and the vertebral column. 868

axillary bud Bud located in the axil of a leaf. 643

axon Elongated portion of a neuron that conducts nerve impulses typically from the cell body to the synapse. 829

b

B lymphocyte Lymphocyte that matures in the bone marrow and, when stimulated by the presence of a specific antigen, gives rise to antibody-producing plasma cells. 764

Bacteria One of the three domains of life containing prokaryotic cells that differ from archaea because they have their own unique genetic, biochemical, and physiological characteristics. 60, 502, 517

bacteriophage Virus that infects bacteria. 221, 267, 510

Barr body Dark-staining body (discovered by M. Barr) in the nuclei of female mammals that contains a condensed, inactive X chromosome. 253

base Molecules tending to lower the hydrogen ion concentration in a solution and raise the pH numerically. 28

basidium (pl., basidia) Clublike structure in which nuclear fusion, meiosis, and basidiospore production occur during sexual reproduction of club fungi. 551

basophil Leukocyte with a granular cytoplasm and that is able to be stained with a basic dye. 762

behavior Observable, coordinated responses to environmental stimuli. 362

benthic division Ocean or lake floor from the high-tide mark to the deepest depths; which supports a unique set of organisms. 463

bicarbonate ion Ion that participates in buffering the blood, and the form in which carbon dioxide is transported in the bloodstream. 805

bilateral symmetry Body plan having two corresponding or complementary halves. 580

bile Secretion of the liver that is temporarily stored and concentrated in the gallbladder before being released into the small intestine, where it emulsifies fat. 788

binary fission Splitting of a parent cell into two daughter cells; serves as an asexual form of reproduction in bacteria. 144, 515

binomial system Assignment of two names to each organism, the first of which designates the genus and second of which is the specific epithet. 490

biodiversity Total number of species, the variability of their genes, and the communities in which they live. 7, 470

biodiversity hotspots Regions of the world that contain unusually large concentrations of species. 471

biogeochemical cycle Circulating pathway of elements such as carbon and nitrogen involving exchange pools, storage areas, and biotic communities. 428

biogeography Study of the geographical distribution of organisms. 286

biological clock Internal mechanism that maintains a biological rhythm in the absence of environmental stimuli. 687

biological magnification Process by which substances become more concentrated in organisms in the higher trophic levels of a food web. 435

biome One of the biosphere's major communities characterized in particular by certain climatic conditions and particular types of plants. 445

biosphere Zone of air, land, and water at the surface of the earth in which living organisms are found. 5, 378, 422

biotic potential Maximum population growth rate under ideal conditions. 381

bipedalism Walking erect on two feet. 347

bird Homeothermic vertebrate characterized by the presence of feathers, having wings often adapted for flight and laying hard-shelled eggs. 632

bivalent Homologous chromosomes, each having sister chromatids that are joined by a nucleoprotein lattice during meiosis; also called tetrad. 161

bivalve Type of mollusc with a shell composed of two valves; includes clams, oysters, and scallops. 600

blade Broad expanded portion of a plant leaf that may be single or compound leaflets. 643

blastocoel Fluid-filled cavity of a blastula. 921

blastocyst Early stage of human embryonic development that consists of a hollow fluid-filled ball of cells. 931

blastula Hollow, fluid-filled ball of cells occurring during animal development prior to gastrula formation. 921

blind spot Region of the retina lacking rods or cones and where the optic nerve leaves the eye. 854

blood Fluid circulated by the heart through a closed system of vessels. 727, 741

blood pressure Force of blood pushing against the inside wall of blood vessels. 749

bony fish Member of a class of vertebrates (class Osteichthyes) containing numerous, diverse fishes, with a bony rather than cartilaginous skeleton. 624

bottleneck effect Cause of genetic drift; occurs when a majority of genotypes is prevented from participating in the production of the next generation as a result of a natural disaster or human interference. 305

brain Ganglionic mass at the anterior end of the nerve cord; in vertebrates the brain is located in cranial cavity of the skull. 827

brain stem In mammals; portion of the brain consisting of the medulla oblongata, pons, and midbrain. 839

bronchiole In terrestrial vertebrates, small tube that conducts air from a bronchus to the alveoli. 803

bronchus (pl., bronchi) In terrestrial vertebrates, branch of the trachea that leads to lungs. 803

brown alga Marine photosynthetic protist with a notable abundance of xanthophyll pigments; this group includes well-known seaweeds of northern rocky shores. 531

budding Asexual form of reproduction whereby a new organism develops as an outgrowth of the body of the parent. 545

buffer Substance or group of substances that tend to resist pH changes of a solution, thus stabilizing its relative acidity and basicity. 29

bursa Saclike, fluid-filled structure, lined with synovial membrane, that occurs near a synovial joint. 871

C

C₃ plant Plant that fixes carbon dioxide via the Calvin cycle; the first stable product of C₃ photosynthesis is a three-carbon compound. 122

C₄ plant Plant that fixes carbon dioxide to produce a C₄ molecule that releases carbon dioxide to the Calvin cycle. 122

Calvin cycle Primary pathway of the light-independent reactions of photosynthesis; converts carbon dioxide to carbohydrate. 119

CAM plant Plant that fixes carbon dioxide at night to produce a C₄ molecule that releases carbon dioxide to the Calvin cycle during the day; CAM stands for crassulacean-acid metabolism. 122

camera-type eye Type of eye found in vertebrates and certain molluscs; a single lens focuses an image on closely-packed photoreceptors. 850

camouflage Method of hiding from predators in which the organism's behavior, form, and pattern of coloration allow it to blend into the background and prevent detection. 408

cancer Malignant tumor whose nondifferentiated cells exhibit loss of contact inhibition, uncontrolled growth, and the ability to invade tissue and metastasize. 152, 258

capillary Microscopic blood vessel; gases and other substances are exchanged across the walls of a capillary between blood and tissue fluid. 742

capsule Gelatinous layer surrounding the cells of blue-green algae and certain bacteria. 60

carbaminohemoglobin Hemoglobin carrying carbon dioxide. 805

carbohydrate Class of organic compounds that includes monosaccharides, disaccharides, and polysaccharides. 37

carbon cycle Continuous process by which carbon circulates in the air, water, and organisms of the biosphere. 430

carbonic anhydrase Enzyme in red blood cells that speeds the formation of carbonic acid from water and carbon dioxide. 805

carcinogen Environmental agent that causes mutations leading to the development of cancer. 258

cardiac conduction system System of specialized cardiac muscle fibers that conducts impulses from the SA node to the chambers of the heart causing them to contract. 747

cardiac cycle One complete cycle of systole and diastole for all heart chambers. 746

cardiac muscle Striated, involuntary muscle tissue found only in the heart. 728

cardiac pacemaker Mass of specialized cardiac muscle tissue that controls the rhythm of the heartbeat; the SA node. 747

carnivore Consumer in a food chain that eats other animals. 423

carpel Ovule-bearing unit that is a part of a pistil. 573, 701

carrier Heterozygous individual who has no apparent abnormality but can pass on an allele for a recessively inherited genetic disorder. 207

carrier protein Protein that combines with and transports a molecule or ion across the plasma membrane. 83, 88

carrying capacity Largest number of organisms of a particular species that can be maintained indefinitely by a given environment. 383

cartilage Connective tissue in which the cells lie within lacunae embedded in a flexible proteinaceous matrix. 727

cartilaginous fish Member of a class of vertebrates (class Chondrichthyes) with a cartilaginous rather than bony skeleton, including sharks, rays, and skates. 623

Casparian strip Layer of impermeable lignin and suberin bordering four sides of root endodermal cells; prevents water and solute transport between adjacent cells. 649, 670

catabolism Metabolic process that breaks down large molecules into smaller ones; catabolic metabolism. 139

catastrophism Belief espoused by Georges Cuvier that periods of catastrophic extinctions occurred, after which repopulation of surviving species took place, giving the appearance of change through time. 284

cell Smallest unit that displays the properties of life; composed of cytoplasm surrounded by a plasma membrane. 56

cell cycle Repeating sequence of events in eukaryotes that involves cell growth and nuclear division; consists of the stages G₁, S, G₂, and M. 150

cell plate Structure across a dividing plant cell that signals the location of new plasma membranes and cell walls. 148

cell theory One of the major theories of biology which states that all organisms are made up of cells; cells are capable of self-reproduction and they come only from pre-existing cells. 56

cell wall Structure that surrounds a plant, protistan, fungal, or bacterial cell and maintains the cell's shape and rigidity. 60, 61, 92

cell-mediated immunity Specific mechanism of defense in which T cells destroy antigen-bearing cells. 768

cellular differentiation Process and developmental stages by which a cell becomes specialized for a particular function. 924

cellular respiration Metabolic reactions that use the energy from carbohydrate or fatty acid or amino acid breakdown to produce ATP molecules. 128

cellular slime mold Free-living amoeboid cells that feed on bacteria by phagocytosis and aggregate to form a plasmodium that produces spores. 539

cellulose Polysaccharide that is the major complex carbohydrate in plant cell walls. 38

centriole Cell organelle, existing in pairs, that occurs in the centrosome and may help organize a mitotic spindle for chromosome movement during animal cell division. 74, 146

centromere Constriction where sister chromatids of a chromosome are held together. 145

centrosome Central microtubule organizing center of cells. In animal cells, it contains two centrioles. 72, 144, 146

cephalization Having a well-recognized anterior head with a brain and sensory receptors. 588, 827

cephalopod Type of mollusc in which a modified foot develops into the head region; includes squids, cuttlefish, octopuses, and nautiluses. 602

cephalothorax Fused head and thorax found in decapods (shrimps, lobsters, crayfish, and crabs). 608, 613

cerebellum In terrestrial vertebrates, portion of the brain that coordinates skeletal muscles to produce smooth, graceful motions. 839

cerebral hemisphere Either of the two lobes of the cerebrum in vertebrates. 840

cerebrospinal fluid Fluid found in the ventricles of the brain, in the central canal of the spinal cord, and in association with the meninges. 839

cerebrum Largest part of the brain in mammals, the cortex receives and responds to sensory information and carries out mental processes. 839

channel protein Protein that forms a channel to allow a particular molecule or ion to cross the plasma membrane. 83

character Any structural, chromosomal, or molecular feature that distinguishes one group from another. 493

character displacement Tendency for characteristics to be more divergent when similar species belong to the same community than when they are isolated from one another. 404

chemical energy Energy associated with the interaction of atoms in a molecule. 98

chemical evolution Increase in the complexity of chemicals over time that could have led to the first cells. 320

chemiosmosis Ability of certain membranes to use a hydrogen ion gradient to drive ATP formation. 107, 118, 135

chemoautotroph Organism able to synthesize organic molecules by using carbon dioxide as the carbon source and the oxidation of an inorganic substance (such as hydrogen sulfide) as the energy source. 516

chemoheterotroph Organism that is unable to produce its own organic molecules and therefore requires organic nutrients in its diet. 516

chemoreceptor Sensory receptor that is sensitive to chemical stimulation—for example, receptors for taste and smell. 848

chitin Strong but flexible nitrogenous polysaccharide found in the exoskeleton of arthropods. 39, 606

chlorophyll Green pigment that absorbs solar energy and is important in algal and plant photosynthesis; occurs as chlorophyll *a* and chlorophyll *b*. 114

chloroplast Membrane-bounded organelle in algae and plants with chlorophyll-containing membranous thylakoids; where photosynthesis takes place. 70, 114

cholesterol One of the major lipids found in animal plasma membranes; makes the membrane impermeable to many molecules. 81

chordate Animals in the phylum Chordata that have a dorsal tubular nerve cord, a notochord, pharyngeal gill pouches and past anal tail at some point in their life cycle. 619

chorion Extraembryonic membrane functioning for respiratory exchange in birds and reptiles; contributes to placenta formation in mammals. 930

chorionic villi sampling Prenatal test in which a sample of chorionic villi cells are removed for diagnostic purposes. 212

chorionic villus Treelike extension of the chorion of the embryo, projecting into the maternal tissues at the placenta. 933

chromatin Network of fibrils consisting of DNA and associated proteins observed within a nucleus that is not dividing. 65, 145

chromosomal mutation Alteration in chromosome structure or number typical of the species. 197

chromosome Structure consisting of DNA complexed with proteins that transmits genetic information from the previous generation of cells and organisms to the next generation. 65, 144

chyme Thick, semiliquid food material that passes from the stomach to the small intestine. 787

ciliary muscle Within the ciliary body of the vertebrate eye, the ciliary muscle controls the shape of the lens. 852

ciliate Complex unicellular protist that moves by means of cilia and digests food in food vacuoles. 537

cilium Short, hairlike projection from the plasma membrane, occurring usually in larger numbers. 74

circadian rhythm Biological rhythm with a 24-hour cycle. 686, 897

cladistic systematics (cladistics) School of systematics that uses derived characters to determine monophyletic groups and construct cladograms. 498

cladogram In cladistics, a branching diagram that shows the relationship among species in regard to their shared, derived characters. 498

class One of the categories, or taxa, used by taxonomists to group species; taxon above the order level. 493

cleavage Cell division without cytoplasmic addition or enlargement; occurs during the first stage of animal development. 920

climate Weather condition of an area including especially prevailing temperature and average daily/yearly rainfall. 442

climax community In ecology, community that results when succession has come to an end. 415

cloaca Posterior portion of the digestive tract in certain vertebrates that receives feces and urogenital products. 626

clonal selection theory States that the antigen selects which lymphocyte will undergo clonal expansion and produce more lymphocytes bearing the same type of receptor. 765

clone Production of identical copies; in organisms, the production of organisms with same genes, in genetic engineering, the production of many identical copies of a gene. 266

club moss Type of seedless vascular plant that are also called ground pine because they appear to be miniature pine trees. 575

cnidarian Invertebrate in the phylum Cnidaria existing as either a polyp or medusa with two tissue layers and radial symmetry. 584

coal Fossil fuel formed millions of years ago from plant material that did not decay. 563

cochlea Spiral-shaped structure of the vertebrate inner ear containing the sensory receptors for hearing. 856

codominance Inheritance pattern in which both alleles of a gene are equally expressed. 188

codon Three-base sequence in messenger RNA that causes the insertion of a particular amino acid into a protein or termination of translation. 237

coelom Body cavity lying between the digestive tract and body wall that is completely lined by mesoderm. 580, 598

coenzyme Nonprotein organic molecule that aids the action of the enzyme to which it is loosely bound. 105

coevolution Joint evolution in which one species exerts selective pressure on the other species. 411, 704

cofactor Nonprotein adjunct required by an enzyme in order to function; many cofactors are metal ions, others are coenzymes. 105

cohesion-tension model Explanation for upward transport of water in xylem based upon transpiration-created tension and the cohesive properties of water molecules. 674

cohort Group of individuals having a statistical factor in common, such as year of birth, in a population study. 384

coleoptile Protective sheath that covers the young leaves of a seedling. 688

collecting duct Duct within the kidney that receives fluid from several nephrons; the reabsorption of water occurs here. 816

collenchyma Plant tissue composed of cells with unevenly thickened walls; supports growth of stems and petioles. 646

colon In humans, the major portion of the large intestine. 791

colony Loose association of cells that remain independent for most functions. 530

commensalism Symbiotic relationship in which one species is benefited, and the other is neither harmed nor benefited. 412

common ancestor Ancestor held in common by at least two lines of descent. 492

community Assemblage of populations interacting with one another within the same environment. 5, 378, 400

compact bone Type of bone that contains osteons consisting of concentric layers of matrix and osteocytes in lacunae. 727, 866

companion cell Cell associated with sieve-tube elements in phloem of vascular plants. 672

competitive exclusion principle Theory that no two species can occupy the same niche. 404

complement system Series of proteins in plasma that form a nonspecific defense mechanism against a microbe invasion; it complements the antigen-antibody reaction. 764

complementary base pairing Hydrogen bonding between particular purines and pyrimidines in DNA. 49, 224

complementary DNA (cDNA) DNA that has been synthesized from mRNA by the action of reverse transcriptase. 267

complete gut Digestive tract that has both a mouth and an anus. 782

compound Substance having two or more different elements united chemically in fixed ratio. 22

compound eye Type of eye found in arthropods; it is composed of many independent visual units. 850

concentration gradient Gradual change in chemical concentration from one point to another. 84

conclusion Statement made following an experiment as to whether the results support or falsify the hypothesis. 10

condensation synthesis Chemical reaction resulting in a covalent bond with the accompanying loss of a water molecule. 36

cone Structure comprised of scales which bear sporangia; pollen cones bear microsporangia and seed cones bear megasporangia. 568

cone cell Photoreceptor in vertebrate eyes that responds to bright light and allows color vision. 853

conidiospore Spore produced by sac and club fungi during asexual reproduction. 549

conjugation Transfer of genetic material from one cell to another. 515, 529

connective tissue Type of animal tissue that binds structures together, provides support and protection, fills spaces, stores fat, and forms blood cells; adipose tissue, cartilage, bone, and blood are types of connective tissue. 726

consumer Organism that feeds on another organism in a food chain; primary consumers eat plants, and secondary consumers eat animals. 423

continental drift Movement of continents with respect to one another over the earth's surfaces. 334

control group Sample that goes through all the steps of an experiment but does not contain the variable being tested; a standard against which results of an experiment are checked. 10

convergent evolution Similarity in structure in distantly related groups due to adaptation to the environment. 495

copulation Sexual union between a male and a female. 902

coral reef Area of biological abundance found in shallow, warm tropical waters on and around coral formations. 464

corepressor Molecule that binds to a repressor, allowing the repressor to bind to an operator in a repressible operon. 249

cork Outer covering of bark of trees; made of dead cells that may be sloughed off. 645

cork cambium Lateral meristem that produces cork. 655

cornea Transparent, anterior portion of the outer layer of the eyeball. 852

corpus luteum Follicle that has released an egg and increases its secretion of progesterone. 909

cortex In plants, ground tissue bounded by the epidermis and vascular tissue in stems and roots; in animals, outer layer of an organ such as the cortex of the kidney or adrenal gland. 649

cotyledon Seed leaf for embryo of a flowering plant; provides nutrient molecules for the developing plant before photosynthesis begins. 644

coupled reactions Reactions that occur simultaneously; one is an exergonic reaction that releases energy and the other is an endergonic reaction that requires an input of energy in order to occur. 100

covalent bond Chemical bond in which atoms share one pair of electrons. 23

cranial nerve Nerve that arises from the brain. 834

creatine phosphate High energy phosphate molecule found in vertebrate muscles used to generate ATP molecules for muscle contraction. 875

crenation In animal cells, shriveling of the cell due to water leaving the cell when the environment is hypertonic. 87

cristae (sing., crista) Short, fingerlike projections formed by the folding of the inner membrane of mitochondria. 71

crossing-over Exchange of segments between nonsister chromatids of a bivalent during meiosis. 162

cuticle Waxy layer covering the epidermis of plants that protects the plant against water loss and disease-causing organisms. 558, 675

cyanobacterium Photosynthetic bacterium that contains chlorophyll and releases oxygen; formerly called a blue-green alga. 517

cycad Type of gymnosperm with palmate leaves and massive cones; cycads are most often found in the tropics and subtropics. 570

cyclic electron pathway Portion of the light-dependent reaction that involves only photosystem I and generates ATP. 116

cyclin Protein that cycles in quantity as the cell cycle progresses; combines with and activates the kinases that function to promote the events of the cycle. 150

cyst In protists and invertebrates, resting stage that contains reproductive bodies or embryos. 526, 591

cytokine Type of protein secreted by a T lymphocyte that attacks viruses, virally infected cells, and cancer cells. 768

cytokinesis Division of the cytoplasm following mitosis and meiosis. 145

cytokinin Plant hormone that promotes cell division; often works in combination with auxin during organ development in plant embryos. 692

cytoplasm Contents of a cell between the nucleus (nucleoid) region of bacteria and the plasma membrane. 60

cytosine (C) One of four nitrogen-containing bases in nucleotides composing the structure of DNA and RNA; pairs with guanine. 223

cytoskeleton Internal framework of the cell, consisting of microtubules, actin filaments, and intermediate filaments. 72

cytosol Semifluid medium between the nucleus and the plasma membrane. 60

cytotoxic T cell T lymphocyte that attacks and kills antigen-bearing cells. 768

datum (pl., data) Fact or piece of information collected through observation and/or experimentation. 10

day-neutral plant Plant whose flowering is not dependent on day length, i.e., tomato and cucumber. 694

deamination Removal of an amino group ($-NH_2$) from an amino acid or other organic compound. 139

decapod Type of crustacean in which the thorax bears five pairs of walking legs; includes shrimps, lobsters, crayfish, and crabs. 608

decomposition The breakdown of organic matter accompanied by the release of inorganic compounds; a means by which nutrients cycle in ecosystems. 423

deductive reasoning Process of logic and reasoning, using "if . . . then" statements. 9

delayed allergic response Allergic response initiated at the site of the allergen by sensitized T cells, involving macrophages and regulated by cytokines. 776

demographic transition Due to industrialization, a decline in the birthrate following a reduction in the death rate so that the population growth rate is lowered. 393

denatured Loss of an enzyme's normal shape so that it no longer functions; caused by a less than optimal pH and temperature. 47, 104

dendrite Part of a neuron that sends signals toward the cell body. 829

denitrification Conversion of nitrate or nitrite to nitrogen gas by bacteria in soil. 432

dense fibrous connective tissue Type of connective tissue containing many collagen fibers packed together; found in tendons and ligaments, for example. 726

density-dependent factor Biotic factor, such as disease and competition, that affects population size according to the population's density. 386

density-independent factor Abiotic factors, such as fire and flood, that affects population size independent of the population's density. 386

deoxyribose Pentose sugar found in DNA that has one less hydroxyl group than ribose. 37

dependent variable Result or change that occurs when an experimental variable is utilized in an experiment. 10

derived character Structural, physiological, or behavioral trait that is present in a specific lineage and is not present in the common ancestor for several lineages. 494

dermis In mammals, thick layer of the skin underlying the epidermis. 731

detrital food web Complex pattern of interlocking and crisscrossing food chains that begins with a population of detritivores. 427

detritivore Organism that feeds on freshly dead or partially decomposed organic matter. 423

detritus Organic matter produced by decomposition of substances such as tissues and animal wastes. 423

deuterostome Group of coelomate animals in which the second embryonic opening is associated with the mouth; the first embryonic opening, the blastopore, is associated with the anus. 598, 618

diaphragm In mammals, dome-shaped muscularized sheet separating the thoracic cavity from the abdominal cavity. 801

diarrhea Excessively frequent bowel movements. 791

diastole Relaxation period of a heart chamber during the cardiac cycle. 746

diatom Golden brown alga with a cell wall in two parts, or valves; significant part of phytoplankton. 533

dicotyledon Flowering plant group; members have two embryonic leaves, (cotyledons) net-veined leaves, cylindrical arrangement of vascular bundles, flower parts in fours or fives, and other characteristics. 573

diencephalon In vertebrates, portion of the brain in the region of the third ventricle that includes the thalamus and hypothalamus. 839

differentially permeable Ability of plasma membranes to regulate the passage of substances into and out of the cell, allowing some to pass through and preventing the passage of others. 84

diffusion Movement of molecules or ions from a region of higher to lower concentration; it requires no energy and tends to lead to an equal distribution. 85

dikaryotic Having two haploid nuclei that stem from different parent cells; during sexual reproduction sac and club fungi have dikaryotic cells. 545

dinoflagellate Photosynthetic unicellular protist, with two flagella, one whiplash and the other located within a groove between protective cellulose plates; significant part of phytoplankton. 533

diploid (2n) number Cell condition in which two of each type of chromosome are present. 145, 160

directional selection Outcome of natural selection in which an extreme phenotype is favored, usually in a changing environment. 306

disaccharide Sugar that contains two units of a monosaccharide; e.g., maltose. 37

disruptive selection Outcome of natural selection in which the two extreme phenotypes are favored over the average phenotype, leading to more than one distinct form. 308

distal convoluted tubule Final portion of a nephron that joins with a collecting duct; associated with tubular secretion. 816

DNA (deoxyribonucleic acid) Nucleic acid polymer produced from covalent bonding of nucleotide monomers that contain the sugar deoxyribose; the genetic material of nearly all organisms. 48, 220

DNA fingerprinting Using DNA fragment lengths, resulting from restriction enzyme cleavage, to identify particular individuals. 269

DNA ligase Enzyme that links DNA fragments; used during production of recombinant DNA to join foreign DNA to vector DNA. 266

DNA polymerase During replication, an enzyme that joins the nucleotides complementary to a DNA template. 226

DNA repair enzyme One of several enzymes that restore the original base sequence in an altered DNA strand. 229

DNA replication Synthesis of a new DNA double helix prior to mitosis and meiosis in eukaryotic cells and during prokaryotic fission in prokaryotic cells. 226

DNA-DNA hybridization Method to determine relatedness by allowing single DNA strands from two different species to join and thereafter observing how well they joined. 496

domain Largest of the categories, or taxa, used by taxonomists to group species; the three domains are Archaea, Bacteria, and Eukarya. 493

dominance hierarchy Organization of animals in a group that determines the order in which the animals have access to resources. 367

dominant allele Allele that exerts its phenotypic effect in the heterozygote; it masks the expression of the recessive allele. 177

dormancy In plants, a cessation of growth under conditions that seem appropriate for growth. 690

dorsal-root ganglion Mass of sensory neuron cell bodies located in the dorsal root of a spinal nerve. 834

double fertilization In flowering plants, one sperm fuses with the egg and a second sperm fuses with the polar nucleus of an embryo sac. 706

doubling time Number of years it takes for a population to double in size. 393

duodenum First part of the small intestine where chyme enters from the stomach. 788

e

ecological niche Role an organism plays in its community, including its habitat and its interactions with other organisms. 403

ecological pyramid Pictorial graph based on the biomass, number of organisms, or energy content of various trophic levels in a food web—from the producer to the final consumer populations. 427

ecological succession The gradual replacement of communities in an area following a disturbance (secondary succession) or the creation of new soil (primary succession). 414

ecology Study of the interactions of organisms with other organisms and with the physical and chemical environment. 378

ecosystem Biological community together with the associated abiotic environment; characterized by a flow of energy and a cycling of inorganic nutrients. 5, 378, 422

ectoderm Outermost primary tissue layer of an animal embryo that gives rise to the nervous system and the outer layer of the integument. 921

ectothermic Having a body temperature that varies according to the environmental temperature. 627

edema Swelling due to tissue fluid accumulation in the intercellular spaces. 760

edge effect Edges around a landscape patch have a slightly different habitat than favorable habitat in the interior of the patch. 481

effector Muscle or gland that receives signals from motor fibers and thereby allows an organism to respond to environmental stimuli. 825

electrocardiogram (ECG) Recording of the electrical activity associated with the heartbeat. 747

electromagnetic spectrum Solar radiation divided on the basis of wavelength, with gamma rays having the shortest wavelength and radio waves having the longest wavelength. 112

electron Negative subatomic particle, moving about in an energy level around the nucleus of an atom. 18

electron shells Concentric energy levels in which electrons orbit. 20

electron transport system Passage of electrons along a series of membrane-bounded carrier molecules from a higher to lower energy level; the energy released is used for the synthesis of ATP. 106, 116, 129

electronegativity The ability of an atom to attract electrons toward itself in a chemical bond. 24

element Substance that cannot be broken down into substances with different properties; composed of only one type atom. 18

elephantiasis A swelling of the limbs due to blockage of lymphatic vessels by parasitic filarial roundworms. 593

embryo Stage of a multicellular organism that develops from a zygote before it becomes free living; in seed plants the embryo is part of the seed. 706, 920

embryo sac Megagametophyte of flowering plants. 562, 706

embryonic disk During human development, flattened area during gastrulation from which the embryo arises. 932

embryonic period From approximately the second to the eighth week of human development, during which the major organ systems are organized. 930

emulsification Breaking up of fat globules into smaller droplets by the action of bile salts or any other emulsifier. 788

endergonic reaction Chemical reaction that requires an input of energy; opposite of exergonic reaction. 100

endocrine gland Ductless organ that secretes (a) hormone(s) into the bloodstream. 724

endocytosis Process by which substances are moved into the cell from the environment by phagocytosis (cellular eating) or pinocytosis (cellular drinking; includes receptor-mediated endocytosis). 90

endoderm Innermost primary tissue layer of an animal embryo that gives rise to the linings of the digestive tract and associated structures. 921

endodermis Internal plant root tissue forming a boundary between the cortex and the vascular cylinder. 649

endometrium Mucous membrane lining the interior surface of the uterus. 908

endoplasmic reticulum (ER) System of membranous saccules and channels in the cytoplasm, often with attached ribosomes. 67

endoskeleton Protective, internal skeleton, as in vertebrates. 864

endosperm In flowering plants, nutritive storage tissue that is derived from the fusion of a sperm cell and polar nuclei in the embryo sac. 706

endospore Spore formed within a cell; certain bacteria form endospores. 515

endosymbiotic hypothesis Possible explanation of the evolution of eukaryotic organelles by phagocytosis of prokaryotes. 64, 328

energy Capacity to do work and bring about change; occurs in a variety of forms. 3, 20, 98

energy of activation Energy that must be added in order for molecules to react with one another. 102

enterocoelom Body cavity that forms by the fusion of a pair of mesodermal pouches from the wall of the primitive gut. 597

entropy Measure of disorder or randomness. 98

environmental resistance Sum total of factors in the environment that limit the numerical increase of a population in a particular region. 381

enzymatic protein Protein that catalyzes a specific reaction. 83

enzyme Organic catalyst, usually a protein, that speeds up a reaction in cells due to its particular shape. 102

enzyme inhibition Means by which cells regulate enzyme activity; there is competitive and noncompetitive inhibition. 105

epidermis In mammals, the outer, protective layer of the skin; in plants, tissue that covers roots and leaves and stems of nonwoody organisms. 645, 731

epiglottis Structure that covers the glottis, the air-tract opening, during the process of swallowing. 803

epiphyte Plant that takes its nourishment from the air because its placement in other plants gives it an aerial position. 450, 671

epistasis Inheritance pattern in which one gene masks the expression of another gene that is at a different locus and is independently inherited. 189

epithelial tissue Tissue that lines hollow organs and covers surfaces. 724

esophagus Muscular tube for moving swallowed food from the pharynx to the stomach. 786

estrogen Female sex hormone that helps maintain sexual organs and secondary sexual characteristics. 909

estuary Portion of ocean located where a river enters and fresh water mixes with salt water. 458

ethylene Plant hormone that causes ripening of fruit and is also involved in abscission. 693

euchromatin Chromatin that is extended and accessible for transcription. 252

euglenoid Flagellated and flexible freshwater unicellular protists that usually contains chloroplasts and has a semirigid cell wall. 534

Eukarya One of the three domains of life consisting of organisms with eukaryotic cells and further classified into the kingdoms Protista, Fungi, Plantae, and Animalia. 502

eukaryotic cell Type of cell that has a membrane-bounded nucleus and membranous organelles; found in organisms within the domain Eukarya. 60

eutrophication Enrichment of water by inorganic nutrients used by phytoplankton; often overenrichment caused by human activities leading to excessive bacterial growth and oxygen depletion. 435, 456

evolution Descent of organisms from common ancestors with the development of genetic and phenotypic changes over time that make them more suited to the environment. 4, 283

excretion Elimination of metabolic wastes by an organism at exchange boundaries such as the plasma membrane of unicellular organisms and excretory tubules of multicellular animals. 811

exergonic reaction Chemical reaction that releases energy; opposite of endergonic reaction. 100

exocrine gland Gland that secretes its product to an epithelial surface directly or through ducts. 724

exon Coding segment of an eukaryotic gene that is expressed; exons are separated by introns. 239

exoskeleton Protective external skeleton, as in arthropods. 864

experiment Artificial situation devised to test a hypothesis. 9

experimental variable Component that is tested in an experiment by manipulating it and observing the results. 10

expiration Act of expelling air from the lungs; exhalation. 801

exponential growth Growth, particularly of a population, in which the increase occurs in the same manner as compound interest. 381

extinction Total disappearance of a species or higher group. 293, 329

extraembryonic membrane Membrane that is not a part of the embryo but is necessary to the continued existence and health of the embryo. 903, 930

f

facilitated transport Passive transfer of a substance into or out of a cell along a concentration gradient by a process that requires a carrier. 88

facultative anaerobe Prokaryote that is able to grow in either the presence or the absence of gaseous oxygen. 516

FAD Flavin adenine dinucleotide; a coenzyme of oxidation-reduction that becomes $FADH_2$ as oxidation of substrates occurs and then delivers electrons to the electron transport system in mitochondria during cellular respiration. 128

fall overturn Mixing process that occurs in fall in stratified lakes whereby the oxygen-rich top waters mix with nutrient-rich bottom waters. 456

falsify To show a hypothesis to be untrue. 10

family One of the categories, or taxa, used by taxonomists to group species; taxon above the genus level. 493

fat Organic molecule that contains glycerol and fatty acids and is found in adipose tissue of vertebrates. 40

fate map Diagram that traces the differentiation of cells during development from their origin to their final structure and function. 926

fatty acid Molecule that contains a hydrocarbon chain and ends with an acid group. 40

feather One of the light, horny epidermal outgrowths that form the external covering of the body of birds and the greater part of the surface of their wings. 632

fermentation Anaerobic breakdown of glucose that results in a gain of two ATP and end products such as alcohol and lactate. 129, 137

fertilization Fusion of sperm and egg nuclei producing a zygote which develops into a new individual. 706, 920

fibroblast Connective tissue cell that synthesizes fibers and ground substance. 726

fibrous root system In most monocots, a mass of similarly sized roots that cling to the soil. 650

filament End to end chains of cells that form as cell division occurs in only one plane; in plants, the elongated stalk of a stamen. 529, 701

fin In fish and other aquatic animals, membranous, winglike or paddlelike process used to propel, balance, or guide the body. 623

first messenger Chemical signal such as a peptide hormone that binds to a plasma membrane receptor and alters the metabolism of a cell because a second messenger is activated. 883

fitness Ability of an organism to reproduce and pass its genes to the next fertile generation; measured against the ability of other organisms to reproduce in the same environment. 288

five-kingdom system System of classification that contains the kingdoms Monera, Protista, Plantae, Animalia, and Fungi. 501

flagellum (pl., flagella) Slender, long extension used for locomotion by some bacteria, protozoans, and sperm. 60, 74, 514

flame cell Found along excretory tubules of planarians; functions in propulsion of fluid through the excretory canals and out of the body. 815

flower Reproductive organ of a flowering plant, consisting of several kinds of modified leaves arranged in concentric rings and attached to a modified stem called the receptacle. 700

fluid-mosaic model Model for the plasma membrane based on the changing location and pattern of protein molecules in a fluid phospholipid bilayer. 80

follicle Structure in the ovary of animals that contains an oocyte; site of oocyte production. 909

follicular phase First half of the ovarian cycle, during which the follicle matures and much estrogen (and some progesterone) is produced. 910

fontanel Membranous region located between certain cranial bones in the skull of a vertebrate fetus or infant. 868

food chain The order in which one population feeds on another in an ecosystem, thereby showing the flow of energy from a detritivore (detrital food chain) or producer (grazing food chain) to final consumer. 427

food web In ecosystems, complex pattern of interlocking and crisscrossing food chains. 427

foramen magnum Opening in the occipital bone of the vertebrate skull through which the spinal cord passes. 868

fossil Any past evidence of an organism that has been preserved in the earth's crust. 324

fossil fuel Fuels such as oil, coal, and natural gas that are the result of partial decomposition of plants and animals coupled with exposure to heat and pressure for millions of years. 430

founder effect Cause of genetic drift due to colonization by a limited number of individuals who, by chance, have different gene frequencies than the parent population. 306

fovea centralis Region of the retina consisting of densely packed cones that is responsible for the greatest visual acuity. 853

frameshift mutation Insertion or deletion of at least one base so that reading frame of the corresponding mRNA changes. 259

free energy Useful energy in a system that is capable of performing work. 100

fructose Hexose monosaccharide frequently found in fruits. 37

fruit Flowering plant structure consisting of one or more ripened ovaries that usually contain seeds. 573, 708

fruiting body Spore-producing and spore-disseminating structure found in sac and club fungi. 549

functional group A specific cluster of atoms attached to the carbon skeleton of organic molecules that enters into reactions and behaves in a predictable way. 35

fungus Saprotrophic decomposer; the body is made up of filaments called hyphae that form a mass called a mycelium. 544

g

gallbladder Organ attached to the liver that serves to store and concentrate bile. 788

gametangia Multicellular sex organs; plants, but not green algae, have gametangia. 559

gamete Haploid sex cell; e.g., egg and sperm. 160

gametophyte Haploid generation of the alternation of generations life cycle of a plant; produces gametes that unite to form a diploid zygote. 559, 700

ganglion Collection or bundle of neuron cell bodies usually outside the central nervous system. 834

gap analysis Use of computers to discover places where biodiversity is high outside of preserved areas. 481

gap junction Junction between cells formed by the joining of two adjacent plasma membranes; it lends strength and allows ions, sugars, and small molecules to pass between cells. 93

gastrovascular cavity Blind digestive cavity in animals that have a sac body plan. 584

gastrula Stage of animal development during which the germ layers form, at least in part, by invagination. 921

gene Unit of heredity existing as alleles on the chromosomes; in diploid organisms typically two alleles are inherited—one from each parent. 4

gene flow Sharing of genes between two populations through interbreeding. 304

gene locus Specific location of a particular gene on homologous chromosomes. 177

gene pool Total of all the genes of all the individuals in a population. 302

gene therapy Correction of a detrimental mutation by the addition of new DNA and its insertion in a genome. 275

genetic disorder An abnormal phenotype often resulting in a medical condition. 207

genetic drift Mechanism of evolution due to random changes in the allelic frequencies of a population; more likely to occur in small populations or when only a few individuals of a large population reproduce. 305

genetic engineering Alteration of genomes for medical or industrial purposes. 229, 258, 270

genetic mutation Altered gene whose sequence of bases differs from the previous sequence. 229

genome Full set of genetic information within an organism or a virus. 251, 267

genomic imprinting Inheritance pattern that differs depending upon the sex of the parent passing it on. 208

genomic library Collection of engineered bacteriophages or viruses that together carry all of the genes of the species. 267

genotype Genes of an organism for a particular trait or traits; often designated by letters, for example, *BB* or *Aa*. 177

genus One of the categories, or taxa, used by taxonomists to group species; contains those species that are most closely related through evolution. 493

geological timescale History of the earth based on correlations between rocks (or the fossils contained in them) and time periods of the past. 326

germ layer Primary tissue layer of a vertebrate embryo; namely, ectoderm, mesoderm, or endoderm. 921

germination Beginning of growth of a seed, spore, or zygote, especially after a period of dormancy. 694

gibberellin Plant hormone promoting increased stem growth; also involved in flowering and seed germination. 690

gill Respiratory organ in most aquatic animals; in fish, an outward extension of the pharynx. 619, 799

girdling Removing a strip of bark from around a tree. 678

global warming Predicted increase in the earth's temperature, due to human activities that promote the greenhouse effect. 430, 478

glomerular capsule Cuplike structure that is the initial portion of a nephron. 816

glomerular filtration Movement of small molecules from the glomerulus into the glomerular capsule due to the action of blood pressure. 818

glomerulus Capillary network within a glomerular capsule of a nephron. 817

glottis Opening for airflow in the larynx. 802

glucose Six-carbon sugar that organisms degrade as a source of energy during cellular respiration. 37

glycerol Three-carbon carbohydrate with three hydroxyl groups attached that is a component of fats and oils. 40

glycogen Storage polysaccharide, found in animals, that is composed of glucose molecules joined in a linear fashion but having numerous branches. 38

glycolipid Lipid in plasma membranes that bears a carbohydrate chain attached to a hydrophobic tail. 81

glycolysis Anaerobic breakdown of glucose that results in a gain of two ATP and the end product pyruvate. 129, 130

glycoprotein Protein in plasma membranes that bears a carbohydrate chain. 82

gnathostome Jawed vertebrates; includes jawed fishes and all tetrapods. 623

Golgi apparatus Organelle consisting of saccules and vesicles that processes, packages, and distributes molecules about or from the cell. 68

gonad Organ that produces gametes; the ovary produces eggs, and the testis produces sperm. 896, 902

granum Stack of chlorophyll-containing thylakoids in a chloroplast. 71, 114

gravitropism Growth response of roots and stems of plants to the earth's gravity; roots demonstrate positive gravitropism, and stems demonstrate negative gravitropism. 685

gray crescent Gray area that appears in an amphibian egg after being fertilized by the sperm, thought to contain chemical signals that turn on the genes that control development. 925

gray matter Nonmyelinated axons and cell bodies in the central nervous system. 838

grazing food web Complex pattern of interlocking and crisscrossing food chains that begins with a population of photosynthesizers serving as a producer. 427

green alga Member of a diverse group of photosynthetic protists that contains chlorophylls *a* and *b* and has other biochemical characteristics like those of plants. 528

greenhouse effect Reradiation of solar heat toward the earth, caused by gases such as carbon dioxide, methane, nitrous oxide, water vapor, ozone, and nitrous oxide in the atmosphere. 431

ground tissue Tissue that constitutes most of the body of a plant; consists of parenchyma, collenchyma, and sclerenchyma cells which function in storage, basic metabolism, and support. 645

growth factor Chemical messenger that promotes the growth of development of particular types of cells. 260

guanine (G) One of four nitrogen-containing bases in nucleotides composing the structure of DNA and RNA; pairs with cytosine. 223

guard cell One of two cells that surround a leaf stomate; changes in the turgor pressure of these cells cause the stomate to open or close. 676

guttation Liberation of water droplets from the edges and tips of leaves. 674

gymnosperm Type of woody seed plant in which the seeds are not enclosed by fruit and are usually borne in cones such as those of the conifers. 568

h

habitat Place where an organism lives and is able to survive and reproduce. 378, 403

habitat corridor Strips of land that allow organisms to move from one fragment of an ecosystem to another or one ecosystem to another. 471

halophile Type of archaea that lives in extremely salty habitats. 520

haploid (n) number Cell condition in which only one of each type of chromosome is present. 145, 160

Hardy-Weinberg law Law stating that the gene frequencies in a population remain stable if evolution does not occur due to nonrandom mating, selection, migration, and genetic drift. 302

heart Muscular organ whose contraction causes blood to circulate in the body of an animal. 744

helper T cell Secretes lymphokines, which stimulate all kinds of immune cells. 768

heme Iron-containing group found in hemoglobin. 805

hemocoel Residual coelom found in arthropods that is filled with hemolymph. 609

hemoglobin Iron-containing respiratory pigment occurring in vertebrate red blood cells and in blood plasma of some invertebrates. 763, 805

hemolymph Circulatory fluid which is a mixture of blood and interstitial fluid; seen in animals that have an open circulatory system, such as molluscs and arthropods. 741

herbaceous plant Plant that lacks persistent woody tissue. 572, 652

herbivore Primary consumer in a grazing food chain; a plant eater. 423

hermaphroditic Type of animal that has both male and female sex organs. 589

heterochromatin Highly compacted chromatin that is not accessible for transcription. 252

heterotroph Organism that cannot synthesize organic compounds from inorganic substances and therefore must take in organic food. 423

heterozygous Possessing unlike alleles for a particular trait. 177

hexose Six-carbon sugar. 37

histamine Substance, produced by basophils in blood and mast cells in connective tissue, that causes capillaries to dilate. 762

HLA (human leukocyte associated) antigen Protein in a plasma membrane that identifies the cell as belonging to a particular individual and acts as an antigen in other organisms. 768

holozoic Obtaining nourishment by ingesting solid food particles. 537

homeobox 180 nucleotide sequence located in all homeotic genes. 929

homeostasis Maintenance of normal internal conditions in a cell or an organism by means of self-regulating mechanisms. 3, 734

homeothermic Maintenance of a uniform body temperature independent of the environmental temperature. 632

homeotic genes Genes that control the overall body plan by controlling the fate of groups of cells during development. 928

Homo sapiens Modern humans. 353

homologous chromosome Member of a pair of chromosomes that are alike and come together in synapsis during prophase of the first meiotic division; a homologue. 160

homologous structure In evolution, a structure that is similar in different types of organisms because these organisms are derived from a common ancestor. 296, 495

homologue Member of a homologous pair of chromosomes. 160

homozygous Possessing two identical alleles for a particular trait. 177

horizons A major layer of soil visible in vertical profile; topsoil is the A horizon. 669

hormone Chemical messenger produced in one part of the body that controls the activity of other parts. 688, 882

host Organism that provides nourishment and/or shelter for a parasite. 410

human chorionic gonadotropin (HCG) Gonadotropin hormone produced by the chorion that functions to maintain the uterine lining. 932

human immunodeficiency virus (HIV) Virus responsible for AIDS. 914

humus Decomposing organic matter in the soil. 668

hybridization Crossing of different species. 714

hydrogen bond Weak bond that arises between a slightly positive hydrogen atom of one molecule and a slightly negative atom of another molecule or between parts of the same molecule. 24

hydrogen ion Hydrogen atom that has lost its electron and therefore bears a positive charge (H^+). 28

hydrolysis Splitting of a compound by the addition of water, with the H^+ being incorporated in one fragment and the OH^- in the other. 36

hydrophilic Type of molecule that interacts with water by dissolving in water and/or by forming hydrogen bonds with water molecules. 26, 35

hydrophobic Type of molecule that does not interact with water because it is nonpolar. 35

hydroponics Technique for growing plants by suspending them with their roots in a nutrient solution. 666

hydrostatic skeleton Fluid-filled body compartment which provides support for muscle contraction resulting in movement; seen in cnidarians, flatworms, roundworms, and segmented worms. 864

hydrothermal vent Hot springs in the sea floor along ocean ridges where heated seawater and sulfate react to produce hydrogen sulfide; here chemosynthetic bacteria support a community of varied organisms. 463

hydroxide ion One of two ions that results when a water molecule dissociates; it has gained an electron and therefore bears a negative charge (OH^-). 28

hypertonic solution Higher solute concentration (less water) than the cytosol of a cell; causes cell to lose water by osmosis. 87

hypha (pl., hyphae) Filament of the vegetative body of a fungus. 544

hypothalamus In vertebrates, part of the brain that helps regulate the internal environment of the body; for example, involved in control of heart rate, body temperature, water balance. 839, 886

hypothesis Supposition that is established by reasoning after consideration of available evidence; it can be tested by obtaining more data, often by experimentation. 9

hypotonic solution Lower solute (more water) concentration than the cytosol of a cell; causes cell to gain water by osmosis. 86

i

immediate allergic response Allergic response that occurs within seconds of contact with an allergen, caused by the attachment of the allergen to IgE antibodies. 776

immunity Ability of the body to protect itself from foreign substances and cells, including disease-causing agents. 762

immunization Strategy for achieving immunity to the effects of specific disease-causing agents. 772

immunoglobulin (Ig) Globular plasma protein that functions as an antibody. 766

implantation In placental mammals, the embedding of an embryo at the blastocyst stage into the endometrium of the uterus. 930

imprinting Learning to make a particular response to only one type of animal or object. 365

inclusive fitness Fitness that results from personal reproduction and from helping nondescendant relatives reproduce. 372

incomplete dominance Inheritance pattern in which the offspring has an intermediate phenotype as when a red-flowered plant and a white-flowered plant produce pink-flowered offspring. 188

incomplete gut Digestive tract that has a single opening, usually called a mouth. 782

independent assortment Alleles of unlinked genes segregate independently of each other during meiosis so that the gametes contain all possible combinations of alleles. 163

induced-fit model Change in the shape of an enzyme's active site which enhances the fit between the enzyme's active site and its substrate(s). 103

inducer Molecule that brings about activity of an operon by joining with a repressor and preventing it from binding to the operator. 250

induction Ability of a chemical or a tissue to influence the development of another tissue. 925

inductive reasoning Using specific observations and the process of logic and reasoning to arrive at a hypothesis. 9

industrial melanism Increased frequency of darkly pigmented (melanic) forms in a population when soot and pollution make lightly pigmented forms easier for predators to see against a pigmented background. 303

inflammatory reaction Tissue response to injury that is characterized by redness, swelling, pain, and heat. 762

inheritance of acquired characteristics Lamarckian belief that characteristics acquired during the lifetime of an organism can be passed on to offspring. 284

inorganic molecule Type of molecule that is not an organic molecule; not derived from a living organism. 34

insect Type of arthropod, the head has antennae, compound eyes, and simple eyes; a thorax has three pairs of legs and often wings; and an abdomen has internal organs. 611

inspiration Act of taking air into the lungs; inhalation. 801

interferon Antiviral agent produced by an infected cell that blocks the infection of another cell. 764

interleukin Cytohine produced by macrophages and T lymphocytes that functions as a metabolic regulator of the immune response. 773

interneuron Neuron, located within the central nervous system, conveying messages between parts of the central nervous system. 829

internode In vascular plants, the region of a stem between two successive nodes. 643

interphase Stages of the cell cycle (G$_1$, S, G$_2$) during which growth and DNA synthesis occur when the nucleus is not actively dividing. 150

interspecific competition Similar species trying to occupy the same niche in an ecosystem compete with one another for a share of resources and in this way the number of niches increases. 404

intestinal enzymes Enzymes, produced by the epithelial cells on the surface of villi, which function in the digestion of small organic molecules. 788

intrinsic rate of natural increase Maximum per capita rate of population increase under ideal conditions. 380

intron Noncoding region of an eukaryotic gene; introns are transcribed but removed from mRNA before mRNA leaves the nucleus. 239

invertebrate Referring to an animal without a serial arrangement of vertebrae. 580

ion Charged particle that carries a negative or positive charge. 22

ionic bond Chemical bond in which ions are attracted to one another by opposite charges. 22

isogamy Sexual reproduction by means of gametes that look alike; there is no definite egg and sperm. 528

isomer Molecules with the same molecular formula but different structure, and therefore shape. 35

isotonic solution Solution that is equal in solute concentration to that of the cytosol of a cell; causes cell to neither lose nor gain water by osmosis. 86

isotopes Atoms having the same atomic number but a different atomic mass due to the number of neutrons. 19

j

jaw Tooth-bearing bone of the head. 623

jawless fish Type of fish that has no jaws, includes today's hagfishes and lampreys. 622

joint Articulation between two bones of a skeleton. 871

jointed appendages Freely moving appendages of arthropods. 606

k

k-selection A favorable life-history strategy under stable environmental conditions characterized by the production of a few offspring with much attention given to offspring survival. 391

karyotype Chromosomes arranged by pairs according to their size, shape, and general appearance in mitotic metaphase. 202

keystone species Species whose activities have a significant role in determining community structure. 480

kidney One of the paired organs of the vertebrate urinary system that regulates the chemical composition of the blood and produces a waste product called urine. 816

kinase Any one of several enzymes that phosphorylate their substrates. 150

kinetic energy Energy associated with motion. 98

kingdom One of the categories, or taxa, used by taxonomists to group species; taxon above phylum (in animals) and division (in plants). 493

kinin Chemical mediator, released by damaged tissue cells and mast cells, which causes the capillaries to dilate and become more permeable. 762

Krebs cycle Cycle of reactions in mitochondria that begins with citric acid; it breaks down an acetyl group and produces CO_2, ATP, NADH, and FADH$_2$; also called the citric acid cycle. 129

l

lactation Secretion of milk by mammary glands usually for the nourishment of an infant. 912

lacteal Lymphatic vessel in an intestinal villus, it aids in the absorption of fats. 789

lactose Disaccharide that contains galactose and glucose; found in milk. 37

lacuna Small pit or hollow cavity, as in bone or cartilage, where a cell or cells are located. 727

ladderlike nervous system In planarians, two lateral nerve cords joined by transverse nerves. 827

landscape A number of interacting ecosystems. 471

large intestine In vertebrates, portion of the digestive tract that follows the small intestine; in humans, consists of the cecum, colon, rectum, and anal canal. 791

larva Immature form in the life cycle of some animals; it sometimes undergoes metamorphosis to become the adult form. 903

larynx Cartilaginous organ located between the pharynx and the trachea; in humans, contains the vocal cords; voice box. 802

lateral line Canal system containing sensory receptors that allow fishes and amphibians to detect water currents and pressure waves from nearby objects. 859

law Theory that is generally accepted by an overwhelming number of scientists. 12

leaf Lateral appendage of a stem, highly variable in structure, often containing cells that carry out photosynthesis. 643

leaf vein Vascular tissue within a leaf. 646

learning Relatively permanent change in an animal's behavior that results from practice and experience. 364

leech Blood-sucking annelid, usually found in fresh water, with a sucker at each end of a segmented body. 606

lens Clear membranelike structure found in the vertebrate eye behind the iris; brings objects into focus. 852

less-developed country (LDC) Country which is becoming industrialized; typically population growth is expanding rapidly and the majority of people live in poverty. 393

lichen Symbiotic relationship between certain fungi and algae, in which the fungi possibly provide inorganic food or water and the algae provide organic food. 519, 553

life cycle Recurring pattern of genetically programmed events by which individuals grow, develop, maintain themselves, and reproduce. 168

ligament Tough cord or band of dense fibrous tissue that binds bone to bone at a joint. 726, 871

light-dependent reactions Portion of photosynthesis that captures solar energy and takes place in thylakoid membranes of chloroplasts; it produces ATP and NADPH. 114

light-independent reactions Portion of photosynthesis that takes place in the stroma of chloroplasts and can occur in the dark; it uses the products of the light-dependent reactions to reduce carbon dioxide to a carbohydrate. 114

limbic system In humans, functional association of various brain centers including the amygdala and hippocampus; governs learning and memory and various emotions such as pleasure, fear, and happiness. 841

limiting factor Resource or environmental condition that restricts the abundance and distribution of an organism. 379

linkage group Alleles of different genes that are located on the same chromosome and tend to be inherited together. 194

lipase Fat-digesting enzyme secreted by the pancreas. 788

lipid Class of organic compounds that tends to be soluble in nonpolar solvents such as alcohol; includes fats and oils. 40

liposome Droplet of phospholipid molecules formed in a liquid environment. 322

littoral zone Shore zone between high-tide mark and low-tide mark; also shallow water of a lake where light penetrates to the bottom. 459

liver Large dark red internal organ that produces urea and bile, detoxifies the blood, stores glycogen, and produces the plasma proteins among other functions. 788

logistic growth Population increase that results in an S-shaped curve; growth is slow at first, steepens, and then levels off due to environmental resistance. 382

long-day plant Plant which flowers when day length is longer than a critical length, i.e., wheat, barley, clover, spinach. 694

loop of the nephron Portion of a nephron between the proximal and distal convoluted tubules; function in water reabsorption. 816

loose fibrous connective tissue Tissue composed mainly of fibroblasts widely separated by a matrix containing collagen and elastic fibers. 726

lung Internal respiratory organ containing moist surfaces for gas exchange. 627, 801

luteal phase Second half of the ovarian cycle, during which the corpus luteum develops and much progesterone (and some estrogen) is produced. 910

lymph Fluid, derived from tissue fluid, that is carried in lymphatic vessels. 755, 760

lymph nodes Mass of lymphoid tissue located along the course of a lymphatic vessel. 760

lymphatic vessel Vessel that carries lymph. 760

lymphocyte Specialized white blood cell that functions in specific defense; occurs in two forms—T lymphocyte and B lymphocyte. 753

lymphoid organ Organ other than a lymphatic vessel that is part of the lymphatic system; includes lymph nodes, tonsils, spleen, thymus gland, and bone marrow. 760

lysogenic cycle Bacteriophage life cycle in which the virus incorporates its DNA into that of a bacterium; occurs preliminary to the lytic cycle. 511

lysosome Membrane-bounded vesicle that contains hydrolytic enzymes for digesting macromolecules. 69

lytic cycle Bacteriophage life cycles in which the virus takes over the operation of the bacterium immediately upon entering it and subsequently destroys the bacterium. 510

m

macroevolution Large-scale evolutionary change; e.g., the formation of new species. 324

macronutrient Essential element needed in large amounts for plant growth such as nitrogen, calcium, sulfur. 666

macrophage In vertebrates, large phagocytic cell derived from a monocyte that ingests microbes and debris. 753, 762

Malpighian tubule Blind, threadlike excretory tubule near the anterior end of an insect hindgut. 611, 815

maltose Disaccharide composed of two glucose molecules; found in the human digestive tract as a result of starch digestion. 37

mammal Homeothermic vertebrate characterized especially by the presence of hair and mammary glands. 634

mantle In molluscs an extension of the body wall which may secrete a shell. 600

mass extinction Episode of large-scale extinction in which large numbers of species disappear in a few million years or less. 329

mast cell A connective tissue cell that releases histamine in allergic reactions. 762

matrix Unstructured semifluid substance that fills the space between cells in connective tissues or inside organelles. 71

matter Anything that takes up space and has mass. 18

mechanoreceptor Sensory receptor that responds to mechanical stimuli, such as that from pressure, sound waves, and gravity. 856

medulla oblongata In vertebrates, part of the brain stem that is continuous with the spinal cord; controls heartbeat, blood pressure, breathing, and other vital functions. 839

megagametophyte In seed plants, the gametophyte that produces an egg; in flowering plants, an embryo sac. 703

megaspore One of the two types of spores produced by seed plants; develops into a megagametophyte (embryo sac). 568, 700

megasporocyte Megaspore mother cell; produces megaspores by meiosis; only one megaspore persists. 703

meiosis Type of nuclear division that occurs as part of sexual reproduction in which the daughter cells receive the haploid number of chromosomes in varied combinations. 160

memory Capacity of the brain to store and retrieve information about past sensations and perceptions; essential to learning. 841

meninges Protective membranous coverings about the central nervous system. 838

menses Flow of blood during menstruation. 910

menstruation Periodic shedding of tissue and blood from the inner lining of the uterus in primates. 910

meristem Undifferentiated embryonic tissue in the active growth regions of plants. 712

mesoderm Middle primary tissue layer of an animal embryo that gives rise to muscle, several internal organs, and connective tissue layers. 645, 921

mesoglea Jellylike layer between the epidermis and the gastrodermis of a cnidarian. 584

mesophyll Inner, thickest layer of a leaf consisting of palisade and spongy mesophyll; the site of most of photosynthesis. 658

messenger RNA (mRNA) Type of RNA formed from a DNA template and bearing coded information for the amino acid sequence of a polypeptide. 236

metabolic pathway Series of linked reactions, beginning with a particular reactant and terminating with an end product. 102

metabolic pool Metabolites that are the products of and/or the substrates for key reactions in cells, allowing one type of molecule to be changed into another type, such as the conversion of carbohydrates to fats. 139

metabolism All of the chemical reactions that occur in a cell during growth and repair. 3, 100

metamorphosis Change in shape and form that some animals, such as insects, undergo during development. 607, 903

metapopulation Population subdivided into several small and isolated populations due to habitat fragmentation. 480

metastasis Spread of cancer from the place of origin throughout the body; caused by the ability of cancer cells to migrate and invade tissues. 153

methanogen Type of archaea that lives in oxygen-free habitats, such as swamps, and releases methane gas. 520

microevolution Change in gene frequencies between populations of a species over time. 302

microgametophyte In seed plants, the gametophyte that produces sperm; a pollen grain. 703

micronutrient Essential element needed in small amounts for plant growth such as boron, copper, and zinc. 666

microsphere Formed from proteinoids exposed to water; has properties similar to today's cells. 321

microspore One of the two types of spores produced by seed plants; develops into a microgametophyte (pollen grain). 568, 700

microsporocyte Microspore mother cell; produces microspores by meiosis. 703

microtubule Small cylindrical organelle composed of tubulin protein about an empty central core; present in the cytoplasm, centrioles, cilia, and flagella. 72

microvillus Cylindrical process that extends from an epithelial cell of a villus and serves to increase the surface area of the cell. 788

midbrain In mammals, part of the brain located below the thalamus and above the pons. 839

mimicry Superficial resemblance of two or more species; a mechanism that avoids predation by appearing to be noxious. 409

mineral Naturally occurring inorganic substance containing two or more elements; certain minerals are needed in the diet. 666, 793

mitochondrion Membrane-bounded organelle in which ATP molecules are produced during the process of cellular respiration. 70, 132

mitosis Process in which a parent nucleus produces two daughter nuclei, each having the same number and kinds of chromosomes as the parent nucleus. 145

molecular clock Idea that the rate at which mutational changes accumulate in certain genes is constant over time and is not involved in adaptation to the environment. 329, 497

molecule Union of two or more atoms of the same element; also the smallest part of a compound that retains the properties of the compound. 22

molt Periodic shedding of the exoskeleton in arthropods. 606

monoclonal antibody One of many antibodies produced by a clone of hybridoma cells which all bind to the same antigen. 774

monocotyledon Flowering plant group; members have one embryonic leaf, parallel-veined leaves, scattered vascular bundles, and other characteristics. 573

monomer Small molecule that is a subunit of a polymer; e.g., glucose is a monomer of starch. 36

monosaccharide Simple sugar; a carbohydrate that cannot be decomposed by hydrolysis; e.g., glucose. 37

monotreme Egg-laying mammal—for example, duckbill platypus and spiny anteater. 634

monsoon Climate in India and southern Asia caused by wet ocean winds that blow onshore for almost half the year. 443

more-developed country (MDC) Country that is industrialized; typically population growth is low and the people enjoy a good standard of living. 393

morphogen Protein that is part of a gradient which influences morphogenesis. 928

morphogenesis Emergence of shape in tissues, organs, or entire embryo during development. 924

morula Spherical mass of cells resulting from cleavage during animal development prior to the blastula stage. 921

mosaic evolution Concept that human characteristics did not evolve at the same rate; e.g., some body parts are more humanlike than others in early hominids. 348

motor molecule Protein that moves along either actin filaments or microtubules and translocates organelles. 72

motor neuron Nerve cell that conducts nerve impulses away from the central nervous system and innervates effectors (muscle and glands). 829

mouth In humans, organ of the digestive tract where food is chewed and mixed with saliva. 785

multiple allele Inheritance pattern in which there are more than two alleles for a particular trait; each individual has only two of all possible alleles. 190, 210

multiregional continuity hypothesis Proposal that modern humans evolved separately in at least three different places: Asia, Africa, and Europe. 353

muscular (contractile) tissue Type of animal tissue composed of fibers that shorten and lengthen to produce movements. 728

mutation Alteration in chromosome structure or number and also an alteration in a gene due to a change in DNA composition. 196

mutualism Symbiotic relationship in which both species benefit in terms of growth and reproduction. 412

mycelium Tangled mass of hyphal filaments composing the vegetative body of a fungus. 544

mycorrhiza (pl., mycorrhizae) Mutualistic relationship between fungal hyphae and roots of vascular plants. 554, 671

myelin sheath White, fatty material—derived from the membrane of neurolemmocytes—that forms a covering for nerve fibers. 829

myofibril Specific muscle cell organelle containing a linear arrangement of sarcomeres, which shorten to produce muscle contraction. 875

myoglobin Pigmented molecule in muscle tissue that stores oxygen. 875

myosin Muscle protein making up the thick filaments in a sarcomere; it pulls actin to shorten the sarcomere, yielding muscle contraction. 875

n

NAD$^+$ (nicotinamide adenine dinucleotide) Coenzyme of oxidation-reduction that accepts electrons and hydrogen ions to become NADH + H$^+$ as oxidation of substrates occurs; during cellular respiration, NADH carries electrons to the electron transport system in mitochondria. 106, 128

NADP$^+$ (nicotinamide adenine dinucleotide phosphate) Coenzyme of oxidation-reduction that accepts electrons and hydrogen ions to become NADPH + H$^+$. During photosynthesis NADPH participates in the reduction of carbon dioxide to glucose. 106

natural killer (NK) cell Lymphocyte that causes an infected or cancerous cell to burst. 764

natural selection Mechanism of evolution caused by environmental selection of organisms most fit to reproduce; results in adaptation to the environment. 4, 288, 306

negative feedback Mechanism of homeostatic response by which the output of a system suppresses or inhibits activity of the system. 734, 885

nematocyst In cnidarians, a capsule that contains a threadlike fiber whose release aids in the capture of prey. 584

nephridium Segmentally arranged, paired excretory tubules of many invertebrates, as in the earthworm. 604, 815

nephron Microscopic kidney unit that regulates blood composition by glomerular filtration, tubular reabsorption, and tubular secretion. 816

nerve Bundle of long axons outside the central nervous system. 834

nerve cord In many complex animals, a centrally placed cord of nervous tissue that receives sensory information and exercises motor control. 619

nerve net Diffuse noncentralized arrangement of nerve cells in cnidarians. 584, 827

nervous tissue Tissue that contains nerve cells (neurons), which conduct impulses, and neuroglial cells, which support, protect, and provide nutrients to neurons. 728

neural plate Region of the dorsal surface of the chordate embryo that marks the future location of the neural tube. 923

neural tube Tube formed by closure of the neural groove during development. In vertebrates, the neural tube develops into the spinal cord and brain. 923

neuroglia Nonconducting nerve cells that are intimately associated with neurons and function in a supportive capacity. 728, 829

neurolemmocyte Type of neuroglial cell that forms a myelin sheath around axons; also called Schwann cell. 829

neuromuscular junction Region where an axon bulb approaches a muscle fiber; contains a presynaptic membrane, a synaptic cleft, and a postsynaptic membrane. 876

neuron Nerve cell that characteristically has three parts: dendrites, cell body, and axon. 728, 829

neurotransmitter Chemical stored at the ends of axons that is responsible for transmission across a synapse. 833

neutron Neutral subatomic particle, located in the nucleus and having a weight of approximately one atomic mass unit. 18

neutrophil Granular leukocyte that is the most abundant of the white blood cells; first to respond to infection. 753

nitrification Process by which nitrogen in ammonia and organic compounds is oxidized to nitrites and nitrates by soil bacteria. 432

nitrogen cycle Continuous process by which nitrogen circulates in the air, soil, water, and organisms of the biosphere. 432

nitrogen fixation Process whereby free atmospheric nitrogen is converted into compounds, such as ammonium and nitrates, usually by bacteria. 432

node In plants, the place where one or more leaves attach to a stem. 643

noncyclic electron pathway Portion of the light-dependent reaction of photosynthesis that involves both photosystem I and photosystem II. It generates both ATP and NADPH. 117

nondisjunction Failure of homologous chromosomes or daughter chromosomes to separate during meiosis I and meiosis II respectively. 203

nonpolar covalent bond Bond in which the sharing of electrons between atoms is fairly equal. 24

nonrandom mating Mating among individuals on the basis of their phenotypic similarities or differences rather than mating on a random basis. 305

nonseptate Lacking cell walls; some fungal species have hyphae that are nonseptate. 545

nonvascular plant Bryophytes such as mosses and liverworts that have no vascular tissue and either occur in moist locations or have special adaptations for living in dry locations. 559

norepinephrine (NE) Neurotransmitter of the postganglionic fibers in the sympathetic division of the autonomic system; also a hormone produced by the adrenal medulla. 833

notochord Cartilaginous-like supportive dorsal rod in all chordates sometime in their life cycle; is replaced by vertebrae in vertebrates. 619, 923

nuclear envelope Double membrane that surrounds the nucleus in eukaryotic cells and is connected to the endoplasmic reticulum; has pores that allow substances to pass between the nucleus and the cytoplasm. 65

nuclear pore Opening in the nuclear envelope which permits the passage of proteins into the nucleus and ribosomal subunits out of the nucleus. 65

nucleic acid Polymer of nucleotides; both DNA and RNA are nucleic acids. 48, 220

nucleoid Region of prokaryotic cells where DNA is located; it is not bounded by a nuclear envelope. 60, 144, 514

nucleolus Dark-staining, spherical body in the nucleus that produces ribosomal subunits. 65

nucleoplasm Semifluid medium of the nucleus, containing chromatin. 65

nucleotide Monomer of DNA and RNA consisting of a five-carbon sugar bonded to a nitrogenous base and a phosphate group. 48, 220

nucleus Membrane-bounded organelle within a eukaryotic cell that contains chromosomes and controls the structure and function of the cell. 65

O

obligate anaerobe Prokaryote unable to grow in the presence of free oxygen. 516

ocean ridge Ridge on the ocean floor where oceanic crust forms and from which it moves laterally in each direction. 321

octet rule An atom other than hydrogen tends to form bonds until it has eight electrons in its outer shell; an atom that already has eight electrons in its outer shell does not react and is inert. 21

olfactory cell Modified neuron that is a sensory receptor for the sense of smell. 848

omnivore Organism in a food chain that feeds on both plants and animals. 423

oncogene Cancer-causing gene. 260

oocyte Immature egg that is undergoing meiosis; upon completion of meiosis the oocyte becomes an egg. 908

oogamy Sexual reproduction in which the gametes are dissimilar; the egg is large and nonmotile and the sperm is small and motile. 528

oogenesis Production of eggs in females by the process of meiosis and maturation. 168

operant conditioning Learning that results from rewarding or reinforcing a particular behavior. 364

operator In an operon the sequence of DNA that binds tightly to a repressor and thereby regulates the expression of structural genes. 248

operon Group of structural and regulating genes that functions as a single unit. 248

orbital Volume of space around a nucleus where electrons can be found most of the time. 21

order One of the categories, or taxa, used by taxonomists to group species; taxon above the family level. 493

organ Combination of two or more different tissues performing a common function. 642, 724, 730

organ system Group of related organs working together. 730

organelle Small, often membranous structure in the cytoplasm having a specific structure and function. 61

organic molecule Type of molecule that contains carbon and hydrogen; it may also have oxygen attached to the carbon(s). 34

orgasm Physiological and psychological sensations that occur at the climax of sexual stimulation. 905

osmosis Diffusion of water through a differentially permeable membrane. 86

osmotic pressure Measure of the tendency of water to move across a differentially permeable membrane; visible as an increase in liquid on the side of the membrane with higher solute concentration. 86

ossicle One of the small bones of the vertebrate middle ear—malleus, incus, stapes. 856

osteoblast Bone-forming cell. 866

osteoclast Cell that causes erosion of bone. 866

osteocyte Mature bone cell located within the lacunae of bone. 866

ostracoderm Earliest vertebrate fossils of the Cambrian and Devonian periods, these fishes were small, jawless, and finless. 622

otolith Calcium carbonate granule associated with sensory receptors for detecting movement of the head; in vertebrates, located in the utricle and saccule. 859

out-of-Africa hypothesis Proposal that modern humans originated only in Africa; then they migrated and supplanted populations of *Homo* in Asia and Europe about 100,000 years ago. 353

ovarian cycle Monthly changes occurring in the ovary that determine the level of sex hormones in the blood. 909

ovary Female gonad in animals that produces an egg and female sex hormones; in flowering plants, the enlarged ovule-bearing portion of the pistil which develops into a fruit. 573, 701, 902

ovulation Bursting of a follicle when a secondary oocyte is released from the ovary; if fertilization occurs the secondary oocyte becomes an egg. 909

ovule In seed plants, a structure that contains the megagametophyte and has the potential to develop into a seed. 560, 701

ovum Haploid egg cell which is usually fertilized by a sperm to form a diploid zygote. 909

oxidation Loss of one or more electrons from an atom or molecule; in biological systems, generally the loss of hydrogen atoms. 106

oxidative phosphorylation Process by which ATP production is tied to an electron transport system that uses oxygen as the final acceptor; occurs in mitochondria. 134

oxygen debt Amount of oxygen required to oxidize lactic acid produced anaerobically during strenuous muscle activity. 137, 875

oxyhemoglobin Compound formed when oxygen combines with hemoglobin. 805

ozone shield Accumulation of O_3, formed from oxygen in the upper atmosphere; a filtering layer that protects the earth from ultraviolet radiation. 327, 436

P

p53 gene Involved in cell division control, the *p53* gene halts the cell cycle when DNA mutates and is in need of repair. 152

paleontology Study of fossils that results in knowledge about the history of life. 284, 324

palisade mesophyll Layer of tissue in a plant leaf containing elongated cells with many chloroplasts. 658

pancreas Internal organ that produces digestive enzymes and the hormones insulin and glucagon. 788, 894

pancreatic amylase Enzyme that digests starch to maltose. 788

pancreatic islet Masses of cells that constitute the endocrine portion of the pancreas. 894

parallel evolution Similarity in structure in related groups that cannot be traced to a common ancestor. 495

parasite Organism that lives off of and takes nourishment from an organism called the host. 410

parasitism Symbiotic relationship in which one species (parasite) benefits in terms of growth and reproduction to the harm of the other species (host). 410

parasympathetic division Division of the autonomic system that is active under normal conditions; uses acetylcholine as a neurotransmitter. 837

parathyroid gland Gland embedded in the posterior surface of the thyroid gland; it produces parathyroid hormone. 890

parenchyma Plant tissue composed of least specialized of all plant cells; found in all organs of a plant. 646

parthenogenesis Development of an egg cell into a whole organism without fertilization. 902

pathogen Disease-causing agent. 760

pattern formation Positioning of cells during development that determines the final shape of an organism. 924

peat Organic fuel that consists of the partially decomposed remains of peat mosses which accumulate in bogs. 562

pectoral girdle Portion of the vertebrate skeleton that provides support and attachment for the upper (fore) limbs; consists of the paired scapula and clavicle. 870

pedigree chart A family tree that uses standardized genetic symbols and shows the inheritance pattern for a specific phenotypic characteristic. 207

pelagic division Open portion of the sea. 462

pelvic girdle Portion of the vertebrate skeleton to which the lower (hind) limbs are attached; consists of the coxal bones. 871

penis Male copulatory organ; in humans, the male organ of sexual intercourse. 904

pentose Five-carbon sugar; deoxyribose is the pentose sugar found in DNA; ribose is a pentose sugar found in RNA. 37

pepsin Enzyme secreted by gastric glands that digests proteins to peptides. 787

peptide Two or more amino acids joined together by covalent bonding. 45

peptide bond Type of covalent bond that joins two amino acids. 45

peptide hormone Type of hormone that is a protein, a peptide, or is derived from an amino acid. 883

peptidoglycan Unique molecule found in bacterial cell walls. 517

perennial Flowering plant that lives more than one growing season because the underground parts regrow each season. 642

perforin Molecule secreted by a cytotoxic T cell that perforates the plasma membrane of the target cell so that water and salts enter, causing the cell to swell and burst. 768

pericycle Layer of cells surrounding the vascular tissue of roots; produces branch roots. 649

peristalsis Wavelike contractions that propel substances along a tubular structure like the esophagus. 786

permafrost Permanently frozen ground usually occurring in the tundra, a biome of Arctic regions. 447

peroxisome Enzyme-filled vesicle in which fatty acids and amino acids are metabolized to hydrogen peroxide that is broken down to harmless products. 69

petal A flower part that occurs just inside the sepals; often conspicuously colored to attract pollinators. 700

petiole Part of a plant leaf that connects the blade to the stem. 643

pH scale Measurement scale for the hydrogen ion concentration. 28

phagocytize To ingest extracellular particles by ingesting them as do amoeboid-type cells. 536

phagocytosis Process by which amoeboid-type cells engulf large substances, forming an intracellular vacuole. 90

pharynx In vertebrates, common passageway for both food intake and air movement, located between the mouth and the esophagus. 786, 802

phenetic systematics School of systematics that determines the degree of relatedness between species by counting the number of their similarities. 500

phenomenon Observable event. 9

phenotype Visible expression of a genotype—for example, brown eyes or attached earlobes. 177

pheromone Chemical messenger that works at a distance and alters the behavior of another member of the same species. 370, 882

phloem Vascular tissue that conducts organic solutes in plants; contains sieve-tube elements and companion cells. 562, 646

phospholipid Molecule that forms the bilayer of cell membranes; has a polar, hydrophilic head bonded to two nonpolar hydrophobic tails. 42, 81

phosphorus cycle Continuous process by which phosphorus circulates in the soil, water, and organisms of the biosphere. 434

photoautotroph Organism able to synthesize organic molecules by using carbon dioxide as the carbon source and sunlight as the energy source. 516

photochemical smog Air pollution that contains nitrogen oxides and hydrocarbons which react to produce ozone and PAN (peroxyacetylnitrate). 433

photon Discrete packet of solar energy; the amount of energy in a photon is inversely related to the wavelength of the photon. 112

photoperiodism Relative lengths of daylight and darkness that affect the physiology and behavior of an organism. 694

photoreceptor Sensory receptor that responds to light stimuli. 850

photorespiration Series of reactions that occurs in plants when carbon dioxide levels are depleted but oxygen continues to accumulate and the enzyme RuBP carboxylase fixes oxygen instead of carbon dioxide. 123

photosynthesis Process occurring usually within chloroplasts whereby chlorophyll-containing organelles trap solar energy to reduce carbon dioxide to carbohydrate. 3, 112

photosystem Photosynthetic unit where solar energy is absorbed and high energy electrons are generated; contains a pigment complex and an electron acceptor; occurs as PS (photosystem) I and PS II. 116

phototropism Growth response of plant stems to light; stems demonstrate positive phototropism. 685

phylogenetic tree Diagram that indicates common ancestors and lines of descent among a group of organisms. 494

phylogeny Evolutionary history of a group of organisms. 494

phylum One of the categories, or taxa, used by taxonomists to group species; taxon above the class level. 493

phytochrome Photoreversible plant pigment that is involved in photoperiodism and other responses of plants such as etiolation. 694

phytoplankton Part of plankton containing organisms that photosynthesize releasing oxygen to the atmosphere and serving as food producers in aquatic ecosystems. 437, 533

pineal gland Gland—either at the skin surface (fish, amphibians) or in the third ventricle of the brain (mammals)—that produces melatonin. 897

pinocytosis Process by which vesicle formation brings macromolecules into the cell. 90

pioneer species Early colonizer of barren or disturbed habitats that usually has a rapid growth and high dispersal rate. 415

pistil Reproductive flower structure composed of one or more carpels; consisting of an ovary, style, and stigma. 573, 700

pith Parenchyma tissue in the center of some stems and roots. 649

pituitary gland Small gland that lies just inferior to the hypothalamus; consists of the anterior and posterior pituitary, both of which produce hormones. 886

placenta Organ formed during the development of placental mammals from the chorion and the uterine wall that allows the embryo, and then the fetus, to acquire nutrients and rid itself of wastes; produces hormones that regulate pregnancy. 635, 903, 934

placental mammal Member of mammalian subclass characterized by the presence of a placenta during the development of an offspring. 635

placoderm First jawed vertebrates; heavily armored fishes of the Devonian period. 623

plankton Freshwater and marine organisms that are suspended on or near the surface of the water; includes phytoplankton and zooplankton. 457, 526

plasma In vertebrates, the liquid portion of blood; contains nutrients, wastes, salts, and proteins. 753

plasma cell Cell derived from a B-cell lymphocyte that is specialized to mass-produce antibodies. 765

plasma membrane Membrane surrounding the cytoplasm that consists of a phospholipid bilayer with embedded proteins; functions to regulate the entrance and exit of molecules from cell. 60

plasmid Self-duplicating ring of accessory DNA in the cytoplasm of bacteria. 60, 266, 514

plasmodesmata In plants, cytoplasmic strands that extend through pores in the cell wall and connect the cytoplasm of two adjacent cells. 92

plasmodial slime mold Free-living mass of cytoplasm that moves by pseudopods on a forest floor or in a field feeding on decaying plant material by phagocytosis; reproduces by spore formation. 539

plasmolysis Contraction of the cell contents due to the loss of water. 87

plate tectonics Concept that the earth's crust is divided into a number of fairly rigid plates whose movements account for continental drift. 335

platelet Component of blood that is necessary to blood clotting. 754

pleiotropy Inheritance pattern in which one gene affects many phenotypic characteristics of the individual. 189

plumule In flowering plants, the embryonic plant shoot that bears young leaves. 711

pneumonectomy Surgical removal of all or part of a lung. 807

point mutation Alternation of one base only in the sequence of bases in a gene. 259

polar body In oogenesis, a nonfunctional product; two to three meiotic products are of this type. 169

polar covalent bond Bond in which the sharing of electrons between atoms is unequal. 24

pollen grain In seed plants, structure that is derived from a microspore and develops into a microgametophyte. 568, 703

pollination In gymnosperms, the transfer of pollen from pollen cone to seed cone; in angiosperms, the transfer of pollen from anther to stigma. 568, 706

pollinator Animal; e.g., bee, that inadvertently transfers pollen from anther to stigma. 573

pollution Any environmental change that adversely affects the lives and health of living things. 477

polygenic inheritance Inheritance pattern in which a trait is controlled by several allelic pairs; each dominant allele contributes to the phenotype in an additive and like manner. 190

polymer Macromolecule consisting of covalently bonded monomers; for example, a polypeptide is a polymer of monomers called amino acids. 36

polymerase chain reaction (PCR) Technique that uses the enzyme DNA polymerase to produce millions of copies of a particular piece of DNA. 268

polyp Small, abnormal growth that arises from the epithelial lining. 791

polypeptide Polymer of many amino acids linked by peptide bonds. 45

polyploid (polyploidy) Having a chromosome number that is a multiple greater than twice that of the monoploid number. 196

polyribosome String of ribosomes simultaneously translating regions of the same mRNA strand during protein synthesis. 66, 241

polysaccharide Polymer made from sugar monomers; the polysaccharides starch and glycogen are polymers of glucose monomers. 38

pond Standing water within a basin. 455

population Group of organisms of the same species occupying a certain area and sharing a common gene pool. 5, 378

population genetics Study of gene frequencies and their changes within a population. 302

population viability analysis Calculation of the minimum population size needed to prevent extinction. 481

portal system Pathway of blood flow that begins and ends in capillaries, such as the portal system located between the small intestine and liver. 748

positive feedback Mechanism of homeostatic response in which the output of the system intensifies and increases the activity of the system. 735, 886

posttranscriptional control Gene expression following translation regulated by the way mRNA transcripts are processed. 251

posttranslational control Gene expression following translation regulated by the activity of the newly synthesized protein. 251

postzygotic isolating mechanism Anatomical or physiological difference between two species that prevents successful reproduction after mating has taken place. 311

potential energy Stored energy as a result of location or spatial arrangement. 98

prairie Terrestrial biome that is a temperate grassland. When travelling east to west in the midwest of the United States, a tall-grass prairie changes to a short-grass prairie. 452

predation Interaction in which one organism uses another, called the prey, as a food source. 406

predator Organism that practices predation. 406

pressure-flow model Explanation for phloem transport; osmotic pressure following active transport of sugar into phloem brings a flow of sap from a source to a sink. 678

prey Organism that provides nourishment for a predator. 406

prezygotic isolating mechanism Anatomical or behavioral difference between two species that prevents the possibility of mating. 310

primary root Original root that grows straight down and remains the dominant root of the plant; contrast fibrous root system. 650

primitive character Structural, physiological, or behavioral trait that is present in a common ancestor and all members of a group. 494

principle Theory that is generally accepted by an overwhelming number of scientists. Also called law. 12

prion Infectious particle consisting of protein only and no nucleic acid. 513

probe Known sequence of DNA that is used to find complementary DNA strands; can be used diagnostically to determine the presence of particular genes. 267

producer Photosynthetic organism at the start of a grazing food chain that makes its own food (e.g., green plants on land and algae in water). 423

product Substance that forms as a result of a reaction. 100

progesterone Female sex hormone that helps maintain sexual organs and secondary sexual characteristics. 909

proglottid Segment of a tapeworm that contains both male and female sex organs and becomes a bag of eggs. 591

prokaryote Organism that lacks the membrane-bounded nucleus and membranous organelles typical of eukaryotes; bacteria and archaea are prokaryotes. 513

prokaryotic cell Lacking a membrane-bounded nucleus and organelles; the cell type within the domain Bacteria and Archaea. 60

promoter In an operon, a sequence of DNA where RNA polymerase binds prior to transcription. 238, 248

proofreading Process used to check the accuracy of DNA replication as it occurs, and to replace a mispaired base with the right one. 229

protein Molecule consisting of one or more polypeptides. 44

protein-first hypothesis In chemical evolution, the proposal that protein originated before other macromolecules and allowed the formation of protocells. 321

protist Member of the kingdom Protista. 526

proto-oncogene Normal gene that can become an oncogene through mutation. 260

protocell In biological evolution, a possible cell forerunner that became a cell once it acquired genes. 322

proton Positive subatomic particle, located in the nucleus and having a weight of approximately one atomic mass unit. 18

protoplast Plant cell from which the cell wall has been removed. 712

protostome Group of coelomate animals in which the first embryonic opening (the blastopore) is associated with the mouth. 598

protozoan Heterotrophic unicellular protist that moves by flagella, cilia, pseudopodia, or are immobile. 535

proximal convoluted tubule Portion of a nephron following the glomerular capsule where tubular reabsorption of filtrate occurs. 816

pseudocoelom Body cavity lying between the digestive tract and body wall that is incompletely lined by mesoderm. 591

pseudopod Cytoplasmic extension of amoeboid protists; used for locomotion and engulfing food. 536

puberty Period of time in life when secondary sex changes occur in humans, marked by the onset of menses in females and sperm production in males. 907

pulmonary circuit Circulatory pathway between the lungs and the heart. 748

pulse Vibration felt in arterial walls due to expansion of the aorta following ventricle contraction. 746

pupil Opening in the center of the iris of the vertebrate eye. 852

purine Type of nitrogen-containing base, such as adenine and guanine, having a double-ring structure. 223

pyrimidine Type of nitrogen-containing base, such as cytosine, thymine, and uracil, having a single-ring structure. 223

pyruvate End product of glycolysis; its further fate, involving fermentation or entry into a mitochondrion, depends on oxygen availability. 129

r

r-selection A favorable life history strategy under certain environmental conditions; characterized by a high reproductive rate with little or no attention given to offspring survival. 390

radial symmetry Body plan in which similar parts are arranged around a central axis, like spokes of a wheel. 580

radioactive isotope Unstable form of an atom that spontaneously emits radiation in the form of radioactive particles or radiant energy. 19

radula Tonguelike organ found in molluscs that bears rows of tiny teeth that point backward; used to obtain food. 600

rain shadow Lee side (side sheltered from the wind) of a mountainous barrier, which receives much less precipitation than the windward side. 443

reactant Substance that participates in a reaction. 100

receptor protein Protein located in the plasma membrane or within the cell that binds to a substance that alters some metabolic aspect of the cell. 83

receptor-mediated endocytosis Selective uptake of molecules into a cell by vacuole formation after they bind to specific receptor proteins in the plasma membrane. 91

recessive allele Allele that exerts its phenotypic effect only in the homozygote; its expression is masked by a dominant allele. 177

recombinant DNA (rDNA) DNA that contains genes from more than one source. 266

red algae Marine photosynthetic protist with a notable abundance of phycobilin pigments; includes coralline algae of coral reefs. 530

red blood cell Erythrocyte; contains hemoglobin and carries oxygen from the lungs or gills to the tissues in vertebrates. 753

red bone marrow Vascularized modified connective tissue that is sometimes found in the cavities of spongy bone; site of blood cell formation. 762, 866

reduction Gain of electrons by an atom or molecule with a concurrent storage of energy; in biological systems, the electrons are accompanied by hydrogen ions. 106

reflex Automatic, involuntary response of an organism to a stimulus. 835

regulator gene In an operon, a gene that codes for a protein that regulates the expression of other genes. 248

relative dating (of fossils) Determining the age of fossils by noting their sequential relationships in strata. 324

renal cortex Outer portion of the kidney that appears granular. 816

renal medulla Inner portion of the kidney that consists of renal pyramids. 816

renal pelvis Hollow chamber in the kidney that lies inside the renal medulla and receives freshly prepared urine from the collecting ducts. 816

renin Enzyme released by kidneys that leads to the secretion of aldosterone and a rise in blood pressure. 821

replacement reproduction Population in which each person is replaced by only one child. 394

replication fork In eukaryotes, the point where the two parental DNA strands separate to allow replication. 229

repressible operon Operon that is normally active because the repressor is normally inactive. 249

repressor In an operon, protein molecule that binds to an operator, preventing transcription of structural genes. 249

reproduce To produce a new individual of the same kind. 4

resource partitioning Mechanism that increases the number of niches by apportioning the supply of a resource such as food and living space between species. 404

respiration Sequence of events that results in gas exchange between the cells of the body and the environment. 798

resting potential Membrane potential of an inactive neuron. 830

restoration ecology Subdiscipline of conservation biology that seeks ways to return ecosystems to their former state. 482

restriction enzyme Bacterial enzyme that stops viral reproduction by cleaving viral DNA; used to cut DNA at specific points during production of recombinant DNA. 266

restriction fragment length polymorphism (RFLP) Differences in DNA sequence between individuals that result in different patterns when DNA is cleaved by a restriction enzyme. 269

reticular formation Complex network of nerve fibers within the central nervous system that arouses the cerebrum. 839

retina Innermost layer of the vertebrate eyeball containing the photoreceptors—rod cells and cone cells. 851

retrovirus RNA virus containing the enzyme reverse transcriptase that carries out RNA/DNA transcription. 512

rhizoid Rootlike hair that anchors a plant and absorbs minerals and water from the soil. 560

rhizome Rootlike, underground stem. 564, 656

rhodopsin Light-absorbing molecule in rod cells and cone cells that contains a pigment and the protein opsin. 853

ribbon worm Marine invertebrate of the phylum Nemertea having a distinctive proboscis apparatus. 588

ribose Pentose sugar found in RNA. 37

ribosomal RNA (rRNA) Type of RNA found in ribosomes that translate messenger RNAs to produce proteins. 236

ribosome RNA and protein in two subunits; site of protein synthesis in the cytoplasm. 60, 66

RNA (ribonucleic acid) Nucleic acid produced from covalent bonding of nucleotide monomers that contain the sugar ribose; occurs in three forms: messenger RNA, ribosomal RNA, and transfer RNA. 48, 220, 236

RNA polymerase During transcription, an enzyme that joins nucleotides complementary to a DNA template. 238

RNA transcript mRNA molecule formed during transcription that has a sequence of bases complementary to a gene. 238

RNA-first hypothesis In chemical evolution, the proposal that RNA originated before other macromolecules and allowed the formation of the first cell(s). 321

rod cell Photoreceptor in vertebrate eyes that responds to dim light. 853

root In vascular plants, the underground organ that anchors the plant in the soil, absorbs water and minerals, and stores the products of photosynthesis. 562

root hair Extension of a root epidermal cell that collectively increases the surface area for the absorption of water and minerals. 562, 645, 670

root nodule Structure on plant root that contains nitrogen-fixing bacteria. 650

root pressure Osmotic pressure, caused by active movement of mineral into root cells; serves to elevate water in xylem for a short distance. 674

root system Includes the main root and any and all of its lateral (side) branches. 642

rough ER (endoplasmic reticulum) Membranous system of tubules, vesicles, and sacs in cells; with attached ribosomes. 67

roundworm Member of the phylum Nematoda with a cylindrical body that has a complete digestive tract and a pseudocoelom; some forms free-living in water and soil and many are parasitic. 593

RuBP (ribulose bisphosphate) Five-carbon compound that combines with and fixes carbon dioxide during the Calvin cycle and is later regenerated by the same cycle. 120

s

sac body plan Body with a digestive cavity that has only one opening, as in cnidarians and flatworms. 588

saccule Saclike cavity in the vestibule of the vertebrate inner ear; contains sensory receptors for static equilibrium. 859

salivary amylase In humans, enzyme in saliva that digests starch to maltose. 785

salivary gland In humans, gland associated with the mouth that secretes saliva. 785

saltatory conduction Movement of nerve impulses from one neurolemmal node to another along a myelinated axon. 830

saprotroph Organism that secretes digestive enzymes and absorbs the resulting nutrients back across the plasma membrane. 516

sarcolemma Plasma membrane of a muscle fiber; also forms the tubules of the T system involved in muscular contraction. 875

sarcomere One of many units, arranged linearly within a myofibril, whose contraction produces muscle contraction. 875

sarcoplasmic reticulum Smooth endoplasmic reticulum of skeletal muscle cells; surrounds the myofibrils and stores calcium ions. 875

saturated Fatty acid molecule that lacks double bonds between the carbons of its hydrocarbon chain. The chain bears the maximum number of hydrogens possible. 40

savanna Terrestrial biome that is a grassland in Africa, characterized by few trees and a severe dry season. 452

scale In fishes and reptiles, a thin flake, many of which cover the body and offer protection. 622

schistosomiasis Disease caused by the blood fluke, a parasitic flatworm of the phylum Platyhelminthes. 590

schizocoelom In protostomes, coelom formed by splitting of the embryonic mesoderm. 599

science Human endeavor that considers only what is observable by the senses or by instruments that extend the ability of the senses. 9

scientific method Process by which scientists formulate a hypothesis, gather data by observation and experimentation, and come to a conclusion. 12

scientific theory Concept supported by a broad range of observations, experiments, and data. 12

sclerenchyma Plant tissue composed of cells with heavily lignified cell walls and functions in support. 646

scolex Tapeworm head region; contains hooks and suckers for attachment to host. 591

seaweed Multicellular forms of red, green, and brown algae found in marine habitats. 531

second messenger Chemical signal such as cyclic AMP that causes the cell to respond to the first messenger—a hormone bound to plasma membrane receptor. 883

secondary oocyte In oogenesis the functional product of meiosis I; becomes the egg. 169

secondary sexual characteristic Trait that is sometimes helpful but not absolutely necessary for reproduction and is maintained by the sex hormones in males and females. 907

sedimentation Process by which particulate material accumulates and forms a stratum. 324

seed Mature ovule that contains an embryo, with stored food enclosed in a protective coat. 568, 708

segmentation Repetition of body units as seen in the earthworm. 580

semen (seminal fluid) Thick, whitish fluid consisting of sperm and secretions from several glands of the male reproductive tract. 905

semicircular canal One of three half-circle-shaped canals of the vertebrate inner ear that contains sensory receptors for dynamic equilibrium. 859

semiconservative replication Duplication of DNA resulting in two double helix molecules each having one parental and one new strand. 226

semilunar valve Valve resembling a half moon located between the ventricles and their attached vessels. 744

seminiferous tubule Long, coiled structure contained within chambers of the testis where sperm are produced. 907

senescence Sum of processes involving aging, decline, and eventual death of a plant or plant part. 692

sensory neuron Nerve cell that transmits nerve impulses to the central nervous system after a sensory receptor has been stimulated. 829

sensory receptor Structure that receives either external or internal environmental stimuli and is a part of a sensory neuron or transmits signals to a sensory neuron. 825

sepal Outermost, sterile, leaflike covering of the flower; usually green in color. 700

septate Having cell walls; some fungal species have hyphae that are septate. 545

septum Partition or wall that divides two areas; the septum in the heart separates the right half from the left half. 744

sessile filter feeder Animal that stays in one place and filters small food particles from the water. 582

seta (pl., setae) A needlelike chitinous bristle of annelids, arthropods, and others. 604

sex chromosome Chromosome that determines the sex of an individual; in humans, females have two X chromosomes and males have an X and Y chromosome. 192, 202

sex-influenced trait Autosomal phenotype controlled by an allele that is expressed differently in the two sexes; for example, the possibility of pattern baldness is increased by the presence of testosterone in human males. 215

sex-linked Allele that occurs on the sex chromosomes but may control a trait that has nothing to do with sexual characteristics of an animal. 214

sexual reproduction Reproduction involving meiosis, gamete formation, and fertilization; produces offspring with chromosomes inherited from each parent with a unique combination of genes. 160

sexual selection Changes in males and females, often due to male competition and female selectivity leading to increased fitness. 305, 366

shoot apical meristem Group of actively dividing embryonic cells at the tips of plant shoots. 652

shoot system Aboveground portion of a plant consisting of the stem, leaves, and flowers. 642

short-day plant Plant which flowers when day length is shorter than a critical length, i.e., cocklebur, poinsettia, and chrysanthemum. 694

sieve-tube element Member that joins with others in the phloem tissue of plants as a means of transport for nutrient sap. 672

sink population Population that is found in an unfavorable area where at best the birthrate equals the death rate; sink populations receive new members from source populations. 480

sister chromatid One of two genetically identical chromosomal units that are the result of DNA replication and are attached to each other at the centromere. 145

skeletal muscle Striated, voluntary muscle tissue that comprises skeletal muscles; also called striated muscle. 728

sliding filament model An explanation for muscle contraction based on the movement of actin filaments in relation to myosin filaments. 875

slime layer Gelatinous sheath surrounding the cell wall of certain bacteria. 60

small intestine In vertebrates, the portion of the digestive tract that precedes the large intestine; in humans, consists of duodenum, jejunum, and ileum. 788

smooth (visceral) muscle Nonstriated, involuntary muscles found in the walls of internal organs. 728

smooth ER (endoplasmic reticulum) Membranous system of tubules, vesicles, and sacs in eukaryotic cells; without attached ribosomes. 67

society Group in which members of species are organized in a cooperative manner, extending beyond sexual and parental behavior. 370

sociobiology Application of evolutionary principles to the study of social behavior of animals, including humans. 372

sodium-potassium pump Carrier protein in the plasma membrane that moves sodium ions out of and potassium into animal cells; important in nerve and muscle cells. 88

soil Accumulation of inorganic rock material and organic matter that is capable of supporting the growth of vegetation. 446, 668

soil erosion Movement of topsoil to a new location due to the action of running water or wind. 669

soil profile Vertical section of soil from the ground surface to the unaltered rock below. 669

solute Substance that is dissolved in a solvent, forming a solution. 85

solution Fluid (the solvent) that contains a dissolved solid (the solute). 85

solvent Liquid portion of a solution that serves to dissolve a solute. 85

somatic embryo Plant cell embryo which is asexually produced through tissue culture techniques. 712

source population Population that can provide members to other populations of the species because it lives in a favorable area, and the birthrate is most likely higher than the death rate. 480

speciation Origin of new species due to the evolutionary process of descent with modification. 310

species Group of similarly constructed organisms capable of interbreeding and producing fertile offspring; organisms that share a common gene pool; taxon at the lowest level of classification. 310, 493

specific epithet In the binomial system of taxonomy, the second part of an organism's name, which may be descriptive. 491

sperm Male gamete having a haploid number of chromosomes and the ability to fertilize an egg, the female gamete. 907

spermatogenesis Production of sperm in males by the process of meiosis and maturation. 168

spicule Skeletal structure of sponges composed of calcium carbonate or silicate. 583

spinal cord In vertebrates, the nerve cord that is continuous with the base of the brain and housed within the vertebral column. 838

spinal nerve Nerve that arises from the spinal cord. 834

spindle Microtubule structure that brings about chromosomal movement during nuclear division. 146

spiral organ Structure in the vertebrate inner ear that contains auditory receptors (also called organ of Corti). 857

spleen Large, glandular organ located in the upper left region of the abdomen that stores and purifies blood. 761

sponge Invertebrate animal of the phylum Porifera; pore-bearing filter feeder whose inner body wall is lined by collar cells. 582

spongy bone Type of bone that has an irregular meshlike arrangement of thin plates of bone. 727, 866

spongy mesophyll Layer of tissue in a plant leaf containing loosely packed cells increasing the amount of surface area for gas exchange. 658

sporangium (pl., sporangia) Structure that produces spores. 539, 546, 560

spore Asexual reproductive or resting cell capable of developing into a new organism without fusion with another cell, in contrast to a gamete. 545

sporophyte Diploid generation of the alternation of generations life cycle of a plant; produces haploid spores that develop into the haploid generation. 559, 700

sporozoan Spore-forming protist that has no means of locomotion and is typically a parasite with a complex life cycle having both sexual and asexual phases. 538

spring overturn Mixing process that occurs in spring in stratified lakes whereby the oxygen-rich top waters mix with nutrient-rich bottom waters. 457

stabilizing selection Outcome of natural selection in which extreme phenotypes are eliminated and the average phenotype is conserved. 308

stamen In flowering plants, the portion of the flower that consists of a filament and an anther containing pollen sacs where pollen is produced. 573, 701

starch Storage polysaccharide found in plants that is composed of glucose molecules joined in a linear fashion with few side chains. 38

statocyst Static equilibrium organs of cnidarians, molluscs, and crustaceans; gives information about the position of the head. 859

statolith Sensors found in root cap cells which cause a plant to demonstrate gravitropism. 685

stem Usually the upright, vertical portion of a plant, which transports substances to and from the leaves. 643

steroid Type of lipid molecule having a complex of four carbon rings; examples are cholesterol, progesterone, and testosterone. 42

steroid hormone Type of hormone that has a complex of four carbon rings but different side chains from other steroid hormones. 883

stigma In flowering plants, portion of the pistil where pollen grains adhere and germinate before fertilization can occur. 573, 700

stolon Stem that grows horizontally along the ground and may give rise to new plants where it contacts the soil (e.g., the runners of a strawberry plant). 656

stomach In vertebrates, muscular sac that mixes food with gastric juices to form chyme, which enters the small intestine. 786

stomate Small opening between two guard cells on the underside of leaf epidermis through which gases pass. 562, 645, 676

stratum Ancient layer of sedimentary rock; results from slow deposition of silt, volcanic ash, and other materials. 324

striated Having bands; in cardiac and skeletal muscle, alternating light and dark crossbands produced by the distribution of contractile proteins. 728

strobilus In club mosses, terminal clusters of leaves which bear sporangia. 565

stroma Fluid within a chloroplast that contains enzymes involved in the synthesis of carbohydrates during photosynthesis. 71, 114

stromatolite Domed structures found in shallow seas consisting of cyanobacteria bound to calcium carbonate. 327

structural gene Gene that codes for an enzyme in a metabolic pathway. 248

style Elongated, central portion of the pistil between the ovary and stigma. 573, 701

substrate Reactant in a reaction controlled by an enzyme. 102

substrate-level phosphorylation Process in which ATP is formed by transferring a phosphate from a metabolic substrate to ADP. 130

sucrose Disaccharide that contains glucose and fructose; found in plants and is refined as table sugar. 37

survivorship Probability of newborn individuals of a cohort surviving to particular ages. 384

sustainable development Management of an ecosystem so that it maintains itself while providing services to human beings. 282

swim bladder In fishes, a gas-filled sac whose pressure can be altered to change buoyancy. 624

symbiosis Relationship that occurs when two different species live together in a unique way; it may be beneficial, neutral, or detrimental to one and/or the other species. 410, 516

sympathetic division Division of the autonomic system that is active when an organism is under stress; uses norepinephrine as a neurotransmitter. 837

sympatric speciation Origin of new species in populations that overlap geographically. 312

synapse Junction between neurons consisting of the presynaptic (axon) membrane, the synaptic cleft, and the postsynaptic (usually dendrite) membrane. 833

synapsis Pairing of homologous chromosomes during meiosis I. 161

synaptic cleft Small gap between presynaptic and postsynaptic membranes of a synapse. 833

synovial joint Freely moving joint in which two bones are separated by a cavity. 871

systematics Study of the diversity of organisms to determine evolutionary relationships and classify organisms. 494

systemic circuit Circulatory pathway of blood flow between the tissues and the heart. 748

systole Contraction period of a heart during the cardiac cycle. 746

t

T lymphocyte Lymphocyte that matures in the thymus and exists in four varieties, one of which kills antigen-bearing cells outright. 764

taiga Terrestrial biome that is a coniferous forest extending in a broad belt across northern Eurasia and North America. 448

taproot Main axis of a root that penetrates deeply and is used by certain plants such as carrots for food storage. 650

taste bud Structure in the vertebrate mouth containing sensory receptors for taste; in humans most taste buds are on the tongue. 848

taxon (pl., taxa) Group of organisms that fills a particular classification category. 492

taxonomy Branch of biology concerned with identifying, describing, and naming organisms. 8, 490

template Parental strand of DNA that serves as a guide for the complementary daughter strand produced during DNA replication. 226

tendon Strap of fibrous connective tissue that connects skeletal muscle to bone. 726, 873

tendril Threadlike extension of a modified leaf or stem used for grasping objects; a means of mechanical support. 686

terminal bud Bud that develops at the apex of a shoot. 652

terminator Specific DNA sequence that signals transcription to terminate. 238

territoriality Marking and/or defending a particular area against invasion by another species member; area often used for the purpose of feeding, mating, and caring for young. 368

testcross Cross between an individual with the dominant phenotype and an individual with the recessive phenotype. The resulting phenotypic ratio indicates whether the dominant phenotype is homozygous or heterozygous. 180

testis Male gonad which produces sperm and the male sex hormones. 902

tetanus Sustained muscle contraction without relaxation. 873

tetrapod Four-footed vertebrates; includes amphibians, reptiles, birds, and mammals. 625

thalamus In vertebrates, the portion of the diencephalon that passes on selected sensory information to the cerebrum. 839

therapsid Mammallike reptiles appearing in the middle Permian period; ancestral to mammals. 628

thermal inversion Temperature inversion that traps cold air and its pollutants near the earth with the warm air above it. 433

thermoacidophile Type of archaea that lives in hot and acidic aquatic habitats, such as hot springs or near hydrothermal vents. 520

thigmotropism In plants, unequal growth due to contact with solid objects, as the coiling of tendrils around a pole. 686

three-domain system System of classification that recognizes three domains: Bacteria, Archaea, and Eukarya. 502

thrombin Enzyme that converts fibrinogen to fibrin threads during blood clotting. 754

thylakoid Flattened sac within a granum whose membrane contains chlorophyll and where the light-dependent reactions of photosynthesis occur. 60, 71, 114

thymine (T) One of four nitrogen-containing bases in nucleotides composing the structure of DNA; pairs with adenine. 223

thymus gland Lymphoid organ involved in the development and functioning of the immune system; T lymphocytes mature in the thymus gland. 761, 897

thyroid gland Large gland in the neck that produces several important hormones, including thyroxine, triiodothyronine and calcitonin. 889

tight junction Junction between cells when adjacent plasma membrane proteins join to form an impermeable barrier. 93

tissue Group of similar cells combined to perform a common function. 724

tissue culture Process of growing tissue artificially in usually a liquid medium in laboratory glassware. 712

tissue engineering Biotechnology which creates products from a combination of living cells and biodegradable polymers resulting in bioartificial organs and implants. 271

tissue fluid Fluid that surrounds the body's cells consists of dissolved substances that leave the blood capillaries by filtration and diffusion. 734, 755

tone Continuous, partial contraction of muscle. 873

tonicity Osmolarity of a solution compared to that of a cell; if the solution is isotonic to the cell, there is no net movement of water; if the solution is hypotonic, the cell gains water; and if the solution is hypertonic, the cell loses water. 86

tonsils Partially encapsulated lymph nodules located in the pharynx. 761, 806

totipotent Cell that has the full genetic potential of the organism and has the potential to develop into a complete organism. 712, 924

trachea (pl., tracheae) Air tube in insects that is located between the spiracles and the tracheoles. 802

trachea Air tube (windpipe) in tetrapod vertebrates that runs between the larynx and the bronchi. 607

tracheid In vascular plants, type of cell in xylem that has tapered ends and pits through which water and minerals flow. 672

tract Bundle of myelinated axons in the central nervous system. 838

traditional systematics School of systematics that takes into consideration the degree of difference between derived characters to construct phylogenetic trees. 500

transcription Process whereby a DNA strand serves as a template for the formation of mRNA. 236

transcription factor In eukaryotes, protein required for the initiation of transcription by RNA polymerase. 254

transcriptional control Control of gene expression during the transcriptional phase determined by mechanisms that control whether transcription occurs or the rate at which it occurs. 251

transduction Exchange of DNA between bacteria by means of a bacteriophage. 515

transfer rate Amount of a substance that moves from one component of the environment to another within a specified period of time. 430

transfer RNA (tRNA) Type of RNA that transfers a particular amino acid to a ribosome during protein synthesis; at one end it binds to the amino acid and at the other end it has an anticodon that binds to an mRNA codon. 236

transformation Taking up of extraneous genetic material from the environment by bacteria. 515

transgenic organism Free-living organisms in the environment that have had a foreign gene inserted into them. 270, 714

transition reaction Reaction that oxidizes pyruvate with the release of carbon dioxide; results in the acetyl-CoA and connects glycolysis to the Krebs cycle. 129

translation Process whereby ribosomes use the sequence of codons in mRNA to produce a polypeptide with a particular sequence of amino acids. 236

translational control Gene expression regulated by the activity of mRNA transcripts. 251

transpiration Plant's loss of water to the atmosphere, mainly through evaporation at leaf stomates. 674

trichinosis Serious infection caused by parasitic roundworm of the phylum Nematoda whose larvae encyst in muscles. 593

trichocyst Found in ciliates, trichocysts contain long, barbed threads useful for defense and capturing prey. 537

triglyceride Neutral fat composed of glycerol and three fatty acids. 40

triplet code During gene expression, each sequence of three nucleotide bases stands for a particular amino acid. 237

trophic level Feeding level of one or more populations in a food web. 422

trophoblast Outer membrane surrounding the embryo in mammals, when thickened by a layer of mesoderm, it becomes the chorion, an extraembryonic membrane. 931

tropism In plants, a growth response toward or away from a directional stimulus. 684

trypanosome Parasitic zooflagellate that causes severe disease in human beings and domestic animals, including a condition called sleeping sickness. 535

trypsin Protein-digesting enzyme secreted by the pancreas. 788

tube foot Part of the water vascular system in sea stars, located on the oral surface of each arm; functions in locomotion. 619

tube-within-a-tube body plan Body with a digestive tract that has both a mouth and an anus. 588

tubular reabsorption Movement of primarily nutrient molecules and water from the contents of the nephron into blood at the proximal convoluted tubule. 818

tubular secretion Movement of certain molecules from blood into the distal convoluted tubule of a nephron so that they are added to urine. 818

tumor Cells derived from a single mutated cell that has repeatedly undergone cell division; benign tumors remain at the site of origin, and malignant tumors metastasize. 152, 260

tumor-suppressor gene Gene that codes for a protein that ordinarily suppresses cell division; inactivity can lead to a tumor. 260

turgor pressure Pressure of the cell contents against the cell wall, in plant cells, determined by the water content of the vacuole; gives internal support to the plant cell. 87

tympanic membrane Membranous region that receives air vibrations in an auditory organ; in humans, the eardrum. 856

typhlosole Expanded dorsal surface of long intestine of earthworms, allowing additional surface for absorption. 605

u

umbilical cord Cord connecting the fetus to the placenta through which blood vessels pass. 933

uniformitarianism Belief espoused by James Hutton that geological forces act at a continuous, uniform rate. 285

unsaturated Fatty acid molecule that has one or more double bonds between the carbons of its hydrocarbon chain. The chain bears fewer hydrogens than the maximum number possible. 40

upwelling Upward movement of deep, nutrient-rich water along coasts; it replaces surface waters that move away from shore when the direction of prevailing wind shifts. 460

uracil The pyrimidine base that replaces thymine in RNA; pairs with adenine. 236

urea Main nitrogenous waste of terrestrial amphibians and most mammals. 814

ureter Tubular structure conducting urine from the kidney to the urinary bladder. 816

urethra Tubular structure that receives urine from the bladder and carries it to the outside of the body. 816

uric acid Main nitrogenous waste of insects, reptiles and birds. 814

urinary bladder Organ where urine is stored. 816

urine Liquid waste product made by the nephrons of the vertebrate kidney through the processes of glomerular filtration, tubular reabsorption, and tubular secretion. 816

uterine cycle Cycle that runs concurrently with the ovarian cycle; it prepares the uterus to receive a developing zygote. 910

uterus In mammals, expanded portion of the female reproductive tract through which eggs pass to the environment or in which an embryo develops and is nourished before birth. 908

utricle Saclike cavity in the vestibule of the vertebrate inner ear; contains sensory receptors for static equilibrium. 859

V

vaccine Antigens prepared in such a way that they can promote active immunity without causing disease. 772

vacuole Fluid-filled membrane-bounded sac that fills much of the interior of a plant cell and contains a variety of substances. 69

variable Factor that can cause an observable change during the progress of the experiment. 10

vascular bundle In plants, primary phloem and primary xylem enclosed by a bundle sheath. 646

vascular cambium In plants, lateral meristem that produces secondary phloem and secondary xylem. 652

vascular cylinder In dicots, the tissues in the middle of a root consisting of the pericycle and vascular tissues. 646

vascular plant Type of plant that contains vascular tissue; e.g., ferns, gymnosperms, and angiosperms. 562

vascular tissue Transport tissue in plants consisting of xylem and phloem. 645

vector In genetic engineering, a means to transfer foreign genetic material into a cell; e.g., a plasmid. 266

vein Blood vessel that arises from venules and transports blood toward the heart. 742

vena cava Large systemic vein that returns blood to the right atrium of the heart in tetrapods; either the superior or inferior vena cava. 748

ventricle Cavity in an organ, such as a lower chamber of the heart; or the ventricles of the brain. 744, 838

venule Vessel that takes blood from capillaries to a vein. 742

vertebral column Portion of the vertebrate endoskeleton that houses the spinal cord; consists of many vertebrae separated by intervertebral disks. 869

vertebrate Chordate in which the notochord is replaced by a vertebral column. 622

vesicle Small, membrane-bounded sac that stores substances within a cell. 66

vessel element Cell which joins with others to form a major conducting tube found in xylem. 672

vestigial structure Remains of a structure that was functional in some ancestor but is no longer functional in the organism in question. 296

villus (pl., villi) Small, fingerlike projection of the inner small intestinal wall. 788

viroid Infectious strand of RNA devoid of a capsid and much smaller than a virus. 512

virus Noncellular parasitic agent consisting of an outer capsid and an inner core of nucleic acid. 508

visible light Portion of the electromagnetic spectrum that is visible to the human eye. 112

vitamin Essential requirement in the diet, needed in small amounts. They are often part of coenzymes. 105, 792

vocal cord In humans, fold of tissue within the larynx; creates vocal sounds when it vibrates. 802

W

waggle dance Performed by honeybees, this action indicates the distance and direction of a food source. 371

water (hydrologic) cycle Interdependent and continuous circulation of water from the ocean, to the atmosphere, to the land, and back to the ocean. 429

water mold Unicellular or filamentous organisms having cell walls made of cellulose; typically decomposers of dead freshwater organisms but some are parasites of aquatic or terrestrial organisms. 540

water potential Potential energy of water; it is a measure of the capability to release or take up water relative to another substance. 673

water vascular system Series of canals that takes water to the tube feet of an echinoderm, allowing them to expand. 619

wax Sticky, solid, waterproof lipid consisting of many long-chain fatty acids usually linked to long-chain alcohols. 40

whisk fern Common name for seedless vascular plant that consists only of stems and has no leaves or roots. 564

white blood cell Leukocyte, of which there are several types, each having a specific function in protecting the body from invasion by foreign substances and organisms. 753

white matter Myelinated axons in the central nervous system. 838

woody plant

woody plant Plant that contains wood; usually trees such as evergreen trees (gymnosperms) and flowering trees (angiosperms). Alternative is a herbaceous plant. 542

X

X chromosome Female sex chromosome that carries genes involved in sex determination; see Y chromosome. 202

X-linked Allele located on an X chromosome but may control a trait that has nothing to do with the sexual characteristics of an animal. 192, 214

xenotransplantation Use of animal organs, instead of human organs, in human transplant patients. 271

xylem Vascular tissue that transports water and mineral solutes upward through the plant body; it contains vessel elements and tracheids. 562, 646, 672

Y

Y chromosome Male sex chromosome that carries genes involved in sex determination; see X chromosome. 202

yolk Dense nutrient material that is present in the egg of a bird or reptile. 903, 920

yolk sac One of the extraembryonic membranes which in shelled vertebrates contains yolk for the nourishment of the embryo and in placental mammals is the first site for blood cell formation. 930

Z

zero population growth No growth in population size. 394

zooflagellate Nonphotosynthetic protist that moves by flagella; typically zooflagellates enter into symbiotic relationships and some are parasitic. 535

zooplankton Part of plankton containing protozoa and other types of microscopic animals. 457, 536

zygospore Thick-walled, resting cell formed during sexual reproduction of zygospore fungi. 546

zygote Diploid cell formed by the union of two gametes; the product of fertilization. 160

Credits

Line Art and Text

Chapter 2

Ecology Focus: Data from G. Tyler Miller, *Living in the Environment*, 1993, Wadsworth Publishing Company, Belmont, CA; and Lester R. Brown, *State of the World*, 1992, W.W. Norton & Company, Inc., New York, NY. p. 29.

Chapter 3

3.9B, C: From R.R. Seeley & T.D. Stephens, *Anatomy & Physiology*, 3rd edition. Copyright 1995 McGraw-Hill Companies, Inc. All Rights Reserved. Reprinted by Permission; **3.19A:** From Peter H. Raven & George B. Johnson, *Biology*, 5th edition. Copyright 1996 McGraw-Hill Companies, Inc. All Rights Reserved. Reprinted by Permission. p. 41.

Chapter 6

6.6: From Peter H. Raven & George B. Johnson, *Biology*, 5th edition. Copyright 1996 McGraw-Hill Companies, Inc. All Rights Reserved. Reprinted by Permission. p. 103.

Chapter 8

Health Focus: Scott K. Powers and Edward T. Howley, *Exercise Physiology*, 2d edition. Copyright 1994 McGraw-Hill Companies, Inc., Dubuque, Iowa. All Rights Reserved. Reprinted by Permission. p. 138.

Chapter 9

9.5: From Peter H. Raven and George B. Johnson, *Biology*, 5th edition. Copyright 1996 McGraw-Hill Companies, Inc. All Rights Reserved. Reprinted by Permission. p. 149; **9.6:** R.G. Kessel and C.Y. Shih, *Scanning Electron Microscopy in Biology: A Student's Atlas on Biological Organization* (1974). Reprinted with Permission of Springer-Verlag, New York. p. 149.

Chapter 11

11.8: From Burton S. Guttman, *Biology*. Copyright 1999 McGraw-Hill Companies, Inc. All Rights Reserved. Reprinted by Permission. p. 182; **11.9:** From Burton S. Guttman, *Biology*. Copyright 1999 McGraw-Hill Companies, Inc. All Rights Reserved. Reprinted by Permission. p. 182.

Chapter 12

12.5: From Burton S. Guttman, *Biology*. Copyright 1999 McGraw-Hill Companies, Inc. All Rights Reserved. Reprinted by Permission. p. 193.

Chapter 13

13.2B: From Robert F. Weaver and Philip W. Hedrick, *Genetics*, 2nd edition. Copyright 1994 McGraw-Hill Companies, Inc. All Rights Reserved. Reprinted by Permission. p. 203.

Chapter 16

Science Focus: Courtesy of Joyce Haines. p. 257.

Chapter 18

18.14: From Burton S. Guttman, *Biology*. Copyright 1999 McGraw-Hill Companies, Inc. All Rights Reserved. Reprinted by Permission. p. 293; **18C:** From Peter H. Raven & George B. Johnson, *Biology*, 5th edition. Copyright 1996 McGraw-Hill Companies, Inc. All Rights Reserved. Reprinted by Permission. p. 294.

Chapter 19

19.13: From Burton S. Guttman, *Biology*. Copyright 1999 McGraw-Hill Companies, Inc. All Rights Reserved. Reprinted by Permission. p. 313; **Science Focus:** Courtesy of Gerald D. Carr, University of Hawaii at Manoa. p. 314.

Chapter 20

20.16: Data supplied and illustration reviewed by J. John Sepkoski, Jr., Professor of Paleontology, University of Chicago. p. 336.

Chapter 21

21.1: From Burton S. Guttman, *Biology*. Copyright 1999 McGraw-Hill Companies, Inc. All Rights Reserved. Reprinted by Permission. p. 342; **21.2:** Redrawn from *Vertebrates, Phylogeny, and Philosophy*, 1986. Contributions to Geology, University of Wyoming, Special Paper 3 (frontispiece and article) by Rose and Bown; and Thomas M. Bown and Kenneth D. Rose, "Patterns of Dental Evolution in Early Eocene Anaptomorphine Primates (Omomyidae) from Bighorn Basin, Wyoming" in Paleontological Society Memoir 23 (*Journal of Paleontology*, Vol. 61, supplement to no. 5). Courtesy of Kenneth D. Rose of The Johns Hopkins University, Baltimore, MD. p. 343; **21.4C:** Reprinted by Permission from Alan Walker; **Science Focus:** Courtesy of Steven Stanley, The Johns Hopkins University. p. 345; **21.9:** From C. Hickman, *Integrated Principles of Zoology*, 9th edition, 1997. Reproduced with Permission of The McGraw-Hill Companies, Inc. All Rights Reserved. Reprinted by Permission. p. 351.

Chapter 22

22.2: Data from S.J. Arnold, "The Microevolution of Feeding Behavior" in *Foraging Behavior: Ecology, Ethological, and Psychological Approaches*, edited by A. Kamil and T. Sargent, 1980, Garland Publishing Company, New York, NY. p. 363; **22.7:** Data from G. Hausfater, "Dominance and Reproduction in Baboons (Papio cynocephalus): A Quantitive Analysis," *Contributions in Primatology*, 7:1–150, 1975. p. 367.

Chapter 23

23.5: From Raymond Pearl, *The Biology of Population Growth*. Copyright 1925 McGraw-Hill Companies, Inc. All Rights Reserved. Reprinted by Permission. p. 382; **23.7B:** Data from W.K. Purves, et al., *Life: The Science of Biology*, 4th edition, Sinauer & Associates. p. 384; **23.7C:** Data from E.J. Kormondy, 1984, *Concepts of Ecology*, 3rd edition, Prentice-Hall, Inc., Figure 4.6, page 107; **23.7D:** Data from A.K. Hegazy, 1990, "Population Ecology & Implications for Conservation of Cleome Droserifolia: A Threatened Xerophyte," *Journal of Arid Environments*, 19:269–82. p. 384; **23.9B:** Data from Charles J. Krebs, *Ecology*, 3rd edition, 1984, Harper & Row; after Scheffer, 1951; **23.11B:** Data from Charles J. Krebs, *Ecology*, 3rd edition, 1984, Harper & Row; after Lack 1966 and J. Krebs, personal communication. p. 387; **23.11C:** Data from Michael Begon, et al., *Population Ecology*, 3rd edition, 1996, Blackwell Science; **23A table:** Data from Charles J. Krebs, *Ecology*, 3rd edition, 1984, Harper & Row. p. 388; **23A:** Data from Karen Arms & Pamela Camp, *Biology*, 4th edition, 1995, Saunders College Publishing. p. 389; **23B:** Data from Charles J. Krebs, *Ecology*, 3rd edition, 1984, Harper & Row.

Chapter 40

40.4: From John W. Hole, Jr., *Human Anatomy & Physiology*, 6th edition. Copyright 1993 McGraw-Hill Companies, Inc., Dubuque, Iowa. All Rights Reserved. Reprinted by Permission. p. 727; **40.10:** From D. Shier, et al., *Hole's Human Anatomy & Physiology*, 8th edition. Copyright 1996 McGraw-Hill Companies, Inc. All Rights Reserved. Reprinted by Permission. p. 735.

Chapter 43

43.7: From Kent M. Van De Graaff and Stuart Ira Fox, *Concepts of Human Anatomy and Physiology*, 4th edition. Copyright 1995 McGraw-Hill Companies, Inc., Dubuque, Iowa. All Rights Reserved. Reprinted by Permission. p. 786; **43.11:** U.S. Department of Agriculture. p. 792.

Chapter 49

49.10: From K.S. Saladin, *Anatomy & Physiology*. Copyright 1999 McGraw-Hill Companies. Reprinted with Permission of The McGraw-Hill Companies. p. 891.

Chapter 50

50.11: From Kent M. Van De Graaff and Stuart Ira Fox, *Concepts of Human Anatomy and Physiology*, 4th edition. Copyright 1995 McGraw-Hill Companies, Inc., Dubuque, Iowa. All Rights Reserved. Reprinted by Permission. p. 912; **50A:** Sexually Transmitted Disease Surveillance, 1997 and 1998. Atlanta: Centers for Disease Control and Prevention. p. 915; **50.2 text art:** From Ruth Bernstein and Stephen Bernstein, *Biology*. Copyright 1996 McGraw-Hill Companies, Inc., Dubuque, Iowa. All Rights Reserved. Reprinted by Permission. p. 917.

Chapter 51

51.8: From Ricki Lewis, *Life*, 3rd edition. Copyright 1997 McGraw-Hill Companies, Inc. All Rights Reserved. Reprinted by Permission. p. 926; **Science Focus:** Courtesy of John Sternfeld, State University of New York College at Cortland. p. 927; **51.10B:** From Burton S. Guttman, *Biology*. Copyright 1999 McGraw-Hill Companies, Inc. All Rights Reserved. Reprinted by Permission. p. 929; **51.16:** Redrawn from Kent M. Van De Graaff and Stuart Ira Fox, *Concepts of Human Anatomy and Physiology*, 4th edition. Copyright 1995, McGraw-Hill Companies, Inc., Dubuque, Iowa. All Rights Reserved. Reprinted by Permission. p. 935.

Photos

History of Biology

Leeuwenhoek, Darwin, Pasteur, Koch, Pavlov, Lorenz, Pauling: © Bettmann/Corbis; McClintock: © AP/Wide World; Franklin: © Cold Springs Harbor Laboratory.

Chapter 1

Opener: © Joe McDonald/Animals Animals/Earth Scenes; **1.2a:** © Mitch Reardon/Photo Researchers, Inc.; **1.2b:** © David C. Fritts/Animals Animals/Earth Scenes; **1.3:** © Francisco Erize/Bruce Coleman, Inc.; **1.5a:** Rainforest: © Barbara Von Hoffman/Tom Stack & Associates; **1.5b:** Toucan: © Ed Reschke/Peter Arnold, Inc.; **1.5 (Orchid):** © Max and Bea Hunn/Visuals Unlimited; **1.5 (Butterfly):** © Kjell Sandved/Butterfly Alphabet; **1.5 (Jaguar):** © BIOS (Seitre)/Peter Arnold, Inc.; **1.5 (Frog):** © Kevin Schafer/Martha Hill/Tom Stack & Assoc.; **1.6a:** © T.J. Beveridge/Visuals Unlimited; **1.6 (Nostoc):** © Eric Grave/Photo Researchers, Inc.; **1.6 (Euglena):** © John D. Cunningham/ Visuals Unlimited; **1.6d (Mushroom):** © Rod Planck/Tom Stack & Assoc.; **1.6 (Rosa):** © Farell Grehan/Photo Researchers, Inc.; **1.6 (Lynx):** © Leonard L. Rue.

Chapter 2

Opener: © Dani/Jeske/Animals Animals/Earth Scenes; **2.1:** © The McGraw-Hill Companies, Inc./Carlyn Iverson, photographer; **2.5b:** © Charles M. Falco/Photo Researchers, Inc.; **2.8a:** © Grant Taylor/Tony Stone Images, Inc.; **2.10a:** © Di Maggio/Peter Arnold, Inc.; **p. 29:** © Frederica Georgia/Photo Researchers, Inc.

Chapter 3

Opener: © Dr. Gopal Murti/SPL/Photo Researchers, Inc.; **3.1a:** © John Gerlach/Tom Stack & Assoc.; **3.1b:** © Leonard Lee Rue/ Photo Researchers, Inc.; **3.1c:** © H. Pol/ CNRI/SPL/Photo Researchers, Inc.; **3.7a:** © Jeremy Burgess/SPL/Photo Researchers, Inc.; **3.7b:** © CNRI/SPL/Photo Researchers, Inc.; **3.8:** © BioPhoto Assoc./Photo Researchers, Inc.; **3.18:** Courtesy Ealing Corporation.

Chapter 4

Opener: © Biophoto Associates/Photo Researchers, Inc.; **4.1a:** © Tony Stone Images; **4.1b:** © Jim Solliday/Biological Photo Service; **4.1c:** © Barbara J. Miller/Biological Photo Service; **4.1d:** © Ed Reschke; **4Aa:** © Robert Brons/Tony Stone Images; **4Ab:** © M. Schliwa/Visuals Unlimited; **4Ac:** © Kessel/Shih/Peter Arnold, Inc.; **4Ba:** © Ed Reschke; **4Bb:** © Biophoto Associates/Photo Researchers, Inc.; **4Bc:** © David M. Phillips/Visuals Unlimited; **4Bd, 4Be:** © David M. Phillips/Visuals Unlimited; **4.3a:** © David M. Phillips/Visuals Unlimited; **4.3b:** © Biophoto Assoc./Photo Researchers, Inc.; **4.4b:** © Alfred Pasieka/Photo Researchers, Inc.; **4.5b:** © Newcomb/Wergin/BPS/Tony Stone Images; **4.7b:** Courtesy Ron Milligan/Scripps Research Institute; **4.7c:** Courtesy E.G. Pollock; **4.8a:** © Warren Rosenberg/Biological Photo Service; **4.10b:** © Richard Rodewald/Biological Photo Service; **4.10c:** © K.G. Murti/Visuals Unlimited; **4.11b:** © S.E. Frederick & E.H. Newcomb/Biological Photo Service; **4.12a:** Courtesy Herbert W. Israel, Cornell University; **4.13a:** Courtesy Dr. Keith Porter; **4.14 (top):** © M. Schliwa/Visuals Unlimited; **4.14 (middle):** © K.G. Murti/Visuals Unlimited; **4.14 (bottom):** © K.G. Murti/Visuals Unlimited; **4.15b:** Courtesy Kent McDonald, University of Colorado Boulder; **4.15c:** From Manley McGill, D.P. Highfield, T.M. Monahan, and B.R. Brinkley, *Journal of Ultrastructure Research* 57, 43–53 pp. 48, 6 (1976) Academic Press; **4.16a:** Sperm: © David M. Phillips/Photo Researchers, Inc.; **4.16b,c:** Flagellum and Basal Body: © William L. Dentler/Biological Photo Service.

Chapter 5

Opener: © Hank Morgan/Photo Researchers, Inc.; **5.1a:** © Warren Rosenberg/Biological Photo Service; **5.1d:** © Don Fawcett/Photo Researchers, Inc.; **5.13b:** Courtesy Mark Bretscher; **5.16a:** Courtesy Camillo Peracchia; **5.16b:** © David M. Phillips/Visuals Unlimited; **5.16c:** From Douglas E. Kelly, J. Cell Biol. 28(1966):51. Reproduced by copyright permission of The Rockefeller University Press.

Chapter 6

Opener: © Patti Murray/Animals Animals/Earth Scenes; **6.1:** © Gregg Adams/Tony Stone Images.

Chapter 7

Opener: © Keren SU/Tony Stone Images; **7.2b:** © Newcomb & Wergin/BPS/Tony Stone Images; **7.2c:** Courtesy Herbert W. Israel, Cornell University; **7.6a:** Courtesy Melvin P. Calvin; **7.7:** © The McGraw-Hill Companies, Inc./Bob Coyle, photographer; **7.9a:** © Jim Steinberg/Photo Researchers, Inc.; **7.9b:** © Charlie Waite/Tony Stone Images; **7.9c:** © Beverly Factor/Tony Stone Images.

Chapter 34

Opener: © Andrew Henley/Biofotos; **34.2b:** © Kjell Sandved/Butterfly Alphabet; **34.3a:** Courtesy of Larry S. Roberts; **34.3b:** © Rick Harbo; **34.4a:** © Alex Kerstitch/Bruce Coleman, Inc.; **34.4b:** © Douglas Faulkner/Photo Researchers, Inc.; **34.4c:** © Michael DiSpezio; **34.5a:** © M. Gibbs/OSF/Animals Animals/Earth Scenes; **34.5b:** © Kenneth W. Fink/Bruce Coleman, Inc.; **34.5c:** © James H. Carmichael; **34.6a:** © Heather Angel; **34.6b:** © James H. Carmichael; **34.7c:** © Roger K. Burnard/Biological Photo Service; **34.8:** © St. Bartholomew's Hospital/SPL/Photo Researchers, Inc.; **34.11a:** © James H. Carmichael; **34.11b:** © Natural History Photographic Agency; **34.11c:** © Kim Taylor/Bruce Coleman, Inc.; **34.11d:** © Kjell Sandved/Butterfly Alphabet; **34.12 (Dragonfly):** © John Gerlach/Tony Stone Images; **34.12 (Walking stick):** © Art Wolfe/Tony Stone Images; **34.12 (Scale):** © Science VU/Visuals Unlimited; **34.12 (Grasshopper):** © Alex Kerstitch/Visuals Unlimited; **34.12 (Beetle):** © Kjell Sandved/Bruce Coleman, Inc.; **34.12 (Lacewing):** © Glenn Oliver/Visuals Unlimited; **34.13 (top):** © Bill Beatty/Visuals Unlimited; **34.13 (lower):** © L. West/Bruce Coleman, Inc.; **34.15a:** © Dwight Kuhn; **34.15c:** © John MacGregor/Peter Arnold, Inc.; **34.16 (Scorpion):** © Tom McHugh/Photo Researchers, Inc.; **34.16 (Crab):** © Zig Leszczynski/Animals Animals/Earth Scenes; **34.16 (Spider):** © Ken Lucas/Planet Earth Pictures Limited.

Chapter 35

Opener: © Merlin D. Tuttle/Bat Conservation International; **35.1a:** © Randy Morse/Tom Stack & Assoc.; **35.1b:** © Alex Kerstitch/Visuals Unlimited; **35.1c:** © Randy Morse/Animals Animals/Earth Scenes; **35.2b:** © Heather Angel; **35.3a:** © Rick Harbo; **35.5:** © Heather Angel; **35.6a:** © Norbert Wu; **35.6b:** © Fred Bavendam/Minden; **35.7a:** © Ron & Valarie Taylor/Bruce Coleman, Inc.; **35.7b:** © Hal Beral/Visuals Unlimited; **35.7c:** © Jane Burton/Bruce Coleman, Inc.; **35.8a:** © Estate of Dr. Jerome Metzner/Peter Arnold, Inc.; **35.9a:** © Suzanne L. Collins & Joseph T. Collins/Photo Researchers, Inc.; **35.9b:** © Joe McDonald/Visuals Unlimited; **35.9c:** Courtesy Dr. Marvalee H. Wake; **35.10a–d:** © Jane Burton/Bruce Coleman, Inc.; **35.13a:** © Bruce Davidson/Animals Animals/Earth Scenes; **35.13b:** © H. Hall/OSF/Animals Animals/Earth Scenes; **35.13c:** © Joe McDonald/Visuals Unlimited; **35.13d:** © Nathan W. Cohen/Visuals Unlimited; **35.14b:** © R.F. Ashley/Visuals Unlimited; **35A:** © William Weber/Visuals Unlimited; **35.15a:** © Kirtley Perkins/Visuals Unlimited;

35.15b: © Thomas Kitchin/Tom Stack & Associates; **35.15c:** © Brian Parker/Tom Stack & Associates; **35.16c,d:** © Daniel J. Cox/Tony Stone Images; **35.17a:** © Tom McHugh/Photo Researchers, Inc.; **35.17b:** © Leonard Lee Rue/Photo Researchers, Inc.; **35.17c:** © Tony Stone Images; **35.18a:** © Leonard Lee Rue; **35.18b:** © Stephen J. Krasemann/DRK Photo; **35.18c:** © Denise Tackett/Tom Stack & Associates; **35.18d:** © Mike Bacon/Tom Stack & Associates.

Chapter 36

Opener: © Richard Thom/Visuals Unlimited; **36.2a:** © Michael Gadomski/Photo Researchers, Inc.; **36.2b:** © Norman Owen Tomalin/Bruce Coleman, Inc.; **36.2c:** © Brian Stablyk/Tony Stone Images; **36.4a:** © Runk Schoenberger/Grant Heilman Photography; **36.4b:** © J.R. Waaland/Biological Photo Service; **36.4c:** © Biophoto Assoc./Photo Researchers, Inc.; **36.5a,b,c:** © Biophoto Associates/Photo Researchers, Inc.; **36.6a:** © J. Robert Waaland/Biological Photo Service; **36.7a:** © George Wilder/Visuals Unlimited; **36.8b:** © CABISCO/Phototake; **36.9:** © Dwight Kuhn; **36.10a:** © John D. Cunningham/Visuals Unlimited; **36.10b:** Courtesy of George Ellmore, Tufts University; **36.11a:** © G.R. Roberts; **36.11b:** © Ed Degginger/Color Pic; **36.11c:** © David Newman/Visuals Unlimited; **36.11d (left):** © Biophot; **36.11d (right):** © Barbara J. Miller/Biological Photo Service; **36.12a:** © J. Robert Waaland/Biological Photo Service; **36.13a:** © Ed Reschke; **36.13b:** © Dwight Kuhn; **36.14a:** © CABISCO/Phototake; **36.14b:** © Runk/Schoenberger/Grant Heilman Photography; **36.16a:** © Ardea London Limited; **36.17a:** © John D. Cunningham/Visuals Unlimited; **36.17b:** © William E. Ferguson; **36.17c,d:** © The McGraw-Hill Companies, Inc./Carlyn Iverson, photographer; **36B:** © James Schnepf Photography, Inc.; **36.18b:** © Jeremy Burgess/SPL/Photo Researchers, Inc.; **36.20 (Cactus):** © Patti Murray/Animals Animals/Earth Scenes; **36.20 (Cucumber):** © Michael Gadomski/Photo Researchers, Inc.; **36.20 (Flytrap):** © CABISCO/Phototake; **36C (Wheat plants):** © C.P. Hickman/Visuals Unlimited; **36C (Wheat grains):** © Philip Hayson/Photo Researchers, Inc.; **36C (Corn plants):** © Adam Hart-Davis/SPL/Photo Researchers, Inc.; **36C (Corn grains):** © Mark S. Skalny/Visuals Unlimited; **36C (Rice plants):** © Scott Camazine; **36C (Rice grains):** © John Tiszler/Peter Arnold, Inc.; **36.Da (both):** © Heather Angel; **36Db (left):** © Dale Jackson/Visuals Unlimited; **36Db (right):** © Bob Daemmrich/The Image Works, Inc.; **36Dc:** © Steven King/Peter Arnold, Inc.; **36Dc (inset):** © Will & Deni McIntyre/Photo Researchers, Inc.

Chapter 37

Opener: © Lawrence Migdale/Photo Researchers, Inc.; **37.1:** © Dwight Kuhn; **37.2a:** Courtesy Mary E. Doohan; **37.2b,c:** Courtesy Mary E. Doohan; **37.6a:** © Dwight Kuhn; **37.6b:** © E.H. Newcomb & S.R. Tardon/Biological Photo Service; **37.7:** © Runk Schoenberger/Grant Heilman; **37Aa, Ab:** © Dwight Kuhn; **37.9a,b:** Courtesy W.A. Cote, Jr., N.C. Brown Center for Ultrastructure Studies, SUNY-ESF; **37.10:** © Ed Reschke/Peter Arnold, Inc.; **37.12a:** © Jeremy Burgess/SPL/Photo Researchers, Inc.; **37.12b:** © Jeremy Burgess/SPL/Photo Researchers, Inc.; Science Focus p. 677: Courtesy G. David Tilman; **37.13a:** From M.H. Zimmerman. "Movement of Organic Substances in Trees. SCIENCE 133 (13 Jan. 1961), p. 667 © AAAS; **37.13b:** © Bruce Iverson/SPL/Photo Researchers, Inc.

Chapter 38

Opener: © Bates Littlehales/Animals Animals/Earth Scenes; **38.1:** © Kim Taylor/Bruce Coleman, Inc.; **38.2a:** © Kingsley Stern; **38.2b:** Courtesy Malcom Wilkins, Botany Department, Glasgow University; **38.2c:** © Biophot; **38.3:** © John D. Cunningham/Visuals Unlimited; **38.4a,b:** © John Kaprielian/Photo Researchers, Inc.; **38.5a,b:** © Tom McHugh/Photo Researchers, Inc.; **38.6a,b:** Courtesy Prof. Malcolm B. Wilkins; **38.7a,b:** © Runk Schoenberger/Grant Heilman Photography; **38.10:** © Robert E. Lyons/Visuals Unlimited; p. 691: Courtesy Donald Briskin; **38.12a–d:** Courtesy Alan Darvill and Stefan Eberhard, Complex Carbohydrate Research Center, University of Georgia; **38.14a,b:** © Kingsley Stern; **38.17a,b:** © Grant Heilman Photography.

Chapter 39

Opener: © Dwight Kuhn; **39.2:** © Michael Viard/Peter Arnold, Inc.; **39Aa:** © Comstock; **39Ab:** © H. Eisenbeiss/Photo Researchers, Inc.; **39Ac:** © Anthony Mercieca/Photo Researchers, Inc.; **39Ad:** © Merlin D. Tuttle/Bat Conservation International; **39.4a:** © Biophoto Assoc./Photo Researchers, Inc.; **39.4b:** © Jeremy Burgess/SPL/Photo Researchers, Inc.; **39.7a (left):** © Joe Munroe/Photo Researchers, Inc.; **39.7a (inset):** © Kingsley Stern; **39.7b (left):** © Ralph Reinhold/Animals Animals/Earth Scenes; **39.7b (right):** © W. Ormerod/Visuals Unlimited; **39.7c (both):** © Dwight Kuhn; **39.7d (left):** © Christopher Lobban/Biological Photo Service; **39.7d (right):** © John N.A. Lott/Biological Photo Service; **39.10:** © G.I. Bernard/Animals Animals/Earth Scenes; **39.11a–f:** Courtesy Prof. Dr. Hans-Ulrich

Koop, from *Plant Cell Reports,* 17:601–604; **39.12a–c:** Courtesy Monsanto; **39.13b:** Courtesy Eduardo Blumwald; **39B,C,D,E:** Courtesy Elliot Meyerowitz/California Institute of Technology.

Chapter 40

Opener: © Zig Leszczynski/Animals Animals/Earth Scenes; **40.2 (Stratified squamous, Pseudostratified, Simple squamous, Simple cubodial):** © Ed Reschke; **40.2 (Simple columnar):** © Ed Reschke/Peter Arnold, Inc.; **40.3a–d:** © Ed Reschke; **40.5a–c:** © Ed Reschke; **40Aa:** © Ken Greer/Visuals Unlimited; **40Ab:** © Dr. P. Marazzi/ SPL/Photo Researchers, Inc.; **40Ac:** © James Stevenson/SPL/Photo Researchers, Inc.

Chapter 41

Opener: © David M. Phillips/Visuals Unlimited; **41.1a:** © Eric Grave/Photo Researchers, Inc.; **41.1b:** © CABISCO/Phototake; **41.1c:** © Michael DiSpezio; **41A:** © Bettmann/Corbis; **41B:** © Biophoto Associates/Photo Researchers, Inc.; **41.12b:** © Manfred Kage/Peter Arnold, Inc.

Chapter 42

Opener: © NIBSC/SPL/Photo Researchers, Inc.; **42.2 (Thymus):** © Ed Reschke/Peter Arnold, Inc.; **42.2 (Spleen):** © Ed Reschke/Peter Arnold, Inc.; **42.2 (Bone marrow):** © R. Calentine/Visuals Unlimited; **42.2 (Lymph node):** © Fred E. Hossler/Visuals Unlimited; **42.6b:** Courtesy Dr. Arthur J. Olson, Scripps Institute; **42Aa:** © AP/Wide World Photo; **42.7a:** © Bohringer Ingelheim International, photo by Lennart Nilsson; **42.9a:** © Matt Meadows/Peter Arnold, Inc.; **42.10:** © Estate of Ed Lettau/Peter Arnold, Inc.; **42.12 (both):** Courtesy of Stuart I. Fox; **42.13:** © Martha Cooper/Peter Arnold, Inc.

Chapter 43

Opener: © Matt Meadows/Peter Arnold, Inc.; **43.8b:** © Ed Reschke/Peter Arnold, Inc.; **43.8c:** © St. Bartholomew's Hospital/SPL/ Photo Researchers, Inc.; **43.9c:** © Manfred Kage/Peter Arnold, Inc.; **43.9d:** Photo by Susumu Ito, from Charles Flickinger *Medical Cellular Biology* W.B. Saunders, 1979.

Chapter 44

Opener: © Bates Littlehales/Animals Animals/Earth Scenes.

Chapter 45

Opener: © Biophoto Associates/Photo Researchers, Inc.; **45.7 (top left):** © R.G. Kessel and R.H. Kardon, *Tissues and Organs: A Text-Atlas of Scanning Electron Microscopy,* 1979, **45.7 (top right and bottom):** © 1966 Academic Press, from A.B. Maunsbach, J. Ultrastruct. Res. 15:242–282; **45.8:** © J. Gennaro/Photo Researchers, Inc.

Chapter 46

Opener: © Dr. Colin Chumbley/SPL/Photo Researchers, Inc.; **46.4:** © Linda Bartlett; **46.5a:** Courtesy Dr. E.R. Lewis, University of California Berkeley; **46.7c:** © Manfred Kage/Peter Arnold, Inc.

Chapter 47

Opener: © Johnny Johnson/Animals Animals/Earth Scenes; **47.1:** © Omikron/SPL/Photo Researchers, Inc.; **47.4a:** © Heather Angel; **47.4b:** © Heather Angel; **47.7:** © Lennart Nilsson, from *The Incredible Machine;* **47.8:** © Biophoto Associates/Photo Researchers, Inc.; **47A:** Robert S. Preston, courtesy Prof. J.E. Hawkins, Kresge Hearing Research Institute, Univ. of Michigan Medical School; **47.10a:** © P. Motta SPL/Photo Researchers, Inc.

Chapter 48

Opener: © Robert Maier/Animals Animals/Earth Scenes; **48.2:** © Michael Fogden/OSF/Animals Animals/Earth Scenes; **48.4 (Hyaline cartilage, Compact bone):** © Ed Reschke; **48.4 (Osteocyte):** © Biophoto Associates/Photo Researchers, Inc.; **48Aa:** © Royce Bair/Unicorn Stock Photo; **48Ab-1,2:** © Michael Klein/Peter Arnold, Inc.; **48.13b:** © Ed Reschke/Peter Arnold, Inc.; **48.14:** © Victor B. Eichler.

Chapter 49

Opener: © A.M. Shah/Animals Animals/Earth Scenes; **49.5a:** © Bob Daemmrich/Stock Boston; **49.5b:** © Ewing Galloway, Inc.; **49.6a–d:** From Clinical Pathological Conference, "Acromegaly, Diabetes, Hypermetabolism, Proteinura and Heart Failure," *American Journal of Medicine,* 20 (1956): 133. Reprinted with permission from Excerpta Medica Inc.; **49.7:** © Biophoto Associates/Photo Researchers, Inc.; **49.8:** © John Paul Kay/Peter Arnold, Inc.; **49.12a:** © Custom Medical Stock Photos; **49.12b:** © NMSB/Custom Medical Stock Photos; **49.13a,b:** "Atlas of Pediatric Physical Diagnosis," Second Edition by Zitelli & Davis, 1992. Mosby-Wolfe Europe Limited, London, UK.

Chapter 50

Opener: © Stephen Krasemann/Tony Stone Images; **50.1:** © Runk/Schoenberger/Grant Heilman Photography; **50.2:** © Anthony Mercieca/Photo Researchers, Inc.; **50.5b:** © Biophoto Assoc./Photo Researchers, Inc.; **50.8b:** © Ed Reschke/Peter Arnold, Inc.; **50A:** © G.W. Willis/BPS/Tony Stone Images.

Chapter 51

Opener (four days): Lennart Nilsson, "A Child is Born," 1990, Delacorte Press, p. 63; **Opener (five weeks):** Lennart Nilsson, "A Child is Born," 1990, Delacorte Press, p. 81; **Opener (three weeks):** Lennart Nilsson, "A Child is Born," 1990, Delacorte Press, p. 76; **Opener (four months):** Lennart Nilsson, "A Child is Born," 1990, Delacorte Press, p. 111 top frame; **51.1:** © David M. Phillips/Visuals Unlimited; **51A–1, A–2:** Courtesy John Sternfeld; **51.9a–c:** Courtesy Steve Paddock, Howard Hughes Medical Research Institute; **51.10a:** Courtesy E.B. Lewis; **51.14a:** © Lennart Nilsson *A Child is Born* Dell Publishing.

Index

Note: Page numbers followed by f refer to figures; page numbers followed by t refer to tables.

ISBN 0-07-252331-X

9 780072 523317

90000